CHRONICLES
of the GRINGOS

Chronicles
of the Gringos

THE U.S. ARMY IN THE MEXICAN WAR, 1846-1848
Accounts of Eyewitnesses & Combatants

Edited, with introduction, commentaries, and notes by

GEORGE WINSTON SMITH
& CHARLES JUDAH

THE UNIVERSITY OF NEW MEXICO PRESS

© THE UNIVERSITY OF NEW MEXICO PRESS, 1968. ALL RIGHTS RESERVED. Manufactured
in the United States of America by The University of New Mexico Printing Plant, Albuquerque.
Library of Congress Catalog Card No. 68-19739. First edition.

ACKNOWLEDGMENTS

We wish to thank the librarians and archivists whose services were so valuable. We should especially like to mention James W. Patton, Carolyn Wallace, Anna Brooke Allan, Ellen R. Strong, Mattie Russell, Virginia R. Gray, William Erwin, Archibald Hanna, Anne Whelpley, Joyce Steerman, Carol Macomber, Ellen Fisher, John T. Thackery, Jr., Elizabeth Farics, James N. Babcock, Myra Ellen Jenkins, Linda Barreras, Ruth Miller, Nicholas B. Wainwright, R. N. Williams II, Stephen T. Riley, Ruth H. Davis, Clifford K. Shipton, Kimball C. Elkins, W. H. Bond, John Lindenbusch, Gretchen Tobey, C. Percy Powell, Peter Ho, Victor Gondos, Sarah Jackson, Elizabeth Ryall, Donald R. Haynes, Frances H. Stadler, Wanda M. Randall, Genevieve Porterfield, and Dorothy Wonsmos.

The research was partially financed by a grant (to G. W. Smith) from the American Philosophical Society. With respect to this subvention the recipient is grateful for the assistance of William B. Hasseltine, Josiah C. Russell, Glenn Sonnedecker and Edwin Lieuwen. We also made use of a typing grant from the Organized Research Fund, University of New Mexico, awarded to Charles Judah.

Those who have given valuable assistance and advice are too numerous to mention individually but we should like to especially acknowledge the help of the following: Myra Ellen Jenkins, Archibald Hanna, Howard Lamar, Edward S. Wallace, David Horne; Gus Blaisdell, editor, and the other efficient staff members of the University of New Mexico Press. Judith Bateman was the cartographer who drew the original maps and William H. Owings assisted with the reproductions. Most of all we acknowledge the indispensable help of Mrs. Helen M. Smith, who has worked with us at every stage of the project, and Mrs. Dorothy Judah. We wish to relieve from any responsibility, however, all other but ourselves for any errors or shortcomings in this book.

Special permission to cite manuscripts was given, as follows: the Robert Treat Paine MSS in the Southern Historical Collection, University of North

Carolina Library, by Mrs. Nell Lockett Miller and Captain Robert N. Miller, United States Navy; the Starr Papers in the Bixby Collection, Missouri Historical Society, St. Louis; a letter in the Getty Papers, State Records Center and Archives, Santa Fe, by Miss Mildred Getty; quotations from the Jenks Beaman Papers and John A. Quitman Papers, Houghton Library, by Harvard College Library; and by the respective depositories indicated in the footnotes.

Authorizations to cite printed materials under copyright have been acquired from Harvard University Press to quote from Emma Jerome Blackwood, ed., *To Mexico With Scott–Letters of Capt. E. Kirby Smith to His Wife;* from Princeton University Press to cite Jacob S. Robinson, *A Journal of the Santa Fe Expedition Under Colonel Doniphan;* and from Yale University Press to quote from Stella M. Drum, ed., *Down the Santa Fe Trail, The Diary of Susan Shelby Magoffin, 1846-1847.*

CONTENTS

ILLUSTRATIONS

FIGURES

ILLUSTRATIONS | xi

EDITORIAL METHOD

Because monotonous repetition would result from placing suspension points at the beginning and end of each excerpt presented, the editors have omitted them in such locations. They have, however, indicated omissions *within* excerpts by two suspension points for any omission of two words or less, and by three suspension points for omissions of more than three words up to paragraph length. An omission of a paragraph or more is indicated by a row of suspension points.

Punctuation—especially commas, semicolons, and periods—has been added wherever necessary to clarify the excerpts, and excessive punctuation (e.g. hundreds of commas) has been removed. Some of the longer paragraphs have been broken up. Capitalization has been altered by reducing a great many common nouns to lowercase. Superscript letters have been lowered, and periods appended to them, as, for example, after abbreviated titles.

Consistent with readability, the editors have kept original spellings. If the rendering of the words prevents understanding, a bracketed *sic* and a correction have been inserted after the word in question. This applies especially to proper and place names. All editorial insertions have been placed in square brackets. In attempting to keep these at a minimum, however, the editors have at times chosen to make corrections of proper names in the footnotes instead of inserting them in the excerpts. If a misspelled word was obviously because of a slip of a pen and if it does not seem to distort the meaning to do so, the editors have silently corrected such slips. The editors have kept the common spelling of Monterey (instead of Monterrey) which was all but universal at the time of the Mexican War.

INTRODUCTION

If the War of 1812 has properly been called the most poorly administered American war, the war with Mexico was certainly a formidable rival. Pinchpenny economy at the expense of the fighting men, political expediency, and bureaucratic insistence that paper estimates rather than field requirements be the measure of the armies' needs were all too prevalent in Washington.

On the battlefront the older generals were campaign hardened but they thought in the past, in terms of 1812 or Indian wars, and they often fought among themselves with a vehemence that might have been better directed against Santa Anna. There were also a number of generals and colonels, appointed as a result of political maneuvering, who were determined to be bathed in military glory during the war and to reap a hero's reward from a grateful constituency when it was over; if natural shrewdness diluted their pretensions, they commanded with instruction manuals in hand and with ears and minds open to the counsel of the young West Pointers on their staffs.

At their worst the enlisted men, both regulars and volunteers, were unworthy of the most incompetent among their officers. Some fled the battlefield, a few mutinied, and thousands deserted to the enemy. Military atrocities against the Mexican civilian population were numerous enough to cause grave concern on the part of the officers, and the punishment was often as brutal as the original crime.

Nor were all the ugly aspects of the war attributable to self-seeking politicians, fumbling bureaucrats, incompetent officers and unworthy troops. Profiteering contractors, business-as-usual purveyors of rotten supplies, cheats and scoundrels, all made their unsavory contributions to the army. If this was the seamy side of the war, there was another, more significant side.

Most of the troops bore themselves well in battle and endured the sickness, hardship and ennui of life in the camps, and on the march there was no more grumbling than might be expected and perhaps less than was sometimes justified. Junior officers led by West Point graduates brought éclat and *professional enthusiasm to the command. This was especially true of the engineers, the light, "flying," artillery and other technicians, many of them from Europe, who were pointing the way towards newer practices in warfare. The two foremost generals, though bitterly criticized by rivals, had very real virtues. Taylor was solicitous of his men's well-being, and warm and informal in his relations with them. In return, though not given to hero worship, the men of Zachary Taylor's army molded him into a heroic figure fit to be president of the United States. Winfield Scott, far less popular than Taylor, was a better tactician and an excellent organizer. Both Taylor and Scott were wise enough to recognize and use the talents of the young professionals on their staffs.*

A proud sense of history was shared by many officers and enlisted men. To-day, because the Mexican War was waged to despoil a weak neighbor of its territory, many Americans feel guilty; but this is a moral judgment rooted in the values of the 1960's rather than one based on those of the 1840's.

True, even in the 1840's there were misgivings. Joel R. Poinsett, a former Secretary of War, wrote Senator Cass of Michigan (May 16, 1846, Poinsett Papers, Vol. 16, Historical Society of Pennsylvania Library, Philadelphia):

I am aware that great ignorance exists in Washington on the subject of Mexico and I am anxious that our arms should be untarnished in a contest with a weaker antagonist and our friends saved from the reproach of rashness.

This concern is over military reputation but others, among them Zachary Taylor and Ulysses S. Grant, doubted that the army had any business in Mexico. Still others opposed the war chiefly on political grounds: it was "Mr. Polk's war," a Democratic-party conflict waged in the interest of the party in power and its dominant slaveocracy. And of course there was Thoreau sounding the call to conscience and civil disobedience.

But the critics, though articulate and earnest and frequently loud, were a minority. In the 1840's the concept of a destiny to be fulfilled was held by the nations of Europe as well as by the United States, and the rationale used to justify empire building—that it was the right and even the duty to subjugate and "civilize" an inferior people—was generally accepted by Americans, including most of those in the army.

Even before the fighting began, a correspondent of President Polk dramatically expressed this opinion when he wrote (John Catron, Nashville, to [James K. Polk], August 16, 1845, Polk Papers, Vol. 90, Library of Congress.):

The English never talk of what they mean to do in India, and their history in India is worth the study of an American statesman at the present juncture. Their policy has been, as acted out by Clive, Hastings and pre-eminently by

Wellesley, to silently draw together at the point to be secured, ample strength to take, and that backed by power to hold—(simply Rob Roy's rule of acquisition) and to fight hard and deadly at the object, if fighting must be done to gain the country—*and then treat.* That history teaches by example is a stale truth, . . . we [will] have read that of India with profit by the time the Texas question is ended.

The Mexicans were an "inferior people" who needed civilizing. Thus many soldiers who had fought in Florida in the Seminole War seemed to regard the peoples of the lower Rio Grande Valley as comparable to the Seminoles— with the exception of the Texas Rangers who remembered the Alamo and Goliad—it was hard for the Gringo to develop the degree of hatred towards the enemy that was to characterize twentieth-century wars. Nevertheless, the Black Legend of Spanish cruelty was remembered: "cowardly," "yellow sneaks," "cruel," and "vindictive" were common epithets. Moreover, the idea of liberation, however mistaken, was sincerely held by many. For these it was a war to free the people of Mexico from the thralldom of an outworn aristocracy and the dead hand of the Roman Catholic Church. This convic-tion received some nourishment from Mexicans. If the people of New Mexico did not welcome the invaders, their loyalty to the mother country was not deep enough to spur them into battle. California was much the same. Even south of the Rio Grande some Mexicans were bitter. One lieutenant wrote (Daniel Harvey Hill Diary MS, entry of [Oct. 20, 1846] Southern Historical Collection, University of North Carolina Library, Chapel Hill.):

Some Rancheros stopped at the Guard-house and I had a long talk with them about their country. The[y] spoke with bitterness of the insolence of the rich, the tyranny of the military and the extortion of the priests. I have observed a bitter spirit of discontent among the lower classes. We are fighting the Army and the Aristocracy not the people of Mexico.

Finally, amidst hardship, sickness, anger and cruelty a sense of romance and adventure flourished. This was particularly true as Scott's army took the historic conqueror's route from Vera Cruz to Mexico City. No phrase rever-berated more loudly than "the Halls of Montezuma," and for a fortunate few Prescott's Conquest of Mexico had appeared at the proper moment to add glamour to the pyramid of Cholula, the snow-covered peak of Orizaba and other natural wonders and monuments of an ancient civilization along the route.
These then are chronicles of the Gringos, who were both the victims and victors of the Mexican War. They are closeups as seen through the eyes of those who lived the war, suffered through it, underwent its privations and

enjoyed whatever satisfaction they derived from comradeship, adventure in a strange land and the sense that they were making history and serving their country. For the most part the chronicles are in the Gringos' own words.

The editors have not written a general history, a textbook account, or a tractarian commentary on the immorality of the Mexican War. Instead they have attempted to recreate it in several dimensions by assembling the eye-witness accounts of the Gringo soldiers and those close to them—the joys and sorrows, excitement and suffering, hopes and fears of the men who fought that war. In many respects the experiences of the Gringos were unique in their epoch, but also running through them is a certain timeless similarity of soldier life familiar to those who have known later wars.

AN ARMY IN THE MAKING

For an aggressive nation which had sustained armed conflicts one or more times every generation since birth, the United States found itself relying upon a limited military force in the autumn of 1845. Along a three-thousand-mile northern border in menacing contretemps with Great Britain, manning seaboard fortifications, holding posts in Florida, on a great arc from the Falls of St. Anthony at the north for fifteen hundred miles through the Indian country to New Orleans, and in newly annexed Texas where more than half the army was stationed, there were only fourteen regiments—two of dragoons, four of artillery, and eight of infantry. The total number of noncommissioned officers, musicians, and privates available for duty was 6,562.[1]

THE PEACETIME ARMY IN 1845

In these scattered forces there was proof to support a statement made by Joel R. Poinsett when he was Secretary of War in 1842: "that [a] natural and well grounded jealousy [is] justly entertained against the existence of a large standing army in our country."[2] After the War of 1812, Congress forced a reduction in the army, which, by 1842, had a skeletonized organization of forty-two privates in its artillery and infantry companies compared to the sixty-four privates which Baron Von Steuben had prescribed for Washington's Army during the War for Independence.[3] When the Secretary of War, William L. Marcy, recommended in December 1845 that the infantry and artillery companies be built up to sixty-eight privates, and those of dragoons to sixty, he thought it wise to explain that if these changes were made the army would still be smaller than it was in 1821, and only 1,740 men greater than in 1808.[4]

1

CONTEMPT FOR THE REGULAR ARMY

Apart from a parsimonious attitude toward the military establishment which marked the Polk administration, it was not surprising that Marcy should be cautious. Nineteenth-century Americans in the "roaring forties" not only were suspicious of standing armies, but they scorned professional soldiers below the gentleman's rank of officer. George Ballentine, a Scotsman who had just enlisted in the American army, noted that this contempt prevailed even when troops presumably were headed for important service in the ranks. Young Ballentine, a weaver by trade from Paisley in the west of Scotland, served in the British army, then came to Philadelphia looking for employment in a carpet factory. Failing to find work there, he tried without success to ship on a whaling vessel, then enlisted in the United States army in the late summer of 1845. After an unpleasant sojourn at the rendezvous for recruits on Governor's Island in New York Harbor, he described his embarkation from New York:

About five o'clock on the evening of the thirty-first August we got on board a sloop belonging to the garrison, which landed us at the custom-house wharf near the battery. There we were met by a crowd of idlers, who gathered round us, curious to have a look at the soldiers who they imagined were ordered to Texas to fight the Mexicans; the most trivial movement of troops being magnified into an event by the rumour of the approaching war with Mexico. . . . The boat was full of passengers, a few of whom occasionally entered familiarly into conversation with the soldiers, and showed their good breeding by various acts of civility and kindness. But we could scarcely help remarking that the majority of them seemed to look upon us in the light of a degraded caste, and seemed to think that there was contamination in the touch of a soldier; for it is a singular fact that though Jonathan is so vain of his military prowess, and a little too apt to boast of the wonderful exploits of those armies of his that can whip all creation so easily, it is only in the collective term, or as an abstract idea; he is exceedingly shy of the individuals who compose it. In reply to some casual observation made by a fellow passenger upon our appearance on board, I chanced to overhear an old fellow of most vinegar-looking aspect drily remark, "Ay, ay! they are a fine set of candidates for the State's prison."

. . . . .

Company I to which I now belonged . . . after having received our draft of twenty recruits, consisted of sixty men, including noncommissioned officers and privates; of these, two were English, four Scotch, seven Germans, sixteen

Americans, and the remainder Irish. Such was its composition at the time I entered, but in the American service a company soon undergoes a change in its component parts.[5]

If on the eve of the War with Mexico the army was small and the enlisted men were held without honor, the martial spirit was nevertheless surging throughout the land. During the 1844 presidential campaign James K. Polk, the Democratic candidate, advocated as part of his expansionist program the annexation of the Republic of Texas, and made it a major issue in his appeal for election. Henry Clay, the Whig candidate, equivocated and went down to defeat. Although American election mandates are notoriously difficult to translate, Polk's victory made it clear that the voters approved his policy of national expansion.

John Tyler, the retiring president, heeded the election verdict and, hoping to harvest at least a measure of profit for himself, hastened to act. In December 1844 he proposed in his annual message that Congress adopt a joint resolution inviting the Republic of Texas into the American Union. The House approved such a resolution in January and the Senate in February. On July 4, 1845 the Texas Convention voted 55-1 for annexation. On December 29, Texas was formally annexed.

As early as 1843, Mexico had threatened that American annexation of Texas would be considered "equivalent to a declaration of war against the Mexican Republic." When the United States invited Texas to join the Union, the Mexican government broke off diplomatic relations. Its minister left Washington in March 1845. Meantime, angry demands for war were voiced in Mexico City, and plans for strengthening the armed forces stationed at Matamoros on the Rio Grande were initiated.

Reacting to the Mexican threats, and in conformity with his own policies, America's new President, James K. Polk, ordered regular army contingents commanded by Bvt. Brig. Gen. Zachary Taylor to Corpus Christi, Texas.[6] This was the nucleus of the army that was to advance from the Nueces to the Rio Grande and from there to carry the war to Monterey and Buena Vista. But it was only the nucleus. The armies that were to fight the Mexican War were barely in the making.

EARLY OFFERS OF VOLUNTEERS

Consequently, even before fighting occurred, the War Department in Washington was showered with letters from potential warriors. In the autumn of 1845, offers that were typical of many others came from Indiana, Ohio, and Kentucky. One of these, from Governor James Whitcomb of Indiana, advised the Secretary of War that a veteran officer who had served in the War of 1812 had organized a company of volunteers known as the "Indiana Riflemen";

By a letter received from Capt. William Walker, of Evansville,[7] in this State, who served as Captain of a company of volunteers from the State of New Jersey in the last war with Great Britain, I am advised that the "Indiana Riflemen," a company of volunteers at that place, & now under his command, has recently been organized for the purpose of offering their services to the U. States in the war between this country & Mexico.

In requesting the Executive of this State in behalf of himself and company to make known this offer as soon as possible to the proper Department, he states that "they are now awaiting orders, & can be ready to march in defence of their country at five minutes notice."

In gladly complying with their request, I beg leave to add that in the event of hostilities between our beloved country & Mexico, or any other power, I entertain no doubt from the spirit already manifested in our midst, that the offer now so promptly & patriotically made will be but an earnest of the thousands of citizen soldiers in this state, who on brief notice, will zealously throng to do battle in their country's cause.[8]

A comprehensive report describing Kentucky's potential volunteers was submitted by Humphrey Marshall. Marshall was an old army man whose career began as a cadet at West Point in 1828, and included service in the Black Hawk War. He resigned in 1833. But on June 9, 1846, he became Colonel of the 1st Kentucky Volunteer Cavalry (Mounted Men) styled "The Hunters of Kentucky"—a tough, colorful regiment far different from the would-be volunteers described by him in his letter of Sept. 14, 1845:

In answer to your inquiries I will proceed to give my opinion as briefly as may be. 1st. Kentucky in case of need could turn out ten thousand good men, but they would be untrained and such as militia usually are when first drawn into active service, involving the Government in much expense to fit them for service. 2d. In ten days Kentucky could march off 1,500 men well trained and drilled, and as perfectly to be depended upon as any regiments of the U.S. Army, as well equipped, and as fit for service immediately as any soldiers in the country. I would answer for the embarkation of this number of effective men directly upon the requisition of the General Government.

To prove the correctness of this assertion, you will remember that since 1839 it has been the practice of our uniformed volunteer companies to assemble at one or more points in the State military encampments from the 1st to the 6th of July each year, there to be drilled according to the latest tactics in the School of the Battalion, and, where their numbers would permit, in the Evolutions of the Line and to perform all the duties of the soldier in field & camp service. This practice has produced these important results. Our Volunteer Corps generally are provided with company chests, tents, havresacks, canteens, camp utensils, knapsacks—in fine every description of camp equipage and not unfrequently with baggage wagons; that they understand the use of all these things, can lay out a camp, pitch & strike their tents; understand camp calls; the duties of sentinels; how to post & retire guards and all of guard duty; and so far as depends upon the soldier are sufficiently advanced to be trusted in any situation. The officers have by their associations become familiar with the drill in the School of the Company & School of the Battalion and from frequent practice are *confident in their discharge of duty*.

Be not surprised when I tell you that from our volunteer companies I can select a full regiment which I would not shrink from trying *to morrow* alongside of any average Regiment of the U.S. Army in every department of military duty. The officers are generally well educated gentlemen and men of property, and the moral force of the *material* far above that of the regular army. Our volunteer companies constituted as I have described would be the force which Kentucky would present in answer to a requisition by the General[9] commanding on the Nueces.[10]

RESPONSE TO WAR

On April 25, 1846, a skirmish between Mexican and United States cavalry occurred, and on May 8 and 9, Americans and Mexicans fought at Palo Alto and Resaca de la Palma. On May 11, President Polk sent a war message to Congress; Congress responded with a declaration that war existed and a call upon the States for 50,000 volunteers.[11]

As word that the United States was actually at war spread throughout the country, the smouldering martial spirit exploded into an enthusiastic response to the call for volunteers. John Blount Robertson, a Tennessean who joined the First Regiment of Tennessee Volunteers, recalled the scene:

Who does not remember what intense interest was elicited by the approach of our little army to the Rio Grande? Every ear was strained to catch the faintest rumor of its issue; but the announcement of the peaceful occupation of the fort opposite Matamoras had partially lulled our apprehensions, and we had begun to laugh at our fears, when suddenly peal after peal bursting upon us told us too plainly that the hour had come. "It has begun!" was the ominous alarm cry of the Revolution, and now again, "It has begun!" needed no commentary: it swept like a tornado through the land; old and young, men and women, felt its influence and caught its spirit, until the vexed and pent-up indignation of twenty millions of people was about to give vent to its impulse. Blood had been shed; Thornton had been captured; Taylor was surrounded; and the war had actually commenced! This, of itself, was enough to raise excitement to its highest pitch; but a thousand distressing rumors served to goad our fears and make anxiety painfully intense. To arms! to arms! came from the mouth and heart of every American freeman. Our soil had been invaded and American blood had been spilled; and this, too, by an aggressor, who had so long refused to mete out to us even-handed justice, and who, instead of granting us indemnity for torts, had taken advantage of our spirit of forbearance to inflict new injuries. It was enough; casuists did not stop to inquire of conscience the lawfulness of war; politicians did not wait to argue its policy; and as for patriots, they only required to know that their country was at war.

. . . . .

Every town and village [of Tennessee] was roused by "the shrill fife and spirit-stirring drum"; the hill-tops and the mountains poured down their thousands—the plains and the vallies were teeming with men, and companies were filled up so fast that it soon became difficult even to purchase a place in the ranks.[12]

In Memphis, Tennessee, Chatham Roberdeau Wheat was possessed by a spirit of exaltation, and if he wrote of it in a melodramatic and half-humorous vein to his friend George Maney, his subsequent career proves him wholly sincere. Wheat was far from the average volunteer. He was a born soldier of fortune or perhaps a born crusader. He had been graduated from college and was studying law when the Mexican War broke out. "Joining up," he fought in Scott's army.

I cannot forbear to address one or two lines to you—now that the blast of war has sounded on my ears. . . . Methinks I can see your noble eye flash with honest indignation at the insults we have received & your arm uplifted high with the stern resolve to wipe it out e'en with your heart's best blood. I had determined to enlist under no other commander than your own noble self, but by the news of this morning I find that no cavalry will be admitted from Tennessee[13]—so I have this morning enlisted under Capt. Porter.[14] The company is principally composed of members of the bar & students of law. Dan Robinson (Godfrey) is one of the latter, and the way he sets his under jaw is death to Mexicans. Morgan Cook is marching his company through the streets—ours will be ready to night—we have an election to night.

Oh! how I wish that I were with you all. I would like to die with you George and be wrapped in the same Star Spangled banner and be borne triumphantly by victorious troops to burial. I would ask for no greater glory—while our spirits should wing their flight to a brighter & a better world where we should enlist under the captaincy of Great Michael and mingle with the hosts of Heaven—and when our comrades on earth should prove triumphant—we would, with Washington & the heroes that have gone before, hang out our banners from the battlements of Heaven & let the shout of our exulting voices ring from arch to arch of heaven's bright canopy.

Suppose the other side of the picture—that we should live & be victorious & gaily enter the city of Mexico & entering the halls of the Montezumas throw our wearied limbs upon a couch of down beneath a canopy of pure gold studded with diamonds & sap[p]hire stones—and call upon her proud daughters to be our cup bearers—& to bring us some of the old Tabernian of which we have so often read and while drinking deep drafts of its oily stream—fight with renewed lustre all our hard won "battles oer again"—then when rich nabobs we returned covered with glory & with bright stars upon our breasts, we would claim a soldier's bride. The rest you may imagine—in either case we are victorious, victorious even in death—how sublime! How pleasing the thought![15]

After the Mexican War was over Wheat practiced law in New Orleans and served in the Louisiana State Legislature, but law and politics were not enough. He joined the Lopez filibuster to Cuba and that of William Walker in Nicaragua; he fought with Garibaldi. And finally, in the Civil War, as a major in the famous Louisiana Tigers' regiment he was wounded at the first battle of Bull Run and killed at Gaines Mill in 1862. And if at burial he was wrapped in the Stars and Bars rather than the Star Spangled Banner, his spirit no doubt winged its way to "enlist under the captaincy of Great Michael."

Sentiments less exalted but fully as fervent were expressed by William Dickinson of Shady Grove, Virginia in a letter which pictured a community celebrating victory when the war was yet young and the casualties had not yet been counted.

I have joined the Volunteers Company that's araising a[t] Henry Co[urt] House [Henry Co., Va.] to go and slay them Mexicans when cal[l]ed for. I am in hopes that there will be an opportunity for us to go. I would be willing to bundle up and start tomorrow morning. . . . We are to have a big day at Henry Co[urt] Ho[use] on the 4th [July 4, 1846]. A Big Barbacue, Balloon ascension &c. &c. in commemoration of that day. And in honour of the Brilliant achievements of our Troops under Genl. Taylor over the force of Mexico.[16]

Dickinson further noted, however, that in many instances enlisting entailed very real material sacrifice. Such was the case of Jubal Early[17] who accepted a commission recommended by Virginia's governor.

One of our County men, Mr. Juble [sic] A. Early has been appointed by the Governor of V[irgini]a Major over the Regiment of Volunteers from this state and he starts today for Richmond in company with Messrs. Shumaker & Wm. A. Martin, who are going with him as we failed in raising a company in this county. Mr. Shoemaker [sic][18] is a talented young lawyer of Rocky Mount and he also has an office from the Gove[r]nor which I do not recollect. Mr. Martin is a young man from Henry & stud[y]ing medicine under Dr. Egan but quits his occupation to go to fight the battles of his country. He is a young man of extraordinary talents. I was present at his taking leave of his aged mother and brothers and sisters on yesterday and I do not think that I ever heard in my life more eloquent remarks than he made on his taking leave of them. There is a great excitement up this way on parting with the above named gentlemen. Mr. Early goes at making a great sacrafise as he was getting a very extensive practice as an attorney though ever since the call upon Va. for Volunteers he has not attended to his profession at all, being so much excited in trying to raise a company to go on to fight. But it is not a new thing with him. He [had] a conspicious [sic] part in the Florida War.[19]

In the early months of the war the cost of volunteering in terms of personal sacrifice did not present serious obstacles to raising enough men. Billboards, mass meetings and parades stimulated recruiting.

In New York City, walls were covered with placards headed "Mexico or Death," and "Ho! for the Halls of Montezuma." The lower house of the New York Legislature at the end of the session (on May 13) adopted a resolution authorizing the Governor to call out 50,000 volunteers from the state.[20] Twenty thousand citizens attended a great mass meeting in Philadelphia. In Ohio, within two weeks, over three thousand men volunteered. Cincinnati alone responded to the call by parading nine hundred volunteers; five hundred of these were in German volunteer companies. Illinois, Kentucky, North Carolina, and the deep South exceeded their quotas. The Nashville Whig announced that a draft would be necessary in Tennessee, but it would be a drawing of lots to see who would have to stay home.[21] In New Orleans, several of the city's fire companies volunteered, and the French, German, and Spanish citizens vied with each other to form regiments. In Indianapolis, Lew Wallace, who was to finish writing his novel "Ben Hur" in the palace of the Spanish and Mexican governors from whence he ruled the conquered province of New Mexico, raised a company of volunteers in two days. Some manufacturing establishments in Louisville temporarily suspended operations "for want of hands, so great is the number of operatives who have joined the army."[22]

The number of volunteers at the beginning of the war was so large in a number of states, that it caused both confusion and embarrassment. Some governors, such as William Owsley of Kentucky, accepted the services of volunteer corps "in anticipation of a call from Washington," and permitted regiments, such as the Louisville Legion, to embark with an "excess" of volunteers. In Ohio, volunteers nearly sufficient to fill an entire regiment beyond the number requisitioned, came to the camps. The State Adjutant General's office had to send many of them home. Three would-be companies from Baltimore took the cars for Washington, determined to report themselves directly to the Secretary of War. They had trouble in finding living accommodations in the nation's capital, but they did manage to secure a muster. An Illinois company, organized in Clark County on the Wabash River, was not so fortunate. It marched some 150 miles to the rendezvous at Alton under the impression that the Governor's secretary had accepted its services. Its Captain, William B. Archer, was "an old and well tried soldier," who had fought in the War of 1812 and the Black Hawk War. A correspondent of the St. Louis Missouri Republican called him a "plain, old fashioned, unassuming man, of sterling worth." At Alton, the Clark County contingent discovered that Governor Thomas Ford had refused it. Ford explained this by saying that while he was in St. Louis receiving companies for the Illinois regiments, his Secretary had been doing the same thing in the Illinois capital: when they compared notes they discovered that they had too many men. Archer, however, hinted that political discrimination was involved. He marched his volunteers to downtown Alton, halted them in front of a hotel, and with "thousands looking on," told his followers that Governor Ford had "swindled them" out of the service. Archer then volunteered as a private soldier in the 2d Illinois Regiment of Volunteers.

UNWILLINGNESS TO ENLIST

But even from the beginning there was dissent. In Michigan, far-distant Mexico and its tropical climate seemed to be an alien field for northern boys who might be needed to fight the British along the Canadian border recently stripped of its garrisons by Mexico-bound regulars. Two days after the declaration of war, G. Mott Williams wrote from Washington to his father in Detroit:

We are at War with Mexico as you will have seen before this. It is supposed that England supplies the means, which is not improbable. The wise heads here are now looking to the aspect of our relations with that power, and the

Oregon question is now involved in greater difficulty than at any former period. No man can see the end of the business in which we are now embarked. Under these circumstances I would dissuade all movements at Volunteering, from our own or the adjoining States having in view a service in Texas & Mexico. It is possible in the first place, that we may want all our own people at home before a twelvemonth and then there is not only more force than requisite in the Southwestern States but the climate of Mexico, I am assured, would prove more fatal to our people, than the force of a dozen such nations as Mexico.[23]

The initial enthusiasm subsided as the war progressed. The causes were varied.[24] The most obvious was that those anxious to fight "joined up" early. But there were other reasons. The war itself was not universally popular. Whigs of the political opposition, suspicious of "Polk's War" from the beginning, saw their doubts confirmed and gained a substantial popular following as the imperial magnitude of the presidential design emerged; antislavery Northerners saw the war as a scheme to extend slavery and increase the power of the "slaveocracy"; many Southerners began to reflect on John C. Calhoun's admonition that Mexican territory was for the South the "forbidden fruit." The combined opponents of the war were not insignificant.[25]

A further reason for refusal to join the army was the period of enlistment. The war was not one of survival or even defense of the national interest and it did not touch the immediate well-being of a great number of Americans. Consequently, many young men though willing to go for a limited period (generally a year), during which they would contribute their share to victory, would not sign up for the duration of the war. In December 1846, this was apparent in Virginia, when David Campbell, a prominent Whig[26] wrote to his cousin in Scott's army.[27]

In my last letter, I believe, I mentioned that a requisition had been made for nine regiments of volunteers of 960 strong each, to be organized and marched immediately.[28] New York has probably by this time sent off a regiment, but no other State has, unless Louisianna has raised hers. I am now very doubtful about Virginia. The volunteers are required to engage for the war. This they object to here.

The new requisition upon Virginia for a regiment of volunteers, to engage for the war, has given very great offence to some of the old democratic farmers here, and I believe elsewhere too. They now say that the war has been badly conducted—agree that the Executive is incompetent to conduct it—and can see no reason why those who first volunteer should do all the fighting. This is a view that will take with the masses—and all who do not want any how to volunteer, will adopt it as their reason for refusing.[29]

Further discouraged by cold and stormy weather, volunteering continued to be "slow business" but, as David Campbell observed, excitement was "gotten up," and nineteen or twenty companies, "at great trouble and expense," finally organized themselves in Virginia by January 1847.[30]

In North Carolina, however, as one Greensboro woman recorded in her diary, recruiting assumed a melancholy aspect at the beginning of 1847:

Tuesday, January 5, 1847 . . . today was a general muster and speeches by Mr. Gorrell and Mr. Henry. General Logan received them in this street and requested all the Volunteers to follow after; as he walked up and down the street, I saw some 6 or 7, bad looking persons following, with poor Jim Laine in front. How many poor creatures have been and are still to be sacrificed upon the altar of pride and ambition. O Lord be pleased to bless our country and visit us not in Judgement, may our president and all who are in authority be directed by wisdom from on high—and may peace be speedily restored to our land.

. . . . .

Sabbath January 10, 1847. This day Capt. Henry[31] and Col. Scales[32] came in town with a company of about 70 men on their way to Mexico, the Company is made up from Stokes, Rockingham and Guilford. They were mustered or sworn in by Lieut. Fremont[33] who dined with us. He was in the battle of Monterey, in May caught Lt. Ringold [sic][34] in his arms when he was shot, received a shot in one of his arms. He is a fine looking young man. The company came marching in with music (the drum and fife) which sounded badly and very sad. It was the first thing of this kind had ever occurred in our streets on the sabbaths. I thought it was a very useless desacration of the Sabbath. May the time come when God's holy day shall be sanctified as it should be.[35]

Resistance to enlistment was met by increased efforts to stimulate recruitment. Posters and broadsides appealed to both patriotism and material interest. In Massachusetts this poster appealed for volunteers to serve under Col. Caleb Cushing in the Massachusetts Volunteer Regiment:

MEN OF OLD ESSEX! MEN OF NEWBURYPORT!
rally round the bold, gallant and lion-hearted
CUSHING! He will lead you to victory and to glory!
Let Essex County have one company in the Regiment
that shall be her PRIDE AND BOAST.

The Company will go into comfortable quarters in about a week, and will sail in the course of two or three weeks. The pay is from 7 to $10 per month—21 dollars in advance; and Congress proposes a bounty of 24 dollars in money, and 160 acres of land. NEWBURYPORT, FEB. 1, 1847.[36]

The reply to such appeals, however, was often disappointing to the recruiters. Such was the case when a young Massachusetts critic, who kept his name anonymous, wrote to the Cambridge Chronicle his reasons for refusing volunteer service:

Neither have I the least idea of "joining" you, or in any way assisting the unjust war waging against Mexico. I have no wish to participate in such "glorious" butcheries of women and children as were displayed in the capture of Monterey, &c. Neither have I any desire to place myself under the dictation of a petty military tyrant, to every caprice of whose will I must yield implicit obedience. No sir-ee! As long as I can work, beg, or go to the poor house, I won't go to Mexico, to be lodged on the damp ground, half starved, half roasted, bitten by mosquetoes [sic] and centipedes, stung by scorpions and tarantulas—marched, drilled, and flogged, and then stuck up to be shot at, for eight dollars a month and putrid rations. Well, I won't.

As to the "bounty," I have not the least doubt *that* will be promptly paid. Many a poor fellow has received it already at Palo Alto, Ransaca de la Plunder, Monterey, and Buena Vista. And no doubt it has and will come to thousands more, in the shape of shot, shell, and *vomito* at Vera Cruz. Much obliged to you, but I have no desire to have my bones picked by the hideous Mexican vultures, landcrabs, and jackalls. Had much rather wait my appointed time, and close my eyes in peace among friends and kindred.

As for yourself [the recruiting officer], I should not wonder if you were a likely sort of a chap. But you are employed at an intensely mean trade, "if you ever noticed it." Human butchery has had its day. Human progress has made mighty inroads upon it within the last half century. And the time is rapidly approaching when the professional soldier will be placed on the same level as a bandit, the Bedouin, and the Thug. You had better quit the business: and in return for your offer and information, if you wish to engage in the woolen manufacture (which is my trade), I will give you all the information and assistance in my power. I am satisfied with my condition. I think a man is more nobly employed, drawing a spinning jack, assisting to clothe his fellow "humans," than even leading an army to slaughter them.[37]

In Pennsylvania the unwillingness of many militiamen to enlist for service in Mexico brought forth this entreaty:

Brigade Inspector's Office, Wilkes-Barre, Nov 23d, 1846

To the Citizen Soldiers of the 2d Brigade, 8th Division Pennsylvannia Militia:

The President of the United States has found it necessary in the prosecution of the war with Mexico, to ask for a regiment of the Volunteers of Pennsylvania. The South and West have cheerfully met his requisition and covered themselves with laurels in the contest. Their bravery and their patriotism were never excelled in the tented field. They rejoiced in the privilege thus extended to them and it is not to be supposed for a moment that the soldiers of Pennsylvania do not glow with the same degree of enthusiasm. They, we are persuaded, are ever ready to serve their country. Their past history attests it, and their future conduct will not tarnish their well earned reputation.

"It may be proper to remark that the law provides for the clothing (in money) and subsistence of the non-commissioned officers, musicians, and privates of volunteers who are received into the service of the United States." For this purpose twenty one dollars will be advanced to each non-commissioned officer, musician, and private, after being mustered into the service, aside from their regular pay and board. "In respect to subsistence before arriving at the place of rendezvous, and for travelling home from the place of discharge, the allowance is fifty cents for every twenty miles distance." Should you be disabled in the service, the government will, as in former instances of a like nature, bountifully provide for you. The requisition is for ten companies, to constitute one Infantry Regiment of volunteers. It is not doubted that from every part of the Commonwealth, the declaration will be heard, "We are ready!"

Our duty is to furnish one of these companies—and no company is complete with less than 80 privates—yet 64 will be accepted. The Wyoming Artillerists, Capt. E. L. Dana,[38] have already tendered their services; and the requisite number being deficient, my object is to urge upon those volunteers within my Brigade, who have any wish to signalize themselves, to offer their services without delay to Capt. Dana, and become regular members of this company. This once done and the ranks full, there is a reasonable hope that this company may be accepted.

The struggle cannot long be protracted. The American Eagle must and WILL spread her pinions in the valleys and on the hill-tops of Mexico! Not a shot has been fired which has not been effective. Not a blow has been struck, which did not redound to the credit of our arms! "Old Rough and Ready" and his battalions, have inscribed upon their arms "onward and right onward!" And when the struggle shall be over, and our Country's honor vindicated, let it be said of the citizen soldiery of the 2nd Brigade, 8th Division, theirs was, in part, the honor of that war, which extended to Mexico the benefits of civilization and civil and religious liberty.[39]

A speech by W. P. Richards of Science Grove, North Carolina, urging the "Volunteers of Davidson" to extend their enlistment appears to have been a somewhat frenetic attempt by the orator (he apparently regarded himself as North Carolina's Tom Paine) to offset decreasing enthusiasm for the war.

TO THE VOLUNTEERS OF DAVIDSON

Fellow Volunteers:

Are you ready? Your country now demands *your service.* She calls upon you to rush to her standard: *to fulfil your obligations as true and noble souled Volunteers.* The North Carolina Regiment is now called for by the Government, and it is for you now to show whether you are true Volunteers—Volunteers who are ready, willing to defend your country,—or whether you will *cowardly* slink from your duty on a quibble of time![40] Can there be a coward in the Davidson Volunteer Company? A man who would desert his country in the hour of danger? A traitor to his country's cause? No, never. There cannot be. No citizen of Davidson can be so base.

Need I to ask, what occasioned you to volunteer yourselves as citizen soldiers to fight your country's battles, whenever and wherever you should be called within the bounds of Mexico? No. I need not repeat that Parades [*sic*], the Mexican monarchist and tyrant, through his tools, and having an ephemerical sway in Mexico, *upon your own soil,* murdered your fellow-citizens, attacked the armies of your country, and waged war against us without any just cause whatever. In self-defence, our Congress declared war existing between the Un. States and Mexico, *by the act of Mexico;* and called upon her brave and patriotic sons to sustain her, in her just and righteous cause. You nobly responded to the call. You volunteered under the Law of Congress, by the Proclamation of your Governor. This law requires each volunteer to serve for twelve months after being called into service, or during the war, unless sooner discharged. But the Government has thought fit to fill her armies with these Volunteers, who are good and true; and who volunteered during the war, and not for twelve months only. The question may probably be raised by some, not overburdened with bravery, as to the length of time for which they volunteered. Some may contend that they volunteered for twelve months only; but no true volunteer—no true patriot can, will, or dare to do it. . . .

There is every inducement that should actuate man, to induce you to stand by your country and your pledge. Your honor, and every thing that is prized by honorable minds, is involved.

If you go, you will get to see the whole Southwest, without the expense incident to traveling. And you will doubtless, independent of your common wages as soldiers, receive a handsome bounty of the choicest lands. Why do I say so? Why, because Mexico will have to pay the expense of the war. She has no money, but she has lands: hence California, New Mexico, &c., will have to pay the forfeit of Mexican madness and barbarity. Here will be large bodies of vacant land; and the ballot-box will instruct Congress, that a portion of them shall pay the defenders of their country. So that the poor, pennyless, but patriotic Volunteer who now stands to his post, may expect, when the time of war is ended (which cannot exceed from 12 to 18 months) to be the owner of a tract of excellent land.[41]

Philadelphia had a different problem. Anti-Catholic riots had occurred there in 1844[42] and it was feared that sending men with families to the war would spark new outbreaks. A letter from Morris Longstreth to James Buchanan on the subject reveals that fear of religious discord was being used to spare the city's volunteers from the necessity of leaving home.

On visiting Philadelphia a day or two since, I found the general joy and enthusiasm damped by the consideration, that should the exigencies of the country demand the actual transportation of the Volunteers to the seat of War, the public peace might be again compromised by a renewal of the deplorable events of May and July 1844. I discovered that men of judgment and sagacity considered that the serpent of religious discord was merely "Scotched, not killed," and that the "Sun," "Eagle" and other native organs were as virulent in their incendiary denunciation of Foreigners and Catholics, as just prior to these fatal Riots. In short, it is feared that the departure of the Volunteers will be the Signal for another outbreak. These opinions and views are I find from occasional intercourse with Catholic Gentlemen, participated in, by them.

My own apprehensions would not, however, have induced me to trouble you on this occasion, had I not been specially enjoined by a distinguished member of the Philadelphia Bar to make this communication, together with the assurance that the Volunteers consisted chiefly of men with familys; and that while as citizen soldiers, against foreign or domestic foes, they are invaluable—their transportation to a remote and unhealthy climate is deprecated, except in the most urgent need. The Pennsylvania contingent might be easily raised from unmarried and ardent young men always, as was well exemplified in the French Conscripts, the most available for Foreign Service.[43]

PROTESTS AGAINST RECRUITING OFFICERS

If the protests of some of its victims are to be credited, recruitment was not always too scrupulous. A letter from a Bostonian, Nathan Burdit, to Col. Caleb Cushing of Massachusetts raised not only the question of how the captain of a company obtained his volunteers but also why he would want such a recruit:

May I crave your attention to the statement of a few facts relating to the enrol[l]ing of my son, George W. Burdit, into Company H of the regiment under your Command, which Company is at present under the immediate command of Captain Barker[44] by whose persuasions my son was induced to enrol[l] himself. He, Captain Barker, first assured him that he could leave his pay ticket with his wife so that she might in his absence draw a portion of his pay.

He next told him that he would not be required to carry a musket, he having a stiff elbow which renders him unable to perform manual exercise in rank and file. He then appointed him Bugler, for which duty he was alike unfit. As a last resource he made him fifer altho he never blew a note of music in his life. He cannot raise his left arm to his head, a fact which any of the Medical Faculty in the City will attest to. Still under all those difficulties my son was willing to go rel[y]ing on the honour of his Captain with respect to the transfer of his pay ticket to his wife than which she has no other means of support. When he put the Captain in mind of this matter he told him that was all nonsense and moreover he must carry his musket as well as others. Such contradictions as those are not becoming a gentleman holding a commission from the United States.

. . . . .

I saw Captain Barker yesterday and he told me that if my son would get from his mother-in-law, Mrs. Badger, a written consent for her two sons to go that in consideration of his lameness he would accept a substitute for him; that shows that he considered him unfit for service. Why not discharge him then at once. I never until within a few days done anything about the matter because I made sure that when the regular [doctor] examined him he would be rejected for he was once refused by the Navy Surgeon.[45]

An appeal from an enlisted man, who insisted he was being forced to serve in the Virginia Volunteer Regiment, has a familiar ring to military historians. The armies and navies of Europe had long been raised in part by impressment of men found in the grog shops. James Miller, a Scotsman "shanghaied" in Norfolk while intoxicated, though not technically impressed, failed to see the difference, and protested bitterly to Lt. Col. Thomas B. Randolph:

The reputed justice and honor of character for which I have heard you [are] distinguished has emboldened me to ask exoneration from the constrained and unjust oppression imposed upon me by Captain John P. Young, of your Regiment,[46] who tore me from my lawful employment, forced me to embark for this distant Country, and now, per might, holds me an involuntary soldier in his company.

In order to enlighten you as to the outrage perpetrated upon my liberty and rights, let me bespeak your patience while I detail a plain and unvarnished tho' tedious narrative of the facts of my hard case as they occurred: I, James Miller was born in Renfordshire, Scotland. When only thirteen years of age

I emigrated to Nova Scotia, and in the town of New Glasgow of that province I served an apprenticeship to the trade of ship carpenter. On the last of Aug. 1846, I left Nova Scotia for Philadelphia, U.S. where I remained only about the space of six weeks, when I sailed in the capacity of second Mate and Carpenter aboard the Barque Ann Hood, bound to New Orleans, which vessel having been forced by distress to enter the Harbor of Norfolk, Virg. to repair damages sustained at sea, I left her by consent of the Captain and engaged myself in employment in the U.S. Navy-Yard at Gosport.

While so employed I first met, on or about the 1st day of Decr. '46, Captain Young, then engaged in raising a Volunteer Company to serve the Government of the U.States in the existing war with the Republic of Mexico. Stimulated by the influence of an unusual quantity of ardent spirits and incited by persuasion I signed a paper purporting to be an enrollment of the names of men about to organize themselves for said service. At the time of signing my name I was under the impression that the term of service was limited to a twelve months [sic]. Not more than ten days thereafter, having maturely reflected on the nature and consequences of the engagement into which I had in part entered and having ascertained the indefinite term for which, upon being mustered into the service, I was expected to enlist, I informed said Capt. Young that circumstances and after consideration had determined me, while yet in my power, to recede from my first intention; therefore I wished him no longer to consider me as a member of the Company certain to consummate the enlistment.*

Subsequently, in the collection of the individuals into Rendezvous, their organization as a Company, election of Officers &c I took no part nor concern. I neither ate, drank, slept nor appeared with them under the guise or semblence of membership. Far from it. I went several times to their quarters, continuing only there long enough at each visit to undeceive the Company as to my ultimate intentions, by declaring unequivocally my disinclination to adhere to my yet incomplete compact with them. When the Company was organized by the election of Officers, in this all important matter, involving as it does the reputation, order, peace and comfort of the soldier, I participated in no manner. Captain Young, having been duly elected and commissioned the head, moved the Company to Richmond, Va. without insisting upon my attendance or the attendance of several other men who recanted after signing. Thinking myself free from further trouble on this score, I continued to labor daily for about eight days following in the Navy Yard.

When, that time elapsed, Capt. Young returned and endeavoured to persuade me to accompany him back to Richmond for the purpose of suffering myself to be mustered into the service of the U. States; but upon my steady

* Thus in text.

refusal to take this last decisive and deciding step, he threatened me with force and violence with so much earnestness of manner as constrained me to accompany him to Richmond, not with any intention on my part of submitting to the proposed order &c., but by the intervention of a writ of habeas corpus to free myself from the entanglement. . . .

I returned to my employment in the Navy Yard pursuing it without molestation for the period of a week more. On the first day of the succeeding week Lieut. John Cook appeared in Portsmouth and descrying [illeg. word] me standing, with some others, my fellow-laborers at the door of my boarding house, he made diagonally across the street for the place where I stood, accosted me as he came up with "well, Miller, you ran away from Richmond and must surrender and go with me." I replied that I had not run away, but had acted in my departure thence according to the advice of a legal friend; that I recognized no authority subsisting in him to control my actions or impel my movements, and that I should not yield obedience to any of his dictates. He swore a mighty oath that he would compel me, following the threat by the act of clutching me by the collar of my coat. By an effort I parried his hold upon my collar, whereupon he instantly drew a revolver-pistol, vociferating oaths that he would take me dead or alive. Yielding to the persuasions of my friends present, and to the force of my necessity, I submitted myself a prisoner first to be led by said Lieut. Cook's order to the jail, wherein the jailer refusing to confine me, I was taken to a tavern and committed to the custody of two men of the Company for the night.

Next morning, I was dragged aboard of a boat landed at Fort Monroe, and closely immuned in the guard house for sixteen days, at the expiration of which time, I was again transported to Richmond reiterating at every suitable opportunity my determination not to consent to be mustered into service. There I was taken before a Capt. Smith[47] who asking me my name and if I was a sound man, received for reply from me that I was "a pressed man" and that I should answer no questions the drift and bearings of which I did not clearly comprehend. Capt. Smith then accosting Lieut. Cook said, "I want to have nothing more to do with this man." Immediately after this, Lieut. Cook [sic] took[48] me away and delivered me to the custody of the City Guard.

On the day following, a writ of habeas corpus brought me before a Judge of the City who at the close of the trial consigned me and my blighted hopes to military domination remarking that if it were not for some order emanating from the Adjutant General's Office then before him, the tenor and purport of which I was before then, and am now, profoundly ignorant, he would feel himself bound to discharge me. My lawyer promised to make one more effort to rescue me, but was frustrated in his humane design by my being hurried next morning, at 5 o'clock, on board of a boat bound to Fort Monroe, and remaining there only one short night, I was chucked aboard a barque, and have been dragged into this lawless land, devoid of any hope of release, but that which I repose in your magnanimity and love of equal justice.[49]

Disillusionment of Recruits

A spirited, if unquestionably jaundiced account of recruitment by means of excessive promises is found in ". . . a Full and Exciting History of the New-York Volunteers," probably written by Albert Lombard and published in 1848. Also included is a description of the sort of men obtained by these means, and the sad tale of their disillusionment.

In the early part of November, 1846, an order from [the] Government was received to raise one regiment of Volunteers for "during the War with Mexico." Accordingly the First Regiment was selected, and Col. Ward B. Burnett,[50] Lt. Col. Charles Baxter, and Major J. C. Burnham were appointed field officers; they selected ten places of rendezvous and issued notices for "able-bodied recruits willing to live or die in defence of our common country," *promising* three months extra pay, or three months advance, and six months clothing, which never went into operation so far as the poor soldier was concerned, except the six months clothing; the *gallant* officers of course, fared a little better.

. . . . .

The drumming up of recruits was commenced, and by the middle of December about eight hundred men enlisted for "better or for worse,". . . and were sent down to Fort Hamilton to *fat* on bread and pork with soft planks for a bed and icy ground to drill on.

Among the troops there were the greatest medley ever congregated together in one regiment during the War. For officers we had barbers, tailors, sportsmen, bar-tenders, politicians, and a *few* gentlemen. For non-commissioned [officers], we had a pretty considerable variety of *decent fellows*—my humble self included—all promised to be made Brigadier Generals or something else before "returning from the wars."

The privates too, were all promised "roast beef and two dollars a day," "plenty of whiskey," "golden Jesuses," "pretty Mexican gals," "safe investments, quick returns," and every thing pictured to the fancy.

The privates were generally smart active men, with the exception of about two hundred totally unfit for service, or scarcely anything else—a fraud on the War Department and a curse to the officers who enlisted them. But anything to fill up the ranks, and ho! for Mexico! Even the U.S. Surgeon held no examination as is usual, and so ordered by the War Department; it is true he passed the *line* in company with Col. Bankhead [sic, Burnett?] eyeing each man and rejecting a number of boys unable to carry a musket, and a few others who looked the "worse for wear," but they were soon thrust into line again by our magnanimous officers. Thus was our regiment composed of rejected boys, men who were diseased and broken down, some lame and blind in one eye, others were sixty-year old *boys*—with many *beautiful* subjects, selected especially "by order" of the commander-in-chief of the First New York Regiment, bound for Mexico, among which were *gentlemen* from the Tombs, ragamuffins from Blackwell's Island, Alms House, and a sprinkling of "Five Pointers"; and a more rascally, *lousy* set was never thrown among decent men. There is no palliation for the officers, their conduct was outrageous! to place men (of no kind of use except for "turkey buzzards") without having them cleansed—and their *lousy, filthy,* and *diseased* rags thrown to the dogs! before putting on new clothes, and allowed to associate with decent men. I say it was outrageous! insulting and degrading to the clean soldier.

The consequence was, that by inattention and indolence on the part of the officers (?) [*sic*] the whole regiment were covered with *vermin* before they left Fort Hamilton, by a few scamps. . . .

The New York Regiment consisted of about eight hundred rank and file, three hundred Americans, the balance Dutch, Irish, French, English, Poles, Swedes, Chinese, Indians, &c., there were not one hundred men and officers ever born in the City of New York in the whole regiment.

. . . . .

In the latter part of November, 1846, a portion of the new recruits met "by order" at Centre Hall, where they were formed into line as straight as a crooked stick, when the "'dashing white sergeant" gave orders to "dress!" "dress by the right!" "dress back on the left!" "steady in the centre!" "heads up!" "front!" &c., &c., but it was of no use, you might as well straighten the sea serpent. Most of them being raw recruits, and some *fresh caught* from the "land of bogs," and of all sizes and sorts. Perhaps they might have been reflecting on that roast beef and "three months advance" at Fort Hamilton, when in came our gallant Colonel, looking like a cropped Canadian pony; three distinct cheers were given—"long live our noble Colonel," "Hurra for roast beef." "Go it Jimmy!" "Down with Santer Ranner," &c., &c. It was several minutes before the Colonel could command silence, when he commenced nearly as follows,

"Fellow soldiers and comrades!" (curious comrades, thinks I, judging from outward appearances), "we have met for the first time together," (long pause) "I am glad to see so many fine looking fellows," (three cheers! hurra for Mexico!) "Yes! with such men I am proud to lead on to Mexico!" (tremendous cheering). "You shall share with me—my bed shall be your bed—my food, your food"— (gammon!)—"In the toils and hardships of war, we will all share alike," (three cheers, that's it! that's the way we do it at Five Points! good! go it!) "Now, my brave fellows, I wish all those who have got nothing to eat, nor hole to lay his carcass in would go to Fort Hamilton, where there's plenty of every thing." (Hurra for that! I'll go!) "I have engaged good quarters, and you can all have good beds, and plenty of roast beef and potatoes." (Nine cheers for that! hurra! hurra! for roast beef and 'taters!) "I now take my most respectful—good night." (Three cheers for Col. Burnett and roast beef! hip! hip! hurra! hurra! hurra! ha! ha!) *By the sergeant*, "attention! company! by the right flank *left face!*" (Music) "March!" And away they do march, up and down like a sheep's hind leg, is a caution to regulars. Thus ends the first interview.

Next morning about two hundred recruits sailed for the Fort in high glee— instead of soft beds they found hard planks, and a thin horse blanket, with a stick of wood for pillow and bolster; and instead of "roast beef and taters," they were glad to get raw pork and hard crackers. O! the horrors of war! The *mean* and *unmanly deception* of the officers. However, many fared better than they had been in the habit of. They were well aware that there were no accommodations provided for them; and to send men in the cold of winter was inhuman, to say the least of it.

Time passed on, and recruiting went on—"come, my dear fellow, won't you *list?* glorious times! roast beef, ice creams, and three months' advance! You can leave your dear wife and children behind with plenty of money and draw part of your pay in your absence. Glorious times! Come take something to drink with me—here's a health to old Zack! Glorious times! plenty to eat and drink—and if you are a pretty good fellow, we'll make a *sergeant* of you. Nothing so happy as a soldier's life—music all day—no *work*—only a *little* drill now and then—that's fun! Come my boy! let's take another glass, and I'll show you your rendezvous. Fine officers—real gentlemen! All we have got to do is—have a fine sea voyage to Vera Cruz (Uncle Sam pays our passage), bombard the City —*swallow* the Castle —and come home again with plenty of gold in our pockets and lots of glory in our bones!" "And so the days would move on, the Sergeant "treating" the green 'uns, bringing them to the rendezvous for exhibition to the worthy Captain or Lieutenant, who would "treat" again, and tell the poor fellow all about the *glory* and *money* he would naturally receive from his good appearance, &c., how good and kind they would be, and in case of sickness it cost *him* nothing, and they would *stick* by him—roast beef and sweet potatoes were nothing to be compared to their promises—every man, too, should be "made a Sergeant or Corporal" and perhaps a Lieutenant should any of them be so lucky as to "shuffle off this mortal coil." (Pity some didn't before they left the Fort, for the benefit of the rising generation.)

. . . . .

Another way of recruiting, never before "written in the bills," and showing great Yankee ingenuity, was to publish an advertisement for "Mechanics and Laborers to go South—good wages and passage free," which brought large numbers to the rendezvous, many were *caught* and deluded by the thrilling and splendid account of a glorious campaign, promising three months extra pay and a *bran* new suit of clothes; after treating &c., the poor fellow was induced to sign the muster roll, and politely invited to take a ride to Fort Hamilton to receive the hospitalities of that great and glorious institution, for the cultivation of *vermin* and manufacturing of great men!

After arriving at the Fort, it was very difficult to ever return, you were treated *so very politely;* and the recruit finds that he has been most egregiously mistaken or hoaxed . . . and very liable to get "into a muss," if he dares to say a word, or even ask Col. Burnett for a *few cents* for his suffering family, or for a small portion of that "five thousand dollars" the City gave for the "aid and comfort" of the poor soldier.

· · · · ·

The men who have been fortunate enough to live, have not forgot [sic] the inducement of "twenty-one dollars" by reason of which they enlisted—many for the purpose of leaving a *mite* at home for their suffering families, in the dead of winter. Here let me charge you, and perhaps a few others, of *direct* and *indirect* ruin and the breaking up of many interesting families, by deception! fraud! and the keeping of monies for your own *private* ends and *speculation,* given by the liberal, honorable, and whole-souled, heart-felt Corporation of the City of New York, for the aid and comfort of those *poor men* who volunteered to fight and die for them and their constituents.

· · · · ·

If it is cruel to *drag* black men from their homes, how much more cruel it is to drag white men from their homes under *false* inducements, and compelling them to leave their wives and children, without leaving a *cent* or any protection, in the coldest season of the year, to die in a foreign and sickly climate! "But," says the reader, "why did they enlist, and leave their families in distress?" The answer is, many enlisted for the *sake* of their families, having no employment, and having been offered "three months' advance," and were promised that they could leave part of their pay for their families to draw in their absence. They, poor duped men, but with patriotic and noble feelings toward their wives and children, sacrificed everything for the *sole* purpose of their support. . . . I boldly pronounce, that the whole Regiment was got up by fraud—a fraud on the soldier, a fraud on the City of New-York, and a fraud on the Government of the United States—and Col. Ward B. Burnett and his *gang* can make the most of it.[51]

QUALITY OF THE OFFICERS

Men undoubtedly were recruited by gaudy promises and deliberate misrepresentation, and in many cases the material thus procured matched the shoddiness of the method. But most of those who went to war went willingly, victims of neither deceit nor misunderstanding.

What kind of soldiers were they?

The answer was given by themselves and their contemporaries. On the whole the regulars, though sometimes bitterly criticized, were judged a competent fighting force.

Their officers were a mixed lot—veterans of the War of 1812, old Indian fighters from the frontier forts, young men fresh from West Point, and appointees from civil life who owed their rank to political "pull." Except for appointment to the General Staff, it was "the established practice for promotion by succession to take place to the grade of Captain, Regiment by Regiment; from the grade of Captain, promotion to the grade of Colonel, . . by succession, corps by corps." But promotions had been slow in coming, and many an able young officer resigned to seek better fortune as a civilian. John Bell, when Secretary of War in the early 1840's, frankly advised the President:

The present condition of the army of the United States, the higher grades of command, with few exceptions being occupied by old men who possess neither the physical nor mental energies necessary to efficient service, forms the most conclusive argument in favor of the principle of selection in all the higher appointments. Promotion by succession in the higher grades it is manifest, if adhered to must in the end result in placing at the head of the Army, and in the principal subordinate commands a succession of imbeciles from age or long service.[52]

This warning, however, went unheeded. When the Mexican War came, the veterans were in the higher ranks and still tended to think in terms of earlier skirmishes. In spite of attempts made before the war to bring American ordnance and tactics more closely in line with those of the French, the regular officers generally distrusted innovations. Zachary Taylor himself had little confidence in light mobile artillery until he witnessed its effectiveness in battle. To his credit, he could learn.

The young men from West Point, many of them lieutenants and captains before their brevets quickly raised them in rank, were often most brilliant. A few lost their lives, some retired at the end of the war never to fight again, but many went on to command the armies of the Union and Confederacy in the Civil War. Among them were Grant, Lee, Bragg, Buell, Meade, Joseph E. Johnston, Hooker, Thomas, and many another. As a group they were conscious of their training, and tended to be a cocky, often haughty, clique, who regarded many of their superiors in command, especially the officers of volunteer troops, with a certain amount of derision. One of them, Cadmus M. Wilcox, described a West Point graduate (probably himself) who joined Taylor's Army of Occupation in the field:

Being well posted in the tactics of the three arms of service, he is at once competent and efficient in drilling enlisted men, either as cavalry, artillery, or infantry, and in charge of details to construct batteries or field fortifications he directs with intelligence, due to his familiarity with the text books in use at the Academy. Subordination, deference, and respect for superior officers have been thoroughly inculcated during his four years' instruction and training at West Point, and to the usages of the service he readily adapts himself.[53]

Although in the end he recalls "the deference and respect" due a superior officer, Wilcox also described the scorn of a West Pointer and his classmates for the errors of the amateurs (volunteers).

While detained at Camargo I saw what was reported at the time in the newspapers as General Pillow's[54] fortifications, with the ditch on the inside. Being recently from West Point, with our minds full of what the text books prescribed in such cases, I and my classmates were greatly amused, and one, Lieut. James Stuart,[55] of South Carolina, mounted on a Texas mustang, and riding at a fast gallop, leaped both parapet and ditch. Probably General Pillow had nothing to do with their construction.[56]

PREJUDICES OF THE REGULARS

Not all the West Point graduates derided those they considered to be their inferiors. Ulysses S. Grant,[57] for example, regarded the volunteers who fought in the Mexican War as excellent soldiers. But Grant probably represented a minority, while young George B. McClellan[58]—who went from West Point classrooms directly to an engineer's company in Mexico, who was destined to precede Grant as a general-in-chief of the Union armies during the Civil War, and who ran against Abraham Lincoln in the presidential campaign of 1864— more nearly reflected West Point's low opinion of volunteers and the rank and file regulars. It was the scorn of the professional for the amateur, of the native-born American for "wretched" immigrants:

I have sure enough resolved to apply for the Engineers, but if there is any truth in the last accounts from Texas, I shall probably go in the Line & what's more be in Texas by the end of next month. The account to which I allude is a rumor, contained in yesterday's paper, to the effect that Genl. Taylor had been defeated with the loss of 700 men[59]—about one third of the Army; if that many have been killed, at least one hundred must have been officers, for great reliance is not placed upon the *present* privates in the Army (they being for the most part composed of these wretched Dutch & Irish immigrants,[60] in time of peace (except the Dragoons who are almost altogether Americans) & as a necessary consequence the officers will have to exert themselves greatly & it is quite certain that no graduate of this Academy will act in a cowardly manner in face of the enemy. . . . I find that the remark I made about the composition of the Army is a little overdrawn, it is not quite so bad, tho' bad enough. . . . The Army (!) of Occupation—1,900 strong, is in front of Matamoras, which is garrisoned by from 7 to 8,000 Mexicans, pretty great odds against troops who have never smelled powder in their lives; all of us have friends among the officers, & the first thing we know may be that about half of them are knocked on the head & that we are to go down & enjoy the same amusement! . . .

The amount of it will be that they will have to dispense with the entire volunteer system, as far as an Army of invasion is concerned, & trust entirely to the regulars. If 7,000 regulars had been at Genl. Taylor's disposal on the Rio Grande, the war would in all probability have been finished at a blow, he would have crushed Arista,[61] & that would have been the end of it.[62]

Concentration of the Army

If, as McClellan surmised, the volunteers were not likely to deliver Taylor from danger, the regulars were almost as unprepared—for the type of campaigning required in a war with Mexico—when the United States army first began to concentrate near Corpus Christi for the "defense of Texas" in the summer of 1845. Widely distributed in small detachments for many years, it was fortunate that the army could again be brought together for battalion and regimental drill before a major campaign had to begin.[63] Even then Brigadier General Taylor undertook these preparations for field service in a leisurely way. Officers who had not seen one another for years greeted old friends as though they were at a fraternity reunion.

These scenes at Corpus Christi were described by John P. Hatch, 2d Lieutenant, 3rd Infantry, later of the Mounted Rifles, brevetted 1st Lieutenant and Captain (Contreras, Churubusco, and Chapultepec), and a Brigadier General, United States Volunteers, in the Civil War:

I find many of my classmates and friends here. . . . You would laugh to see some of the dragoon officers, their hair hanging down their backs, immense mustaches, and beards six or eight inches long. And dressed in the most fantastic style. Nearly all the officers here wear whiskers and mustaches, or rather they never let a razor touch their faces. I consider myself very fortunate in being sent here, for it is very probable that I may not see so many regulars together in twenty years. Many old officers have never before seen so many troops at one time. We must have over three thousand men. My regiment [Third] is one of the best in the service, if not the very best and there is a great deal of regimental pride in it. There is a very good feeling among the officers; most of us mess together. We have a large thatched mess house, with tired table furniture, plates, pitchers, tumblers, all tin, iron spoons, &c., but we live very well as there is an abundance of game here and the beef the best in the world, fish of the finest quality.[64]

Two weeks later, he continued his description in another letter:

The different parts of the Army vary much in the state of discipline. Some of them have not been together for many years. The Fifth [Regiment], for instance, which is all together for the first time in nine years; this of course has prevented them learning the batallion drill, and as the officers had no occasion to practice they had forgotten all their tactics. . . . We have a fine drill ground about a quarter of a mile from the Camp; a hundred and fifty or two hundred acres have been cleared by the soldiers and the land lies beautifully. The Third & Fourth have been drilling together there, and next week we expect that the Eighth and a Regiment of Artillery will drill with us.[65]

MISGIVINGS OF THE REGULARS

Enthusiasm for a campaign against Mexico did not always prevail among the officers of the regular army. A matter-of-fact acceptance of duty, or a determination to do what needed to be done, apart from their own personal feelings, was not an uncommon attitude. Lt. Col. Ethan Allen Hitchcock,[66] Scott's acting inspector general during the climactic campaign to take Mexico City, was more outspoken in his antiwar opinions. In a letter which dealt largely with his stillborn study on Spinoza and Swedenborg, Hitchcock informed his strongly antiwar, New England correspondent, Theodore Parker, of his dislike for the "abominable war."

I take this occasion . . to say that I coincide with you in your views of this abominable war in which our country is engaged with Mexico. From my own observations in the country and from knowledge derived from reliable sources, I could, if I had time, give you much that might be new to you & go to confirm your opinions as you have publicly expressed them. I confess, humble as I am, I wish not to fall a victim to this war without entering my protest against the war itself as unjust on our part & needlessly & wickedly brought about against the plain intentions of the Constitution giving certain powers to Congress. I am here, not from choice, but because, being in the Army, it is my duty to obey the orders of the constituted authorities of the government until the people shall see fit to change those authorities. Our government, as a government, can only exist by admitting this principle. As an individual, I condemn, I abominate this war—as a member of the government I must go with it until it shall be brought back to a sense of justice, though I think I shall feel this obligation less if I can conduct [myself] well in some fair field.[67]

MILITARY SNOBBERY

The volunteers complained repeatedly of what they regarded as favoritism shown the regulars. Thus, Col. William B. Campbell of the 1st Regiment of Tennessee Volunteers, writing from a camp near Jalapa, declared that the volunteers, regardless of their merit, would never receive justice from the regular officers of the army:

Nor would I ever again take a command in the army unless it was in the regular service, as there is so strong a feeling of jealousy & opposition to the volunteers, that while the command & controul of the army and all its departments is in the hands of regular officers, justice will never be done to the Volunteers. The whole of the officers of the regular army seem to regret that the battle of Buena Vista was fought by volunteers & say it will break down the army & seem not to rejoice in the success of our arms in the hands of any but regulars. And Volunteers have hard places, have fewer comforts or conveniences than regulars & when any thing is done all the praise is given to the Regulars. I will never enter the service again as a volunteer unless it be to defend my native land & my own hearth stone.[68]

From the rank and file of the regulars another angry critic accused Major General Scott of favoring the elite from West Point at the expense of the other career soldiers. Samuel Henry Starr had enlisted as a private and won promotion to Sergeant of the G Company, 4th Art., October 26, 1837; then had transferred to Co. A, Engineers, on June 23, 1846. In spite of his pessimistic forecast, he did become a 2d Lt., July 13, 1848, a 1st Lt. in 1851, a Captain in 1858, and retired with the rank of Colonel in 1870. He received three brevets during the Civil War.

I have given up the idea of winning that *Sword* as I deem it impossible, for although I should, unaided and alone *surround* the whole Mexican Army and take them all prisoners of war, Santa Anna included, it would not be deemed a deed worthy of remark, being done as it would be, by a man not a graduate of West Point. Much dissatisfaction is the consequence of the taking of Vera Cruz. Many like myself think their efforts worth a passing remark who have not been remembered by the Com[mander] in Chief, he wishing perhaps, to gather all the laurels for his own front that he may ride upon the backs of the gulled citizens into the Presidential chair.[69]

Ten New Regiments of Regulars

Grave as other problems might be, the most serious one was that of numbers. It was obvious, late in 1846, that something must be done to recruit the strength of the regular army. For, in spite of vigorous recruiting measures, such as lowering physical requirements and paying $2.00 per head to those who brought in acceptable recruits, the results were unsatisfactory.[70] In December, the Secretary of War admitted in his annual report that the regular army was 7,000 below its authorized strength.[71] To an economy-minded Congress, however, it still seemed more desirable to call upon the States for more volunteer regiments which could be quickly demobilized once the war was over.[72] When the President asked for ten additional regiments of regulars, political motives immediately clouded the debate. One Whig wrote: "whole regiments will be filled with Polk democrats."[73] After much indecision, especially in the Senate, Congress finally passed the so-called Ten Regiment Bill on February 11, 1847. This authorized ten new regiments of regulars to serve for the duration of the war, but no longer.[74] Each recruit was promised one hundred acres of public land if he received an honorable discharge. Since few regular officers would be willing to sacrifice their careers by transfer to a regiment which would disappear at war's end, the ten regiments were often commanded by less efficient appointees.[75] Some of them were "very young men, and men of very little general information."[76] Others were, in the parlance of a later war, "retreads" who had served in the regular army and then resigned to enter civilian life, but who again were willing to accept commissions.

Although the recruits were "generally very good looking men,"[77] the experienced regulars contemptuously referred to them as "raw levies." In commenting upon the quality of the 3rd Dragoons, one of the ten new regiments, Col. William S. Harney, commanding the Cavalry Brigade, wrote to General Scott's adjutant:

The third Dragoons was placed under my command on the 10th day of July, at Puebla. The officers and men [were] all perfectly ignorant of every thing like military instruction and discipline. Since which time I have done my utmost to induce the officers to learn their duties and to instruct their men, but up to this time with little effect. The officers are nearly all gentlemen and the men are as fine material as any in the Army—but, the officers want a disposition to learn their duties, and they appear to possess no pride of profession and no pride in their Companies. Under these circumstances it will take a very long time to render either officers or men at all efficient.[78]

Raphael Semmes, then a lieutenant in the navy, but destined to become the commander of the Alabama in the Civil War, regarded the officers of a contingent of the "new regiments" as more skilled in political than in military maneuver:

General [Franklin] Pierce arrived [at Puebla] in command of two thousand five hundred men, including a detachment of three hundred marines, under [Lieutenant] Colonel [S. E.] Watson. These men, with the exception of the marines, all belonged to the ten new regiments, which had been authorized by Congress soon after the commencement of the war [sic, February 11, 1847]. Many of the officers of these corps were very *hard-looking citizens*, who, apparently, required much drilling and "breaking in," to be rendered serviceable. Their uniforms looked as though they had been made by the "tailor of the village" whence the appointed came; they sat their horses awkwardly, and wore their arms and spurs, like very clever country gentlemen, who might have figured, on a race course, or at an election, but who had evidently had but little acquaintance with barracks or battlefield. The most shameful disregard of the claims of the "old officers" had been practiced in filling up these new regiments, and a general disgust was the consequence—not that these officers expected civilians to be entirely excluded, but they thought themselves entitled to at least a share of the appointments. They forgot, for a moment, that they were not politicians, entitled to be conciliated and "sopped," but the patriotic defenders of their country, removed from the precincts of the ballot-box.[79]

Despite the many shortcomings of their "raw levies" the regulars did become a fighting force to admire. Long hours of drill and efficient organization produced troops, such as Worth's 2d Division which, by the time it had been through the Battle of Monterey, impressed even the volunteers. One of these was Capt. John R. Kenly, of Company E, Baltimore and Washington Battalion,[80] who wrote:

During the morning, I heard that General Worth's Division[81] would be ordered to turn the works on the west of the town [Monterey], and was about marching. I stepped over to its camp and saw it leave; the men were in excellent spirits, and that division of regular troops presented an appearance which will never be effaced from my mind. It was thoroughly military and soldierlike; they looked so clean, their arms and accoutrements in such beautiful order, that all my enthusiasm for soldiers was greatly gratified. The artillery battalion[82] especially attracted my attention; the red-legged infantry (as they were called from the broad red stripe running down the seams of their blue pantaloons) never on dress parade appeared to better advantage.[83]

PROFICIENCY OF THE REGULARS

Maj. Gen. Winfield Scott in a despatch to William L. Marcy, the Secretary of War, described the matter-of-fact efficiency of a regular army regiment as it performed the tasks of camp life, in sharp contrast to the careless, less proficient volunteers in his army:

A regiment of regulars, in 15 minutes from the evening halt, will have tents pitched & trenched around, besides straw, leaves or bushes for dry sleeping; arms & ammunition well secured & in order for any night attack; fires made, kettles boiling, in order to [have] wholesome cooking; all the men dried, or warmed, & at their comfortable supper, merry as crickets, before the end of the first hour. . . . Volunteers neglect all these points; eat their *salt* meat raw (if they have saved any at all) or, worse than raw, *fried*—death to any Christian man the fifth day; lose or waste their clothing; lie down wet, or on wet ground—fatal to health, &, in a short time to life; leave arms & ammunition exposed to rain, mud & dews; hence both generally useless & soon lost, & certainly hardly ever worth a cent in battle, &c., &c., &c. In a short time the ranks are thinned, the baggage wagons & hospitals filled with the sick, & acres of ground with the graves of the dead! . . . I mean *in the field* . . . the want of the touch of *the elbow* (which cannot be acquired with the best instructors in many months); the want of the sure step in advancing, falling back & wheeling; . . . the want of *military* confidence in each other, & above all, the want of reciprocal confidence between officers & men.[84]

CONTROVERSIAL VOLUNTEERS

The volunteers[85]—who with practically no training, little discipline and shaky organization, found themselves undergoing the privations and perils of war— were a storm center, assailed as "vile volunteers" by regulars and staunchly defended by their own officers. For a fair estimate of their services, their rowdiness, their frequent petulance, unwillingness to accept discipline, vagaries in appearance and other shortcomings should be balanced against the ennui of camp life, the horrors of ill-conceived marches, the diseases they were exposed to, the blunders of their commanders and their own courage on the battlefields.

In appearance they were a nondescript lot. The law of May 13, 1846, calling forth the volunteer regiments, specified that in clothing they need not be uniform with the other corps in the United States army. So instead of the blue jacket and trousers of privates in the regular army, dress varied from company to company, or from regiment to regiment.[86] The Baltimore Battalion[87] was fortunate enough to be attached to a regular army division, and proudly donned the regular blues. Others "had some curious looking uniforms and hats." One observer, an enlisted man who signed his name "DAN" in a letter to the Charleston Mercury, described the Palmetto Regiment of South Carolina on parade as "Ragamuffinism." He went on to say: "Imagine some seven hundred men, composing ten companies, each company with the exception of the Charleston and Richland, adorned with red, blue, green, check, and white, shirts over their unmentionables, Kilmarnock caps, or white cotton skull hats, of the old Grimes cut, protecting their seats of knowledge from the pelting of the pitiless storm; while their lower extremities are encased in every variety of boot, shoe and stocking!"[88] The "Hunters of Kentucky"[89] tried for the picturesque in dress as well as name:

The cavalry regiment of Col. Humphrey Marshall, mustering 1,000 strong, are represented as a body of martial men. They are generally athletic men, riding splendid horses, and their picturesque dress imparts to them a romantic appearance. The hat particularly is very fanciful. It is a drab beaver with a broad brim, ornamented with several gold stars, and looped up with gold lace in the three cornered fashion of the Revolution. They all wear their beards unshorn with boots over the legs of their trousers, reaching above the knee, armed with huge spurs on the heel and faced with red morocco.[90]

Perhaps the most striking of all the volunteers in appearance were those commanded by Col. Alexander W. Doniphan.[91] An awestruck young observer, who had recently arrived in New Orleans, described them as they appeared at the end of an odyssey that had taken them from Missouri to Santa Fe, down the Rio Grande valley to El Paso, then to Chihuahua, to Saltillo, Matamoros and finally to New Orleans.

The greatest attraction in the city at present is Col. Doniphan and his Regiment of Missouri Volunteers, who are called "Lions" here, but in my opinion they look more like Rocky Mountain Bears than New Orleans or any

The Volunteer

other sort of "*Lions*" that I have ever seen. Col. Doniphan looks like a "host" himself. He is six feet four inches high—weighs about two hundred and forty to sixty pounds—raw-boned—has fingers about nine inches long—feet in proportion—his hair is sort of sandy red and sticks out something like Porcupine quills, and his men say that he is not afraid of the Devil or the God that made him. His men, a great many of them, look more like giants than men, being from six feet to six feet four inches and a half in height. If you can imagine a man about six feet two to four and a half inches high, and well proportioned, with a deer skin (hair on) hunting shirt and pantaloons, the seams fringed with the same material cut into strings, and a bear skin stretched over his face with nothing but eyeholes cut in it, you can see a large portion of Doniphan's Regiment. They are swaggering about the verandah and St. Charles with an air of the most perfect *non chalance* of any set of fellows you ever saw.[92]

Raw Volunteers at their Rendezvous

A war bill rushed through Congress and enacted into law on May 13, 1846 gave President Polk authority to use the army, navy and militia forces against Mexico, and called for "not more than 50,000 volunteers." Brig. Gen. John E. Wool,[93] who had won fame at the Battle of Plattsburg in the War of 1812, was assigned to a general supervision of the various points of rendezvous in the Mississippi Valley to which thousands of volunteers flocked—at Alton (Illinois), Cincinnati, Louisville, and other hastily organized reception centers. In a report to Secretary of War Marcy, written at the end of the first week in June, Wool revealed much of the hectic, unplanned assembling of the volunteers as they crowded into the rendezvous camps:

About one thousand volunteers called for from the State of Ohio are now assembled at this place [Cincinnati], and some five or six hundred men are expected in the course of this week. The whole quota called for will probably be concentrated in the course of ten days. The most of the Volunteers now here, and expected, although not perfectly organized into companies as required, have been, by order of the Governor of the State, mustered into the service of the United States. It appears in raising the companies the men as they were enlisted took the *required oath*, &, when the company was completed as to numbers, without reference to its organisation, was considered mustered into the service of the United States. When all are concentrated, the Governor will organise them into Regiments, and turn them over to myself, for the United States. Such is the present state of the Volunteers of Ohio. It will probably exceed two weeks before the whole will be organised into Regiments and ready to be received into the Service. . . .

The three Regiments required from Kentucky, will, it is reported, assemble at Louisville to-morrow, and will be inspected and mustered into the service by Colonel Croghan.[94] Immediately after which, he will be sent to Memphis to inspect and muster into the service the troops of Tennessee, where, it is reported, the three Regiments will assemble.

After inspecting the troops at that place, Colonel Croghan will proceed and muster the Mississippi Regiment to be assembled at Vicksburg. Colonel

Churchill has been sent to inspect and muster into the service the troops of Indiana and Illinois. Quarter Masters and Commissaries of Subsistence have been sent to all the rendezvous of the different states to supply the Volunteers as they arrive at the rendezvous with subsistence and Quarter Master stores.

Colonel Yell,[95] on his way to Arkansas, called on me this morning. He said the President had directed him to call on me for instructions in regard to the movement of his Regiment. I told him my instructions did not extend to his Regiment, and that I presumed he would receive instructions direct from Washington. I, however, told him he had better get his Regiment prepared to march as soon as he could. In the mean time I would write to Washington on the subject.

I have written to the Adjutant General and informed him of the conversation I had with Colonel Yell.

I shall leave for Louisville to-morrow afternoon, and for such other places beyond as I may find my presence necessary when I reach there, taking care to return to Cincinnati in time to receive the Ohio Regiment. . . .

P.S. I have heard nothing from Lt. Colonel Talcott[96] on the subject of arms & equipments to be furnished the Volunteers. They ought to be sent to the several rendezvous as soon as practicable. Most of the Volunteers are anxious to go to Mexico.[97]

The volunteers fell short of the perfect image of a military man. Samuel Ryan Curtis, serving as adjutant to the governor of Ohio was dismayed, if not discouraged, when he greeted raw recruits at Columbus:

Such a gathering of awkward boys you never saw mixed—mixed up together. . . . You ought to see them when the first order was given—"right face"! You have seen little Henry perform under my command. Well he is a veteran soldier compared to some of these. I hope you won't show this to any one. Our "Ohio volunteers" would regard it as reproachful. They ought not to be offended at it. No doubt they are as expert as I was, when I first took post at West Point. It must have [been] a laughing sight for the old Cadets. I remember the time well. It was on the east side of the North Barracks and I stood so straight my back bowed in more than 9 inches, no doubt of it.[98]

A "German eye" view of the recruits was recorded by Alexander Konze (also spelled Conze),[99] a German immigrant and well-known writer for the German-language press in Milwaukee who volunteered, then reported to a typical rendezvous. His view of his brothers-in-arms was on the whole benevolent but he could not help contrasting the disorder and sloppiness of the

American citizen-soldiers with the neatness and discipline of German mili-
tary life. But he did not despair. Some of the Americans were growing beards.

As you know, Alton is the concentration camp for the Illinois volunteers,
and believe me, the spot is not badly chosen. Easily accessible by the water-
ways of the Mississippi and the Illinois, in close proximity to a large city like
St. Louis, and beautifully located, all these factors render it an excellent
gathering-place. About thirty companies have arrived thus far, and the Baker
Regiment[100] of Springfield is being expected to-day. Several divisions are
quartered in the town itself, the great majority of the soldiers, however, have
gone into camp about a mile out of Alton.

Life within and without the town [Alton] has plenty of liveliness and activity, yet nevertheless one finds in this place where thousands of young, and
for the most part uneducated, fellows have been confined to a relatively small
area, none of those excesses and debaucheries which make a camp of European
troops so disagreeable to the spectator. Discipline is enforced very mildly, and
yet the customs of the people accomplish greater things here than do laws
and strict regulations elsewhere. It is the blessing of a free Constitution that
under it man learns how to govern himself, and does not grow accustomed
to look up to a man higher up who will subdue his passions through slavish
fear. Regarded from the purely militaristic standpoint, the prospect would of
course look less bright. My brothers-in-arms are thus far, at least, no experts in
the art of dealing with weapons, and their uniforms mere makeshifts. Colonels
wandering about in shabby frocks [sic, schnipel] and in very inadequate
trousers of a color no longer distinguishable are no longer a novel sight; many
a captain is commanding his company with drawn walking stick, indeed, I
even saw one with his shirt-sleeves rolled up leading his men into the presence
of the colonel. The officers to whom blind Fortune has granted a sabre the
least bit respectable seem to be well conscious of this advantage; for they do
not tire in bending its blade, testing its edge, and in making comparisons. How
provincial some of these war-lords look and act only the actual spectator can
determine. But there are officers and whole companies who already have a
fairly martial air, and on the whole, the physiques of the soldiers are powerful
and strong. I sometimes feel myself humiliated, as it were, when some backwoodsman seven feet tall strides by me; but I take consolation from the
thought that on the battle-field the advantage will be on my side.

The uniforms, which differ with every company, consist of short jackets or
coats, usually blue or gray with red or yellow facings. The cloth is light sum-
mer-goods, rarely broadcloth. I have seen practically nothing but muskets used
as arms; a few companies are fitted out with fairly long rifles and daggers that
would not look out of place in a museum of curiosities. To every six men there
is a tent which looks very pretty at a distance, but which could gain a great

deal in attractiveness if were roomier and cooler. The hill where the tents have been pitched is covered with beautiful oak-trees, so that there is no lack of shade. The whole encampment presents a picture that would be a welcome subject for the brush of a painter, provided that the artist were not a lover of music. For then the heart- and ear-rending notes coming from the drums and flutes played by unpracticed hands and lips would soon drive him away from his pleasant work.

The destination of the Illinois troops, as far as is known at present, is to be the Rio Grande, and Senator Semple[101] is expected in a few days to take charge of the brigade. The company to which I have the honor of belonging is the first of Belleville, St. Claire County, called the Texan Guards. Among its 94 members there are only 19 Americans, the rest being Germans. Among the officers, only the first lieutenant is a native. Since our former Captain Morrison has been appointed major, the captaincy is filled by Julius Raith, likewise a German, so that the heroic deeds which the Texan Guards are determined to carry out will redound to the honor of the German name, and to the humiliation of the natives. Among the members of the company there are splendid and highly educated persons, whom Major Morrison[102] characterized pretty well, when he said to me, "They sit upon a log and talk metaphysics." In closing I wish to tell you about one fact which seems to me to be of no small moment in its historical significance—the Americans are beginning to grow mustaches, and some of them already have pretty good specimens. I welcome this phenomenon as a sign of the decline of that rigid puritanism which is the curse of our adopted fatherland. My heartiest greetings to the Milwaukeeites.[103]

LACK OF DISCIPLINE AMONG VOLUNTEERS

In general, opinions as to the conduct of the volunteers varied, but there was agreement that they lacked discipline. This probably was inevitable in a "citizen's army" raised during a period when rugged individualism was a fact rather than a nostalgic and somewhat worn political slogan. One officer pointed out that many of the recruits in the Baltimore Battalion "had been sailors, others members of fire-companies, fishing clubs, etc., and they were a wild, frolicsome, reckless set, full of fun and hard to keep in camp. . . ."[104] A "free American" was not transformed into a disciplined soldier by the act of enlistment. They might ". . . fight like tigers to sea [sic] the stars and stripes wave upon the walls of Mexico. . . ."[105] But when there was no fighting to do they were impatient of restraint.

Even before they left their points of rendezvous, tales of "their lawless propensities" appeared in Cincinnati and Louisville newspapers, from which they were reprinted in stories like this one from Niles' National Register:

Camp Washington [Cincinnati]. We are glad to learn there is a prospect of one or two regiments of the volunteers getting off this week. The sooner they are removed the better. A state of things has existed at the camp for the last few days which is highly disgraceful to all concerned. On Sunday a spirit of insubordination (aided by the spirit of alcohol) existed which no friend of law and order desires to be repeated. The troops had been paid during the morning, two months' wages in advance, and there appeared to be no lack of means about the camp whereby they could spend their money.

We are sorry to note a riotous and rowdy disposition manifested by the citizen soldiery volunteered into service. The corps at Louisville have had several rows of disgraceful character, in which knives, pistols, and other southern chivalries were put in requisition. Mr. Marshall,[106] late a[n] M.C., came very near losing his life in attempting to prevent one of these outrages upon the citizens.

The Louisville *Journal* of June 29 says—"There was another disgraceful row between some of the volunteers and citizens about dusk last evening, on Green street. We learn that a man named Davis was so seriously beaten by the volunteers that his life is despaired of. The police were promptly on the spot, and the citizens gathered in large numbers, highly incensed at the volunteers. Pierce Butler, esq.,[107] and Colonel McKee[108] addressed the crowd, after which they dispersed. One of the volunteers, the principal actor in the scene, was put in jail."[109]

SELECTION OF VOLUNTEER OFFICERS

A sense of equality, absent in the regular army, contributed to the problem of discipline. Officers were superior in rank but not superior in fact. This sentiment was augmented by the fact that through the regimental level they might, according to state laws, be elected by the men themselves, and if there was a hint that the men's privilege was to be nullified by political maneuvering, protest was likely to follow.

The St. Louis Republican complained when a former member of Congress, Sterling Price, organized a regiment in Missouri, and was accused of forcing his own election as Colonel by the intimation that the regiment should be disbanded if the result did not favor him. There was political rancor in this,[110] but officers of three Illinois regiments also discovered that the Polk administration and members of Congress considered military commissions to be synonymous with patronage favors. The St. Louis newspaper reported the experience of the Illinois regiments as follows:

We learn that a full meeting of the officers of the three Regiments of Illinois volunteers remaining at Alton, was held on Sunday evening, at which the subject of appointments connected with the Illinois volunteers was considered. A formal protest was signed and forwarded to the President against the appointment of such officers on the recommendation of members of Congress, and a list of men whom they desired to fill those offices was, at the same time, made and forwarded. We apprehend that this has been in the main, labor lost, as the long list of nominations and confirmations which we publish to-day shows that both members of Congress and the President have been before-hand with them. Nearly all these offices have been filled.[111]

The election of officers sometimes resulted in hard feelings and cries of fraud not unlike those raised by the losers in civil elections. For example, in the 2d Indiana Regiment of Volunteers, Col. Joseph Lane, who first commanded, was promoted to Brigadier General and assigned control of the Indiana Brigade. An election was held at Camp Whitcomb near New Albany in which Capt. W. L. Sanderson of the Spencer Grays received the highest vote, but Capt. Walker's company, because its clerk failed to make out a return, did not have its vote counted. Capt. William A. Bowles was declared Colonel, but three companies refused to sign certificates of election, and his commission was withheld. Later, another election was held after the regiment had reached Mexico (Brazos Santiago) and Bowles was elected, but he could not take command until he received his commission.[112] An election incident which probably was unique in its consequences was the "revolt" of a company from Covington County, Mississippi. When the election of a first lieutenant of the regiment went against them they abandoned the army and went home, only to be sent back by another fund raised by citizens of their county. General Scott allowed them to remain as "amateurs" who were more or less on their own. It was a novel solution and the company became known as the "do as they please" company. The story was told by Kenneth McKenzie, a Mississippian and one of the "Covington County boys" who joined in the revolt but did not go to Mexico with the company. This account was written in a letter to Duncan McLaurin of North Carolina:

You did not know how our Volunteers got into the service for less time than twelve months or during the war. I think I can clear up that matter. I shall give you a detail from the beginning of our body. We met several times in our own county [and] made as many as we could, then we went to the county seat of Laurence, Monticello [and] made a few. We rec'd. information of 30 men being in readiness to join us at Gallman the county seat of Copiah, there we filled out the company. By express order of Gov. Brown we were ordered to march to Jackson without any officer, where we were to go into an Election of officers. We elected Adjt. Gen. Ben[jami]n C. Buckly, Capt. by aclamation the Cov[ington] co[unty] boys claimed the 1rst Lieut.'s place but by fraud we were choused out, we revolted and broke the company, fraud practiced by the dignity [sic dignitary] of a high minded aristocratic democratic state, Gov. Brown. I was an eyewitness to his fraudulent partiality. The Gov. was told of it plentifully. We all came home dissatisfied. There was several thousand dollars raised in the county for the benefit of the Cov[ingto]n volunteers of which the before mentioned boys accepted. I was for going but my constitution being known to all my friends, father and mother particularly.* The boys are on their own hook but were recd. by Gen. Scott for any length of time as do as they pleas fellows, and when they want to quit they come to New Orleans at the expense of the Government.[113] I am not with them in boddy, but in spirrit and tell you, I have a silent tear in lifes locality in sympathy for their sufferings and a broken cord within my heart for those they leave behind.[114]

A postscript to the incident was written by Kenneth McKenzie's brother, Daniel C. McKenzie, then in Mexico:

After I wrote to you from Tampico, Gen. Scott arrived there on application to whom we were permitted to enter any portion of the Volunteer Army as Amateurs for any length of time we chose with the chance of drawing rations as others, with all the privileges of non-commissioned officers i.e. we could buy anything in the Quartermasters department in the way of food which is not allowed privates. We paid our transportation, received no pay, did no soldiers duties except fight when we saw the enemy. . . . I was in but one fight while I staid in Mexico that at Vera Cruz and that a skirmish, tho a pretty hard business I would call it. 16 Georgians and 7 of us contended against 2 Reg[i]m[en]ts of the tawny creatures commanded by Gen. [Juan] Morales.[115]

EVALUATION OF VOLUNTEERS AS SOLDIERS

Characteristic of the conflicting verdicts rendered on the volunteers were those of Lt. Thomas Williams, 4th Artillery, and Maj. Luther Giddings of the Ohio Volunteers. Williams adjudged them totally without merit:

The army is in good heart & anxious to go ahead. Some of the volunteers, however, don't know the butt from the muzzle of a musket, but the regulars will take care of them. If the brave volunteers should all run at the first fire, they will nevertheless come out heroes. Such paltry matters as reputation are all arranged by the letter writers now-adays.

* Thus in text.

It is a notorious fact with the army here, that the Baltimore Volunteers, who have been lauded & received the thanks of the legislature of Maryland for their conduct at Monterey—could scarcely be brought into action—the majority skulked off & left the body of their Colonel behind. Depend upon it, Militia won't do. How should they—they want *everything* that constitutes the soldier. Surely no sensible civilian can believe that the *coat* makes the man.

This is the vulgar idea though. And demagogues propagate it to get votes. If the country dont stop sending out volunteers our debt will soon be swelled to that of Gr. Britain. They are useless, useless, useless,—expensive, wasteful—good for nothing.[116]

THE TEXAS RANGERS

Maj. Luther Giddings of the 1st Ohio Volunteers saw the volunteers, especially the Texas Rangers, in a far different light. In a book published five years after the end of the war he wrote:

The volunteer army . . . was composed chiefly of young men who had just attained the age at which the enthusiasm of youth and vigor of manhood are united. The "Young Guard" of Napoleon did not contain in its ranks more energy, valor, and daring than was to be found in that youthful mass. There were soldiers in various regiments whom I had known when "we were boys together," who contemplated the prospect of an arduous campaign with more pleasure than they ever did a recitation in Thucydides or Juvenal. To many of them, a battery was a more agreeable object than a black-board, and I am convinced that some of my old schoolmates would have assaulted a bristling *tete de pont* with more alacrity than they had aforetime evinced in demonstrating the *pons asinorum*.

Many adventurous spirits who had failed to obtain desirable places in the Infantry and who were determined to participate in the war even as privates, attracted by the loose discipline and hazardous service of the Texan Cavalry, had become Rangers. There were two regiments of Texan troops with the army, commanded by Colonels Hays[117] and Wood,[118] comprising the brigade of General Henderson.[119] Their knowledge of the character of the enemy and of the military frontier acquired in their long border struggle rendered them valuable auxiliaries in the invasion. . . . The character of the Texan Ranger is now well known by both friend and foe. As a mounted soldier he has had no counterpart in any age or country. Neither Cavalier nor Cossack, Mameluke nor Mosstrooper are like him; and yet, in some respects, he resembles them all.[120]

Of all the volunteers the Rangers were the most controversial, but there was general agreement that they were unkempt, undisciplined, brutal towards

PLATE I. *Volunteers for Texas*

PLATE II. *Bird's-eye View of the Camp of the Army of Occupation near Corpus Christi, Oct. 1845*

*the Mexicans, devastating as guerrillas and invaluable as scouts. Brantz Mayer
in his* History of the War Between Mexico and the United States, *published
in 1848, described the mounted Texans:*

TEXAN RANGERS, . . . were the bold and reckless children of the
frontier who lived forever in warlike harness prompt to suppress the savage
raids of the Indians and mongrel Mexicans who harassed the settlements of
western Texas in the neighborhood of the Guadalupe, La Vaca and San
Antonio. Organizing themselves in regular companies for mutual protection
along a ravaged border, they were continually prepared alike for camp or
battle, and opposed themselves to the enemy at the outpost barriers of
civilization.

It must not be supposed that men whose life is passed in the forest, on the
saddle, or around the fire of a winter bivouac, can present the gallant array
of troopers on parade, hence the Texan Ranger is careless of external appearance, and adapts his dress strictly to the wants of useful service. His first care
is to provide himself with a stalwart and nimble horse, perfectly broken and
capable of enduring fatigue in a southern climate. His Spanish saddle, or saddle frame, is carefully covered with the skins of wild animals, while, from its
sides depend some twenty or thirty leatheren thongs to which are attached all
the various trappings needed in the woods. No baggage is permitted to accompany the troop and encumber it in the wilderness. A braided *lariat* and a
cabaros of horse-hair are coiled around his saddle-bow, the latter to be un-
wound at nightfall and laid in circles on the ground to prevent the approach
of reptiles which glide off from the sleeper when they touch the bristling hair
of the instrument, while his horse, tethered by the long and pliant *lariat*
trailing along the ground, wanders but little from the spot where his master
reposes.

Stout buckskin leggings, hunting shirt, and cap, protect the ranger's body
from the sharp spines of aloes, or the briars and branches of the matted forest.
His weapons, next to his horse, exact his attention. His long and heavy rifle
carries from fifty to sixty bullets to the pound; around his waist is belted a
bowie knife or home made hanger, and sometimes a brace of revolving pistols
is added to this powerful armory. Across his right side are slung his pouch of
balls and powder-horn, and the strap by which they are suspended is widened
or padded over the shoulder to relieve the weight and pres[s]ure of his gun. A
practised shot, he can hit his mark unerringly in full career. He may be called
a "picked man," though not in the sense of the phrase as ordinarily used in
military affairs. Nevertheless he is a choice soldier, for none but men of equal
stamp and hardihood find their way to the border and congregate naturally for
the hazardous life they endure.[121]

Virtues and Defects of the Volunteers

S. Compton Smith was a surgeon[122] with General Taylor's army in Mexico. After the war he delivered a balanced judgment on the virtues and defects of army volunteers, including the Rangers:

The first volunteer forces, which, in obedience to the requisitions on the different States, hastened to the reënforcement of General Taylor, were made up of altogether different materials from those troops who were sent to the country towards the close of the war.

The first were impelled by generous and not mercenary motives. They were the culled men of the country; and were mostly young men,—the majority of them from the best ranks of society—men of education and refinement. Gentlemen were as often found in the ranks with musket or rifle on shoulder as amongst the officers; and not unfrequently was it the case that the private on duty as sentinel saluted his commanding officer, whom he would scarcely have recognized at home. They were brave, proud-spirited fellows, with just vanity enough to feel that all the eyes and hopes of the country were fixed upon them. And each individual had a due sense of his responsibility to his country, and counted himself, and justly so, a host in himself. Such were the rifle regiments of Texas and Mississippi, the infantry and rifle regiments of Louisiana from the South, and the forces raised in the States of Kentucky, Tennessee, Illinois, Indiana, and Ohio from the North. It is also true that many other volunteer regiments who arrived in the country soon after the taking of Monterey were made up of good materials; and, in the majority, were well officered.

Of all the southern volunteers of General Taylor's division, the Mississippians and Texas Rangers most distinguished themselves. They were in all the battles of that line, after those of Palo Alto and Resaca de la Palma. At Monterey and Buena Vista, these gallant troops were cruelly cut up. Hardly one-tenth of the members of those veteran regiments were returned to their homes, and those with shattered constitutions. The first Rangers from Texas, of whom I have already spoken, were the genuine, brave, and hardy pioneers of that young and rising State. They were the men of Goliad and San Jacinto—men whose greatest sport was an open prairie-fight with the untamable Camanches. They had measured arms with the Mexicans, and had a just appreciation of them. They knew their weakness, and how to take advantage of it.

But some of the so-called Texas Rangers who came into the country at a later period were mostly made up of adventurers and vagabonds whose whole object was plunder. Like Falstaff's ragamuffins, they were—"such as, indeed, were never soldiers; but discarded, unjust serving-men,—younger sons to youngest brothers;—revolted tapsters, and hostlers trade-fallen;—ten times more dishonorable and ragged than an old-faced ancient!"

The gang of miscreants under the leadership of "Mustang Grey"[123] were of this description. This party, in cold bood, murdered almost the entire male population of the rancho of Guadalupe—where not a single weapon, offensive or defensive, could be found! Their only object being plunder.[124]

Roads to War

When the army—regulars and volunteers, officers and privates, heroes and scoundrels—was assembled it had to be moved to the theater of war. The troops went chiefly by water down the rivers to the Gulf, or directly from the eastern ports by sea to Brazos Santiago, Tampico, and Vera Cruz. Some traveled by land across Texas or down the Santa Fe Trail to New Mexico and thence across the deserts to the Pacific; others took the long sea route around Cape Horn to California.

Occasionally experiences on the way were singular: "We caught 2 sharks as we came over the gulf & after chopping their flesh up like beef steak & seasoning it well, I never ate better flesh of any kind."[125] Other incidents, though natural enough in themselves, were somewhat curious for an army: "I wrote you at New Orleans that we should reach Aransas on the fourteenth. . . the first night we were on the Gulf I was informed that Mrs. Roth (a camp woman of my company) was sick. Poor thing! I gave her my stateroom, and by morning she was delivered of a son. This was the second birth on the route. The Mothers are now both well, and doing their regular washing for the men."[126]

Shark steaks and newborn babes were exceptional. More characteristic was the voyage down the rivers to New Orleans. It was no pleasure cruise, but for the curious, the river and the life on its banks were sources of lively interest. Of course there was some dissatisfaction, generally because of conflict between the officers and privates. Each had grievances against the other and each was no doubt justified to some degree. The source of irritation was more in the system than in the soldier.

On arriving in New Orleans, near the end of the river road, the troops were encamped below the city until they could be loaded on seagoing vessels that would carry them to Tampico, Vera Cruz or the Texas gulf ports. Discord tended to increase during the layover. The reason was uncomplicated: the men wanted to go to town, the officers restricted the privilege. There were some complaints about camp conditions, but these were minor—the lure of the city was the chief grievance.

Capt. John W. Lowe of Company C, Fifth Regiment of Ohio Volunteers,[127] set forth the trials of an officer on a riverboat loaded with soldiers. Company

C struck tents and went aboard the steamer Trenton *on September 22, 1847.*
His letter was written September 26; he had been en route only four days.

. . . The Boys are very careless of themselves and are therefore suffering
very severely from their imprudence; this morning I have 12 men on the sick
list, principally fever and ague & dysentary, nothing as yet very serious; we are
yet above Memphis, Tennessee, and I fear we may get worse as we go South,
yet I hope for the best. We have not had one word of news about the negotiations for peace since I left you a[t] Cincinnati, so I cannot indulge in any
speculations as to when we will get back.

. . . My duties are very complicated, very trying to my patience and occupying all my time. You may imagine faintly what I have to endure by re-
membering that I have 80 wild, thoughtless, careless boys to look after with
as much care as you would look after the members of your family. I have
been seated in my stateroom about ¾ of an hour writing this letter and have
had at least 15 if not 20 calls on me of this character. First Bill Davis came
with "Captain, I want my shaving tools. I lent them to Lieut. Howard[128] and
he can't find them." I send him off, and here come[s] another "Captain, Robt.
Townsley is shaking with the ague, will you please give an order for a state
room for him." Well, that is attended to and here comes another, "Captain,
Turner has had no breakfast this morning and wants some thing to eat." This
case is attended to but here comes George Croshaw "Captain, will you please
give me a sheet of paper I want to write home." "Certainly, George, here it is,
but what do you want Ritchey?" "W[ell?], Captain I am almost dead with
the tooth ach[e], will you [plea]se request the Doctor to pull it?" "Certainly
John, there is the Dr., he will fix it." "What do you want Wilson?" "Why
Captain, somebody has stolen my cup and plate." "Well, my dear fellow I
cannot help that, you must take care of yourself." "Well, Blair, what do you
want?" "Why, Captain, the Mississippi water don't agree with me—I am
afraid I am going to be sick!" "Go get a tumbler of water & we'll give you
some paregoric." Well, [that is do?]ne and my door is closed and I take my
pen again to [wri]te when here comes a knock. "Walk in—what's the matter?"
"Why, Captain, I want to borrow a couple of dollars of you to buy socks
when we get to Memphis." "You do? Have you no socks?" "No Sir." "Didn't
I pay you $8 at Cincinnati to get cl[othes?]?" "Yes, but I bought a *pair of*
pistols with my money."

Thus it goes on from day to day. I bear it like a phi[los]opher because it
keeps me from thinking about home; but when I desire to be alone for
meditation it is somewhat annoying. The boys are very rude but not as
troublesome as was expected. There is one matter on which I desire you to be
guarded—it is this: before we left Cincinnati I bought a small burning brand
to mark my name on our tent's poles, axe handles, boxes &c; the brand is just

J. W. Lowe. The boys got it in my absence and branded their carpet bags (the leather parts), the fronts of their caps, the handles of their bowie knives, &c., &c., so if any reports should reach you that anyone is killed, with any thing marked with my name, don't conclude that it is your husband, but merely that they belonged to my Company. This may save you some pain.[129]

Vexations En Route

Captain Lowe had written in vexation at the irresponsible conduct of his charges. Alexander Konze, a German volunteer from Wisconsin, speaking for the privates, was more than vexed; he was angry and contemptuous:

Our trip down the Mississippi came off fairly rapidly and successfully, although we did have to contend with all sorts of hardships. The narrow space to which we were confined, the heat reigning in most parts of the boat, the warm river water which we had to drink to quench our thirst, and above all the disgraceful conduct particularly of the higher officers toward their subordinates, made the journey not a very pleasant one. Our worthy superiors, who but recently possessed a knowledge of military science as limited as could be expected from an honest Philistine, seemed at least to have fixed the idea into their heads that the common soldier is a being far below them, whose woe or weal does not merit any particular attention. These gentlemen, raised to their positions by the votes of the soldiers, enjoyed life in their saloon, while their fellow-citizens and comrades were subjected to all the disagreeable conditions of a steerage. Allow me to state a specific instance which will describe a little more closely the spirit that had taken possession of our superiors.

On the steamers it was strictly prohibited for the privates to take any spirituous liquors whatever at the bar, while the officers drank to their hearts' content, although they were not in need of stimulant or of refreshment as much as we were. The only thing which their graces allowed us to drink was lemonade, i.e. ice-water made sour with the slices of lemon that the officers in their cabin had used in their lemonade. And for this disgusting drink the poor soldier had to pay 10 cents per glass, the same price that the officer was paying for the best claret punch or Madeira. That my dreams of a Republican army soon dissolved amid these circumstances, you may imagine, but the ever-changing scenes round about me and my intercourse with some of my excellent countrymen alleviated my disappointment somewhat. In New Orleans we poor fellows recovered again from the hardships of our Mississippi trip. The delightful southern fruits, the fiery wines, the delicious oysters, how good they tasted to the palate accustomed to pork!

We encamped about four miles from the city upon the battle-field where

Packenham [sic][130] fell with his brave fellows, and our commander, General Wool,[131] to protect the flower of the youth of Illinois from the dangers of a lively sea-port town, had commanded that none of the volunteers were to leave camp, and in one of his orders he pompously announced that the time of picnics had now ceased, and that the serious life of the warrior was beginning. We took the warning of old excellency so much to heart that many of us were to be found spending more time in the city than in the camp, and the officers, forced by a bread and coffee famine, and themselves eager for the flesh-pots of New Orleans, could and would not enforce obedience. After a sojourn of several days, and after we had succeeded in placing the first laurels round our temples by killing an alligator who had been bold enough to cause us uneasiness in the midst of our tents, we boarded several steamers and sailing-vessels and sailed for La Bacca, [sic, LaVaca].[132]

A Private's Journey to War

John Kreitzer, a private in the 1st Pennsylvania Regiment of Volunteers (Infantry), departed with that regiment from the Broad Street station in Philadelphia on December 9. His diary[133] was perhaps too idyllic, but it is a record of what was certainly one of the more pleasant journeys to the battlefields—across Pennsylvania by railroad coach and canal boat, then down the Ohio River and the Mississippi to New Orleans.

Wednesday, December 9th 1846

. . . At 8 o'clock the cars started and the crowd sent forth Huzza after huzza and was heartily responded to by our party. The cars now increased in speed and the city of brotherly love was no more to be seen. Nothing of importance occurred along the road except that w[h]erever the cars stopped the people had their stores closed and so were the taverns. Owing to the first detachment and especially the Rowdy Gang known as the Killers whose behavior was any thing but that of a soldiers, we arrived at Lancaster at 2 O'clock and were met there by Fathcr [illeg. word] Wilt who accompanied us untill we arrived at Harrisburgh which was at 7 o'clock. We were escorted to the armory of the Harrisburg Rifle Co. w[h]ere we partook of a colation served up by the citizens. After doing Justice to the table and ourselves we were formed and marched to the Basin where the canal boats were. But owing to some difficulties which transpired about the arrangements, we were again marched to the armory w[h]ere we for the first time took a soldier's bed on the floor. But there was very little sleeping done by our fellows for they got up and promenaded the streets of Harrisburg all night singing & cutting [up] at a great rate. Eurich, Ahl, Danner & myself got a bed of the landlord and took a good sleep.

Thursday, December 10th 1846

. . . We left Harrisburg just as daylight was dawning. On our journey we passed the towns [sic] of Greensburg[134] and arrived at Clark's Ferry w[h]ere we had to pull the boat across the river by a rope and it was snowing as hard as ever I seen it. . . . Today it has been very cold, snowing very hard, and I find the people very friendly up in those cold regions and would have been more so had it not been for the outrages committed by the Killers all along the Canal. The people say that they came and took just what they wanted from their stores without paying, and if they spoke of their rights they threatened their lives.

Friday, December 11th 1846

This morning at daylight we arrived at the borough of Lewistown. We were formed in double file and marched to the Public House of Mr. Isenbise w[h]ere we had the best meals, victuals, that I ever had. After Breakfast . . . was over we gave three cheers for the citizens of Lewistown and three for our landlord. It was returned by the citizens that made the little borough echo. We then left for the boat and when the boat moved off, cheer after cheer rent the air untill a curve in the canal hid Lewistown and its inhabitants from our view. . . . Today one of our company fell into the canal, and it was very cold which made poor Henry shiver like leaves.

Saturday, December 12th 1846

. . . To day although snowing, blowing and very cold I could not stay in the Boat for the river was full of wild ducks and those were strange sights to me as well as the lofty peaks of the Blue Mountain and Jack's Mountain which were capped with snow. On our passage to day another boat with Capt. Moorehead's [sic][135] company aboard came along side and tried to pass us; so our fellows got out fastened two other ropes to the boat and pulled untill we left them out of sight—they doing the same.

. . . . .

Friday, December 18th 1846

This morning all our fellows were up by daylight preparing for the Election to day. Every man is going to do his duty to day in trying to elect our Capt. to the rank of Colonel if we can possibly do it. If not, we are willing to submit to the majority. At six O'clock the election opened and fighting was the order of the day. Our fellows fought like dogs if any one said ought against the Captain. It was kept up by the party's concerned the whole day. In the evening when the polls closed every thing appeared favourable for the election of Capt. Small.[136] That was the opinion of the majority of the officers.

But to our disappointment when the returns were read off it resulted in the choise [sic] of F[rancis]. M. Wincoop [sic, Wynkoop],[137] S[amuel]. W. Black, Left. Col. and J. W. [sic, Francis L.] Bowman for Major. The evening was spent by all the fellows in drinking, fighting, and c[a]rousing around the city much to their disgrace.

. . . . .

Sunday, December 20th 1846

This morning we formed and proceeded to the Presbyterian church and there listened to an excelent sermon. The greatest decorum prevailed among the soldiers. . . .

Monday, December 21st 1846

This morning we were up at an early hour. All hands were busy in packing up their knap sacks, for our departure from [Pittsburgh] at ten O'clock we formed and marched to the wharf and embarked on board of one of the finest steamboats that runs the river, and known by the name of the Messenger. Company B[138] also came on board with us. When all things were ready we pushed off amid the deaf[e]ning cheers of both parties. The cannons sent forth their peals that shook the earth. . . .

Tuesday, December 22nd 1846

This morning when I awoke I did not know where I was, to hear the steamboat plunging through the ice. But I soon found w[h]ere I was on the broad but beautiful Ohio River. Every thing has gone off first rate so far, no disturbance of any kind has occurred of a serious nature. The river is very high and full of ice which is very favourable to us. There is very few wild ducks to be seen up this far. The weather is very cold and has been snowing the best part of the day. But the fellows are all anxious to see the scenery, which is truly grand. True the ground is covered with snow yet there is sights along the shore that should not be missed seeing. The evening closed by the party playing cards. . . . . . [sic]

Wednesday, December 23rd 1846

This morning some fellows came in and reported to the rest that there were several Deers on the opposite bank, some of us hurried to the deck and seen them as they were leaving, bounding through the thickets. The River is full of wild ducks and floating ice. We passed a great many towns along the shore and some are beautifully situated and promise to sell well hereafter. Many places along the shore they had the American flag flying in honor of us, and many places we received the wave of white handkerchiefs from the door of the humble cottage on the shore, no doubt from some of the fair, who had a near and dear friend in the Army. The weather is cold, but not so cold as it has been. All has passed off well so far and the scenery around is getting more interesting every day.[139]

ORDEAL OF THE MISSISSIPPI RIFLES NEAR NEW ORLEANS

In some instances the road to the war was not only more agonizing but more deadly than the battlefield. Such a case was that of the 2d Regiment of Mississippi Rifles. A soldier of the regiment later said that "sixty out of the eight hundred and fifty died and nearly all of the rest were sick, some lost their eyesight," because of the suffering they endured in New Orleans. Dr. Thomas N. Love, the regimental surgeon, described it in a bleak report:

Six months after our regiment had entered the service we had sustained a loss of 167 by death, and 134 by discharges. This is enough to awaken anxious enquiry into the causes which have produced such destruction in our ranks. It shall therefore be my object in this communication to give a short history of the epidemics with which we have been afflicted, and in the same connection give a history of the troops, their condition, privations, sufferings, the weather, climate, and all the circumstances which had more or less influence upon the health of the men.

The ten companies of volunteers . . . met at Vicksburg, between the 2d. and the 16th of January 1847. During the march of the respective companies from their residences to the place of rendezvous the weather was most delightful—equal to Indian summer. Most of them left home without having provided themselves with sufficient clothing, intending to appropriate in this way the money which [the] Government allowed them for this purpose. But few of them were provided with wollen [sic] clothes and hardly one in ten with flannel. The Governor of the State had rented ware-houses which were fitted up and appropriated as barracks for the companies as fast as they assembled. These were very uncomfortable for men lately accustomed to feather beds and warm buildings. . . .

The officers appointed for the purpose of organizing the regiment selected an encampment 2½ miles above Vicksburg, which in honor of a gallant officer they named "Camp McClung." The men were rapidly mustered into service; not having been subjected to a close inspection the result was that many weak, infirm, and broken in constitution had entered the army. Indeed many had volunteered for the purpose of restoring their health. As fast as they were mustered they marched to the camp, which proved to be a very injudicious selection, situated upon a low bank of the river, exposed to a wide sweep of the north and west winds. Before the men had fairly pitched their tents or became rested from the fatigues of the march, the weather became very inclement. The whole encampment was covered with mud and water. The blankets and clothing of the men were saturated with water. The young soldier's couch was made upon the damp and chilling earth, rife with disease and death. Add[ed] to these misfortunes, they were suddenly placed upon the diet of camp life.

On the 10th of Jan. one of the most remarkable changes in the weather occured I remember ever to have witnessed. The previous night the windows of the very heavens seemed to have been opened, and torrents of rain came like a flood over the encampment. Early in the morning the cold north wind came sweeping down from the broad bosom of the Mississippi, bringing with it a storm of sleet and hail. The situation of the troops now became truly distressing. The inclemency of the weather was such that it was impossible to furnish them provisions and wood sufficiently or regularly. Some muffled themselves up in their dripping blankets and huddled together in their cold and comfortless tents; some hovered over the smoking fires, calmly submitting to the pitiless peltings of the storm, and others, with their wet and frozen blankets close around them, wandered forth through the streets friendless, homeless and houseless. Language fails to give an adequate idea of the sufferings of our men. They felt, "as if the very marrow of their bones was congealed."

These causes, which I have briefly enumerated:—fatigue, exposure, insufficient food and clothing, were soon followed by the most remarkable and disastrous effects—influenza, rheumatism, pneumonia, and a disease more formidable than them all—*cold plague*. In this condition the regiment embarked on board steamboats for New Orleans. Our men were here prostrated by dozens; unprovided with medicines, or even a shelter, they were compelled to seek that comfort which their friends could best procure for them. The situation of the troops became so distressing that they were removed as fast as possible to the Battle Ground below New Orleans. All but two companies were transported upon the 13th & 14th of January. Two companies had taken quarters in Vicksburg and were not transported until the 18th. The citizens of Vicksburg no doubt remember well the eccentricities of a Captain who marched his company about the streets day and night, through mud and water, the result of which was subsequently manifested in a greater proportion of mortality among his men than almost any other company.

During the transportation of the troops to the Battle Ground, their sufferings if possible were increased. Every day we had more or less rain; the cold wind shifting from every point of the compass. The men were crowded upon steamboats, with their wet tents and damp blankets piled about them, poorly provided with shelter and no conveniences for cooking. It was distressing to go among them at night and hear the incessant coughing of hundreds, and the lamentations of the sick, suffering with cold and calling for the simplest wants.

It was during showers of rain and blasts of cold wintry winds that they erected their encampment upon the Battle Ground, and upon an earth saturated with water they made their beds. One hour the sun shown out beautifully, the next the soldiers were seen muffled in their blankets, turning from the cold wind, and the next they were found huddling in their tents from the torrents of rain. Not a dry foot of land was to be found in the whole encampment. The heat of the fevered patients vaporized the dampness of the blankets, creating in their tents a dense, suffocating steam.

In this condition medical treatment was unavailing, and not until the seal of death had fixed the destiny of many a brave soldier did our Government officers pretend to offer the least assistance, and at last it was only to the dying soldier they gave a scanty couch of straw within the walls of a cheerless building, far more comfortable however than was our former condition. Many of our sick had already sought lodgings at their own expense in private hospitals and boarding houses. When comfortable quarters were not allowed by officers whose duty it was to procure them, our officers very justly granted permission to their men who were sick to seek for themselves lodgings in the city. The removal of the sick to the hospitals was a distressing scene. On one occasion more than fifty were taken to Dr. Luzenberg's Hospital.[140] They were first taken in cabs to the river, then crowded into the cabin of a small towboat, then again into cabs to be transported to the rail-road and thence into the cars, and before they were safely lodged in the hospital it was midnight; many of them apparently suffering with severe inflammatory rheumatism, and every effort to move them was uttered an involuntary scream of agony.*

The next step was to remove the troops upon the transports, for which we had waited impatiently for several days. Here our sick list continued to increase. The situation of the troops was but little better than in camp. In the holds of three ships were crowded nearly 800 men. Their tents, blankets, and clothing still very damp, the weather being so inclement that it was impossible to dry them. The berths were made of green pine plank which were as cold and hard as marble. Upon these our sick men were confined. They were not even allowed straw matrasses [sic] although they were earnestly required and demanded, and could have been procured for one dollar a piece. I have seen the sick soldier in his delirium, raging with madness and writhing under the terrors of disease, tear his flesh upon the rough sides of his rugged couch.

At length all our sick were removed from the ships to the hospital and on the 30th of January we were sailing fast from the scene of desolation, with the

* Thus in text.

sanguine hope that we had left behind us the scourge. Indeed, we had left behind *eighty* of our men that were destined never to join us again. But our brightest hopes were soon at an end. The dark cloud of disease still hovered over us. The holds of the ships offered scenes distressing to the most callous heart. The evaporation from the dampness of the blankets and tents settled in great drops upon the ceiling. The holds of the ships were soon crowded with the sick. The effluvia was intolerable. The attendants were young and inexperienced. The sea became rough and the companions of the sick were no longer able to give their kind attention. They had nothing to eat which a peevish appetite would crave. . . . Through the long dark night the rolling ship would dash the sick man from side to side bruising his flesh upon the rough corners of his berth. The wild screams of the delirious, the lamentations of the sick, and the melancholy groans of the dying, kept up one continual scene of confusion. We had a long tedious voyage—four weeks we were confined to the loathsome ships and before we had landed at the Brasos, we consigned twenty-eight of our men to the dark waves.[141]

Hardships experienced in camps near New Orleans by the volunteers on their way to war led to charges that the military establishment was discriminating against the citizen-soldiers. The Matamoros American Flag[142] later published an article which had even wider implications—that the sufferings of the volunteers were an affront to democracy:

A writer in a late number of the New Orleans *Jeffersonian* complains of the distinction shown between the volunteer and regular troops in the enlistment of the latter in that city. He says:

No sooner does a regiment or company, or part of a company of recruits for the regular service arrive, than they are placed in comfortable houses at the barracks, where their comfort and health and wants are attended to; but, on the other hand, our volunteers who freely rush to the field at their country's call, are placed in open sheds, without floors, without yards, or any of the comforts and conveniences of life.

The complaints of the writer are, no doubt, justified by existing facts, for we have observed as much—even more—ourselves, and have often been led to ask, from whence has been derived the rule for making this distinction? We can think of no selfish or mercenary motive that could possibly influence the volunteer in exchanging the comforts and ease of home for the privations and dangers of war, which would justify such a distinction, and we are pleased to find that the subject is arresting public attention. Our entire military system is defective—festering with corruption—and the sooner Congress abolishes it and builds up an establishment more consonant with the pure principles of our government, the better.[143]

Sea Voyage to Mexico

Diaries, journals, and letters recounting the days on the Atlantic or Gulf of Mexico have much in common. Seasickness, storms, awe at the grandeur and limitless expanse of the ocean, and the marine life seen from the decks, are recurrent themes. Of course there were complaints. Quarters were cramped, and the troops were often bored, but some thrilled to the great adventure. Such a volunteer was William Watts Hart Davis, a young Pennsylvanian who went to Massachusetts during 1846 to study law at Cambridge. In December he enlisted in the Regiment of Massachusetts Volunteers. Aided by the political influence of his father, a Democratic officeholder in Philadelphia, and that of John W. Forney, a prominent newspaper publisher, he received a commission and became Col. Caleb Cushing's aide. A letter from Boston, written to his mother, described the embarkation of his regiment:

The Regiment went on board the transport on Tuesday at noon and will soon be ready to sail. I am going in the Ship Remittance, a large vessel of seven hundred tons burden. The accommodations will be very good. We have two good cabins on the upper deck with good berths in them for sleeping. We have about three hundred on board the ship which makes quite a large family. When every thing becomes nicely fixed and arranged in order, we will be as comfortable [sic] suited as one could ask to be on ship board. It was a pretty sight to see the soldiers going on board. We marched by companies, some companies with, and some without arms. Quite a crowd followed us through the streets, and thousands collected around our ship, from whence cheer upon cheer went up for our safety and success. . . . Our destination is the Brazos at the mouth of the Rio Grande, though we do not land there, only wait for further orders. We then expect to go either to Tampico, Tuspan or Vera Cruz w[h]ere I suppose we will land, and join in the active campaign, and maybe assist in the reduction of Vera Cruz. . . . We had some difficulty with one company the day we embarked, and had to threaten force before we could get them to go on board the transport. When they refused to go the Col. [Cushing] ordered a detachment of 80 men with loaded muskets to go to their Quarters, and if necessary compel them to move at all hazard. Seeing things wore a serious aspect they thought it more wise to change their minds, and they concluded to go on board. The disturbance all arose from some misunderstanding, which was increased by some evilly disposed persons.

Our company is the Senior Company on board, and our Captain (Crownin-shield)[144] has been appointed to the command of the men on board the ship, which is considered quite a compliment. I staid on ship board on Thursday night, and had command of the ship until next day nearly noon. During Thursday night some of the men behaved badly, and I had two sergeants handcuffed and placed in prison for safe keeping. They will be court martialed, and should be severely punished. I marched our own Company on ship board. My residence is yet on shore, and it will continue so until a day or so before we sail, when I will go on board bag and baggage. I find quite all my time occupied in the duties of my office, and no time for attending to the duties of my company. The Lieut. Col.[145] goes out in our ship; the Col.[146] in a smaller vessel.[147]

Naive yet sensitive, young Davis gave his impressions of the journey at sea, its novelty, miseries, and excitement.

We left Boston on Tuesday Feb[ruar]y 23, and anchored the same evening in Nantucket roads nine miles below the city. The next morning we put to sea with a strong westerly wind in company with another ship which had two companies on board. We sailed in company with her for two days, then lost sight of her, and have not seen her since. The weather was good and the wind fair until Saturday morning when it commenced blowing hard from the N.W. and by noon it had increased into a perfect gale. It lasted thirty-six hours. You cannot imagine the fierceness of the wind. Our ship seemed only a nut shell, and was tossed about at the mercy of the wind and waves. . . . During the fiercest [part] of the storm we came nigh losing one of the officers of our company, Lt. Cremony.[148] He went forward to secure some fresh beef on the top of the forward cabin. The ship tossed so much that he couldn't hold on. He and every thing on the cabin was thrown down and nothing but his catching to the rigging prevented him from going over board & into the sea. He received a heavy fall and came limping into the cabin.

. . . . .

You would naturally inquire how I spend my time at sea. I divide it between my regular daily duties and reading and keeping my journal. My regular duties are considerable without being arduous. Some think I must give direction about everything from the government of the ship to the making of the meals. I am now reading my military books so I will know my duties when I arrive upon the shores of Mexico, and not have to ask A or B what I must do nor how to do it. The drums beat at daylight for the men to rise, and the duties cease at 10 when all must retire and lights be put out. The music sounds beautifully upon the waters as it is borne upon the wings of the gentle zephers.

Tomorrow is Sunday, when we are to have the church service read to the men from the Quarter deck, and all turn out in full uniform neat and clean. There will be something very solemn in a religious meeting at sea, far different from one of the same kind on shore. This service we will continue as long as we are upon the waters.

. . . . .

We have 18 officers and 300 men on board which makes quiet [sic, quite] a large family for one wooden house. The men do all their own cooking, washing &c. and will soon become quiet [sic, quite] domestic in their habits. The officers all mess at the same table, and although we have not the richest living 'tis good and I think we will grow fat upon it.

You would laugh to see us sometimes when we sit down to eat. The ship will make a sudden lurch and we have to hold on by one hand to the table to keep from falling and with the other hand hold our plates to prevent them from being gently emptied into our laps. Sometimes we have to take our plates and cups and sit around different places flat on the deck as the only manner by which we can manage to take a peaceable meal. . . . We are now within two days sail of the island of Saint Domingo, which we expect to see on Sunday evening or Monday morning. We pass between Domingo and Cuba, and then steer to the westward until we arrive at our point of destination. We are sailing for the Brazos, from whence we expect to go to the island of Lobos below Tampico.[149]

So an army, neither of monsters nor of saints but of ordinary American males was recruited, assembled, trained in a meager fashion and moved to the theater of war. Fighting was underway before most of them enlisted.

THE TAYLOR CAMPAIGN:
CORPUS CHRISTI TO BUENA VISTA

Taylor at Corpus Christi

During the nine months preceding the war, while the Polk administration made a final effort to realize its expansionist ambitions by diplomacy, Bvt. Brig. Gen. Taylor was establishing the base from which the invasion of northern Mexico could be launched.

On August 15, 1845, Taylor reported his activities to President Polk:

After a careful examination, for the most part personal, of Aransas and Corpus Christi bays, I have settled upon this point, west of the Nueces River, as the most favorable for present occupation, and have pushed forward the troops and supplies as rapidly as our means of transportation would permit. . . .

I am gratified . . . that the troops are more healthy than could reasonably be expected, considering their great exposure and the inferior quality of the water on the coast.[1]

Martial Enthusiasm of General Worth

In spite of hardships and bungling, the morale of some of the men, though undoubtedly not all, was high. A letter written November 1, 1845 expressed a warlike spirit, hungering for battle for the sake of battle, as well as defense of country in "a war which to all appearances was to be forced upon us." Bvt. Brig. Gen. William Jenkins Worth,[2] soon to become one of the most controversial luminaries of the war, wrote this bombastic missive. Having served creditably in the regular army for many years, he now saw new vistas opening before him. In effect he was documenting De Tocqueville's shrewd analysis of warlike aspirations in a democratic nation's army. De Tocqueville had observed:

In democratic armies, the desire of advancement is almost universal: it is ardent, tenacious, perpetual; it is strengthened by all other desires, and only extinguished with life itself. But it is easy to see, that, of all armies in the world, those in which advancement must be slowest in time of peace are the armies of democratic countries. . . .

We thus arrive at this singular consequence, that, of all armies, those most ardently desirous of war are democratic armies, and of all nations, those most fond of peace are democratic nations; and what makes these facts still more extraordinary is, that these contrary effects are produced at the same time by the principle of equality.[3]

Worth's revelation of his ambitions was as follows:

Coming hither, as we all have with alacrity and high aspirations added to the natural professional hope of once & again participating in a war which to all appearances was to be forced upon us, the result of which was never for a moment doubted as respected the honor of our country or the eclat of the service, you can well imagine as you will sympathize in the depression accompanying the conviction that this is to be "the be all and the end all"—that all these pleasant fancies are to evaporate in smoke. Ye Gods is it not enough to drive one mad that this, the first opportunity in the past, as it will probably be in the next 30 years when and where the military have had the opportunity beyond peradventure or cavil, and that too in due subordination of position in the legal constitutional and popular relation, to play a leading part in the great orchestra of the great National Drama, by promptly and vigorously displaying this really well appointed and high spirited force upon the Rio Grande! Assembled too it has been with surprising vigor and rapidity and good fortune to boot, from the most remote corners and angles of our broad domain how bravely and surely would it then & there have dictated, aye, that's the word—a speedy settlement of all the open questions between the two governments, handsomely clearing away the rub[b]ish—the debris of years of notes and protocols from the path of your "statesmen by [pattent?] and politicians by trade"—but the time is going if not gone by—the great result is not, will not be achieved—why, time and circumstances will show—our gallant old general does not feel authorised or instructed to take a step in advance—what a misfortune the instructions had not been more specific and in accordance with the tone & spirit of the day! Why Mexico matters [?] now? Have not our

Anglo Saxon race been land stealers from time immemorial and why shouldn't they? When their gaze is fixed upon other lands the best way is to make out the deeds: in this instance had our Eagles been perched upon the banks of the Rio Grande the Mexicans would have posted to Washington and solicited the honor of paying for recording the papers.

Well here we are digesting our disappointment as best we may with little wood and execrable water—500 or 1/8th on the sick list and that number I apprehend to be duplicated when the northers sett in, but what is that to us 'whose duty tis to die'! My own conclusions are that the Northern Democracy who reluctantly want the measure to effect a (nameless) specific object, having attained the which will say "we agreed to annex Texas as she was, not as she would be—Having secured that object call off your Troops—pass not the Nueces." But the Rubicon has been passed, one step more toward Rome adds not to the indignity if any we have committed toward our neighbors—oh what a glorious chance—all circumstances so admirably conspiring in the internal affairs of Mexico where all is confusion worse confounded!—for the like of us it is the last [throw?]. Before another we shall be alike beyond the reach of praise or lampooning—unless perchance, which is not unlikely, England means to keep this pot, to use a culinary phrase, simmering, until her own questions are settled, or failing in that use the Mexican ports or . . . to annoy our South & meantime, having the right of way, stretch over to California and so hang charmingly on the flank of our march to Oregon!

I must add before closing that our Corps is strongly represented and now, as always, up to their work. Well may you be proud of them.[4]

MARCH TO THE RIO GRANDE

The belligerent Worth was soon gratified. By January 1846, approximately one half of the United States forces were at Corpus Christi.[5] Having received orders to advance, on March 8 the army moved toward the Rio Grande. Taylor's immediate objective was Point Isabel on the Gulf of Mexico, about 150 miles southwest of Corpus Christi (196 miles by the route taken) and less than ten miles from the mouth of the Rio Grande. It was sheltered by long, narrow Padre Island but was handicapped as a port by water so shallow that all supplies had to be taken to shore by lighters. Nonetheless, Point Isabel and nearby Brazos Island provided the best available ports and served throughout the war as supply bases for Taylor's army in northern Mexico.[6]

After eleven days of marching the Americans made their first contact with the Mexican military. At the Arroyo Colorado, Mexican officers encountered the vanguard of Taylor's army and threatened that any attempt to cross the river would be met by force. General Taylor gave the order to cross the river. His troops did so on March 20 without meeting opposition. After his supply train had caught up with him, Taylor resumed the march. On March 23 the army reached the road running from Matamoros to Point Isabel. There the force divided. Worth, with the greater part of the infantry, turned towards Matamoros while Taylor led the supply wagons to Point Isabel. Having established his base at Point Isabel, Taylor rejoined Worth.

Confrontation at Matamoros

On March 28 the Americans reached the Rio Grande and began the construction of Fort Texas (later Fort Brown)[7] which took a month to build, under

MAP OF NORTHERN MEXICO

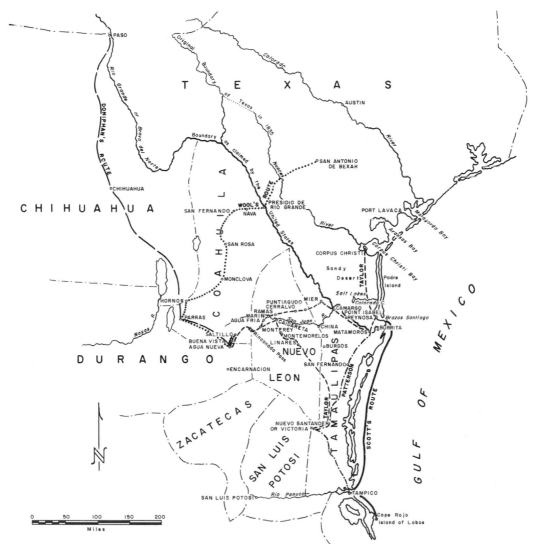

the direction of Capt. Joseph King Fenno Mansfield of the Engineers.[8] Across the river was Matamoros, occupied by Mexican troops under General Pedro de Ampudia.[9] A letter written by Lt. John P. Hatch to his sister reported American activities and problems.

We arrived at this place a week yesterday and have been quietly encamped upon the bank of the Rio Grande. There has yet been no opposition to us and there probably will be none. Genl. Taylor will certainly take the town as soon as they fire a gun. Meanwhile the actions of the two armies are perfectly comical. They are both engaged in erecting batteries on their respective sides of the river and so near each other that we can almost converse between them, but not a shot is fired; the men work without any attempt to conceal themselves. Many of the officers and men bathe in the river. Sometimes parties from each side will be bathing opposite each other. We are still uncertain what course the Mexicans intend to pursue against us. It is thought by many that they intend as soon as they receive enough troops to attack us. They have at present more than we have but they expect three thousand more and as they will have about three to our one they think they would be able to fight us. We would not ask to fight a smaller number than this and I have not the slightest doubt that we would then thrash them so that they would never again dare to look an American in the face. They, day before yesterday marched their troops down to the batteries they had erected and had them (the batteries) consecrated. Two priests threw waters by the pail full upon them, the troops all kneeling. I rather think this must have been done, because they had nothing but nine pounders in them. Our eighteen pounders arrived to day and are to be placed in a battery that has been erected for them. It is intended to direct them upon the town as soon as the Mexicans will give us the slightest chance.

Today one of our men, deserted a few days since, returned, and I have just heard his story. Genl. Worth sent for him a few days ago and told him that he could do his country good service if he chose, but that he would leave it entirely to him and he need not do it unless he wished. He said that he wanted him to desert, to go to Matamoros and ascertain the number of their troops, a description of them, their defences, no. of guns, quantity of provisions, &c. The Genl. told him he would have the reputation of a deserter, would run the risk of being shot by our guard in going over and by theirs in coming back, besides the chance of being hung as a spy. He said he would take his chances. Today he returned. He says they have 3,500 troops, five hundred of them are cavalry and are fine troops, the remainder are good for nothing, a miserable half-starved set of wretches. They have about thirty pieces of artillery none larger than a nine-pounder, many of them twos and fours; they have two mortars. Their soldiers get but one meal a day and that very poor. . . . . He says also that they are not to attack us until they get seven thousand men and then they will surround us *and not let any of us escape*. He thinks, however, that any one of our regiments would have no trouble in taking the town.

I don't believe they can raise seven thousand men and even if they had them I think they would be afraid to attack us. If they should be so rash they will repent it bitterly. We yesterday had two alarms that show how anxious our men are for a little brush. The first one was in the afternoon. A soldier attempted to desert and was seen by two picket guards; both of them were at some distance from him, one above the other below him. The guards commenced firing at him and about twenty shots were fired; he was at some distance from both guards and his head alone was above the water. He was killed. In camp we heard the firing and from the number of shots began to think that our pickets might be contending with the advanced guard of the enemy and that they were almost upon us. The men as soon as they heard the long roll gave three cheers and ran for their equipments. They were formed immediately and showed the greatest eagerness for a fight. The second alarm was in the night. Another man attempted to desert and met a similar fate. There was no alarm given this time but the men got up and put on their equipments and were ready for immediate action had it been given.

April 6th. Last night there was a small rencontre between one of our pickets and a boat load of Mexican soldiers who had come over to this side; it is supposed that one of their men was killed; they retreated across the river. There was no alarm in our camp but the Mexicans were on the alert, sent the men to the guns and appeared to think that we would attack them. I begin to think there is great danger that some little affair of this kind will bring on a general fight before long. . . . We have very few officers in the third brigade and a great deal of duty to attend to. Guard duty and fatigue duty fall just as heavy on us as on other brigades although they have many more officers.[10]

On April 12, Ampudia demanded that the Americans withdraw to the Nueces, and upon Taylor's refusal took the position that a state of war existed. Although Taylor did not believe that the Mexicans would "do anything" he ordered a naval blockade and a stoppage of all supplies to Matamoros. Meantime there was progress on the construction of Fort Texas and the defenses at Point Isabel.

Siege of Fort Brown

The guess that Ampudia would not do anything proved correct, but he was superseded by Mariano Arista, who was more aggressive. On the twenty-fourth (April), Mexican cavalry crossed to the east bank of the Rio Grande. Taylor sent a small force of dragoons against them. On the twenty-fifth the

Matamoros, from Fort Brown

Americans were surrounded, and after a brief fight, in which several were killed, surrendered. Other than desultory sniping this was the first fight of the war.

On April 30 the Mexicans again crossed the river, this time below Matamoros, endangering both the fort and Point Isabel. To meet the threat Taylor left five hundred men to defend the fort and led the rest of his army (about 2,000 men) to secure Point Isabel.[11] On May 4 the Mexicans started a bombardment of the fort. The commander, Maj. Jacob Brown,[12] was mortally wounded (the fort was subsequently named after him) and Capt. E. S. Hawkins[13] took command. After the siege was over he wrote a report, a portion of which follows:

I have the honor to report that on the morning of the 6th instant, during the third day of the bombardment of this fort, its gallant commander, Major Brown, received a severe wound, which caused his death at two o'clock on the 9th instant. I immediately assumed command, and have the honor to report the result of the bombardments since seven o'clock p.m., on the 4th, at which time Captain Walker[14] left with a report of the result up to that time. At nine o'clock p.m. on the 4th, firing of musketry was heard in our rear, about three or four hundred yards distant, and apparently extending a mile up the river; the firing very irregular. This continued until half past eleven o'clock p.m. The garrison was under arms, batteries and defences all manned, and continued so during the night. On the 5th instant, at five o'clock, a.m., the fire was recommenced from the enemy's batteries, which was immediately returned from the 18-pounder battery and 6-pounder howitzer, placed in embrasure on the southeast bastion. The firing was kept up one hour, receiving during that time about fifty round shot and shells from the enemy. The batteries on both sides ceased firing at the same time. Our expenditure of ammunition was thirty rounds of both caliber.

At eight o'clock a.m., Valdez, a Mexican, came in and reported that a party of dragoons had been driven back from the prairie to the point, and also a party to the fort; that he had seen thirty deserters from Arista's army, who stated that the Mexicans were without subsistence stores, that they were tired, and left for their homes; that it was stated in the Mexican camp that Arista had received an express from Mexico informing him that another revolution had broken out in Mexico, and that he could receive no support from the Government. At nine o'clock a.m. it was reported that a reconnaissance of officers, escorted by mounted men of the enemy, was going on in rear, within eight hundred yards of the fort; and that other parties, mounted and infantry, were at the same distance, extending from the bend of the lagoon to the river. Lieutenant Hanson,[15] 7th infantry, asked permission to take the dragoons and go and look at them. This was granted, and in an hour he returned, reporting that the enemy was establishing a battery at the crossroads; his appearance among them created great alarm, and they were soon concentrated at a distance under cover of their work. Every man at work to-day strengthening the defences. Several parties of cavalry and infantry seen to-day occupying our old encampment. At eleven o'clock p.m. musketry was heard in our rear, from bend of lagoon to the river. The troops all are at their places in the bastions during the night.

Wednesday, May 6.—At five o'clock a.m. the cannonade commenced from the lower fort and mortar battery. Many round shot and shells thrown until six o'clock, when there was a cessation of firing. During the last hour the shot and shells were well directed, bursting in all directions in the interior of the fort, tearing our tents to pieces, and injuring several horses. At half past six o'clock the signal 18-pounders were fired, at which the enemy opened their batteries in our front and rear, and the cannonade continued from two mortars and a howitzer in front, and a mortar established at or near the crossroads in rear until ten o'clock a.m., when our gallant commander received a mortal wound from a falling shell. Large mounted parties and infantry were seen at this time in rear. At seven o'clock one mortar was playing upon us from town and two from the rear. At ten o'clock a small party of infantry crept up in ravine and fired musketry; but, being out of range, the fire was not returned. At half past ten o'clock a.m. several parties of infantry and mounted men were seen surrounding us in rear. Several rounds of canister were fired from Lieutenant Bragg's[16] battery, which soon dispersed them. Several were afterwards heard to have been killed. Immediately afterwards, and until half past twelve o'clock p.m., we received a continual shower of shells from the enemy's batteries. At two o'clock five shells were thrown. At half past four o'clock p.m. a white flag was shown at the old buildings in rear, and a parley sounded by the enemy. Two officers advanced and were met by two officers of my command, who brought me the document marked A, signed by General Arista, allowing me one hour to reply.

This document being considered one of great importance, I deemed it necessary to convoke a council, consisting of all the company commanders in my command, and laid it before them. They unanimously concurred with me in the reply, a copy of which is the accompanying document marked B. This document was despatched in the allotted time, and shortly after its reception the enemy's batteries opened upon us with a continual shower of shot and shells until sunset. The night was passed very quietly, but constant vigilance was exercised in the command; every man kept at his post, as an attack was confidently expected in the morning.

. . . . .

Saturday, May 9. . . . Two p.m. Major Brown died, and in a short time we heard the reëngagement between the armies. Quarter to six, quite a number of Mexican cavalry and a few infantry were seen in the retreat. At this time we received a heavy fire of round shot and shells. From the time the battle commenced, and continued to increase, an 18-pounder and 6-pounder were fired in the direction of the upper ferry; when, finding it difficult to distinguish between friend and foe, the firing was discontinued.[17]

PALO ALTO AND RESACA DE LA PALMA

Taylor reached Point Isabel on May 2. During the next five days his troops labored on the fortifications there,[18] then began a march toward Matamoros.[19] Approaching Palo Alto, a water hole about sixteen miles on their march, they were confronted by a Mexican force under General Arista. On May 8, Taylor attacked; following an afternoon of hard fighting, the enemy retreated only to take up a stronger defensive position the next day at Resaca de la Palma, or Resaca de Guerrero, a shallow ravine some eight miles from Palo Alto. Taylor again ordered an attack and drove the Mexicans from the field.

Lt. Jeremiah Mason Scarritt of the Engineers was with Taylor's army in both engagements.[20] His report to Col. Joseph G. Totten,[21] the Chief of Engineers, written on May 12 while the details were still fresh in his mind, gives a thorough description of the tactics and strategy:

PLATE III. *Battle of Palo Alto*

PLATE IV. *Battle of Resaca de la Palma*

General Taylor at the Battle of Palo Alto

You doubtless by this time have heard some intelligence of our fights of the 8th & 9th as I acted the part of Asst. Aid[e] to Gen. Taylor in both engagements, and the only one of our corps present. I thought it would be gratifying to our officers to have something in detail. Our fort opposite Matamoros was sufficiently completed on the first of May to permit the body of the army to move. It was left under the command of Major J[acob] Brown, with the 7th Infantry, 4 eighteen-pdrs. & 2 six-pdrs. & 2 howitzers. The whole force amounted to about 500 men. Capt. Mansfield was left in the fort. The Army reached Pt. Isabel about 2,200 strong. We remained at this place until 3 o'clock on the 7th strengthening the defences and loading our train. On the 7th we moved out with our original force ac[c]ompanied by a train of about 200 waggons and carrying two 18-pdrs. on travelling carriages—these were drawn by oxen and remained with the train. On the night of the 7th we encamped at eight miles from Pt. Isabel. On the 8th when about 15 miles from Pt. Isabel and one mile this side of the position called "Worth's Camp" our line of battle was formed—the command was halted, and the train closed —this was done in consequence of the report of our advance that the enemy was seen in front and appeared to be advancing.

In this order the force advanced until it came to the water hole at Gen. Worth's camp—there it was halted, the men refreshed with rest and water, and the train parked. From this position the enemy were distinctly seen distant about two miles and his long black lines at times fringing the horizon and then projected upon the wood seemed an overwhelming force for our small army. When the men were well refreshed the line was again formed and we advanced until our right flank came within one half mile of their left—their batteries then opened upon us—we halted—formed square—laid down in the grass—and put our guns to work in reply. The side sketch will give about the position of the two forces when the fight commenced. The Mexicans had about 800 cavalry on each flank—10 pieces of artillery disposed as represented of which there were eight 4-pdrs. and two 9-pdrs.—he had also about 4,000 regular Infantry and Artillery and 2,000 rancheros who did not appear, being in the wood as I suppose. We had about 1,800 bayonets, 250 cavalry—two batteries of 4 guns each, and the two 18-pdrs. which was [sic] brought into line. The 18-pdrs. opened upon the cavalry on the left, with round shot. Duncan advanced[22] some 50 yards and Ringgold some short distance in front and opened upon different points of the line. The distance was so great that solid shot was used, at first. The enemies' cavalry on the left soon found their position too uncomfortable to maintain long so that he moved off by the left flank, followed by the two pieces of Artillery nearest. The head of this column was soon seen through the wood demonstrating an attack either on our right flank or on the train—their cavalry followed the broken line. The 5th Inf[antry] were moved into the wood for the purpose of protecting our right and the 3rd withdrawn, so as to cover more effectually the train. The 5th was a square by the time the lancers reached the wood—the latter charged the square but were repelled with the loss of ten killed—they then withdrew out of musquetry [sic] range and continued their march toward our train. The appearance of the 3rd checked this demonstration and their retreat commenced. In the mean time two of Ringgold's guns had been ordered into the wood on the left of the 5th. They reached their position just as this long line of cavalry had commenced their retreat—these guns did great damage to their two pieces of artillery which they never opened, and hastened the retreat of the horsemen. Whilst this was going on, Capt. May[23] with his squadron made a demonstration on their lines, but he found their batteries so strongly supported by infantry and cavalry that he considered it hopeless to expect success from an attack of 65 dragoons. Such was the situation of things until the close of the first part of the fight, when the smoke of the guns and of the burning prairie which had been fired by the burning wads created a cloud so dense that it was impossible to see each other. The fight had commenced at 2 o'clock, and it was about 4. The firing on both sides ceased and we had an intermission of about an hour.

As their cavalry had not returned to their position after their repulse we advanced the 5th to the place occupied by their left, brought up the 2 18-pdrs., advanced Ringgold and the Art[iller]y batallion as represented. We then recommenced the fire which they immediately answered. Duncan finding that the smoke intercepted his view moved to the left and front and thus obtained a very near and deadly fire upon their lines. They made a movement to the right with their cavalry but Duncan's fire was too galling for them to endure and they fell back in some confusion. An assault was also attempted by the cavalry on the art[iller]y batallion but a couple of discharges of grape from the 18-[pounders?] and of musketry from the square dispersed them entirely. Night set in and the firing ceased at 7 o'clock.

Our troops were brought up and encamped upon the ground occupied by our 18-[pounders] with the train compactly parked in [the] rear. The damage done us was not great—three of our men were killed outright upon the field and 47 wounded of whom some six or seven died during the night. We had two officers severely and one slightly wounded. Major Ringgold received a four pr. shot through both thighs without injuring a bone—he has since died. Capt. John Page had his lower jaw carried away—he's still alive but it were a mercy that he were dead.[24] Luther[25] received a slight wound in his leg. The dragoons lost 9 horses—two or three officers were unhorsed—and many narrow escapes were made. Bliss[26] was unhorsed—but not hurt. The damage done

Fall of Major Ringgold

the enemy we could not learn that night and no one would hazard a guess. We all thought that he had got enough to slightly sicken a Mexican stomach but we confidently expected to see something more of him either during the night or the next day.

We were not quite satisfied with what we had done—the train had tied us down and prevented all advance and the feeling and opinion was that the next day the train must look out for itself. I felt perfectly satisfied that if either army had attempted an advance it would have been defeated. The interval that separated us was half a mile of prairie covered with long grass making it very difficult to move through. The Artillery was so numerous and so well served on both sides that no column could have survived in an attempt to advance. . . .

On the morning of the 9th [General Taylor?] directed me to secure the train in the best manner possible. The two 18-pdrs. were left and the 12-pdrs. on truck carriages were got out of the waggons and placed at my disposal. By 12 o'clock, I had the train so that it could resist any attack of cavalry—come in what direction it might and it would have required very steady cavalry to have marched upon it. The army had left early in the morning and was carefully advancing toward the point at which the enemy was last seen. . . .

Gen. Taylor determined to advance more rapidly. Taking some part of his train and leaving the rest in position, we again took up the order of march. When we had marched about 8 miles, the Gen. received intelligence from his advanced scouts that the enemy had taken position in the *chapparal* or thick brush which abounds in this country. The road was almost the only open country about. We had 100 men acting as skirmishers—50 were thrown on each side of the road. Ridgley's [sic] battery[27] was ordered to take position in the open space—the 5th was thrown in open order on the left to clear the woods of the light troops and support the artillery and the 3d, 4th, & 8th were disposed of in the same manner for the same purpose. Duncan was then brought up—then May's squadron and he received an order to charge their batteries which he did in the most gallant manner, capturing Gen. La Vega[28] at his guns. The Mexicans rallied and retook their pieces—the 5th retook and retained them—the 4th took some cannon I think as did the 8th. After the loss of their cannon the Mexicans made a determined stand on their right but they had two batteries of artillery on their flank and the 8th in their front. They broke and made but little resistance afterward. We captured eight pieces of cannon—500 stand of arms—a large quantity of ammunition—about 400 mules with their pack[s],—all of their camp furniture, Arista's private papers, numerous colors, &c., and in short the rout was complete and nothing saved their army but their great speed and the exhausted state of our men. We took prisoner, 14 officers and about 200 men—and killed on the field about 300. The Mexicans acknowledge a loss in the two fights of 1,000 men and 48 offi-

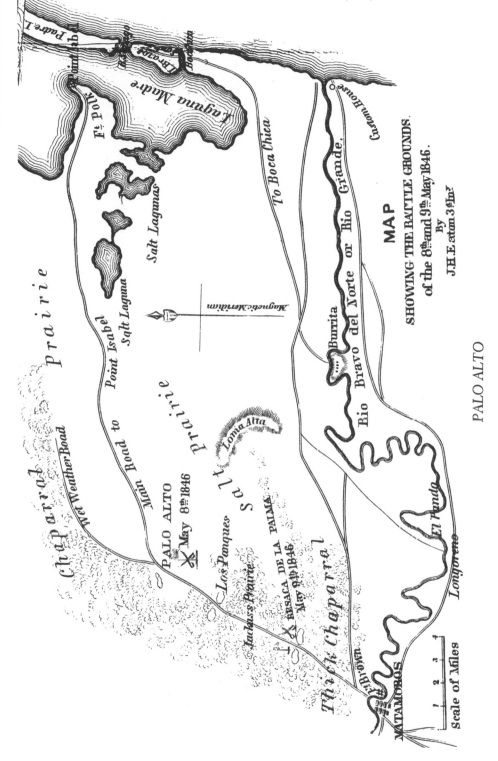

MAP

SHOWING THE BATTLE GROUNDS.
of the 8th and 9th May 1846.
By
J.H.Eaton 3d Inf.

PALO ALTO

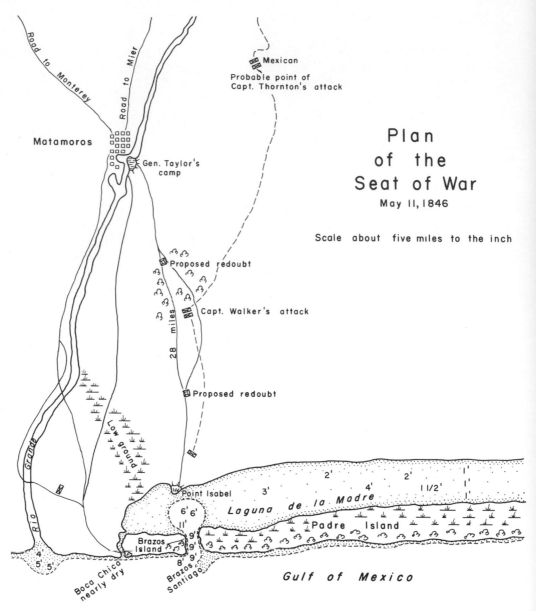

Road to Monterey

Road to Mier

Mexican
Probable point of
Capt. Thornton's attack

Matamoros

Gen. Taylor's
camp

Plan
of the
Seat of War
May 11, 1846

Scale about five miles to the inch

Proposed redoubt

Capt. Walker's attack

28 miles

Proposed redoubt

Low ground

Rio Grande

Point Isabel

2'
3'   4'   2'   1'
1 1/2'   1'

Laguna de la Madre

6' 6'
1'   Padre   Island

Brazos
Island   9'
9'

4   9'
5' 5'   8' 9'

Boca Chica
nearly dry

Brazos
Santiago

Gulf of Mexico

10 miles from Brazos to Rio Grande
5 miles from Brazos to Point Isabel

ISABEL TO MATAMOROS

cers. Our whole loss in the two is 100 killed and wounded. . . . There was a great deal of personal gallantry shown and the most enthusiastic and determined spirit both in officers and men. But the light artillery was the back bone of our success. I will not dwell on this fight for it demonstrates only the efficiency of our artillery and the daring of our officers and men.[29]

Edmund Kirby Smith,[30] *who was to distinguish himself as a Confederate general in the Civil War, wrote an account of the immediate military consequences.*

You may now banish all concern for our safety. The war is pretty much over, two thousand men were it our policy could with ease march to the City of Mexico—never were a people so completely cut up—so panic-struck, as the Mexicans now are—all their energies, all their resources have been expended in one grand effort—for more than a year they have been preparing for this occasion. They have staked their all upon the turn of a die, and at one fell swoop they have been laid perfectly helpless. In the battle of the 8th which lasted from ½ past two P.M. till dark, the Mexicans acknowledge the loss of 500 killed besides the desertion of a large body of Cavalry and two pieces of Artillery. Our loss was between 40 and 50 killed and wounded. This great disparity in loss is owing to the destructive effect with which our Artillery was served, the schrapnel shells sometimes bursting in the very midst of their columns. On the 9th we attacked them in their entrenchments, when with a reinforcement of near 2,000 they confidently expected our destruction. We stormed their works, captured all their Artillery, and entirely routed a force of 7,180 regular troops—500 with their priest were drowned in crossing the Rio Grande. Our men expected no quarter, and fought with perfect desperation—it was hand to hand conflict—a trial of personal strength in many instances, where the bayonet failed, the fist even was used—but in moral courage as well as personal strength—we were far their superiors, and have given them a lesson, which ages cannot remove. We lost 180, killed and wounded in the two actions of Palo Alto and Resaca de la Palmo [sic]. The Mexicans acknowledge a loss of 2,500 in the same.[31]

OCCUPATION OF MATAMOROS

Following the battles of Palo Alto and Resaca de la Palma, General Arista, having vainly sought a truce, evacuated Matamoros. Left defenseless the civilian authorities surrendered the town. Lt. Jenks Beaman described the surrender and occupation, and in doing so revealed the mixed contempt and jealousy with which the professional soldier regarded the volunteer as well as a yearning that the regular's heroism be duly recognized.

Unfinished Cathedral, Matamoros

After the Battle of the 9th of May we remained on the field so gloriously won until 2 o'clock p.m. of the 12th burying the dead, taking care of the wounded (both of our men and Mexicans) and sending our prisoners & captured property to Point Isabel. We then marched to our *old* ground opposite Matamoras for which we had been fighting so hard. Arrived there, we encamped. On the morning of the 17th Genl. Taylor ordered us to be ready to march, at 2 o'clock, up the River to cross, for the purpose of taking Matamoras. There we thought the enemy would give us a hard fight as the town is strongly fortified, and we had a large river to cross in flat & small boats to reach it, but about 11 o'clock (before we got under way), a "parley" was sounded from the Mexican side, to which we replied, and a boat with three of Genl. Arista's officers came over.

They acknowledged in their Genl.'s name that they had been badly whip-[p]ed, and had been sent by him to ask for an Armistice—which Genl. Taylor most peremtoraly declined them, telling them that they had commenced the war that he (Genl. T.) had laid two months under the very museles of their guns, while they were collecting all their resorces—and all the time assuring them that he should not fire the first gun, and that now they had commenced the war by two most bloody battles, he should attack Matamoras, as a *defen-*

sive move (to protect his posts on this (the Texas) side of the River). They then asked the Genl. upon what terms he would except [*sic*] the City if it was surrendered to him. He replied, "That they must leave all their arms & munitions of war, and *all public property of all kinds*, belonging to their government, excepting provisions enough to take them to Monterey. They promised him an answer at 3 o'clock, till which time he waited and the answer not arriving, we commenced our march up the river and marched three miles [and] halted, and as soon as it was dark commenced crossing our army. At day light on the morning of the 18th, we had several pieces of Artillery & 600 men over —and were crossing the rest.

About 8 o'clock the Alcalda, Prefect &c (Civil authorities) came and asked to see Genl. Taylor—and then reported that Genl. Arista and Army had the night previous evacuated the city—and asked that private property might be respected. Genl. Taylor told them that it should not only be respected but *guarded* for them—that he should take "Military possession" of the place, and, of course, take all public property belonging to Mex[i]co—but their citizens could pursue their ordinary vocations without fear of interuption. If it was necessary for him to give them any orders he would give them through the Civil Authorities, but should himself enforce them if they did not—& then orderded us who had not crossed to march back to the bank opposite. M[atamoros], and we crossed right in to the city. We broke open all their customs houses, arsinals & other public buildings, in which we captured about 3,000 stand of arms, and a large amount of amunition.

In this country the trade in the articles of cigars & tobacco are government monopolies, and consequently these articles were contraband & legal captures & in the customs houses we found the greatest quantity of both. Tell Jocl just to imagine his store packed *full* of cigar boxes from the floor to the sealing and he will have some idea of the quantity of cigars we found in one house, all of which we captured and issued to our soldiers, and as they are not done smoking them yet we begin to think that our war is to end in *smoke*. We have just received the Declaration of War and the way the Volunteers are pouring in is beyond description. But, thank God, the Regular army *alone* had whip[p]ed 4 times their numbers twice, and taken their depot & City of near 10,000 inhabitants before one of them reached us. It is to be hoped now that Congress will give us the credit of being ready & willing to do our duty at the *risk* of our *lives*, and let the Military Academy alone for the present. To that institution the U.S. is indebted for the two signal victories of the 8th & 9th in which the killed & wounded of the enemy was nearly equal to our numbers in the action. On the 9th bayonets were crossed, & men killed in large numbers by the sword, bayonet, & lance, and that is hard fighting such as we but seldom *even read of*. After taking possession of the City, Genl. Taylor sent a command of 200 mounted men to pursue Arista, which they did for 70 miles, when they came within about 10 miles of him retreating with 4,000 troops, and cut off a small portion of his rear guard taking 20 men (with their guns) prisoners, and then returned as they had orders to do lest they might "catch a Tartar."

Matamoras is a very large place, much larger than I had ever expected. It has contained 15 or 20 thousand inhabitants—but is much deserted at present, not having more than 6 or 8 thousands now & those of the lowest order. All of the ladies & respectable & we[a]lthy people having left at the first indication of the war.[32]

From Matamoros to Camargo

Taylor was compelled to wait at Matamoros before moving the army up the Rio Grande to Camargo, where he would establish his next base. There were too few riverboats and not enough pilots who knew the Rio Grande channels; wood was scarce and what there was was too green for the boats' boilers; heavy rains had made roads impassable and flooded the river.

General Taylor also had doubts about the war itself and its consequences. On July 14 he wrote:

I feel confident that our ambitious views of conquest & agrandisement at the expense of a weak power will only be restrained & circumscribed by our inability to carry out our view, & in six or eight months if the Mexicans hold out that long, we will be fully as anxious to make peace as they are; for by that time we will have expended with very little effect or purpose all the money in the treasury, when our govt. will have to resort to loans & taxation to carry on the war; a course never palatable to our people.[33]

But in spite of transportation difficulties and a troubled mind he advanced. On July 6 the main body of troops began to leave Matamoros; on the fourteenth the advance regiment occupied Camargo. The first move in that direction occurred on June 6 when Lt. Col. Henry Wilson[34] with his four companies of infantry (1st Infantry), Price's company of Texas Rangers,[35] and two of the guns from Bragg's artillery company, under the command of Lt. George H. Thomas,[36] marched to Reynosa (sixty miles). This was ostensibly in response to an appeal from Reynosa for help against the Comanches and Canales'[37] band of irregulars. Wilson entered the town without opposition, but a few days before Canales had called upon the citizens to maintain their allegiance and a great many had fled or remained aloof when Wilson encamped in the plaza. This was on July 11. The Mexican army offered no resistance, but for the regiments of Taylor's army that were unable to get trans-

portation on steamboats the advance was nonetheless beset with hardship. A correspondent of the New Orleans Picayune called it "this horror march." John R. Kenly, the "Maryland Volunteer," pictured the horrors:

August 15 [1846].[38] Left Matamoras, to march with the brigade to Camargo, distant from 130 to 150 miles, by what was called the mountain road.

Our march was over desert rather than a mountainous country; from the time we left the Rio Grande at Matamoras until we struck the San Juan River on the 23d of August, not a stream, rivulet, brook, or spring, did we see or hear of, the only water to be had being found in ponds or tanks as they were called, in which rain-water had been collected for the use of the cattle. We suffered very much, and our march was more that of a routed army of stragglers than the advance of a well-organized brigade.

The distance from Matamoras to Camargo, by my calculation, was one hundred and thirty miles, and of this we marched seventy-eight miles in four days' continuous marching . . . This would have been excellent marching over good roads, but through the country of our route it was a shameful mismanagement, and reflected but little credit upon all concerned in the movement. The excuse was that our guides had misled the commanding officer, being themselves ignorant of the scarcity of water, and of the very road which we traveled. We marched in the middle of the day, with a burning sun overhead, and burning sand beneath our feet; not a drop of rain had fallen in this section of the country for months, and the dust raised by the tramp of so many men hung over our heads with smothering denseness from which there was no escape. When we reached a pond, which was nothing but a hog-wallow, men and horses rushed pellmell frantically into it, all semblance of rank and organization forgotten and disregarded.

At noon of the third day . . . I fell in the road utterly broken down, and I saw men toward night frantically digging with their bayonets in the dry bed of a water-course in the vain hope of finding water beneath the surface, but all was as dry as the arid country around. For miles our command was straggling along, day after day, some reaching camp long after nightfall, inviting attack by their looseness of array, and scorning the commands of superior officers, through the utter demoralization which prevailed. Curses and imprecations loud and deep were heard, and a vindictiveness was manifested, rarely I expect ever shown by American troops. I saw men fall down in convulsions on this march, frothing at their mouths, clutching the sand with their hands, and left to lie until nature and the shadows of night restored them to consciousness and strength. Kentuckians, Ohio men, and Baltimoreans, were all mixed together; the strongest and best walkers pressing to the front, the weak and the weary lagging behind. No word of encouragement, none of command, was heard, perhaps none was needed, for all who were able to march could be found at the tanks, and to reach the river was the leading, the only, object of that brigade on its memorable march to Camargo.[39]

ON TO MONTEREY

After evacuating Matamoros without a fight the Mexican army withdrew to Monterey where, under General Mejia[40] (to be replaced in September by Ampudia), it was reinforced for a decisive stand against the invader. Monterey, the capital of the state of Nuevo Leon, was the political and economic nerve center of northern Mexico. It was also the Americans' next objective.

Following the occupation of Camargo, General Taylor paused while he organized transportation and accumulated supplies. In August he ordered the American advance.[41]

Still flushed with the victory at Resaca de la Palma, and not anticipating much resistance, the army would soon discover that it had underestimated the Mexicans. In a letter written to his mother, E. Kirby Smith provides an insight into the spirit of the army as it broke camp:

The 8th [Regiment] and Artillery Batallion have received Orders to commence the movement towards Monterey this afternoon,[42] the 5th and 7th to hold themselves in readiness for the march on the morrow—these two Brig-[a]des under Gen. Worth, constitute the 2nd Division. The 3rd, 4th, 1st and 2nd under Twiggs[43] form the 1st Brig[a]de[44] which moves on Twiggs arrival. We are all busily engaged in making our preparations for crossing the mountains—and in fine health and excellent spirits, the camp resounds with the merry hum of our voices—jokes and hilarity circle round—whilst with that carelessness, that recklessness of the future, which seems inherent with a soldier's life, all seem busyly engaged, with their mules, mustangs and Mexicanos Amigos, in preparing for some pleasure excursion. Nor will we be disappointed in soon engaging in the grand ball which comes off at Monterey, for the Gen. sitts cross-legged in his tent, as grum as an old bear—sure indications of the coming storm. We are on the point of leaving a beautiful camp, which streaches for [more] than a mile along the banks of the San Juan; but without regret, for we all long after the mountain winds, the bracing breezes of the Sierra. The Mexicans have not yet recovered from the panic of the 9th and though they have been making preparations for our reception at Monterey, have been concentrating large reenforcements & collecting stores and munitions of War, I really believe we will enter the city without opposition.[45]

Lt. Ulysses S. Grant of the 4th Infantry discussed the logistical difficulties of the march from Camargo to Monterey. Mexican pack mules were not the least of the problems.

PLATE V. *Valley toward Saltillo*

PLATE VI. *Heights of Monterey from the Saltillo Road*

When Camargo was reached, we found a city of tents outside the Mexican hamlet. I was detailed to act as quartermaster and commissary to the regiment. The teams that had proven abundantly sufficient to transport all supplies from Corpus Christi to the Rio Grande over the level prairies of Texas, were entirely inadequate to the needs of the reinforced army in a mountainous country. To obviate the deficiency, pack mules were hired, with Mexicans to pack and drive them. I had charge of the few wagons alloted to the 4th infantry and of the pack train to supplement them.[46] There were not men enough in the army to manage that train without the help of Mexicans who had learned how. As it was the difficulty was great enough. The troops would take up their march at an early hour each day. After they had started, the tents and cooking utensils had to be made into packages, so that they could be lashed to the backs of the mules. Sheet-iron kettles, tent-poles and mess chests were inconvenient articles to transport in that way. It took several hours to get ready to start each morning, and by the time we were ready some of the mules first loaded would be tired of standing so long with their loads on their backs. Sometimes one would start to run, bowing his back and kicking up until he scattered his load; other would lie down and try to disarrange their loads by attempting to get on the top of them by rolling on them; others with tent-poles for part of their loads would manage to run a tent-pole on one side of a sapling while they would take the other. I am not aware of ever having used a profane expletive in my life; but I would have the charity to excuse those who may have done so, if they were in charge of a train of Mexican pack mules at the time.[47]

Maj. Luther Giddings of the 1st Ohio Volunteer Regiment described the march from Camargo to Monterey (about 156 miles), as well as the city and its environs as seen from a camp outside it.

In my last letter from Camargo, I informed you that our army was about moving upon Monterey, at which place we expected to meet the Mexican forces. We left Camargo on Sunday, Sept. 6, halted three days at Seralvo [sic], and encamped before the walls of Monterey on Saturday, 19th Sept. The first days of the march were void of interest; the road passing through a wilderness of thorns, broken in places by immense chasms, hundreds of feet deep. In these ravines alone, often miles apart, the heated and toilworn soldiers found water offensive to every sense. At Mier, the town so celebrated in the history of Texas border warfare[48]—we caught the first glimpse of the distant mountains, and the following day, encamped on a pure, transparent mountain stream, called the Arroya Mier, the murmuring of whose waters made every heart bound with delight. As we approached the mountains the country improved, and our camps were usually upon the banks of pleasant streams and amid groves of olive trees, whose branches were loaded with both flowers and fruit. The whole of the vast region between the gulf and the mountains, seems to be thinly populated. On some days of the march, we did not pass a rancho or see a ranchero (farmer) the only visible traces of man and his religion, being the cross, which was erected upon almost every hill, and in every valley. Upon many of these holy emblems were inscriptions in Spanish, requesting the prayers of the clergy for him who died or was murdered there.

At Marin—two days' march from Monterey—our army was concentrated, it having hitherto marched by divisions. . . . We marched the next day to San Francisco, a small village about 10 miles from Monterey, and which like all those through which we had previously passed, was deserted by all its inhabitants, who were not too poor to move away.

The following day (Saturday, Sept. 19th) was the last march which many of our brave men performed. Our regiment was in the rear upon that day, and ere we had fairly left San Francisco, we heard the report of heavy artillery in the direction of Monterey. Supposing that the advance guard was engaged with the enemy the shout was—"Quick time! Forward!" and for six miles the men ran, quickening the pace at every report, until we met a dragoon going to the rear, who informed us that the firing was from the town upon the mounted Texans,[49] who had ventured within range of the enemy's guns. The American army of invasion, about 6,000 strong—horses, foot, and artillery—encamped that morning in a beautiful grove of live oaks, about 3 miles from the city;—a more suitable spot for a pic nic [sic] could not be found in the vicinity of our own Dayton. I am informed that this camp ground of the invaders (and from which I now write) is a place much resorted to by the elite of Monterey.

. . . . .

Monterey contains about 15,000 inhabitants, and is situated at the base of a lofty range of rugged mountains, called the Sierra Madre. A branch of [the] San Juan river divides the city in unequal parts, the larger and better portion being between the river and the base of the mountain. A gently ascending slope, covered in places with chaparral—with here and there a field of corn or sugar cane, spreads itself before the town. The road by which our army approached, descends over this plain into the centre of the city. Standing upon the elevated grounds, midway between our camp and town, but little of the latter can be seen. It is embowered in trees—a spire or white wall being, in some places, all that is visible through their branches.

In front of the city, and about one fourth of a mile out, upon the plain, stands, solitary and alone, an immense fort, covering 3 or 4 acres of ground. It is built of solid masonry, with bastions, ditches, &c.—and is one of those strong holds which, in the opinion of our military engineers, can only be taken by what they call regular approaches. This fort is pierced for 32 guns, and commands every avenue to the city, over the plain upon the east. It throws both shot and shells from its walls; and it was this fort (named afterwards by our boys—"The Old Colored Gentleman"—from its dingy appearance) that fired upon our advanced division on the day of our arrival.

In the rear, or west of the city, rises, ridge after ridge, and peak over peak, the lofty Sierra Madre. On the north of the city is a deep gorge in the mountain, through which is the road to Saltillo and Mexico. This pass and the approaches to Monterey upon that side, are defended by a series of batteries placed upon peaks jutting out from the sides of the great Sierra, and by a strong and elevated fortress, located about half way between the pass and town—known as "the Bishop's palace." It was through this pass alone, that the Mexican army could receive reinforcements or retreat with safety. The city was protected on the south, by a chain of small forts (six I think in number,) extending from the foot of the mountain out to the plain.

In addition to these immense exterior defences, almost every street and square of the city was barricaded, and raked by field pieces, and every house (being built in the old Mexican style, with thick walls and stone roofs) was a fortress. These fortifications of Monterey (the position and strength of many of which we learned by cruel experience) were occupied by at least 10,000 regular Mexican troops, and defended by forty or fifty pieces of heavy artillery. It will thus be seen that Monterey is one of the strongest places on the continent.[50]

The Battle of Monterey

The American force, six thousand strong, reached the outskirts of Monterey on the morning of September 19. Taylor spent the rest of the day planning his attack on the strongly fortified city defended by a Mexican army of seven thousand men. The plan finally chosen called for a flank attack from the west led by General Worth while Taylor directed a frontal assault. The battle was joined on Monday, September 20; it lasted for three days.

Captains William S. Henry[51] and Electus Backus[52] described their experiences as participants in the frontal attack. Backus' account was recorded in his Journal.

Sept[ember] 20th [1846]. The General's [i.e., Taylor's] manner & appearance this morning indicated nothing but confidence—he had reached the desired point, & had his enemy in position. He despatched Genl. Worth at 11 A.M. to gain the Saltillio [sic] road, & cut of[f] the enemies retreat & supplies in that direction, & to capture several works that crowned the heights at the west of the town. Our engineers were indefatigable in gaining information during the day, but numerous bodies of lancers watched their movements, & made them cautious. An immense plain north of the town was raked by the Artille[r]y from the Citadel, & from 3 redoubts, at the eastern extremity of the town, and the streets were barricaded & defended by artille[r]y, Infantry and lancers.

Sept[ember] 21st [1846]. The troops were early under arms, & prepared to execute the orders of old Rough & Ready, in whose judgement & skill they placed the most implicit confidence. The 1st & 3rd Regts. of Infantry, and the Baltimore Battallion,[53] all under the command of Col. Garland,[54] were first put in motion, and advanced towards the town, but soon left the main road—by inclining to the East. Our line was formed on the edge of the plain, perhaps 3/4's of a mile from town, & the guns from the Citadel opened upon us immediately, & with some effect. Soon after, the batteries at the east end of the town commenced their fire, & we advanced rapidly in line, towards the City. Maj. Mansfield & Capt. Williams[55] were far in our front, with Mr. Kinney[56] as a guide, & endeavering to ascertain the most accessible point, & two or three companies of skirmishers were sent in advance to protect the reconnoisance. A message was sent back by Mr. Kinney, requesting Col. Garland to change his point of direction more to the right. In this partial change of direction, I observed that the Baltimore Battallion (the left of the line) did not reta[in] its position, & [I] saw nothing mor[e] of it as a Battallion during

Battle of Monterey

the day—& I am under the impression that it never recovered its organization after its line was once broken. I sa[w] many individuals of the Battallion, both officers and men, in town during the day, but they were without organization.

Soon after ou[r] change of direction we approached an unfinished battery, from which our skirmishers had driven a few of the enemy, & having passed over it, we entered the town by a street running south, & which led nearly in the direction of one of the Mexican batteries, on the south side of the creek. Our movement down this street was by the right flank, the 3d Infy. being in front, followed by the 1st. Near the foot of this street, where it is intersected by an artificial ditch filled with running water, it makes a slight change of direction and at this point the enemies' battery, over the creek, was visible, and distant about 150, or 200 yards. Fort Diablo was some 200 yards farther east, & was connected with this battery by a breast work—which was lined with Infy. as well as the adjacent buildings. In this position the 3d Infy. recd. a discharge of grape from the batteries, and of small arms from the trenches, which produced terrible havoc in its ranks. The 1st Infy. was halted, when its right had reached the ditch, was faced to its front (left), and ordered to move forward. At the same moment it recd. a fire of musketry in front, from an enemy concealed behind houses, walls, & shrubbery. Our forward movement soon brought the enemy from his concealment, and sent him backward. When we had moved some hundred yards or more, & cleared our front, I looked for a superior officer of the regt., or brigade for instructions—& finding myself the senior present, I directed the troops to cross the ditch on our right, & advance. A few yards brought us to a tannery, filled with the enemy, who opened their fire on us—but were soon destroyed or dispersed.

Having secured this tannery, I mounted its flat roof, & directed the men to follow me. And now for the 1st time I had a fair view of the enemy & his works. At about 120 yards in our front (East) was a large distillery, having a strong flat roof, facing north—& on this roof was posted probably 200 Mexicans (Infy.)—having a breastwork of sand bags on the north side. Some 30 yards north of this distillery, was a redoubt, defended by 5 pieces of artillery, & by Infantry, which was overlooked by the Infy. posted on the distillery. These defences all looked to the north, & we had passed them so far as to be obliquely in the rear. Fort Diablo was now directly on my right (south) distant about 250 yards—but there was some shrubbery intervening which covered us from their sight. Having placed my men on the roof of the tannery, which was protected by a stone battlement about 2 feet in height, I directed them to open their fire upon the enemy on the roof of the distillery, who were without a covering on their left flank. The effect was visible in a moment of time. The roof was cleared in a few shots, and the enemy retreated across the creek to Fort Diablo—and soon after, a party of perhaps 30, women & children, issued from the yard of the distillery, and proceeded to the same place

—about 20 men led & followed this domestic caravan. Our men were ordered not to fire upon the women, but in the mellee one was killed by accident.

About this time Maj. Mansfield came up to my position & stated that we would find it necessary to fall back & I understood him to say we had gone too far with our small force. He returned towards the 3d where I had last seen Col. Garland, and in a moment after Maj. Lear[57] of the 3d came up to my position and stated also that we should be compelled to fall back. He returned towards his Regt. & after making a few steps, recd. a ball in his face, from the effect of which he died a few weeks after. Maj. Mansfield had been wounded at nearly the same time & place. I now heard the command *"Retire in good order"*— but not knowing from what authority it proceeded, I retained my position. I soon saw the troops falling back, & ordered my men down from the roof into the yard. Capt. Lamotte[58] had recd. a severe wound in his left arm near the shoulder, & was lying in rear of a small building adjoining the tannery. I asked Capt. Scott[59] to take my handkerchief, & bind up the wound, knowing him to have some skill in surgical operations, & designed moving to the rear as soon as we could remove Capt. Lamotte.

While this operation was being performed, the fire of redoubt No. 1 & Fort Diablo was renewed, & I became satisfied that our troops were advancing again towards the redoubt. I therefore sprang up again on the tannery, followed by Capt. Scott & our men, & now discovered that the gorge of the redoubt was open, offering us a fair shot into a crowded mass of men, & artillery, & mules. A piece of Artillery was turned upon us, & fired one or two shots without damage, when our men poured a deliberate fire into the open gorge. The effect was electrical. Before our muskets were loaded, the enemy was in full retreat for Fort Diablo, & dismounting from the building.[60] We pursued him to the creek to cut off his retreat or capture prisoners. To my surprize I found the creek deep & rapid at the point where I struck it, though at 60 yards below the water is not above two feet deep & the stream much broader. One of my Sergeants endeavored to jump the stream, & fell into the middle of it, & then clambered up on the opposite bank. I threw him his musket, & formed my men close to the bank opposite him, & directed him to advance a few steps, & endeavor to bring out some Mexicans who had dropped down behind the bushes near the creek. He did so & some 20 Mexicans surrendered to him as prisoners. At this moment, my men called to me that there was a large body of Mexicans in our rear. I ordered Sergt. Kearney to return across the stream, and sprang to an eminence some ten or 12 steps distant to see where the enemy was approaching. My men pointed in the direction of the redoubt No. 1 & I now discovered that they were pointing to the Volunteers who were just approaching the redoubt, & cheering most vociferously. My prisoners thus escaped, with the exception of 3 or four, sent to the rear. The Mississippi & Tennessee volunteers soon left the captured Fort & advanced to my position.[61]

PLATE VII. *View of Monterey from the Heights South of the City*

PLATE VIII. Storming of Monterey—Attack on the Bishop's Palace

Capt. William S. Henry recalled the battle in his volume of impressions on the war published in 1847:

September 23d. From our camp we had the pleasure of hearing General Worth open upon the town from the castle about 7 o'clock. A report was circulated that the enemy were attempting to escape. The whole command was immediately under arms, and marched almost within range of the enemy's guns. So many commanding points were in our possession that we were momentarily in expectation of their capitulation. It was cheering to see Worth pouring it into them, and that, too, with their own pieces and ammunition. The rapid discharge of small-arms at the eastern end of the city gave notice that the engagement had again commenced. The regiment of Texas cavalry under Colonel Woods [sic, Wood] had dismounted, and, with the Mississippians under Colonel Davis were sharply at work. The Mississippians at daybreak took possession of Fort Diablo (from which we had received such a destructive fire on the 21st and 22d), without any resistance, the enemy having abandoned it, taking with them their guns during the night. General Quitman was in command. These troops fought most gallantly, driving the enemy before them from house to house, their rifles picking them off wherever a Mexican's body or head presented itself.

Bragg's battery was ordered into the city, and the 3d Infantry was ordered to support it. When we got within range of the guns of the citadel, the battery crossed the field of fire at full gallop; not one was injured. The 3d took a more circuitous route, and came up under cover. When we arrived the city had been cleared of the enemy on a line with and within two squares of the Cathedral which is situated in the main Plaza, and in which they had been concentrated. General Quitman,[62] General Henderson, General Lamar,[63] Colonel Wood, and Colonel Davis all displayed distinguished gallantry; several of their men were wounded, and some few killed. Bragg's battery and the 3d Infantry dashed in among them, and shared the fight for the remainder of the day. The firing was very severe, but nothing compared to that on the 21st, except at one street running directly from the Cathedral. To cross that street you had to pass through a shower of bullets. One of Bragg's pieces played up this street with very little effect, as the weight of metal was entirely too light. Sergeant Weightman, Bragg's first sergeant, worked his piece like a hero, and was shot through the heart while aiming his gun. The Mexicans whenever the piece was pointed at them would fall behind their barricade, and at that time we could cross without a certainty of being shot; as soon as it was fired, their balls (as if bushels of hickory nuts, were hurled at us) swept the street. Our men crossed it in squads. "Go it, my boys!" and away some would start; others would wait until the enemy had foolishly expended at space their bullets, and then they would cross.

General Taylor was in town with his staff, on foot, walking about, perfectly regardless of danger. He was very imprudent in the exposure of his person. He crossed the street in which there was such a terrible fire in a walk, and by every chance should have been shot. I ran across with some of my men, and reminded him how much he was exposing himself, to which he replied, "*Take that ax and knock in that door.*" When we commenced on the door the occupant signified, by putting the key in and unlocking it, if we had no objection, he would save us the trouble. It turned out to be quite an extensive apothecary-shop. The proprietor, Doctor San Juan (there are more St. Johns in this country than stones), was a very respectable-looking Esculapius, and

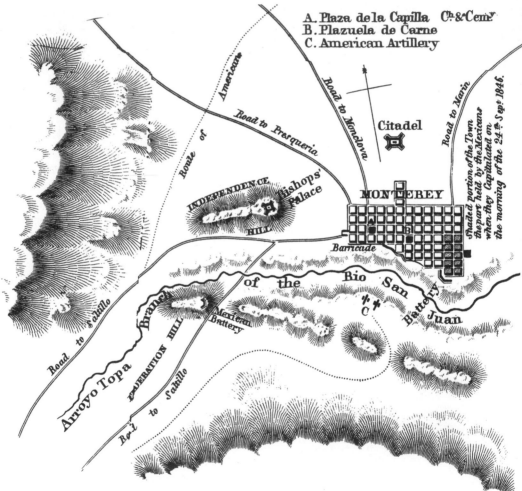

MONTEREY

offered us some delicious, ripe limes and cool water. I took some of the former, but declined the latter, as it was hinted it might be poisoned. One of the men, not so sensitive, made himself a *governor* lemonade, and told me it was "*first rate,*" and advised me to take some. The doctor said Ampudia was in the Plaza with four thousand men, and that two thousand were in the citadel. The house on the opposite corner had been broken open. It was a grocery store; in it the men found bread and other edibles. Bursting open another door, we came upon five rather genteel-looking women, with some children, and one or two men. They were on their knees, each with a crucifix, begging for mercy. As soon as they saw me, the cry was, "Capitano! capitano!" I reassured them by shaking hands, and, by the expression of my countenance, signified there was no danger. They appeared very grateful to find their throats were not to be cut. Although we are fiercely fighting, and the blood of our officers and men has freely flowed, yet not one act of unkindness have I heard reported as being committed by either regular or volunteer.

General Taylor, finding the field-pieces of little use, ordered us to retire to camp as soon as the volunteers had withdrawn. Their withdrawal was ordered upon the supposition that General Worth would commence throwing shells into the city in the afternoon. The mortar was sent to him yesterday. It was a difficult matter to get the volunteers out; they were having their own fun. The enemy sent in a flag of truce today, asking a cessation until the women and children could be removed. The general, of course, declined; such a degree of politeness should not have been expected at this late hour. The flag is a good symptom; their time is drawing near. I hardly think they will hold out another day. It is reported many were leaving the heights with pack-mules this morning. Had not General Worth taken possession of the Saltillo road, I question whether many would not have been off yesterday. Thus far they have fought most bravely, and with an endurance and tenacity I did not think they possessed.

On our march back to camp, I was very much amused at a remark of an Irishman: "Faith, boys, we have had a Waterloo time of it; three days' fighting! The French fought against the combined powers of Europe; we are the combined powers of Europe and America! We have a little of all among us, and *the whole* can't be bate!"[64]

Worth's Flank Attack at Monterey

Lt. Edmund Bradford of the 4th Artillery was with Worth's force that attacked the Mexican flank. He wrote a vivid account of the fight:

Now that I am somewhat settled I will try and give you some description of the battles. On the 19th the whole Army arrived in sight of Monterrey and encamped about 2½ miles from the town. Several reconnoitering parties were sent out in different directions to ascertain the position of the enemy. Genl. Taylor called together the commanding Generals of Divisions and Brigades to hold a council. The next morning the 1st Division (composed of two batteries of Artillery, 200 mounted Texans, the Arty Batallion, the 5th, 7th & 8th Infy) were ordered to take with them two days provisions and one blanket for each man. The Division was under the command of Genl. Worth. We left Camp about 12 o'clock and marched on the road to Montery [sic] about a mile; we then struck off the road to the right, passing through chapparal and corn fields to the left of the town. We were sheltered from the fire, from the Fort, in front of the town by a low ridge. About 5 o'clock P.M. the column was halted, and Genl. Worth and a party of Texans went out to reconnoitre our position. A mile in our advance we could see there was a battery of the enemy planted on the top of a very high hill which commanded the road on which we were marching. Below the battery and on the same hill there was a large fortified building called the Bishop's palace. Beyond this was another hill about the same height with a battery on the top, and a stone fort lower down, both of which commanded the road. After remaining in the road for some time, we heard a fire opened on the reconnoitering party. The fire was returned by the Texans and was kept up about half an hour; during this time several shells were thrown from the top of the hill, but fortunately they all passed too high.

Just as the sun was setting a heavy shower of rain came up which drenched us to the skin and in this condition we were obliged to remain all night. I had fortunately a dry blanket to wrap myself up in. We were not permitted to make any fires to cook or to dry ourselves.

The next morning, the 21st, we rose before day light, and commenced our march. We now knew we were to storm the two heights and take the guns of the enemy, thereby cutting off their retreat by the Saltillo road. Just as the day broke we could hear the enemy sounding their reveille with the greatest confidence. So soon as we came in range of the shot from the first hill, the enemy opened on us with shells; we were exposed to their shots for at least half an hour and during the whole march not a single shell struck near enough [to] the column to do any injury. We could distinctly hear them whiz over our heads and burst in the hill on our right. About 7 o'clock A.M. we heard a firing of musketry in our advance between the Mexicans and our skirmishers. Our Batallion was immediately formed in line of battle and charged towards the place. I could distinctly see the enemy running in every direction. In the charge we passed over the dead bodies of several men and horses. Lances, pistols, holsters &c were lying in every direction. The force of the enemy was estimated at 300 cavalry supported by a column of Infantry. As they retired, our batteries opened on them with shells, making great havoc. I have since ascertained one single shell killed and wounded thirty Mexicans. Some five or six of the enemy were left dead on the field where they attacked us and amongst them was a Colonel of Cavalry said to be the bravest man in the Army. On our side we had one Texan wounded. None of the regulars were touched.

The Division was then formed in the road, and Capt. Smith[65] & Capt. Scott[66] sent out with their companies to reconnoitre. The 1st Brigade was ordered to march into a corn field in order to have a flank fire on any troops which might make a sally from the castle. Whilst we were lying in the field the enemy opened a heavy fire on us from two guns on the 2nd hill. The men we ordered to lie flat on the ground. In this position we remained for 1½ hours, the balls passing a few feet over our heads; one shower of grape fell in and about my company in every direction, but struck no one. At this time we received an order to march out of the reach of the shot. In doing this we were exposed to full view for half an hour and I assure you they took advantage of us. One shot struck the ground about 20 feet from me on my left and ro-choccd [sic, ricocheted] over the company in front of me. Another struck Capt. [Henry] McKavis [sic, McKavett][67] on the left side, passing through his body. He was killed instantly. We now took up another position expecting an attack from the enemy. Col. Duncan's battery was formed in the road, the Arty Batallion on its right and occupying a hedgefence. Lieut. Ma[c]kall's[68] battery was placed on the left and rear of Col. Duncan and the 8th Infy on the left of Lieut. Ma[c]kall; on the left of the 8th was stationed the 2nd Brigade, composed of the 5th & 7th Infy and commanded by Genl. Smith. Three companies of the Arty Batn and two companies of Texans were ordered to join Capt. Smith for the purpose of storming the 2nd hill. The command started about 12½ o'clock P.M.

After they had been gone half and [sic] hour the 7th Infy were ordered to support them. At 1 o'clock we saw the firing from the hill and the Mexicans advancing down it. From this we thought our men were being repulsed and another regiment was sent forward. The enemy kept up firing for half an hour without a gun being fired by our men; about ¼ 2 o'clock we saw the firing commencing by our troops and the Mexicans running up the hill. We then raised such a shout as I have hardly ever heard. In a few minutes Capt. Smith was on the top. He had followed them so fast that they had not had time to carry off one of their guns. This gun was immediately captured and turned on them. The very first shot made with it struck the other gun (which they had placed in the fort) directly on the muzzle breaking it off.

Just at the [sic, that] time the 2nd Brigade charged the Fort and drove the enemy from it. The guns were now turned on the castle on the opposite hill and an incessant firing kept up between the two forts. In storming the height our side lost but one man killed and a few wounded. Amongst the wounded were three officers—their wounds are all slight. On the morning of the 22nd Capt. Scott's, Lieut. Ayers'[69] and my company of the Arty. Batn., three companies of the 8th Infy and the Texans received orders to storm the 1st hill and castle. We started at 3 o'clock in the morning and reached the foot of the hill just as the day began to appear. I suppose we were discovered from the castle as four rockets were thrown up at different times. As we commenced ascending the hill, a heavy fog enveloped the top of it, which prevented the enemy from discovering our exact position. When we came within fifty yards of the summit, the enemy commenced their fire; our men did not return it until we were almost on the top; we then opened our fire and charged at the same time. The enemy retreated very rapidly and we pursued them half way to the castle and the[n] came back to our position on the summit. We planted the American flag amid a shower of bullets from the castle and gave it three cheers. The Mexicans made a sally from the castle and were immediately repulsed.

My company was ordered to move forward to support Capt. Vinton,[70] who had command of the advance which was stationed about 150 yards from the castle. In moving forward I had one man killed instantly. So soon as we gained our position I ordered my men to lie flat on the ground and to cover themselves as much as possible. We laid in this position eight hours, during the whole of which time the shot of the enemy were passing over and around us in every direction. At one time the enemy moved their position so as to obtain a raking fire on us. I immediately moved my position, and ordered the men to do the same. One six pound ball struck so near me that it threw the dirt on me.

Being seperated [sic] from the main body and not knowing what was going on, I began to fear we would be obliged to retire. Just then I heard the voice of Lieut. Roland[71] saying "clear the way gentleman [sic] I am going to fire" and I assure you I have never heard a more agreable sound. In a few moments, I heard the whiz of a shell over my head, and from the cheering on the top of the hill I knew it had been fired with good effect. The enemy returned the fire with a six pounder from the castle but without doing any harm.

After the firing had been continued an hour, we heard the sound of the trumpets of their cavalry who were coming up the hill to charge us; the advance was ordered to close in on the ridge of the hill and charge them. As the right of my company closed up I could see a body of lancers coming up. We immediately fired on them and made them retreat; the company on my left charged down the hill towards the castle followed by mine. In running down, I could see the top of the castle lined with men. Lieut. Ayers of the 3rd Arty was the 1st officer in the castle, and I was the second. Lieut. Ayers, handed down the colors. The men lined the castle in an instant, and commenced firing at the retreating Mexicans. I ran round the castle to the fort in its front and there found a large howitzer. I got some of my men together and ran it into [the] battery, we then found it was spiked, but in a few minutes the spike was driven in and we opened on the retreating enemy with their own guns and ammunition. In a very short time they had all disappeared. We captured one howitzer, one 18-pounder and two six-pounders and a very large quantity of amunition—lances &c. We found and buried 20 Mexicans, on our side the loss was not large. We had not more than six killed and about 15 [possibly 25—not clear] wounded. We took prisoner a Mexican Captain, who had been wounded in the foot. The American flag was hoisted on the earth immediately. In my company I had one killed and two wounded. One of them was struck in the centre of the forehead, he came to me and asked me to let him fall out. I gave him my handkerchief and told him to put it round his head and go to the doctor. That night the man came up to me perfectly well. The ball which struck him was spent and merely broke the skin.

The next day, the 23d we marched into the town; we advanced very cautiously expecting every moment to be fired on from the houses. My company with two others formed the reserve—; as we went along we broke the doors of every house we passed so as to be able to get into them, in case we should be obliged to retreat. When we had penetrated the city about a mile, the enemy opened on us with grape and musketry. The men were immediately put in the houses, and then the work of cutting from house to house commenced. We seized on all the crowbars and pickaxes we could find. The stone of which the houses are built is so soft that we could cut through a wall two feet thick in 20 minutes. By dark our troops had advanced to within one square of the main plaza, where the cathedral is. Just before dark, a ten inch mortar was planted by Maj. Munroe[72] in a grave yard at the end of the city. It opened about dark, the shell fell in the yard of the house in which I was and burst throwing the dirt over me. The second shell was thrown better and fell in the plaza amongst the enemy. The next morning the 24th the firing commenced as usual. About 8 A.M. a flag of truce was sent in by Genl. Ampudia to Genl. Taylor asking to capitulate. During the whole day Genl. Taylor and Genl. Ampudia were agreeing on the terms. At 3 o'clock P.M. Genl. Taylor made his last offer and gave Ampudia one hour to consider it. The Genl. agreed that the Mexicans should march with their muskets, sabres and six pieces of field artillery. At the end of the hour we all thought we should be obliged to commence fighting again, but when the flag returned we were told that Ampudia had agreed to the terms. That night at 10 o'clock the stipulations were signed. By them, all hostilities are to cease for eight weeks or until the two Genls. were able to hear from their respective countries. Neither Army is to advance beyond a certain line half way between this and Saltillo. Ampudia mentioned that a minister had been sent to the United States to make a treaty of peace.[73]

BATTLEFIELD HEROISM AT MONTEREY

Not all the heroism at Monterey belonged to the warriors. An American soldier bore witness to a different, and perhaps higher, order of devotion.

Hungry and cold I crept to one corner of the fort to get in the sunshine and at the same time to shelter myself from the bombs that were flying thick around me. I looked out, and, some two or three hundred yards from the fort, I saw a Mexican female carrying water and food to the wounded men of both armies. I saw her lift the head of one poor fellow, give him water, and then take her handkerchief from her own head and bind up his wounds; attending one or two others in the same way, she went back for more food and water. As she was returning I heard the crack of one or two guns, and she, poor good creature, fell; after a few struggles all was still—she was dead! I turned my eyes to heaven and thought, "Oh God, and this is war!" I cannot believe but that the shot was an accidental one. The next day, passing into another fort, I passed her dead body. It was lying on its back, with the bread and broken gourd containing a few drops of water. We buried her amid showers of grape and round shot, occasionally dodging a shell or twelve pounder, and expecting every moment to have another grave to dig for one of ourselves.[74]

ARMISTICE AFTER MONTEREY

On September 25 the American army entered Monterey, reportedly to the tune of "Yankee Doodle."

In some quarters Taylor was criticized for granting the enemy an armistice. President Polk was among the critics. He believed the Mexicans should have been compelled to surrender their army as well as Monterey. His cabinet concurred and the Secretary of War dispatched a letter ordering the termination of the armistice. The order reached Taylor on November 2. He obeyed, sending word to Santa Anna, now the Mexican commander,[75] that the armistice would end November 13, but he resented the presidential criticism, disagreed with its reasoning and felt that further fighting in northern Mexico was useless. He stated all this in a letter of November 9 published in the New York Express:

I do not believe the authorities at Washington are at all satisfied with my conduct in regard to the terms of the capitulation entered into with the Mexican commander, which you no doubt have seen, as they have been made public through the official organ, and copied into various other newspapers. I

PLATE IX. *Monterey from Independence Hill, in rear of the Bishop's Palace*

PLATE X. *Monterey from a Housetop in the Main Plaza*

have this moment received an answer (to my despatch announcing the surrender of Monterey, and the circumstances attending the same), from the Secretary of War, stating that "it was regretted by the President that it was not deemed advisable to insist on the terms I had proposed in my first communication to the Mexican commander, in regard to giving up the city,"— adding that "the circumstances which dictated, no doubt justified the change."

Although the terms of capitulation may be considered too liberal on our part by the President and his advisers, as well as by many others at a distance, particularly by those who do not understand the position which we occupied (otherwise they might come to a different conclusion in regard to the matter), yet, on due reflection, I see nothing to induce me to regret the course I pursued. The proposition on the part of General Ampudia which had much to do in determining my course in the matter was based on the ground that our government had proposed to his to settle the existing difficulties by negotiation (which I know was the case, without knowing the result), which was then under consideration by the proper authorities, and which he (Gen. Ampudia), had no doubt would result favorably, as the whole of his people were in favor of peace. If so I considered the effusion of blood not only unnecessary, but improper. Their force was also considerably larger than ours: and from the size and position of the place we could not completely invest it; so that the greater portion of their troops, if not the whole, had they been disposed to do so, could, any night, have abandoned the city at once, entered the mountain passes, and effected their retreat,—do what we would. Had we been put to the alternative of taking the place by storm (which there is no doubt we should have succeeded in doing), we should, in all probability, have lost fifty or a hundred men in killed, besides the wounded, which I wished to avoid, as there appeared to be a prospect of peace, even if a distant one. I also wished to avoid the destruction of women and children, which must have been very great, had the storming process been resorted to. Besides, they had a very large and strong fortification a short distance from the city, which if carried with the bayonet, must have been taken at a great sacrifice of life; and, with our limited train of heavy or battery artillery, it would have required twenty or twenty-five days to take it by regular approaches.

That they should have surrendered a place nearly as strong as Quebec, well fortified under the direction of skillful engineers,—their works garnished with forty-two pieces of artillery, abundantly supplied with ammunition, garrisoned by 7,000 regular and 2,000 irregular troops, in addition to some thousand citizens capable of (and no doubt actually), bearing arms and aiding in its defence,—to an opposing force of half their number, scantily supplied with provisions, and with a light train of artillery,—is among the unaccountable occurrences of the times.

I am decidedly opposed to carrying the war beyond Saltillo in this direction, which place has been entirely abandoned by the Mexican forces, all of whom have been concentrated at San Luis Potosi; and I shall lose no time in taking possession of the former as soon as the cessation of hostilities referred to expires,—which I have notified the Mexican authorities will be the case on the 13th inst., by direction of the President of the United States.[76]

Lull for Regrouping

Although the armistice was ended officially on November 15, fighting did not resume immediately. There was a lull in the war while strategy was considered in both Washington and Mexico City and orders issued for the regrouping of troops in the field. A week before the date set for the termination of his armistice, Taylor issued Orders No. 139 which directed the occupation of Saltillo (across the line of demarcation) by the following troops: Lt. James Duncan's battery, the Artillery Battalion (eight companies), the 8th Infantry, the 5th Infantry, and Capt. Blanchard's company of Louisiana Volunteers, all under General Worth. To Saltillo also, Taylor ordered the 1st Ohio and 1st Kentucky Volunteer Regiments, then placed Maj. Gen. William Orlando Butler in charge of all the troops on that line—from Saltillo back to Point Isabel.[77] The army at Saltillo was joined, in December, by another force, one commanded by Brig. Gen. John Ellis Wool, who had marched from San Antonio via Monclova and Parras. From Saltillo the advance probed forward to Encantada, Agua Nueva and Rinconada Pass.

After ordering the 2d Dragoons (except for two companies) to join Butler at Saltillo, Taylor left in Monterey the 4th and 7th Infantry Regiments, two companies of the 3d Artillery, and two companies of Mounted Rifles and then marched with the 1st Infantry to Montemorelos on his way to Victoria. He was closely followed by Quitman's brigade of the Volunteers' Old Field Division (now broken up) composed of the Georgia, 1st Mississippi and 1st Tennessee Regiments. At Montcmorclos the 2d Infantry and 2d Tennessee Regiment joined them for the march to Victoria. On January 4, Taylor entered that city, but he did not remain there for long. Instead he returned to Monterey after the Polk administration decided that the bulk of his army—most of his regulars and some of his volunteers—should be transferred to Scott's new expedition, then being formed for a campaign against Vera Cruz. From Monterey, Taylor went to Saltillo, where he became involved in the operations that led up to the Battle of Buena Vista. In February 1847, despite a repeated order that he remain strictly on the defensive, he moved forward again, this time to Agua Nueva, south of Saltillo. There he awaited events.

Wool's March

Meanwhile, at the same time as Taylor's campaign, another American force, the "Army of the Center," led by Brig. Gen. John Ellis Wool, had invaded Mexico. Starting from San Antonio, the original objective of this attack was Chihuahua, lying to the west of Taylor's theater of operations and south of New Mexico, but news that a Mexican army was assembling for an attack on Taylor led to a change of plans. A correspondent of the Boston Evening Post *sent back an account of Wool's entire campaign, or as it is frequently and perhaps more aptly called, "Wool's march."*

General Wool landed from the gulf on the 2d of August last [i.e., August, 1846], at La Vaca, Texas, with the first and second regiments of Illinois foot, commanded [by] Cols. John J. Hardin[78] and Wm. H. Bissell,[79] and soon after took up the march for San Antonio de Bexar, one hundred and fifty miles to the north. Here he was joined by Col. Yell's mounted regiment from Arkansas, and by that of Col. Marshall,[80] of Kentucky; by Capt. Washington's[81] well drilled company of flying artillery, eight pieces, from Carlisle in Pennsylvania and by Major Bounneville's [sic, Bonneville's][82] battalion of regular infantry. Col. Harney,[83] with four companies of dragoons, was also attached to this division. . . . The two months passed in this delightful region, were well spent in drilling for active service.

On the 26th of September, two days after the capitulation of Monterey, the advance under Colonel Harney, marched for the Rio Grande, followed soon after by General Wool, who left Colonel Churchill,[84] the inspector, and Colonel Bissell to bring up the rear, as they began to do on the 14th of October. The whole army, at this time, was two thousand six hundred strong. We, of the advance, marched to the Rio Grande, two hundred miles in twelve days, resting one, for General Wool to join us.

. . . Crossing the present boundary between our country and Mexico, on the 12th day of October, we set foot on the soil of the enemy. Thence we marched a distance of four hundred miles to the city of Parras, on the southwestern confines of this state and near to a lake of the same name, passing through and taking peaceable possession in our circuitous route of the cities of Presidio del Rio Grande, Nava, San Fernando, Santa Rosa, Monclova, the ancient capital of this state and Parras, which we reached on the 6th December ult. These cities contain, each, a population of from five to fifteen thousand souls, except Nava, which numbers about two thousand. Monclova and Parras are quite wealthy and exhibit fine specimens of Spanish art and refinement. We spent some time at nearly all of them, with pleasure and profit, viewing much of Mexican manners and customs and enjoying an apparently cordial intercourse with the citizens. . . .

The country bordering the Rio Grande where we crossed it, and for a considerable distance into Mexico, west and south, is low, level, very fertile and well watered by streams or irrigating canals. It already supports a large population, and contains the cities of Presidio, Nava, and San Fernando; the last two, situated forty and fifty miles west of the river, struck me as quite flourishing.

The land between the Nueces and the Rio Grande, for nearly a hundred miles, except a few fertile prairies, is divided into sandy deserts and marshy *chaparrals*, almost as difficult of access as the jungles of India. It will be the haunt only of savages and wild beasts for many generations, if not forever. . . .

The effect of our long marching, of the strict discipline enforced by our general, and of the exercise taken in drill was most salutary upon the health of the army. After a professional and sedentary life in the bilious atmosphere of the Mississippi, the campaign had a most renovating effect. The army lay encamped at Monclova three weeks, during which period our rear came up, and Gen. Wool was ordered to co-operate with General Taylor at Monterey, instead of marching upon Chihuahua, which up to this time had been our destination. Eleven days brought us to Parras, two hundred miles farther into the country, where supplies were abundant. Here we lay in camp eleven days, in friendly intercourse with the people, of whom many are not destitute of moral worth and intelligence. The American sharpers among them, *soi-disant* gentlemen, engaged in trade and marrying fortunes, struck me with more disgust than the most degraded Mexicans. Many of the better classes of natives commanded my highest esteem. . . .

But these halcyon days soon passed over our heads, and more stirring scenes were at hand. General Worth, who lay at Saltillo, one hundred and twenty miles north of east from us, with a thousand regulars, on the 16th of December received intelligence which he credited, that Santa Anna was within three days' march of him with 30,000 men, and was advancing. He despatched expresses to Monterey and Parras for aid, promising to hold out one day against any force, and requesting us to reinforce him on the fourth day. General Taylor had gone to Victoria, but General Lane hastened to Saltillo with two regiments. General Wool received the news in the evening of the 17th, and in less than two hours the whole army was on the march. On the 21st we reinforced Worth, but no enemy was present. For three nights in succession on this march, which we accomplished in three days and a half, the army was roused at one o'clock in the morning to resume the advance. The cavalry and artillery called us the sleep-walkers, and complained that we were killing off their horses. The spirit displayed by the men, their alacrity, cheerfulness, and patience, were most admirable. Expecting, as they did, to meet the enemy every hour, their demeanor inspired the staff and all other officers with confidence in the result. Volunteers as they were, and, as compared with regulars, but imperfectly disciplined, they suddenly assumed a bearing and readiness in obeying orders, not altogether unworthy [of] the old guard of Napoleon.

This march was a fitting prelude to the battle of Buena Vista. On the 21st of December, we sat down at Agua Nueva, a small *rancho* or town, twenty-one miles south of Saltillo, and near the great pass in the mountain leading to San Luis Potosi, the seat of the Mexican power. Here we passed Christmas, watching [for] the appearance of the enemy in this pass and two smaller ones, a few miles distant on each side of us. New Year's day was spent at Encantada, nine miles nearer to Saltillo; we still [were] watching, however, and enjoying the luxury of frequent false alarms. We soon after took up our fighting position at the *Rancho*, or Ranch, of Buena Vista, five miles from the city, and prepared to defend the pass two miles in advance of our camp.[85]

Prelude to Buena Vista

The threat which brought Wool hurrying to Taylor's support was posed by Santa Anna. Following the battle of Monterey, Santa Anna had consolidated his position as master of the country; in September he began to assemble at San Luis Potosí an army that was to reach 25,000. San Luis Potosí lay directly west of Tampico, where American troops were being assembled for transport to Vera Cruz, and about midway between the latter and Monterey. Thus Santa Anna could choose his target. The choice was determined by a letter from Scott to Taylor that fell into Mexican hands and was delivered to him. It revealed not only the overall American strategy but also that Taylor's forces had been greatly weakened. The Mexican general decided to crush Taylor before the landing at Vera Cruz could be staged. On February 2, 1847, he started the march north; on the twenty-first he reached La Encarnacion, thirty-five miles from Taylor's headquarters at Agua Nueva.

Taylor, who had at first doubted that the Mexicans were actually approaching, knew that his location at Agua Nueva was indefensible and retreated to Buena Vista Ranch where his outnumbered army took up a strong defensive position.

Santa Anna soon overran a small force that had been left at Agua Nueva to guard supplies that could not be moved (they were burned), and brought his army face to face with Taylor's on February 22. He gave the American general one hour to surrender; when the demand was rejected he attacked. It was the beginning of the fiercest battle of the war and the one in which the Americans came closest to defeat:

On the morning of the 21st [February 1847] it was confirmed that a large Mexican force was marching to attack us, and orders were issued to march immediately. All the troops now struck tents and were ready to go. Many were the conjectures as to where our destination was, and some said that we were about to retreat to Saltillo. Directly the whole army is in motion and off, except the Arkansas Cavalry under Col. Yell, who was ordered to remain at Agua Nueva to guard some stores that were left there until wagons could return for them.

Col. McKee, Second Kentuckians, with one section of Artillery, were kept at Encantada for the purpose of assisting Col. Yell in his retreat should the enemy come upon him. About three miles from Encantada, the First Illinois Regiment, under Col. Hardin, was kept to guard what was termed the pass. Gen. Wool proceeded to Buena Vista and there encamped. Gen. Taylor continued to Saltillo along with Lieut. Col. May's squadron Second Dragoons and Capt. Sherman's[86] and Capt. Bragg's Batteries of Third Artillery.

During the evening Col. Yell was joined by the Kentucky Cavalry and a squadron of the First Dragoons, under command of Col. Marshall, and wagons to take in the remainder of the stores, with orders for Col. Yell, that if the enemy came upon him to destroy all that remained. Accordingly the wagons were loaded as rapidly as possible, but about midnight the piquets were fired upon and came running in except the one at rancho San Juan, which was ten miles distant. A man was accordingly started for that station, but was never heard of afterwards.

Such an alarm as there was we never before witnessed. Wagons were running in every direction; some became locked together and the teamsters did not wait to part them but ran away, supposing the enemy to be just upon us. Some of the men had lost their horses and were in a dilemma. We had broken open some barrels containing sour crout in the evening, and we observed an old German filling two haversacks. He, meantime, had lost his horse and was in an unpleasant situation, but would not lose his crout. We saw him with his two haversacks around his neck, and asked him why he did not leave it and take care of his clothes? "Oh, py sure," said he, "dish ish besser dan de clothes, and if I could find dat ole hause of mine, I would run away faster as dunder and blitzen!"

In the mean time the rancho was set on fire, as was also a large stack of wheat, which sent a lurid glare upon the darkness of the night. It looked awfully grand and sublime, indeed, and had the Mexicans been within six hundred yards they would have been almost compelled to halt and admire the scene.

The troops were formed fronting the rancho, but far enough back, so as not to be seen by any who came that way, but within proper gun shot. In this position we remained about two hours. . . .

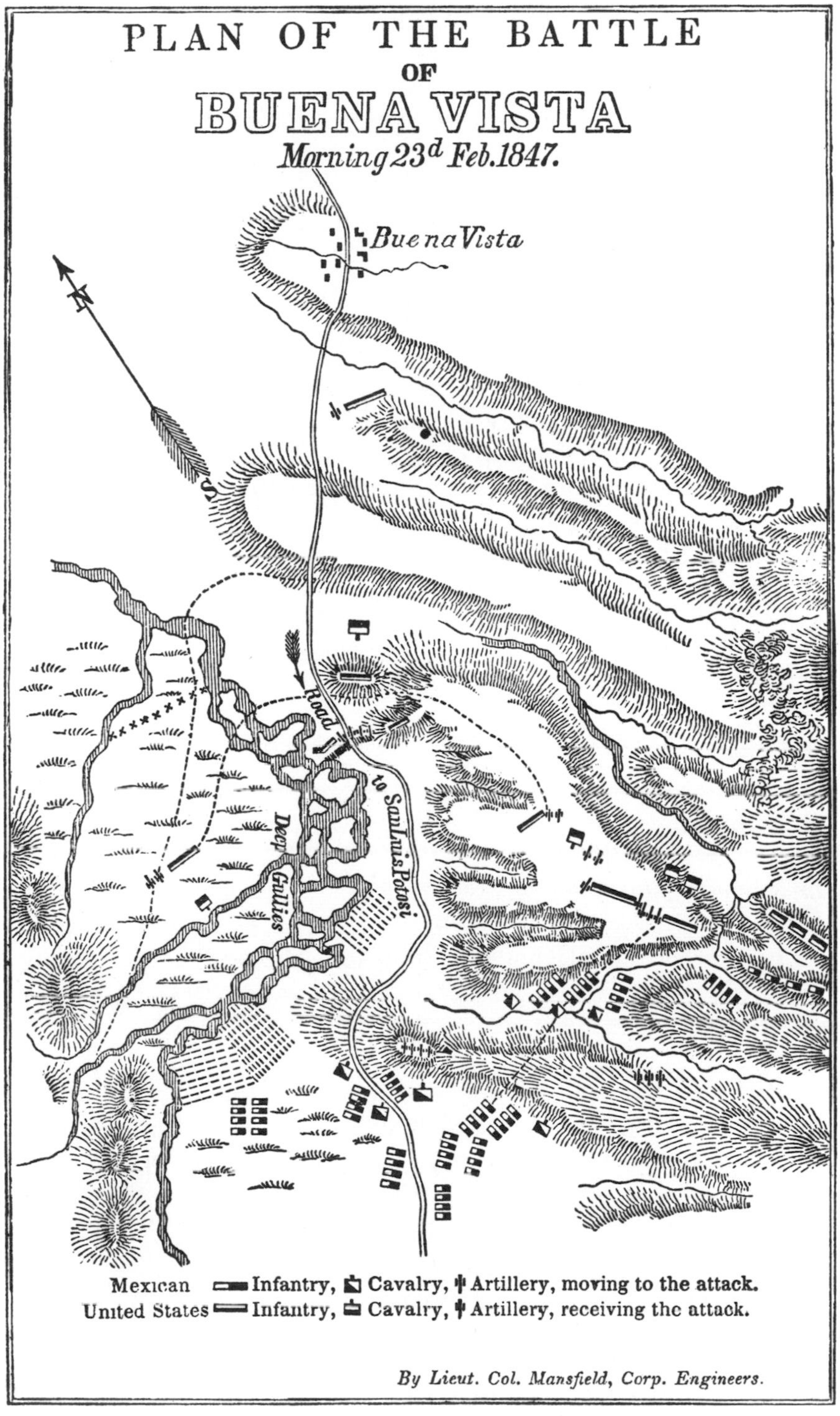

PLAN OF THE BATTLE
OF
BUENA VISTA
Morning 23d Feb.1847.

Buena Vista

Mexican ⊏══ Infantry, ▟ Cavalry, ⫯ Artillery, moving to the attack.
United States ══ Infantry, ⊐ Cavalry, ⫯ Artillery, receiving the attack.

By Lieut. Col. Mansfield, Corp. Engineers.

Orders were now given to march off in good order; but good order there was none. Away went the volunteers, helter, skelter! all the crying out to halt was of no consequence, and had the Mexicans indeed surrounded us, they could not have withstood the charge. When we arrived at Encantada, Col. McKee came out and accompanied us in.

We arrived at Buena Vista about 4 o'clock, A.M., and in a few minutes every man was snugly ensconced in his blanket. . . .

About 9 o'clock the alarm was given that the enemy was in sight. This we could judge from the movements of the First Illinois Regiment, which was stationed at the pass, where they had thrown up a parapet or breastwork, on top of which stood the gallant Suckers cheering him as he approached. . . .

In a few moments the whole army was in line and marched off to meet the foe. Great was the ambition and valor manifested that morning, as the drum and fife stirred up that old fashioned and enthusiasm-giving air, Yankee Doodle; it seemed to inspire every man with new vigor and courage for the affray. The time long looked-for by the boys of the Central Division (now termed the "Sleepy Column,") was rapidly approximating, and they were eager to improve it and come up to it to a man. We have no doubt Gen. Wool looked with feelings of pride on that little band, who had shared the toil and suffering of a six months' march through a barren country with him.[87]

TAYLOR'S INFLUENCE AS COMMANDER

If there was disorder on the eve of battle there was no panic. This was partly because of the army's faith in Taylor. There was carping in Washington since Taylor was suspected (rightly) of presidential ambitions, and his fellow officers sometimes deplored his tactics and lack of skill in the logistics of war, but the men had confidence in "Old Rough and Ready," confidence that he, and hence they, "could not be whipped." An anecdote of Taylor's war council on the night of the 23rd of February was sent to the Cincinnati Chronicle:

Gen. Taylor has gained more influence over his army than any other general, save Napoleon, that ever lived. There is not a man of them, I suppose, who ever thinks of any thing else than success, when Taylor leads them in battle. A certain conviction rests upon the mind of the soldier that old Rough and Ready cannot be whipped, and it nerves his arms and strengthens his heart to do and dare more than he could with any less feeling of confidence. It was that sort of feeling which animated our little army when they saw the glittering arms of the countless host of Santa Anna pouring its thousands through the gorges of the mountains [at Buena Vista]. . . .

One of the camp rumors is, that on the night of the 23rd at a council of his officers, it was debated as to whether they should fall back on Monterey, or risk an engagement with the enemy in the morning. The council was uncertain and somewhat divided, and after a long debate, in which the opinion of the majority inclined against an action, old Rough and Ready rose from his place and said, "Well, gentlemen, the council is adjourned to meet *after* the battle. In the morning we will *feel* the enemy."[88]

The Fighting at Buena Vista

Brigadier General Wool wrote a lengthy report of the Battle of Buena Vista. In one part (omitted below) he paid special tribute to the artillery: "Without our artillery we could not have maintained our position a single hour." Later he wrote in a letter, published in the American Whig, that if a major part of Taylor's army had not been transferred to Scott's command before the Battle of Buena Vista, if indeed Scott had only left Taylor with one regiment of regular infantry, "General Santa Anna's army would have been annihilated."

About 9 o'clock, our picket stationed at the Encantada, three and a half miles distant, discovered the enemy advancing. Word was immediately des-

Battle of Buena Vista

patched to the commanding general at Saltillo, and I ordered the troops at Buena Vista forthwith to be brought forward.

Captain Washington's battery was posted across the road, protected on its left by a commanding eminence, and on its right by deep gullies. The 2d Kentucky infantry, commanded by Col. McKee, was stationed on a hill immediately in rear of Washington's battery. The six companies of 1st Illinois regiment, commanded by Col. Hardin, took post on the eminence on the left, and two companies, under Lieut. Col. Weatherford,[89] occupied the breastwork on the right of Washington's battery. The 2d Illinois regiment[90] was stationed on the left of the Kentucky regiment. The Indiana brigade, commanded by Brig. Gen. Lane,[91] was posted on a ridge immediately in rear of the front line, and Capt. Steen's[92] squadron in reserve in rear of the Indiana brigade. The Kentucky regiment of cavalry, under the command of Col. Marshall, and the Arkansas regiment, under the command of Col. Yell, were stationed to the left of the second line towards the mountains. Shortly afterwards the rifle companies of these two regiments were dismounted, and with the cavalry companies of the Kentucky regiment and a battalion of riflemen from the Indiana brigade, under Major Gorman, under the command of Col. Marshall, were ordered to take post on the extreme left and at the foot of the mountains.

These dispositions were approved by the major-general commanding, who had now returned from Saltillo, bringing with him Lieut. Col. May's squadron of the 2d dragoons, Capt. Sherman's and Bragg's batteries of artillery, and the Mississippi regiment of riflemen.

The enemy had halted just beyond cannon shot and displayed his forces on either side of the road, and commenced pushing his light infantry into the mountains on our left. At the same time, indications of an attempt on our right induced the commanding general to order the 2d Kentucky infantry and Capt. Bragg's battery, with a detachment of mounted men, to take post on the right of the gullies, and at some distance in advance of Captain Washington's battery in the centre.

Capt. Sherman's battery was held in reserve in rear of the second line.

The enemy was now seen pushing his infantry on his right towards the heights, showing evidently an intention to turn our left in order to get possession of the key to our position—the eminence immediately on the left of Washington's artillery—and thus open a free passage to Saltillo.

Col. Marshall, with his regiment, the Arkansas riflemen, under Lieut. Col. Roane,[93] and the Indiana rifle battalion under Maj. Gorman,[94] was charged with meeting this party, and checking their movement on our left. Brigadier General Lane with the 2d Indiana regiment, and a section of Capt. Washington's artillery, under Lieut. O'Brien[95] (since captain of the quartermaster's department), was ordered to the extreme left and front of the plain which was terminated by a deep ravine, extending from the mountain to the road, with orders to prevent the enemy from coming around by the base of the mountain.

At 2 o'clock, as the enemy's light infantry were moving up the side of the mountain and in the ravines, they opened a fire on our riflemen from a large howitzer posted in the road; and between 3 and 4 o'clock, Col. Marshall engaged the Mexican infantry on the side of the mountain, and the firing continued on both sides at intervals until dark. In this our troops sustained no loss, while that of the enemy is known by a subsequent inspection of the ground, to be considerable. After the firing had ceased, the major-general commanding again returned to Saltillo to see to matters at that place, and to guard against General Miñon[96] and his cavalry, taking with him the Mississippi regiment and squadron of the 2d dragoons.

The troops remained under arms during the night in the position they occupied at the close of the day. About two o'clock A.M., of the 23d, our pickets were driven in by the Mexicans, and at the dawn of day the action was renewed by the Mexican light infantry and our riflemen on the side of the mountain.

The enemy had succeeded during the night, and early in the morning, in gaining the very top of the mountain, and in passing to our left and rear. He had reinforced his extreme right by some 1,500 to 2,000 infantry.

Major Trail,[97] 2d Illinois volunteers, was ordered, with his battalion of riflemen, to reinforce Colonel Marshall, who was engaged in holding the right of the enemy in check.

The enemy now opened a fire upon our left from a battery planted on the side of the mountain near where his light infantry had commenced ascending it—every thing now indicating that the main attack would be against our left.

The 2d Kentucky infantry and Bragg's battery of artillery were, by instructions given to Major Mansfield, ordered from the extreme right, and Sherman's battery ordered up from the rear to take post with Colonel Bissel[1]'s regiment (2d Illinois volunteers) on the plateau which extends from the centre of the line to the foot of the mountain, the sides of which were now filled with the Mexican infantry and our riflemen, between whom the firing had become very brisk. About this time the major-general commanding was seen returning from Saltillo with the Mississippi regiment and the squadron of 2d dragoons; and shortly after he arrived and took his position in the centre of the field of battle, where he could see and direct the operations of the day. At 8 o'clock, a large body of the enemy, composed of infantry, lancers, and three pieces of artillery, moved down the high road upon our centre, held by Capt. Washington's battery and the 1st Illinois volunteers, but were soon dispersed by the former. The rapidity and precision of the fire of the artillery scattered and dispersed this force in a few minutes with considerable loss on their side and little or none on our own.

In connexion with this movement, a heavy column of the enemy's infantry and cavalry and [the] battery on the side of the mountain moved against our left, which was held by Brigadier General Lane, with the 2d Indiana regiment, and Lieutenant O'Brien's section of artillery, by whom the enemy's fire was warmly returned, and, owing to the range, with great effect, by Lieutenant O'Brien's artillery. General Lane, agreeably to my orders, wishing to bring his infantry within striking distance, ordered his line to move forward. This order was duly obeyed by Lieutenant O'Brien. The infantry, however, instead of advancing, retired in disorder; and, in spite of the utmost efforts of their general and his officers, left the artillery unsupported, and fled the field of battle. Some of them were rallied by Colonel Bowles,[98] who, with the fragment, fell in the ranks of the Mississippi riflemen, and during the day did good service with that gallant regiment. I deeply regret to say that most of them did not return to the field, and many of them continued their flight to Saltillo.

Lieutenant O'Brien, being unsupported by any infantry, and not being able to make head against the heavy column bearing down upon him with a destructive fire, fell back on the centre, leaving one of his pieces, at which all the cannoneers and horses were either killed or disabled, in the hands of the enemy. Seeing themselves cut off from the centre by the flight of the 2d Indiana regiment, and the consequent advance of the Mexican infantry and cavalry upon the ground previously occupied by it, the riflemen, under the command of Colonel Marshall, retreated from their position in [sic, on] the mountain, where they had been so successfully engaged with the enemy, to the other side of the dry bed of a deep and broad torrent that is immediately in rear of our position. Here many fled in disorder to the rear. Some of them were subsequently rallied and brought again into action with their brave companions; other were stopped at the hacienda of Buena Vista, and there reformed by their officers.

The enemy immediately brought forward a battery of three pieces, and took a position on the extreme left of our line, under the mountain, and commenced an enfilading fire on our centre, which was returned with so much effect upon the advancing column of the Mexicans, containing near 6,000 infantry and lancers, that it forced them to keep to the upper side of the plateau close under the side of the mountain; and instead of turning to the left and advancing on our centre against the heavy fire of so much well served artillery, continued its course perpendicular to our line on the extreme left, crossed over the bed of the dry torrent in the direction taken by our retreating

PLATE XI. *Battle of Buena Vista*

PLATE XII. The Island of Lobos, Scott's Rendezvous Prior to the Attack on Vera Cruz

riflemen, keeping all the while close to the foot of the mountain. Colonels Marshall and Yell, with their cavalry companies, Colonel May, with the squadron of the 1st and 2d dragoons, and Capt. Pike's[99] squadron, Arkansas regiment, in connexion with a brigade of infantry, formed of the Mississippi regiment, the 3d Indiana (Colonel Lane) and a fragment of the 2d Indiana regiment, under Colonel Bowles' and Bragg's artillery, and three pieces of Sherman's battery, succeeded in checking the march of this column. The Mississippi regiment alone, and with a howitzer under Captain Sherman, moved against some 4,000 of the enemy, and stopped them in their march upon Saltillo. A large body of lancers from this body, formed column in one of the mountain gorges, and advanced through the Mexican infantry to make a descent on the hacienda of Buena Vista, near which our train of supplies and baggage had been parked. They were gallantly and successfully met by our mounted men, under Colonels Marshall and Yell, and the attacking column separated—part returning to the mountain under cover of their infantry, and a part going through the hacienda. Here the latter were met by a destructive fire from those men who had left the field in the early part of the action, and had been rallied by their officers. Colonel May's dragoons and a section of artillery, under Lieutenant Reynolds,[100] coming up at this moment, completed the rout of this portion of the enemy's cavalry. The column that had passed our left and had gone some two miles to our rear, now faced about and commenced retracing their steps, exposing their right flank to a very heavy and destructive fire from our infantry and artillery, who were drawn up in a line parallel to the march of the retreating column, of whom many were forced on and over the mountains and many dispersed.

General Santa Anna seeing the situation of this part of his army, and no doubt considering them as cut off, sent in a flag to the major general commanding to know what he desired. The general asked me to be the bearer of his answer, to which I cheerfully assented, and proceeded immediately to the enemy's battery under the mountains to see the Mexican general-in-chief. But, in consequence of a refusal to cease firing on our troops, to whom the news of the truce had not yet been communicated, and who were actively engaged with the Mexican infantry, I declared the parley at an end, and returned without seeing General Santa Anna or communicating the answer of the general commanding.

The Mexican column was now in rapid retreat, pursued by our artillery, infantry, and cavalry, and notwithstanding the effect of our fire they succeeded, for the greater part, favored by the configuration of the ground, in crossing the bed of the torrent and regaining the plateau from which they had previously descended.

While his was taking place on the left and rear of our line, our centre, under the immediate eye of the commanding general, although it suffered much in killed and wounded, stood firm and repelled every attempt made upon it.

The Mexican forces being now concentrated on the left, made a bold move to carry our centre by advancing with his whole strength from the left and front. At this moment Lieutenant O'Brien was ordered to advance his battery and check this movement. He did so in a bold and gallant manner, and maintained his position until his supporting force was completely routed by an immensely superior force. His men and horses being nearly [all] killed and wounded, he found himself under the necessity of abandoning his pieces, and they fell into the hands of the enemy. From this point the enemy marched upon the centre, where the shock was met by Colonel McKee, the 1st Illinois under Colonel Hardin, and the 2d under Colonel Bissell, all under the immediate eye of the commanding general. This was the hottest as well as the most critical part of the action; and at the moment when our troops were about giving way before the greatly superior force with which they were contending, the batteries of Captains Sherman and Bragg coming up most opportunely from the rear, and under the immediate direction of the commanding general, by a well directed fire checked and drove back with great loss the enemy who had come close upon the muzzles of their pieces. A part of the enemy's lancers took our infantry in flank and drove them down the ravine in front of Captain Washington's battery, who saved them by a well-directed and well-timed fire from his pieces.

This was the last great effort of General Santa Anna; the firing, however, between the enemy's artillery and our own continued until night.[101]

War Psychology after Buena Vista

An officer in Taylor's army described the bitter aftermath of battle:

At one time during the night, we returned over the ground on which was made our first charge. We there saw the mangled bodies of our fallen comrades, and although animated by the excitement of the fierce contest . . . yet I think there was not a heart among us which did not for a moment cease to beat on beholding that horrible scene. But for his straw hat, and a few other articles of clothing which the ruffians had left on him, I should have failed to recognize the body of young Eggleston. He was shot, stabbed, and otherwise abused. . . .

After the battle, I rode over the whole field. Parties were engaged in burying the dead—but there were still hundreds of bodies lying still and cold with no covering save the scanty remnant of clothing which the robbers of the dead found too valueless to take from them. I saw the human body pierced in every place. I saw expressed in the faces of the dead almost every passion and feeling. . . . Some seemed to have died defending their lives bravely to the last, while others evidently used their last words in supplicating for mercy. . . .

Passing on from this part of the bloody ground, I went over to the plain literally covered with the dead bodies of those who had so recently been our foes. The scene was horrible enough, God knows—but was divested of some of its horrors by the fact that not one of the Mexican soldiers was either robbed or stripped of his clothing, nor was there the least appearance of the bodies having been abused after being wounded. This, indeed, speaks much for the "barbarous volunteers of the United States of the North," as the Mexicans style us.[102]

During the night of the twenty-third, Santa Anna withdrew his troops from the field and prepared for the long march back. The war would be continued and concluded by Scott's army as it battled its way from Vera Cruz to Mexico City, but in northern Mexico the major fighting was over—the men who remained would serve as an army of occupation.

Mexican Barbarity

MANIFEST DESTINY: WAR IN THE WEST

However defined—real or chimerical—manifest destiny inevitably became involved in the war with Mexico. From the state papers of President Polk to the chronicled thoughts of the Gringos in the field, it was a powerful spur. The decisive battles were fought at Monterey, Buena Vista, Cerro Gordo, Churubusco and Chapultepec; the ultimate strategic objective was Mexico City. But the grand prize sought and won by the victors was not the land lying between the Rio Grande and the Nueces. It was a vast empire stretching from Texas to the Pacific Ocean. The battles in this territory were minor engagements compared to those fought by Taylor and Scott. On the whole the journeys to the West Coast were more trying than the fields of combat; the plains and deserts a greater peril than the Mexicans.

Manifest Destiny and California

In the early summer of 1845, before American troops under Bvt. Brig. Gen. Zachary Taylor had arrived at Corpus Christi, and ten months before the first skirmishes on the Rio Grande, the Polk administration through the Navy Department communicated in a prophetic vein with Commander John D. Sloat, commanding in the Pacific. Nominal homage was paid to peace but eyes already were fixed on San Francisco and "other Mexican ports" should Mexico "be resolutely bent on hostilities." Occupying the ports should not be difficult inasmuch as they were virtually defenseless. With this in mind, George Bancroft, Secretary of the Navy, instructed Sloat:

106

Your attention is still particularly directed to the present aspect of the relations between this country and Mexico. It is the earnest desire of the President to pursue the policy of peace; and he is anxious that you, and every part of your squadron, should be assiduously careful to avoid any act which could be construed as an act of aggression.

Should Mexico, however, be resolutely bent on hostilities, you will be mindful to protect the persons and interests of citizens of the United States near your station; and, should you ascertain beyond a doubt that the Mexican government has declared war against us, you will at once employ the force under your command to the best advantage. The Mexican ports on the Pacific are said to be open and defenceless. If you ascertain with certainty that Mexico has declared war against the United States, you will at once possess yourself of the port of San Francisco, and blockade or occupy such other ports as your force may permit.

Yet, even if you should find yourself called upon by the certainty of an express declaration of war against the United States to occupy San Francisco and other Mexican ports, you will be careful to preserve, if possible, the most friendly relations with the inhabitants; and, where you can do so, you will encourage them to adopt a course of neutrality.

Should you fall in with the squadron under Commodore Parker, you will signify to him the wish of the department that, if the state of his vessels will admit of it, he should remain off the coast of Mexico until our relations with that power are more definitively adjusted.[1]

Project for Conquest of New Mexico

Such a policy as Bancroft outlined for California might have defensive rather than aggressive implications. But California alone was not enough. The Adjutant General of the United States Army, Roger Jones,[2] made more aggressive plans. Nine months before Congress declared war on Mexico and ten months before Kearny's expedition to Santa Fe was launched, Jones requested Major Richard Bland Lee,[3] Commissary of Subsistence in St. Louis, to work out the details of a plan for the conquest of New Mexico. In doing so Lee submitted proposals on September 4, 1845 which anticipated the Kearny expedition of 1846. He wrote:

Your letter of the 21st ultimo, owing to some unaccountable delay of the mail only reached me on the 2d inst., several days previous to which, the map of Texas was received. This map, so far as relates to New Mexico, is very imperfect, and cannot be relied upon as the basis of military operations. I send you a map taken from Gregg's book "The Commerce of the Pra[i]ries,"[4]

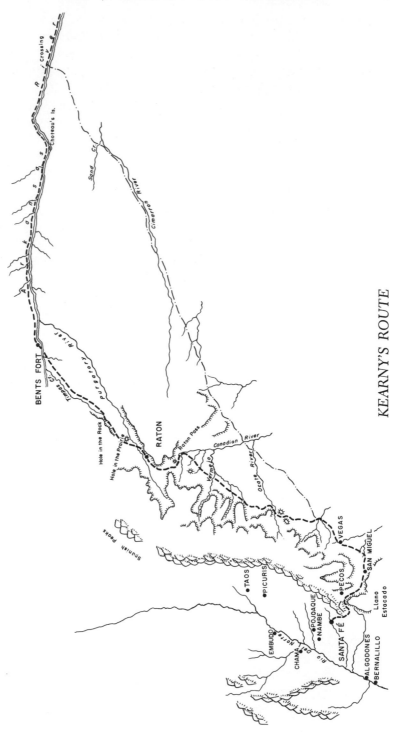

KEARNY'S ROUTE

which lays down with great accuracy the position of Santa Fe and Toas [sic, Taos], with the several routes and distances. I have dotted with red ink the rout[e]s most available for an Army encumbered with Artillery and baggage train. And in red lines, the country occupied by several tribes of Indians. The Utaw's [sic, Utaws,] Apache & Navijo tribes are at this time at war with New Mexico. . . . Santa Fe cannot be occupied many days by a force of mounted men for want of forage. So very limited and scarity [sic, scarce] is the supply that all the stock, even to the horses of the Mexican Dragoons are driven to the mountains and vallies for subsistence, ranging from twelve to sixty miles. It will therefore become necessary in case of the invasion of Santa Fe to establish a depot at some point beyond the reach of the enemy and favourable grazing of animals. The most fav[o]urable position I know of is Bent's Fort (Fort William), distant 550 miles from Independence and 250 from Santa Fe.

Should a movement upon Santa Fe be determined upon during the present season, no time is to be lost, and the first of November should find the troops on the march beyond the settlements, and as much sooner as practicable. I respectfully suggest the following plan of organization and of operation.

The Army should consist of two Corps, one of regular troops, and one of Volunteers, to be arranged as follows. The Corps of Regulars to be composed of one Company of Artillery, two of Dragoons, and four of Infantry. The Corps of Volunteers to be composed of two companies of Dragoons, four of Infantry and three of Rifle. Each Corps should be commanded by a Lieut. Col. and the Army by a Collonel [sic]. The Staff should consist of an Adjt. Genl. with the rank of Lieut. Col. as Chief of the staff. There should be a Commissary to act as Quartermaster & Commissary to the Command, and one A[s]st. Com. to each Corps. It would also be well to have an Engineer or Topographical Officer. The whole command should be limited to one thousand men, including teamsters and other camp followers. The Company of Artillery should be armed with two brass twelve pounders, and two twenty-four pounder howitzers, with fifty rounds for each gun, 20 of round shot and 30 of canister. To lessen the weight of transportation, hollow shot would answer for the how[i]tzers. There should also be a traveling forge.

With this force, should the President deem me competent and worthy of the command, I would undertake the conquest of Santa Fe within sixty day[s] from leaving the settlements. The Army should rendesvous as speedily as possible at or near sapling groves about ten miles from Westport on the Missouri river. The most favourable point for debarkation. The mounted men should be thrown forward as soon as possible to take position at the Pawnee fork of the Arkansas, distant about 300 miles from Independence, accompanied by as many wagons as possible and the beef cattle and sheep intended for subsistence. Here they should recruit the animals and await the arrival of the main body. Upon the arrival of the main body at Pawnee fork, the army should take up the line of march along the north side of the Arkansas river until reaching a point a short distance beyond Choutrous [sic, Chouteau's] Island, 510 miles from Westport and 60 miles below Bent's Fort. Here the heavy wagons should proceed to the Depot to be established at Bent's Fort and the Army cross the Arkansas, and following a small creek heading south west, strike the Cimeron [sic, Cimarron] at the upper spring, a point nearly intersecting the three routes accessible to wagons, by the middle route distant 225 miles from Santa Fe, and by the northern and southern routes 260 miles.

Here the Commander of the expedition can with some degree of certainty arrange his plans, and if possible, will doubtless take the southern route in order to pass unobserved the settlements of the Mora, Vegas, and San Jose. The first settlement he would then encounter is San Miguel distant 48 miles from Santa Fe. By a cautious approach and a night march this settlement might be passed without discovery, and all the avenews [sic] to Santa Fe guarded. The next settlement, the Pecas [sic, Pecos], should be approached and passed in like manner, and the City taken by supprise, or before any formidable resistance could be organised. Thus, a single [operation] would begin, and end the war, for the fall of Santa Fe must be regarded as the conquest of New Mexico.

Should it be found impracticable to subsist the annimals [sic] at Santa Fe, the Mounted force and the train should fall back upon the Mora, and there establish an intermediate post between the main Army and the depot at Bent's Fort. This would be a favourable posit[i]on to open communications with the Arapahoe Indians and through them, with the Apache, Utaw and Navijo tribes, the three latter of which are at war with New Mexico.

It is important that the Indian tribes should be conciliated, and made to comprehend the power as well as the liberality of the Government. The Commander of the expedition should therefor[e] have at his disposal about ten thousand dollars worth of Indian goods—guns, powder, ball E[tc.] to bestow as presents. First impressions with Indians are strong and lasting.

An Indian agency should also be established at Bent's Fort, and an Agent appointed familiar with the tribes. . . .

The following estimates will give some idea of the probable cost of the expedition.

PROVISIONS

125,000 pounds of flour & hard bread at 8 ounces, per ration (quite
         enough) (rations) 250,000
    100 barrels of pork at 6 ounces per ration 60,000
 24,000 pounds of sugar—(full allowance) 200,000

12,000	pounds of coffee	200,000
200	bushels of salt	320,000
10,000	pounds of soap	250,000

1,000 pounds of candles ⎤ To be issued at
500 gal. of vinigar ⎬ discretion, by order
1,000 gal. molasses ⎫ of the Commander.
10,000 pounds of rice ⎦
500 beef cattle on the hoof
500 sheep on the hoof

The estimated cost of the whole being $18,000

> Estimate of transportation & forage and the cost—
> 56 large ox wagons for subsistence
>   storcs to carry 4,000 pounds each.
>
> 44 large ox wagons for corn to
>   carry at the start 90 bushels each.
>
> 40 six mule wagons two to each
>   and ten for other purposes.
>
>   1,000 oxen
>   300 mules
>   4,000 bushels of corn—at estimated
>   cost not exceeding $50,000. . . .

P.S. I have just finished this rough sketch in time for the mail and have no time to make a fair copy without losing a day, which I beg you to receive as my apology for sending it. R.B.L.[5]

Lee wrote out the plans and specifications for the Santa Fe Expedition on such short notice and so hastily that he did not even copy the original draft or send it to his own commanding officer, Brig. Gen. George Gibson,[6] Commissary General, before dispatching them to Jones.[7] That this document was relevant to the conquest of New Mexico, however, is obvious from a letter which Jones sent to Lee in May 1846. It was as follows:

Your interesting letters of the 4th of Sept., in reply to mine of August 21, 1845, when we thought war might come with Mexico, are very opportunely referred to at this time, which fact I feel bound to tell you. A movement will be made from the frontier of Missouri along the route to Bent's Fort—which you say is about 250 miles short of Santa Fé. The force will chiefly consist of Volunteers—with 2 or 3 Companies of the 1st Dragoons—the whole to be commanded by Col. Kearney [sic].[8] I wish your known wishes upon this subject could be gratified, but I do not see how you can be spared from your own proper department—if you *could* be.[9]

ORIGINS OF THE KEARNY EXPEDITION

The same day that Jones was alerting Richard Bland Lee, a confidential letter from the United States Senate (written apparently by Thomas Hart Benton) went out to Col. R. Campbell, aide to the governor of Missouri. Soon this appeared in the St. Louis Missouri Republican. It announced the Kearny expedition to protect the trade route to Santa Fe and beyond.

WASHINGTON, MAY 14, 1846.

Dear Sir: The morning papers will let you see that the state of war was declared to exist yesterday, between the United States and Mexico. Our first care in this sudden change in our relations with that country was to try and take care of our Santa Fe trade. For this purpose, it will be proposed to the people of New Mexico, Chihuahua and the other internal provinces, that they remain quiet and continue trading with us as usual, upon which condition they shall be protected in all their rights and be treated as friends. To give effect to this proposition and to make sure at all events, of protection to the persons and property of our traders (besides the proclamation of the President to that effect) Col. Kearney will start immediately with 300 Dragoons,[10] to be followed as quick as possible by 1,000 Mounted Volunteers from Missouri,[11] and with authority to engage the services, if necessary, of all the Americans, in that part of the world. This military movement will be to make sure of the main object, to wit: peace and trade, to be secured peaceably if possible, forcibly if necessary. For unless they accept these conditions, the country will have to be taken possession of as a conquest. This, however, we hope will not be necessary, as it will be so obviously to the interest of the inhabitants of that part of Mexico (too far off from the Central Government to have any effect on general hostilities), to enjoy the benefits of peace and trade, with the full protection of all their rights of person, property, and religion.[12]

To the west, in Kansas, news that the country was at war stirred Fort Leavenworth into hectic activity. Reports, only half-believed, that Indians, Mexicans, and Mormons had attacked American soldiers added to the furor.

There is a great deal of excitement here, at present, about Mexico &c. The 1st Regiment has been ordered from this place to Santa Fe. Rich the Sutler at this Post has been ordered to go. He has gone to St. Louis to purchase a large stock of goods to take out. I expect to go with him. The Regt. will start in two weeks. 800 Volunteers go with them from Platte. One of Col. Fremont's[13] men came in today with the news that all his men had been cut off by a party of Indians & Mexicans in the mountains . . . we believe about one half.[14]

Meantime, in Washington, President Polk left no doubt that he wanted the territories about to be occupied to become part of the United States as soon as possible. He wrote the following paragraphs and sent them to Secretary of War Marcy so that they might be incorporated in the latter's instructions to Colonel Kearny. Scratching out and interlining indicate the President's concern over his message.

After you shall have conquered & taken possession of either New Mexico & Upper California, it will be necessary that you should establish a temporary civil Government in each of these Provinces abolishing all arbitrary restrictions which may exist at present so far as this can be done with safety. In performing this duty, it would be wise & prudent to continue in their employment all such of the existing officers as are known to be friendly to the United States & will take the oath of allegiance to them. The duties at the Custom Houses ought at once to be reduced to such a rate as may be barely sufficient to maintain the necessary officers, without yielding any revenue to the Government. You may assure the people of these Provinces, . . . that, a free Government will be provided for them, with the least possible delay, similar to that which at present exists in the Territories of the United States. They will then be called upon to exercise the rights of freemen in electing their own Representatives to the territorial Legislature.

This will be a very important duty & much must necessarily be left to your discretion. In yr. whole conduct you will act in such a manner as best to conciliate the inhabitants & render them friendly to the United States.[15]

Colonel Kearny's force of more than 1,600 men was "The Army of the West." It marched out of Fort Leavenworth on June 27, 1846, crossed the great plains to Bent's Fort and then turned southward toward Santa Fe. Coming along close behind Kearny, and soon to catch up with him, was Lt. Jeremy Gilmer, a young engineer who was both observant and articulate as he journeyed about five marches in Kearny's rear. Gilmer carried with him Kearny's commission as brigadier general, issued on June 30. In a letter to the Headquarters of the Engineers in Washington, Gilmer wrote a description of the soldiers' march through the Comanche country in the summer of 1846:

On the 12th inst. I wrote to you from Leavenworth informing you that I was about to leave that place for Santa Fe in company with Major Swords[16] and Lieut. Ingalls.[17] We got off at 3 P.M. and came to our first encampment at dusk—making some 19 miles the first day. We were all in fine spirits, and hoped from the fair start which we had made, that we would soon reach our destination and get our "squint" at the bloody Mexicans, but alas, the next morning our baggage waggon upset and broke the axel tree. This accident caused us to lose nearly one day's march. We were not discouraged by this mishap, and determined by greater exertions to gain lost time. The following day our waggon broke again. . . . This was repaired as soon as possible, and on we came, and we travelled pretty well for a day or two, but we were destined to meet with another accident. The 7th day, the new axel which we had put in, being of green wood, sprung & broke. A second one was put in, and this point has been reached without further accident. On the day before yesterday, we came up with 7 commissaries waggons with provisions for the Army. They have good teams and are not very heavily loaded—hence Major Swords has decided to keep them in company with us until we reach the crossing of the Arkansas. Notwithstanding all our misfortunes, we have averaged more than 20 miles per day and we hope to do better for the future. From teamsters, and others returning, we have learned that Col. Kearny is some 5 or 6 marches in advance; troops doing well, and that he was going by the way of Bent's Fort, high up on the Arkansas. At that place we shall join. The Army will be able to advance from that point as early as the 18th or 20th proximo (probably).

We are now coming to the Camanche country—also to the ranges of the buffalo. We have burnished our arms, and intend to give our red friends a warm reception if they honor us with a visit. At night our eight waggons are formed around us, enclosing an area sufficiently large for a small camp, and sentinals are posted. Very few Indians have been seen, however, for some time by any one passing the road, and it is probable they will not attempt to attack us. As to the buffalo . . . Ingalls and I have decided to give them one chase when we find them. They are said to be abundant, but some little distance from the road, being kept off by the troops which have gone in advance. We shall have some fresh meat, notwithstanding, in less than 48 hours.

On the 21st, we met Mr. [George T.] Howard & Julian May returning to the U. States from the vicinity of Santa Fe. It was their opinion that Armijo, the Gov. of Santa Fe, would not be able to offer much resistance to our advance, and that Genl. Kearny would take possession of the town immediately. Armijo will have to depend upon such troops as he can raise in the northern Provinces. These would be very inferior soldiers, even should he succeed in concentrating them, which is very doubtful. This is only surmise, however, and it is possible we may have a brush before paying our respects to the Dons of Santa Fe, and our devotions to their fair daughters. We are all curious to know what is to be the direction of our army after leaving Santa Fe—whether to the west thro' Northern Mexico, or south towards Chihuahua.

We have been highly favored on our march thus far, so far as the weather is considered. We had no rain on us until yesterday, fresh breezes and air cool. On yesterday, however, the temperature rose and the sun came down hot— the thermometer in the heat of the day as high as 85° and a shower in the afternoon. This morning is warm, but not oppressive.

The express that last reached us brought the news of Col. Kearney's promotion. We carry his commission with us.[18]

CAMPAIGN IN NEW MEXICO

On August 18, Kearny entered Santa Fe unopposed. After fifty-two days of marching New Mexico had been won. The final days of the "conquest" produced excitement founded on rumors and designs for battle, but there was no battle. An officer with Kearny recorded these days in his diary:

Sunday, August 16. Started[19] at the usual hour, and at seven miles came to the village of St. Miguel,[20] built like the others, of sun-burned brick, and with flat roofs. After much delay the Alcalde and Padre were found, and presented to General Kearney, but it was evident that they did not relish an interview with him. This village contains a respectable church and about two or three hundred houses. The general expressed a wish to ascend one of the houses, with the priest and Alcalde, and to address the people of the town, informing them of the object of his mission. After many evasions, delays, and useless speeches, the Padre made a speech, stating that "he was a Mexican, but should obey the laws that were placed over him for *the time*, but if the general should point all his cannon at his breast, he could not consent to go up there and address the people."

The general very mildly told him, through the interpreter, Mr. Robideau, that he had not come to injure him, nor did he wish him to address the people. He only wished him to go up there and hear him (the general) address them. The Padre still fought shy, and commenced a long speech which the general interrupted, and told him, he had no time to listen to "useless remarks," and repeated that he only wanted him to go up and listen to his speech. He consented. The general made pretty much the same remarks to the Alcalde and people, that he had made to the people of the other villages. He assured them that he had an ample force and would have possession of the country against all opposition, but gave them assurances of the friendship and protection of the United States. He stated to them that this had never been given them by the government of Mexico, but the United States were able and would certainly protect them, not only in their persons, property, and religion, but against the cruel invasion of the Indians. That they saw but a small part of the force that was at his disposal. Many more troops were near him on another road (some of which he showed them a mile or two distant) and that another army would, probably, be through their village in three weeks.

After this, he said, "Mr. Alcalde, are you willing to take the oath of allegiance to the United States." He replied that "he would prefer waiting till the general had taken possession of the capital." The general told him, "it was sufficient for him to know that he had possession of his village." He then consented and with the usual formalities, he said, "You swear that you will bear true allegiance to the government of the United States of America." The Alcalde said, "provided I can be protected in my religion." The general said, "I swear you shall be." He then continued, "and that you will defend her against all her enemies and opposers, in the name of the Father, Son, and Holy Ghost-Amen."

The general then said, "I continue you as the Alcalde of this village, and require you, the inhabitants of this village to obey him as such. Your laws will be continued for the present, but as soon as I have time to examine them, if any change can be made that will be for your benefit, it shall be done." After shaking hands with them he left. The Padre then invited him to his house, and gave him and his staff refreshments; and after sundry hugs, jokes and professions of friendship, with an expression from the general, that, "the better they became acquainted the better friends they would be," and an invitation to the Padre to visit him at Santa Fe (which he promised), we left the village. The Padre was evidently the ruling spirit of the village, and the Alcalde was under great restraint by his presence. The visit to the priest, and the frank and friendly manner of the general had the desired effect, and I believe they parted the best of friends, and have no doubt that the inhabitants of St. Miguel will soon be as good democrats as can be found in Missouri.

The Alcalde informed the general that 400 men left the village to join the Mexican army, but that two hundred had returned home.

Soon after leaving this village an express arrived from Santa Fe, informing the general that a large force would oppose his march 15 miles from that place, in a deep ravine. It was headed by an individual known as Salazar.[21] That Gen. Armijo[22] refused to command them, and said he would defend the town. The same information was soon after brought by Puebla Indians, who said there was a large force of their people among the Mexicans, armed with bows and arrows; that their people had been forced into the service, and their chiefs would not permit them to take their guns.

As it is not more than two days march to Santa Fe, if we have a fight it will probably be to-morrow.—Marched 17 miles.

Monday, Aug. 17.—Started at the usual time. Our picket guard took a prisoner, the son of the noted Salazar,[23] well remembered by the Texan prisoners for his cruelties to them. He stated that the Mexican army had left

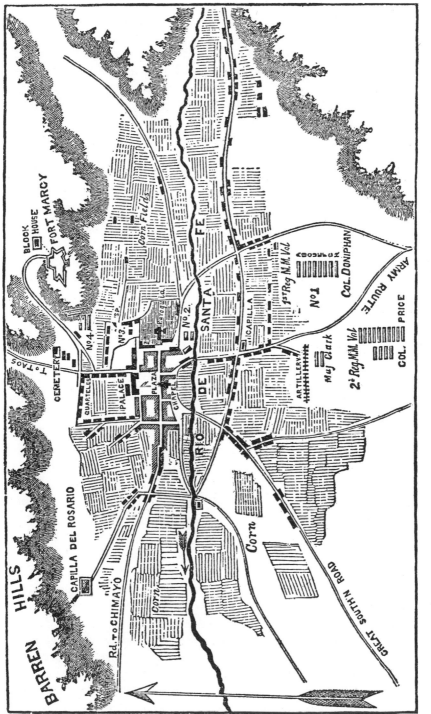

SANTA FE

the cannon and gone home. The general told him he would keep him a prisoner, and if he found that he had told him falsely, he would hang him. We soon met others from Santa Fe, who congratulated the general on his arrival in the country, and their deliverance from the tyrannical rule of Armijo.

They further said, that Armijo had taken one hundred dragoons and his cannon, and gone this morning towards Chihuahua. We passed to day the ruins of the ancient town of Pecos. I visited it with some Mexicans, and an interpreter, who gave me a full account of it. It was said to have been built long before the conquest. It stands on an eminence. The dwellings were built of small stones and mud; some of the buildings are still so far perfect as to show three full stories. There were four rooms under ground, fifteen feet deep and twenty-five feet across in a circular form. In one of these rooms, burned the "holy fire," which was kindled many centuries before the conquest; and when the Pecos Indians were converted to the Catholic faith they still continued their own religious rites, and among them the "sacred fire," which never ceased to burn till seven years since, when the village was broken up. The population is probably one thousand. The church is large, and although in ruins, was evidently a fine building. It was built after the conquest. The eastern roof of the main building is still good—it is filled with birds. As we came in front of it the Mexicans took off their hats, and on entering the building we did the same.

The general learned to-day that Salazar had been in command at the cannon, and that he had passed around us and gone to St. Miguel, the town we passed yesterday. The general sent him word that he had his son a prisoner, and would treat him well, if the father remained peaceable, but if he took up arms, or excited the people to resistance, he would hang him.

We encamped at 3 P.M., on the Pecos creek, in excellent grass, where there was a beautiful farm well watered—distance to-day fifteen and three quarter miles.

An abundance of vegetables have been brought into camp this evening, and we have fared better than since we left Missouri. Bread, coffee, and bacon are excellent articles of food, when accompanied with other little "fixings" which ladies can only provide us with, but of themselves, after a few weeks, campaigners become a little tired.

An American gentleman has just arrived in camp from Santa Fe; he left at 12 M. to-day, and says that after the governor's abdication, the Alcaldes held a meeting, and gravely discussed the propriety of tearing down the churches to prevent their being converted into barracks, and that the American citizens interfered and assured them that they had nothing to fear on that subject; and thereby saved the churches. A lady also sent for him this morning, and asked him if he did not think it advisable for her to leave the town, with her daughters, to save them from dishonor. He advised her by all means to remain at home, and assured her that she and her daughters were in no danger from the approach of the army.

Most of the respectable people of the town have left, and many country people are going to town for protection.

Tuesday, August 18.—Started as usual and at six miles came to the cannon, where the Mexican army under Armijo had been assembled. There had been 3,000 troops there, but it seems that the nearer we approach them, the fewer they became, and when we passed through they had all gone. The position they chose was near the lower end, and it was one of great strength. The passage was not more than forty feet wide—in front they had made an obstruction with timber, and beyond this, at 300 yards distance, was an eminence in the road, on which their cannon had been placed; and it was thought by us, that their position was equal to 5,000 men. We reached the hill which overlooks Santa Fe at 5 P.M. Major Clark's[24] artillery was put into line, and the mounted troops and infantry were marched through the town to the Palace (as it is called) on the public square, whether [*sic*, where] the general and his staff dismounted, and were received by the acting governor and other dignitaries and conducted to a large room.[25]

A private in the Missouri Mounted Volunteers also described the hardships and excitement of the final thrust through the mountains into Santa Fe:

You will see by the date of this letter that we have at length arrived at the long sought for place—Santa Fee. On the 18th, Genl. Kearney took formal possession of the capital of the province without having fired a single gun. On the next morning I with half of my company was sent to this place[26] on detached service.

Our march after the date of my last letter to you was the same unvaried monotony untill within five days travel of Santa Fee—when the whole army was thrown into a state of excitement by the arrival of a flag and letter from Gov. Armijo. In the letter the Gov. informed Genl. K. "that he had advanced as far into the Mexican territory as he could with safety—and that he called upon him to retire immediately—but if he did not that he would meet him at the Vigas a stream about 20 miles off and give him battle." To this Genl. K. made a characteristic reply, that he would meet Gov. A. at the Vigas.

You can well immagine the excitement created in camp by the interchange of *civilities*. Every one expected a fight [for] certain. And sure enough the next day the enemy advanced to within three miles of our encampment determined to oppose our passage through a narrow gap in the mountains.

On the next morning after this disposition of the enemies forces, Genl. K. marched out of his camp, in battle order, both himself and every man in the army, from the nature of the ground and reported strength of the enemy (about 2,000 strong) anticipating a bloody battle. My company being armed with the Hall Rifle and bayonet was unmounted to act as Infantry and as such attached to the battallion of Infantry. About ten o'clock we moved out of camp in the following order, the Genl. with 500 dragoons in front, the battalion of Infantry with my company attached, about 200 next, the artillery next with two batteries of five pieces each—then followed the Regt. of Missouri Volunteers under Col. Doniphan[27]—800 strong—and in the rear the baggage train with a strong rear guard—this was the order of march. As to the constituents of the army I must say that [I] never have seen men engage in anything with finer spirits or more alacrity than this army marched off with on this morning. And as to my own company the officers (with all modesty) and men where in as fine spirits as I have even seen them—every fellow at his post—determined that Franklin County should not be unknown to *fame*. We each of us strip[p]ed off our coats, shouldered our Rifles, and marched off—at double quick time to enter upon our career as soldiers.

As I said before, the enemy were posted at a gap in the mountains about three miles from our camp on the direct road to Santa Fee. This gap is formed by two mountains of the same range approaching to within 150 feet of each other suddenly terminating in [a] steep precipice—leaving a gorge through which the road passed. To within [a] half mile of this gap the army was marched, when the Genl. determined that the infantry should scale the mountain on the right, pass in rear of the enemy, and cut off their retreat. So as the order was given we commenced the ascent of an allmost perpendicular mountain side, covered with rocks, about 400 feet high, and after hard puffing and scratching gained the summit. We immediately commenced our descent on the other side and in a few minutes were in the valley below, formed the company, marched up to the pass—and to our chagrin and surprise found it occupied by the dragoons—the enemy having suddenly recollected—

"that he that runs away
will live to fight another day"

but this was not the termination of the fatigues of the day as we were compelled to make a march on foot of 12½ miles in hope of overtaking the Spaniards—the result of which was that every fellow had blistered feet and wearied leggs, and when we again mounted our horses did so with profound gratitude to the providence that provided us such good friends.

Thus ended the first great battle of this campaign. We next marched to the town of San Magil [sic, Miguel] within fifty miles of Santa Fee—at which place we learned that Gov. Armijo with a force of 3,000 men occupied the narrow Pass[28] between that point and Santa Fee and the only gap in the mountains through which it was possible for our army to pass—the pass being about twenty miles from Santa Fee. We continued our march, each day

hearing of the position and strength of the enimy [sic]—and on the 17th encamped within 4 miles of the pass. Here again we expected to have had a
battle, but on the evening of the 17th there arose a contest in the camp of the
enimy as to the supreme command, the result of which was that the enimy
dispersed without attempting to oppose our passage.

On the 18th we struck tents and marched off not knowing certainly
w[h]ether we should have a fight or not but yet prepared for every contingen-
cy. As we advanced, the mountains seemed to be gradually approaching each
other untill at length they seemed to have placed themselves in front of us,
an impassible barrier, hundreds of feet in height and almost perpendicular.
Here by turning the point of a mountain you are suddenly thrown into a pass
through which the road was just wide enough for a waggon to pass or four
men abreast and about ¼ of a mile [in] lenght [sic], each side of the pass
having walls of rock, perpendicular hundreds of feet high—and entirely impossible for us to ascend. It was at this pass the enemy had made preparations
to resist our passage, and it seems to me if they had availed themselves of the
natural advantages of the place, thrown up a barricade, and upon it planted a
battery—with one sixth of their force they could have effectually resisted every
effort of ours to pass—but instead of doing so, although they doubled us in
numbers, and were possessed of five excellent pieces of artillery under the
effe[c]ts of fear and discord, after throwing up a few brush as a breast work—
dispersed without firing a solitary gun in defence of their homes.

That evening as I have said in the first part of my epistle we took peaceble
[sic] possession of Santa Fee.

The people of this section [of] the country in our first appearance were
the most abjcct contemptible looking objects I ever saw. They had been
frightened allmost to death by the stories the priests and rich (for they are
the two classes that rule the country) had told them of the barbarian[s] that
were marching against them, but now after we have mingled a few days with
them, they begin to look a little more cheerful and assume somewhat the appearance of men. They supposed our force was much larger than it is and say
that if they had known we were so weak they would have fought us. Gov
Armijo sent Genl. Kearney word that he intended attacking his forces and
contending for the country, that when he dispersed his army he supposed that
we were in overpowering numbers, but that since we have come into the country he is satisfied that he can drub us—but it is the general impression that he
cannot collect a force sufficient to effect anything of importance although it is
pretty certain that he will make the effort.

Yesterday a Spaniard came into our camp and informed the Lt. Col., Ruff,[29]
that Armijo had concealed all of his cannon in a little village about 1½ miles
from the camp, and forthwith we started with two companies about 70 men
in strength in search of them but before we arrived at the town Capt. Fisher

[sic][30] of St. Louis with a small body of men had them in possession. They proved to be very excellent brass peices [sic]—six pounders, and constitute the whole of the enimies formidable armament—and depriving Armijo of one of his great dependents in a struggle for the supremacy of the country.[31]

OCCUPATION OF SANTA FE

Kearny entered Santa Fe on August 18 as a conqueror. A staff officer[32] wrote a letter describing the dramatic scene to the St. Louis Reveille:

On went the Dragoons and Rangers, until at length we emerged from the stunted pines and cedars into full view of the valley in which the terminus (for the present) of our long and arduous march is situated, and of the country beyond to the western range of mountains. Reaching a hill immediately south-east of the city and from which the tops of the public buildings were visible, the General halted, and waited some two hours for the artillery; during which time the Stars and Stripes were observed unrolled in the hands of a Sergeant, and certain inquiries were overheard to be made of American citizens as to the best means of hoisting it on the palace of the Armijos. We also understood that preparations were making to fit up the palace for the occupancy of the General, and that, in all probability, his intention expressed at Bent's Fort, *to be in Santa Fe on the 18th of August* with his whole army, would be made good. The sun, which had been obscured in the morning, was beaming forth gloriously, but *going down* a great deal faster than the artillery was coming *up*.

Some few of the Mexican citizens, prompted by curiosity, came out in their white shirts and wide breeches, with those everlasting big hats on, and looked with gaping wonder on the advanced corps of the "Army of the West." Mr. Thurston [sic],[33] standing about 6 feet 6 in moccasins, and other Americans, including our never-tiring friend, Col. Owens,[34] of Jackson, were standing in groups about, while the General held conversation with that prime old soldier, who never missed a roll-call, Maj. Sumner[35]—and old Fitzpatrick,[36] with his venerable silver head, and keen grey-blue eye, looked on as perfectly at home as when guiding us over the plains, with never-erring memory and sagacity. Horses went to sleep, for not a spear of grass was in sight, and men wondered what would come next—declared the subsistence wagons *would not* come up—and speculated on the price of bread and cards in Santa Fe.

At length the artillery appeared—the bugle call to horse, and into the town we marched, with drawn sabres, and taking as much care of the little urchins in the streets as we would on parade in St. Louis—and, by the way, children are everywhere the same, when soldiers or any other show are on the tapis. The General took his position with his guard in the plaza or great square before the palace, where he claimed the capital and country of the Alcalde for the American Union, and administered the oath of allegiance, while Major Sumner marched us through several streets, and the American flag was hoisted over the palace, saluted by the deep voices of Major Clark's artillery from the hill where we had halted. We were then marched out to the hill again, where we found that the wagons of our company *had not* come up, and that the prospect for supper was no longer *dubious*, but decidedly bad; while our poor horses, tired beyond measure, had no hope of a single blade of grass to stand between them and starvation.

Well—supper or not—here we are in Santa Fe—AND NEW MEXICO IS OURS![37]

This was the shout of the victors. But what of the people of Santa Fe, who watched the conquering army sweep into their capital? The same correspondent had this to say about their feelings a few days later:

Our march into the city, I have already told you, was extremely warlike, with drawn sabres, and daggers in every look. From around corners, men with surly countenances and downcast looks regarded us with watchfulness, if not terror; and black eyes looked through latticed windows at our column of cavaliers, some gleaming with pleasure, and others filled with tears. Strange, indeed, must have been the feelings of the citizens when an invading army was thus entering their home—themselves used only to look upon soldiers as plagues sent to eat out their substance, burn, ravage and destroy—all the future of their destiny vague and uncertain—their new rulers strangers to their manners, language and habits, and, as they had been taught to believe, enemies to the only religion they have ever known. It was humiliating, too, to find their city thus entered, without a gun having been fired in its defence; and we thought that humble, mortified pride, was indicated in the expression of more than one swarthy face. As the American flag was raised, and the cannon boomed its glorious national salute from the hill, the pent-up emotions of many of the women could be suppressed no longer, and a sigh of commiseration, even for causeless distress, escaped from many a manly breast, as the wail of grief arose above the din of our horses' tread, and reached our ears from the depth of the gloomy-looking buildings on every hand.[38]

And what impression did Santa Fe make on the newly arrived conquerors? Some observations were to be found in a letter which M. L. Baker, a traveler en route to Mexico, sent back East:

I am much disappointed in this country. It is bare of wood and water, mountainous and the only parts they can cultivate is a few of the valleys that are watered by springs and small streams from the Mountains. The houses of town and country are built of mud brick dried in the sun, are one story high and have no windows, so when the door is shut the room is dark at mid-day. However, they are very warm in winter & cool in summer. The roofs all flat. They raise corn, wheat, onions, no potatoes, have thousands of goats, sheep, some cattle, plenty of asses & mules with some fine pony horses. The silver and gold mines seem to be plenty and no doubt before long Yankee skill & perseverance will bring many to light, as yet undiscovered. The Americans have heretofore been afraid to hunt for and work the mines on account of the Indians, who have been the real masters of the country. But the American Dragoons will soon learn them to keep quiet.

They have no mills for grinding wheat except some small hand concerns, and they have to use the sieve or what is commonly done eat bran and all. They kill-dry both corn & wheat. They have some apples & peaches as well as melons and their grapes equal those I saw in France. They are fond as a nation of *dancing* and have *Fandangos* every night in town & country, and the way the Mexican *senora* dances would be a caution to a Broadway belle. The beauty of Mexican ladies is not *genirally* [sic] great, but in some cases is extraordinary fine and brilliant. They become women very young and marry early, but fade and become old & haggard in proportion. Indian blood is almost universally mixed throug[h]out the population & the language is far from the pure Spanish. I have given you some few ideas of this country & people but cannot dwell at length on the subject now. You know I must have something to talk about when I see you. I suppose you are anxious to know when that may be. I cannot say for certainty when, for I start the 25th of this month to go some hundreds of miles south into the Country, to Chiwauwau and then west into *California*, to *Monterey*, about 1,400 miles off. This is the most healthy country in the world, and I am much larger and heavier than ever before. It rains only in the spring & fall. You would laugh to see what a complexion I have, burnt to the colour of mahogany and wear immense moustachios.[39]

KEARNY IN THE RIO GRANDE VALLEY

Having established his command in Santa Fe, Kearny led a detachment down the Rio Grande Valley to visit the Indian pueblos and Spanish towns. At first this phase of the occupation went smoothly. The Mexicans did not welcome their "deliverers" and many were reluctant to take the oath of allegiance, but the American prophets of manifest destiny had calculated correctly when they assumed that the people of New Mexico and California would be unwilling to shed much blood. A captain with Kearny wrote an account of his visit to the Rio Grande communities:

On the 2d instant, [September] General Kearny, with about eight hundred men, left this town on an excursion south. We went to a village called Tonie [sic, Tomé], about one hundred miles distant. We struck the Rio Grande twenty seven miles from this place [i.e. Santa Fe], at a village called San Domingo, inhabited by the Puebla [sic] Indians. Our reception at this village was quite a grand affair; the principal men and braves of the tribe met us six miles from the town, and escorted us in; the braves were mounted on their best horses, and dressed in the most gaudy apparel, and armed and equipped in the same manner as when they go out for the purpose of fighting. When the general passed the head of their columns, they fired off their guns, and then one file on each side of our companies proceeded to the rear, and then wheeled and came down to close our line at the top of the speed of their horses, yelling and going through all the manoeuvres of a regular charge; they met again at the head of our columns, fired at each other with their pistols, made passes with their lances, and then filed off, and returned to the head of our companies. This was repeated several times, to the great admiration and astonishment of all who witnessed it. I have never seen better horsemen anywhere, and from what I could discover, I should take them to be formidable in battle, if properly armed.

They are fine looking men, and much superior, in every respect, to the Mexican population. They have a very fine village, most splendid vineyards, and appear to be much more comfortable, in every respect than the Mexicans. When we got into the village, we were invited into the priest's house, where a most sumptuous repast was set out, consisting of the best grapes I ever saw, melons, apples, cakes, and with liquor sufficient to wash them down.

There is at this town quite an extensive church, to which is attached the priest's house, where he keeps his wives or concubines. The priest at this place has four—two of them are quite good-looking. After our repast, the general made a speech to the citizens, who appeared quite well pleased. They then escorted us out of town, and we went on our way rejoicing, with full stomachs, and every man with just liquor enough in him to make him feel patriotic. This was the only Indian village we visited.

After we left San Domingo, we passed through villages every eight or ten miles, until we reached the village of Tonie. Most of them, however, were quite small, and the inhabitants, with the exception of two or three men in each, are a poor miserable set.

The only villages on the Rio Grande, that we visited worthy of note, are San Domingo, San Philippe [sic, Felipe], Albuquerque, and Tonie [sic Tomé]. Albuquerque was the residence of Armijo.[40] We halted a short time at the place, going and returning. Gen. Kearney called on the late governor's wife, and passed an hour or two, as he told me, very pleasantly. She is said to be an intelligent woman, and deported herself with much propriety. Her husband (Armijo), it is said, has gone to the Passo [sic El Paso], and it is supposed will continue on to the city of Mexico.

The people near the town of Tonie and the inhabitants of the different villages, have heard of our intended visit, and the general so arranged our marches as to bring us to this town the evening before the anniversary of their patron Saint—a great day with the inhabitants of that region of country; and I assure you it was a great day not only with them, but to all who were present. There was an immense concourse of people, men, women, and children, Mexicans, Indians, and white folks. They had prepared fire-works, which were gotten up in a very good style, the town was illuminated, they had a theatre—that is, a play in the open yard, which appared to be well received by the inhabitants. They also had a fandango, which was not only crowded, but jammed and crowded to over-flowing. The *beauty* and fashion were there, and, to my astonishment, I found some of the women quite handsome. During the day there was mass said, and the Virgin Mary was paraded around the streets followed by the principal men of the town, and also by Gen. Kearney and his staff, with lighted candles in their hands.

The priest at Tonie[41] [sic] joined in the waltz, and appeared as jovial and as much disposed to participate in all the amusements as any one else. The country south of this place (Santa Fe) along the Rio Grande, is much better than any portion of the province I have yet visited; yet in my judgement, no Missourian would ever think of locating any where here for the purpose of cultivating the soil. The province has been overrated, and our government has been grossly imposed upon and deceived, as to its resources, commerce, &c. I have not seen anything since my arrival here that would excite the least desire for me to reside here. To sum up the whole in a few words, the Mexicans are physically, mentally and morally an inferior and "low flung" race.[42]

RISING TENSIONS IN NEW MEXICO

By the end of September, General Kearny was satisfied that his mission in New Mexico was accomplished. It was time to get on with the war. He decided to divide his forces into three parts. One would remain in New Mexico under the command of his successor, Col. Sterling Price; a second force led by Colonel Doniphan, Missouri lawyer by profession and warrior by nature, would occupy Chihuahua, south of the Rio Grande. Kearny himself, following his original instructions from Secretary of War Marcy would lead an expedition southwest across the desert to aid the United States Navy in the conquest of California. He advised the Adjutant General of the United States Army that he would start for California on September 25.

Although Kearny was correct in assuming that he had successfully carried out the assignment to "conquer" New Mexico, his successor, Colonel Price, *was to encounter grave troubles. In a letter written only four days after the general's departure, Lt. Jeremy F. Gilmer, a young engineer, reported from Santa Fe. He was unsparing in his criticism of the undisciplined American troops and hinted that relations between the soldiers and townspeople were not cordial. Tensions seemed to be rising:*

All the boys here are volunteers, numbering more than 1,700 men—and a sweet set of boys are they. All do as they please, and demonstrate to the Spaniards daily, that they belong to the freest and "smartest people in creation." The men are about as good as their officers—none have learned enough of military matters to know that they are ignorant. The Com[m]anding officer has ordered daily drills of the companies—also an officers drill each day. The order is observed to some extent—particularly on those days when his most dutiful "subs" do not find it too inconvenient. We have had some improvement, however, within the last two weeks over the former state of things. The guards have been made larger, and sentinals posted in all proper places. A gun is fired at 10 o'clock in the evening, and no one is permitted to be in the street after that hour without the countersign,—neither citizen or soldier. If this system be kept up, it will be the means of preventing many of the rows and street fights, which unfortunately have occured too often.[43]

A correspondent of the Missouri Republican reported further details of a deteriorating situation:

About a fortnight ago, Ambrosio Armijo, was taken prisoner by Capt. Burgwin,[44] of the U.S. Dragoons, at Albuquerque, with two other Mexicans.— On Ambrosio (brother to the General of that name) was found a treasonable correspondence with Gen. A[r]mijo, and letters were found on his person and in the rifle barrel of one of the other Mexicans, informing Gen'l. A. that all in this province was ripe for a revolt, and needed but the assistance of some military display from below, in order to break out on the shortest notice. What will be done with the traitors, I knew [*sic*, know] not. I learn that Don Ambrosio is as great a simpleton as his worthy brother is a coward, and the whole matter may well be a fanciful invention of the old gentleman, to while away his dreary hours. Others, however, think that Ambrosio has been used only as a tool, in this contemplated plan for insurrection, and that the matter is entitled to more consideration than I am inclined to give it.

It is clear that the Mexicans here are very much discontented, and the further south you go, the more this will become apparent. The clergy are our enemies, for reasons too obvious, and too palpable to need mentioning here; the wealthier classes dislike our government, because the liberal principles of its institutions break down their power; the patriotic must needs feel mortification and pain, at seeing our people domineering in their homes; and the lower classes lived too long in a state of abject slavery, dependence, and ignorance, to be at once capable of appreciating the benefits conferred on them by the change of government. All are dissatisfied—the rich, the poor, the high and the low; and the Pueblos are the only people here, whose protestations of fidelity can be believed; but they are content indeed. But notwithstanding these facts, which would seem to bode evil, and entitle these plans of intended insurrections to some importance, I cannot be made to believe, that these people are either so hardy or so foolish, to attempt any thing in the shape of revolt; and must place these and all similar attempts, at once under the broad head of Mexican braggadocio.[45]

THE TAOS REBELLION

Although the author of the foregoing report noted unrest among the Mexican people neither he nor other Americans realized its gravity: even as he wrote a general uprising was being planned. The plot was discovered in mid-December but the leaders escaped. After the artillery under Major Clark left Santa Fe to join Doniphan, the situation exploded in February. Colonel Price reported to the Adjutant General in Washington:

I have the honor to submit to you a short account of the recent *revolution* in this territory, and a detailed report of the operations of the forces under my command consequent upon the rebellion.

About the 15th of December last I received information of an attempt to excite the people of this territory against the American government. This rebellion was headed by Thomas Ortiz and Diego Archuleta. An officer, formerly in the Mexican service, was seized, and on his person was found a list of all the disbanded Mexican soldiers in the vicinity of Santa Fe. Many other persons, supposed to be implicated, were arrested, and a full investigation proved that many of the most influential persons in the northern part of this territory were engaged in the rebellion.[46] All attempts to arrest Ortiz and Archuleta proved unsuccessful, and these rebels have, without doubt, escaped in the direction of Chihuahua.

After the arrest above mentioned, and the flight of Ortiz and Archuleta, the rebellion appeared to be suppressed; but this appearance was deceptive.

On the 14th of January, Governor Bent[47] left this city for Taos. On the 19th of the same month, this valuable officer, together with five other persons, were seized at Don Fernando de Taos by the Pueblos and Mexicans, and were murdered in the most inhuman manner the savages could devise. On the same day, seven Americans were murdered at the Arroya Honda, and two others on the Rio Colorado.

. . . . .

It appeared to be the object of the insurrectionists to put to death every American and every Mexican who had accepted office under the American government.

News of these events reached me on the 20th of January; and letters from the rebels calling upon the inhabitants of the Rio Abajo for aid, were intercepted. It was now ascertained that the enemy was approaching this city, and that their force was continually being increased by the inhabitants of the towns along their line of march.

In order to prevent the enemy from receiving any further reinforcements in that manner, I determined to meet them as soon as possible. Supposing that the detachment of the necessary troops would weaken the garrison of Santa Fe too much, I immediately ordered up from Albuquerque Major Edmonson,[48] 2d regiment Missouri mounted volunteers, and Captain Burgwin, with their respective commands, directing Captain Burgwin to leave one company of dragoons at this post, and to join me with the other. Major Edmonson was directed to remain in Santa Fe.

. . . . .

On the 24th of January, at half-past one, p.m., our advance (Captain St. Vrain's[49] company) discovered the enemy in considerable force near the town of Cañada, their position at that time being in the valley bordering the Rio del Norte. Preparations were immediately made by me to attack them; and it became necessary for the troops to march more rapidly than the ammunition and provision wagons could travel, in order to prevent the escape of the enemy, or to frustrate them in any attempt they might make to occupy commanding positions. As I entered the valley, I discovered them beyond the creek on which the town is situated, and in full possession of the heights commanding the road to Cañada, and of three strong houses at the bases of the hills. . . . So soon as the wagon train had been brought up, I ordered Captain Angney[50] to charge with his battalion of infantry, and dislodge the enemy from the house opposite the right flank, and from which a warm fire was being poured on us. This was done in the most gallant manner.

A charge was then ordered to be made upon all the points occupied by the enemy in any force. Captain Angney, with his command, supported by Lieutenant White's[51] company, charged up one hill, while Captain St. Vrain's company turned the same, in order to cut off the enemy when in retreat. The artillery, supported by Captains McMillen [sic],[52] Barber,[53] and Slack,[54] with their respective companies, at the same time took possession of some houses (enclosed by a strong corral densely wooded with fruit trees, from which a brisk fire was kept up by the enemy), and of the heights beyond them. Captain Halley's[55] company was ordered to support Captain Angney. In a few minutes my troops had dislodged the enemy at all points, and they were flying in every direction. The nature of the ground rendered pursuit hopeless; and it being near night, I ordered the troops to take up quarters in the town. The number of the enemy was about fifteen hundred. . . .

On the 27th I advanced up the Rio del Norte as far as Luceros, where, early on the 28th, I was joined by Captain Burgwin, commanding company G, 1st dragoons, and company A, 2d regiment Missouri mounted volunteers, commanded by Lieutenant Boone.[56] Captain Burgwin's command was dismounted, and great credit is due to him and his officers and men for the rapidity with which a march so long and arduous was performed. At the same time Lieutenant Wilson,[57] 1st dragoons, who had volunteered his services, came up with a 6-pounder, which had been sent for from Cañada.

My whole force now comprised 479 rank and file. On the 29th, I marched to La Joya, where I learned that a party of sixty or eighty of the enemy had posted themselves on the steep slopes of the mountains which rise on each side of the cañon, or gorge, which leads to Embudo.[58] Finding the road by Embudo impracticable for artillery or wagons, I detached Captain Burgwin in that direction, with his own company of dragoons and the companies commanded by Captain St. Vrain and Lieutenant White. This detachment comprised 180 rank and file.

. . . . .

The rapid slopes of the mountains rendered the enemy's position very strong, and its strength was increased by the dense masses of cedar and large fragments of rock which every where offered them shelter. The action was commenced by Captain St. Vrain, who, dismounting his men, ascended the mountain on the left, doing much execution. Flanking parties were thrown out on either side, commanded respectively by Lieutenant White, 2d regiment Missouri mounted volunteers, and Lieutenants McIlvaine [sic][59] and Taylor,[60] 1st dragoons. These parties ascended the hills rapidly, and the enemy soon began to retire in the direction of Embudo, bounding along the steep and rugged sides of the mountains with a speed that defied pursuit. The firing at the pass of Embudo had been heard at La Joya, and Captain Slack, with twenty-five mounted men, had been immediately despatched thither. He now arrived and rendered excellent service by relieving Lieutenant White, whose men were much fatigued. Lieutenants McIlvaine and Taylor were also recalled; and Lieutenant Ingalls was directed to lead a flanking party on the right slope, while Captain Slack performed the same duty on the left. The enemy having by this time retreated beyond our reach, Captain Burgwin marched through the defile, and debouching into the open valley in which Embudo is situated, recalled the flanking parties, and entered that town without opposition, several persons meeting him with a white flag.

Our loss in this action was one man killed, and one severely wounded, both belonging to Captain St. Vrain's company. The loss of the enemy was about twenty killed and sixty wounded.

Thus ended the battle of the pass of Embudo.

On the 30th, Captain Burgwin marched to Trampas,[61] where he was directed to await the arrival of the main body, which, on account of the artillery and wagons, was forced to pursue a more southern route. On the 31st I reached Trampas, and being joined by Capt. Burgwin, marched on to Chamisal[62] with the whole command. On the 1st of February, we reached the summit of the Taos mountain, which was covered with snow to the depth of two feet; and on the 2d, quartered at a small village called Rio Chicito [sic, Chiquito] in the entrance of the valley of Taos. The marches of the 1st and 2d were through deep snow. Many of the men were frostbitten, and all were very much jaded with the exertions necessary to travel over unbeaten roads, being marched in front of the artillery and wagons in order to break a road through the snow. The constancy and patience with which the troops bore these hardships, deserve all commendation, and cannot be excelled by the most veteran soldiers.

On the 3d, I marched through Don Fernando de Taos, and finding that the enemy had fortified themselves in the Pueblo de Taos, proceeded to that place. I found it a place of great strength, being surrounded by adobe walls and strong pickets. Within the enclosure and near the northern and southern walls, arose two large buildings of irregular pyramidal form to the height of seven or eight stories. Each of these buildings was capable of sheltering five or six hundred men. Besides these, there were many smaller buildings, and the large church of the town was situated in the northwestern angle, a small passage being left between it and the outer wall. The exterior wall and all the enclosed buildings were pierced for rifles. The town was admirably calculated for defence, every point of the exterior walls and pickets being flanked by some projecting building. . . .

After having reconnoitred the town, I selected the western flank of the church as the point of attack; and about 2 o'clock, p.m., Lieutenant Dyer[63] was ordered to open his battery at the distance of about 250 yards. A fire was kept up by the 6-pounder and the howitzers for about two hours and a half, when, as the ammunition wagon had not yet come up, and the troops were suffering from cold and fatigue, I returned to Don Fernando.

Early on the morning of the 4th, I again advanced upon Pueblo. Posting the dragoons under Captain Burgwin about 260 yards from the western flank of the church, I ordered the mounted men under Captains St. Vrain and Slack to a position on the opposite side of the town, whence they could discover and intercept any fugitives who might attempt to escape towards the mountains, or in the direction of Don Fernando. The residue of the troops took ground about 300 yards from the northern wall. Here, too, Lieutenant Dyer established himself with the 6-pounder and two howitzers, while Lieutenant Hassandaubel [sic][64], of Major Clark's battalion light artillery, remained with Captain Burgwin, in command of two howitzers. By this arrangement a cross-fire was obtained, sweeping the front and eastern flank of the church.

All these arrangements having been made, the batteries opened upon the town at nine o'clock, a.m. At 11 o'clock, finding it impossible to breach the walls of the church with the 6-pounder and howitzers, I determined to storm that building. At a signal Capt. Burgwin, at the head of his own company, and that of Captain McMillin, charged the western flank of the church, while Captain Angney, infantry battalion, and Captain Barber and Lieutenant Boon[e], 2d regiment Missouri mounted volunteers, charged the northern wall. As soon as the troops above mentioned had established themselves under the western wall of the church, axes were used in the attempt to breach it; and, a temporary ladder having been made, the roof was fired. About this time, Captain Burgwin, at the head of a small party, left the cover afforded by the flank of the church, and penetrating into the corral in front of that building endeavored to force the door. In this exposed situation, Captain Burgwin received a severe wound which deprived me of his valuable services, and of which he died on the 7th instant. Lieutenants McIlvaine, 1st United States dragoons, and Royall[65] and Lackland,[66] 2d regiment mounted volunteers, accompanied Captain Burgwin into the corral; but the attempt on the church door proved fruitless, and they were compelled to retire behind the wall.

In the meantime small holes had been cut into the western wall, and shells were thrown in by hand, doing good execution. The 6-pounder was now brought around by Lieutenant Wilson, who at the distance of two hundred yards, poured a heavy fire of grape into the town. The enemy during all this time kept up a destructive fire upon our troops. About half-past three o'clock the 6-pounder was run up within sixty yards of the church, and after ten rounds, one of the holes which had been cut with the axes was widened into a practicable breach. The gun was now run up within ten yards of the wall— a shell was thrown in—three rounds of grape were poured in the breach. The storming party—among whom were Lieutenant Dyer of the ordnance, and Lieutenants Wilson and Taylor, 1st dragoons, entered and took possession of the church without opposition. The interior was filled with dense smoke, but for which circumstance our storming party would have suffered great loss. A few of the enemy were seen in the gallery where an open door admitted the air, but they retired without firing a gun. The troops left to support the battery on the north were now ordered to charge on that side. The enemy abandoned the western part of the town. Many took refuge in the large houses on the east, while others endeavored to escape toward the mountains. These latter were pursued by the mounted men under Captains Slack and St. Vrain, who killed fifty-one of them, only two or three men escaping.

It was now night, and our troops were quietly quartered in the houses which the enemy had abandoned. On the next morning the enemy sued for peace, and thinking the severe loss they had sustained would prove a salutary lesson, I granted their supplication, on the condition that they should deliver up to me Tomas [Baca]—one of their principal men, who had instigated and been actively engaged in the murder of Governor Bent and others. The number of the enemy at the battle of Pueblo de Taos was between six and seven hundred. Of these, about one hundred and fifty were killed—wounded not known. Our own loss was seven killed and forty-five wounded. Many of the wounded have since died.[67]

MISGOVERNMENT IN SANTA FE

Suppression of the Taos Rebellion ended the conquest of New Mexico but problems of occupation remained. Colonel Price would not or could not control his troops. As a consequence those who chose to looked for and, abetted by the worst elements of Mexican population, found trouble. A correspondent of the St. Louis New Era observed: "When [Col. Price was] in command here the place was a perfect bedlam; no order in the streets and public places —no discipline among the troops—everything at loose ends. . . ."[68] The St. Louis Missouri Republican added these details:

We have been assured, indeed, by persons who passed the winter at Santa Fe, that all military discipline, all regard for propriety [sic], was lost, by the regiment under the immediate command of Col. Price. It was a common occurence, not restricted by any order of the Colonel, to see *officers* of his regiment dealing *Monte* at the gambling hells of Santa Fe, and the *privates* of their companies betting their money on the turn of the card.[69]

A reporter for the same St. Louis newspaper was even more severe in his criticism:

We arrived at Santa Fe on the 25th of June, after a trip of 58 days from Independence, losing 51 head of oxen, stolen by the Indians, on Coon Creek, and some 20 were lost for want of grass between Las Vegas and this place. And lo! when we arrived at the goal of our destination, and domiciled in a mud-house in the great City of Santa Fe, and look around at men and manners, we see the most miserable state of society that exists upon the wide globe. Lewdness in both sexes exhibits itself in the most glaring and shameless forms, and walks abroad at midday, as if the human family had dwindled down to nothing more than brute intellect and to less than savage refinement. True, there are many of the officers and privates of Col. Price's regiment who are gentlemen, and hold themselves aloof from the vices and dissipation that are so contagious, and of which the very atmosphere seems composed, but alas! for the large majority, they have expended more than the amount of their wages and are, indeed, a reckless ragamuffin band, a disgrace to the name of American soldiers, and will return to Missouri, a miserable, ragged set, with morals corrupted, and will, ere long, be a great accession to our State Penitentiary.[70]

El Brazito

While troubles were beginning to build for Price in Santa Fe, Colonel Doniphan left on November 17, 1846 with a part of his force for the Navajo country in the western part of the territory. At Ojo Oso he made a treaty with the tribe on November 22, then united his command and marched down the Rio Grande to Valverde where he prepared for a thrust toward Chihuahua. On December 12 he launched his expedition. His first objective was El Paso (or Passo). Although his troops grumbled, the intrepid Doniphan moved

BATTLE OF EL BRAZITO

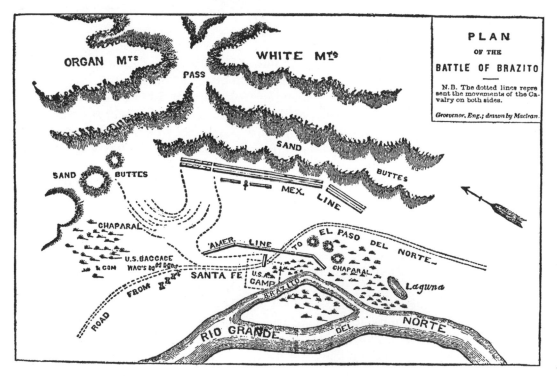

to enter the Mexican city without artillery, since that arm, which would join his force later under Major Clark, had not caught up with him. Mexican troops, many of them Paseños exceeding one thousand in number, barred his way at El Brazito thirty miles north of El Paso. On Christmas Day, 1846, the Battle of El Brazito was fought.

BATTLE OF SACRAMENTO

Two days later, Doniphan occupied El Paso where he remained throughout January 1847. In early February he started for the city of Chihuahua, two hundred and thirty five miles due south. Fifteen miles north of that goal, at the Sacramento River, the Mexicans made a stand. This time their resistance was more determined. William H. Richardson, a private soldier under Doniphan, wrote a detailed account of the Battle of Sacramento:

The pass of the Sacramento is formed by a point of the mountains on our right, their left extending into the valley, so as to narrow the valley about one and a half miles. On our left was a deep, dry channel of a creek, and between these points, the plain rises abruptly about 50 or 60 feet. The road passes down the centre of the valley, and in the distance we had a full view of the Mexican army. On the point of the mountain, they had a battery of 4 guns, so elevated as to sweep the plain. On the left, there was another battery commanding the road with 6 pounders and rampart pieces mounted on carriages. Their cavalry was drawn up in front of their redoubts in the intervals of four deep.

When we had arrived near their entrenchments, our columns suddenly diverged to the right so as to gain the elevation which the enemy endeavoured to prevent by moving forward with 4 pieces of cannon and 1,000 cavalry. But our movements were so rapid that we not only gained the eminence, but were formed in order for their reception. Our company (Capt. Hudson's)[71] now dismounted, and every eighth man was detailed to hold horses and mules. It fell to my lot to hold 8 mules. The action now commenced by a brisk fire from our cannons, doing considerable execution at the distance of twelve hundred yards, killing fifteen of the enemy, and disabling one of their guns. Our fire was briskly returned from 14 pieces of artillery, sending ragged balls and heavy copper ore. But being badly aimed they struck the ground about forty or fifty yards before us, and rebounding passed over our heads without harm except slightly wounding two men and killing several horses and mules in the rear. Our guns were so well aimed as to compel the enemy to fall behind the breastworks. We resumed our march in our former order, diverging as much as possible to the right to avoid a heavy battery and their strongest redoubts which were on our left near the common road. After marching as

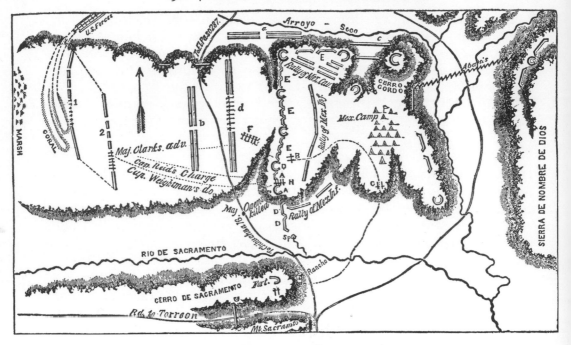

BATTLE OF SACRAMENTO

far as we thought it prudent without coming in range of their heavy battery, Capt. Weightman[72] of the artillery was ordered to charge it with two 12 lb. howitzers, to be supported by the cavalry under Captains Reid, Parsons[73] and Hudson. We then remounted and charged the battery from right to left with a brisk and deadly fire from our rifles. We then advanced to the very brink of their redoubts, and drove them out with our sabres.

The enemy now fell back on their centre battery, where they made a desperate rally, and gave us a shower of balls and copper ore which whizzed over our heads without doing us any injury except wounding several men and killing a few mules and horses. Major Clarke [sic, Meriwether L. Clark] was ordered to commence a heavy fire upon this battery which being well directed together with the rapid advance of our columns put them to flight over the mountains in utter confusion, leaving all their cannons and the ground strewed with their dead and wounded. Thus ended the battle of Sacramento which commenced about 3 o'clock, and ended about sun-set. The enemy numbered 4220 rank and file, and lost 300 killed, 500 wounded, beside 40 prisoners. The American force consisted of 924 effective men, 1 killed, 11 wounded. Our success is to be attributed entirely to the superior skill of our commander. Had he not taken advantage of position in keeping out of range of their redoubts and batteries, we should all have shared a common fate, as the black piratical flag was captured, together with a wagon load of that formidable weapon, the lariat, which was intended to tie us all to our saddles in case of a defeat.

The Mexicans lost 10 pieces of artillery, varying from 5 to 10 lbs. and 7 one lb. culverines. One of the cannon is very valuable, being composed of silver and brass melted together. They also lost all their baggage, ammunition, &c., and provisions enough to last us 3 months were found in their wagons, together with $4000 in specie. It was gratifying to see the soldiers shaking hands with their officers after the engagement and tendering their congratulations to their commander for his skill and bravery displayed on this memorable occasion.

The surgeons are now busily engaged in administering relief to the wounded Mexicans, and it is a sight to see the pile of legs and arms that have been amputated. The cries and groans of the poor fellows are distressing in the extreme. It is a fact, worthy of note, that the atmosphere here in this mountainous region is so perfectly pure and clear that a cannon shot can be seen coming when it is a considerable distance off by leaving a blue streak in the air. Many a soldier saved his life in the battle by dodging the balls as they came forward. When a flash would be seen from the enemy's battery, you could hear the soldiers cry out—"Watch the ball boys!—here comes a ball boys," and they invariably avoided them, or the slaughter must have been

Charge of Captain Reid at Sacramento

very great. I saw a ball coming in the direction where I was, when immediately falling off my mule, it passed just over my saddle without injury.

Our rapid movements seemed to astonish the enemy. Our 4 pieces of flying artillery, discharging five times in a minute volleys of grape and canister with chain shots, would rake the enemy's redoubts and cut roads through their lines, while our 12 lb. howitzers throwing a constant shower of bombs into the middle of their entrenchments, and the unerring aim of our Mississippi Rifles, acting in concert, cast terror and dismay among the cowardly and unprincipled foe. Our men acted nobly, and in the hand to hand fight in the redoubts they fought to desperation. Lieutenant Sprawl [sic][74], our 2d Lieutenant, a man over six feet high with bared arms, and without his hat, his long hair and beard streaming in the wind, with sword in hand, was charging the enemy at every point when a ball struck his splendid charger and he fell. But seizing his carbine he kept up with us on foot. Another of our men, being unhorsed and fighting near me was attacked by a Mexican who was about to lance him, and the poor fellow's gun being discharged, he picked up a rock, and throwing it, struck his enemy on the head, which felled him to the earth, when he knocked his brains out with a butt of his gun. These were but common occurrences in that hard contested fight, where we had to contend with nearly five to one.

. . . . .

[March] 2nd.—Placed on mounted guard to precede the army, whose entrance in[to] the city [Chihuahua] will take place to-day. Came 10 miles; saw the spire of the cathedral towering in the distance, with peculiar feelings of delight. A merrier group could scarcely be pictured than our worthy Col. Mitchell and his escort. We entered the beautiful city of Chihuahua about 12 o'clock, and proceeded immediately to the plaza or public square. The inhabitants are polite, and manifest in various ways the utmost complaisance and regard to our soldiery. Of course we see the fairest specimens of the Mexican character here, and they afford us evidences of superior intelligence, comfort and industry. While the soldiers were scattered in various directions, seeking refreshments, I took a walk alone, and seated myself in a quiet nook, fronting the cathedral. It is an imposing structure of white marble. It was about fifty years in building—the production of a gold mine, and cost *three million dollars.* . . . The tones of the bell are grand. It strikes the hour, and can be heard at a great distance. At sun down Col. Doniphan arrived in town with the rest of the Command, all in fine order. The band was playing Washington's March—just as we reached the public square, the tune was changed to Yankee Doodle, when there was a general huzzah. We then marched through the town and took up our quarters on the outskirts.[75]

According to Susan Magoffin, the wife of a Santa Fe and Chihuahua trader, the Missourians' occupation of Chihuahua was something less than inspiring to see:

We arrived at Chihuahua on the 4th April [1847]; here we found Col. Doniphan's command occupying the city, and a beautiful sight they have made of it in some respects. Instead of seeing it in its original beauty as I thought to have done twelve months since, I saw it filled with Missouri volunteers who though good to fight are not careful at all how much they soil the property of a friend much less an enemy. The good citizens of Chi. had never dreamed I dare say that their loved homes would be turned into quarters for common soldiers, their fine houses many of them turned into stables, the rooves made kitchens of, their public *pila* (drinking fountain) used as a bathing trough, the fine trees of their beautiful *alamador* (*alameda*—public walk) barked and forever spoiled, and a hundred other deprivations equal to any of these, but yet all has been done; Chihuahua was quite an indifferent looking place when I saw it. We took a comfortable house a square off from the plaza, as none could be had in it, and spent three weeks in it as pleasantly as we could under the circumstances; the families all had left, so I of course saw none of them.[76]

Doniphan's Odyssey

Doniphan's men stayed in Chihuahua until April, when they began a six-hundred-mile march toward a meeting with Taylor's army near Saltillo. Frederick Adolph Wislizenus (1810-1889) was a native of Germany who had migrated to the United States in 1835. He was a medical practitioner in southern Illinois and led an exploring expedition to the Rocky Mountains in 1839. In the spring of the year that the Mexican War broke out, Wislizenus left St. Louis on a scientific expedition to northern Mexico and, as planned, to upper California. When he arrived at Chihuahua he was held prisoner for six months, until the arrival of the American troops. He then abandoned his journey and accepted a position in the medical department of the Army, accompanying Doniphan via Saltillo and Monterey to the United States. His account, like that of his fellow scientist, Josiah Gregg, is full of observations on the geography, natural history, and statistics of Mexico. In his diary one can follow the day by day experiences of the Missourians on their remarkable trek:

On April 5, 1847, 600 men, with 14 cannon, left Chihuahua for that purpose, while about 300 men, with some pieces of artillery, were left behind for the safekeeping of the city. As there was at that time a want of surgeons in the regiment, an appointment to that effect was offered to me, which I accepted. I left Chihuahua with the troops, moving towards the south. . . . and a day was at last fixed for the final departure of the whole regiment, if the express sent to General Wool should not return up to that time. Our route in that case would have been by Presidio del Norte and the Red river, to Fort Towson. But in due time Mr. Collins made his appearance. In about 30 days he had travelled, with a mere handful of men, about 1,000 miles through a hostile country, with no other passports but their rifles.[77] In going out, his party consisted of but 12 men; on his return it was increased to about 40. The gallant Squire was received in Chihuahua with enthusiastic joy. He brought us definite orders from General Wool to march at once, and on the most direct road to Saltillo. Within two days our troops were on the march. Colonel Doniphan, before he left, called the Mexican authorities of the place and made them promise to treat the American residents of Chihuahua in a decent manner, and threatened them, in case of disorder, with a return of the American troops and a severe chastisement. The Mexicans promised everything. Many American and other foreign residents, however, had so little confidence in Mexican faith, that they preferred to accompany the army.

. . . . .

May 12.—Starting this morning for *San Juan*, our vanguard discovered three armed Mexicans running from us. After a short steeple-chase through the chapparal, the Mexicans were made prisoners, and, as no plausible account could be elicited from them, taken along to our night camp in San Juan Bautista, a rancho on the Nasas, 15 miles from San Lorenzo. The road to-day was sandy, and mountain chains towards west, south, and east. The Nasas contained here plenty of running water again.

. . . . .

May 13.—We travelled to-day 25 miles, from San Juan to *el Pozo*.

. . . . .

I had been riding ahead this morning, and reached Pozo early, though not in time to take part in a skirmish between our vanguard and a party of Indians. When I arrived, some Mexicans were engaged in lazoing several dead bodies of Indians and dragging them into a heap together. The skirmish had taken place under the following circumstances: Two days before, a party of Lipan Indians, upon one of their predatory excursions, had stolen from a hacienda near Parras several hundred mules and horses, and killed several men. The proprietor of the hacienda, Don Manuel de Ibarra, applied to Captain Reid,[78] of our regiment (who was then ahead of us with Lieut. Colonel Mitchell's[79] party), for aid against these Indians. The captain, one of our most gallant officers, took but eight men along, and, accompanied by the Don himself, went back to el Pozo, where the Indians, on their march to the mountains, had to pass, being the only watering place in that neighborhood. There they hid themselves in a corral, to wait for the arrival of the Indians. Quite un-expected, about 20 men of our vanguard came very early this morning to el Pozo, and increased their party to 30 men. Soon afterwards the Indians ap-peared—from 40 to 50 warriors. When our men rushed on horseback out of the corral to attack them, the Indians (probably supposing them to be Mexi-cans) received them with sneering and very contemptous provocations, and their confidence in their bows and arrows was increased when the Americans firing their rifles from horseback, killed none at the first charge. But as soon as our men alighted, and took good aim with their rifles, the Indians fell on all sides. Nevertheless, they fought most desperately, and did not retire till half of them were either dead or wounded. But at last they had to run for their lives, and to leave all their dead and all their booty behind.

Besides the stolen stock, thirteen prisoners, Mexican women and children, whom they had carried along, were retaken and released from the brutality of their savage masters. Fifteen Indians were lying dead on the field. On our side, Captain Reid was wounded by some arrows, but not dangerously. Most of the dead Indians had fine blankets; some even carried gold; all were armed with bows and arrows, and a few with elegant shields of leather; and the "medicine-man," who was foremost in the action, and fought most bravely, wore a head-dress of feathers and horns. Our men, of course, took of these curiosities whatever they liked, and the Mexicans stripped them of the rest, and dragged their bodies together. The fallen Indians were all of medium size, but well proportioned and very muscular; their skulls and faces bore all the characteristics of the Indian race, but their skin looked whiter than I have ever seen it in Indians. The dead bodies were lying there all day; neither Americans nor Mexicans seemed to care about them, and their burial was no doubt left to the wolves. I saw, therefore, no impropriety in taking another curiosity along for scientific purposes—to wit, the skull of the medicine man, which I have, since my return, presented to that distinguished craniologist, Professor Samuel G. Morton, of Philadelphia. In relation to the tribe of Lipans, I could only ascertain from the Mexicans that they live in the moun-tains of the Bolson, extend their stealing and robbing excursions very far south, and have the reputation of being a most brutal and cruel set of Indians, though brave in battle.

El Pozo (the well) is a hacienda, belonging to Don Manuel de Ibarra, and consists of but one large building, in which many families live. The place is distinguished for its ingenious water-works. It consists of a deep and very spacious well, from which the water is drawn by mule power. . . . On the threatened invasion of General Wool, the Mexicans, amongst other prepara-tions of defence, had proposed to fill up this well on the approach of the American army, to expose them to starvation for want of water. This would certainly have proved a most wanton destruction, as the Mexicans must have found out by this time that a Jornada of 50 miles is not capable of stopping an American army.

. . . . .

May 20.—Made 22 miles to-day, from Vequeria to *San Juan.* . . .

We encamped at San Juan, a place renowned by the battle fought here in the revolutionary war against Spain. At present, nobody lives here. On a hill of limestone stands a deserted rancho, and below is a green spot, with fine spring-water, and some miry places around it. Here we camped. General Wool's camp is about 15 miles from here, in Buena Vista.

May 21.—As we expected to meet General Wool to-day, there was a general brushing up this morning in the camp; but as it was impossible to create something out of nothing, we looked as ragged as ever. In the marching line, too, an improvement was tried. Usually, during the march, the men selected their places more according to fancy than military rule, and it was not uncommon to have our line stretched out to five miles, or three-fourths of the regiment marching in the vanguard. But, to day, to my utter astonishment, the heroes of Sacramento fell into regular line, and marched so for nearly half an hour, till the spirit of independence broke loose, and the commanding voice of Colonel Doniphan had to restore order again. However, after about 10 miles march over the plain, we arrived in "*Encantada,*" where some Arkansas troops were encamped. According to orders from headquarters, we encamped here also. The battle field and General Wool's camp at Buena Vista were five or six miles from here, and visits were soon exchanged between the two camps. With some friends from the Illinois regiments, I rode in the afternoon over the battlefield and to General Wool's camp.

. . . . .

May 22.—The General, with his staff, rode to-day to our camp to review our regiment. A salute was fired, and he expressed himself highly satisfied with the martial appearance of the great marching and fighting regiment of Missouri, though he seemed not to admire our uniform. We received orders to march from here to Saltillo, Montcrcy, and Matamoros.

. . . . .

On *May 23,* in the morning, we left Encantada, passed by the battlefield and General Wool's camp, and marched through Saltillo and six miles beyond it before we encamped. In Wool's camp the old American cannon belonging to our regiment were left, while the conquered Mexican pieces were taken along as trophies, to Missouri.[80]

Doniphan and his men were in Monterey during May; early in June a writer described them in the Matamoros American Flag *as they passed down the Rio Grande:*

The unshorn beards and goat and deer skin clothes of many of them reminded us of descriptions we have read of the inhabitants of some of the countries of the Russian empire. They stopped in town a couple of hours. Col. Doniphan is a stout, rough featured, good natured looking sort of a man. He brought along with him Clark's battery, and ten pieces of cannon captured at Sacramento. The sick, &c., forty or fifty wagons, with several hundred mules, were turned over to the quarter master.[81]

Colonel Doniphan and seven companies of the Missouri Volunteers went on to a heroes' welcome in New Orleans after an odyssey which had covered over three thousand miles of mountains, plains and parched desertland. They had fought one skirmish, El Brazito, and one fierce battle at Sacramento.

SANTA CRUZ DE ROSALES

As in many of the Mexican cities conquered but not adequately garrisoned, new threats sprang up in Chihuahua. The threat seemed important enough for Price to reoccupy Chihuahua in March 1848, and then to move in pursuit of General Trias sixty miles southeast of there, where he fought some eight hundred Mexican troops, and entered the town of Santa Cruz de Rosales. It was a fatiguing march but a decisive skirmish. Lt. Alexander Brydie Dyer, described it to Maj. Jubal Early who was with the army under General Wool:

You will doubtless be surprised to hear that I am within striking distance of you and coming by the way of New Mexico where I have been ever since fall before last. We reached here on the 7th of last month having marched with about 300 [? or 200] men nearly 300 miles in less than ten days in the hope of surprising Genl. Trias[82] in his capital but he anticipated us and fled with his troops, cannon &c &c on the previous day. On the 8th Genl. Price started with less than 200 men in pursuit of him and before daylight of the 9th pressed him so closely, that he was compelled to seek safety in the town of Santa Cruz de Rosales, where he resolved to fortify himself and give battle to us. As our force was less than one fourth that of the enemy, who had eight guns and nine heavy wall pieces, 2 of the Guns being 32-pdr. howrs. and one nearly a 12-Pdr. gun, whilst he occupied a strong position we determined not to attack him unless he should attempt to escape until we were reinforced. An express was sent to hasten forward Love's[83] battery which reached us on the morning of the 16th at day light having marched more than 200 miles in four days and nights, and 65 miles in the last 20 hours. At 10 A.M. we opened the attack an[d] at dark had entire possession of the town.[84]

CALIFORNIA: DESIGN FOR CONQUEST

On September 25, 1846, while Doniphan still was in New Mexico and the Taos Rebellion was four months in the future, Kearny left Santa Fe for California with three hundred men. This was in obedience to confidential orders he received before leaving Fort Leavenworth and was part of the Polk administration's grand design for conquest.

However clear the design might be in Washington, the situation in California was confused. Communications were slow and Commander Sloat, whose instructions ordered action only when he knew "beyond a doubt" that a state of war existed, hesitated to act. But if Sloat was irresolute, John C. Frémont was waging a war of sorts of his own.

FRÉMONT'S ADVENTURE

Frémont, Brevet Captain of United States Topographical Engineers and son-in-law of the influential United States Senator Thomas Hart Benton of Missouri, had arrived in December 1845 with 62 men at the station of Capt. John Sutter in northern California. His official assignment was to explore the Oregon country but Frémont habitually consulted his own judgment (or ambition) rather than his orders, and in this case he decided to ignore his orders. Instead of proceeding to Oregon he left his men at Sutter's station and went to Monterey (California) where he asked for and received permission from the Mexican Comandante, General José Castro, to remain in the interior of California throughout the winter. This was in January. In February, without further consulting Castro, he moved with his men to the coast; by early March he was in the Salinas Valley, twenty-five miles from Monterey. The Mexican commandant reacted by ordering the Americans out of the province. Frémont at first refused, then reconsidered, and left California to establish headquarters at Klamath in Oregon. Here he remained until May when Lt. Archibald H. Gillespie of the United States Marine Corps arrived with a letter of introduction from Secretary of State Buchanan and a packet of family letters from Senator Benton.

Lieutenant Gillespie had left Washington in October 1845. His primary concern was with Commander Sloat at Mazatlán and with the American consul, Thomas O. Larkin, in Monterey. He was to deliver to them orders, which he had memorized, confirming a written one already despatched by sea. The orders were oral because Gillespie's route was across Mexico—with whom the United States was still at peace—and a message dealing with war and conquest would be embarrassing if it fell into the Mexican hands. The lieutenant completed the first part of his mission, repeated his orders to Sloat, and departed from Mazatlán for Monterey by way of the Sandwich Islands. Arriving at Monterey[85] he delivered his message to Consul Larkin, then continued to Klamath and Frémont, to whom he delivered letters including one from Senator Benton.

Frémont read and pondered over his father-in-law's message and decided, through characteristic reasoning, that it was a call to arms. He explained himself in a letter to the senator:

When Mr. Gillespie overtook me in the middle of May, we were encamped on the northern shore of the Greater Klamath Lake. Snow was falling steadily and heavily in the mountains, which entirely surrounded and dominate[d] the elevated valley region into which we had penetrated; in the east, and north, and west, barriers absolutely impassable barred our road; we had no provisions; our animals were already feeble, and while any other way was open, I could not bring myself to attempt such a doubtful enterprise as a passage of these unknown mountains in the dead of winter. Every day the snow was falling; and in the face of the depressing influence exercised on the people by the loss of our men, and the unpromising appearance of things, I judged it inexpedient to pursue our journey farther in this direction, and determined to retrace my steps, and carry out the views of the government by reaching the frontier on the line of the Colorado river.

I had scarcely reached the lower Sacramento, when General Castro,[86] then in the north (at Sonoma, in the department of Sonoma, north of the bay of San Francisco, commanded by General Vallejo), declared his determination immediately to proceed against the foreigners settled in the country, for whose expulsion an order had just been issued by the governor of the Californias. For these purposes Castro immediately assembled a force at the Mission of Santa Clara, a strong place, on the northern shore of the Francisco bay. You will remember how grossly outraged and insulted we had already been by this officer; many in my own camp, and throughout the country thought that I should not have retreated in March last. I felt humiliated and humbled; one of the main objects proposed by this expedition had been entirely defeated, and it was the opinion of the officers of the squadron (so I was informed by Mr. Gillespie) that I could not again retreat consistently with any military reputation.

Unable to procure supplies elsewhere, I had sent by Mr. Gillespie [to] Captain Montgomery,[87] commanding the United States ship of war Portsmouth, then lying at Monterey, a small requisition for such supplies as were indispensably necessary to leave the valley; and my animals were now in such a state that I could not get out of the valley, without reaching the country which lies on the west side of them in an entirely destitute condition.

Having carefully examined my position, and foreseeing, I think, clearly, *all* the consequences which may eventuate to me from such a step, I determined to take such active and anticipatory measures as should seem to me most expedient to protect my party and justify my own character. I was well aware of the grave responsibility which I assumed, but I also determined that, having once decided to do so, I would assume it and its consequences fully and entirely, and go through with the business completely to the end. . . .Castro's first measure was an attempt to incite the Indian population of the Joaquin and Sacramento valleys, and the neighboring mountains, to burn the crops of the foreigners and otherwise proceed immediately against them. These Indians are extremely numerous, and the success of his measure would have been very destructive; but he failed entirely. On the 6th of June I decided on the course which I would pursue, and immediately concerted my operations with the foreigners inhabiting the Sacramento valley.

A few days afterwards, one of Castro's officers, with a party of 14 men, attempted to pass a drove of 200 horses from Sonoma to Santa Clara, via New Helvetia, with the avowed purpose of bringing troops into the country. On the 11th they were surprised at daylight on the Cosume river by a party of twelve from my camp. The horses were taken, but they were [the men] dismissed without injury. At daybreak on the 15th, the military fort of Sonoma was taken by surprise, with 9 brass pieces of artillery; 250 stand of muskets, some other arms, and a quantity of ammunition. General Vallejo,[88] . . . and some others were taken prisoners, and placed at New Helvetia, a fortified post under my command. In the meantime a launch had reached New Helvetia with stores from the ship Portsmouth, now lying at Yerba Buena, on Francisco bay. News of General Castro's proceedings against me in *March* had reached Commodore Sloat at Mazatlan at the end of that month, and he had immediately despatched the ship Portsmouth to Monterey, with general instructions to protect American interests in California.

These enterprises accomplished, I proceeded to the American settlements on the Sacramento, and the Rio de los Americanos, to obtain reinforcements of men and rifles.

The information brought by Mr. Gillespie to Captain Montgomery, in relation to my position, induced that officer immediately to proceed to Yerba Buena, whence he had despatched his launch to me. I immediately wrote to him, by return of the boat, describing to him fully my position and intentions, in order that he might not, by supposing me to be acting under orders from our government, unwittingly commit himself in affording me other than such assistance as his instructions would authorize him naturally to offer an officer charged with an important public duty; or, in fine, to any citizen of the United States.

Information having reached me from the commanding officer at Sonoma, that his post was threatened with an attack by a force under Gen. Castro, I raised camp on the American fork on the afternoon of the 23d, and, accompanied by Mr. Gillespie, at two in the morning of the 25th, reached Sonoma, with 90 mounted riflemen, having marched 80 miles. Our people still held the place, only one division of Castro's force, a squadron of cavalry, numbering 70 men, and commanded by Joaquin de la Torre (one of his best officers) having succeeded in crossing the straits (Francisco bay). This force had attacked an advanced party of twenty Americans, and (was) defeated with the loss of two killed and two or three wounded. The Americans lost none.

This was an unexpected check to the Californians, who had announced their intentions to defeat our people without firing a gun; to beat out their brains with their "*tapaderos*," and destroy them "*con cuchillos puros*." They were led to use this expression from the circumstance that a few days previous they had captured two of our men (an express), and after wounding, had bound them to trees, and cut them to pieces while alive, with an exaggeration of cruelty, which no Indian would be capable of.

In a few days de la Torre was driven from the country, having barely succeeded in effecting his escape across the straits, the guns (six large and handsome pieces) spiked at the fort on the *south* side of the entrance to Francisco bay, and the communication with the opposite side entirely broke off, the boats and launches being either destroyed or in our possession. Three of Castro's party having landed on the Sonoma side in advance, were killed near the beach; and beyond this there was no loss on either side.

In all these proceedings, Mr. Gillespie has acted with me. We reached Sonoma again on the evening of July 4, and in the morning I called the people together, and spoke to them in relation to the position of the country, advising a course of operations which was unanimously adopted. California was declared independent, the country put under martial law, the force organized and officers elected. A pledge, binding themselves to support these measures, and to obey their officers, was signed by those present. The whole was placed under my direction. Several officers from the Portsmouth [were] present at this meeting.

Leaving Captain Grigssby [sic][89] with fifty men in command of Sonoma, I left that place on the 6th, and reached my encampment on the American Fork in three days. Before we arrived at that place, Gen. Castro had evacuated Santa Clara, which he had been engaged in fortifying, and with a force of about 400 men, and two pieces of artillery, commenced his retreat upon St. John's, a fortified post, having 8 pieces of artillery, principally brass. . . . We were electrified by the arrival of an express from Captain Montgomery, with information that Commodore Sloat had hoisted the flag of the United States at Monterey, and taken possession of the country. Capt. Montgomery had hoisted the flag at Yerba Buena, and sent one to Sonoma, to be hoisted at that place. One also was sent to the officer commanding at New Helvetia, requesting that it might be hoisted at his post.

Independence and the flag of the United States are synonomous terms to the foreigners here (the northern, which is the stronger part, particularly), and accordingly I directed the flag to be hoisted with a salute the next morning. The event produced great rejoicing among our people. The next day I received an express from Commodore Sloat, transmitting to me his proclamation, and directing me to proceed with the force under my orders to Monterey. The registered force, actually in arms, under my orders, numbered two hundred and twenty riflemen, with one piece of field artillery, and ten men, in addition to the artillery of the garrison.[90]

The impact of Frémont's unauthorized activities is controversial. They certainly did not change the course of history but whether he softened or stiffened Californian resistance is debatable. Perhaps a wry letter from naval lieutenant Archibald MacRae[91] to his brother reduces the episode to something resembling its proper proportions.

I do not know that I can give you a very correct idea of what has taken place on this side in the war line. Such as it is it is at your service.

It appears that in the early part of the year Col. Frémont arrived and encamped with about seventy-five followers within twenty miles of Monterey; he then sought and obtained permission of the Governor of California to remain in the country until his men had time to recruit themselves. Not long afterwards the Governor suspecting that he "know'd what Col. Frémont was arter [sic, after] and that he wasn't arter fire" determined that he shouldn't have it "unless he was stronger than he (the Govnr.) was" and therefore notified the Col. that he must quit the country or be whipped.

Demonstrations were made on both sides of decidedly warlike character, but as neither would knock the chip off of the other's shoulder, nothing was done except calling each other "You are another" and as neither party understood what the other meant, each thought it was something terrible and quietly took themselves off in contrary directions, the Californians—like the King of France's Army—having marched up the hill, marched down again, and Col. Frémont marched for the Oregon. About this time a Lieut. Gillespie of the Marine Corps arrived on a mysterious mission, pursued and overtook Fremont's party, and returned with them to California, where they were joined by another party of American settlers, who having understood that the California Government had issued a proclamation requiring all Americans to leave the country immediately (which was the case) had risen, fought one little battle in which two men and four horses were killed, taken possession of the town of Sonoma and hoisted a Bear Flag intending to establish an independent Government if the United States did not annex them. With this force Frémont remained passive for a while until by the arrival of the Ships of War from Mazatlan news was learned of the existence of war; active measures were then taken on all sides to secure the Territory.[92]

Occupation of California

While Frémont marched and countermarched in California Commander Sloat waited at Mazatlán for news. The instructions from the Secretary of the Navy, George Bancroft, delivered orally by Gillespie and eventually confirmed by the written orders which had travelled by sea around Cape Horn, included the following:

You will henceforth exercise all the rights that belong to you as commander-in-chief of a belligerent squadron.

You will consider the most important public object to be to take and to hold possession of San Francisco, and this you will do without fail.

You will also take possession of Mazatlan and of Monterey, one or both, as your force will permit.

If information received here is correct, you can establish friendly relations between your squadron and the inhabitants of each of these three places. . . .

When you cannot take and hold possession of a town, you may establish a blockade, if you have the means to do it effectually, and the public interest shall require it.

With the expression of these views, much is left to your discretion as to the selection of the points of attack, the ports you will seize, the ports which you will blockade, and as to the order of your successive movements.

A connexion between California, and even Sonora, and the present government of Mexico, is supposed scarcely to exist. You will, as opportunity offers, conciliate the confidence of the people in California, and also in Sonora, towards the government of the United States; and you will endeavor to render their relations with the United States as intimate and as friendly as possible.

It is important that you should hold possession at least of San Francisco, even while you encourage the people to neutrality, self-government, and friendship.

You can readily conduct yourself in such a manner as will render your occupation of San Francisco, and other ports, a benefit to the inhabitants.[93]

On May 31 Sloat got word of the battle of Palo Alto but still hesitated. When he learned on June 7 that the United States fleet was blockading Vera Cruz on the Gulf of Mexico his doubts were finally resolved. The next day he left Mazatlán. A little more than seven weeks later, in a letter to the Secretary of the Navy, he reported on the occupation of the northern California ports:

I have the honor to report that on the 7th June I received, at Mazatlan, information that the Mexican troops, six or seven thousand strong, had, by order of the Mexican government, invaded the territory of the United States north of the Rio Grande, and had attacked the forces under General Taylor, and that the squadron of the United States were blockading the coast of Mexico on the gulf.

These hostilities I considered would justify my commencing offensive operations on the west coast; I therefore sailed on the 8th, in the *Savannah*, for the coast of California, to carry out the orders of the department of the 24th June, 1845, leaving the *Warren* at Mazatlan, to bring me any despatches or important information that might reach there. I arrived at Monterey on the 2d of July, where I found the *Cyane* and *Levant*, and learned that the *Portsmouth* was at San Francisco, to which places they had been previously ordered to await further instructions.

On the morning of the 7th, having previously examined the defences and localities of the town, I sent Captain Mervine[94] with the accompanying summons to the military commandant of Monterey, requiring him to surrender

Capture of Monterey, California

the place forthwith to the forces of the United States under my command. At 9h. 30m. a.m., I received his reply stating he was not authorized to surrender the place, and referred me to the commanding general of California, Don José Castro.

Every arrangement having been made the day previous, the necessary force (about 250 seamen and marines) was immediately embarked in the boats of the squadron, and landed at 10 o'clock, under cover of the guns of the ships, with great promptitude and good order, under the immediate command of Captain Wm. Mervine, assisted by Commander H. N. Page, as second.

The forces were immediately formed and marched to the customhouse, where my proclamation to the inhabitants of California was read, the standard of the United States hoisted, amid three hearty cheers of the troops and foreigners present, and a salute of 21 guns fired by all the ships. Immediately afterwards, the proclamation, both in English and Spanish, was posted up about the town, and two justices of the peace appointed to preserve order and punish delinquencies, the alcaldes declining to serve.

. . . . .

On the 6th of July, I despatched orders, by sea, to Commander Montgomery, to take immediate possession of the bay of San Francisco, &c.; and, on the 7th, a duplicate of that order, by land, which he received on the evening of the 8th; and at 7 a.m., of the 9th, he hoisted the flag at San Francisco, read and posted up my proclamation, and took possession of that part of the country in the name of the United States.

. . . . .

On the 23d, my health being such as to prevent my attending to so much, and such laborious duties, I directed Commodore Stockton to assume the command of the forces and operations on shore; and, on the 29th, having determined to return to the United States via Panama, I hoisted my broad pendant [sic] on board the *Levant* and sailed for Mazatlan and Panama, leaving the remainder of the squadron under his command.[95]

Commander Sloat's account is factual, presumably accurate and, as official communications are apt to be, colorless. Once again Lieutenant MacRae's letter to his brother gives a lively account not only of Sloat's activities in northern California but also those of his successor, Commodore Stockton.

The Naval Forces under Commodore Sloat landed in the face of a hot sun and took possession of Monterey and San Francisco, meeting with no other loss than that of two men who took the first opportunity of getting drunk, and quietly stowing themselves away in a pig sty, while the military force galloped up and down the country on horse back proclaiming every where that they were looking for Genl. Castro and his Army; this was done so that Castro might have no idea of their movements and therefore would not guard against a surprise.

The war having progressed so far the aged hero Commodore Sloat thinking that he had gained laurels enough gave up command of the squadron to Commodore Stockton and proceeded to the U.S. where I believe he expects to be received in triumph by the Roman citizens. After Commodore Stockton took command he despatched the vessels down the coast and took possession of all the towns on the sea coast of upper California; besides which he arrested the French Consul at Monterey in consequence of his writing some very insolent letters protesting against our taking possession of the country; this may give us trouble. No blood has been spilled on this side, nor have the hostile forces ever been near each other except in two instances, the first on the occasion spoken of on the preceding page, and the last at the town of Angels (Pueblo de los Angeles). It was known from some very bombastic proclamations of Genl. Castro that he was at that place with nearly all his force—some five hundred men—in consequence of which the Congress proceeded to San Pedro (a small port 30 miles from the Pueblo) landed about 400 men and marched up. But unfortunately the General left a few hours before the Commodore arrived, and so no one had an opportunity of distinguishing himself, and what is still worse, it is said that Castro's five hundred cavalry made so much dust in their retreat that it was impossible to distinguish any one else.

I have said that no blood has been spilled but here I am mistaken or rather had forgotten. Two troops of mounted men the command of which was given to two Pursers for God knows what reason, not being able to amuse themselves in any other way have been cooly shooting down some peaceful and friendly Indians. This occurred just before we left and therefore I do not know the full particulars, but all accounts agree upon the fact that deliberate murders have been committed upon a number of men who under the impression that they were to be put to death when ordered to arrange themselves in a line in front of the troop committed the very grave offence of attempting to escape, and who committed no other fault.

At present all Upper California (which extends from our Southern boundary to San Diego in Lat. 32° 40′ N) is in our possession, and the Mexican Coast is blockaded at all of its principal ports.

. . . . .

The country of California is not what it has been cracked up to be, although it is very good; the only two places I have been to are Santa Barbara and Monterey. The land immediately around the former is level but about five miles back mountainous. The soil there, as well as at Monterey, is rich and about the consistence of clay or rather lighter, indeed it is very much

San Francisco Bay

like clay for they build with mammoth bricks made of it. The great curse of the land is the multitude of ground squirrels that there are on it. Around Santa Barbara the ground is completely honeycombed by them, and I believe they ruin the crops in many instances. About Santa Barbara there is little or no wooded land but around Monterey there is quite a heavy growth of the short leaf pine; for this I think the land would suit a North Carolinian.

It is said that the best land in the Territory is on the Sacramento (Sacrament) River, which empties into the Harbour of San Francisco; this from all accounts is a very fine stream running through a fertile and well wooded country for about three hundred miles, and emptying as it does into one of the finest bays in the world there can be no doubt that it will be the focus of all emigration.

The land in the Bay of San Francisco is in most places mountainous and barren, so that when a city is built there, which there certainly will be, it will be dependent on the Sacramento. The climate is very temperate; even in mid-winter it is scarcely ever cold enough for a fire—and is very dry, which however is rather a disadvantage than not, for they frequently suffer very much for water. Wheat, corn, potatoes, melons &c., &c., are raised very easily and very abundantly, and the wheat and potatoes (Irish) are said to be of a very excellent quality. Agriculture is however but little attended to, the raising of cattle and horses occupying almost entirely the attention of the people. The horses are about equal to our North Carolina horses, but the cattle are very superior, and although the whole country wears a burned and barren aspect they are always fat. I believe they live on wild oats which are said to grow very abundantly and to be equal to our cultivated ones. Monterey is quite a little town, having I should suppose about two thousand inhabitants; the houses are generally single storied, built of the large mud bricks I spoke of, and tile roofed; the mud bricks or "adobes" keep them always dirty. Santa Barbara is rather smaller than Monterey and very much such another place.

It may appear singular to you that with so little force as we have employed out here the country could be taken possession of so quietly. But it is not at all so. The country is very thinly populated and the few Californians in it are divided in their political relations into three or four factions, so that any small number of resolute men—and such are those who are with Capt. Frémont— can do what they please. Besides this the number of Americans now in the territory is not much inferior to the number of Californians and the Americans are a hardy, brave set of men, used to handling fire arms from their infancy. As for the towns on the coast, all put together would not be a match for one good frigate.[96]

Stockton's ambitions were as boundless as Sloat's were limited. He dreamed not only of completing the conquest of northern California, but of proceeding from there to Acapulco from which port he would lead his troops to the gates of Mexico City to join in the final American assault and triumph.

The latter part of Stockton's vision proved unrealistic but his activities in California proceeded so smoothly that on August 28 he reported to the Secretary of the Navy that his mission was accomplished.

You have already been informed of my having, on the 23d of July, assumed the command of the United States forces on the west coast of Mexico. I have now the honor to inform you that the flag of the United States is flying from every commanding position in the territory of California, and that this rich and beautiful country belongs to the United States, and is forever free from Mexican dominion.

On the day after I took this command, I organized the "California battalion of mounted riflemen" by the appointment of all the necessary officers, and received them as volunteers into the service of the United States. Captain Frémont was appointed major, and Lieutenant Gillespie captain, of the battalion.

The next day they were embarked on board the sloop-of-war *Cyane*, Commander Dupont,[97] and sailed from Monterey for San Diego, that they might be landed to the southward of the Mexican forces, amounting to 500 men, under General Castro and Governor Pico,[98] and who were well fortified at the "Camp of the Mesa," three miles from this city.

A few days after the *Cyane* left, I sailed in the *Congress* for San Pedro, the port of entry for this department, and thirty miles from this place, where I landed with my gallant sailor army, and marched directly for the redoubtable "Camp of the Mesa."

But when we arrived within twelve miles of the camp, General Castro broke ground and ran for the city of Mexico. The governor of the territory, and the other principal officers, separated in different parties, and ran away in different directions.

Unfortunately, the mounted riflemen did not get up in time to head them off. We have since, however, taken most of the principal officers; the rest will be permitted to remain quiet at home, under the restrictions contained in my proclamation of the 17th.

On the 13th of August, having been joined by Major Frémont with about eighty riflemen, and Mr. Larkin,[99] late American consul, we entered this famous "City of the Angels," the capital of the Californias, and took unmolested possession of the government house.

Thus, in less than a month after I assumed the command of the United States force in California, we have chased the Mexican army more than three hundred miles along the coast; pursued them thirty miles in the interior of their own country; routed and dispersed them, and secured the Territory to the United States; ended the war; restored peace and harmony among the people; and put a Civil government into successful operation.[100]

Revolt and Reconquest

Stockton proved to be too optimistic. About a month after he reported conquest, peace and harmony, the people of Los Angeles revolted, laid siege to the small garrison that had been left there, and forced it to surrender on September 23. This was the only serious military reversal the United States forces suffered in California.

The shocking news reached Stockton in San Francisco. He immediately proceeded southward and occupied San Diego. Frémont, having landed at San Diego from the U.S.S. Cyane on July 29, returned to Monterey to raise reinforcements. He did not move at once toward Los Angeles but fought a skirmish on November 14, 1846 in the Salinas Valley. Reinforcements, however, were on the way by land and by sea, although one of these elements was not to arrive in California until the fighting was over and the other contributed little to the recapture of Los Angeles.

In September 1846 the Seventh New York Infantry, commanded by Col. Jonathan D. Stevenson and consisting of about 1,000 men, left New York Harbor on the long voyage around South America. The storeship Lexington preceded the regiment, carrying on board a company of flying artillery and twenty guns of large calibre together with arms and ammunition for a new fortification. Stevenson's men were provided with articles of husbandry—a printing press and other articles to "civilize the land and the natives of whatever region they may light upon." Even editors were allowed to embark with the expedition. Mutiny and other disasters plagued them on the way but eventually the New York Regiment arrived in California.[101]

KEARNY'S MARCH TO CALIFORNIA

The relief, moving toward San Diego from the east, was a band of about 100 dragoons led by General Kearny, who had left Santa Fe on September 25, 1846, two days after Californians had driven the Americans out of Los Angeles. The general reported upon his march from Santa Fe to California in a despatch to the Adjutant General of the Army:

As I have previously reported to you, I left Santa Fe (New Mexico) for this country on the 25th September, with 300 of the 1st dragoons, under Maj. Sumner. We crossed to the bank of the Del Norte at Albuquerque (65 miles below Santa Fe), continued down on that bank till the 6th October when we met Mr. Kit Carson, with a party of 16 men on his way to Washington city, with a mail and papers: an express from Commodore Stockton and Lieut. Colonel Frémont, reporting that the Californias were already in possession of the Americans under their command; that the American flag was flying from every important position in the territory, and that the country was forever free from Mexican control; the war ended, and peace and harmony established among the people. In consequence of this information, I directed that 200 dragoons, under Major Sumner, should remain in New Mexico, and that the other 100, with two mounted howitzers, under Captain Moore,[102] should accompany me as a guard to Upper California.

. . . . .

On the 2d December, [we] reached Warner's ranche (Agua Caliente), the frontier settlement in California, on the route leading to Sonora. On the 4th, [we] marched to Mr. Stokes' rancho (San Isabella), on the 5th were met by a small party of volunteers, under Capt. Gillispie [sic],[103] sent out from San Diego by Commodore Stockton, to give us what information they possessed of the enemy, 600 or 700 of whom are now said to be in arms and in the field throughout the territory, determined upon opposing the Americans and resisting their authority in the country. Encamped that night near another rancho (San Maria) of Mr. Stokes' about 40 miles from San Diego.[104]

BATTLE OF SAN PASQUAL

Before he reached San Diego, however, Kearny fought an engagement in which his band of one hundred was in serious jeopardy near a little Indian village some forty miles east of San Diego. This was the battle of San Pasqual. John M. Stanley,[105] of Cincinnati, who accompanied Kearny's force, described it in the following letter:

From two Californians who were captured the hostile state of the country was ascertained; and the little band, without provisions save their horses, and almost destitute of water, pushed on their route.

On the morning of the 4th of December we resumed our march, Gen. Kearny having previously sent an express to San Diego to inform Commodore Stockton of his arrival in the country, and on the 5th we met Capt. Gillespie and Lieut. Beall [sic],[106] U.S.N., with an escort of thirty-five men. After making a late camp, General Kearny heard that an armed body of Californians were encamped about nine miles from us. Lieut. Hammond,[107] with a small party was sent out to reconnoitre. He returned about 12 o'clock, with the intelligence of a camp in the valley of *San Pasqual,* but learned nothing of the extent of the force, although it was thought to be about sixty.[108]

At 2 o'clock on the morning of the 6th the reveille sounded, and at 3 our force was formed in the order of battle and the march resumed. We arrived about daylight at the valley—the enemy were encamped about a mile from the declivity of the mountain over which we came, and, as Lieut. Hammond had been discovered on the night previous, the Californians were waiting in their saddles for our approach. From a misapprehension of an order, the charge was not made by our whole force, or with as much precision as was desirable; but the Californians retreated, on firing a single volley to an open plain about half a mile distant. Capt. Johnson [sic][109] and one private were killed in this charge. . . . The retreat of the enemy was followed with spirit by our troops, skirmishing the distance of half a mile. When they reached the plains, our force was somewhat scattered in the pursuit. The Californians, taking advantage of this disorganization, fought with desperation, making great havoc with their lances. It was a real hand-to-hand fight, and lasted half an hour. They were, however, driven from the field, with what loss we could not learn.

We camped on the field and collected the dead. At first Gen. K[earny] thought to move on the same day. The dead were lashed on mules, and remained two hours or more in that posture. It was a sad and melancholy picture. We soon found, however, that our wounded were unable to travel. The mules were released of their packs, and the men engaged in fortifying the place for the night. During the day the enemy were in sight, curvetting their

BATTLE OF SAN PASQUAL

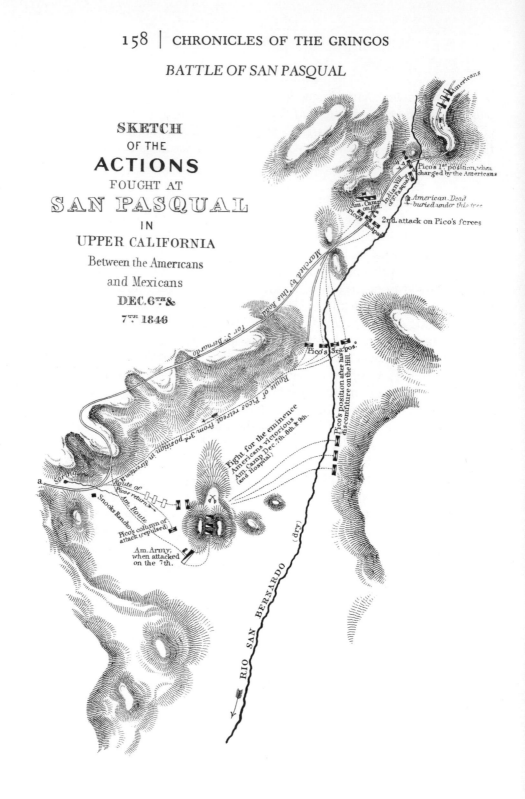

SKETCH
OF THE
ACTIONS
FOUGHT AT
SAN PASQUAL
IN
UPPER CALIFORNIA
Between the Americans
and Mexicans
DEC. 6TH &
7TH 1846

Americans

Pico's 1st position, when
charged by the Americans

American Dead
buried under this tree

2nd. attack on Pico's forces

Am. Camp
on Com.

Indian Vill.
of Pasqual

Pico's outpost

Marched by this Road

Route for St. Bernardo

Route of Pico's retreat from 3rd position in direction

Pico's 3rd pos.

Pico's position after his
discomfiture on the hill

Fight for the eminence
Americans victorious
Am. Camp Dec. 7th, 8th & 9th.
(and Hospital)

Spring

a

Route of
Pico's return

Snooks Rancho

Am. Route

Pico's column of
attack repulsed.

Am. Army,
when attacked
on the 7th.

RIO SAN BERNARDO (dry)

horses, keeping our camp in constant excitement. Three of Capt. Gillespie's volunteers started with despatches to Com. Stockton. The dead were buried at night, and ambulances made for the wounded; and the next morning we started, in face of the enemy's spies, being then about 38 miles from San Diego. In our march we were constantly expecting an attack. Spies could be seen upon the top of every hill—but with a force of one hundred men, many of whom were occupied with the care of the wounded, we did not leave our trail.

We had travelled about seven miles, when just before sunset we were attacked. The enemy came charging down a valley—about one hundred well mounted men. They were about dividing their force, probably with a view of attacking us in the front and rear, when Gen. Kearny ordered his men to take possession of a hill or hut on our left.

The enemy, seeing the movement, struck for the same point reaching it before us, and as we ascended they were pouring a very spirited fire upon us from behind the rocks. They were soon driven from the hill only one or two being wounded on our side. Here, therefore, we were compelled to encamp and also to destroy the more cumbersome of our camp equipage. A white flag was sent by Senor Pocos [sic, Andrés Pico], the Californian commandant, and an exchange of prisoners effected—our bearers of despatches having been intercepted by the enemy. We were more fortunate in getting an express through to San Diego for a reinforcement, and at the expiration of four days, during which we lived on the meat of mules, horses and colts, without bread or other condiment, we were joined by a reinforcement of two hundred men, and on the 11th of December resumed our march. Not a Californian was to be seen as we proceeded, and on the 12th of December we reached San Diego, and received from the officers a hearty welcome. Thus, my friend, you have the *finale* of an overland journey across the continent, a distance of one thousand and ninety miles from Santa Fe.[110]

TAKING OF LOS ANGELES

Kearny's battered forces arrived in San Diego on December 12. Frémont failed to arrive at all (he showed up at Los Angeles two days after the town had been recaptured)[111] but by the end of the month Kearny decided to attack with the forces available. He advanced from San Diego on December 29 with about six hundred dragoons, marines and sailors.[112] Kearny's topographical engineer, Bvt. Capt. William H. Emory, now appointed his Chief of Staff, reported this brief campaign:

January 6. [1847]—To-day we made a long march of 19 miles to the upper Santa Anna, a town situated on the river of the same name. We were now

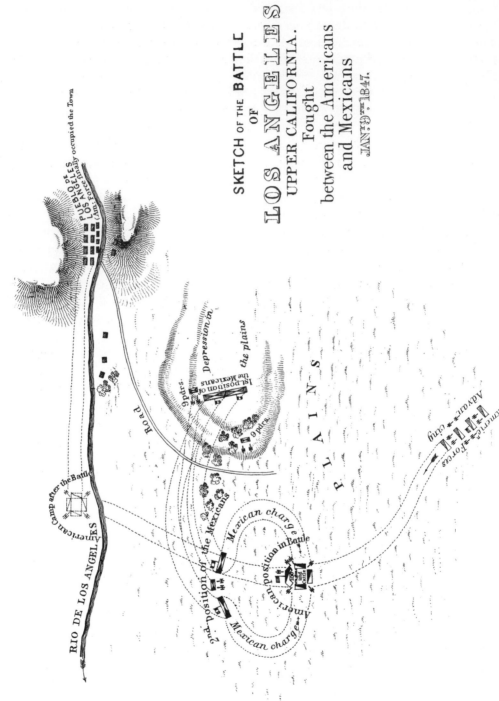

SKETCH OF THE BATTLE
OF
LOS ANGELES
UPPER CALIFORNIA.
Fought
between the Americans
and Mexicans
JANᵧ 9ᵀᴴ 1847.

PUEBLO DE LOS ANGELES
(Am: Force finally occupied the Town

Road

RIO DE LOS ANGELES

American Camp after the Battle

Depression in the plains

1st position of the Mexicans

9 pdrs.

9 pdrs.

P L A I N S

Mexican charge

2nd position of the Mexicans

American position in Battle

Mexican charge

American Forces

Advancing

near the enemy, and the town gave evidence of it. Not a soul was to be seen; the few persons remaining in it were old women, who, on our approach, had bolted their doors. The leaders of the Californians, as a means of inciting their people to arms, made them believe we would plunder their houses and violate their women.

. . . . .

January 8.—We passed over a country destitute of wood and water, undulating and gently dipping towards the ocean, which was in view. About two o'clock we came in sight of the San Gabriel river. Small squads of horsemen began to show themselves on either flank, and it became quite apparent the enemy intended to dispute the passage of the river.

. . . . .

The river was about 100 yards wide, knee-deep, and flowing over quicksand. Either side was fringed with a thick undergrowth. The approach on our side was level; that on the enemy's was favorable to him. A bank fifty feet high, ranged parallel with the river at point blank cannon distance, upon which he posted his artillery.

As we neared the thicket, we received the scattering fire of the enemy's sharp-shooters. At the same moment, we saw him place four pieces of artillery on the hill, so as to command the passage. A squadron of 250 cavalry just showed their heads above the hill, to the right of the battery, and the same number were seen to occupy a position on the left.

The 2d battalion was ordered to deploy as skirmishers, and cross the river. As the line was about the middle of the river, the enemy opened his battery, and made the water fly with grape and round shot. Our artillery was now ordered to cross—it was unlimbered, pulled over by the men, and placed in counter battery on the enemy's side of the river. Our people, very brisk in firing, made the fire of the enemy wild and uncertain. Under this cover, the wagons and cattle were forced with great labor across the river the bottom of which was quick sand.

Whilst this was going on, our rear was attacked by a very bold charge and repulsed.

On the right bank of the river there was a natural banquette, breast high. Under this the line was deployed. To this accident of the ground is to be attributed the little loss we sustained from the enemy's artillery, which showered grape and round shot over our heads. In an hour and twenty minutes our baggage train had all crossed, the artillery of the enemy was silenced, and a charge made on the hill.

Half-way between the hill and river, the enemy made a furious charge on our left flank. At the same moment, our right was threatened. The 1st and 2d battalions were thrown into squares, and after firing one or two rounds, drove off the enemy. The right wing was ordered to form a square, but seeing the enemy hesitate, the order was countermanded; the 1st battalion, which formed the right, was directed to rush for the hill supposing that would be the contested point, but great was our surprise to find it abandoned.

The enemy pitched his camp on the hills in view, but when morning came he was gone. We had no means of pursuit, and scarcely the power of locomotion, such was the wretched condition of our wagon train. The latter it was still deemed necessary to drag along for the purpose of feeding the garrison intended to be left in the Ciudad de los Angeles, the report being that the enemy intended, if we reached that town, to burn and destroy every article of food. Distance 9.3 miles.

January 9.—The grass was very short and young, and our cattle were not much recruited by the night's rest; we commenced our march leisurely, at 9 o'clock, over the "Mesa," a wide plain between the Rio San Gabriel and the Rio San Fernando.

Scattering horsemen, and small reconnoitring parties hung on our flanks. After marching five or six miles, we saw the enemy's line on our right, above the crest made by a deep indentation in the plain.

Here Flores[113] addressed his men, and called on them to make one more charge; expressed his confidence in their ability to break our line; said that "yesterday he had been deceived in supposing that he was fighting soldiers."

We inclined a little to the left to avoid giving Flores the advantage of the ground to post his artillery; in other respects we continued our march on the Pueblo as if he were not in view.

When we were abreast of him, he opened his artillery at a long distance, and we continued our march without halting except for a moment to put a wounded man in the cart, and once to exchange a wounded mule hitched to one of the guns.

As we advanced, Flores deployed his force, making a horse shoe in our front, and opened his nine-pounders on our right flank, and two smaller pieces on our front. The shot from the nine-pounders on our flank was so annoying that we halted to silence them. In about fifteen minutes this was done, and the order "forward" again given when the enemy came down on our left flank in a scattering sort of charge; and notwithstanding the efforts of our officers to make their men hold their fire, they, as is usually the case under similar circumstances, delivered it whilst the Californians were yet about a hundred yards distant. This fire knocked many out of their saddles and checked them. A round of grape was then fired upon them, and they scattered. A charge was made simultaneously with this on our rear with about the same success. We all considered this as the beginning of the fight but it was the end of it. The Californians, the most expert horsemen in the world, stripped the dead horses on the field, without dismounting, and carried off

BATTLE OF RIO SAN GABRIEL

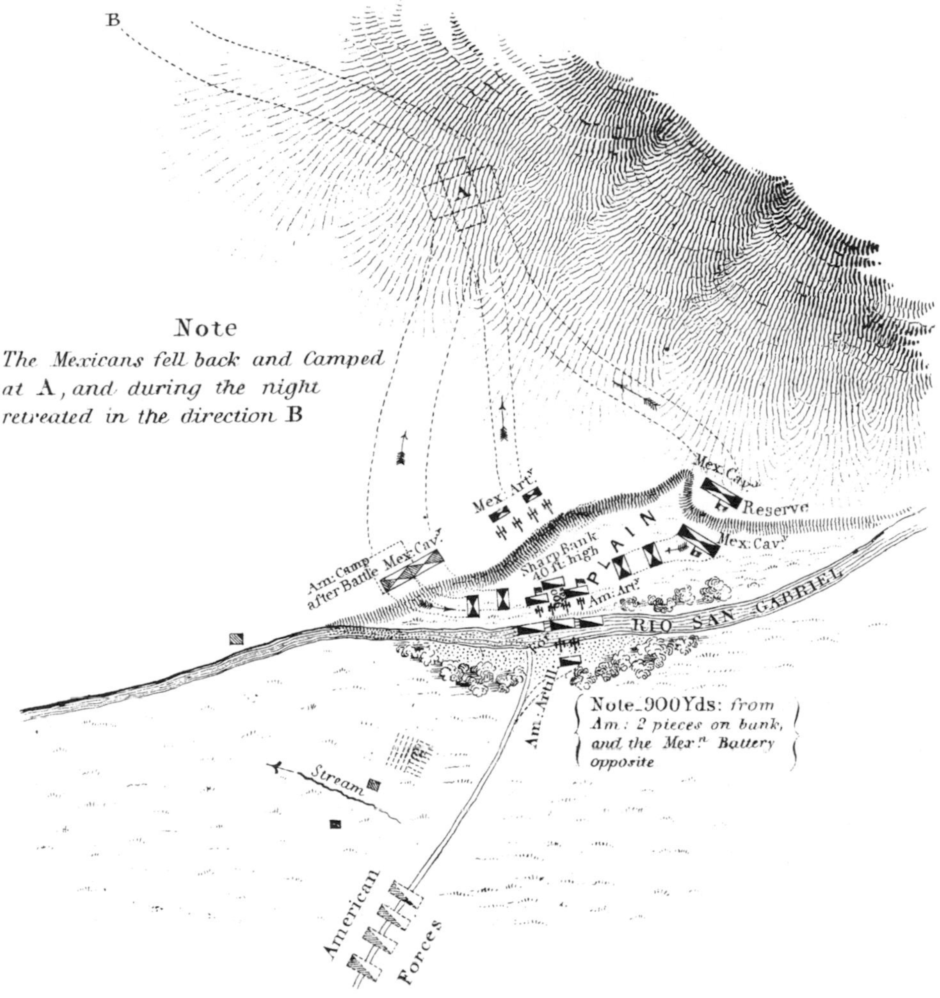

B

Note
*The Mexicans fell back and Camped
at A, and during the night
retreated in the direction B*

Mex. Cav.ᵞ

Reserve

Mex. Cav.ᵞ

Mex. Art.ᵞ

PLAIN

Am: Camp
after Battle Mex: Cav.ᵞ

Sharp Bank
40 ft. high

Am: Art.ᵞ

Am: Artillery

RIO SAN GABRIEL

Note_900 Yds: *from
Am: 2 pieces on bank,
and the Mexᵗ Battery
opposite*

Stream

American Forces

SKETCH of the PASSAGE
OF THE
RIO SAN GABRIEL
UPPER CALIFORNIA
by the
Americans,_discomfiting
the opposing Mexican Forces
JANUARY 8ᵀᴴ 1847.

most of their saddles, bridles, and all their dead and wounded on horseback to the hills to the right.

It was now about three o'clock, and the town, known to contain great quantities of wine and aguardiente, was four miles distant. From previous experience of the difficulty of controlling men when entering towns, it was determined to cross the river San Fernando, halt there for the night, and enter the town in the morning with the whole day before us. The distance to-day, 6.2 miles.

After we had pitched our camp, the enemy came down from the hills and 400 horsemen with the four pieces of artillery drew off towards the town, in order and regularity, whilst about sixty made a movement down the river on our rear and left flank. This led us to suppose they were not yet whipped, as we thought, and that we should have a night attack.

January 10.—Just as we had raised our camp, a flag of truce borne by Mr. Celis, a Castilian, Mr. Workman, an Englishman, and Alvarado, the owner of the rancheria at the Alisos, was brought into camp. They proposed, on behalf of the Californians, to surrender their dear City of the Angels, provided we would respect property and persons. This was agreed to; but not altogether trusting to the honesty of General Flores, who had once broken his parole, we moved into the town in the same order we should have done if expecting an attack.

It was a wise precaution, for the streets were full of desperate and drunken fellows who brandished their arms and saluted us with every term of reproach. The crest, overlooking the town, in rifle range was covered with horsemen engaged in the same hospitable manner. One of them had on a dragoon's coat, stolen from the dead body of one of our soldiers after we had buried him at San Pasqual.

Our men marched steadily on until crossing the ravine leading into the public square when a fight took place amongst the Californians on the hill; one became disarmed, and to avoid death rolled down the hill towards us, his adversary pursuing and lancing him in the most cold-blooded manner. The man tumbling down the hill was supposed to be one of our vaqueros, and the cry of "rescue him" was raised. The crew of the Cyane, nearest the scene, at once, and without any orders, halted and gave the man that was lancing him a volley; strange to say he did not fall. Almost at the same instant but a little before it, the Californians from the hill did fire on the vaqueros. The rifles were then ordered to clear the hill, which a single fire effected, killing two of the enemy. We were now in possession of the town; great silence and mystery was observed by the Californians in regard to Flores; but we were given to understand that he had gone to fight the force from the north, drive them back, and then starve us out of the town. Towards the close of the day we learned very certainly that Flores, with 150 men, chiefly Sonorians and desperadoes of the country had fled to Sonora, taking with him four or five hundred of the best horses and mules in the country, the property of his own friends. The silence of the Californians was now changed into deep and bitter curses upon Flores.[114]

The battle of San Gabriel ended the fighting in California. Two days later, January 10, 1847, Los Angeles was reoccupied by the American troops. The conquest of California had been achieved; manifest destiny was triumphant.

THE VERA CRUZ EXPEDITION

Strategic Problems after Monterey

By late September 1846, Taylor had a firm grip on Monterey, and New Mexico had as anticipated "fallen off the tree" with a minimum of shaking. In California also Polk's objectives were being achieved. Many of the people back home thought the war should be over, but the Mexicans still showed no sign of acknowledging defeat. With Santa Anna consolidating his power and Taylor's supply line strung out precariously from Monterey to Brazos Santiago the position of the invaders in Nuevo Leon was by no means an enviable one. A correspondent of the New Orleans Picayune assessed the situation:

There never was a nation so much mistaken as ours in regard to that of Mexico. I mean in respect to its military resources. The people are warlike, and have an abundant supply of munitions of war. Our battles with them improve them as soldiers. Our invasion is held by them in abhorrence, and has united all classes in determined resistance against us. The battles of Palo Alto, Resaca de la Palma, and of Monterey were battles with their *frontier* army. From this place onward, if we have to march on further in this direction, we shall meet with their *home* army, made up of hardy mountaineers and a better class of soldiery. So far I consider we have not injured their nation, but done it a *service*, by defeating their old officers, thus causing their army to be placed under the direction of younger, more ambitious, braver, and more accomplished generals. In fact, so far from the war being ended, it has just commenced.

Our position is critical. Our supplies at Camargo, 180 [sic] miles distant, must be wagoned to this place. This long line has no protection. The ranchero

166

troops, numbering near 2,500 are behind us as guerillas, and if they choose to act, our trains must be cut off. Although this is a rich valley, its supplies are inadequate to our wants, except in beef, for any length of time. Our army, or the effective part of it, is too diminutive to meet a strong force. It is weak, physically, for it has now been in campaign over thirteen months, with scanty clothing and much hardship and exposure. The volunteers are numerous, but, with the exception of those regiments commanded by late officers of the army, without discipline. I suppose our whole army will muster, when all arrive from below, 9,000 men for duty, and we hear the Mexicans have one on the advance to meet us of 30,000 men. I am convinced, and so is every officer of the army, that we have done wrong and committed an irreparable error in leaving the Rio Grande to march in this direction.

To end this war a more vital blow must be struck nearer the Mexican capital; and that is, Vera Cruz should be taken by the way of Alvarado. We are now over 700 miles from the city of Mexico, with a vast desert to traverse. In a word, to make peace *economically* with Mexico some things must be undone, and our government must commence again. Discharge your volunteers, and raise your regular force to thirty or fifty thousand men. We have the fullest expectation of the most active guerilla war against us. Move where we will, the mountains and passes afford every facility to carry it on successfully and most disastrously for us. Our army as now situated, can be compared to the French in Spain, when Joseph was driven out.[1]

Bvt. Maj. Gen. Thomas S. Jesup,[2] no friend of Taylor's, pointed to a precarious dispersion of American military forces as a violation of a primary maxim of war:

The army in Mexico is cut up into small detachments, in place of being concentrated as it should be; and it offers a fine opportunity for the "Napoleon of the South," as he styles himself, to strike several successive blows which if struck promptly and energetically would be successful if the Southern possess any of the qualities of the Northern Napoleon. But I imagine the Mexican is deficient in most of the qualities that distinguished the Corsican chief.[3]

The Polk administration had no intention of going on the defensive. Instead, it resolved to carry the war into the heart of Mexico and to dictate peace from the enemy's capital. Although he was far from Washington and certainly not within the inner circle of strategists, Bvt. Maj. Gen. John Anthony Quitman no doubt expressed his government's point of view when he wrote to the Secretary of the Treasury:

Your prominent position in the administration, and our long and intimate acquaintance, induces me to address you without reserve upon some matters of the highest interest to the country and to the present administration. . . . I have very lately been informed that officers high in rank have recommended the policy of ceasing further offensive operations, of holding on to the conquered Mexican provinces, and standing on the defensive. This policy would in my opinion be disastrous if not disgraceful to the country, and would result in protracting and adding to the expenses of the war, to say nothing of the contempt of our national character which it would engender in Europe and even in Mexico.

National insult is at least one cause of the war. Will the occupation of territory unimportant in a revenue point of view to Mexico, compel her to atone for national insult? Will not such a policy tend to prolong the war? It will soon be known to Mexico. Under it, secure from attack she need not even defend her salient points in advance of our line, and may quietly & safely await the development of her resources, until on her part some favourable blow may be struck. All the occupied points of our defensive line, being equally accessible to her, she may choose her own time and season to throw upon any one of them an overwhelming force and cut off our garrisons or defeat our detatchments [sic]. Suppose in pursuit of this policy we occupy the line from Tampico, through Victoria, Lenaris [sic, Linares], Monterey or Saltillo & Monclova to S[ant]a Fe—25,000 men would be required—5,000 at Tampico—5,000 at Victoria—5,000 at Monterey & Saltillo—5,000 at Monclova to Santa Fe—and at least 5,000 to protect the depots & transportation in rear—and even then Tampico & Monterey would be exposed to the whole force of the Mexican army before relief could be had from other points.

If however we have an efficient army of but half this force *in the field*, threatening Potosi or any other vulnerable point in advance of our line, it would most effectually cover the whole stragetic [sic, strategic] line in rear of its movement, and force the enemy to concentrate his forces & meet us in the field, or uncover the way to his capital. I do not intend positively to designate Potosi as the proper objective point to our opcrations, but to give my opinion that the war should be prosecuted by penetrating the country on some practicable line, with an adequate force, say 12,000 men well equipped.

From the information I have been able to pick up, I have no doubt such a force could take Potosi against 30,000 Mexicans. The obstacles in the way are said to be deficiency of permanent supplies of water. I have no doubt this is exaggerated. At least I am satisfied it can be overcome in several modes, which I will not weary you with detailing. With such an enemy as we have to contend against, we can never succeed in impressing them with respect for our power and national character, except by dealing upon them hard blows. We can only obtain their respect, through their fears. Besides this mode of prosecuting the war would be better suited to the character of the provisional force we have in the field, to ardent and energetic dispositions of the people of the United States, and would be more in consonance with our pretensions, or rather claims, as one of the principal powers of the civilized world. Besides, the heavy expenses incident to a war, are calculated to have the most serious effects upon the administration in power, unless they are compensated by brilliant results. The field is in my opinion open for these, if judiciously planned. . . . Should this campaign be wasted in inactivity, the same expense and loss will have to be encountered before a proper force can be placed in the field. Be assured Mexico will never make peace, upon any terms which an administration can accept, until she has received some harder blows.[4]

Several possible routes for an advance were considered: the one from Monterey through San Luis Potosí would be rejected because of distance and difficult terrain. Taylor himself took a dim view of such an advance. He wrote:

I do not intend to carry on my operations . . . beyond Saltillo, deeming it next to impracticable to do so. . . . From Saltillo to San Luis Potosi, the next place of importance on the road to the city of Mexico, is three hundred miles—one hundred and forty badly watered, where no supplies of any kind could be procured for men or horses. I have informed the War Department that 20,000 efficient men would be necessary to insure success if we moved on that place (a city containing a population of 60,000 where the enemy could bring together and sustain, besides the citizens, an army of 50,000) a force which, I apprehend, will hardly be collected by us with the train necessary to feed it, as well as to transport various other supplies, particularly ordnance and munitions of war.[5]

GENESIS OF THE SCOTT EXPEDITION

Another point d'appui for a penetration of Mexico became available when Commodore David Conner[6] and the navy took Tampico during November 1846; military occupation of that port followed this move. On January 4, Taylor entered Victoria after a march from Monterey, and although he soon returned to his base near Saltillo to counter an advance by Santa Anna that culminated at Buena Vista, Taylor thus opened the way for overland reinforcement of Tampico, and its use as a staging depot for further offensive operations. But a direct attack upon Mexico City from Tampico was hardly feasible[7] *because of unfavorable topography. That left one other possibility: an amphibious operation against Vera Cruz and an advance along Cortez' historic invasion route, and even this seemed to be a hazardous gamble. Arthur Campbell, a prominent Whig in Washington, expressed these doubts:*

Polk is at the head of affairs and he will remain there for two years to come & he is as obstinate as old Calvin or Jno. Knox. I have no doubt but him [sic] and his advisers are very anxious for peace—but not without getting a large slice of Mexico to pay for the expenses of the war or in other words to preserve their popularity. Now this is what Mexico is not yet prepared to give—and it will not be easy to force her to do so by our arms. You may be mistaken in supposing that an army can be marched from Tampico against an opposing force of any strength to the City of Mexico or even far into the interior of the country. I understand that the head of the War Dept. says that it cant be done. The mountain passes between Tampico and the interior of Mexico makes it impossible or nearly so. We have no correct map of Mexico and very few of our scientific men have ever traveled much through the country. Mexico some pretty good judges here now think is the most difficult country perhaps in the whole world naturally for an invading army to march through. To march an army from Monterey to the City of Mexico would perhaps be like Napoleon's campaign to Moscow and if we had possession of Vera Cruz the same difficulties though not so formidable present themselves. These are the views of some of our wise folks here now at all events. I suppose that Genl. Taylor & his officers know more about Mexico now—than all the balance of the people of the U States put together. And if they cant divin[e] ways & means to bring the Mexicans to terms. I am sure that Polk & his cabinet cant.[8]

The invasion of Vera Cruz seemed to offer the best hope of success. As Lt. William T. Withers[9] *wrote from Monterey: "We want Vera Cruz and Vera Cruz we must have it, if the war continues. Once in possession of this we would soon settle the matter. If we cannot take it, I do not see how we are to get at the City of Mexico."*[10] *President Polk and Secretary of War Marcy came to the same conclusion—it would be the sea-land route to Mexico City.*[11] *Maj. Gen. Winfield Scott, the general-in-chief, finally would have his chance to lead the campaign, although neither Polk nor Marcy liked him.*[12] *Most of Taylor's regulars and even some of his volunteers would be transferred to Scott's command for the expedition.*

Scott plunged into the business of putting an army together. He revealed his plans in a letter to Commodore David Conner, then in command of the blockading squadron off the Gulf Coast of Mexico.

Plate XIII. *The U.S. Frigate Mississippi*

PLATE XIV. *Castle of San Juan de Ulua & City of Vera Cruz*

You have, no doubt, been informed by the Navy Department that I am ordered to Mexico, and of the probability of our becoming, as soon as practicable, associated in joint operations against the enemy. I look forward with great pleasure to that movement. I shall do all in my power to render the combined service cordial and effective. Of your hearty reciprocation I am entirely confident. This is the beginning of a correspondence which the objects in view will render frequent on my part, and I hope to hear often from you in reply, and on all matters interesting to the common service.

You are aware of the point near which our more intimate association will take place. I hope to be ready for the descent at a very early day in the month after the next. Every effort will be made to get afloat off the Brazos San Iago, and off Tampico, in time, the necessary number of troops. I have estimated twelve or fifteen thousand, besides the numbers you may be able to supply from the blockading squadron, to be highly desirable; but you may expect me, if I can get afloat, in time to meet you early in February, ten, eight, or even five thousand men. The land force is expected from the Atlantic coast, the Ohio and Mississippi rivers, all new volunteers to be added to regulars and volunteers to be withdrawn from Major General Taylor.

I have appointed the 15th of the next month for the assemblage of all intended for the particular expedition I am to conduct, off the two points mentioned above; but do not hope that more than three regiments of the new volunteers will be up so early. I shall, therefore, have to draw more largely upon the forces already on and beyond the Rio Grande. I am aware of the usual return of the black vomit, early in April, at the proposed point of our joint operations, and hence shall not be able to wait for the largest number of land troops I deem desirable. This number will greatly depend on the force we may expect to oppose our descent from the open sea. I mean a Mexican army, *in the field*; not the garrisons and guns of any city or fort.

I embark to-day for the Brazos, and hence write in haste. Thence I may go up to Camargo for a few days, but wherever I may be, your despatches will follow me rapidly. Perhaps you may appropriate some steamer to our frequent correspondence. What my means of that sort may be at the Brazos, I cannot yet precisely know. Occasionally I may find a steamer for the purpose, at least as far as your vessels off Tampico.

Upon information just obtained, I think it quite probable that I may appoint the roadstead between the Island of Lobos and the main, some fifty or sixty miles beyond Tampico, as a general rendezvous for the transports and other vessels with troops and supplies destined for the expedition in question. If a good harbor, as reported, it will serve and mask my views admirably. Please give me information on the subject, although I may be compelled to act to some extent before I can hear from you.[13]

Scott Takes the Field

In mid-February, Scott was able to leave Brazos Santiago. On the nineteenth he arrived at Tampico where he received a "thundering reception" from troops who awaited the next move—a move about which the Mexicans appeared to be well informed. A reporter described the scene in Tampico:

Major General Scott, and suite, embarked from the Rio Grande in the steamer Massachusetts, and reached Tampico on the evening of the 19th February. He met with "a thundering reception," of course. Landing next morning he proceeded to Gen. Patterson's head quarters,[14] and received the attention due to a commanding officer and the welcome of his friends. He found about 9,000 men at Tampico, preparing to embark. Four brigades, under Genls. Twiggs, Pillow, Shield[s],[15] and Quitman, were to embark on the 20th and 21st.

The scene in and about Tampico, is stated to be stirring in the extreme. Reviews of troops, in regiments and brigades, were daily taking place; vessels were continually arriving with goods, merchandize, military stores, &c. &c., the American population were all in intense excitement, regarding coming events. Every thing announced action, in its utmost intensity. All quiet, with regard to the enemy, in the interior.

. . . . .

To give you some idea of what is expected to be done, I will show you a portion of what is going down in the way of munitions: First, there are some 100,000 rounds of heavy ammunition; rockets, shells and an enormous supply of all sorts of combustibles, with 40 mortars and columbiads—some of them ten inches calibre; from 10 to 20 24-pounders; 3 field batteries, consisting of six- and twelve-pounders, and twelve- and twenty-four pound howitzers. With all these go the sappers and miners and the pontoon train. . . .

There is not a Mexican in this whole country who does not know that our troops are going to Vera Cruz, while in the United States, and even here, our own people are all in the dark. Santa Anna manages to keep himself well advised of our movements. I almost venture to say that he now knows as much of our plans and intentions, and of our strength and numbers in the field as any of those who are at headquarters, in Washington city. Despatches of the greatest moment are sent through the enemy's country, almost totally unguarded, and, like weak and straggling forages, and mules and wagons without good and strong escorts, they fall into the hands of our foes.

All the forces now here, except the Louisiana volunteers,[16] the Baltimore battalion, and one company of artillery will be on the way to Vera Cruz in a short time. Those that I have named will be left here, under the command of Col. Gates,[17] to garrison the city.

Every thing indicates a movement upon Vera Cruz, which place, so far from being abandoned by the Mexicans, appears to be making efforts for defence. Men, women and children are said to be labouring on the works for defence, making ditches, removing sand banks, &c. Additional troops have arrived, and it is stated that Santa Anna has advanced $75,000 of his personal estate for the immediate exigencies of the place.[18]

General Scott left Tampico almost immediately (on February 20) for Lobos Island, ten miles off the coast and about sixty miles south of Tampico. Here the American fleet was assembling for the last stage of the journey to Vera Cruz. From Lobos Island, Scott wrote to Secretary of War Marcy:

I left the Brazos the 15th, and Tampico the 20th instant, having done much official business at the latter place in a delay of some thirty hours.

But a small part of the transport engaged at New Orleans, under my orders of December 28, 1846, to receive troops at the Brazos and Tampico, had reported at the two placcs, and not one of the ten ordered by your memorandum of the 15th of that month, and the whole were due at the Brazos on the 15th of January.

Leaving orders at both places to supply deficiencies, by taking up any craft-ships, brigs, and schooners—that might chance to be in the way, I hastened to this first general rendezvous, where, as I had heard, the small pox had broken out among the volunteers. I was also anxious to learn what had become of the 2d Mississippi volunteers,[19] which regiment I knew had sailed from New Orleans (without its arms) for the Brazos in January, its place of debarkation, under my general orders No. 6, of the 30th of that month. By the strangest misapprehension or fatality, consequent on obeying a *prior* instead of a *later* order received, I found one of the transports of this regiment off Tampico, and the other two here, neither having called off the Brazos, where the three ships had been long, in our difficulties, relied upon to receive other troops.

The several detachments of the Mississippians were, as I successively came up with them, ordered back to the Brazos; but, considering the accidents and delays on this terrible coast, the ships cannot be up with me again, with troops, in time for the descent. Indeed, the season has already so far advanced, in reference to the usual return of the yellow fever on this coast, that I can now only wait a day or two longer for Brevet Brigadier General Worth, delayed as above, and for part of the regulars, yet behind with the great body of old volunteers, from Tampico. . . . I cannot wait more than forty-eight hours for any body, except Brevet Brigadier General Worth, and Duncan's and Taylor's[20] horse artillery companies, or for anything behind; and two-thirds of the ordnance and ordnance stores, and half the surf-boats, are yet unheard of, although Adjutant General Jones reported to me, on the 23d ultimo, that all those objects had been then shipped, and were under way for the Brazos; and so he wrote, as I understand him, that I might soon expect the ten transports, in ballast, from Atlantic ports, ordered by you, as arranged with me.

Perhaps no expedition was ever so unaccountably delayed—by no want of foresight, arrangement, or energy on my part, as I dare affirm—under circumstances the most critical to this entire army; for every body relied upon, knew from the first, as well as I knew, that it would be fatal to us to attempt military operations on the coast after, probably, the first week in April, and here we are at the end of February.

Nevertheless, this army is *in heart*; and, crippled as I am in the means required and promised, I shall go forward, and expect to take Vera Cruz and its castle in time to escape, by pursuing the enemy, the pestilence of the coast.

. . . . .

We find this harbor, against *northers*, even better than I had anticipated. One has now been blowing some forty hours, and has brought down all the vessels ready to sail, that were outside of the bars at the Brazos and Tampico. The next will take the fleet to Anton Lizardo,[21] whither I am sending off ships with surf boats, in order that the latter may be launched, under the care of the navy, and held ready for my arrival.

Captain Saunders,[22] of the United States sloop-of-war St. Mary's has rendered me most valuable services in general, besides landing and re-embarking volunteers. The island has afforded them the means of healthy military exercises, and tolerable drinking water. The few surf boats launched are admirably adapted to the purposes for which they were intended.[23]

A more cheerful note from Lobos Island was sounded by a correspondent of the Philadelphia North American, who, unburdened by the responsibility for winning a war, was free to enjoy its tropical splendor:

This letter is written upon the most delightful tropical island ever trodden by adventurers from any clime.

The Island of Lobos is a lovely little spot, formed entirely of coral, about two miles in circumference, twelve miles from the Mexican shore, about sixty miles from Tampico, and some 130 from Vera Cruz. It is covered (or was before we landed) with a variety of trees and shrubs, the highest of the former perhaps twenty-five feet high, and these are so thickly covered with vines that one can hardly get through them. There is hardly a tree or shrub, or plant growing here I have ever before seen.—Banyan trees spreading over large spaces of ground, their limbs forming props as they pierce into the earth and take root, while the tops thickly thatched with evergreen vines, form most beautiful arbors.—Lemon, lime, fig, palm, cane, and a hundred other species of wood are growing with all the freshness and beauty of the Indies. There is plenty of water to be had by digging four to six feet. It is brackish and sweet, but we are getting used to it, and like it nearly as well as ship water. Fish and sea fowl we have in profusion. With these we have delightful sea air, that fourteen hours out of the twenty-four makes the place delightfully pleasant.

It will be difficult, I imagine, to convince you, who will read this scrawl beside great coal fires, that we are literally roasting during a portion of the day. The sun is so hot that our faces and arms are blistered if exposed but a few minutes. To-day, by Fahrenheit, in the shade, I scored 92°. The universal remark among the volunteers is, "If this is *winter*, what will summer be?"[24]

Temper of Scott's Army

But what of the men who were going into battle? What were their thoughts as they awaited the campaign? Their hopes and fears? Capt. John R. Vinton,[25] 3d Artillery, had few misgivings. He was in many respects a model officer, a career soldier who would die before Vera Cruz on March 22. In a revealing letter to his mother he wrote of the expedition from the deck of Scott's flagship, the steamer Massachusetts, off Lobos Island:

We are now under the lee of this little island riding safely at anchor in spite of winds or waves. Forty odd vessels are also anchored here awaiting orders for a movement toward Vera Cruz, which will be issued as soon as the rear division arrives,—perhaps in two days from this time. Five thousand troops will be landed at one time,—perhaps at Anton Lizardo,—perhaps at Sacrificios Island;[26] a second line will follow it so as to make the movement safe, no matter what force the Mexican General may bring against us. Our armament is very powerful and I do not believe that Vera Cruz can stand our attack or bombardment two days without capitulating. Gen. Scott & his staff are all on board this vessel,—with whom I have constant & very friendly intercourse,—so that I am able to hear all the plans & projects from first sources. Nothing can be more pleasant than everything is here, for one anyways interested in military operations. I have never seen service in a siege, so that whatever we may have to do in this line will be new to me. The weather is delightful, our troops in good health & spirits, and all things look auspicious of success. I am only afraid the Mexicans will not meet us & give us battle,—for, to gain everything without controversy after our large & expensive preparations would look like supererogation,—and besides would give us officers no chance for exploits and honors.

. . . . .

My confidence in the overruling providence of God is unqualified. So that I go to the field of action fully assured that whatever may befal[]l will be for the best. I feel proud to serve my country in this her time of appeal;—and should even the worst,—death itself—be my lot, I shall meet it cheerfully,— concurring fully in the beautiful Roman sentiment, *"Dulce et decorum est, pro patria mori."*[27]

AMPHIBIOUS OPERATIONS

The fleet weighed anchor on March 2, 1847 with between twelve and thirteen thousand soldiers aboard. Three days later it was off Anton Lizardo, a point about fourteen miles south and east of Vera Cruz. This phase of the amphibious operation was recorded by Capt. Electus Backus in his journal:

MARCH 2D. [18]47. Off Lobos Island.

About 30 Vessels of the flotilla sail[e]d this day for Anton Lizardo. The breeze was fresh from the east, & in attempting to get under way, the Othello fell back, & nearly came in collision with a large ship at anchor. We therefore anchored for the night, but finding our vessel drifting, the ship in our rear paid out 60 or 80 fathoms of cable to keep clear of us.

MARCH 3D.

The wind hauled round to S.W. light & some 20 vessels in harbor commenced getting under weigh. A large ship sail[e]d a little ahead of us, but in attempting to pass to windward of her, we fell on to her & were in a dangerous position for several minuits. We backed our sails, & fell off & got clear of her. Wind light & baffling. Many vessels which sailed yesterday are still in sight. The steamer Alabama arrived from the north, & passed on her way to Anton Lizardo.

MARCH 4TH [18]47.

[At] 2. A.M. the wind hauled round to N.W. fresh-sails flying & a little rain in the early part of the day. At 12. the sun came out, & soon after we had a beautiful view of the mountains, bearing S.W. & distant so[me] 15 or 20 miles. We had a beautifull view—some 10 or 12 sail in sight, most [of] to day, & making about 8. knots. At sun set we were 25. miles north of Vera Cruz & the wind light.

MARCH 5[T]H.

This morning at 4. a large steam boat passed ahead of us—but did not hail. At day light we made the land, & [with]in about 4. miles off Anton Lizardo.

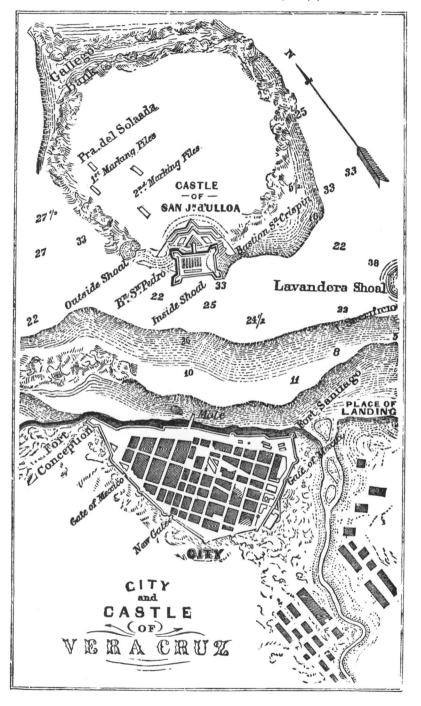

CITY
and
CASTLE
(OF)
VERA CRUZ

We had outsailed nearly all the squadron. At 9. a.[m.] we passed the reef, & were inside the harbor. There is about 30 sail at anchor, & nearly as many in sight in the offing. A report reached us this evening that Genl. Taylor has whipped Santa Anna.

MARCH 6TH.

A few men landed this morning & were fired on—& came off again. There are about 70 sail in port. Genls. Scott, Worth, & Smith,[28] with staff officers sailed for Sacrificios in the Steamer *Champion* to reconnoitre—& had a salute from San Juan of 15. shots which passed in their immediate neighborhood.[29]

The Island of Sacrificios mentioned by Backus was three miles from Vera Cruz and the point from which the assault was to be launched on March 9. The reconnaissance phase of the operation lasted for two days and was described by Bvt. Maj. George Archibald McCall:[30]

Yesterday the General-in-Chief, with the Generals of his army corps, viz., Twiggs, Worth, Patterson, Quitman, Pillow, and General Totten, of the Engineers, their staffs and the engineers, &c., made a reconnoissance in a small steamer, along the coast from this point to the town. While off the castle, after we had just lunched very comfortably through the hospitality of the naval officer who commanded the steamer, our little vessel was saluted by the Mexicans with one of their heavy Paix[h]an guns. We were then at the distance of one mile and a half, and the shell falling short, Commodore Conner, who was of the party, and of course regulating the movements of the boat, ordered the steam to be stopped, to the end, as it were, to let them have a fair trial of their skill in gunnery. We lay thus before the castle until they had fired about eight or nine shells, some of them passing some thirty feet above our heads and exploding afterwards; others exploding before they reached us, until they began to calculate the charge and the length of the fuse with considerable accuracy, and to scatter the fragments of the shell around the boat. The Commodore then in his gentle manner remarked to the General-in-Chief, "that he thought we might now proceed," and the latter assenting, we continued our course, followed by three or four parting shells. The castle is certainly a very strong work, and I doubt very much whether it would be practicable to take it with any naval force that we could bring before it. Our work must be done with shells, for they have sent out no guns of calibre as great as those in the castle.

Their force is variously estimated, and there is no means of ascertaining what numbers we shall have brought against us. But about that we do not feel much concern.

The probability is, that we shall effect a landing to-night, opposite the Island of Sacrificios, at a point between two and three miles below the town. There is a ridge of sand-hills about half a mile from this point, running in rear of the town to within the distance of five hundred or four hundred yards of it. On this, as our first parallel, batteries will be established.[31]

LANDINGS AT VERA CRUZ

This was to be the most significant amphibious operation yet carried out by American armed forces. The critical phase, which began on March 9, was the establishment of the beachhead less than three miles south of Vera Cruz which Past Midshipman (later Admiral) William G. Temple discussed in a memoir:

In anticipation of the arrival of the transports off Vera Cruz, the frigate *Potomac* and the sloops-of-war *Albany* and *John Adams* were stationed in the vicinity of Isla Vcrdc (some five miles to seaward of the city), with orders to put an officer on board each vessel as she arrived, to pilot her in to the anchorage at Anton Lizardo; or should the number of officers prove inadequate to this duty, to furnish the masters of the transports with such sailing directions as would enable them to pass inside of the Blanquilla Reef to the anchorage. The naval squadron under the command of Commodore Conner, and the transports having on board the troops and their equipment under the command of Major-General Scott, were thus concentrated at the anchorage between the Island of Salmadina and Point Anton Lizardo, a distance of some ten or twelve miles to the eastward of Vera Cruz.

As fast as those transports having on board any of the surfboats arrived, the boats were launched under the direction of a lieutenant of the squadron, their equipment inspected, and everything belonging to them fully prepared for service; after which they were hauled up on the landward side of the island, and arranged and numbered by divisions—each division consisting of ten boats, taken from all the different sizes.

In the mean time a speedy debarkation was resolved upon, it being important that a landing should be effected before "a norther" should come on, as that would delay the operation for several days. . . . The choice [of a landing place] lay principally between Point Anton Lizardo, opposite which the squadron and transports lay anchored, and the beach directly abreast the island of Sacrificios. The great objection to the first of these two was the distance (about fifteen miles) that the troops would have to march before reaching the point of attack, while at the same time the road led through deep, loose sand, and involved the passage of one or two considerable streams.

As to the mere landing, however, it was deemed quite as good as that near Sacrificios. The selection of this last-named point obviated the difficulty already mentioned, being within two and a half miles of the city walls; although it had its own disadvantages. The exceedingly confined space afforded here for a secure anchorage rendered it dangerous in the then season of northers to bring up many of the transports. It was therefore suggested to transfer all the troops from the transports to the men-of-war and steamers, and after their debarkation to order up from Anton Lizardo such transports with provisions and stores as might first be required, which in turn might make room for others till all should be landed.*

In view of all these considerations, the beach near Sacrificios was deemed the most eligible point, and the debarkation was appointed to take place on the 8th of March. General orders were therefore issued on the 7th by the commodore and the commanding general, prescribing the necessary arra[n]gements.

The surf-boats were apportioned for use among the following men-of-war, as follows: Frigate *Raritan*, fifteen; frigate *Potomac*, twenty; sloop-of-war *Albany*, ten; sloop-of-war *St. Mary's*, ten; steamer *Princeton*, ten; and these vessels were directed to furnish to each boat, so apportioned to them, a crew of seven seamen, and a junior or petty officer to command it. Each division of ten boats was commanded by a lieutenant, and in some instances was divided between two of that grade, the general direction of the whole remaining always with the senior. Captain Forrest, commanding the frigate *Raritan*, was ordered to superintend the whole operation.

The officers detailed for this duty were sent on shore the day previous to the debarkation, and the boats allotted to their respective ships pointed out to them, as they lay ranged and numbered on the beach so as to avoid confusion and an indiscriminate seizure of the boats when they should come with their crews at daylight to launch them. The boats' anchors were stowed in the sterns of the boats, with their hawsers coiled clear for running, and the coxswains were instructed, in case the landing should be effected in a heavy surf to drop the anchor from the stern outside the breakers, and to pay out the hawser as the boat went in, so that after the troops should have jumped out in shoal water, the boat could be warped out again through the breakers, without having received any injury from thumping on the beach.†

* Subsequent to the landing, however, the transports were ordered to Sacrificios in too great numbers; and a gale of wind coming on from the north, about forty vessels were blown upon the beach.

† This precaution, however, proved unnecessary at the time of landing, from the smooth state of the water, but at a later period while landing heavy articles in a surf, it was resorted to with great success. It should be remembered while reading these instructions that the boats were built with both ends alike.

Two of the largest-sized surf-boats were assigned to carry the officers and men of a company of ninety men and upward, two of the middle size to a company of eighty men and upward, two of the smallest to a company under eighty officers and men. Each of these boats, therefore, would hold a platoon (half company) and officers, together with its own crew. The platoons were directed to supply any deficiency of oarsmen in their respective boats, but at the same time to *land* with their companies.

The troops were ordered to be in readiness for the following distribution among the different men-of-war and steamers, to take passage from Anton Lizardo to Sacrificios.

The first line, under Brevet Brigadier-General Worth, consisting of the First Brigade of Regulars and Captain Swift's company of sappers and miners,[32] to be received on board the frigate *Raritan*, and the steamers *Princeton* and *Edith*. The field batteries of Captain Taylor and Lieutenant Talcott[33] (also attached to this line and to be *landed* with them) to be towed up, in their respective transports, by the steamers *Massachusetts* and *Alabama*.

The second line, under Major-General Patterson, consisting of the First Brigade of volunteers, commanded by Brigadier-General Pillow, and the South Carolina Regiment of volunteers* (all of the Second Brigade that had yet arrived out), to be received on board the frigate *Potomac* and the steamers *Alabama* and *Virginia*.

The reserve, under Brigadier-General Twiggs, consisting of the Second Brigade of Regulars, to be received on board the sloops-of-war *Albany* and *St. Mary's*, the brig *Porpoise*, and the steamers *Massachusetts*, *Eudora*, and *Petrita*.

.   .   .   .   .

Every man of the army was directed to take in his haversack bread and meat (cooked) for two days, and the vessels of war were ordered to supply the troops with water and provisions, while on board.

A system of signals had been arranged beforehand by the general-in-chief, by which the transports were to indicate the number of boats required by each one to take from them the troops they had on board. They were to hoist a flag at the fore for each boat required to receive the first line, and to haul them down as the boats arrived alongside. In like manner at the main for the second line, and at the mizzen for the reserve.

All the preliminary arrangements were thus completed on the evening of the 7th, but the next morning there were indications of a norther, and the movement was postponed. At sunrise on the morning of the 9th, the officers

---

* The South Carolina Regiment, finding themselves crowded out of the vessels assigned to their transportation, asked and received permission of Captain Sands, of the steamer "Vixen," to take passage in his vessel.

and men detailed for that duty were sent from the men-of-war to launch and man the surf-boats. Those divisions of boats manned by the *Raritan* and *Princeton* were assigned to the transfer of the first line, going for them whenever a transport had flags flying at the fore, and taking them to the vessels of war and steamers, according to the hereinbefore-mentioned distribution. In like manner those divisions manned by the *Potomac* were assigned to the transfer of the second line, and those by the *Albany* and *St. Mary's* to the reserve.

Each of the frigates received on board between twenty-five and twenty-eight hundred men, with their arms and accountrements; the sloops received about nine hundred each, and the smaller vessels numbers in proportion.

When all were transferred, the fifteen boats belonging to the *Raritan* were taken to the steamer *Spitfire*, to be towed to Sacrificios; the steamer *Vixen* went alongside the *Potomac*, and took in tow the twenty boats belonging to her; the *Albany* sent her ten to the steamer *Eudora*; the *St. Mary's* ten were sent to the steamer *Petrita*; and the *Princeton* took in tow her own ten. At the same time the vessels so sending them detailed two lieutenants and two midshipmen to remain on board the towing steamers and look out for their boats, together with two seamen for each boat, who were to remain in them and steer them during the tow.

This part of the movement was completed very successfully about eleven o'clock A.M.; and a few moments thereafter the squadron and such of the transports as had been selected for the purpose got under way for Sacrificios, the general-in-chief on board the steamer *Massachusetts*, and the commodore of the squadron in the frigate *Raritan*.

The weather was very fine, with a fresh yet gentle breeze from the southeast, and a perfectly smooth sea. The passage to Sacrificios occupied between two and three hours. Each vessel came in and anchored in the small space previously allotted to her, without the slightest disorder or confusion, the anchorage being still very much crowded, notwithstanding the number of transports that had been left behind.

The debarkation commenced on the instant. Each vessel reclaiming her surf-boats from the steamer that had towed them up, sent them to receive the first line. The *Princeton* was ordered to take a position abreast the landing place, and as near the shore as possible; and the surf-boats were directed after receiving their quota of soldiers to rendezvous astern of her, and to form there in a double line ahead according to regiments and companies and in prescribed order of battle, the two head boats holding on to each quarter of the *Princeton*, [the] other two holding on to them, and so on, with the regimental flag flying in the head boat of each regiment.

In the mean time, while this work of transfer and arrangement was going on, the steamers *Spitfire* and *Vixen*, and the five gunboats *Petrol*, *Bonita*,

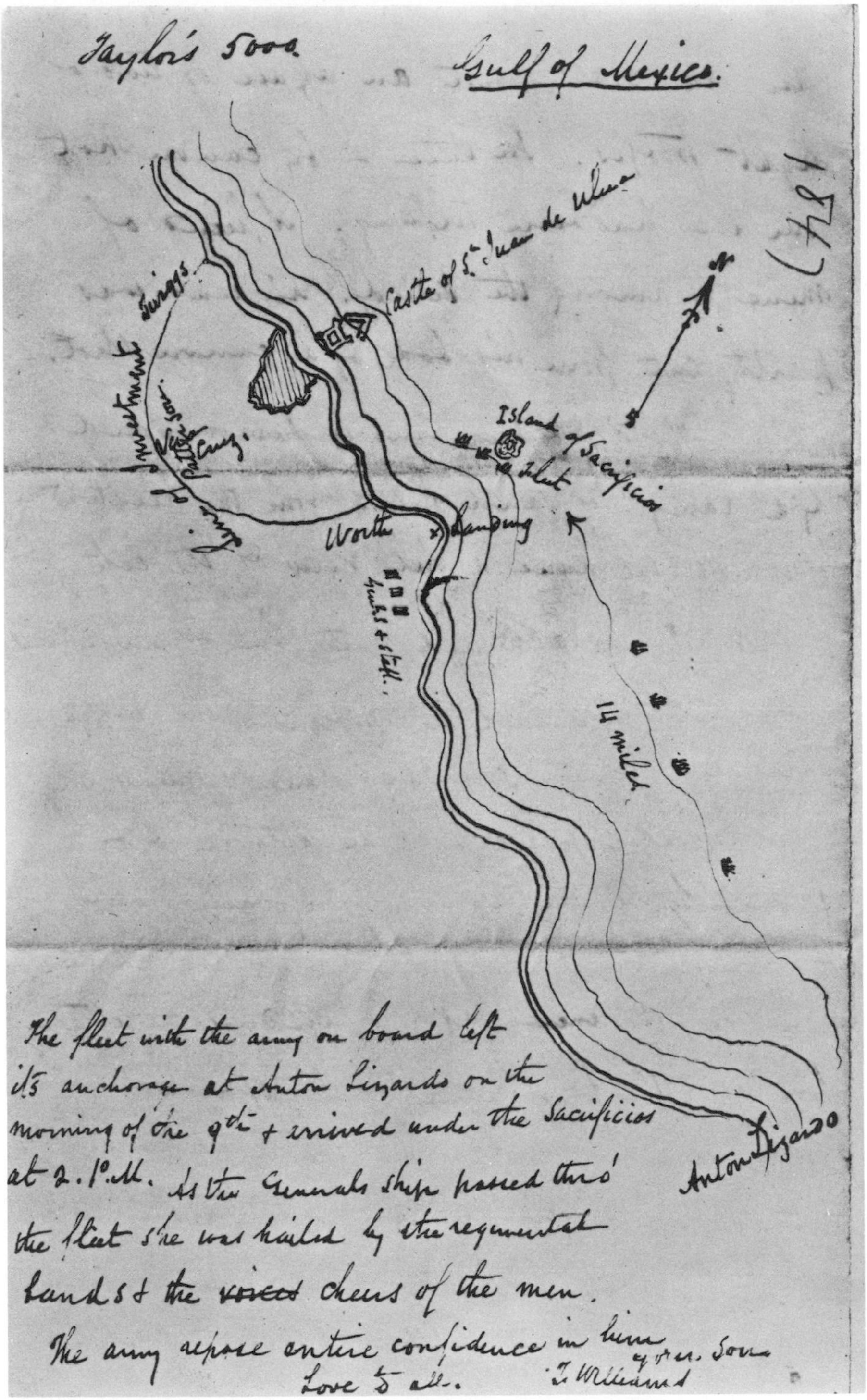

Taylor's 5000   Gulf of Mexico:

Castle of S^a Juan de Ulua

Investment

Twiggs

King Patterson

Vera Cruz.

Worth

Landing

Island of Sacrificios

Islet

Sacks & Lith.

14 miles

(478)

Anton Lizardo

The fleet with the army on board left
it's anchorage at Anton Lizardo on the
morning of the 9th & arrived under the Sacrificios
at 2.1 P.M. As the Generals ship passed thro'
the fleet she was hailed by the regimental
bands & the ~~voices~~ cheers of the men.

The army repose entire confidence in him
Love to all.   your Son
T. Williams

PLATE XV. Letter with Map of Vera Cruz & Anton Lizardo

PLATE XVI. *Naval Bombardment of Vera Cruz*

Reefer, Falcon, and *Tampico* were ordered to anchor in a line parallel with and as close in to the beach as they could get, to cover the landing with their guns if necessary. These vessels were armed chiefly with 32-pounder shell-guns, and were of such light draft (from five to eight feet) that they were enabled to take positions within good grape range of the shore.

When all was prepared, the boats cast off from the *Princeton* and from each other, squared away in "line abreast," and pulled in together to the beach, where the troops landed without the slightest opposition. The boats immediately returned to the vessels for the second line of the army, and afterwards for the reserve, and without waiting to form again in order of battle they continued to pour the troops upon the beach in successive trips as fast as they could come and go. At some places the loaded boats grounded on the bar or false beach, some twenty yards from dry land, and the troops had to wade through waist-deep water to get ashore. This occurred in comparatively few instances, however, and aside from the inconvenience of these few wettings, not an accident of any kind occurred throughout the whole operation. No enemy appeared to dispute the ground, and General Worth had the satisfaction of forming his command upon the neighboring sand-hills just before sunset. The landing commenced about the middle of the afternoon, and before ten o'clock that night upward of ten thousand men, with stores and provisions for several days, were safely deposited on the beach.

The steamer *New Orleans,* with the Louisiana Regiment of volunteers, eight hundred strong, arrived at Anton Lizardo just as the squadron had been put in motion for Sacrificios. She joined them, and her troops, together with the marines of the squadron (who formed a battalion under the command of Captain Edson of the Marine Corps),[34] were landed with the others. Other troop-ships came in subsequently, so that on the 24th of March the field-return showed a total of twelve thousand six hundred and three men.

In the mean time, also, the transports were ordered up successively from Anton Lizardo, and whenever the weather would permit the surf-boats (still manned and officered from the squadron) were constantly employed in landing artillery, horses, provisions, stores, etc. For the sake of unity and system in this work, an officer was stationed on the beach, having the general superintendence of the whole, and all the officers in charge of surf-boats were directed to report to him for further orders immediately on landing. In addition to this, the business of landing the different articles was assigned to different vessels, so that the division of boats belonging to one ship attended to getting the horses ashore, those of another the forage, another the provisions, and so on. At sunset each day the boats were moored head and stern near their respective vessels, and on the appearance of a norther they were hauled up on the Island of Sacrificios.

In landing the horses and mules, if brought out in a small vessel having light draught, they were thrown overboard as near the beach as the vessels could safely get; if in a large vessel, they were first put on board the steamer *Petrita*, which went alongside to receive them, and taken as far in as possible, and in either case they were afterwards made to swim ashore in tow of the surf-boats. In this way nearly five hundred were got ashore in one day by a single division of boats.

In landing the field artillery, two surf-boats lashed side by side and with a platform of plank laid athwart their gunwales were brought alongside the transport having the batteries on board, and two field pieces were lowered into them, ready mounted and with limbers and ammunition boxes, as in the field. This plan, however, was abandoned after the first trial, and the guns with their cais[s]ons and carriages were lowered directly into single boats, whose bottoms were protected simply by a few plank laid fore and aft in them. On reaching the shore, two gangway-planks were laid, from the bows towards the beach, sufficiently wide apart for the wheels to travel upon, and with side battens upon them to prevent the wheels from slipping off; by means of these the guns were disembarked and were dragged through the surf with such rapidity that not a cartridge was wet in the ammunition boxes.

As the bottoms of the boats were made of white pine, and therefore comparatively frail, great care was required in landing the siege train to prevent their bilging. In addition to the loose plank in the bottom of the boats, therefore, it was ordered that they should be kept always afloat by being anchored outside the surf and dropped in as far as safe. The guns were then hoisted out of the boats by means of tripods and taken up on large timber-wheels for transportation.[35]

Vera Cruz Invested

The beachhead secured, General Scott turned to plans for Vera Cruz. The city was walled, garrisoned by about five thousand men, and so far as the invaders knew, well supplied. Any direct attack upon the harbor was certain to be a formidable task because of the fortress of San Juan d'Ulloa which guarded it. Scott decided to forego a frontal assault in favor of besieging the city and its reduction by artillery fire. This would be slower and it was desirable to get the troops off the low-lying, disease-breeding beach as quickly as possible; moreover, it would cause greater havoc in the city, as well as civilian suffering and deaths. But it would save the lives of American soldiers and reduce the possibility of failure. Scott had his critics. Was the bombardment, with its toll of civilian casualties, necessary? Could not naval action have forced the entrance to Vera Cruz? David Glasgow Farragut, naval hero of the Civil War, and others thought so.[36] Scott, however, defended his decision in his Memoirs:

The city of Vera Cruz and its castle, San Juan de Ulloa, were both strongly garrisoned. . . .

The walls and forts of Vera Cruz, in 1847, were in good condition. Subsequent to its capture by the French under Admiral Baudin and Prince de Joinville, in 1838,[37] the castle had been greatly extended—almost rebuilt, and its armament about doubled. Besides, the French were allowed to reconnoitre the city and castle, and choose their positions of attack without the least resistance—the Mexicans deprecating war with that nation, and hence ordered not to fire the first gun. Of that injunction the French were aware. When we approached, in 1847, the castle had the capacity to sink the entire American navy.

Immediately after landing, I made, with Colonel (soon after Brigadier-General) Totten, and other staff officers, a reconnoissance of the land side of the city, having previously reconnoitred the water front. This was at once followed by a close investment, so that there could be no communication between the garrisons and the interior. The blockade, by Commodore Conner, had long before been complete. Grave deliberations followed. From the first my hope had been to capture the castle under the shelter of, and through the city. This plan I had never submitted to discussion. . . .

In my little cabinet, however, consisting of Colonel Totten, Chief Engineer, Lieutenant-Colonel Hitchcock, acting Inspector-General, Captain R. E. Lee,[38] Engineer, and (yet) First Lieutenant Henry L. Scott,[39] acting Adjutant-General—I entered fully into the question of storming parties and regular siege approaches. A death-bed discussion could hardly have been more solemn. Thus powerfully impressed—feeling Mr. Polk's halter around my neck, as I expressed myself at the time—I opened the subject substantially as follows:

"We, of course, gentlemen, must take the city and castle before the return of the *vomito*—if not by head-work, the slow, scientific process, by storming—and then escape, by pushing the conquest into the healthy interior. I am strongly inclined to attempt the former unless you can convince me that the other is preferable. Since our thorough reconnoissance, I think the suggestion practicable with a very moderate loss on our part.

"The second method, would no doubt be equally successful, but at the cost of an immense slaughter to both sides, including non-combatants—Mexican men, women, and children—because assaults must be made in the dark, and the assailants dare not lose time in taking and guarding prisoners without incurring the certainty of becoming captives themselves, till all the strongholds of the place are occupied. The horrors of such slaughter, with the usual terrible accompaniments, are most revolting. Besides these objections, it is necessary to take into the account the probable loss of some two thousand, perhaps three thousand of our best men in an assault, and I have received but half the numbers promised me. How then could we hope to penetrate the interior?" "For these reasons," I added, quoting literally, "although I know our countrymen will hardly acknowledge a victory unaccompanied by a long butcher's bill (report of killed and wounded) I am strongly inclined—policy concurring with humanity—to 'forego their loud applause and aves vehement,' and take the city with the least possible loss of life. In this determination I know, as Dogberry says truly of himself, I 'write me down an ass.'"

My decided bias in favor of proceeding by siege, far from being combated, was fully concurred in. Accordingly Colonel Totten, the able chief engineer, and his accomplished assistants, proceeded to open the trenches and establish the batteries deemed necessary, after, by a general sweep, every post and sentry of the enemy had been driven in.[40]

BOMBARDMENT OF VERA CRUZ

Lt. Thomas Williams of the 4th Artillery summarized the army's operations through March 13. By then Scott had established his line of investment around the city:

The army effected its landing about 3 miles south of the city of Vera Cruz without opposition on the 9th & 10th instants. The landing was made under the guns of our fleet in broad day light. The day was fine, & as the sun shone upon the arms of our men the effect was brilliant & grand. Our line of investment around the city was completed the 11th instant. We now only await the landing of our mortars & heavy guns near at hand to complete *the work.* If our batteries were in position a week or ten days would give us possession of the city & castle.

If the line of investment were a regular curve it would be 5 miles long, but, as it winds over hills & thro' woods it is a good deal longer.

Our effective force is about 12,000 regulars & volunteers. The vol. are commanded by Maj. Genl. Patterson of Philadelphia & the regulars by Generals Worth & Twiggs. The enemy's force in the city & castle numbers from our latest information 5,000 men. Two thirds of this force regulars. They are well provided with heavy batteries & all the materials of defence. We are informed that they are poorly fed & may run out of water. We have already cut off some of the latter supply. Since the hour of our landing the enemy's shells & round shot have been liberally dispensed towards us. And every day has brot about an affair or two of light troops. In these & by can[n]on shot our loss has been trifling. A friend of mine is among the killed. His head was partly cut from his body by a cannon shot.

Bombardment of Vera Cruz and Castle

The City of Vera Cruz is surrounded by a range of sand hills from the heights of which we have a full view of the city. These hills are occupied by the line of investment.

At 3 o'clock this morning we were aroused by the sounds of cannon & musketry. This was supposed to be an attack but proved to be the firing of fire balls from the walls of the town to light up the ground in advance, the enemy apprehending an attack from us. We have rumors of the approach of troops from Alvarado marching to the relief of city &c &c.[41]

Brig. Gen. David E. Twiggs, commanding the Second Division, wrote an account of the part played by his command in the short but sharp engagements as they established the siege ring around Vera Cruz:

I have the honor to report the occurrences in which my brigade has been concerned since the commencement of the march from the place of debarkation until now.

The brigade took up the line of march on the morning of the 11th instant—the regiment of mounted riflemen leading. After passing the position of the 1st brigade, the 1st squadron of riflemen, composed of the companies of Captains Loring[42] and Mason,[43] under the command of Major Sumner, 2d dragoons, was sent forward as an advanced guard. On crossing the railroad, the advanced guard took the direct way over the hills, but this being impassable for the artillery, the rest of the brigade, with the pieces was obliged to make a detour to the left. On passing the position of General Pillow's brigade, Brevet Captain Alburtis,[44] 2d infantry, and one private of riflemen, were killed by a round shot, and two privates wounded. Major Sumner, having passed some distance beyond the position occupied by the volunteers, was opposed by the enemy's light troops, whom he drove off, and halted near a small ranch, when the rest of the brigade joined him, and proceeded to clear the ground to be occupied by my brigade.

The advance drove the enemy's skirmishers before it, receiving without loss their fire, until it arrived at the Orizaba road. On passing the road, a party of horsemen were perceived stationed on it to our left. Captain Sanderson's[45] company mounted riflemen was detached to attack them—being supported by Captain Simonson's[46] company of the same regiment. He drove them off, killing two captains—one of lancers, and the other of the auxiliary guard of Jalapa, named J. Platos. In this affair, Private Weller, of Captain Sanderson's company, was severely wounded in the thigh by an escopette ball.

Having driven these parties all off, the brigade took its position in line, extending as far towards the Jalapa road on the beach as the strength of the brigade would allow, and bivouacked till the morning of the 13th, when we took up the line of march towards the sea—Major Sumner again commanding the advanced guard, composed of the left wing of the rifle regiment. Making a considerable detour to the left, to avoid some ponds of water, I arrived about noon on the great road leading to the city of Mexico. On coming out here, Lieutenant [sic] Roberts'[47] company mounted riflemen leading, a party of mounted men was discovered. After a short skirmish the enemy were dispersed, my men receiving no injury. The head of the column arrived at its present position on the beach at the village of Vergara, about two and a half miles from Vera Cruz, a few minutes after 12 o'clock.

I would commend to particular notice the conduct of Major Sumner, 2d dragoons. His skill and coolness inspired those under his command with the fullest confidence, and gave to them the bearing of old soldiers. The officers and men of all the companies engaged gave entire satisfaction.

An important mail, which I had the honor to transmit to the head-quarters of the army this morning by Captain Taylor, was taken last night by Captain Magruder,[48] 1st artillery, who was in command of one of the supporting companies sent out yesterday morning to skirmish in the front of my brigade towards the city. The mail carrier was shot at, and is supposed to have been wounded. His horse, hat, and cloak were left on the ground at the place where he was fired at, and the mail along with these effects. Captain Magruder deserves praise for his zeal and good conduct in this affair.[49]

With his forces positioned, Scott demanded the city's capitulation on March 22. After the Mexicans rejected the ultimatum the artillery opened fire. In the midst of the bombardment, Lt. Edmund Bradford, by the light of a lantern, recorded many observations on the siege in his journal. These were in turn transcribed in a letter to his sister on March 27:

On the 19th the enemy threw at the men working in the trenches 167 shot and shells without injury to a single man. It is almost miraculous how they escaped for some of the shells would fall in the midst of companies and then burst throwing the fragments in every direction. Whenever a shell [falls] near a body of men they immediately drop flat on the ground and remain in that position until it has burst—in this way they avoid being struck. The trenches have been opened to within half a mile of the walls of the city. . . .

On the 20th the company to which I belong was detailed for picket duty. We marched from our camp to a position about 800 yards of the walls. The company was hidden from the view of the town by a ridge of sand hills, and although we could see every thing going on about the city, we could not be seen by them. The firing in the trenches was kept [up]—very briskly all day, both from the town and castle but without injuring any one. Early in the morning a party of Mexicans came out of the town to drive in some cattle. They were seen by the volunteers and fired upon, wounding two of them, whereupon they immediately retreated back to town. About 5 o'clock P.M. a French bark which had run the blockade attempted to run out again, and was chased and was captured by the U.S. brig. Porpoise and steamer Hunter. In coming in to Sacrificios a norther came up and blew ashore both the French bark and the steamer Hunter. Both are wrecks. Owing to the severe norther which blew almost all day, the firing from the town and castle did not commence until 5 o'clock P.M. It was kept up all night at intervals. Com. Perry[50] arrived in the Mississippi and is to relieve Com. Conner in command of the squadron. The Navy officers are rejoiced in the change. They say they will now have something to do.

On the 22nd Genl. Scott sent in to the town a summons to surrender. Genl. Morales returned an answer "that he had heroes placed by the Government in command of the town and castle with the means to defend it," and that he should do so as long as possible, and that he regretted that it was necessary that the blood of women and children should be shed. At 4½ o'clock P.M. our mortars opened a heavy fire on the town which was answered by a brisk fire from both town and castle. Capt. Vinton 3rd Arty was killed by a shell which came through the top of the parapet. There was not a single wound to be seen in his body.

9 o'clock P.M. I was called off from my letter by an order to go with my company to the trenches and I am now writing in the trenches by the light of a magazine lantern. I will again take up my journal. On the 23rd my company Capt. Bainb[ridge][51] and Lieut. Miller[52] were ordered to the trenches to serve the 24 po[under?] battery. When we arrived there we found the guns had not been [put?] into position, neither was the battery finished. We worked all night mounting the guns and running them into battery. The mortars from our side kept up an incessant fire all night which was returned by the enemy from the town. At night we cared nothing for the shells as we could see them in the air a long time before they reached the trenches and thus we were enabled to avoid them. The round shot we could always get rid of by keeping close under the embankment. During the 23rd but one man was wounded. About 9 o'clock A.M. on the 24th the battery of six heavy guns, which the navy had established on a hill which overlooked the town, opened. The fire from this battery soon silenced two of the enemy's batteries and produced great destruction among the buildings in town. Several of the men at the mortar batteries were slightly wounded. At 7 o'clock P.M. we were relieved and marched back to our camp, not a single one of our men having been hurt.

On the 25th the 24-pounder battery opened on the city. In the afternoon a flag was sent in to Genl. Scott requesting him to allow the women and children and foreigners to leave the city. This the Genl. refused as a matter of course. At 4½ o'clock P.M. the firing from the town and castle ceased owing

PLATE XVII. Landing of the Troops at Vera Cruz

PLATE XVIII. *Naval Battery during the Bombardment of Vera Cruz, March 24-25, 1847*

to a flag having been sent in. About 2 o'clock A.M. on the 26th our guns again opened on the town. The Mexicans fired three guns and then sounded a parley. Our side kept up the fire until 7 A.M. not know[ing] that a flag had been sent in from the city. The city and castle agreed to surrender on the same conditions which were granted at Monterey. This the Genl. refused and told them they must surrender unconditionally.[53]

Lt. Col. Francis S. Belton,[54] commanding the mortar batteries, entered fully into the drama of the siege even while he saw cherished cultural landmarks crumbling about him:

It is a beautiful seige! [sic]—not a man here, that is not in high hopes. The lines and trenches are very safe—all yesterday's fire—& 60 shot & shell last night, have done no damage—but to their own beautiful gem of a church in the cemetery. I was in it yesterday afternoon. A beautiful chaste altar stands in the center under the dome—which was shelled thro' & thro'. The splendid crucifix on the altar seems a high work of art. I could see it imperfectly by the mortar and lime falling down, the crown of thorns was displaced and fell below. The candles in the sticks (*not* of silver & gold) were broken, 4 shot holes thro the doors and other ruin around. Every wall has traces of shot & also the magnificent entrance. I hear the steamers are also to batter the town from under Point Hornos. . . . The Spitfire the morning after our first landing—threw shells into the plaza so says the Vera Cruz paper— and it will be done again. Steptoe has a 12-Pdr. & 2, 24-Pdr. Howitzers at the north side of the town where the 2nd Brigade & 1st & 4th Arty. lay. . . . I keep open, to give (if I hear) the result of the summons at 5 P.M. The summons went in and the reply was that General Morales was entrusted with ample means for the defence and it would be persisted in to the last extremity. The batteries then opened on both sides and the fire continued with great vigor for 1½ hours. 2 steamers (Vixen & Spitfire) & 4 gun boats, participated. . . . I write at 10 a.m. 23 March—and have been up all night, was relieved at dawn. I kept firing shells all night and from the time of the opening of the batteries at 5 P.M. to my leaving the battery this morning—some 600—10 inch shells have been thrown into the city—nine out of ten bursting. The navy boats opened for an hour before breakfast & gave them an additional dose. The enemy's fire is slack. We shall have by night 6, or 8-24 & 4 or 6, 8-inch Paixhans in battery at another two points—and I think they must surrender tomorrow. We are in high spirits. I am quite well but hard worked—and I feel from knowing how to take care of myself, as safe in the trenches as at home. So dismiss all fears for my safety. I shall run no idle risks. . . . 13 more mortars just arrived.[55]

MEXICAN NARRATIVE OF THE SIEGE

Experiences and emotions within the city were far different from those of the men in Scott's army. A "Mexican Narrative of Events at the Heroic City of Vera Cruz, While Besieged by the American Army" was published in Jalapa during 1847, and reprinted in the American press:

How horrible is the scene we are attempting briefly to describe! What sympathizing heart can behold it without his eyes filling with the bitterest tears of grief? We would rejoice to conceal from Mexico this event, with the origin of our melancholy abandonment, and the causes of such serious and lamentable misfortunes to the country—but we are compelled to announce to the entire world, what was our true position, during those days of barbarous conflict, without any relief, which this city sustained, and her disastrous end.

. . . . .

When the squadron of the enemy appeared, bearing the invading army, all our points of defence were at once covered with our veterans and the National Guard. From this first moment, the service was constant, with the greatest vigilance—citizens excused by the law, ran to the common defence, and few were found without their gun, to assist; all worked and ate their ration in the line, moment[ari]ly expecting the assault, and, agreeably to their oath, resolved, at the cost of their lives, to defend their families and their country.

But days and dark nights passed, and the enemy did not approach our walls; remaining concealed behind his works, he was not anxious to measure arms with us—nor venture upon an uncertain deed of arms, selecting as was most agreeable to him, and most in accordance with his character, the barbarous manner of assassinating the unoffending and defenceless citizens, by a barbarous bombardment of the city in the most horrible manner, throwing into it 4,100 bombs, and an innumerable number of balls of the largest size, during nights and days, directing his first shots to the powder magazine, to the quarter of hospitals of charity, to the hospitals for wounded, and to the points he set afire, where it was believed the public authorities would assemble with persons to put it out; to the bakers' houses designated by their chimnies, and during the night raining over the entire city bombs, whose height was perfectly graduated with the time of explosion, that they might unite in falling, and thus cause the maximum destruction—but such infamous proceedings indicated from the first day the cowardice of the enemy.

His first victims were women and children, followed by whole families perishing from the effects of the explosion, or under the ruins of their dwellings. In a short time the hospitals were crowded with the wounded, the dead being simultaneously buried—with the exception of those unknown, who could not be taken from under the ruins. The bombs entered the walls of the church of Santo Domingo, killing the unfortunate wounded, frightening away the nurses and doctors; who after arriving with haste and risk at the church of San Francisco and the chapel of the third order, encountered the same dismal fate; as well as at the hospitals of Belen and of Loreto, where it is well ascertained one bomb assassinated nineteen innocent persons. In all quarters perished unfortunate persons, seeking a shelter from this frightful desolation, while the wounded, retaining strength enough to raise themselves, were flying as cripples and sprinkling the streets with their blood.

At the second day of the bombardment, we were without bread or meat, reduced to a ration of beans eaten at midnight beneath a shower of fire, and the light issuing from the projectiles. By this time all the buildings from La Merced to the Parraquia were reduced to ashes, and the impassable streets filled with ruins, stones and projectiles. The citizens had progressively removed to the claleta side, where up to this time less destruction had happened, taking shelter in the streets and entries, in such numbers that there was only room to stand on their feet.

But the third day the enemy alternately scattered their shot, and now every spot was a place of danger. This was the actual condition of the desolate families, suffering so much anguish, without advice, hope, sleep or food, solely engaged in preserving their lives, yet more aggravated by the reflection of the uncertain fate of their sons and brothers, remaining on the fortifications, who in return sympathized with this condition of their parents, known to be subjected to the explosion of every bomb upon their own habitation. Most of the families whose houses had been destroyed, had lost every thing, all the property remaining to them was the clothes on their backs, because what the flames did not consume, was buried under the ruins. Hundreds of persons, as well as fathers of numerous families of children, heretofore relying upon certain incomes, to-day find themselves without a bed to lie upon, without covering or clothing to shelter them, and without any victuals.

The principal bake houses no longer existed, no provisions could be had, and we were without any retail shops—the garrison and part of the population feeding upon rice and beans collected by the municipal authorities! ! ! Let it be remembered that we had been blockaded one year, causing general poverty; that our rich and benevolent men, who could have consoled many and relieved more, were absent, and our real situation can be best ascertained by all those knowing Vera Cruz to live on her commerce, which had been already dead so many months. In the midst of such a multitude of horrors, desolation and sorrow, with the hospitals full of wounded without attendants; the dwellings filled with unburied dead corpses, no food, breaches in the walls, the damage of the strongest and best defended works, with an expiring stack of cannon cartridges, from the constant reply of them for the enemy, the commanding general surrounded with such appeals and misfortunes, felt his courage stimulated, and declared his resolution to defend the post, so long as there remained alive ten men to the accomplishment of this object—the officers of the line and the municipal authorities assembled for consultation, and the majority judged it proper to save the lives of the innocent citizens assailed by the enemy, whose death did not improve their condition.

We are yet ignorant of the exact number of our killed and wounded; but by the best data we have obtained, estimate both at not less than one thousand persons. The damage done to dwellings and edifices is five or six millions of dollars, which cannot be repaired for many years.[56]

A correspondent of the New Orleans Delta confirmed the horrors of the bombardment as he gave details on the weight of metal thrown into the city:

The Mexicans variously estimate their loss at from 500 to 1,000 killed and wounded, but all agree that the loss among the soldiery is comparatively small and the destruction among the women and children is very great. Among their killed is General Felix Valdez, an officer of some celebrity.

At the time of the surrender the Mexicans had but two days' ammunition and three days' subsistence, which accounts for their generally withholding their fire during the night.

During the bombardment our army have thrown the following number and size of shot:

	Army Battery	
3,000	ten-inch shells	90 lbs. each
500	round shot	25 lbs. each
200	eight-inch howitzer shells	68 lbs. each
	Navy Battery	
1,000	Paixhan shot	68 lbs. each
800	round shot	32 lbs. each
	Musquito fleet	
1,200	shot and shell averaging	62 lbs. each
	Making in all 6,700 shot and shell, weighing	463,600 lbs.

The destruction in the city is most awful—one-half of it is destroyed. Houses are blown to pieces and furniture scattered in every direction—the streets torn up, and the strongest buildings seriously damaged.[57]

To Scott's Inspector General, Lt. Col. Ethan Allen Hitchcock, the bombardment was a demonstration of military efficiency, but nonetheless a sickening butchery of helpless women and children:

I am in Camp (Washington) some 2½ miles from Vera Cruz, and we moment[ari]ly expect the return of our Commissioners, Generals Worth & Pillow and Col. Totten, with the Articles duly signed by the Mexicans, surrendering both the city of Vera Cruz & the celebrated Castle of St. Juan D'Ulloa. . . . On the 24[th], a heavy battery of guns (6) landed from the navy, opened fire and the day following. The 25th—another heavy battery of 24s commenced fire and more mortars being placed in position the firing during the night of the 25th was very destructive—perfectly terrific—nothing can exceed its horrors. The enemy commenced firing the day after we landed and continued to fire every day, but with very little effect. They ceased firing usually at night and on the night of the 25[th] they scarcely fired at all. Our mortars on the contrary (13 in number) poured in a perfect stream of shells into all parts of the City, the very thought of which makes me now shudder. The shells were filled with several pounds of pow[d]er & at night might be seen by their burning fuzes making their passage from the mortars—sometimes 3 or 4 at a time—through an immence [sic] arc, rising very high and then descending into the denoted City & probably falling, 4 out [of] 5, into some house through the roof would there burst with an awful explosion, destroying whole families of women & children. It is horrible to think of.

The enemy sent a white flag the morning of the 25th at daylight and all day yesterday & today have been concerned in negociating but we understand that the city & castle are both agreed to be surrendered on our own terms. . . .

I must add that we have lost but two army officers (Captains Alburtis & Jno. R. Vinton) and a midshipman (Shubrick)[58] with 5 or 6 soldiers & as many seamen. Our approach and our active proceedings have been conducted under the direction of scientific Engineers & everything has proceeded according to known rules of the Art of War. Hence the loss has been very slight—of course I mean comparatively—no loss in this infamous war is slight. We have not acted neighborly towards our weak brother.[59]

VERA CRUZ OCCUPIED

The bombardment lasted from March 22 to March 26. Terms were agreed upon the next day. In a letter to his sister, Lt. Peter V. Hagner,[60] after briefly describing the surrender and departure of the Mexican troops, gave an account of Vera Cruz on the second day after occupation:

My previous letters will have told you that we are in possession of Vera Cruz City & dependencies. On the 29th the garrisons of the different forts & the Castle marched out to a plain near the city selected by the Genl. and there between two of the Divisions of the Army stacked their arms, gave their parole—not to fight during the War—& then march off—southwards. Capt.

H. & his officers were appointed to receive the arms. We stood at a white flag in the large open space and upon the head of the Mexican column, reaching our position—it was halted & the arms stacked. We then took an Inventory—Compy by Compy—over 4,000 muskets—swords, colors. musical instruments &c. &c. Then we marched into town—took possession of the vacated Forts—fired salutes—marched in review before the Genl. posted on a balcony in the Plaza—and then commenced the business of putting things to rights.

Genl. Worth, as Gov. is bringing everything into order as fast as possible in a dirty Spanish town now nearly one third destroyed—full of rubbush—streets piled up with barricades or cut up by our shot & shells—houses shattered terribly in every street—few lazy half-clothed, dirty inhabitants, the most [of them] having left the city or hid themselves, as soon as our lines were opened to them. There seems to be no bad feeling towards us—among them. As soon as they get over their fright, they cluster around us and look as amiable as is desirable. The ordnance officers had then to visit all the forts & the Castle to take inventories of their munitions & supplies. Such immense supplies of guns & ammunition I had no idea that they possessed.

There are 12 forts around the city—connected by walls—these are armed with more than 100 peices [sic] of heavy artillery, brass & iron, plenty of shells, cartridges, Balls to each fort. Besides these there are 250 old peices & 25 or 30 good—scattered through the city—with munitions—small arms—military equipments, everywhere. This kept us till night—nearly, when we got dinner at a restaurant & returned to our camp here.

Today I have been completing the visitation in the City and also at the famous castle of San Juan. It is a fine old fort—indeed old, very old, but in good military preservation—and it has been infinitely assisted in its protection by skilful Engineers. Barricades, piles of sand bags—at every corner. There are mounted here 130 heavy peices—and enormous supplies of munitions & materials. This people have spent all their means for years past in purchasing mil[i]t[ar]y weapons & have given them up with only half a struggle. They fired at us for three weeks—we fired at them for 78 hours—when they surrendered every thing they had *at hand*—230 mounted guns, in strong Forts—we had 23 guns in the trenches behind sand bags—which we had to haul through deep sand under their fire nearly two miles. But alas for them, they had a city attacked, which offered many points for injury. We had only men & material which could be injured and by good engineering—in such cases, these are much protected. We get plenty of trophies, you see many of these fine old brass peices from Spain—and peices of ordnance—old Bombards by name—which must have been made as early as 1620. We get too, many fine peices of our own muskets—made at West Point Foundry for several years past with thousands of shot, shells, &c. &c. &c. & English guns—equally well supplied & of the latest patterns.

They have been very leniently dealt with and the consequence is that except the arms & guns—and ammunition, they have managed to leave but little public property of much use. The city is paved—built of coral stones & cement—might be made clean & healthful, but is now filthy—& will soon be sickly, unless we can prevent it by speedy policing.

The public establishments are large and costly. We take possession of such of these as we need for storehouses. The private houses are like all Spanish houses, prisons on the outside, within cool and airy. Every thing is as much respected and quiet—is as well preserved—even on this the 2nd day as in every city in the country. The people can hardly believe their own senses yet I suspect—as soon as they find out this order is to be continued, they will gladly hurry back. The city has few or no gardens and as our lines were around them for three weeks they had consumed the most of their fresh provisions, they had plenty of rice & mutton apparently. The poor say they are suffering—and the Genl. has ordered provisions to be distributed. We go to their restaurants in the mean time & pay $1—for a poor dinner—or in the markets pay a picayune for an onion. I don't want to go there—sooner than absolutely necessary. . . . We shall soon move towards the interior. I learn there we will have a more agreeable country & a more pleasant time, I hope.[61]

American Fleet Saluting the Castle at Vera Cruz

SCOTT'S INVASION:
VERA CRUZ TO MEXICO CITY

SCOTT PLANS AN ADVANCE

*With a base secured at Vera Cruz, General Scott made plans for the advance
on Mexico City. As usual, he was beset with difficulties: supply was inadequate and slow in arriving; the volunteers, though becoming soldiers, still
gave trouble, and the one-year term of enlistment for many of them had or
was about to expire; and there were the problems of relations with the civilian population common to armies of occupation. But in spite of his worries
the general was optimistic, and confident that he would be in Mexico City
during the summer if the enemy did not make peace on American terms before that time. He reported it all in one of his "hasty" letters (his letters all
seem to have been hasty and lengthy) to the Secretary of War:*

My hasty report, of the 29th ultimo, made you acquainted with the capture of this city and the castle of San Juan d'Ulloa.

. . . . .

This army was detained some six weeks at the Brazos and Tampico, waiting for water transportation that had been, in good time, specifically required, and it is now delayed by the non-arrival of a sufficient number of
wagons and teams.

. . . . .

The chief quartermaster here reports 180 wagons and teams as ready for
the road, and 300 wagons, without teams, afloat. He supposed many of both
to have been lost in the recent heavy storms on this coast, and I have reported,

198

heretofore, that many of our artillery and cavalry horses perished on board vessels, in the same weather. In this neighborhood, notwithstanding every effort, we are not likely to supply the tenth part of our wants in horses, mules, and oxen. Towards Jalapa (sixty [nine] miles), the chances of success are much better.

I am now organizing a movement of three or four brigades upon Jalapa, and have only waited for the arrival of two steamers, from Tampico, with mules for some sixty additional wagons. In the mean time the city and camps remain free from signs of malignant fever, and we may hope will continue healthy for weeks longer.

It is evident that the movement of any adequate force, without the necessary supplies being well assured, might cause a return to our water depots, which would be much worse than standing fast for a time. When I commence a march, I shall wish it to be continuous—with such short delays, only, as may be necessary to occupy the National Bridge and Jalapa, 30 and 60 miles off, respectively. At present, I apprehend no serious resistance this side of Perote, (90 miles) if there, provided I can find draught animals for a small siege train.

. . . . .

Being, by the default of others, thrown upon this coast six weeks too late, in respect to the *vomito*, I have been made to feel the deepest solicitude for the safety of the army.

Tampico is not less unhealthy than Vera Cruz, and Tuspan is considered the worst of the three places.

There is no practicable route for wagons from Tampico to San Luis de Potosi, except by Victoria and Monterey; but one by the beach, through Tuspan, might be opened, at the expense of great labor and time, from Tampico to Perote, or to some other point in the national road, hence to the capital. That long line of communication, yet to be opened, in great part, is, of course, out of the question, and it could not be shortened by making Tuspan the depôt, for two reasons: 1. That harbor is the most difficult of access, and, 2. When reached it is the worst for health. I might add, it is further from Jalapa, Perote, and the centre of the enemy's resources, than Vera Cruz.

Our depôts, therefore, must of necessity, be at this place. The harbor is the best on the coast, and hence to the capital, is the best road in the country.

With proper care, I do not apprehend any great mortality in the garrisons . . . to be left in this city and the castle of San Juan de Ulloa, nor among the hired people of the quartermaster's and commissary departments, because we shall principally, if not only, occupy the water front of the city, separated from the inhabitants and open to the sea breezes.

. . . . .

Points have been made in one of the old volunteer regiments here, which may, possibly, be propagated throughout the seven,[1] to this effect: 1. That the regiment is entitled to be discharged in time to reach home by the end of its year's service; and, 2. That as the regiment was all the sickly season, last year, exposed to the *malaria* of the Rio Grande, it is now entitled to a discharge before it shall again be more exposed to fever here, and at New Orleans, on its way home. Far from entertaining such claims, I have taken measures to silence them, and to prevent their spread among other regiments.

The seven old volunteer regiments with me, now become respectable in discipline and efficiency, cannot fail to give us much trouble when the time for their discharge, and transportation back to their homes, shall arrive. I am looking to that time, and hope for the previous arrival of the regiments recently authorized by Congress. With a reinforcement of eight or ten thousand men, from that source, and recruits for the old regiments, at any point not beyond Puebla, I shall, I think, take the capital in all the summer, if not earlier stopped by a treaty of peace, or such terms for an armistice as will insure one.

The inhabitants of this city, under the excellent government of Brevet Major General Worth, are beginning to be assured of protection, and to be cheerful. Those in the vicinity have suffered more from green recruits, who much dilute the regular companies, and from volunteers. My last orders, No. 87, herewith, against outrages, have rallied thousands of good soldiers to the support of authority. In the meantime, claims for damages, principally on the part of neutrals, through their consuls, have been many. I am without

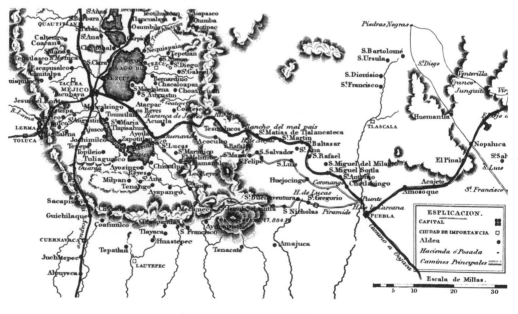

SCOTT'S INVASION

authority or means to indemnify, and can only feel and deplore the disgrace brought upon our arms by undetected villains.

. . . . .

In the act of writing, the arrival, by water, of 180 mules is reported, and I also learn that, besides an equal number from Tampico, to-morrow we may hope to obtain some two hundred from the country around us. These additions to our road train will greatly aid the forward movement intimated above.[2]

ON THE NATIONAL HIGHWAY TO MEXICO CITY

On April 8 Scott issued general orders for the march inland from Vera Cruz. The first objective was Jalapa, sixty-nine miles to the northwest on the National Highway to the City of Mexico. The road was better than most of those encountered by General Taylor's army in northern Mexico: the numerous bridges were durable, made of stone, and the highway was, as one foot soldier observed, "coped the whole way as our side walks in New York are." But the first eight or ten miles were heavy with sand, and the march was up hill. William Higgins, a volunteer, found himself "nearly used up with fatigue"[3] at the end of the first day. George Ballentine, a Scotsman with the regulars, became dismayed at the irregular system of marching, but fared well enough. He blamed the troubles of those who fell by the way on their poor physical condition and lack of discipline. Ballentine wrote in his Autobiography:

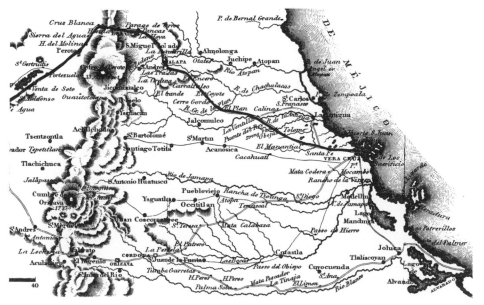

General Twiggs, who rode at the head of the division, committed a great error in permitting the men in front to walk too quick on this day's march. The consequence of this was that a great many of the men being weak from the effects of diarrhoea could not keep up, and slipped off the road into the thickets, which after leaving Santa Fé began to offer an inviting shade, and in which many of them lay down and deliberately resolved on staying behind the division. When we reached the place where we were to encamp for the night, a small stream about five miles from Santa Fé, the rear of the column was several miles behind, the men straggling along the road at their own discretion; and when the rolls were called at sunset, about a third of the men were absent, not having come up. We bivouacked under the trees by the roadside, the grass was deliciously soft and elastic, and, after a supper of coffee, biscuit, and pork, Nutt made us some aquadiente punch, after quaffing a bumper or two of which we lay down, and slept very comfortably until roused by the *reveille* next morning about four o'clock.

We had warm coffee before starting in the morning, our cooks, who had no other duties to perform on a march, except cooking, always getting up sufficiently early to have coffee ready before the hour of starting. On the rolls being called this morning, there were between three and four hundred men still absent according to current report. Although there was no great danger for these men, as they would go in small bodies for mutual protection, and each man besides being well armed had three days' provisions in his havresac; yet one could scarcely help thinking that it was a strangely irregular system of marching, which, carried on to much greater extent, would have a fatally destructive effect on the discipline of an army. We marched considerably slower today, resting more frequently, and taking care that none of the men straggled to the rear.[4]

SANTA ANNA AT CERRO GORDO

Jalapa, Scott's initial objective, stands upon a height, slightly above four thousand feet. Nearly seventy miles away were Vera Cruz and the Gulf. The city was walled, and the church near the west gate could have been converted into a fortress. Santa Anna made preparations to block Scott's army as it moved toward the city.

After his withdrawal from Buena Vista on February 23, Santa Anna had returned to San Luis Potosí, some four hundred and fifty miles north of Mexico City. There he rested his army, and also received the news of a revolt in the capital. Hastening south, he restored order, further consolidated his power, and reorganized his forces. On March 31, only five weeks after Buena Vista, he issued a ringing pronunciamento to the Mexican people in which he called for heroic measures.

Santa Anna

In making energetic plans for a defense of the invasion route into the heart of his country, Santa Anna decided not to make a stand at Jalapa. He chose the hamlet of Cerro Gordo instead, twenty-one miles to the southeast. Near it, Cerro Gordo Pass was a narrow, four-mile gap between almost perpendicular hills—it also was known as the Devil's Jaws—in these, as in a vise, the Mexican general proposed to crush Scott's army.

Scott Prepares for Cerro Gordo

Three miles east of Cerro Gordo the road from Vera Cruz crossed the Rio del Plan.[5] General Twiggs' division reached the crossing on April 11, and was joined by Major General Patterson's volunteer division the next day; General Scott arrived on the fourteenth.

Scott's camps at Plan del Rio were located where the tierra caliente rose to meet the lofty uplands; from there the National Highway looped through the hills, and defiled by a long, narrow, tortuous gorge, to the hamlet of Cerro Gordo. Cutting transversely across the route there were deep ravines on whose banks Santa Anna had placed artillery strongly supported by infantry detachments. The Mexican advance position (right flank) was anchored on the edge of a five-hundred-foot precipice overlooking Rio del Plan, but the strongest Mexican concentration was about one-half mile east of Cerro Gordo village, on El Telégrafo, a hill which sloped gradually toward the west and thrust out an escarpment some five to six hundred feet high facing the east. It commanded all approaches; the highway bordered its southern flank. Near El Telégrafo, slightly northeast of it, was another, lower height known as La Atalaya. The main body of Mexican troops was at Santa Anna's base camp, on level ground, close to Cerro Gordo hamlet. A battery of five guns defended it.

Reconnaissance by Scott's engineers indicated that if a force departed from the National Highway about half way from Plan del Rio to Cerro Gordo and followed a rough-hewn road constructed along a trail to the right or north of the highway, the Mexican positions might be turned on their (i.e. the Mexican) left flank, and the Mexican base camp opened to direct attack. Scott's plan called for Twiggs' division to lead in such a turning movement, to be followed by Shields' brigade[6] and Worth's division. In his plans, Scott did not provide for a direct assault upon El Telégrafo. Scott, however, did order Brig. Gen. Gideon Pillow with his brigade of volunteers to leave the National Highway and move southward toward the river (just out of range of all but one of the Mexican batteries), until he enveloped the Mexican right or advance positions closest to the American camps. Instead, with Pillow mismanaging the maneuver, Pillow's brigade moved toward the strongly placed guns and then stopped; it might have been in serious trouble had not the tide of battle favored the Americans elsewhere. The turning movement around the Mexican left flank succeeded, but not quite as planned. Shields' brigade, skirting La Atalaya and circling north of El Telégrafo, finally descended upon the Mexican camp, but not until Shields himself had been critically wounded, and not soon enough to cut off Mexican retreat along the highway to Jalapa. The outcome of the battle, however, was decided by two brigades of Twiggs' division in assaults on La Atalaya and El Telégrafo. On April 17, Harney's brigade took La Atalaya and the next morning stormed up the east face of El Telégrafo. While this action was going on, Riley's brigade attacked Mexican defenses on a lower spur of El Telégrafo (on the west side of that hill), then swept on into the Mexican base camp less than half a mile beyond. With their morale shattered by these developments, the Mexican center and right gave way, and the retreat was on.

General Scott gave a general résumé of the battle in his report to the Secretary of War, dated at Jalapa, April 23, 1847:

Resolving, if possible, to turn the enemy's left, and attack in rear, while menacing or engaging his front, I caused daily reconnoissances to be pushed, with the view of finding a route for a force to debouch on the Jalapa road and cut off retreat.

The reconnaissance begun by Lieutenant Beauregard,[7] was continued by Captain Lee, engineers, and a road made along difficult slopes and over chasms—out of the enemy's view, though reached by his fire when discovered—until, arriving at the Mexican lines, further reconnaissance became impossible without an action. The desired point of debouchure, the Jalapa road, was not therefore reached, though believed to be within easy distance. . . .

Twigg's division, reinforced by Shield's brigade of volunteers, was thrown into position on the 17th, and was, of necessity, drawn into action in taking

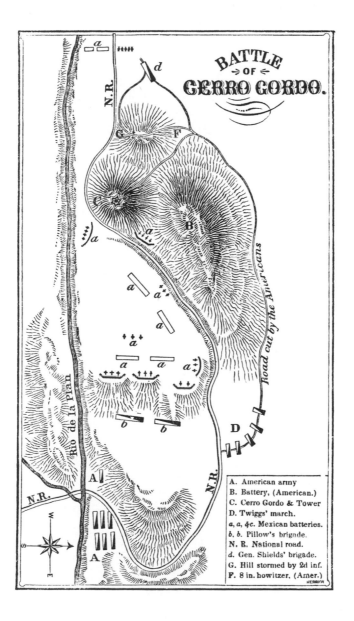

BATTLE OF CERRO GORDO.

A. American army
B. Battery, (American.)
C. Cerro Gordo & Tower
D. Twiggs' march.
a, a, &c. Mexican batteries.
b, b. Pillow's brigade.
N. R. National road.
d. Gen. Shields' brigade.
G. Hill stormed by 2d inf.
F. 8 in. howitzer, (Amer.)

up the ground for its bivouack and the opposing height for our heavy battery. It will be seen that many of our officers and men were killed or wounded in this sharp combat—handsomely commenced by a company of the 7th infantry under Brevet First Lieutenant Gardner,[8] who is highly praised by all his commanders for signal services. Colonel Harney coming up with the rifle regiment and first artillery (also parts of his brigade) brushed away the enemy and occupied the height-on which, in the night, was placed a battery of one 24-pounder and two 24-pound howitzers, under the superintendence of Captain Lee, engineers, and Lieutenant Hagner, ordnance. These guns opened next morning, and were served with effect by Captain Steptoe[9] and Lieutenant Brown, 3d artillery,[10] Lieutenant Hagner (ordnance), and Lieutenant Seymour, 1st artillery.[11]

The same night, with extreme toil and difficulty, under the superintendence of Lieutenant Tower,[12] engineers, and Lieutenant Laidley,[13] ordnance, an eight-inch howitzer was put in position across the river and opposite to the enemy's right battery. A detachment of four companies, under Major Burnham,[14] New York volunteers, performed this creditable service, which enabled Lieutenant Ripley,[15] 2d artillery, in charge of the piece, to open a timely fire in that quarter.

Early on the 18th, the columns moved to the general attack, and our success was speedy and decisive. Pillow's brigade, assaulting the right of the entrenchments, although compelled to retire, had the effect I have heretofore stated. Twigg's division, storming the strong and vital point of Cerro Gordo [sic, El Telégrafo] pierced the centre, gained command of all of the entrenchments, and cut them off from support. As our infantry (Colonel Riley's brigade)[16] pushed on against the main body of the enemy, the guns of their own fort were rapidly turned to play on that force (under the immediate command of General Santa Anna), who fled in confusion. Shield's brigade, bravely assaulting the left, carried the rear battery (five guns) on the Jalapa road, and aided materially in completing the rout of the enemy. . . .

The moment the fate of the day was decided, the cavalry, and Taylor's and Wall's[17] field batteries were pushed on towards Jalapa in advance of the pursuing columns of infantry—Twigg's division and the brigade of Shields (now under Colonel Baker)[18]—and Major General Patterson was sent to take command of them. In the hot pursuit many Mexicans were captured or slain before our men and horses were exhausted by the heat and distance.[19]

. . . . .

Our whole force present, in action and in reserve, was 8,500, the enemy is estimated at 12,000, or more. About 3,000 prisoners, 4 or 5,000 stands of arms, and 43 pieces of artillery were taken. By the accompanying return, I regret to find our loss more severe than at first supposed, amounting in the two days to 33 officers and 398 men—in all 431, of whom 63 were killed. The enemy's loss is computed to be from 1,000 to 1,200.

I am happy in communicating strong hopes for the recovery of the gallant General Shields, who is so much improved as to have been brought to this place.[20]

Two hills, La Atalaya and El Telégrafo (called "Cerro Gordo" in all of the field reports)[21] were to decide the fortunes of the battle. As one officer described it: El Telégrafo "towering high above all the other summits, was crowned with a tower from which floated the Mexican ensign; around the summit of the mountain was formed a breast-work for 5,000 infantry, and between this and the tower . . was planted a battery of artillery."[22] The Mexican Third Infantry was on the crest of El Telégrafo, but La Atalaya was more lightly held. As Twiggs' division advanced along the crude road which the pioneers had hacked out for the flanking march, the Mexicans sent strong reinforcements to La Atalaya. Near there they attacked Lt. Gardner of the 7th Regiment; the fighting soon brought in the rest of Harney's 1st Brigade, which took La Atalaya and began an abortive attack on El Telégrafo. After hard fighting the Americans fell back but still held La Atalaya. That rainy night General Shields' volunteers and other troops dragged heavy artillery pieces up the side of La Atalaya, and mounted them to fire upon El Telégrafo. An artillery officer in Shields' brigade told the story of this exhausting feat:

It was determined to bivouac where we then [Shields' brigade] lay for the night,[23] and resume the offensive in the morning. Reinforcements were sent for, and a heavy 24-pounder was ordered up from below. This gun and our section of [two] 24-pound howitzers were to be dragged up to the summit of the mountain carried by our men during the day, with a view to cannonade the tower, lines and batteries on "Cerro Gordo" [sic, El Telégrafo] early next morning. Five hundred volunteers[24] dragged up the 24-pounder from below and reached our bivouac, at the base of the mountain it was intended to decorate at about 7 o'clock in the evening.

The night that followed was the most distressing one to me I have ever passed. The whole division was worn out and exhausted, having been under arms from dawn of day, oppressed by fatigue, hunger, and worse than all, thirst. Water was scarce and the canteens had all been emptied before night set in. The "new road" over which we had marched was but a rough rocky path, from which the pioneers had time only to clear the trees and bushes— plunging now into a deep ravine, rising again up a precipitous, rocky steep, with scarce level space sufficient for breathing before the undulations of the ragged mountain side would call again for the exertion of all our strength.

Well—with men thus enfeebled and indisposed to work, the guns were to be dragged, up a steep, rocky mountain side, without a road, a path, or even a land mark to indicate the direction we must take through the dismal darkness of the night. A fire was kindled at the foot of the mountain, and taking this for the starting point we were to ascend in a perfectly straight line. Five hundred men manned the drag ropes of the 24-pounder at about 9 o'clock, reliefs of 500 men each following in rear of the gun, to take the places of the first detachment when their strength should be exhausted. Such a time of hard, grinding toil and persevering labor as then followed for six successive hours I hope never again to look upon, much less take part in.

Many of our strongest men gave out from utter exhaustion of all their force; others were overcome by thirst and others from various causes. Then while fresh parties were coming up, the wheels of the heavy gun carriage were to be chocked, braced and chained—every precaution taken to prevent the gun from running backward down the mountain, crushing everything in its course. Water was to be brought from a small muddy pool, half a mile distant, to relieve the fainting. Some fell down, unable to stand, and by the time the last gun was dragged up—I should judge about 3 in the morning— the track over which they had passed was strewn with tired, exhausted and sleeping men from the top to the base of the mountain. The fatigue was greater than I could well bear—being indisposed at the time and without my usual strength and robustness. I would have given every thing I possessed in the world to have the delicious sweet enjoyment of lying down to rest. Several times I found myself stretched out upon a rock or in the road, wherever I might chance to be, and just about yielding to the irresistible impulses of exhausted nature—but no—with pain in every muscle and bodily agony, I roused myself up—shook off the stupor creeping over my senses and resumed the toilsome task. . . .

At last our guns were all dragged to their respective positions upon the mountain height. Thirty men worked until morning in scraping together enough earth from the barren soil to make a breastwork for the 24-pounders. Our two howitzers were left without the slightest protection in front. I was awakened early in the morning by a sweet, plaintive, melancholy strain of music. It was the Mexican reveille on "Cerro Gordo," [sic, El Telégrafo] opposite to our position, and from summit across to summit about 80 yards. I jumped up, crept along through the bushes that masked our position and saw a beautiful spectacle in the rosy morning light; the main body of the Mexican army were turning out at reveille; the lancers—the chivalry of Mexico—were there, with their lances and streaming pennons; the Zapadores (sappers), the artillerists drawn up beside their guns, and far down the mountain slope were assembled in groups, by hundreds and thousands, the Mexican infantry.

Storming the Heights of Cerro Gordo

It was a beautiful morning. Turning and moving a little to the left, I saw far below me the Jalapa road and the batteries that guarded it. Here too the Mexican reveille was given to the breeze, and the soldiers were turning out from their grass-thatched huts. Still further to my left and almost in rear were unmasked and exposed to view all the remaining lines of the Mexican defences; and the mountain we occupied commanded all their batteries except the one on Cerro Gordo [El Telégrafo], which still frowned down upon us. Little did the men who held that height suppose that in one hour a 24-pounder and two 24-pound howitzers would open upon them from amidst the clouds.[25]

On the morning of the eighteenth, Col. William S. Harney and his 1st Brigade[26] assaulted El Telégrafo. Harney's description of the fight was in his report dated, April 21, 1847 at Jalapa:

The [mounted] rifles and 7th infantry slept on the hill [La Atalaya], and to that point were brought, in the night, a 24-pounder and two 24-howitzers, which at 7 o'clock in the morning, commenced a cannonade on the enemy's fortification on the Cerro Gordo. Early in the morning I was reinforced by four companies 1st artillery, under Lieutenant Colonel Childs,[27] and six companies, 3d infantry, under Captain Alexander,[28] and I immediately gave directions to the different commanders to prepare their troops for storming Cerro Gordo [El Telégrafo]. The rifles were directed to move to the left in the ravine and to engage the enemy; and I instructed Major Loring that, as soon as I had discovered that he had commenced the attack, I would move forward the storming force which I was about to organize. The 7th infantry was formed on the right, the 3d infantry on the left, and the artillery was formed in rear of the infantry, with orders to support it. Observing that a large force was moving from the left on the main road, towards the Cerro Gordo, I deemed it prudent to advance at once, and immediately ordered the charge to be sounded without waiting for the fire of the riflemen.

The enemy poured upon my line a most galling fire of grape, cannister, and musketry from different positions around the hill; but my troops advanced intrepidly and as steadily as on a parade day. I cannot speak too ardently of their animation, zeal, and courage under such trying circumstances, and without which they never could have surmounted the natural and artificial obstacles which opposed their progress. Around the hill, about sixty yards from the foot, there was a breastwork of stone, which was filled with Mexican troops, who offered an obstinate resistance, continuing to fire until the troops reached the breastwork, and where for a few moments bayonets were crossed. Beyond this and immediately around the fort, there was another work, from which our advance was again obstinately opposed; but the troops immediately surmounted it, carried the fort, pulled down the Mexican flag, and planted our colors amid the proud rejoicings of our troops.

Agreeably to instructions, the rifles moved to the left, where they became engaged with a succoring force, but which they held in check, notwithstanding a most galling fire from the enemy's entrenchments and from the musketry in front. After the enemy's cannon had been captured, I directed Captain Magruder to take charge of the pieces and to direct their fire upon the enemy, which he executed with zeal and ability. It is also due to Lieutenant Richardson to state that, as soon as he came into the fort, he took possession of one of the enemy's guns, and with his men promptly turned it with great effect upon the enemy. I also directed Lieutenant Colonel Plympton,[29] at the same time, to move with his regiment into the Jalapa road to cut off the enemy's retreat, which he promptly executed, and maintained his position until the forts and forces of the enemy had surrendered.[30]

A private in the Sappers and Miners (Company A, Engineers) who served under Harney that day, and was "personally engaged in the hottest of the action," gave more intimate details in a letter to his parents:

In the evening we succeeded after a great deal of labor, in getting our 24-pounder and two howitzers, and two other pieces of cannon on this hill. A detail was made from our party (about fifteen of us), to plant them. All but the three men thus detailed slept on the battle ground.[31] This was the night of the 17th. It was a shocking sight to behold the poor wounded riflemen and some artillery and infantry, about 100 in number, lying on the ground, with legs shot off, arms gone, and cut in every part, some with both legs and arm gone, some shot through the breast and other parts of the body, some just alive, all waiting for the surgeons who were busily engaged in dressing the wounds. We were obliged to encamp or rather lie down here, and notwithstanding the groans of the wounded and dying, and the rain which was falling fast, we slept soundly, such was our fatigue.

In the morning we were awakened early, and ascended the hill to our battery, and assisted in planting our guns. It was a very exposed position, in full range of the enemy's battery, and just concealed by a small growth of chapparel. We had a fair view of the enemy's battery through the trees, where they could be seen busily at work getting ready to fire upon us. We got the guns ready and were ordered a little way down the hill, out of the direct range of the enemy's cannon. We had just got a position where we considered ourselves safe, when the enemy opened their battery upon us. The grape and canister flew over our heads like hail-stones, striking a few feet from us, tearing up the ground and cutting down the bushes, and throwing the stone into the air in every direction. I saw one ball strike into the body of mounted

Scott Complimenting Colonel Harney

riflemen, killing six poor fellows, and wounding three or four others. It is a surprising fact that some regiments will get cut up, and others, more exposed, escape with but little loss through a whole campaign. A strange fatality seems to follow some regiments, while others escape.

Our battery opened upon the enemy about 8 A.M., and continued to fire for half or three-quarters of an hour, when the charge was sounded. Colonel Harney, of the dragoons, had command, and Lieutenant Smith[32] volunteered the services of his 10 men (all that were here as at that time the others being engaged in cutting a road, and with Gen. Pillow's command in another direction), and we rushed on with the other troops, preceded by our gallant Lieutenant.

We descended the hill on which was our battery, under a heavy fire of grape, cannister and musketry from the enemy, about five times our number. You have seen a hail-storm, and witnessed the falling of the hail-stones, accompanied by rain—then you have an idea of our situation. The shots fell around us, cutting down the low bushes, and passing through the clothes of some, and cutting down others of the brave fellows that were on to the charge. You can imagine my feelings—I thought of home and friends—and then such was the excitement of the moment, that all fear was done away. I looked—expecting to see some one of our brave little band fall—but they marched on after their brave officer until we reached the foot of Cerro Gordo [sic, El Telégrafo], where we rested but a moment to breathe, and then charged up the almost impassable height. The officers were obliged to use their swords for canes to help them up the hill, as did the soldiers their muskets. They fired briskly upon us, cutting down one after another; but still we pushed on, excited and maddened to a complete frenzy—that madness insensible to fatigue or even fear. We met them at the point of the bayonet, and drove them out of their fortifications, and then turned their own guns, these already loaded for us, upon them, making great destruction. I almost forgot to say that a reinforcement of some 10,000 or 12,000 Mexicans[33] were seen advancing toward this hill, which spurred us on to take the fort. We turned their guns upon their batteries and upon the advancing foe, which silenced their battery and caused them to scatter in every direction. . . .

After we had secured the position of the hill, and planted the flag of our country on the walls, we proceeded down the hill and found a quantity of sappers and miners' tools, which we took and placed a guard over. We took several prisoners—among whom was an aid[e] of Gen. LaVega, who was wounded in the thigh, and several other soldiers. Lieut. Smith then showed himself to be not only a soldier, but a true gentleman, and a friend to humanity. He ordered this officer (who, by the way, could not repeat English), to be placed in a comfortable position, took his own blanket, wrapped him up,

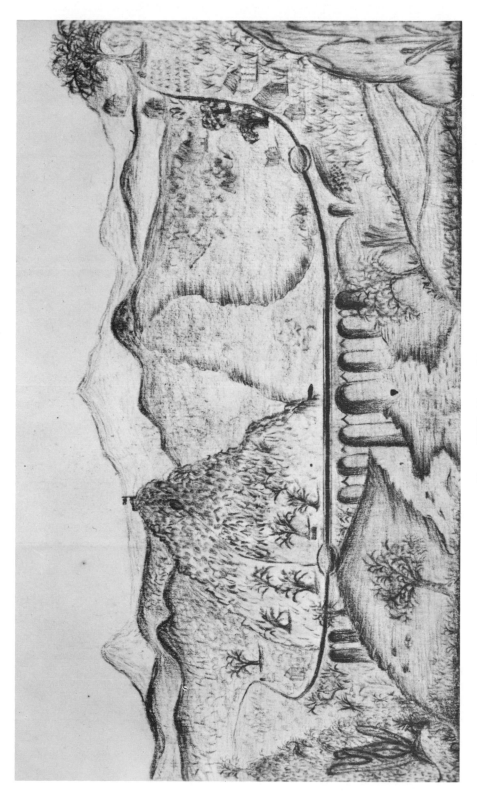

PLATE XIIX. *Puente Nacional*

PLATE XX. *Santa Anna Declining a Hasty Plate of Soup at Cerro Gordo*

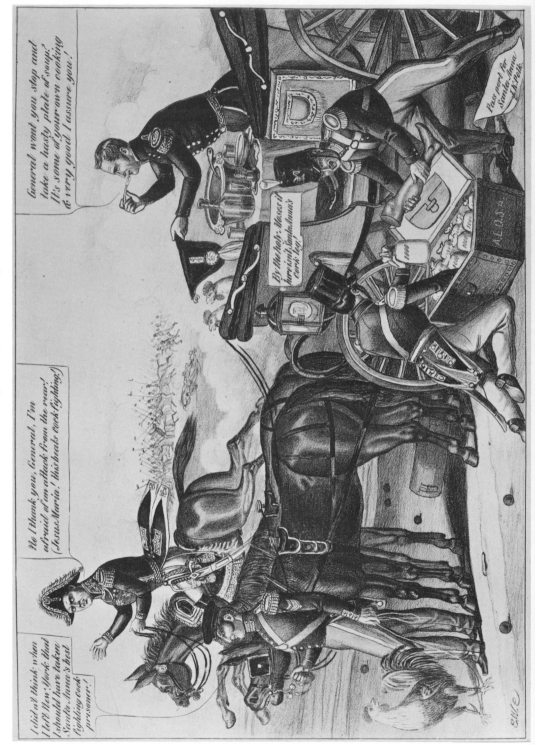

placed a guard over him and the other wounded prisoners, and proceeded himself in search of a physician. Nothing could equal the praise that was bestowed upon him and his men, by the suffering officer. He was a perfect gentleman—we no longer looked upon him as an enemy. . . . We pressed on until we came to Encerro, about eight miles from Cerro Gordo, where we encamped for the night. A great number of prisoners were taken and brought into camp that night, but all but the soldiers were set at liberty again. In the morning we started for Jalapa, and after marching 10 miles through a most beautiful country, we reached Jalapa about 12 A.M.[34]

All was not glory for Scott's army. That Brig. Gen. Gideon Pillow's brigade (Patterson's division) failed to carry out its assignment was evident from an eyewitness account published at Jalapa soon after the battle:

Gen. Pillow's brigade consisted of four regiments; the First and Second Tennessee, and the First and Second Pennsylvania. The plan of attack was that the Second Tennessee, under Col. Haskell,[35] and First Pennsylvania, under Col. Wynkoop, should form the storming force; to be supported by the other two regiments, Second Pennsylvania and First Tennessee. The First Pennsylvania moved in advance towards the point of attack.[36] They were halted by Gen. Pillow (in person) about a half mile from their position, and Col. Wynkoop was ordered to make a detour through the chaparrals, in order to reach the ground without observation. At that time Col. Haskell was almost in position, and, although, our regiment, the First Pennsylvania was hurried on at a trot, they did not and could not attain their position until after the fire opened on Col. Haskell.

Col. Wynkoop, before leading off his regiment, desired to know from Gen. Pillow when he should make the charge, and was ordered distinctly to take his ground and remain there until he received the signal, or an order from Gen. Pillow through an officer. The signal was to be a single bugle note. He took the position designated.

Our right extending into the low brushwood, skirting the chaparrals, was not distant from the enemy's batteries more than seventy-five yards, when a crashing fire of musketry, canister and grape was opened upon us whilst filing into place; and the only reason by which I explain the fact that our loss was only twelve men wounded, and of these but two mortal, was the elevation of the enemy's cannons, the grape almost entirely passed over our heads. The men had received orders not to fire, and not a trigger was pulled. In this position we remained two hours; our men glaring upon the faces of the enemy, and not permitted to move. We received neither the signal nor the orders to charge, and were compelled to stand there like stones, cursing and impatient. I know that Col. Wynkoop sent several officers to ask whether he might not charge, and every man in the regiment knows that all the officers, from the Colonel down, were chafing at the delay. The first intimation we received was an order to retire, and when we reached the ranch at the main road we there learned, for the first time, that Col. Haskell had charged and been repulsed. Our regiment obeyed orders to the letter. The Generals will, I am sure, testify to that fact. It was the last to leave its position, remained firm under the fire, and did not (as some might suppose from the statement in your paper) retreat; perhaps had we charged we might also have been repulsed, but, as that privilege was denied us, we think it unjust to imagine for us such an event.

BY AN OFFICER WHO WAS THERE.—[37]

The bombardment of El Telégrafo opened about seven o'clock on Sunday morning, April 18; the charge followed hard upon it. By ten o'clock Santa Anna's army was in flight. Santa Anna with Generals Canalizo and Almonte escaped, together with six or eight thousand men. But five Mexican generals (Pinzón, Jarero, La Vega, Noriega and Obando) were captured and General Vazquez was killed. Lt. Col. Ethan Allen Hitchcock wrote a factual summary on the outcome and significance of the battle:

I think proper to remark, with regard to the operations at Cerro Gordo, that by turning the left flank of the enemy and storming the principal hill occupied by him [i.e. El Telégrafo], which was done under your personal observation on the morning of the 18th inst., his force was divided, all the batteries east of the hill being separated from the main body of the army encamped on the Jalapa road west of the hill. All of the positions of the enemy were commanded by this hill which was believed by the Mexicans to be inaccessible to our troops.

The hill being stormed & taken, the main body of the enemy, commanded by Santa Anna in person, fled in utmost confusion and but a very few were taken prisoners. Many of the troops in the batteries made their escape at the same time, in the adjacent hills, throwing away their arms. A Mexican officer assured me that no less than 1,500 thus escaped from one single battery. Of those in the batteries who laid down their arms, surrendering at discretion, more than a thousand continued to escape on their march from the field of battle to Plan del Rio, some five miles or more, along a circuitous road bordered by woods & ravines—and hence, the number of prisoners on parole is reduced to about 3,000 men exclusive of officers: yet, although this may not be the place for the expression of an opinion, I feel warranted in saying that the defeat was as complete as it was unexpected by the enemy—that he was utterly destroyed, captured, or routed, spreading terror & consternation throughout the country.[38]

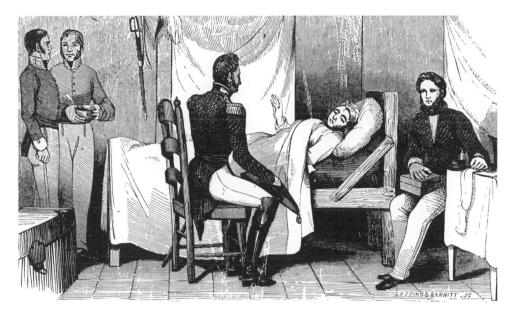

Scott Visiting General Shields

AFTERMATH OF CERRO GORDO

A correspondent of the Vera Cruz American Eagle travelled the National Highway from Vera Cruz to Jalapa in the wake of the victorious army. At the site of the battle he found appalling carnage, then overtook the retreating Mexicans and witnessed the distribution of the booty. He recorded this in his firsthand account of the aftermath:

Yesterday, at noon, I left the encampment near Sierra Gorda [sic] simultaneously with the thousands of Mexican prisoners who had been released on parole, and who were wending their way to their different homes, or to some place from whence they may again be forced to take up arms against us. I believe their line, extended as it was along the road, was full five miles in length. The Guardia Nacionale was the only corps that maintained any order in their march—the residue trudging along as best they could, and in most admirable disorder.

We rode over the road on which they marched with much difficulty, turning our horses heads twenty different ways in the space of half an hour, to avoid riding them down. They were less sad than men under similar circumstances would generally be, and cracked many a joke at their own expense. This was in the early part of the march. But towards sunset, when they had measured 18 or 20 miles of the journey—most of them in their bare feet—they became quite silent and sad, and the effects of the fatigue of the day, combined with previous privations, told sensibly upon them.

I felt much interest in the numerous camp women—those devoted creatures who follow them through good and evil—and it grieved me to see them, worn down with fatigue, moving at a snail's pace, their heavy burthens almost weighing them to the earth. The woman of sixty or more years—the mother with her infant wrapped in her rebosa—the wife, far advanced in that state that "women wish to be who love their lords,"—the youthful señorita frisking along with her lover's sombrero upon her head; even to the prattling girl who had followed padre and madre to the wars—could all be seen at one view moving along—and barring the hardships of the tramp, unconscious of the existence of misery in this world.

These women, like the Indians, are the slaves of the men—a slavery they submit to under the all-powerful influence of affection. In addition to their bedding and wearing apparel, they pack upon their backs the food and the utensils to cook it in, and worn out as they are by the toils of the day, whilst their husband or lover sleeps, they prepare his repast.

. . . . .

When the Mexicans first surrendered, it was about their dinner hour. In one of their forts the camp kettles were taken from the fire, and the rations were being proportioned out, when the order for surrender came from the second in command—so they had to march out without their dinners. That evening, although large quantities of food had been served out to them by our commissaries, they were picking up old bones, stale pieces of bread, and everything that could be eaten. Yesterday, on the march, they would run up to a beef, killed the day before by our advance, and cut off every piece that could be obtained, as eagerly as though they were half famished.

From the foot of Sierra Gorda [sic, El Telégrafo] to Santa Anna's hacienda, the roadside was lined with dead Mexicans, and horses. At and near the rancho where Gen. Twiggs overtook the retreating enemy, they lay thick around, and a more horrible scene it would be difficult to picture. Mexicans lay dead in every direction; some resting up against trees, other with legs and arms extended, and occasionally a lancer laying with his arm upon the charger that received his death wound from the same volley which ended the career of his rider. Some of the [sic, those] passing through would occasionally halt to view the features of the deceased, and then, mending their gate, regain their place by the side of those who were more fortunate in the fight.

At the place above cited was to be seen all the property, other than munitions of war taken from the enemy. In one place, arranged in good order, were all the pack saddles, then the pen containing mules, the provisions next, comprising rice, beans, bread, pepper, *pilonceos* [sic peloncillos], garlic, &c.,

PLATE XXI. *Battle of Cerro Gordo*

PLATE XXII. *View of Cerro Gordo with Genl. Twiggs' Division Storming the Main Heights*

piles of shoes, knapsacks, and all the paraphernalia of a Mexican camp. Capt. Robt. Allen, A.Q.M., stopped for a moment, and gave orders as to the removal of those things.

The muskets taken from the enemy were being broken on stones as I passed the spot where they were. They were of no earthly use to us, and hence the summary mode of disposing of them.

J. H. P.[39]

JALAPA OCCUPIED

After Cerro Gordo—Jalapa. There all could agree, notwithstanding the hardships of the campaign, that they had arrived at one of the most fascinating cities in Mexico. A correspondent of the Boston Advertiser captured much of the color and excitement in his "Letters From Mexico":

JALAPA, MEXICO, APRIL 30, 1847.

As you approach the city, for several miles, the country becomes more open, as well as somewhat more mountainous; and on the cleared spaces upon the slopes of the hills are pastured many fine droves of cattle and sheep. Still, there are few cultivated fields; save here and there a little patch on which the ranchero produces maize and vegetables enough for his own subsistence. Occasionally you meet "burros," the diminutive donkeys of the country, loaded with three or four bushels of charcoal in small packages of not much more than a quart each, and driven usually by little boys, of a size quite in proportion to that of the beast and cargo. But there are few signs of being near a city of any size, till one is close upon it. Notwithstanding its being "a city set on an [sic] hill," the town is pretty effectually "hid" from travellers coming from Vera Cruz. Finally, at the end of a long hill, you find yourself in the environs, and Jalapa is before you.

The outskirts of the city strike one at first sight as very different from those of the towns we have heretofore occupied. Here are few or none of the usual mud and cane hovels, occupied by dirty, lazy looking Indians. Most of the dwellings are substantially built of brick or stone, covered with plaster; the people had an air of neatness and intelligence as we saw them seated in front of their houses at the close of the day, very different from the lounging, listless manner so common among the lower Mexicans. The gardens attached to each house showed that not only industry but a considerable degree of taste had been concerned in their cultivation. We passed many little patches or groves of plantains and bananas, whose tall stalks and broad green leaves contrasted somewhat strangely with the large yellow flowers of the plain Yankee-looking *pumpkin vines*, growing in many instances side by side with these tropical plants, like the honest rustic who finds himself in the society of nobles but puts on his Sunday suit, and "holds up his head with the best of them."

Among clusters of roses, pinks, carnations and flowers to me unknown, I observed in many of the gardens a beautiful blossom much resembling our purple convolvulus, or "morning glory," but much larger. This, I believe, is the vine whose root affords the well-known medicine, *Jalap*,[40] produced in great abundance here, and named from the town.

But before descending into the city, you pause and survey the scene stretched before you and at your feet.

On the side of a steep hill, sloping towards the south, rise one above another the houses of the city, with their nearly flat, red, tiled roofs—most of the houses are stuccoed and whitewashed—in some instances painted yellow —but the immense number of trees interspersed among them, in the gardens (one of which is attached to almost every house, or at least a great proportion) prevents the otherwise painful effect of such a mass of white, and gives a beautifully rural appearance to the general view of the city, which also from this circumstance seems much smaller than it really is, as you perceive on actually getting into it. Among the dwellings and trees, rise here and there the domes and towers of the various churches—some of them venerable look-

Jalapa

ing piles of dark stone and quaint architecture, visible everywhere, like the traces of the religion taught in them, of which in this land one can never lose sight.

The valley to the South of the town is filled with the most charming culti-vated fields, interspersed with woods, hillocks and shrubbery—among which, surrounded by extensive lawns, are two white buildings, like the residences of gentlemen of taste and fortune; and such I had imagined them, till I was in-formed—alas! for romance! that they are *factories*.

Beyond the immediate vicinity of the town, to the South, West and North, rises a chain of lofty mountains, apparently within a few miles, so clear is the atmosphere of this region, but in reality at a much greater distance. These mountains combine beauty and grandeur of scenery in the highest degree. The eye rests on an endless variety of little sunny slopes, and nooks in the hills, covered with the richest tropical verdure, and rising one above another, till the view is almost imperceptibly carried up to the towering crags of their summits, which seem to form an impassible barrier between the lands on this side and those beyond.

In the Southwest, towers the peak of Orizaba—covered with perpetual snow, shining in the brilliant sun-light. If one unacquainted with its actual distance were asked what he supposed that distance to be, he would probably give it at about ten miles, at most. It is, in fact, somewhat more than forty miles from the city.

But while you are gazing at the scene, you become aware that you are in a different atmosphere from that in which you have been travelling. A feeling of vigor, to which you have been a stranger, pervades your whole frame. The change is singular as it is sudden. I may be thought to exaggerate; but nothing can be more delightful than the transition from the hot, enervating, sultry air of the "tierra caliente," at once into that of which Mr. Thompson,[41] in speak-ing of this place, remarks, "It is impossible for one who has never visited the table lands of Mexico, to conceive a climate so Elysian." There is not a day in the year when one could say 'I wish it were a little warmer, or a little colder.' It is never warm enough to take off your coat, rarely cold enough to button it."

At length, not tired of the scene, but reminded by the setting sun that "man cannot live upon air," our travel-worn party descended into the city, and found that it abounded in more substantial comforts, as you shall hear more particularly in my next.

· · · · ·

JALAPA, MAY 3D, 1847.

At the close of my last epistle, I was about introducing you into this city, after having taken a general external view of the place and its environs.

On entering it, and proceeding towards the central part, you find the streets well paved, sloping towards the middle, and furnished with good side walks of flat stone. They are in general not wide, not inconveniently narrow, there being usually sufficient room for two wagons abreast. The houses present an air of comfort; many of them are in modern style, some with pretensions to good architecture, and many are painted in the most fanciful style. They are mostly two stories high, and around the outside of the second floor is in most cases a balcony, upon which the windows open, all in the form of folding doors. The floors, both in the first and second story, are of brick, as are many of the staircases. A common style of building is with an arched entrance, leading to a court yard in the centre, from which is an ascent to the second floor.

The streets are filled with people, giving the place the appearance of being densely populated. The town has about 12,000 inhabitants, but the number is now nearly doubled, by the great numbers who left Vera Cruz when that city was threatened by our troops. These being chiefly persons of respectability, one meets a large proportion of well dressed persons. You pass gentlemen in large broadcloth cloaks, thrown over the shoulder a l'Espagnol—now and then a Mexican officer, mingled with tradesmen and country people in short jackets or blankets; women in coarse mantles, with baskets of produce on their heads; boys selling cakes and candy, and the only thing which reminds you of being in an enemy's country is meeting here and there a soldier, or crowds of slovenly looking volunteers, or passing a sentry in his pipe-clayed belts, quietly pacing in front of the quarters, his burnished musket glancing in the sun, or ringing as he salutes a passing officer. The streets are often crowded with large wagons, conveying the subsistence and stores of the army; little Mexicans horses, gaily caparisoned, the saddles often mounted with silver; droves of pack mules, in strings of five or six, the halter of each tied to the braided tail of his "illustrious predecessor," and donkeys almost entirely concealed beneath immense bundles of straw or forage.

Among this varied throng we made our way to our quarters, previously secured by a friend who had gone before, and paid due compliment to the chickens, vegetables and other dainties, which we had long known only in memory. The various church bells, which seemed to be constantly sounding, hardly served to interrupt our rest, and we fell asleep, quite confirmed in our "love at first sight" of Jalapa.

The next morning we visited the Plaza, occupied generally more or less as a market, where we saw exhibited for sale the most various productions. This place is about the size of that in your city called Bowdoin square, I believe at the junction of Cambridge and Green streets; it . . has a considerable slope to the south, and is overlooked on one side by a large church, whose external style, a most barbarous composite, "without form or comeliness," carries one back to the middle ages; on the others, it is surrounded by houses and shops, many with porticos in front, and the former barracks of the National Guard, or militia. In the centre is a fountain somewhat scantily supplied with water.

But it is on Sunday that the plaza should be seen, and the view is then most animated. This is the principal market day, and the whole place is covered with the venders of comestibles, seated flat on the pavement, each by his or her little stock, which they bring on their backs from the country. These people have strongly marked Indian features, and dark complexions; the men dress in jackets or blankets, wide trowsers, and large straw hats; the women in a light upper dress of cotton (camisa) with or without a coarse "rebosa" or shawl, and skirts usually of brilliant colors.

There is just room enough to pass between the lines of traders, and inspect their stock. The article which seems to be brought in greatest abundance, is the red pepper—but you find besides the greatest variety of others. One woman has perhaps a dozen chickens and a turkey; another a few cabbages; heads of splendid lettuce and greens, among which I observe the flowers of the pumpkin vine, which are much prized for the table—next is a man with a lot of plantains, bananas and oranges, and a little basket of eggs. Near him you find a peck or two of turnips and onions. A woman recommends to you her pine apples and melons—piles of beans, green peas and lemons, and baskets of blackberries fill up the gaps—fine tomatoes are abundant—and beside the fruits I have mentioned, others whose names are quite unknown to us. Many beautiful bouquets are offered for sale; and on the outskirts of the crowd, are billets of wood, each a load for a man or woman, and little packages of charcoal. So you can buy your dinner, and just fuel enough to cook it every day. Meats are sold elsewhere. In the neighboring shops, are exposed rice, sugar and corn, and milk, which the venders assure you is from the cow (an important fact, in this region of goats and asses), and not watered. Next to the variety of produce, you are struck by the very small quantities in which everything is brought for sale.

On Sundays too, one sees what is a rare sight on other days,—the ladies of Jalapa, picking their way across the market place to the church. Many are of unmixed Castilian descent, and quite beautiful. I know if you were here you would follow some of them into the church—very well, the bells are ringing with redoubled energy, and there goes the padre,—the corpulent gentleman in the blue gown and broad brimmed white hat- . . . .

As you come out of the church, you see a crowd in the portico opposite— that is a little market in itself, but of commodities quite different from those in the middle of the plaza. I have no time now to show you half of it.

I know not when I can send to you again, as it is expected that the communication between this place and Vera Cruz will soon be cut off. It is necessary to send very large escorts now.

. . . . .

JALAPA, MAY 6TH, 1847.

As we came out of the church, with the account of which I terminated my last epistle, I was prevented by want of time from introducing you to the little market under the portico on the opposite side of the plaza. But here I am yet, having been disappointed in my hope of an opportunity of following the advance of the army, the advance not having taken place. About midnight of the 3d inst., the order was countermanded,—from information received, as I hear, that the twelve months' volunteers would not re-enlist in any great number, and the consequent necessity of dispensing with those troops in any forward movement. This order was followed by another, in pursuance of which several of these regiments left the city today for Vera Cruz, thence to embark for New Orleans, there to be mustered out of service.[42] The men started apparently in high spirits, and quite satisfied with the amount of "soldiering" they have done. The departure tomorrow of another detachment, will give me an opportunity of sending this letter, for which I hardly hoped. A large train set out for Vera Cruz on the 3d inst. with an escort of picked men, which it was supposed would be attacked in returning.

As it is understood that an advance will soon be made to Puebla, and perhaps farther, I do not despair of being able ere long to write to you from that place, and possibly from the capital itself. An American who arrived last night from the city of Mexico, reports that there are no troops on the road to oppose the march of our army, and that no preparations have been made for resistance in the city—most of the people seeming convinced that it is useless to attempt farther opposition.[43]

THE TOWN AND FORTRESS OF PEROTE

After their defeat at Cerro Gordo, the Mexicans retreated through Jalapa along the National Highway to the town of Perote—about thirty miles from Jalapa and beyond. Within a mile of the town stood a stone fortress which commanded the road. Maj. Gen. William J. Worth, ordered by Scott to lead the advance against the town and fortress, reported on his mission:

I have the honor to report for information of the general-in-chief, that my division occupied the castle and town of Perote at 12 m., to-day, without resistance—the enemy having withdrawn the night before last, and yesterday evening—leaving Colonel Valasquez [sic], as commissioner on behalf of the Mexican government, to turn over the armament of the castle, consisting of fifty-four guns and mortars, iron and bronze, of various calibres, in good service condition, eleven thousand and sixty-five cannon balls, fourteen thousand three hundred bombs and hand grenades, and five hundred muskets.

In the retreat hence, the enemy carried away no materiél of war. No force has passed, embodied, except some 3,000 cavalry, in deplorable plight, headed by the recreant Ampudia.[44] The infantry, some two thousand, passed in small bodies, generally without arms. The few having any, sold them, whenever a purchaser could be found, for two or three rials. The route [sic] and panic is complete, and the way opened. A stand may be made at Puebla, but doubted. These are the fruits of the victory at Cerro Gordo.

I have received already some 300 cargoes (6 bushels each) of corn, perhaps 50 (300 lbs. each) of flour; and much more may be had, both here and at Tenestipec, two leagues in advance, whither I sent a detachment of cavalry to-night; all at fair prices. The alcaldes of Perote and the neighboring haciendas are in full activity, and manifest laudable zeal, assisted by the padres in aiding us. At a brief interview, I fully possessed them of the general's sentiments in all respects.

The current of disfavor seems strongly against Santa Anna, whose whereabouts are not known; supposed to be in the mountains.

I pray the general may have the means of moving rapidly; while the terror is on, our rear may be left with slight guards.

It is not doubted many mules may be obtained hereabouts. Shall such as are procured be sent to Jalapa, or retained here? I engaged some few en route, and ordered them to the rear.

The fortress affords quarters for 2,000 troops and their officers, with ample store-houses, hospitals, &c., &c., and a supply of good water within the walls.

The Generals Landero[45] and Morales,[46] confined in Perote for the affair at Vera Cruz, as also some American prisoners, were allowed to go at large on the retirement of the garrison. I have several of the latter belonging to the South Carolina regiment, captured near Vera Cruz.[47]

March to Puebla

Nelson McClanahan, a Tennessee volunteer, wrote of the forward movement from Jalapa to Perote, and, from there, on to Puebla. At Puebla the army had advanced some 190 miles from Vera Cruz, and was within 80 miles of the City of Mexico. Perote itself was of little consequence, but the fortress was of considerable interest to Scott's soldiers. It was a prison during the War for Texas Independence as well as during the Mexican War. While fighting the war against the Texans, Santa Anna had sent a group of prisoners to Perote. They attempted to escape but failed. To discourage repetition, their captors had forced them to draw beans. Most of these were white but some were black. Those who drew the black beans were executed.[48] *McClanahan had this episode in mind when he visited the fortress and described it, together with other aspects of the march:*

After leaving Jalapa a short distance the face of the country is entirely changed from what it is around Jalapa, for instead of the large oaks, you see nothing but stunted pines, and the fine wide and level road becomes very narrow and rough and is "up hill" from Cerro Gordo to within seven miles of Perote, where it first enters the vall[e]y of Mexico. . . . I will not attempt to describe it, but will only say that I doubt very much whether there is another such seenery [sic] on the ground. We marched and camped *in the clouds* nearly the whole route between Jalapa and Perote, and they were sometimes so thick that a man could not see ten steps before him.

We halted at Perote 2 days, and I have never been as glad in all my life as I was to see Perote, but once, and that was *to get away from there!* We arrived there after dark a short time, having marched from La Hoya that day and I do declare that I came nearer freezing at Perote on *the last day of July* than I ever did in the States on the last day of January. The march was the first long one that we had attempted, and I, to be as much unencumbered as possible, had taken off my coat in the morning and put it in the wagon, which did not come up until about nine o'clock, and there I stood shivering (officer of the guard) without coat, blanket, or a particle of fire; the wind having a fair sweep for seven miles in one direction and so far that you couldn't see the end in another came whistling around the corners of the old gray walls of [the] Castle, and seemed to go thro' every stich of my clothing and the clouds of fine white sand (worse than the beach at Vera Cruz) that it raised had the appearance, for the world of a snow storm; and had I been in a comfortable bed where I could have peeped out, I would have been almost ready to swear that it was the dead of winter. But, the next morning I saw immense fields of corn and wheat growing, and about 9 o'clock it is so intolerable hot that a man had to stay in his tent for shade. This . . . is not strange for Mexico. . . . 3 or 4 days ago we had ice in the quarters 1/16 of an inch thick and on the same day I eat green peas for dinner!

The Castle at Perote is an immense concern and its exterior is precisely the same as that at Vera Crus [sic]. It is situated about a mile from the town, in the Valley, and when I first beheld the "Stars and Stripes" floating above it, I thought it a most grand affair, but, on approaching nearer, it presents a scene of the most melancholy grandeur that I ever saw; its gray, grizzly walls, the large number and size of the cannon that are grimacing up on its parapets, some having been there so long that the carriages have rotted from under them, all combined, give it the appearance of having been there since time "whereof the memory of man runneth not to the contrary." The interior of the Castle is most beautiful, and everything extremely well fitted for the uses they are put to. The chapcl, in the Castle, is one of the richest, and the grave of Guadaloupe Victoria,[49] one of Mexico's first Presidents, also in the Castle, is one of the most grand affairs that I ever saw. . . . I also saw . . . the cross upon which the unfortunate Mier prisoners who drew in the celebrated "black bean lottery," were shot, and many fragments of their bones were still lying there, the larger part having been carried away by individuals, and buried together. I also saw, for the first time in my life, waggons loaded with dead bodies, some rapped [sic] in blankets, and others almost naked; some with swollen legs, arms, & heads &c, &c., being mostly wounded and broken down soldiers who were left to die.

The city of Perote is just a little the filthiest, most smoky, dusty, or murky place that I ever saw, or that I ever want to see again, and were it not for the Castle it would not be known as a city. It is the only town in Mexico that I have seen where the houses have either slanting roofs, like our own, or where they are covered with timber. The houses are covered with boards which are fastened down by wooden pegs instead of nails. After leaving Perote, the road runs directly thro' the vall[e]y to Puebla, and in many places for a day's march at a time it is the most horrid that I ever saw, the sand being ankele deep in many places, and not a square inch of shade to be seen in a whole day's march. There are no fences in the valley, and [through the] whole extent of it, from Perote to the City of Mexico, with the exception of about fifteen miles (on the 3d day's march from Puebla), seems to be one continued field of corn, wheat and other grain. We reached Puebla on the 7th of August.[50]

ENTRANCE INTO PUEBLA

As Worth led Scott's advance into Puebla, he skirmished briefly against cavalry that Santa Anna sent out to meet him. But the Mexicans withdrew and the city was occupied without an engagement. Worth reported on this to Scott:

I have the honor to report, for information of the general-in-chief, that the forces under my command, including the brigade of Major General Quitman, took military possession of this city at 10 o'clock to-day.

Halting yesterday at Amosoque, to await the junction of General Quitman (for which purpose I had shortened the marches of the leading brigades the two previous days), I found my position suddenly menaced, at 8 o'clock, a.m., by a large body of cavalry. This force approached somewhat stealthily by a road on our right, unknown to us. A rapid examination as it unmasked itself exhibited, as was supposed, some 2,000; but, from accurate information obtained here, 3,000 cavalry of the line, unsupported either by infantry or artil-

Puebla

lery, and moving a mile on our right and toward the rear, led to the conclusion that it was a *ruse* to attract attention in that quarter, while the real attack was to be looked for on the high road in front, or a movement on General Quitman, who might have been supposed the usual day's march in the rear. It was presently reported that a heavy column was actually approaching on the main road; thus it became necessary, while directing a portion of the force against the visible enemy, to guard our large train, reserve ammunition, &c., packed in the square against the invisible.

The 2d artillery, with a section of Duncan's battery, under the brigade commander, Colonel Garland; the 6th infantry, under Major Bonneville, with Steptoe's battery, was promptly moved and so directed as to take the enemy in flank; the head of his column having now reached a point opposite the centre of the town, and distant about half a mile. The batteries soon opened a rapid and effective fire. After some twenty five rounds, the entire column broke, without attempting to charge or firing a shot, and hastily fled up the sides of the convenient hills. Only one company of infantry (of the 6th) was enabled, from distance, to deliver its fire. The broken column was seen to reunite and resume its march in direction of General Quitman's approach. The

2d artillery and 8th infantry, with two sections of the light batteries, were put in its track, when the enemy again swerved to the left and disappeared in the hills. Two miles distant General Quitman was met by the last named detachments. He had already discovered the enemy, of whose proximity their firing had admonished him, and promptly taken his order of battle. The discomfited enemy reached Puebla late at night, and evacuated the place at four in the morning. We took some prisoners and found a few dead. The enemy acknowledge a loss of 89 killed and wounded. General Santa Anna conducted the enterprise.

. . . . .

It is understood the force which retired from this city the day before yesterday, and to-day, is to take post at Puenta del Tesmaluca, distant twelve leagues on the road to the capital, where it is proposed to fortify. Our reception was respectfully and coldly courteous, but without the slightest cordiality. Incessant occupation has not allowed me a moment to look into the resources in way of supply; but Mr. ---- -- says breadstuff will be had in abundance, less of beef, and perhaps liberal quantity of small rations.[51]

In 1847, Puebla, with a population of 80,000, was the second largest city in Mexico. It was a handsome place, 7,000 feet above sea level. Scott's soldiers found the people to be somber and unfriendly, but they did not resist when the troops moved into their city. H. Judge Moore of the Carolina Regiment arrived there on May 15, immediately behind the van of the invading force, and described the scene as the occupation began:

About ten o'clock, we reached the summit of a high hill which overlooks the city of Puebla, and from which we had a beautiful view of the castles, domes, and spires of that ancient and beautiful city of the angels, while in the magnificent array of churches, theatres, colleges and convents, with mosque and minaret, and [a] thosuand steeples, it seemed to sleep in silent but princely grandeur upon the soft velvet bosom of the green valley that lay beneath our feet. And at 12 o'clock precisely, on Saturday, the 15th day of May, 1847, the van of the invading army of the North, with the gallant and intrepid Worth at its head, entered in triumph and without opposition the south gate of the city of Puebla, and marched to the Grand Plaza fronting the Cathedral, where they stacked their arms, and supplied themselves with water from the fountain. This fountain appears to have been formed out of beautifully carved basaltic stone, surmounted by some half dozen full life likeness[es] of a species of dogs or tigers, with wide extended mouths, out of which the water spouted in every direction into the basin below.

I thought I had seen large masses of human beings before, but I never saw a shoreless sea of living, moving, animated matter, composed of crowding thousands of men, women and children, ebbing and flowing like the agitated waves of the ocean. From the time that our lines entered the outer gate, till we reached the Grand Plaza, every street, lane and alley, door, window and house top, were crowded and jammed with solid columns of human beings, to the depth of two squares in every direction, as far as the eye could reach.

As I cast my eyes round, I almost shuddered for the fate of our little army, although I saw no arms or warlike implements of any kind, nor any thing like a military organization, yet the immense cloud of hostile citizens that hovered round our little band in dark and portentous gloom, was altogether sufficient to have crushed our whole force into utter annihilation, without the aid of any other arms than clubs and rocks. And it was not on account of any good feelings which were cherished for us on their part that they did not avail themselves of the advantages which circumstances had thrown in their way, by which they could have completely demolished the advance of the army of invasion, before succor could possibly have reached them. For I afterwards learned that all they wanted was a bold and daring leader who could have given direction and impetus to public feeling, and led the already excited populace in a united and organized body against the heart of the invading foe. None of us doubted that the spirit was there; the bitter feeling of enmity and hatred which they had been taught to cherish from the time the first hostile gun was fired on the banks of the Rio Grande, was then burning in their bosoms like the pent up fires of their own volcanic mountains; and they longed for an opportunity of quenching those fires with the warm heart's blood that might flow from the stricken bosoms of a slaughtered American army.

But no modern Moses rose up to lead them forth—no martial clarion's thrilling notes sounded to the charge—no battle cry peals it[s] thunder tones upon the patriot's ear, urging the infuriated hosts of Anahuac's[52] chivalry against the serried columns of the advancing foe. The flower of their army had fallen—their bravest and best troops had gone down before the wasting and murderous fire of the Anglo-Saxon, like grass before the reaper—their favorite chieftain had been routed, and was then on the wing, flying for safety with a few panic stricken troops that had rallied around their leader in his fallen fortunes, bending his hurried steps towards the capital, not even daring to look behind him.

The city of Puebla contains nearly one hundred thousand inhabitants,[53] ten thousand of whom at least were able to bear arms; and these, backed and supported by a hostile population of eighty thousand, were standing quietly by, and looking on when the gates of the city were opened, and an army of four thousand two hundred men entered the angel-trod streets of this celestial city, and took peaceable possession of it without firing a gun. Many of the citizens and foreign residents, in speaking afterwards of our entry into the city, acknowledge themselves perfectly astonished at the cool and careless indifference that seemed to characterize every movement of the American army while such imminent danger encompassed them on all sides. They actually stacked their arms in the plaza and marched off to the fountain to get water, and then passed on to the market to buy bread and fruit, while those who remained to guard our arms lay down and went to sleep, and at the same time we were surrounded in every direction by hostile thousands of bloody-minded foes, who were anxiously waiting an opportunity to wreak their vengeance upon the invaders of their soil. But this very spirit of apparent rash and reckless imprudence might have eventually proved our strongest safe-guard, as it had a tendency to teach our enemies the light in which we viewed the prowess of their arms, and the unbounded confidence we had in our own skill and courage which always rose paramount to the thickening dangers that surrounded us.[54]

DOMINGUEZ AND HIS SPY COMPANY

The invading army stayed in Puebla from May 15 to August 7 while Scott numbered his problems and grievances, but took consolation from the fact that Santa Anna's lot was worse than his own.

It was in Puebla that the robber chief Manuel Dominguez entered the service of the Americans. As related by Ethan Allen Hitchcock, the tale of Dominguez was in some respects a Mexican version of Robin Hood. Hitchcock called him a respectable merchant who was robbed and ruined by those who should have protected him. Embittered, he became the leader of a band of highwaymen who had "perfect understanding with each other by signs as infallible and secret as those of masonry," and lived upon the spoils they took, but did not commit murder. In the reminiscences of his military career, Hitchcock (as Inspector General) described how Dominguez came to be employed by him in Scott's army:

Puebla, 5th June, [1847] A.M. I have taken into service a very extraordinary person—a Mexican, rather portly for one of his profession, but with a keen, active eye and evidently 'bold as a lion' or an honest man. He has been a very celebrated captain of robbers and knows the band and the whole country. I have engaged him to carry a letter to the commanding officer at Jalapa, and if he performs the service faithfully, I shall further employ him.

. . . . .

Puebla, 20th June. [1847]. The Mexican robber-chief Dominguez, whom I sent with a letter of General Scott's to Jalapa and Vera Cruz on the 3d, has got back here bringing a return despatch from Colonel Childs. . . . Through this man I am anxious to make an arrangement to this effect: that, for a sum of money yet to be determined, the robbers shall let our people pass without molestation and that they shall, for extra compensation, furnish us with guides, couriers, and spies.

Puebla, 23d June, [1847]. The robber Dominguez is a very curious and interesting man. When General Worth first arrived here, some person pointed out this man as a great robber and desired that he might be seized. He was living quietly with his family here, the people fearing him or the laws being powerless in regard to him. General Worth arrested him, but, after a few days, sent to him saying that he was arrested on complaint of his own people, and, giving him to understand that he had no friends among the Mexicans, offered to take him into our service. The plan took, and when General Scott arrived, he at once sent Dominguez to me.

I tried him and found him faithful. When I settled with him, paying him about $110, including his outfit, I suggested his bringing into our service the whole band of professional robbers that line the road from Mexico to Vera Cruz. He assented, but frankly spoke of the difficulty of giving security for their good faith and honesty. I told him to think the matter over and we would talk again.

The next day, Major Smith's interpreter (Mr. Spooner)[55] recognized our Dominguez as the fellow who had robbed him on the highway! Dominguez took $5 from him and gave him a pass of protection from other robbers.

Last evening we saw Dominguez again and engaged five of his men at $2 a day, with himself at $3 a day. I told Dominguez to find out how many men he can control on the road. He thinks some 300. I have ordered the five men in different directions for information.

· · · · ·

[Puebla] 26th June [1847]. This morning I brought twelve from the city prison into the presence of my Dominguez and saw a most extraordinary meeting. Dominguez met some of his friends for the first time for years—men with whom he had doubtless been engaged in many an adventure, perhaps highway robbery. They embraced and swore eternal fidelity to each other and to the United States. I remanded them to prison, saying that I would report their cases to the General and ask their release.

June 28th. And I did report to the General, who ordered their release. I distributed about $50 among them and last evening I arranged with Dominguez that he should forthwith enroll about 200 of them. They are to be formed into companies and to operate under the orders of the General. We are to pay $20 a month to each man and they find everything. Each man counts, in fact, two for us, for if we did not employ them the enemy would; so that one detached from the enemy and transferred to us makes a difference of two in our favor. Dominguez says he will bring over the guerillas to our side or seize their chiefs and bring them prisoners to our general, etc., etc.[56]

Lt. Henry Moses Judah, 4th Infantry, also had a meeting with the Dominguez Spy Company in the summer of 1847. He recorded it in his journal:

[August] 17th [1847]. . . . My Regt. was taken to a house [in San Augustín] occupied by a gentleman Spaniard. Four cos. of it including my own, were quartered under the balcony surrounding the inner courtyard; the sons of the kind looking Philadelphia-like gentleman were highly prepossessing in appearance and manners. They gave us officers a very good room, and insisted upon getting us supper, which they did. About dusk I was detailed to command Co. "D" quartered farther down the street. Lieut. R. being off[ice]r of the day. After eating some supper I had my things sent down there, and upon going myself found that there were no rooms for the officers and three of us had to sleep on the inner porch around the court yard. The Mex[ican] spy co. were quartered in the same building, and had brought their horses up on the porch, and left the end of it for us; horses & of[fice]rs were crowded so closely that they ran against and kicked my bed several times during the night; had I been without a cot I should have been trampled under their feet.

The following is the history of this co. Soon after reaching Puebla—Gen. Worth was informed that the most renowned robber chief of Mexico, Dominguez, was in the city, that he had committed seven murders, and been under sentence of death three times but by means of money and the fears of his prosecutors for their lives, had escaped justice. Gen. Worth had him arrested. This Captain of robbers is a very fine looking man with a good face and nothing indicating cruelty in it. He can command by a sign, 10,000 men on the road from Mexico to Vera Cruz; he can give you a passport which will carry you in perfect safety over the worst infested road, and has made a great deal of money by these passes given to rich merchants for the conveyance of rich goods and money along the several highways. When Gen. Scott arrived, he entered into an arrangement with him requiring his services for his life. The Chief promised to raise Gen. Scott a company of 100 Mexicans (principally robbers) who should continue in his service during this war, as a sort of spy or ranger company. These men were to convey Gen. Scott's despatches &c., and render any service required. Gen. Scott asked him what security he could give him that he would perform what he promised. *My word* replied the robber and up to this time most faithfully has it been kept.[57]

Gen. Scott appointed a man named Spooner from Virginia who has been a robber in this country under Dominguez for some time captain of the co. and two foreigners the Lieuts. Dominguez merely goes along with the co. as general superviser &c. This co. led the way for Capt. Ruff to San Juan, where they killed so many guerrillas, and took a very active part in the slaughter. They carry lances, escopets, swords and pistols, are well mounted, and well dressed. Whenever they want a horse or clothing they go to any person of their own countrymen, and in a very polite manner take what they want, apologizing in a regular robber style. Dominguez says he never killed a man in his life and I do not believe he ever did. These men with whom I was quartered, appeared to be a happy reckless set.[58]

However valuable their services may have been to Scott's army, the Spy Company became notorious everywhere. Dr. Elisha Kent Kane,[59] then an Assistant Surgeon in the United States Navy, but later to gain fame as an American arctic explorer, wrote to the commanding general of the United States forces in Mexico City about the cold-blooded violence of Dominguez and his band:

On the 6th. of Jany., while proceeding to the City of Mexico, accompanied by an escort of Lancers under Col. Domingues, we fell in with a body of Mexican troops crossing the National Road near Nopaluca [sic, Nopalucan]. In the action which ensued Generals Gaona[60] and Torrejon, Major Gaona and two captains were taken prisoners, together with thirty-eight rank and file. I would now respectfully present to your notice the following facts which I am able to sustain by satisfactory testimony, viz.

1. That, after the formal surrender of the Mexican party, Domingues with his Lieutenants, Rocher and Paladios, and others, did, in cold blood attempt to sabre the prisoners.

2. That an American Officer upon interposing his person was similarly menaced and assaulted, receiving thereby an injury of a most serious character.

3. That, by the consent and with the participation of Domingues, the personal effects of the prisoners, including horses, clothing, watches, money and swords, were distributed among the Lancers—Domingues taking to himself the elegantly caparisoned animals of the General Officers—valued at more than *Three Thousand Dollars.*

4. That the Mexican Officers—two of them Generals of high rank were ignominiously mounted upon horses without bridles, and that when at Nopaluca, they were promiscuously huddled together in one room, destitute of food or clothing; and that Domingues, in answer to the urgent remonstrances of the American Officer before-mentioned, *refused* to restore, even temporarily the blankets or other clothing which he had stolen. The prisoners—three of them dangerously wounded—were thus obliged to sleep uncovered upon a stone floor during a night of extreme cold. I would further state as not coming under my own personal knowledge, but sustained by undoubted testimony.

5. That more than thirty-six hours after the capture, when the prisoners were deprived of American protection, Domingues did order them to be

shot, which order, after having been given to his troops was only withheld from execution by an appeal from Genl. Torrejon holding out threats of punishment from the authorities of the United States.[61]

Preparations to Enter The Valley of Mexico

Lt. Raphael Semmes of the United States Navy, who accompanied Scott's army during the last phase of its campaign, described the preparations for a movement on the City of Mexico while Scott was at Puebla in the summer of 1847:

We are growing somewhat tired of our inactivity. Puebla begins to lose the charm of novelty, and we are anxious to be moving toward the "Halls of the Montezumas," that terminus of the campaign which each one has pictured to his imagination in such glowing colors, and which is to repay us for so much tedious delay, and for so much toil and hardship; the said toil and hardship, so far as the officers are concerned, who are mostly mounted, and have baggage-wagons *ad lib.*, to carry their wardrobes and comfortable bedding, consisting in performing a very interesting tour, in a very unique and interesting country! We had hoped to hold our "revel" in the Halls on the coming fourth of July; but that hope we have now abandoned, as it will be impossible for our reinforcements to be up in time.

But as we cannot be marching, we are doing the next best thing, drilling and preparing our troops for the march. The city of Mexico, which once invited us with open gates to enter it, is now being converted into a citadel by the indefatigable Santa Anna, and we shall have to fight one or more battles to capture it. We have two beautiful drill grounds in the vicinity of Puebla, and they are as classic as they are beautiful—one of them being situated on the road to *Tlascala*,[62] and the other in full view of *Cholula*. The snow mountains look down upon them both, and they are covered with the most velvety green sward.

There is a regiment constantly on drill in one or the other of these plains; and once or twice a week there is a division review, at which the general-in-chief is sometimes present. When General Worth or Twiggs drills his division, half the town flocks out to witness the splendid spectacle. The veterans of these divisions (the 1st and 2d of regulars) which have hitherto borne the brunt of the war, and are expected to bear it again, perform their various evolutions with the ease and accuracy of so much machinery under the guidance of their skillful officers; and nothing can exceed the *coup d'oeil* presented by a review of one of these famous corps. The magnificent plain with its storied associations; the transparency of the brilliant atmosphere, unknown to, and

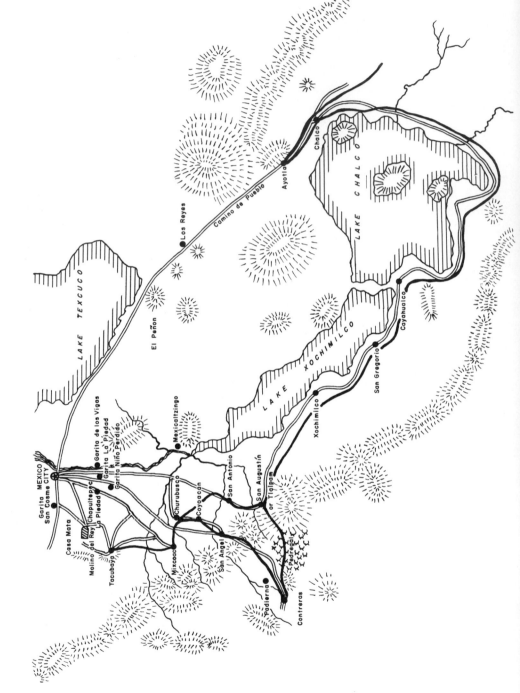

almost inconceivable by a dweller in low-lands; the solid phalanx as it is moved hither and thither at will; the glitter of bayonets, the flutter of pennons, and the soul-stirring music of the bands all form a picture which the imagination may conceive, but which the pen, or at least my pen, refuses to commit to paper.

I always connected these military displays—fancifully, no doubt—with the history of Cortez and his exploits. But our situation was somewhat similar. With a handful of men, we had, like him, boldly thrown ourselves into the interior of the country. We had not burned our ships, but we had suffered our retreat to be cut off in case of disaster; and we were now preparing to march against the same city of Mexico which he had conquered, and from nearly the same place; as he had marched on his great expedition, first from Tlascala, and then from Cholula. Science and skill, and the nature of weapons considered, our great predecessor, as compared with his enemy, had had greatly the advantage of us; for his invading force, Tlascalans and other Indian allied included, amounted, at times, to from twenty to forty thousand men; his allies being at least equal, if not superior as soldiers to the enemy. We expected to move with ten thousand, all told! If beaten, he could fall back upon Tlascala, which sturdy little republic had become his faithful friend and confederate in the war; but if we should be beaten our total destruction would be inevitable.[63]

El Peñon Bars the Way

On the morning of August 7, "amid the waving of banners and exciting rattle of drums,"[64] Twiggs' first division led the way toward Mexico City, while Twiggs' advance division marched steadily toward the capital of Mexico for sixty miles, to the town of Ayotla. There he paused for several days. Ayotla lay twenty miles from the goal. Ahead on the highway, about three miles away, was the town of Los Reyes. Beyond that another two miles stood El Peñon.[65] This fortified hill, dominating the highway about nine miles from the great city, was at a point where the road turned from its northwestward course almost straight west along the southern shore of Lake Texcuco. Part of the way it ran on a causeway flanked by marshes and ditches which often overflowed in the rainy season. The large, shallow lake was just northeast of Mexico City.

South of Ayotla there was another lake—Lake Chalco—at the eastern end of which was the town of Chalco and a small fort; on the west, Lake Chalco was connected by a canal-like channel with Lake Xochimilco, a long, irregularly shaped body of water which extended toward the northwest almost to Mexico City.

When the advance division paused to reconnoiter, the first problem which had to be considered was the feasibility of an assault upon El Peñon. If the *main highway was to be followed, the fortress could not be bypassed. For a reconnaissance of El Peñon, Scott chose his brilliant engineer-soldier, Captain Robert E. Lee. Lee's report on El Peñon, although matter-of-fact in tone, indicated something of that officer's thoroughness, accuracy, and daring. It was as follows:*

In compliance with your orders, accompanied by Capt. Mason[66] & Lt. Stevens[67] of the Corps of Engrs., I proceeded on the road to the City of Mexico to examine the approaches to & the defenses of the Piñon [sic, El Peñon] &c. The road as far as Los Reyes, about 4 miles distant is bounded on either side by cultivated fields. From that point it is open to the right to Lake Tescuco [sic, Texcuco]. About 1½ miles farther is a bold spring which flows into Lake Tescuco & whence commences the causeway leading to the Piñon, with a ditch on each side. About ½ mile from this spring the water washes the causeway on both sides & extends apparently entirely around the Piñon. The distance from the firm land in front to the foot of the hill is about 1,300 y[ar]ds & to the top about 1 mile. About 300 yds in advance of the Piñon & the same distance in rear of a bridge in the causeway, is a three gun battery across the road. The embrazures were distinctly visible, but no guns were apparent. The foot of the Piñon was enveloped as far as could be seen by a trench for musketry. After crossing the road it was terminated on the extreme left by a field battery, in which I discovered no guns.

Another field work, situated at the foot of the hill on the right side, & well to the rear, limited my view in that direction. The crest of the hill was surmounted by three batteries at different elevations though nearly on the same straight line. There was in addition a breastwork about half way down the hill flanking the road, & two smaller breastworks apparently placed to defend the ascent of the hill where it was the most easy. I discovered no guns on any of the works on the hill. The communications from the different points on the hill appeared easy & protected & the communication around the foot of the hill practicable for cavalry. The water surrounding the Piñon did not appear more than a foot or two deep, though I was informed by some Indians that near the base of the hill it was 5 feet deep. The bottom of the lake I was told was firm. I saw numerous troops both foot & horse on & around the hill, but had no means of ascertaining their number. I saw nothing that would render an assault *impracticable*.

After examining the Piñon as far as practicable, I proceeded about a mile on the road to Mexicalcingo [sic, Mexicaltzingo]. As far as examined it was hard & firm & well defined. Before reaching the low ground I was recalled by the Commander of the escort. I learned from the Indians in the neighborhood that it was a good road the whole way & not more than a league long. It was, however, defended in the vicinity of Mexicalcingo & the bridge at that place broken. It passed entirely without the reach of the batteries of the Piñon & the point where it left the main road furnished good encamping ground, & is provided with wood, water & some shelter.[68] The village of Los Reyes furnishes no particular facilities for defense, & no shelter for troops.[69]

Although Lee did not report that an attack on El Peñon was impossible, it was largely because of his observations, supported by the findings of other engineers, that Scott decided his army should follow another line of operations. Possibly as a feint, boats were collected as if to ferry the army across island-dotted Lake Chalco. The other divisions, however, soon followed by Twiggs' backtracking force, marched through the town of Chalco, around the eastern end of the lake, and continued over primitive roads along the south shoreline of Lake Chalco and Lake Xochimilco to the town of Xochimilco (about mid-point on that lake's southern shore), and then turned off toward the west and the attractive resort town of San Augustín. There they were only about twelve miles due south of Mexico City.

BATTLE OF CONTRERAS

On August 18, while part of Scott's army was poised at San Augustín ready to advance, Captain Lee next examined the roads to the Pedregal, a field of sharp volcanic rocks which lay to the left. The divisions of Twiggs and Pillow fol-

Storming of Contreras

lowed, picking their way through the lava and ravines, as the Mexicans at-
tacked them and opened the Battle of Contreras on August 19. The climax
came the next day when Riley's brigade swept into General Valencia's[70]
camp. Lt. Richard S. Ewell, of the 1st Dragoons, wrote an account of the
battle's early stages:

I really think one of the most talented men connected with this army is
Capt. Lee, of the Engs. By his daring reconnaissances pushed up to the cannon's mouth, he has enabled Genl. Scott to fight his battles almost without
leaving his tent. His modest, quiet deportment is perfectly refreshing compared with the folly & bombast of the Genls. & officers by Prest. Polk.

. . . . .

This Company has generally been Gen. Scott's escort & we have had the
luck to be in tolerably exciting scenes more than once on that account. One
part of our duties was to accompany the Engrs. on reconnoitering trips when
a small force only was required, & on the 18th of August we were sent out
with Capt. Lee to examine the road towards the Pedrigal. This, you know, is
the name given to a stream of lava several miles across, which in times past,
ran from the mountains almost half across the valley & in cooling broke up in
the most beautiful combination of sharp rocks, pits, &c. . . .

We were at St. Augustine,—the Avenue to the city goes through the Fortification at St. Antone [sic, San Antonio], & on the left of the road is the
Pedrigal & [on] the right a lake. We wished to cross the Pedrigal about the
arrow head to turn the other works &, as I said before, our Drags. & several
hundred Infy. under Col. Graham[71] escorted Capt. Lee somewhere towards
the arrow head, but not across the Pedrigal. When we got to the edge, the
Dragoons were a few hundred yards ahead of the In[f]y., & about 200 Mexicans, stuck away in the cracks & behind rocks began firing on us, quite to my
surprise for it was the first time I had been under fire. It was some time before I could clearly comprehend, but presently a horse in ranks tumbled over
shot through the heart & I could hear the bullets striking the ground around
us & singing over our heads. A path led a short distance into the Ped. &
Capt. Kearny[72] let me take one half the Compy that was up & gallop down
the path as far as I could where I dismounted leaving the horses in a hollow
safe with a guard & I had the gentlemen Mexs in rear & flank. They did not
fire at me after I started. Capt. K. brought up the remainder & Col. Graham's
Infy came up & sent a Compy on the opposite side. But the Mex. had retreated as soon as they found 30 men on fair terms with them leaving 8 or 10
dead & about as many pris[on]ers.

The next day our army began to take up positions, entering the Ped. at the
very spot where we had the skirmish. The evening of the 19th we went out
with Genl. Scott & staff who stood on a hill over-looking the scene of opera-

tions. Nearly all the army was in the lava crossing to the other side by four or 5 different routes which Valencia from his works kept up an incessant fire of heavy artillery upon the different columns, now & then blazing away with his 6,000 muskets as though our troops were within 50 yds (a Mex. fashion) & then by way of change throwing a shell across at the Genl. or at the cavalry but fortunately without harm, though they sometimes fell among us. The Mex. were so surprised at not being at once driven off that they thought a great victory was gained & commenced a jubilee that night, among other things their bands would strike up "Hail Columbia," play about half through it & then suddenly stop. Valencia brevetted some of his officers & was crazy with joy. St. Anna knew something more of the Yankees & ordered Valencia that night by an Aid[e] to strike his pieces & retire. "Pshaw! pshaw!," said the latter, "Tell St. Anna to go to Hell, I have saved the Republic." A fight of ten minutes the next morning as utterly destroyed his army as though each man had been summoned to the other world.[73]

Even closer to some phases of the engagement than Ewell (and who, like Ewell, was brevetted for bravery in the battle) was Lt. Daniel Harvey Hill, who wrote a forthright account in his journal:

Aug. 18th [1847]. Morning, we passed through the singularly picturesque town of Cayahualco. The houses are built of volcanic rock & the most of them thatched with the reed called bagies. Rude walls of stone enclosed the narrow streets on each side and in the yards were lovely & magnificent groves of the thick-foliaged olive. A mile or two beyond Cayahualco, we passed through a smaller town in all respects very like it, called San Gregorio. The Volunteers had been here the night before & had committed the most shameful depredations. For five miles we saw continuous groves of the olive. That road was most horrible & as the train was in front of us, we were much delayed by it & on an average did not advance more than three hundred yards at a time without a halt. The Mexicans had obstructed the road in several places by rolling down immense rocks from the hills & it required much labor to remove these obstacles. I climbed up one of the hills & for the first time saw the great City of Mexico some 15 miles distant. The view was of course imperfect, but I saw enough to satisfy me of its splendor and beauty.

We only marched eight miles but I am more fatigued now than I have been after a march of twenty-five. The road was truly horrible, if a man made the least false step he was sure to be plunged over his hips in the mud. To make the matter worse, a piercingly cold rain poured down in torrents upon us for hours & being without shelter we of course got thoroughly drenched to the skin. We at length reached the once famous town to Xochimilco an immense city in the time of Cortez, now a town of some two thousand inhabitants but not more than two hundred of these remain. The vile Volunteers & raw levies have been here & the inhabitants have fled to escape from these savages. We learned to our great surprise on arriving here that the works on this side of Mexico [City] are represented to be excessively strong and can only be taken with heavy loss. Reconnaisances have been made by Worth's Division during the last two days. Unfortunately the gallant Capt. Thornton,[74] 2d Dragoons was killed whilst escorting with his company the Engineer officers on their tour of reconnaissance. The enemy fired at us this morning repeatedly from the hills & then ran. We continued our march paying but little attention to them. I suppose that our Division will not move tomorrow.

Aug. 23d. Pueblo of Coyoacan. The last four days have been full of danger, hardship and suffering. On the morning of the 19th we moved at 8 o'clock from the village of Zochimilco & about 10 A.M. we reached San Augustine de las Cuevas or Tlálpam. Here all the wagons of the divisions were halted and we all, officers & men, took each a blanket and one day's rations in our haver-sacks & then moved off, taking the advance of the whole American Army. Our expedition was looked upon as one of the most forlorn & desperate character and the troops of the other Divisions at San Augustine (Pillow's and Quitman's) came to the roadside & bade us farewell. San Augustine is a large & beautiful town & I do not think that I ever have seen so many fruit trees as were there. The vile Volunteers had committed the usual excesses & the lovely town was in good part deserted. I observed three beautiful girls seated in a window, calmly looking at us as we passed and the sight gratified me no little, though I expected so soon to be on the field of blood.

We advanced for several miles over an exceedingly bad road which in many places had just been made by our pioneers and at length came in sight of a Fort on the heights of Padierna which completely commanded the road that we were pursuing. Genl. Twiggs here mysteriously disappeared and that con-summate fool Genl. Pillow assumed command of our division and detached our brigade (Riley's) composed of the 4th Artillery, 2d & 7th Infantry in all (1,100 men) to get between the Fort at Padierna and the City of Mexico, whilst he made an attack upon the work in front with the mountain howit-zers & Magruder's battery of four 12-Pounders. Certainly of all the absurd things that the ass Pillow has ever done this was the most silly. Human stupid-ity can go no farther than this, the ordering of six and twelve pounders to batter a Fort furnished with long sixteens, twenty-fours and heavy mortars!! Sage general, the Army appreciates you if the country does not.

Our light batteries were cut to pieces in a short time and some of our best officers & men killed or mortally wounded. In the meanwhile our Brigade crossed over boggy cornfields & deep ravines, clambered over sharp volcanic rock called Pedregal until we reached the main road to Mexico. There our regiment surprised a party of Lancers, killed four, wounded others & put the whole to flight. Soon after a splendid looking body of Cavalry issued from the Fort and from an adjacent height began to taunt our regiment (then far in advance of the rest of the Brigade) & banter us to come there.

Whilst Col. Riley appeared to be hesitating whether to accept the taunting challenge or not we saw four long columns of soldiers, Foot & Cavalry, advancing from the City. The whole of our brigade had by this time come up, and we were moved off to the little village of San Geronimo still nearer to the Fort but still just at the foot of the hill occupied by the Lancers from the Fort. We were in the little village for hours partially hid from the enemy by the dense growth of fruit trees though occasionally having a man struck by grape from the Fort. We were then ordered up a deep, rugged ravine apparently with the design of attacking the Fort by attacking it at the gorge. When within a few hundred yards of it, a body of Cavalry made their appearance on our right while the Fort in front sent forth shot & shells in the greatest profusion; however only a few of our troops were hit as we sheltered ourselves in the ravine. An officer of the Lancers dashed at our brigade alone with his drawn sword & almost reached us before he was shot. I saw a Mexican a short time before show almost equal courage.

We remained in the ravine where we had gone for shelter [a] quarter of an hour and then we heard that 'twas decided not to attack the Fort at that time and we moved off seemingly with the intention of attacking the troops which had come out from the City. Our brigade was now halted when just beyond musket range of the Mexicans and we now learned that the whole of Twiggs' division had come up & a portion of Pillow's. A Council of War was now held as to the advisability of giving battle to the Mexican troops in front whilst a strong Fort was so near in our rear. The result of the consultation was to countermarch once more & occupy the village for the night, it being now after dark. We have since learned that the force which came out from the City was 10,000 strong under the command of General Santa Anna in person. Whilst awaiting the decision of the General, a young Rifle officer came up to me & told me of the shameful mismanagement of the fool Pillow & that [a] battery had been cut to pieces & his regiment (the Rifles) completely dispersed. Soon after the Rifles defiled pa[st] and there were not one hundred men among them all. We had scarcely got into our position when it began to rain very hard and continued to do so all night. We had no shelter except such as was afforded by the trees & were all soon drenched to the skin.

Before two o'clock we were aroused & t'was whispered that a night attack upon the Fort was to take place and as our arms were not to be relied upon in the tremendous rain that it was to be carried by the bayonet alone. Our men were formed in silence and we moved on led by Lt. Tower of the Engineers. The night was so dark that 'twas scarcely possible to see the hand before the face & the path was muddy & slippery. A man of F Company of our regiment neglected to keep "closed up" & lost his place thereby misleading the whole brigade in his rear. We wandered about for hours not knowing where we were. At length we got upon the right trail and succeeded in reaching the rendezvous at daylight. Finding it so late our arms were got ready for firing and we moved on to the Fort which was reached about half an hour after sunrise. The enemy was expecting us though he was taken somewhat by surprise as all his preparations had not still been completed. He therefore threw out an Advance corps to check us until more cannon could be brought to bear on our column. This corps poured a heavy fire into us before we had completed our deployment. Riley's brigade constituted the entire storming column and our regiment[75] led the column.

We returned the fire of the advance Corps with deadly effect & then marched forward, the enemy falling back before us. Cannon now opened upon us, charged with grape & cannister, but owing to the fright of the gunners did but little injury. My company carried the colors and in consequence suffered more severely than any other as the standard drew the enemy's fire. The day before whilst in San Geronimo, the top of the colors was knocked off. This morning, the tassel carried off by a cannon shot and soon after the color bearer was killed. Our advance was steady under a heavy but far from destructive fire as the Mexicans took no aim. After fighting for half an hour we discovered that the enemy's Infantry & Cavalry were in full retreat leaving the artillerists still at their guns. We received a discharge of grape when within twenty yards of the muzzles of the cannon. Capt. Drum[76] of our Regt. captured two guns which proved to be the very guns that Lt. O'Brien of our Regt. lost at Buena Vista.[77] I succeeded in capturing three guns which the enemy were just abandoning. The enemy was now completely routed & was retreating in disorder towards Mexico [City]. The 1st Brigade of our division and a portion of Pillow's division now intercepted the retreat by getting across the road. Shot down in front and rear the helpless Mexicans hid themselves in gullies & ravines, in the cornfields and under the rocks.

The result of our victory was five hundred killed, near a thousand wounded, four General officers & more than a thousand men prisoners of war, twenty two, (22), splendid pieces of artillery and munitions of war almost beyond belief. The loss of our brigade though the storming column was very trifling, the 4th Artillery leading lost but thirty-seven—fourteen of these belonged to my company. More than a fourth of my company were therefore cut down though composed entirely of recruits.[78]

A more intimate account, which supplements that of Hill and Ewell, was written by Lt. William Montgomery Gardner, 2d Infantry, who served in Riley's Brigade at Contreras:

The night of the 18th we halted in a small town called Ochomilco [sic, Xochomilco]. I slept that night in a church where I was more annoyed by fleas than I have ever been before. Early next day we set out little expecting before evening to be engaged. On our right flank as we faced the enemy was Santa Ana with between 10 & 12,000 men and 2 light pieces. On our left Genl. Valencia with 27 pieces of can[n]on many very heavy and a force of 6 to 8,000 veterans. . . . About 7 or 8 o'clock it commenced to pour down torrents but I was more fortunate than my companions. Having been ordered out on Picket we were fortunate enough to discover a house, the residence apparently of a Padre but entirely deserted. We selected this as the Head-quarters of the G'd t[h]rowing out our pickets from this point. We found the Padre's larder well lined. The Capt. and I supped that night on stewed chickens, honey, chocolate, brandy and water and hard bread. The Capt. and I alternated about bedding up and as we found mattresses, pillows and blankets we had nothing to complain of in point of lodgings.

I had scarcely taken my first nap, when an engineer officer and Twiggs Adjutant Genl. came to the picket for a guard to protect their reconnaissance. I took command of a few men and started out in the most unpleasant night I almost ever saw. I then for the first time heard that we were to storm . . at just before day[light] a work containing about 30 guns and defended by 6 to 8,000 men. The storming party [was] to be [the] Riley Brigade. Altho' I was confident that we would suffer terribly in this affair still I felt quite relieved for the idea of our being canonaded all the next day without being able to return a shot was rather too much for my equanimity, if I was to be killed I wanted [it] to be while at close quarters and not have my head knocked off by an enemy [a] half mile distant.

About three o'clock in the morning or perhaps a little later the three Regiments composing Riley's command had started for their position on the left flank of Valencia's camp and in rear of it. We reached our position as day was dawning. There we remained probably 30 minutes. The enemy had not all this time discovered us.

When it was broad daylight we formed columns of attack. There were two columns by division, one composed of the 4th Artillery with 6 cos. of my Rgt. The other of 7th Infty. with 4 Compys. [of] my Rgt. Just imagine to yourself 900 men, for the columns of attack did not contain quite that number, attacking an entrenched camp with 27 pieces of ordnan. and at least 8,000 Infantry, to say nothing about *lancers*. I thought that at least two thirds of our numbers would be swept down before we could be able to use our bayonets. The enemy did not perceive us until we had pushed on to the most serious obstacle in our progress, viz. a deep barranca containing about two feet of water. As we got over that we saw a devil of a hub[b]ub in their camp, the men run[n]ing to arms, the mounting of horses &c. it was a complete surprise. Just before getting to the top of the hill, down the other side of which was the enemy's camp, we halted for a minute for the men to close up. When we reached the top, [we] halted a second time to allow the men to blow a minute. Here we received a volley from the enemy's Infantry t[h]rown hastily out to oppose us. We did not return a shot but stood up as if they were throwing apples instead of lead at us. We marched towards them still under heavy fire of musketry, for some twenty or thirty yards, then halted, and deployed column. During all this time we had not fired a shot and men were dropping in our ranks at every moment. I admire the coolness of our men during this trying time even more than their headlong impetuosity after the word *charge* was given. When we had deployed into line of battle, we gave them a volley, and then made a head long rush, the enemy could not stand this more than twenty minutes. They then broke. We pursued with relentless feroc[ity].

In conclusion I state upon my personal responsibility, that no troops excepting the 7th and 2nd Infantries and 4th Artillery had any thing to do with the storming of Contreras. The other regiments participating in the *chace* but not in the *fighting.* Genl. Pillow slept five miles or thereabouts from the field of Battle also Genl. Twiggs. Genl. Smith—Genl. Shields I know were with us, as to the rest of the Genl officers I cant say.[79]

CHURUBUSCO

While the Battle of Contreras was being fought, Worth's division of Scott's army lay a short distance to the right of the engagement, well within sound of the guns. No sooner had Valencia's camp been taken and his force routed, than the 2d Division (Worth's) was in motion toward Santa Anna's main position at San Antonio. Supported by most of Twiggs' division, Worth then fought the second major battle to clear the way into Mexico City. This was the Battle of Churubusco. Captain Ephraim Kirby Smith[80] described the bloody fighting at Churubusco in a letter to his wife:

I hardly know how to commence a description of the events of the last three days. My brain is whirling from the long continued excitement and my body sore with bruises and fatigue—but I will try to . . . record things as they happened. On the nineteenth we still lay near San Antonio. . . . Quitman held San Augustine and we kept the enemy in check at San Antonio. Our battalion[81] strengthened by two companies from the Sixth, under Captain Hoffman,[82] and two from the Eighth, under Brevet Major Montgomery,[83] went far to the right reconnoitring. We passed over the same route as on the eighteenth but took no pains to conceal our march among the lava crags and

Charge at Churubusco

ravines as before, but showed ourselves to the enemy wishing them to believe we still threatened their position at San Antonio. . . .

As soon as the result [of the Battle of Contreras] was known to General Worth, the Second Brigade of his division with our battalion were put in motion to endeavor to turn the position at San Antonio. For two hours we ran over the rocks moving by a flank, the enemy in a heavy column marching parallel to us and almost in gun shot, until the head of the Fifth Infantry pierced their line and the fight began at a quarter before twelve. . . . The point where our troops pierced the retreating column of the enemy was on the road from San Antonio to Mexico near a hacienda where the left of their line of defences terminated. Our battalion when the firing began must have been near a half mile to the rear. The "double quick" was sounded and the whole advanced at a run. We soon reached the road and turned in hot pursuit. This road is a broad, stone causeway with corn fields and pastures on each side of it, divided by broad ditches filled with water from three to six feet deep,—the corn tall and very thick. It was soon seen as we rushed along the road that the enemy was only retreating to a fortified position which constituted their second line of defences at Churubusco. . . .

Along the road to this point I had seen no wounded or dead American, though on either hand and in the road were many dead Mexicans. I saw one colonel lying in the ditch shot through the heart. We had advanced on the road less than a mile when we were ordered into the fields to assault the right of the enemy's position,—I am speaking of our battalion. We soon formed line in an open field behind the thick corn in our advance. The escopet balls were whistling over our heads, though at long range, and occasionally a cannon ball sang through the corn as it tore its path along in our front.

At this time the battle was fiercely contested on our left and front. . . It must have been about half-past twelve. Immediately in front of us, at perhaps five hundred yards, the roll of the Mexican fire exceeded anything I have ever heard. The din was most horrible, the roar of cannon and musketry, the screams of the wounded, the awful cry of terrified horses and mules, and the yells of the fierce combatants all combined in a sound as hellish as can be conceived. We had not from our battalion as yet fired a gun, but now rapidly advanced, all apparently eager to bring the contest to a hand to hand combat in which we knew our superiority.

We could not tell what was before us—whether the enemy were in regular forts, behind breastworks, or delivering their fire from the cover afforded by the hedges and ditches which bordered the road and fields,—all was hidden by the tall corn.

We soon came out of it into a crossroad near some small houses, where we were exposed to a dreadful cross fire, which could scarcely be resisted. Many had fallen and the battalion was much scattered and broken. The grape round shot and musketry were sweeping over the ground in a storm which strewed it with the dead and dying. I found it extremely difficult to make the men stand or form, but finally succeeded with my own company which was at once ordered to charge under my brave Lieutenant Farrelly. I was occupied reorganizing the three other companies, the colonel and many of the officers and men not appearing when arose the most fearful time of the battle. My men were just formed and I had ordered the charge which I was about to lead, when the dreadful cry came from the left and rear that we were *repulsed*. A rush of men and officers in a panic followed, running over and again breaking my little command. I, however, succeeded in disentangling them from the mass, composed of a great portion of the Eighth, Sixth, and Fifth Infantry, with some artillery. I shouted that we were *not* repulsed—to charge—and the day would be ours. Our colonel, C. F. Smith,[84] now joined us, and the cry throughout was: "Forward!"

Up to this time we were not aware that the other divisions of the army were engaged, but we now learned that Twiggs and others were pressing them on the left and had been fighting them an hour or more. Before this we had discovered we were under the fire of two forts, one a bastion front *tete du pont* flanking, and being flanked by a larger work, built round an extensive convent. Now as the whole army shouted and rushed to the assault, the enemy gave way, retreating as best they could to Mexico. They were pursued by all, hundreds being shot down in the retreat, our dragoons charging after them to the guns at the gate of the city, where they were stayed by a tremendous discharge from the battery covering the entrance. . . .

As soon as the battle terminated and the pursuit ceased, I went back, tired and sore as I was, to collect the dead and dying of our battalion and did not return until night. The field presented an awful spectacle—the dead and the wounded were thickly sprinkled over the ground—the mangled bodies of the artillery horses and mules actually blocking up the road and filling the ditches. . . . In my own company I found two dead and fifteen wounded. Lieutenant Farrelly[85] received two shots, one in the breast and one in the arm. In the battalion there was in the aggregate fifty killed and wounded out of about two hundred and twenty engaged; in our entire division, three hundred and thirty-six; in the whole army, one thousand fifty-two. Seventy-four officers were killed and wounded, thirteen killed on the field. . . . I was in the thickest of the fight for more than an hour, and my feet by grape and cannon were twice knocked from under me.

The loss of the enemy must be immense. We have taken between two and three thousand prisoners, seven generals, and thirty-seven large guns. Their officers say, in killed, missing, and captured, they have lost over five thousand. They acknowledge that they had twenty, some say thirty thousand, in the fight. It is a wonderful victory and undoubtedly the greatest battle our country has ever fought, and I hope will bring peace. At all events, the great city is at our mercy, and we could enter it at any hour.[86]

THE TACUBAYA ARMISTICE

Contreras and Churubusco (August 20), brought the invading army to within a few miles of Mexico City. Scott established his headquarters at Tacubaya. But his troops were tired out, had suffered severe casualties, and were in no condition for an immediate attack upon the capital. Instead, Scott demanded the capitulation of the city, and began to negotiate an armistice on August 21. Santa Anna's army was in far worse condition than Scott's so the Mexican general grasped at a breathing spell. Negotiations could proceed with the Chief Clerk of the State Department, Nicholas B. Trist, who accompanied Scott's army. On the twenty-fourth, terms for an armistice were agreed upon. Scott regarded this as a preliminary step to Mexican surrender; Santa Anna used it to prepare for further resistance. From the day it was made, the Tacubaya armistice was destined to become one of the most controversial decisions made during the campaign for Mexico. George Wilkins Kendall, brilliant editor of the New Orleans Picayune, who accompanied Scott's army, called it Scott's greatest mistake. He argued in defense of this position:

The greatest error of the campaign in the valley of Mexico was purely of a political nature—was in granting the ill-advised armistice at Tacubaya. Viewed in whatever light it may be, it was a mistake. After Churubusco had fallen, and the capital was completely at the mercy of the invading army, this great advantage, purchased with the blood of over one thousand men, was relinquished under the vain or delusive hope that such an unbounded stretch of magnanimity would obtain the important desideratum of peace. That General Scott was performing an act which he deemed would meet with the approval of the Government and people at home, is certain; that both himself and Mr. Trist thought they were carrying out the wishes of the cabinet at Washington, nervously anxious to secure a peace, the author has no right to question. It had been the policy of the American Government, from the day when General Taylor crossed the Rio Grande at Matamoros to exercise all magnanimity towards the Mexicans—to follow up hard blows by soft words—to raise olive branches above the smoke of stricken fields—in short, to endeavor to coax a proud enemy, while smarting under the disgrace of defeat, to agree to terms of peace, and this while the very terms offered ever looked towards what they contended was an unjust dismemberment of domain and a loss of national honor.

Farther than this, entirely mistaking the character of the Mexican people, the policy had obtained of addressing them proclamations from time to time—well written, it is true, affluent in truth, and abounding with wholesome advice—yet at the same time exasperating in their nature, and always entirely failing in their object. One of these proclamations generally followed every victory gained by the Americans, and reached the enemy while yet sore under the effects of recent discomfiture. More unbefitting seasons could not have been chosen thus to address one of the most haughty and arrogant races of the earth, and it is more a matter of surprise that such appeals were made than that the Mexicans would neither hear nor heed offers so mortifying to their self-pride. The hope was of course entertained that there was a large party in Mexico anxious to make peace with the United States, but even this was never proved. That there were a few wealthy men in the country opposed to the war is doubtless true; their opposition, however, was of a nature so purely selfish that they did not dare avow themselves openly, and one great effect of the peace manifestoes and proclamations was to procrastinate the war up to a moment when the enemy were really unable longer to continue the struggle.

The policy of the home government, so long and so zealously persisted in, may have had its effect upon General Scott's action after the battle of Churubusco. The victories of the morning of the 20th of August, achieved over such superior numbers, and opening, as they did, the gates of the Mexican capital to his soldiers, would, he doubtless thought be highly gratifying to the American people at large, and the news of these brilliant successes, followed by a treaty of peace, would be hailed by the entire nation with joy and acclamation. Such a consummation was worth something to effect—the thanks of a grateful people to one ambitious of political distinction, mingled with the proud satisfaction of having earned them, General Scott, or any other man in his position, would hazard much to obtain—and hence the excuse for the halt of his victorious army outside the city when it was virtually taken, the after armistice, and unsuccessful attempts to procure the settlement of peace. . . .

Had not General Scott considered the chances of obtaining peace as highly favorable, he would not have relinquished the immense military advantage the immediate possession of the capital would have given him—would not have allowed his enemy to retain a position where he could so easily organize new resistance. . . . General Scott resigned every advantage the victories of Contreras and Churubusco had given him, and threw into the hands of his wily and unprincipled adversary the only weapon he could wield with the least hope of success—that of diplomacy.[87]

An opposite argument, defending and indeed praising Scott for the Tacubaya armistice, was written by one of his brilliant young engineers, Maj. Isaac Ingalls Stevens (later Major General of Volunteers, killed at the Battle of Chantilly in 1862), in a review of the war published in 1851:

This armistice is the subject of severe animadversion . . . and Gen. Scott is held up as endangering the safety and sacrificing the lives of his gallant troops for the selfish object of winning popular favor and reaching the grand object of his life—the Presidency.

We deem this a most unjust and illiberal view of the whole transaction. It requires but a very cursory examination of the page of history to learn that almost all the treaties of peace, resulting from the issue of arms, have first been preceded by an armistice, and this armistice has not unfrequently been proposed by the victorious party. An armistice is a least a most desirable preliminary to a treaty of peace, though not absolutely essential. . . . It will not be denied that our government and people were exceedingly anxious to bring difficulties to a close. Every one was looking to the campaign of Scott to conquer a peace. This expression was in everybody's mouth. Peace was the great object desired by all, and more grateful to all than the most splendid achievements of arms. Is not this fact the simple, obvious explication of Gen. Scott's whole course? Was it not his plain and obvious duty to let no opportunity slip that should promise to secure the accomplishment of this object?

Personally, had he not more to gain by his triumphal entry into the magnificent city of the Astecs [sic], than by forbearing to enter for the sake of a peace, the negotiating of which was to redound to the honor of another?

The course pursued by General Scott in entering into the Tacubaya armistice will form one of the brightest pages of the history of our country. Through all time it can be referred to as convincing proof of the moderation, of the sincerity, and of the magnanimity of the government he represented. And when we consider the fact that Commissioners on both sides *did* meet, and that the negotiations at one time were all but successful; that Santa Anna himself had almost determined to sign the treaty, and that he deliberated long before he concluded to make a second appeal to arms, we consider General Scott to be entirely vindicated in his course.

We speak thus in general terms of the armistice. In reference to details, we think a mistake was made in not insisting upon the surrender of Chapultepec. But we do not consider this serious cause of censure, when we reflect, how utterly prostrate in the dust was the enemy, and how strong in himself and his gallant troops was the victorious General. . . . We have only to hope that in our future wars our armies shall have the guidance of a chief of equal skill and valor in the shock of battle, and of equal magnanimity to a conquered foe.[88]

BREAKDOWN OF THE ARMISTICE

The Tacubaya armistice, however interpreted, did not end the war. Within a few days after it was signed, incidents leading to charges of violation began to occur. Tensions mounted until, on September 7, Scott declared it to be abrogated. The next day, Worth attacked Molino del Rey, and "in nine short days, Santa Anna and his army were driven fugitives from that valley [of Mexico.]" From Scott's headquarters, Lt. Pierre Gustave Toutant Beauregard, of the engineers, scrawled into his diary cryptic notices of the incidents which occurred, from the signing of the armistice to the resumption of the war:

[August] 21 [1847]. We then marched to Tacubaya—Headquarters at the Bishop's Palace—. . . An armistice was then offered to Santa Ana [sic]. [August] 22. The day was passed in discussing the terms of the armistice—Genls. Quitman—Smith & Pierce on our side & Gen. Mora[89] & [Quijano?][90] on the side of the Mexicans. [August] 23—The same as on 22d. [August] 24—The armistice was concluded & signed this day. The object being to enable Mr. Trist to enter into negociations with Mex. Commissioners. [August] 25—The Mex.—Coms.—were Genl. Mora—2—3 [sic, Quijano]. [August] 26—Mr.

PLATE XXIII. Assault at Contreras

PLATE XXIV. *Battle of Molino del Rey*

Trist went this day into the city to treat with the Commisrs. A train of wagons were sent also to bring out money, provisions &c—but not allowed to enter on acct. of Capt. Wayne[91] going in uniform. Santa Anna sending an apology.

[August] 27.—The wagons entered the city but were no sooner in than a mob commenced stoning the waggons killing & wounding several, the authorities being unable to quell the mob, Santa Anna sending again an apology.

[August] 28.—The wagons were not this day sent in but arrangements were made for bringing out the money & provisions, only a small amt. of the former was brought out.

[August] 29.—Another arrangement was made to bring out these articles in boats to Mexicalcingo but nothing was done on this subject, except a little at night. The army is this day out of provisions, except flour & fresh beef. The whole thing appears to be a humbug & stronger measures will soon have to be adopted.

[August] 30.—Everything still in the same condition. Rumours of every description afloat considerable difficulty is experienced in getting out provisions from the city. This day a train of mules was sent in under Mr. Argon's [sic Aragon] direction & brought some out with some money. Sent off a letter.

[August] 31.—Things bear the same appearance. The Engr. officers were sent out to make a survey of the battlefield.

Sept. 1st.—The survey was this day concluded. The peace stock is on the rise. [September] 2d.—Things bear still the same appearance. The armistice not being very strictly kept by the Mexicans. The authorities sending in daily apologies. [September] 3d.—Genl. Scott has this day removed his h-q- from the bishop's palace to the Square in the town, & dined at our house. The armistice continues to be broken by the enemy, & daily apologies sent. [September] 4.—The Genl. & Mr. Trist continue to be sanguine of peace but the whole thing seems to be a humbug. [September] 5.—The same as yesterday. [September] 6.—News has this day come in that the authorities sanction the violation of the armistice. Working night & day with strong forces on the works of Chapultepec, Tacubaya road, San Cosmo, [sic Cosme] & the Genl. has sent in to Genl. Santa Anna to inform that the truce would cease by tomorrow at 12 h m unless ample apology & satisfaction is given for said violation.

[September] 7th.—The apology was not given & the armistice was ended at 12 h, & preparations were made for an attack on the Molino de los Reyes near Chapultepec. We were ordered to commence our reconnaissance. I was ordered to go with Genl. Pillow to make a night reconnaissance about Piedad & the Gerita [sic] of San Antonio— a d-d humbug.[92]

MOLINO DEL REY

Beauregard's diary for September 8 began with the laconic remark that "Genl. Worth attacked the Molino & carried it after a severe loss of officers & men." The Molino del Rey, less than a mile northwest of Tacubaya, was a group of stone buildings, including one used for a flour mill and another for a foundry; a half mile farther to the northwest was Casa Mata, which at one time had been a powder magazine. Santa Anna decided to anchor part of his force on this complex, and to key his defense of Mexico City upon it and the Castle of Chapultepec, half a mile to the east of the Molino. The Battle of Molino del Rey, September 8, has been called the "most dreadful shock of arms of the whole war." When, after its capture, the foundry was found to contain no machinery for the boring of cannon, the American troops withdrew. It had been, for all of its cost, a partial attack; a full commitment of Scott's army (six brigades instead of three) might have resulted in the immediate capture of Chapultepec. Lt. Raphael Semmes, with Scott's army, later wrote a colorful and factually accurate account, although he was biased against Scott:

The reconnoissances of the engineers showed that the enemy's left rested on a group of strong stone buildings (El Molino), at the western slope of Chapultepec and about half a mile from the base of the hill; that the right of his line rested on another stone building, called Casa-Mata . . . situated at the foot of the ridge, that slopes gradually down from the heights above the village of Tacubaya to the plain below, and distant from the first building about one-third of a mile; that these two buildings were more or less connected by irregular dikes, planted with the maguey, affording excellent cover for infantry; and that the enemy's field-battery occupied a position, midway between the two buildings, supported by infantry on either flank, lying *perdue* behind the dikes. Both Molino del Rey and Casa Mata were filled with infantry, the long *azotea* of the Molino, in particular, affording them an excellent position from which to pick off our troops as they advanced.

The military reader perceives of course, that the weak point of the enemy's position, as here described, was his center. Worth's order of battle was as follows:—Garland's brigade was ordered to take position on the right (our right), strengthened by two pieces of Drum's battery, to look to El Molino, as well as to any support which might be attempted to be sent to this position from Chapultepec, under whose guns it partially was. This brigade was to place itself also so as to be within supporting distance of Huger's battery,[93] of twenty-four-pounders, which was directed to take position on a ridge between Tacubaya and El Molino within about six hundred yards of the latter, which it was designed to shake somewhat previous to the assault. An assaulting party of five hundred picked men and officers under Major Wright, of the 8th infantry (Worth's own regiment), was posted on the ridge, to the left of the battering guns, to force the enemy's center. McIntosh's brigade (Colonel Clarke,[94] its regular commander, being sick), with Duncan's battery was assigned to a position still farther to the left, opposite the enemy's right, to look to our left flank, to sustain the assaulting column of Wright,[95] if necessary, or to attack the enemy himself (the ground being favorable), as circumstances might require. Thus, to recapitulate briefly, the enemy's left, center, and right, were opposed respectively by Garland, Wright, and McIntosh;[96] Huger being with Garland and Duncan with McIntosh. Cadwallader's brigade was held in reserve in the rear of our line and within easy supporting distance of any part of it. . . .

We were astir, at headquarters, at half-past two A.M. on the morning of the memorable 8th [of September], and the various columns being reported ready, they were put in motion at about three, on their respective routes. It was not yet light, as we moved out of Tacubaya; but the troops took up their positions, with the utmost precision according to the order of battle without the slightest mistake being made. We of the staff rode along in silence, the general only exchanging an occasional word with the engineer as to the route;

we seemed to have a sort of presentiment of the bloody tragedy which was to be enacted. The night was perfectly clear, but without moon, and the sun afterward rose in all his glory, over the battle field to light up the work of carnage and death.

At the earliest appearance of dawn in the east, Huger opened with his heavy pieces, which, for awhile, gave forth the only sounds that broke in upon the perfect silence of the field. Chapultepec seemed fast asleep, and it was some minutes before it could be aroused into returning our fire. When Huger had fired a few rounds at Molino, and this place was supposed to be somewhat shaken, Wright, with his storming party—under the guidance of Mason and Foster[97]—rushed gallantly forward to assault and pierce the enemy's center. He was met by a most appalling fire of musketry, and grape and canister, which at once revealed to General Worth the formidable numbers he had opposed to him. Nothing daunted, however, he rushed on, driving infantry and artillerymen, at the point of the bayonet, but at terrible loss. The ground, as before remarked, formed a gradual slope down the enemy's lines, and it was down this slope (forming a slightly inclined plane) that our brave fellows were compelled to march without so much as a twig to shelter them; while the enemy lay concealed behind the dikes and maguey plants, or was protected by the walls and parapets (around the azotea) of the Molino.

The enemy's field-battery was taken and the guns immediately trained upon his retreating masses. Before, however, they could be discharged, the enemy, perceiving that he had been dispossessed of this strong position by a mere handful of men, rallied and returned to the charge, aided by a tremendous fire of musketry from the troops in and on the top of the Molino—within pistol shot. Eleven out of the fourteen officers who composed the command —the gallant major and his two engineers among the number—were shot down by this murderous fire; and the rank and file suffered in proportion. The remainder were of necessity driven back, and the enemy regained possession of his pieces, bayoneting the wounded with a savage delight! This was a critical moment with us. . . . [Worth] did not once think of falling back . . but ordered Smith's light battalion[98]—which had been so terribly cut up at Churubusco, and was now under the command of Captain Kirby Smith, the gallant lieutenant-colonel being sick—and the right wing of Cadwallader's brigade to advance promptly to the support of the repulsed storming party. This order was executed in gallant style, and the enemy (being now hard pressed by Garland on his left) gave way in the center, and his battery was captured a second time.

In the meantime, Garland's brigade, sustained by the battery of the gallant Captain Drum, assaulted the enemy's left, and after an obstinate and severe contest drove him from the strong works of the Molino. The battering guns under Captain Huger were now advanced to the captured position, and were opened, together with the enemy's own guns, on his broken and retreating forces. While these operations were progressing on the enemy's left and center, Duncan's battery opened on his right, and the 2d brigade, under McIntosh, was ordered forward to the assault of this point. The direction of this brigade soon caused it to mask Duncan's battery—the fire of which, for a moment, was discontinued—and the brigade moved steadily on to the assault of the Casa-Mata, which instead of being an ordinary stone house, as had

MOLINO DEL REY

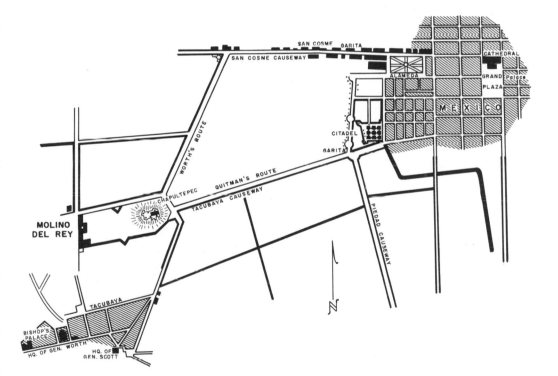

been supposed by the engineers, proved to be a citadel, surrounded with bastion intrenchments and impassable ditches—an old Spanish work, recently repaired and enlarged. The reconnoissance had been as close as possible, and this mistake as to the character of the work had been unavoidable—the work being situated in low ground and the lower portions of it being masked by dikes and maguey plants.

While McIntosh was moving forward to assault this formidable work, a large body of cavalry (it afterward appeared from the official reports of the enemy, that there were four thousand of them, under Alvarez)[99] was seen approaching us on our extreme left, as with a view of charging us on that flank, or endeavoring to turn and envelop that position. As soon as Duncan's battery was masked, as before described, by the interposition of McIntosh's brigade between him and the Casa-Mata, he was ordered to change front, to hold the enemy's cavalry in check, which he did rapidly, moving a little farther to the left. The Voltigeurs, under Colonel Andrews,[100] were sent to support him; and Major Sumner[101] with his two hundred and seventy dragoons was ordered also to place himself in position near by, to profit by events, and pursue, if opportunity should invite, the enemy's retreating forces.

In taking up this position, the gallant major, in order to avoid some ditches which impeded his march, was forced to pass within pistol shot of the Casa-Mata, when [sic, where] his command suffered considerably; the enemy knocking several of his dragoons from the saddle, and the affrighted and wounded horses careering wildly over the field. One of the enemy's brigades (two thousand, under Alvarez himself) moved boldly forward (Duncan purposely withholding his fire to invite it) until it had come within good canister range, when the gallant lieutenant-colonel opened upon it one of those exceedingly rapid and terrible fires for which his battery was so celebrated. The enemy could not withstand the shock, but was first checked, and then thrown into confusion, the front of his column recoiling in disorder upon its center, and this again upon its rear, until the whole mass commenced a disorderly retreat. The 2d brigade, under Andrada [sic], which[102] was forming to support Alvarez, was involved in the disorder and retreat of the 1st, and the whole four thousand horse disappeared from the field. While Duncan was in the midst of these operations, General Worth dispatched an aid-de-camp to him, to direct him to be "sure to hold the enemy's cavalry in check". . . .

Let us now return to McIntosh, whom we left advancing upon the Casa Mata. As his gallant brigade came within easy musket range, the enemy opened a most destructive fire upon him, cutting down officers and men in fearful profusion. But McIntosh was a man whom danger never daunted, and he moved on amid this storm of balls until he was cut down mortally wounded. The brigade, under the lead of the gallant Martin Scott,[103] continued on, however, until it reached the very slope of the parapet that surrounded the citadel. By this time Scott himself was shot dead; his next in command, Major Waite,[104] was knocked down, badly wounded, and a large proportion of the gallant fellows were destroyed. A momentary recoil, and some disorder ensued, and the *remainder* of the brigade now fell back for support upon Duncan's battery, which, having repulsed the enemy's horse . . had by this time returned to its former position. Duncan being now at liberty to renew his fire opened again upon the Casa-Mata . . . and in a few minutes thereafter we had the satisfaction of seeing the enemy abandon this stronghold. . . . Upon reaching the Molino, which was no molino—mill— at all, no vestige could be found of furnace, tools, or any other apparatus for the casting of cannon. . . .

Having been directed to withdraw our troops to Tacubaya, wagons were sent for, and the mournful task was commenced of collecting our dead and wounded, which occupied us for several hours—the enemy, all the while firing at us from Chapultepec.[105]

ASSAULT UPON CHAPULTEPEC

After the fight at Molino del Rey, the Castle of Chapultepec still stood between the invading army and Mexico City. During the night of September 11, Scott's artillery began its bombardment of the 200-foot-high castle; the Mexican artillery men replied with effect. On the hill, the military college suffered considerable damage, and some of the Mexican batteries were knocked out. But, on September 12, Scott realized Chapultepec could be carried only by assault. While the troops of Quitman and Pillow attacked from the west, a storming party led by Captain Casey[106] (supported by other elements), struck from the southern approaches. By nine thirty in the morning, Chapultepec had fallen. Scott's official report was criticized by some of the regular army officers because it seemed to them to give too much prominence to the volunteers of Quitman and Pillow. Nevertheless, it was a comprehensive, well-written, and lucid account of the complex storming operations:

The victory of the 8th at the Molinos del Rey was followed by daring reconnoissances on the part of our distinguished engineers—Captain Lee, Lieutenants Beauregard, Stevens, and Tower—Major Smith, senior,[107] being sick, and Captain Mason, third in rank, wounded. Their operations were directed principally to the south, towards the gates of Piedad, San Angel (Niño Perdido), San Antonio, and the Paseo de la Viga.

This city stands on a slight swell of ground near the centre of an irregular basin, and is girdled with a ditch in its greater extent—a navigable canal of great breadth and depth—very difficult to bridge in the presence of an enemy, and serving at once for drainage, custom-house purposes, and military defence; leaving eight entrances or gates over arches, each of which we found defended by a system of strong works that seemed to require nothing but some men and guns to be impregnable.

Outside, and within the cross-fires of those gates, we found to the south other obstacles but little less formidable. All the approaches near the city are over elevated causeways, cut in many places (to oppose us) and flanked on both sides by ditches, also of unusual dimensions. The numerous cross-roads are flanked in like manner, having bridges at the intersections recently broken. The meadows thus chequered are, moreover, in many spots under water or marshy; for, it will be remembered, we were in the midst of the wet season though with less rain than usual, and we could not wait for the fall of the neighboring lakes and the consequent drainage of the wet grounds at the edge of the city—the lowest in the whole basin.

After a close personal survey of the southern gates, covered by Pillow's division and Riley's brigade of Twiggs', with four times our numbers concentrated in our immediate front, I determined on the 11th to avoid that net-work of obstacles, and to seek by a sudden inversion to the southwest and west less unfavorable approaches.

To economize the lives of our gallant officers and men, as well as to insure success, it became indispensable that this resolution should be long masked from the enemy; and again, that the new movement when discovered should be mistaken for a feint, and the old as indicating our true and ultimate point of attack.

Accordingly, on the spot, the 11th, I ordered Quitman's division from Coyoacan to join Pillow *by day light* before the southern gates, and then that the two major generals, with their divisions, should *by night* proceed (two miles) to join me at Tacubaya, where I was quartered with Worth's division. Twiggs, with Riley's brigade and Captain Taylor's and Steptoe's field batteries—the latter of 12-pounders—was left in front of those gates to manoeuvre, to threaten, or to make false attacks in order to occupy or deceive the enemy. Twiggs's other brigade (Smith's) was left at supporting distance in the rear, at San Angel, till the morning of the 13th, and also to support our general depot at Mixcoac. The stratagem against the south was admirably executed throughout the 12th and down to the afternoon of the 13th, when it was too late for the enemy to recover from the effects of his delusion.

The first step in the new movement was to carry Chapultepec, a natural and isolated mound of great elevation, strongly fortified at its base, on its acclivities and heights. Besides a numerous garrison, here was the military college of the republic, with a large number of sub-lieutenants and other students. Those works were within direct gun-shot of the village of Tacubaya, and until carried we could not approach the city on the west without making a circuit too wide and too hazardous.

PLATE XXV. *Storming of Chapultepec*

PLATE XXVI. Scott's Army Storming the Castle of Chapultepec

In the course of the same night (that of the 11th) heavy batteries within easy ranges were established. . . .

To prepare for an assault, it was foreseen that the play of the batteries might run into the second day; but recent captures had not only trebled our seige [sic] pieces, but also our ammunition; and we knew that we should greatly augment both by carrying the place. I was, therefore, in no haste in ordering an assault before the works were well crippled by our missiles.

The bombardment and cannonade, under the direction of Captain Huger, were commenced early in the morning of the 12th. Before nightfall, which necessarily stopped our batteries, we had perceived that a good impression had been made on the castle and its outworks, and that a large body of the enemy had remained outside, towards the city, from an early hour to avoid our fire, and to be at hand on its cessation in order to reinforce the garrison against an assault. The same outside force was discovered the next morning, after our batteries had reopened upon the castle, by which we again reduced its garrison to the *minimum* needed for the guns.

Pillow and Quitman had been in position since early in the night of the 11th. Major General Worth was now ordered to hold his division in reserve, near the foundry, to support Pillow; and Brigadier General Smith, of Twiggs's division, had just arrived with his brigade from Piedad (2 miles), to support Quitman. Twiggs's guns, before the southern gates, again reminded us, as the day before, that he with Riley's brigade and Taylor's and Steptoe's batteries was in activity, threatening the southern gates, and there holding a great part of the Mexican army on the defensive.

Worth's division furnished Pillow's attack with an assaulting party of some 250 volunteer officers and men, under Capt. McKenzie,[108] of the 2d artillery; and Twiggs's division supplied a similar one, commanded by Captain Casey, 2d infantry, to Quitman. Each of those little columns was furnished with scaling ladders.

The signal I had appointed for the attack was the momentary cessation of fire on the part of our heavy batteries. About eight o'clock in the morning of the 13th, judging that the time had arrived by the effect of the missiles we had thrown, I sent an aid-de-camp to Pillow, and another to Quitman, with notice that the concerted signal was about to be given. Both columns now advanced with an alacrity that gave assurance of prompt success. The batteries, seizing opportunities, threw shots and shells upon the enemy over the heads of our men with good effect, particularly at every attempt to reinforce the works from without to meet our assault.

Major General Pillow's approach, on the west side, lay through an open grove filled with sharp shooters who were speedily dislodged; when, being up with the front of the attack, and emerging into open space at the foot of a rocky acclivity, that gallant leader was struck down by an agonizing wound.

The immediate command devolved on Brigadier General Cadwalader in the absence of the senior brigadier (Pierce) of the same division—an invalid since the events of August 19.[109] On a previous call of Pillow, Worth had just sent him a reinforcement—Colonel Clark's [sic] brigade.[110]

The broken acclivity was still to be ascended, and a strong redoubt, midway, to be carried, before reaching the castle on the heights. The advance of our brave men, led by brave officers, though necessarily slow, was unwavering, over rocks, chasms, and mines, and under the hottest fire of cannon and musketry. The redoubt now yielded to resistless valor, and the shouts that followed announced to the castle the fate that impended. The enemy were steadily driven from shelter to shelter. The retreat allowed not [sic, no] time to fire a single mine without the certainty of blowing up friend and foe. Those who at a distance attempted to apply matches to the long trains were shot down by our men. There was death below as well as above ground. At length the ditch and wall of the main work were reached; the scaling-ladders were brought up and planted by the storming parties; some of the daring spirits first in the assault were cast down—killed or wounded; but a lodgment was soon made; streams of heroes followed; all opposition was overcome, and several of the regimental colors flung out from the upper walls, amidst long-continued shouts and cheers, which sent dismay into the capital. No scene could have been more animating or glorious.

Major General Quitman, nobly supported by Brigadier Generals Shields and Smith (P. F.), his other officers and men, was up with the part assigned him. Simultaneously with the movement on the west, he had gallantly approached the southeast of the same works over a causeway with cuts and batteries, and defended by an army strongly posted outside to the east of the works. Those formidable obstacles Quitman had to face with but little shelter for his troops or space for manoeuvring. Deep ditches, flanking the causeway, made it difficult to cross on either side into the adjoining meadows, and these again were intersected by other ditches. Smith and his brigade had been early thrown out to make a sweep to the right in order to present a front against the enemy's line (outside), and to turn two intervening batteries near the foot of Chapultepec.

This movement was also intended to support Quitman's storming parties, both on the causeway. The first of these, furnished by Twiggs's division, was commanded in succession by Capt. Casey, 2d infantry, and Captain Paul,[111] 7th infantry, after Casey had been severely wounded; and the second, originally under the gallant Major Twiggs, marine corps, killed, and then Captain Miller,[112] 2d Pennsylvania volunteers. The storming party, now commanded by Captain Paul, seconded by Captain Roberts[113] of the rifles, Lieutenant Stewart [sic],[114] and others of the same regiment, Smith's brigade, carried the two batteries in the road, took some guns with many prisoners, and drove

Chapultepec

the enemy posted behind in support. The New York and South Carolina volunteers (Shields' brigade) and the 2d Pennsylvania volunteers, all on the left of Quitman's line, together with portions of the storming parties, crossed the meadows in front, under a heavy fire, and entered the outer enclosure of Chapultepec just in time to join in the final assault from the west.[115]

A close-up description by a member of Casey's storming party was written in the journal of Daniel Harvey Hill:

We are now in the City of Mexico after a hard day's fight on yesterday. On the evening of the 11th we returned to La Piedad and I got a quiet night's rest. We heard that night that Chapultepec was to be the real point of attack and that a feint was to be made on the Niño Perdido causeway. Long before dawn on the morning of the 12th our whole Division was under arms (Smith's brigade having come up the night before), and Steptoe's Battery began to fire about daylight on the works near the Niño Perdido. This was intended to be a feint or diversion whilst the real attack was made against the Fortress of Chapultepec. It proved to be a most abortive diversion indeed. Our troops should have been displayed along the causeway at every cost so as to make the enemy believe that we meditated an attack upon the works at Candelaria.[116] Instead of which we were kept carefully concealed lest forsooth we should be injured by the enemy's artillery. The whole object of the diversion was defeated by the too great caution of Genl. Twiggs. We lost but one man by the cannonade and as we afterward learned the loss of the enemy was also trifling, not exceeding three or four killed and a few wounded. At first the enemy was deceived by our feint and large bodies of Infantry & Cavalry hastened from other points to strengthen the position of Candelaria, but discovering that the calibre of Steptoe's Battery was light and seeing that no Infantry was displayed they began to suspect a trick. In the course of half an hour, our heavy batteries opened upon Chapultepec and then all the enemy's reinforcements for Candelaria were marched off towards that point in the greatest haste.

During the most of the day, our Division was kept under arms & we were for want of better occupation idly looking at the bombardment of the Castle of Chapultepec. We all felt satisfied that the building was rendered untenable but knew that there was too much shelter behind the walls that encircled the hill and under the projection of the hill itself for the enemy to have sustained much injury. Affairs now looked dark and gloomy in the extreme. Chapultepec was regarded to be impregnable and the Engineers thought it madness to attempt the storming of Candelaria. There was deep depression among us also, the fruitless victory of the 8th, attended with the loss of so many of our best officers and men had a very dispiriting influence upon us all and in a great degree destroyed our confidence in our Commanders.

That evening a call was made for a storming party from our Division to consist of 13 officers and 250 men. This body was to cooperate with a similar corps selected from Genl. Worth's Division. These parties to be sustained by several Regiments of Volunteers and raw levies under the command of Genls. Pillow, Quitman & Shields. As the leading storming party "the forlorn hope" was expected to suffer very much and strong incentives were held out to induce us to volunteer. To the officers were promised an additional grade by brevet, to sergeants, commissions as second Lieutenants, to corporals, promotion to sergeancies, to privates that their names should be borne on the regimental books forever and to receive pecuniary rewards also. I volunteered & was placed in command of the detachment from the 4th Artillery consisting of thirty as gallant spirits as ever breathed. We left La Piedad about 5 P.M. on the 12th, the whole storming party from our division under command of Capt. Casey, 2d Infantry. On reaching Tacubaya we were supplied with pickaxes and scaling ladders and then at a late hour we got into quarters within short range of the enemy's guns.

Early on the morning of the 13th, we advanced down the main road to attack the Fortress in front whilst the storming party from Genl. Worth's

Division attacked it in rear. A very strong building used as a Military College placed upon a very rugged, steep hill surrounded by two thick walls twelve feet high and defended by strong works in front constituted the famous Fortress of Chapultepec. Our column of attack had moved but a short distance down the main road when we were exposed to a heavy fire of Artillery & escopotery, which we were unable to return with effect, from their concealed position and from the shorter range of our arms. Capt. Casey was wounded early in the action and the command of our storming party devolved upon Capt. Paul, 7th Infantry. An attempt was now made to turn the enemy's batteries by the left but owing to some misunderstanding, we who were leading were not followed by a sufficient number of our men to carry the plan into execution. We then returned and the officers of our party endeavored in vain to get the supporting column of Marines to aid us in charging the advanced batteries of the enemy. We then dashed forward along the road and drove the Mexicans before us with great slaughter. The other storming party had in the meanwhile gained the height from the opposite side and when we entered the enemy's advanced works, the Stars and Stripes were flying from the highest point of the Castle.

The havoc among the Mexicans was now horrible in the extreme. Pent up between two fires they had but one way to escape and all crowded toward it like a flock of sheep. I saw dozens hanging from the walls and creeping through holes made for the passage of water & whilst in this position were shot down without making the least resistance. Our men were shouting give no quarters "to the treacherous scoundrels" and as far as I could observe none was asked by the Mexicans. I collected my little party and for more than a mile was far in advance of all our troops in the chase of the enemy. They frequently formed across the road, but a few well directed shots from my little party put them promptly to flight again. 'Twas a sublime and exalted feeling that which we experienced whilst chasing some five thousand men with but little more than a dozen. Capt. Magruder's Battery at length came up and was supported by my party and a detachment of the 14th Infantry under Lieut. Morgan [117] and a detachment of the storming party under Lt. Bee,[118] 3d Infantry. The Lancers attempted to charge upon the Battery but were repulsed by a few rounds of grape and cannister. After we had pursued the enemy a mile & [a] half when the Division of Genl. Worth arrived and then hearing that the storming party had been recalled, Lt. Bee and myself returned to our respective Regiments.

The storming of Chapultepec is looked upon as the most brilliant operation of the whole war. The enemy was in the strongest position he has ever occupied and was twelve thousand strong with ten pieces of cannon, the whole force being under command of Santa Anna in person. The two storming parties consisted of two hundred & fifty men each and the supporting column was near two thousand strong. This column from what I saw & have since heard must have behaved badly, the Marines I know did so.[119] The enemy's loss was 1,000 killed and wounded and some 500 prisoners. Among these latter were Generals Bravo[120] & [Monterde?].[121] The whole of our Army I understand as well as the whole of the Mexican not engaged in the fight were looking on with almost breathless interest during the hour & a half that the bloody struggle lasted. All felt that upon its issue depended the triumph or defeat of the American arms, the fate of the campaign & the gain or loss of the grand City of Mexico. The enemy fought under the dispiritment caused by a guilty conscience from the consciousness of breach of faith & by the remembrance of so many defeats. We on the contrary were sustained by a sense of the uniform rectitude of our conduct & were encouraged by the prestige of so many victories.[122]

Via the Causeways into Mexico City

From Chapultepec, two roads led into the City of Mexico. The most direct of these routes was the Tacubaya causeway which passed through the garita of Belén some two miles away. An aqueduct ran down the center of the causeway, with a carriage road on either side of it. The causeway was a "high and massive stone structure." The other road, more circuitous than the Tacubaya causeway, entered the city through the suburb and garita of San Cosmé. It was along these two causeways that Scott's army advanced immediately after the capture of Chapultepec. There was still fighting to be done as the invaders pushed into the City. George W. Kendall in Mexico City reported this final action of the campaign to the New Orleans Picayune:

Another victory, glorious in its results and which has thrown additional lustre upon the American arms, has been achieved to-day by the army under Gen. Scott. The proud capital of Mexico has fallen into the power of a mere handful of men compared with the immense odds arrayed against them, and Santa Anna, instead of shedding his blood as he had promised, is wandering with the remnant of his army no one knows whither. . . .

Gen. Quitman, supported by Gen. Smith's brigade, took the road by the Chapultepec aqueduct towards the Belén gate and the Ciudadela; Gen. Worth, supported by Gen. Cadwalader's brigade, advanced by the San Cosme aqueduct towards the garita of that name. Both rout[e]s were cut up by ditches and defended by breastworks, barricades, and strong works of every description known to military science; yet the daring and impetuosity of our men overcame one defence after another, and by nightfall every work to the city's edge was carried. Gen. Quitman's command, after the rout at Chapultepec, was the first to encounter the enemy in force.

PLATE XXVII. Castle of Chapultepec

PLATE XXVIII. Attack on the City of Mexico

Midway between the former and the Belén gate, Santa Anna had constructed a strong work; but this was at once vigorously assaulted by Gen. Quitman, and aided by a flank fire from two of Duncan's guns, which Gen. Worth had ordered to approach as near as possible from the San Cosme road, the enemy was again routed and in full flight. They again made a stand from their strong fortifications at and near the Belén garita, opening a tremendous fire not only of round shot, grape, and shell, but of musketry; yet boldly Gen. Quitman advanced, stormed and carried the works, although at great loss, and then every point on this side of the city was in our possession. In this onslaught two of our bravest officers were killed—Capt. Drum and Lieut. Benjamin.[123]

Meanwhile Gen. Worth was rapidly advancing upon San Cosmé. At the English burying ground the enemy had constructed a strong work. It was defended by infantry for a short time, but could not resist the assault of our men. The affrighted Mexicans soon fled to another line of works nearer the city, and thus Gen. Worth was in possession of the entrance to San Cosmé. As his men advanced towards the garita, the enemy opened a heavy fire of musketry from the house tops, as well as of grape, cannister, and shell from their batteries, thus sweeping the street completely. At this juncture the old Monterey game, of burrowing and digging through the houses, was adopted. On the right, as our men faced the enemy, the aqueduct afforded a partial shelter; on the left, the houses gave some protection; but many were still killed or wounded by the grape which swept every part, as well as by the shells which were continually bursting in every direction. About 3 o'clock the work of the pick-axe and the crow-bar, under the direction of Lieut. G. W. Smith, of the sappers and miners, had fairly commenced, and every minute brought our men nearer the enemy's last stronghold.

In the meantime two mountain howitzers were fairly lifted to the top of one of the houses and into the cupulo [sic] of the church, from which they opened a plunging and most effective fire, while one of Duncan's guns, in charge of Lieut. Hunt,[124] was run up under a galling fire to a deserted breastwork, and at once opened upon the garita. In this latter daring feat, four men out of eight were either killed or wounded, but still the piece was most effectively served. The work of the miners was still going on. In one house which they had entered, by the pick-axe, a favorite aid[e] of Santa Anna's was found. That great man had just fled, but had left his friend and his supper! Both were well cared for—the latter was devoured by our hungry officers; the former, after doing the honors of the table, was made a close prisoner. Just as dark was setting in, our men had dug and mined their way almost up to the very guns of the enemy, and now, after a short struggle, they were completely routed and driven [out] with the loss of everything. The command of the city by the San Cosmé route was attained.

During the night Gen. Quitman commenced the work of throwing up breastworks and erecting batteries, with the intention of opening a heavy cannonade upon the Ciudadela with the first light this morning. At 10 o'clock at night Gen. Worth ordered Capt. Huger to bring up a 24-pounder and a 10-inch mortar to the garita or gate of San Cosmé, and having ascertained the bearings and distance of the grand plaza and palace, at once opened upon those points. The heavy shells were heard to explode in the very heart of the city. At a little after midnight Major Palacios, accompanied by two or three members of the municipal council of the city, arrived at Gen. Worth's headquarters, and in great trepidation informed him that Santa Anna and his grand army had fled, and that they wished at once to surrender the capital! They were referred to the commander-in-chief, and immediately started for Tacubaya; but in the mean time the firing upon the town ceased.

At 7 o'clock this morning Gen. Scott, with his staff, rode in and took quarters in the national palace, on the top of which the regimental flag of the gallant rifles and the stars and stripes were already flying, and an immense crowd of blanketed leperos, the scum of the capital, were congregated in the plaza as the commander-in-chief entered it. They pressed our soldiers, and eyed them as though they were beings of another world. So much were they in the way, and with such eagerness did they press around, that Gen. Scott was compelled to order our Dragoons to clear the plaza. They were told, however, not to injure or harm a man in the mob—they were all our friends.

About five minutes after this, and while Gen. Worth was returning to his division near the Alameda, he was fired upon from a house near the Convent of San Francisco. Some of the cowardly Polkas [sic],[125] who had fled the day previous without discharging their guns, now commenced the assassin game of shooting at every one of our men they saw, from windows, as well as from behind the parapets on the azoteas or tops of the houses. In half an hour's time our good friends, the leperos, in the neighborhood of the hospital of San Andres and the church of Santa Clara, also commenced discharging muskets and throwing bottles and rocks from the azoteas. I have neglected to mention that just previous to this Col. Garland had been severely wounded by a musket, fired by some miscreant from a window.

For several hours this cowardly war upon our men continued, and during this time many were killed or wounded. It was in this species of fighting that Lieut. Sidney Smith[126] received his death wound. The division of Gen. Twiggs in one part of the city, and Gen. Worth in another, were soon actively engaged in putting down the insurrection. Orders were given to shoot every man in all the houses from which the firing came, while the guns of the different light batteries swept the streets in all directions. As the assassins were driven from one house they would take refuge on another; but by the middle

Entrance of the Army into the Grand Plaza at Mexico City

of the afternoon they were all forced back to the barriers and suburbs. Many innocent persons have doubtless been killed during the day, but this could not be avoided. Had orders been given at the outset to blow up and demolish every house or church from which one man was fired upon, the disturbances would have been at once quelled.[127]

MEXICAN VERSION OF SCOTT'S ENTRADA

The Mexican version of events, from Molino del Rey to the American occupation of the capital was given in a letter from a merchant living in Mexico City to a Spanish commercial house in New York City. It was taken to Orizaba, and thence to Vera Cruz, where F. M. Dimond, the collector of the port, received it and forwarded it to the United States:

On the morning of the 14th, before day light, the enemy, with a part of his force, commenced his march upon the city.

Our soldiers, posted behind the arches of the aqueducts and several breast works which had been hastily thrown up, annoyed him so severely, together with the trenches which he had to bridge over, that he did not arrive at the gates until late in the afternoon. Here he halted and attempted to bombard the city, which he did during the balance of the day and the day following, doing immense damage. In some cases whole blocks were destroyed and a great number of men, women and children killed and wounded. The picture was awful. One deafening roar filled our ears, one cloud of smoke met our eyes, now and then mixed with flame, and amid it all we could hear the various shrieks of the wounded and dying. But the city bravely resisted the hundreds of flying shells. It hurled back defiance to the blood thirsty Yankee, and convinced him that his bombs could not reduce the Mexican capital.

The enemy then changed his plan, and determined to enter the city, where we prepared to meet him, having barricaded the streets with sand bags and provided on the house tops and at the windows all who could bear arms or hurl missiles, stones, bricks, &c., on the heads of the enemy. Before General Scott had fairly passed the gates he found the difficulty of his position. A perfect torrent of balls and stones rained upon his troops. Many were killed and more wounded. Still he kept advancing until he gained the entrance of two streets leading directly to the Plaza. Finding that he could not oppose himself to our soldiers, who were all posted out of sight, and that he was losing his men rapidly, Gen. Scott took possession of the convent of San Isidor, which extends back to the centre of a block, and at once set his sappers and miners to cutting a way directly through the blocks of buildings. In some instances whole houses were blown up to facilitate his progress; but after several hours he again emerged into the street, and finally regained the Plaza with great loss. On entering the Plaza a heavy fire was opened on him from the palace and cathedral, which were filled and covered with our patriotic troops. Finding himself thus assaulted, the enemy drew out his force in the Plaza and opened a cannonade on the palace and Cathedral, firing over one hundred shots, which did immense damage to the buildings and caused a severe loss of killed and wounded.

Seeing further resistance useless, our soldiers ceased firing, and on the 16th of September (sad day!) the enemy was in possession of the Mexican capital. Though we inflicted havoc and death upon the Yankees, we suffered greatly ourselves. Many were killed by the blowing up of the houses, many by the bombardment, but more by the confusion which prevailed in the city, and altogether we cannot count our killed, wounded and missing since the actions commenced yesterday at less than 4,000, among whom are many women and children. The enemy confesses a loss of over 1,000, it is no doubt much greater. What a calamity! But Mexico will yet have vengeance. God will avenge us for our sufferings.[128]

The Sacking of Huamantla

The capture of Mexico City insured the victory of the United States and made possible the Treaty of Guadalupe Hidalgo by which Mexico ceded five-twelfths of her territory. But the fighting was not quite finished by the occupation of the Mexican capital. Santa Anna fled from Mexico City with a remnant of his army and attempted to cut the supply line of Scott's army to Vera Cruz. His first move was to attack the American detachment left in Puebla—his futile attack there was to be known as the "siege of Puebla." Then, moving toward Perote from Puebla, he met a force commanded by Brig. Gen. Joseph Lane, and fought the Battle of Huamantla, in which he was again defeated. Huamantla was fought on October 9, 1847. Lt. William D. Wilkins,[129] 15th Infantry, wrote a perceptive account to his parents:

We left Jalapa on the morning of the 2nd of October. Our train was the largest that had ever went "up" since Gen. Scott marched from Vera Cruz. It consisted of a regiment of Volunteers from Ohio, another from Indiana, eight hundred recruits, commanded by Capt. Heintzleman [sic],[130] eight pieces of artillery, commanded by Lieut. Pratt, three cavalry companies, and our old train, commanded by Maj. Lally. The whole, about 4,000 strong, with a train of 200 waggons. The whole force was under the command of Brig. Genl. [Joseph] Lane of Indiana. . . . [At] the redoubtable fortress and miserable half ruined, gloomy town of Peroté . . we halted for a couple of days, for intelligence had arrived that Santa Anna had left Puebla, where he had for 28 days besieged Col. Childs, and reduced him to great extremities, and was waiting for us, with 8,000 men at the strong pass of El Peñal, 27 miles from Puebla. . . .

[At Peroté] we received a reinforcement of Col. Wynkoop's battalion, the celebrated Capt. [Samuel H.] Walker's Comp'y of mounted rangers, and three pieces of Artillery. Two days march brought us to the hacienda of Veragua, 12 miles from El Peñal. Here we received intelligence that Santa [Anna] had gone from the Pass to Huamantla, 6 miles off the road, with the intention of falling on our [rear] when the train was laboring through the Pass. Gen. Lane immediately decided to leave the train [where] it was, under guard of the Ohio Regt, and Capt. Heintzleman's command, and march, with the rest of [his] force, about 3,000 strong to meet Santa Anna.

We started on the morning of the 9th and it was a beautiful sight, as our long line drew up, in battle array, on the plain in front of the Hacienda. The banners of the different regiments were stripped of their coverings, and flung to the breeze, amidst resounding cheers, and as we moved off by platoons of companies the different brass bands discoursed most martial melody. I must confess I was affected by the scene and its concomitants, and felt savage enough to fight a legion of Mexicans single handed. At about noon we arrived in sight of Huamantla, a beautiful town, charmingly situated, with a population of about 8,000. As we drew near, a beautiful sight presented itself. We had taken Santa by surprise and he sent out 2,000 lancers to arrest us while he drew off his Artillery. They were beautifull[y] [un]iformed, handsomely mounted, and as their long line gallopped out of town, their long pennons and bright lances shining in the sun, drew up in line, and charged our van, we all held our breath with excitement.

Suddenly a small body of horse broke from our ranks, headed by a tall cavalier, and dashed like a thunderbolt into the midst of the glittering Mexicans. They wavered a moment, then broke, and fled in confusion into the town, followed by all our cavalry. It was Walker with his Rangers who performed this gallant feat, and with 80 men dispersed 2,000 lancers. Our cavalry followed them pell mell into the town, received a fire from six pieces of Artillery, charged upon and captured three of them (Walker cutting off the head of a Mexican officer who was about firing his piece), taking Col. La Vega (a brother of the Gen's.) Maj. Iturbide, an aide of Santa Anna's and two other officers prisoners, and driving the enemy from the Plaza. But this success was dearly purchased by the death [of] the gallant Walker, who fell, pierced by two escopette balls, whilst re-forming his Company in the [Plaza]. He was, in the opinion of all who knew him, the bravest and most dashing officer in our army, a perfect [MS torn here—word missing], a man who seemed to be devoid of fear, and who could and would lead his company against any opposing [force].

Meanwhile our Infantry proceeded on a smart run across the fields in front

PLATE XXIX. *General Scott Entering Mexico City*

PLATE XXX   *Death of Captain Walker at Huamantla*

of the city, hoping [to int]ercept the retreat of the Mexicans, and to cut off and capture the rest of their Artillery. But they had st[out?] legs for us, and got out of town a few minutes before we got in. We rushed up the streets to the [MS torn here—word missing] where we met Gen. Lane, who told us to "avenge the death of the gallant Walker, to break open [MS torn here—word missing] house, and take all we could lay hands on."

And well and fearfully was his mandate obeyed [by us]. Grog shops were broken open first, and then maddened with liquor every species of outrage was committed. Old women and girls were stripped of their clothing—and many suffered still greater outrages. Men were shot by dozens while concealing their property, churches, stores and dwelling houses ransacked. The [word illegible] run with shouts, screams, reports of fire arms and the crash of timber and glass as the troops batte[red] down the doors and windows. Even the streets were strewn with different articles which had be[en] thrown away to make room for more valuable plunder. The Plaza presented a singular sc[ene]. It had been beautiful, was surrounded by handsome buildings, encircled by a row of poplars, and a superb fountain playing in the centre. But now "Grim visaged War" had taken possession of it. Three or four large wagons filled with captured ammunition stood in the centre, and our troops were destroying the fragments and strewing them around the square. Dead horses and men lay about pretty thick, while drunken soldiers, yelling and screeching, were breaking open houses or chasing some poor Mexicans who had abandoned their houses and fled for life. Such a scene I never hope to see again. It gave me a lamentable view of human nature, stripped of all disguise and free from all restraint, and made [me] for the first time, ashamed of my country.

We left Huamantla late in the evening, and marched all [night] to our former encampment. And such a march. Half our men were drunk. . . . When we arrived in camp, near 200 men were missing, who lay along the road, unable from intoxication to move. However they were nearly all brought in the next day. The amount of plunder taken by our men was very large. One man took $1,500 in gold, and several men of my Comp'y had from 40 to 60 dollars apiece, besides silk, shawls, jewelry etc. During the fray, I captured a handsome pony, from which a Lancer had just been dismounted, and found a handsome mantle strapped to the saddle. These constitute all my plunder, but one of my brother officers has near $500 worth of gold plate. We left our camp on the 10th and, passing through El Peñal[131] (which is no great affair) arrived at Puebla on the 12th.[132]

Six days after the rape of Huamantla, Santa Anna resigned his command of the Mexican army. Except for minor actions and guerrilla warfare the fighting was over.

LIFE IN THE CAMPS

The story of the Mexican War is more than a retelling of the campaigns; it also was the chronicles of the soldiers in the camps. Lacking the spectacular, often filled with boredom, camp life nevertheless made up many experiences of the Gringo soldier, for like his G.I. descendant of later wars he too soon learned how to "hurry up and wait" in the camp routine. Not everything in the camps was dull, for experiences varied with time and place. Camp life in Ohio during the first flush of enthusiasm differed sharply from that on rain-sodden ground near New Orleans; encampment at tropical Tampico was a dissimilar experience from mountainous Santa Fe, as the lower Rio Grande contrasted to the idyllic setting near Monterey. The differences, moreover, were not only those of season and geography. Discipline was one thing under General Wool but quite another with Taylor in command. The camp of a regiment of regulars had a different tone from that of free and easy volunteers. Most importantly, men translated the same experiences in separate ways. Lt. George B. McClellan found a soldier's career the best of all possible lives, while Capt. John W. Lowe of Ohio wrote: " . . . never my children as you value your happiness, indulge the thought of being soldiers: the boys have to submit to everything that is hard, and virtue & morality are strangers to the camp . . . ."[1]

If there were differences there were also similarities. Certain themes recur. Wherever they might be, routine, drill, ennui, recreation, recollections of home, and complaints were characteristic of the camps. Sickness and death seldom were wholly absent—sacrifice, brutality, comradeship, hostility, laughter and anger all came out.

In the beginning most of the camps which mushroomed into being—at

272

Alton in Illinois, New Albany (Indiana), Louisville, Cincinnati, Nashville, and St. Louis, to name some of the more important—were primarily depots for the assembling of troops. Often they lacked adequate shelter and were even short of food. Rowdy recruits rampaged through nearby towns. After the barest rudiments of organization, they were moved on to Mexico.

General Scott's original intention was to hold the mass of recruits in training camps at healthy locations instead of sending them to the Rio Grande, where they would be of little value to Taylor and would suffer from disease. Taylor, in Scott's opinion, would not move out of the lower Rio Grande Valley until September or October 1846. But the term of enlistment was for only a year, and pressure from newspapers and politicians was strong for a forward movement of the army. The volunteers' ardor might cool in drawn-out training exercises. Camps of instruction, therefore, would be set up in Mexico, and serve also as convenient staging areas for the troops. At first these were between Point Isabel and Matamoros—along the lower Rio Grande, afterward at various other locations. Early in the war such camps received the name of some field officer—e.g., Camp Belknap, or some current hero, such as Camp Page, or bore the label of a regiment or even a company.

Another type, base camps, soon were surrounded by more permanent installations built by the combat troops under the supervision of engineers and frequently with Mexicans as laborers—Fort Brown (across from Matamoros), Fort Polk (at Point Isabel), Fort Marcy (at Santa Fe), the base camps at Tampico and at Vera Cruz (Camp Washington at Vergara) are examples of this type of permanent encampment. Camps at Walnut Grove near Monterey, at Saltillo, Buena Vista, Jalapa, Perote, Puebla, San Augustín, and Tacubaya clustered about headquarters of the generals, though in some of these places the troops were billeted in permanent buildings rather than in tents. As the armies marched and fought their way into Mexico, the encampment might be for a night, a week, or for months. Late in the war the camps became centers for occupation, isolated and drab; without the excitement of combat, the troops served their time, stagnated in idleness, and even mutinied.

Rendezvous Camps

At first, as the troops poured into the camps near home, life was not at all bad. Samuel R. Curtis described conditions during the halcyon days at Camp Washington, near Cincinnati, in June 1846:

I am getting a long line of tents, all new and clean. They make a very pretty show. But my troops, yet ununiformed, have a very unsoldierlike appearance.

We have only 5 or 6 hundred mustered in, but hear of the gathering marching clans in all directions. We have our camp now very well policed, and everything has quite a nice and beautiful appearance. We were visited today by a party of Ladies who furnished the officers and Cincinnati Cadets with ample provisions of ice cream, cake, strawberries, and every luxury of the country. I have a hat full of splendid flow[e]rs which were presented to the Commandant. They were kind, generous and noble spirited ladies who were visiting their brothers and sweethearts before their leaving for the war. We had a delightful pick-nick but I could only take a snatch at it for my constant duties keep me always on the move. I wish you had been here. You would have enjoyed it not withstanding your objections to the war. I should like at any rate that you had these beautiful bouquets for I have no earthly use for them.[2]

Two days later, still enthusiastic, he continued in another letter:

Our camp is the most of all the elite of the city. The most distinguished and best men of Cincinnati have called on me, and shown me many special acts of kindness and attention. . . . I shall have lots of old friends around me. Our ranks are full of lawyers, doctors, merchants and every condition, volunteer[e]d, many of them as private soldiers. I could almost form a regiment of Majors, Colonels, and Generals.

Our dress parades are becoming very pretty. The splendid coaches and gay attire of ladies and gentlemen make a gay and beautiful picture. Sunday they crowded round camp all day by thousands. I think that 20 or 30 thousand persons must have visited us. The Governor and some of his family will probably come down next week.[3]

But the new soldier's initial experience of camp life was not always a medley of kind ladies, flowers, strawberries and "pick-nicks." As the camps edged closer to the theaters of war and the problems of logistics became more difficult, the festive notes celebrating a soldier's life were muted, while angry ones increased in volume:

CAMP WOES AT CORPUS CHRISTI

The field-toughened regulars of Zachery Taylor's little "Army of Occupation," which assembled at Corpus Christi in the summer of 1845, never experienced the naive courtesies that Curtis' volunteers basked in at Cincinnati. There was, nevertheless, a period of mismanagement arising from a lack of preparation, even at Corpus Christi, which caused angry complaints and suffering among Taylor's regulars. The mistreatment of the men at Corpus Christi was savagely attacked in an article by Lt. Daniel Harvey Hill, 4th Artillery, later to become famous as a lieutenant general in the Confederate Army, which the young officer published anonymously in the April 1846 issue of the Southern Quarterly Review. In criticizing living conditions in Taylor's camp, Hill wrote:

It . . becomes our painful task to allude to the sickness, suffering and death, from criminal negligence. Two-thirds of the tents furnished the army on taking the field were worn out and rotten, and had been condemned by boards of survey appointed by the proper authorities in accordance with the provisions of the army regulations on that subject. Transparent as gauze, they afforded little or no protection against the intense heat of summer, or the drenching rains and severe cold of winter. Even the dews penetrated the thin covering almost without obstruction. Such were the tents, provided for campaigning in a country almost deluged three months in the year, and more variable in its climate than any other region in the world, passing from the extreme of heat to the extreme of cold within a few hours. During the whole of November and December, either the rains were pouring down with violence, or the furious "northers" were shivering the frail tentpoles, and rending the rotten canvass [sic]. For days and weeks, every article in hundreds of tents was thoroughly soaked. During those terrible months, the sufferings of the sick in the crowded hospital tents were horrible beyond conception. The torrents drenched and the fierce blasts shook the miserable couches of the dying. Their last groans mingled in fearful concert with the howlings of the pitiless storm.

Every day added to the frightfulness of the mortality. The volley over one grave would scarce have died on the air when the ear would again be pained by the same melancholy sound. One procession would scarcely have been lost to sight when the solemn tread of the dead-march would announce another. At one time, one-sixth of the entire encampment were on the sick report, unfit for duty, and at least one half were unwell. Dysentery and catarrhal fevers raged like a pestilence. The exposure of the troops in flimsy tents, and *their being without fires,* aggravated these diseases if they did not superinduce them. The encampment was on the edge of a vast prairie, sparsely covered with little "mottes" of muskeet trees. To obtain a sufficiency of wood from these "mottes," for cooking and camp fires, required a large number of excellent teams and wagons. But this did not accord with the peculiar notions of economy entertained by our Quarter-Masters' Department, whose policy is to save pence, if possible, and squander pounds any how—to require a strict accountability for empty cornsacks, worth six cents a piece, whilst chartering condemned steamboats at hundreds per day. . . .*

As the winter advanced, . . . the encampment now resembled a marsh, the water at times being three and four feet in the tents of whole wings of regiments. All military exercises were suspended, the black gloomy days were passed in inactivity, disgust, sullenness and silence. The troops, after being thoroughly drenched all day, without camp fires to dry by, lay down at night in wet blankets on the well soaked ground. We have seen them bouyed up with the hope of a fray, cheerful and hopeful, when certain death seemed to impend over them. But without occupation, without excitement, without the prospect of meeting the foe; to sit, day after day, and week after week, shivering in wet tents, and listening to the low wail of the muffled drum, as fellow-soldiers, perhaps beloved companions, were carried to their last resting place, was not this enough, more than enough, to try the discipline and fortitude of the best troops in the world? If, under such painful and trying circumstances, the "mercenary soldier" murmured not, and was prompt, cheerful and zealous, in the discharge of duty, of what stern stuff must his revilers be made! If the men who at tattoo lay gasping for breath in the sultry night air, and found, at reveillee [sic], their wet blankets frozen around them, and their tents stiff with ice,* uttered no word of complaint, we certainly must confess that the "bone and sinew," the "sovereigns" themselves, could scarcely have excelled these "hireling soldiers" in manly fortitude, inflexible firmness, and unmurmuring obedience.[4]

Base Camp near Point Isabel

Conditions in the camps were not always as miserable as those which Hill described at Corpus Christi. But the complaints continued, and, at their worst, the camps were unbearable. When landings near the mouth of the Rio Grande led to the setting up of base camps close to Point Isabel, tents on the treeless margins of the Gulf were exposed to the howling northers; the men drilled under the blazing sun in knee-deep sand, and drank brackish water from holes dug in the beach. Lt. Thomas Ewell[5] described the volunteers' hardships at Camp Page, one of these camps.

We are in perfect purgatory here, & Major [Edwin V.] Sumner would be chief devil anywhere. He keeps us all day marching, running, & drilling as

---

* The *Dayton*, whose explosion killed two officers and nine soldiers, was chartered for one hundred and thirty dollars per day, though she had been condemned as highly dangerous *eight* years before.

† The "northers" were always preceded by oppressive sultriness in the atmosphere; the change then was frequently in a single night from 90° Farenheit to far below the freezing point.

skirmishers (which you know is very fatiguing), through sand knee-deep, & the cause of my having liesure to write to you to-day is that the weather is so bad that we can't drill. Yesterday there was a sweltering heat—we lolled our tongues out at drill—we panted in the shade—we rushed by shoals into the sea but then found no relief for in the words of the Poet

> "The sun's perpendicular rays
> Illumined the depths of the sea,
> And the fishes beginning to sweat
> Cried "D—n it how hot we shall be!"

but in an hour last night every thing was changed. Admiral North came down in a hurricane, & now the sand is drifting about like snow—the tents are taking unto themselves wings & flying away, & there is a nose-nipping coldness. We are very uncomfortable for more reasons than one. The last Norther we were washed out of our tents by the sea. However tis an ill wind that blows no good. A great number of turtle[s] wcrc blown ashore, so numbed with cold that they were easily taken, & calipee & calipash some what consoled us for our disaster. If this wind continues long we can again sing, "We're afloat, we're afloat on the fierce rolling tide." Old Sumner has had one good effect on us—he has taught some of us to pray who never prayed before for we all put up daily petitions to get rid of him.

. . . . .

The water here unless well qualified with brandy has a very peculiar effect on one,—it opens the bowels like a melting [fat?]. Gen. Scott came to see us the other day. He complimented Major Sumner very warmly on our improvement & especially on the extraordinary vigilance of our scouts—who, as he said, were peering at him from behind every bush as he approached the camp. To those aware of the disease prevalent here, the mistake of the general is extremely ludicrous. When we go to drill, the men have to leave the ranks by dozens, & as the plain is bare as a table, make an exposé of the whole affair. The effect is unique as they squat in rows about a hundred yards from the battalion & when we deploy as skirmishers, we run right over them.

I have been on my knees almost all day, don't think I am afflicted with an untimely attack of piety,—but the fact is, chairs & tables are luxuries unknown in camps, I have to kneel by the side of a box to write.[6]

CAMP LIFE ON THE LOWER RIO GRANDE

After Taylor had marched to the Rio Grande and won his battles at Palo Alto and Resaca de la Palma, Lt. Col. Henry Wilson (on May 17) with a detachment of three hundred regulars and a slightly larger force of volunteers, moved from *Point Isabel* to a small cluster of buildings known as *Burrita* (some nine miles up the Rio Grande). Rising from a low bluff near the river, one officer said that it "looked marvellously like half a dozen old log stables tumbling down."⁷ Wilson marched into this hamlet without opposition; it was the first place to be occupied by Taylor's army on the right bank of the Rio Grande. Within a few weeks, as the volunteers began to arrive in large numbers, Taylor established camps across the river from Burrita. He believed that the salubrious sea breezes would make it a good place to drill the green troops. After heavy rains, however, the flooding Rio Grande turned the surrounding low lands into sloughs; the roads became muddy tracks; clouds of mosquitoes enveloped the camps and the warm river had to serve for drinking water.

Benjamin Franklin Scribner, an Indiana volunteer, adjusted to camp life at Camp Belknap better than many of his companions. In a series of letters he gave perceptive insights into the common soldier's psychology—his pleasures and discomforts:

The company [Spencer Greys] left the mouth of the Rio Grande on the 3d inst. [i.e., August 3, 1846], except one of the lieutenants and myself, who were sent up the day before with eight men to guard the commissary stores. We arrived at this place, Camp Belknap, fourteen miles below Matamoros in the night and remained on duty in the rain and mud with no shelter for twenty-six hours. When the regiment arrived, we exchanged the duty of sentinels for that of pack horses. We carried our baggage and camp equipage nearly a mile through a swamp into the chaparel situated on a slight elevation or ridge. It is universally admitted that a chaparel cannot be described. . . .

At a short distance it is indeed beautiful, resembling a well cultivated young orchard. Upon a near approach we find the largest trees do not exceed in size the peach or plum tree. These are very crooked and ill-shaped, with pinnate leaves somewhat resembling the locust. They are called musquite trees, and are scattered about at irregular distances. The intervals are filled up with a kind of barren-looking undergrowth, which meets the branches of the former. Prongs of this bush, with sharp steel-colored thorns, shoot out in all directions, commencing just above the surface of the ground. The rest of the chaparel is composed of all kinds of weeds, thickly interwoven with briars, and interspersed with large plats of prickly pear and other varieties of the cactus family. . . . Two days occupied in clearing it away, preparing for an encampment, will give any one a clear idea of its character. . . .

Our encampment is beautifully situated upon a grassy ridge, bounded in front by the Rio Grande, opposite Barita [sic, Burrita], and in the rear by a vast plain bedecked with little salt lakes. Now if you think this is a romantic spot, or that there is poetry connected with our situation, you need only

A Camp Washing Day

imagine us trudging through a swamp, lugging our mouldy crackers and fat bacon (for we are truly living on the fat of the land), to become convinced that this is not a visionary abode, but stern reality. I have yet encountered but little else than sloughs, thorns, and the "rains and storms of heaven," and consequently have not appreciated the clear nights and bright skies of the "sunny South." At present we have finer weather, and it is said the rainy season is nearly over.

I hope that by speaking freely of things as they are, I am not conveying the idea that I am discontented. Notwithstanding the attractions of home, and the greatness of the contrast when compared with these scenes, I never yet have regretted the step I have taken. We sometimes think it hard to bear with the ignorance and inattention of our field officers. The badly selected ground and our frequent want of full rations may possibly not be attributable to their ignorance and neglect, but they are certainly the ones to whom we look for redress. Other regiments around us [which are] better officered fare very differently. I visited another corps the other day, and to my surprise found that they had for some time been drawing an excellent article of flour, good pickles, and molasses. This was the first time I knew that such things could be obtained, except from the sutlers who charged seventy-five cents per quart for the last-mentioned article.

The more I see of our boys the stronger is my impression that a better selection could not have been made. Our messmates are all well chosen, and had we no other difficulties than those incident to a soldier's life, a happier set of fellows could not be found. The plans we form to enliven not only succeed with ourselves, but attract other companies. Our quarters are frequently sought by them to listen to our music and look upon our merry moonlight dances.

I am sometimes struck with the patience and philosophy exercised, even while performing the humiliating drudgery of the camp. In my own case I do not know whether it is owing to my selection of companions or not, but I have never realized the exhaustion and fatigue a description of our manner of procuring water and provisions would indicate. I have just returned from one of these expeditions, and will here give you a faithful description of the schemes resorted to in order to lighten our burdens.

Another and myself set out with two iron camp-kettles swung upon a tent pole. Walking about half a mile up the ridge, we came to the crossing place —the narrowest place of the slough which ebbs and flows with the tide. This is unfit to drink on account of possessing the essence of weeds, distilled by the combined action of water and sun. In this clime he trifles not, but sends his rays down with earnestness and energy. Well, after struggling through the tangled weeds with water nearly to the waist, we in due time arrived at the bank of the river, dipped up our water and sat down to rest. We found but little inconvenience in getting water from the stream as it was filled to the top of its banks. The country here of late has been almost inundated. The oldest residents say such a flood has not been before for thirty years. If there is fatigue in going with empty buckets, you may readily conceive what is the effect of filled ones returning. The pole was kept continually twisting by the swinging motion of the kettles, it being impossible to keep them steady on account of the irregularities of the road. The difficulties of the journey were greatly augmented by the depth and tenacity of the mud which kept us plunging about, and to our great consternation, causing us to spill the precious liquid.

From this description you may think we had a cheerless trip. It was not so. All was characterized by good humor. We started out crying the lead, "a quarter less twain," until we exhausted the vein; then turning military, the command was given, "guide right, cover your file leader, left, left, left," &c. The novelty of the scenery and *genial influences* of the sun—for I know of no other cause—gradually excited our minds as we proceeded through the quiet wave, and inspired us to more noble and exalted demonstrations. Glory became the subject of our song. Touching quotations from the poets, and inflamed, impressive recitations from ardent, patriotic orators and statesmen were resorted to, expressive of the high aspirations with which we set out upon this glorious campaign. We then in lower tones spoke of the realization of these day-dreams. With feelings thus awakened we continued our wade.

. . . . .

You say you often wonder what I am doing. I will give you our daily order of exercises. We are aroused at daylight by the reveille, and have a company or squad drill for two hours; after which eight men and a sergeant, or corporal, are detailed for guard. Company drill again at four o'clock and regimental at five. The intervals are filled up in getting wood, water and provisions, cooking and washing. Hunting parties go out sometimes and kill fowls, cattle, wolves and snakes. One day last week mess No. 14 served up for dinner a rattlesnake seven feet long.

. . . . .

[September] 7th . . . The regiment has just been mustered by Captain Churchill[8] for two months' pay. I have been gloomy and low-spirited all day. When I reflect upon my situation here in contrast with that at home, I can hardly realize that I am the same person. Everything appears like a dream, and I almost believe I am acting a part in which my own character is not represented. I am thrown among the temptations of camp, but do not think the effect will be demoralizing, or its impressions lasting. The more I see of vice and dissipation, the firmer I believe a moral and virtuous life constitutes the only sure guarantee of happiness.

. . . . .

[September] 20th . . . After breakfast this morning, I went to the sutlers, and bought a large box of sardines and some claret, as a little treat for the mess. Our captain and lieutenants were invited to partake, and toasting my birth-day they all wished me success.

. . . . .

[December] 10th—At last we have departed from camp Belknap. The place that a few months ago contained 8,000 souls, is now without an inhabitant. I left this beautiful spot with mingled emotions of pain and pleasure. Here we had light duties, we had opportunities to hear from home, and other sources of comfort. On these accounts I confess I left camp Belknap with regret. But on the other hand it could be no longer said, they still remain away from active duty and scenes of glory. I thought of the upper camp and wonders in other lands. On these accounts I left our old encampment with feelings of delight.

We transported ourselves, our camps and equipments to the river bank; but how heavily many an hour passed away before the arrival of a steamboat. We several times laid in provisions and cooked them for the trip, and several times we eat [sic] up our provisions before we started on our trip. It is said man is a poor economist in domestic matters, and indeed our conduct on this occasion seems to prove it.[9]

Another well-balanced sketch of camp routine came from a young Tennessean, John R. McClanahan, who wrote from another Rio Grande camp—this one the "Camp of the Avengers." While yearning for the comforts of home, this Tennessean nevertheless was eager to "experience all the varieties of soldier's life."

Although we have undergone many privations and some hardships, it is nothing more than we expected and came prepared for. . . . The temperature of the atmosphere here changes very little night or day, and although many of our boys sleep on the bare earth, and occasionally in wet clothes, such a thing as a cold has not been known in our company. Our daily routine of discipline consists in rising at day-break to answer to roll call. We then repair to our *toilet*, rig up in our uniform and parade at sunrise for drill. After drilling [for] one hour we return to camp, lay aside our rigging and take breakfast. After breakfast we amuse ourselves in various ways—some rambling over the country, some cleaning their guns, some reading, some sleeping, some singing, some washing, some sunning their clothes, and others indulging in vague speculations as to what will be the final termination of the war &c., &c.. Dinner, of course, is not neglected at its proper time. Thus the day passes off until an hour by sun, when we again rig up for drill. We return at sun set, lay off our accoutrements, and go to supper. Supper over, we collect about in squads, seat ourselves upon the ground, converse upon various subjects, sing songs, tell tales, chew our tobacco, smoke our pipes, &c. until nine o'clock when we are again called out to answer our names. This being over, we spread our blankets, stretch our musquito bars, crawl under, and retire for the night. Thus passes away our time.

As for myself I diet principally upon crackers and coffee, having had as yet, but little appetite for meat. Our cooking utensils consist of two iron pans, one frying pan, and one large iron bucket. . . . We have Haywood and Dick Hays' servent along who wash for several of us. On one occasion I did my own washing, in order that I might experience all the varieties of a soldier's life. For Nan's gratification, you may tell her this. We have no use here for starch and irons. It needed not your mention to remind me of your vegetables and milk. I have often thought of them, as well as your cool well water and fruit. I have occasionally had an opportunity of buying a little goat's milk from the Mexicans which is all I have tasted since I left home. Fleming Willis, who is in my mess, says the next time you have your table spread with vegetables, soups, milk, &c., you must set a plate for him, and if he should not happen to come, you can let some one else eat his share. A few moments before I received your letter, he and I were lying stretched out upon our backs in our tent, enumerating the various dishes we would like to have for dinner, but I believe I put him to silence by mentioning a good peach cobbler with cool sweet milk. He gave it up and said no more until I read your letter.[10]

Lt. John Forsyth, an adjutant in the regiment of Georgia Volunteers, and in civilian life the editor of the Columbus (Georgia) Times, described the "myriads of crawling, flying, stinging and biting things!" which infested the lower Rio Grande camps:

This country is distinguished, above all other particulars by its myriads of crawling, flying, stinging and biting things. Every thing you touch has a spider on it. We are killing them all day in our tents. We never dare draw on a boot or put on a hat or garment without a close search for some poisonous reptile or insect crouching in their folds or corners. It is wonderful that we are not stung twenty times a day. Yesterday morning, while standing up at breakfast (we never sit at meals for the want of the wherewith to make a seat), I felt some strange thing crawling up my leg about the knee. It did not take me long to seize it with my hand and to disrobe. Looking into the leg of my off-drawn drawer, I beheld a villainous looking creature of black and yellow, with a long bony tail. I called my mess to look at it, when Dr. Hoxey,[11] who has been before in this reptile country, pronounced it a Mexican scorpion, and told me for my comfort that it was as poisonous as a rattlesnake. His sting was out, and no doubt when I clenched him in my hand he struck out at my clothes, instead of in at my flesh. 'Thinks I to myself' there's an escape.

Besides these we have spiders, centipedes, hordes of flies, and every thing else that crawls, flies, bites, and makes a noise. A gang of locusts have domiciled themselves in our camp, and keep up a sleepless clatter all night. To this is joined the music of frogs and the barking of prairie dogs. A few nights since a panther came smelling up to the lines of our sentries. All these small nuisances are universally pronounced in camp as death to one's patriotic emotions, and a right hard fight with the enemy, to be followed by a riddance of this pestilent country, would be hailed by the whole regiment as a consummation of too much happiness. But here we are to stay fighting his insects and vermin, with no present prospect of finding their masters (our enemy), for whose special use and appropriate comfort they seem to have been formed by Nature. Some few of our officers profess to be enamored of this country. The air here, near the seacoast, is certainly fine, and one is at a loss to account for the sickness; but, aside from that, I would willingly forego the possession of all the rich acres I have seen to get back from this land of half-bred Indians and full-bred bugs.[12]

BOREDOM IN CAMP LIFE

No discomfort in the camps had a more devestating effect upon morale than boredom. Prescott described its corrosive influence well when he wrote of another army of invasion—that of Cortez—as it occupied Mexico, centuries earlier: "There is no situation which tries so severely the patience and discipline of the soldier as a life of idleness in camp, where his thoughts, instead of being bent on enterprise and action, are fastened on himself and the inevitable privations and dangers of his condition.[13] Lt. Simon Doyle,[14] of an Illinois cavalry company languishing in a "stinken hole" of a camp near Matamoros—while listening for rumors of the armies which might be fighting in the interior—gave a fresh testimonial to Prescott's observation:

Nothing of importance has transpired in this region since my last, every thing is perfect peace and quiet, no signs or even rumer of a force of the enemy advancing upon the country this side of the mountains.

It is rumered here that the forces now at this post and a portion of those above here will concentrate at Victoria soon and occupy that place under command of General Taylor. This I hope may be true, stil[l] I doubt it, at least I fear it will not be the case, for you may depend I am sick and tiard of this place and this sort of servis. You may say that we are now seeing fine times and enjoying the sweet of the soldier life. This may be so but I would very willingly exchange my present situation for that of more active service, in this exchange perhaps you say I would be cheated. Well I am perfectly willing to try it. I did not come here with a desire to lay around such a stinken hole as this nor even a deasent town if such there be in Mexico. I wish to see some of the country, and experience some of the *hardships* of warfare. I came to Mexico with that expectation, and I do not wish to return disappointed, and further more we would undoubtedly enjoy much better health, for in the first place I am satisfied that a goodly portion of bodily exertion is absolutely requisite for the enjoyment of health as well also as temperance in eating and were we upon a march throug[h] the country the *boys* would not be able to satisfy their *fals* apetites upon pies, cakes and the rich fruits of this climate which they use here to excess consequently they would enjoy as a general thing better health than when lying still at any point.[15]

STAMPEDE ON THE RIO GRANDE

Overcome by the apathy which pervaded the camps along the lower Rio Grande, the volunteers baked in their tents, and wished for a break in the monotony—anything to "wind up the chain of excitement." A march up and down the river's banks, or "a few false alarms" would be better than no activity at all. And false reports of advancing Mexicans sometimes did chase away the "blues." These rumors precipitated the long roll of the drums, the scurrying of troops to positions, and other details of the typical "stampede." Chaplain Lewis Leonidas Allen[16] described one of these alarms near the Brazos:

The respective regiments performing their various evolutions and drills—the sound of music—the command of the officers—the moving of the baggage trains—cooking, and now and then, eating, drinking, laughing and joking, all combined to enliven the scenes, and keep off that most abominable disease, in common parlance called the *blues*, which is apt to attack and sink the spirits of young volunteers. Before leaving the Brazos Island, I may as well give a brief description of the ever memorable battle of the sand hills. So long as memory holds its empire in its proud citadel, the rough hand of time will never erase the impressions stamped upon the scene which transpired upon that night.

The St. Louis Legion, together with the Louisville,[17] and the 6th Regiment of the Louisiana volunteers,[18] were encamped on a line with each other. A hot, sultry day had passed. A dewy night had wrapped her broad curtain around the Island. The lanterns were hung out from the stupendous dome of Heaven—the moon looked dimly down through the breaks of a dark cloud —while a few fleecy and scattering ones moved slowly and gradually along. The sentry had been placed at his post, to mark his lownly [*sic,* lonely] round, while the soldiers retired to their tents, and were wrapped in sweet forgetfulness—forgetting the toils of the day, and the turmoils of a camp.

Suddenly the picket fired. This was the signal of alarm. The long roll was beat—that awful, mournful summons, so well understood by the soldier. In a moment every man was upon the grasp of his arms, mustering into his proper place. The officers were hurrying to and fro, giving their orders, and in less time than it has taken me to tell the story, every man was ready to do his duty, or die for his country. It was reported that a large force of Mexicans had crossed the Rio Grande, at or near its mouth, a distance of eight or ten miles from us, and were marching to give us battle, kill, or take us all prisoners, and take possession of the Island. Our courage, of course, was wrought to the *sticking point.* Every man evinced a disposition to sell his life as dear as possible. Detachments were sent out along the beach to reconnoitre carefully and report. Col. Eastern [*sic*][19] was cool and collected. Lieut. Col. Kennett[20] displayed the same ardent desire to do his duty, and Dr. Johnson[21] found his soul inspired with a noble ambition to be in the front ranks among his fellow-soldiers, and almost forgot his saws and p[l]asters. Young Emmett and Chapall, . . who had been appointed orderlies to Col. Easton and Kennett, were seen marching deliberately along the lines, with their swords and pistols girded on, evincing a desire to have a part in the matter. Every thing being ready, the word of command was given. Every soldier could almost hear his heart beat; and no doubt some were thinking of dying a noble death as martyrs for their country.

Well, as I said, we were ready, willing, anxious, and determined. When— how shall I describe it? Language is too meagre to give a proper idea of the awful scene which followed. The future historian must record the deeds of valor, and chivalry, and noble patriotism. Imagine our mortification and chagrin when you learn that news came that there was not a single foe to be seen upon the Island. Our ardor, of course, sunk suddenly down to thirty degrees below zero, and we soon began to breathe easily again. It appears that Col. Bailie Peyton,[22] commanding the 5th Regiment of Louisiana volunteers, and who was stationed at Burita, had heard a cannonading during the day from some quarter, and he supposed that it came from the enemy, and consequently despatched a messenger with the intelligence that we might be prepared to defend ourselves. Thus the matter ended without smoke. Happily too, there were no lives lost, and the Surgeons and Chaplains had no duties in their lines to perform. Thus ended the battle of the sand hills.[23]

Pillage of Mexican Villages

Because of the heat, drill periods in the Rio Grande camps often were early in the morning or in the cool of the evening. Except for those who were busy with special details, the volunteers found themselves idle for many hours each day. With time to spare and muskets in their hands, they soon made a shambles of Burrita and the surrounding countryside. As at many another Mexican village, the people soon fled from the marauders. A regular officer on his way to join his regiment in Taylor's army during the summer of 1846, wrote in his diary: "We reached Burita [sic, Burrita] about 5 P.M., many of the Louisiana volunteers were there, a lawless drunken rabble. They had driven away the inhabitants, taken possession of their houses and were emulating each other in making beasts of themselves."[24] Another officer, Col. Balie Peyton of the Fifth Regiment of Louisiana Volunteers sent details of these outrages to Brigadier General Taylor.[25] These complaints were statements made by the residents of Burrita:

Bernardo Garza, a respectable citizen of Burrita making complaint against the 6th Regiment,[26] under the command of Col. Featherston [sic]: That on the night of the 25th, and morning of the 26th, his house, occupied as a bakery in Burrita, was pulled down and consumed for fire wood by the soldiers of the 6th Regiment. That from the 22nd inst. to the present time the fence around his corn field has been used by the soldiers for fire wood, his corn cut & taken from the field near and below Burrita, watermellons used & destroyed. And his frequent complaints to the officers in the fort were unavailing.

Antonio Treneria, also a respectable citizen of Burrita, complains that his corn field, immediately opposite to Burrita has been entered and destroyed by the soldiers of the 6th Regiment from the 21st up to the present time. That he has a partner in the corn field who has made frequent complaints to the officers of the 6th Regiment but that the trespasses are continued.

They further state to their own personal knowledge that there have been seven houses belonging to the citizens of Burrita torn down and destroyed by the soldiers of the 6th Regiment within the last three or four days, also several fences which were placed around lots, & one garden. That several families, citizens of Burrita, have left the place with their property since the 6th Regiment has been stationed in that place, in consequence of the destruction of property, and the fears excited by the conduct of the soldiers of that Regiment. That many others have sent their property to the country for the purpose of saving it from destruction, and all those who remain do so with the hope of saving their houses, & other property, and are labouring under great apprehension and alarm.

O. F. Janes, an American, who has been a citizen at Burrita for three years, an[d] intelligent, and who has the reputation of being a truthfull man, states that he has been in Burrita since the place has been occupied by the 6th Regiment, that he has heard the above statement of Bernardo Garza & Antonio Treneria, and the facts as stated by them are to his own personal knowledge true. Many other cases of a similar character, not stated by them and frequent complaints by the citizens to him of like abuses when he would refer them to the officers of the 6th Regiment, but no effective measures were adopted by the said officers to restrain the soldiers.[27]

Riot among the Georgia Volunteers

It was during the last day at Camp Belknap, while the volunteer regiments were boarding river boats for Camargo, that more serious violence erupted among them. Only a month before, the colonel of the Georgia regiment, Henry R. Jackson, boasted of his command's "admirable discipline."[28] The regiment divided for the move up the river, with the Colonel going on the second of three boats; four companies under the command of Lt. Col. Thomas Y. Redd remained behind to take passage on the third steamer. Two of these companies became involved in a fight which developed into a riot involving not only the Georgians but an Illinois regiment as well. A staff officer wrote an account published in the Savannah Republican:

A cloud of impenetrable gloom has suddenly obscured the bright sky that has hitherto cheered and gladdened us. Our joy is changed into grief—our mirth into mourning; and it is with feelings of profound humiliation and despondency, that I resume my pen to give an account of the tragic occurrence that took place at Camp Belknap on the night of the 31st ult. . . . As I was yesterday ordered to Gen. Pillow's head quarters, to take down the ex parte statements of several gentlemen who were present at the rencontre, which were made on honor, and of course impartial, I believe that the issue will show that what follows is substantially true.

Major Williams[29] not having returned from Comargo, the command of the left battalion and rear detachment of the regiment devolved on Lt. Col. Redd. It was composed of four companies, the Jasper Greens, Capt. McMahon;[30] the Kenesaw Rangers, Capt. Nelson;[31] the Fanning Avengers, Capt. Sargent,[32] and the Canton Volunteers, Capt. Byrd [sic].[33] They had all deposited their baggage on board the steamer Corvette, bound for this place, and were being assigned to their respective places on the boat, preparatory to embarkation early on the following morning.

To the two first named companies, which were the only ones implicated in the row that followed, were assigned the upper deck. Whilst coming aboard, the Greens took their station on the right of the boiler deck, and the Rangers on the left—each at the head of a gangway, that led from the centre below to the right and left of the deck above. About one third of each company were still ashore; between whom a difficulty arose that soon became a general melee, which continued for some minutes, during which the "Rangers," entirely unarmed, received heavy blows from the "Greens," who were armed to the teeth with clubs, pistols, knives, &c.—Eight or ten of the former were quite severely wounded, and a few of the latter slightly. It was finally quelled by the interposition of Lieut. Col. Redd and other officers.

In the meantime, Capts. McMahon and Nelson came below to aid in suppressing the row—leaving strict orders with the guards of the gangway to allow no one to pass them. They were, however, soon overborne, and new fuel was added to the flame that was raging below; but the darkness preventing a ready recognition of each other, and the officers of the four companies being present, and using their utmost to restore peace, the battle finally ceased, though hard and loud words were still freely interchanged. Capt. Nelson, with great presence of mind, ordered his men ashore and Capt. McMahon his above orders which were generally obeyed. Capt. McMahon followed his men, and finding them still disposed to continue the fight with a few "Rangers" who still remained on the upper deck, was using his utmost efforts to separate his men, sword in hand, to retire to the quarters which they first occupied on the right.

In the meantime, Col. [Edward D.] Baker,[34] of the Illinois volunteers, the gentleman who resigned his seat in congress to take command of the regiment, returning with a detachment of twenty or twenty-five men from the burial of one of his soldiers, heard the row that was going on, and generously hastened to the boat, and offered his services to Col. Redd. They were accepted, and Col. B. imprudently, but with the best intentions, hastened with his men to the upper deck. He there found Capt. McMahon with his back towards him, earnestly engaged, as before stated, in keeping his men to their place on the right. Col. Baker advanced at the head of his detachment, sword in hand, and called upon the "Greens" to surrender. The captain immediately turned round, and placing himself in a fencing attitude, said to the colonel, "d--n you, measure swords with me;" and immediately commenced thrusting and parrying. They fought furiously for a moment, until Col. Baker's friends, thinking the contest with so athletic a man unequal, pressed him back three or four steps, when a pistol shot from one of the "Greens," aimed at his head, took effect, and the ball passed through his neck from near the ear behind, and knocked out two of his upper fore teeth. As he fell, the lieutenant to command, ordered his men twice to charge bayonet, and run the captain through. They did so, and one of the bayonets entering his mouth and passing through his cheek, overthrew him. As he fell, the cry was raised that he was killed, and his men immediately commenced a furious assault upon those from Illinois, and continued it until about one half the latter were wounded, of whom the lieutenant, and one soldier died the next day.

About the time the colonel fell, Corporal Whalen of the "Greens," who was standing at one of the gangways, stabbing the "Rangers" with his bayonet as they attempted to pass up, was shot through the heart by a musket ball and three buckshot, aimed from below, and died instantly.[35]

EFFICIENCY OF THE REGULARS

Everything was not disorder. As the army concentrated at Camargo and the neat rows of white tents lay before him, the efficiency and martial airs of the regulars impressed one Ohio volunteer officer who wrote an idyllic description of their encampment:

A stroll through the encampment on the morning after our arrival at Camargo, afforded me, a raw volunteer, much pleasure and instruction. It was the first of any magnitude and by far the most beautiful one I had ever beheld. Never before, indeed, had I seen a battalion of our regular troops either in camp or garrison. But there in the same field were horse, foot and artillery; not in great force, it is true, but perfect in all their appointments and discipline. Four light batteries of six guns each, a few squadrons of dragoons, and four brigades of infantry (comprising the divisions of Twiggs and Worth),[36] in all about three thousand men, comprised the regular army of General Taylor.

The tent of every officer and private was pitched in its proper place, so that knowing a man's rank and company, his quarters could be almost as easily found as any number in the streets of our principal cities. In front of the camp was a vast and well smoothed parade-ground; along the edge of which was a row of fading fires at which breakfast had just been prepared. The long lines of white canvas and stacks of burnished arms, interspersed with um-brageous rose-wood and mesqueet trees; troops of splendid horses standing with the calm dignity of veterans at their pickets; batteries of artillery, their bright muzzles gleaming from beneath tarpaulins like watch-dogs peering from their kennels; these assisted in forming one of those impressive martial spectacles that swell the veins and give fresh vigor to the step. Militia camps and parades I had often witnessed, but though every man wore the lace, and feathers, and gaudy trappings of a Field Marshal, they presented but a sorry mimicry of war. Here, however, was Mars himself; in repose, yet armed cap-a-pie and ready for action. The very calmness and order that pervaded the camp would have told plainly enough that it was no holiday affair even if many of the quiet men around us had not exhibited upon their persons and bronzed faces the marks of recent battle.[37]

COMPANY AND BATTALION DRILLS

Company and battalion drills often were daily events, with regimental dress parades in the evening, and reviews did much to raise morale. A young staff officer of the Massachusets Volunteers wrote of a review staged for General Wool: "It was a fine spectacle. After the review they performed many evolutions for the General. The firing of Cannon, rattling of ammunition waggons, together with the charging of cavalry, and rattling of sabres, caused me to imagine the reality of a battle. It would do you good to see our horse artillery drill. They move over the ground like lightning, and with great accuracy too. They are the strongest arm of our service." Drill, however, even of the horse artillery, could be hectic, slap-dash, and dangerous when young officers ordered inexperienced men to mount and perform at full gallop. An Englishman serving under Scott late in the war recalled such an experience.

Three months after we had taken possession of the City of Mexico the mounted company of artillery belonging to General Patterson's division[38] was ordered, along with a considerable body of infantry, to Tulucco [sic], and the battery to which I belonged was transferred to that division in its place. . . .

As the summary method in which a number of the men of our battery were taught riding is tolerably characteristic of the go-ahead way of doing these [sic] sort of things in the United States army, it deserves mention. When our company, which had been previously acting as infantry, was converted into a light battery, our captain had some difficulty in finding a sufficient number of men who could ride well enough to act as drivers. Thereafter, whenever any of these drivers fell sick, or got confined in the guard-house, or happened to be deficient through any other casualty; as it was impossible to get on without drivers, the first cannoneers whom the lieutenant chanced to cast his eyes on were ordered to put on the spurs, take the whips, and mount in the absent drivers' places. No remonstrance, or excuse of incapacity, would obtain a moment's attention. "Not a word, sir; if you can't ride now, you can't learn too soon," the lieutenant would sternly reply to the indignant mutterings of his victims, who, as they reluctantly clambered into their saddles, looked as lugubriously [sic] as if they expected nothing less than fractures, dislocations, or sudden death.

Our drill ground was a fine level plain on the outside of the city, between Guadaloupe [sic] and Penon. . . . Our drill was mostly performed at a brisk trot, warming occasionally into a gallop; and as we seldom went out without firing blank ammunition, and many of the horses, as we were continually changing them when new trains came up, were as new to the business as the men, accidents of a serious kind were constantly dreaded. Our horses were perpetually rearing or kicking until their legs got over the traces, when, if the battery happened to be moving rapidly at the time, and the piece, or caisson, where such an occurrence took place, was not promptly halted, the position of these newly mounted and unskilled riders was sufficiently dangerous to check any propensity to laughter which their awkwardness could scarcely fail sometimes to provoke.

But on such occasions these novices were not alone in danger, the other riders belonging to the same piece or caisson were in almost as much; nothing being more common than to see horses and riders in some alarming predicament, frequently all down in a heap together; and nothing more suprising than the few really serious accidents resulting from such frightful-looking contretemps. On these dismaying occasions, while the anxious and alarmed spectator expected momentarily to behold some poor fellow brought out of the mélée with squelched ribs, or a cloven skull—behold! the horses and drivers had somehow got on their legs again, the traces were unhooked and extricated in a trice, and in a very few seconds the riders were mounted, and, whipping up on a fierce gallop to resume their place in the battery, already half a mile ahead.

Indeed it was a matter of frequent surprise to us all, and seemed only a little short of the miraculous, that no fatal accidents, few even that could be called serious, had occurred in these strange, hap-hazard, break-neck-looking drills of ours; fewer indeed than in some well-disciplined batteries that drilled in our vicinity. For our singular good fortune in this respect, we certainly considered no gratitude was due to a foolish and hot-headed young second lieutenant who commanded and drilled the battery for several months after our troops entered the city, our first lieutenant having been killed in action at Churubusco, and our captain having obtained sick leave and returned to the States. This lieutenant used to get into a great passion, and curse and swear most awfully, when, something being materially wrong, a piece or caisson, had halted for the purpose of rectifying that which happened to be amiss without having received an order from him to that affect. . . . "If a horse gets over the trace, or even if you see a rider fall, you have no right to halt; drive on though you should crush the fool to [a] mummy; it will be a warning to others to take care, and mind better what they are about." Such were the instructions which he repeatedly gave to the non-commissioned officers and men of our company, who luckily possessed more humanity than their officer.[39]

DAILY BEATS AND CALLS

Whether or not drills were efficient, one cure for the soldiers' troubles was to keep them busy. As the campaigns progressed in 1846, the commanding generals' orders prescribed more fully the daily beats and calls. In particular, Brig. Gen. John Ellis Wool became famous as one of the strictest disciplinarians in the army. His orders provided a model for others (especially the inexperienced volunteer officers) to emulate. After the Battle of Buena Vista, when inactivity on the "northern line" contributed to low morale, Wool reissued his previous camp regulations and ordered them read to all the troops of his command. Chaos might have been the alternative, but strict discipline, combined with the monotony of camp routine, enforced upon volunteers whose officers were often as undisciplined as their men, were combustible elements which might lead to mutiny. Wool's Orders No. 326, issued at Buena Vista on June 22, 1847, are reproduced here.

1. The following extracts from orders & Regulations heretofore issued to the Troops of this Division are reiterated with the view of impressing them more fully both on officers & men.

The daily beats & signals will be as follows

Reveille	4½ 00	A.M.
1st Fatigue Call for the police of Camp	5 00	A.M.
Peas upon the Trencher (Breakfast call)	6 00	A.M.

Surgeons Call	7½ 00	A.M.
1st Call for Guard Mounting	8 00	A.M.
Morning Drill	9½ 00	A.M.
Roast Beef (Dinner)	12½ 00	M.
2d Fatigue Call for Police of Camp	3 00	P.M.
Afternoon Drill (for 1½ hours)	4½ 00	P.M.
Retreat at ½ an hour before sunset		
Tattoo	8½ 00	P.M.
Taps	9 00	P.M.
Officers Taps	10 00	P.M.

The signals for each of the above calls will be made by the orderly Buglers at Hd.Qrs. & will be immediately responded to by the music of the various Regiments & Corps.

At Reveille, Breakfast, Dinner, Tattoo Roll calls, the various Companies will be formed on their Company Parade Grounds, and the rolls called by the 1st Sergeants superintended by an officer, to whom the absentees (if any) will be reported, and who will report the state of the Company to the Adjutant of the Regiment for the information of the Colonel or Commanding Officer. At Drills & Parade (which will be at Retreat) all the Officers & men of the Regiment except such as are on other duty, or are specially excused by the Surgeon on account of sickness, will be present. Officers absenting themselves without being so excused—will be reported to Head Quarters & men who may absent themselves will be confined.

Besides the Drills provided for the men as above, there will be a daily drill of the Volunteer Officers & non. Comd. Officers at such times as the Commanding Officers of Regiments may designate.[40]

A DIVISION IN CAMP NEAR TAMPICO

Within the limits set by the official regulations, camp life might be, and often was, both orderly and peaceful. A private in a Tennessee regiment described such a scene on February 7, 1847, as the division of Maj. Gen. Robert Patterson lay in camp near Tampico.

This was a most lovely day; and the sun shone pleasantly on the beautiful river, on the green hills opposite, on the city in the distance, on the camp and the plain. It was warm, pleasant, bright and still. Before the sea breeze rose, not a breath of air was stirring; and every sound was distinct. The flags over the city, and those on the lofty masts of the shipping near it, drooped motionless from their staffs; the screams and chattering of the numbers of parrots of brilliant plumage in the forests opposite the camp came with distinctness across the calm surface of the water. Upon the river, here and there, were long canoes, the paddles of which now and then dipped in the surface glided them quietly on; while the little undulations from their movements caused the rays of the morning sun to dance, as it were, on its bosom. . . .

The city and the camp were still. In the former, the bells calling the people to "mass" had ceased their tones, and in the latter, the drums, the fifes, the bugles, and the instruments of the bands were all silent; for, a wonder, Sunday had been recognized, and there was no drill, no parade, no movements. The long line of succeeding infantry sentinels that extended in front of the entire brigade at regular intervals from the bridge on the left towards the town, down to the bend of the river on the right, seemed as if struck with the stillness and beauty of the scene before and around them, and were motionless also. They leaned on their muskets, at their posts along, from space to space.

. . While all is thus reposing, let us turn our attention to the tents, and see at what the boys are engaging themselves; for at all times when they are at leisure their occupation and movements are about the same, and a glance at this leisure day shows for all.

Let us walk round in the cavalry regiment. The horses are still; tied with their long lariats; they seem dozing in the pleasant sun. At the line of tents nearest to us you observe the captain's marquee, with a crowd around it, sitting on the bales of hay and bags of corn, that have been sent for the use of the company. They are engaged in conversation with respect to our next probable movements.

At the first tent in the line we will stop and look in. We see a couple of the men sitting down in the little space, amid carbines, swords, pistols, blankets, &c., engaged in writing letters on pieces of barrel heads, which are placed across their knees. . . .

Leaving them, another step or two brings us to the second tent. The flap is closed, and the tent is, as it were, shut up. Let us open it, and enter: There is but one man within, and he is mending his bridle; the whole bottom of the tent is filled with baggage and arms. In comes a comrade, who, in a low voice, asks him "if he has got anything." He nods, "Hand it out, then." He drops his bridle, and reaching over, pulls out, from under the blankets, a bottle of brandy, and sells the other a dram, for a bit; but it is done in a very quiet manner, for it is contrary to the regulations of the camp.

At the third tent, we find some of the boys asleep, and a couple cooking behind it; they have been up in town and bought some beef and vegetables, and having borrowed a camp-kettle from another mess, are trying their hand at making soup for a rarity. They have got some light bread from the bakery, some pepper, and several little articles, and they seem as much engaged in making their soup as though it was to be of immense advantage to them. . . .

At the next tent, crowded at its door with bags of oats, are within, several seated on a blanket, playing "old sledge," while another has got a novel, which has been read about the camp until it is hardly readable, and is passing away the time in deciphering it.

At another tent the fire is kindled, and a chap is pounding coffee with the muzzle of his carbine, and is quarreling all the time with his mess-mates about the cooking, declaring that it is not his day in turn, &c., and swearing that hereafter he will cook for himself alone, &c., &c. In this tent are the mess-mates, some of them asleep, others endeavoring to mend up their uniforms and other clothing, and keeping up the dispute with the one who is cooking.

In the next, you see a water bucket with a full supply of water, and a pan of fried pork, and hard bread, to which the boys of the mess are about to apply themselves for a dinner.

In the succeeding tent, a general cleaning of arms is going on; for one of the mess has been lucky enough to get hold of a little sweet oil, and all of them are availing themselves of the opportunity; and with much conversation and many tales to one another they appear to pass the time very pleasantly.

In the next one are many collected to hear a man who is telling amusing tales, and many a loud laugh comes from there. After he is done, another sings a song in high glee. Let us peep in: They have got several bottles of brandy cherries, and they insist upon our taking some of them. (These are procured from the sutler, who, as he is not allowed to sell spirits, thus evades the restriction, and his brandy cherries go off like hot cakes).

We will go on. At the next, we see more writing letters, sewing, &c., and several at a game of euchre. At the next, we find all engaged in a general dressing and cleaning up, having had their clothing returned from the Mexican washerwomen who have made it look new. They are evidently much pleased with their change in appearance. In front of this tent, as well as of several others that we have passed, down the line, you observe many of the men spending much time and pains in rubbing and currying their horses; and in the meanwhile they are talking to them, and patting them, and so accustomed have the horses become each to his rider during the long march that he knows him as far as he can see him, and will express it by neighing, and if loose, will come up to him. A horse could not be driven from near the camp, and it takes them but one feed to learn them their particular place; and, if turned loose, they will each come to it at night. These men are devoting their leisure time to the attention required by their horses, and they could spend it in no better way.

. . . . .

We have now passed down one line of tents, or one company; each company in the regiment, and each one of the regiments of the brigade, will be found engaged in nearly the same ways. It is so all over the camp. Let us now look along the shore of the river near to which our walk down the line of tents has brought us. Here, we find seated on the low bank, many groups of men, who are looking on the beautiful scene before them, of the peaceful river, with the vessels passing up and down; for the sea breeze now gently blows, though the surface of the water is yet unruffled. They are watching the porpoises, who throw their large backs out of the water, blow, and then disappear. An enormous turtle occasionally appears. Passing along, we see other men catching crabs in the shallow water; these are very numerous, and with a short pole, a line with a piece of meat on it, and little dip net, one man catches from twenty to thirty in an hour. Others we see, walking the shore, apparently in thought; though there are not many of these, most having laid aside the task of thinking, as a continual job, to be taken up on their return home. Now, reader, we have given you a sample of the crowded camp when in a state of rest and quiet. Of course, we have not mentioned all particulars, but enough to furnish you a definite and correct idea of the way in which we employ our time when off duty; and knowing it upon one day, you know it upon all.[41]

DONIPHAN'S VOLUNTEERS IN CAMP

Susan Magoffin, wife of a western trader, who journeyed with Colonel Doniphan and his Missouri Volunteers on their march into Chihuahua, found anything but peace in their camps. She wrote: "What an everlasting noise these soldiers keep up, from early dawn till late at night they are blowing their trumpets, whooping like Indians, or making some unheard of sounds, quite shocking to my delicate nerves." George F. Ruxton, an English traveler, was even more critical than Mrs. Magoffin after he visited Doniphan's camp at Valverde on the Rio Grande.

The volunteers' camp was some three miles up the river on the other side. Colonel Doniphan, who commanded, had just returned from an expedition into the Navajo country for the purpose of making a treaty with the chiefs of that nation, who have hitherto been bitter enemies of the New Mexicans. From appearances no one would have imagined this to be a military encampment. The tents were in a line, but there all uniformity ceased. There were no regulations in force with regard to cleanliness. The camp was strewed with the bones and offal of the cattle slaughtered for its supply, and not the slightest attention was paid to keeping it clear from other accumulations of filth. The men, unwashed and unshaven, were ragged and dirty, without uniforms, and dressed as, and how, they pleased. They wandered about, listless and sickly-looking, or were sitting in groups playing at cards, and swearing and cursing, even at the officers if they interfered to stop it (as I witnessed). The greatest irregularities constantly took place. Sentrics, or a guard, although in an enemy's country, were voted unnecessary; and one fine day, during the time I was here, three Navajo Indians ran off with a flock of eight hundred sheep belonging to the camp, killing the two volunteers in charge of them, and reaching the mountains in safety with their booty. Their mules and horses were straying over the country; in fact, the most total want of discipline was apparent in everything. These very men, however, were as full of fight as game cocks, and shortly after defeated four times their number of Mexicans at Sacramento, near Chihuahua.[42]

SORDID "CAMP MISERY"

One of the worst camps was "Camp Misery" on the outskirts of Jalapa, where Scott's army stopped after Cerro Gordo. Sgt. J. Jacob Oswandel of the 1st Pennsylvania Volunteers described it:

Wednesday, April 21, 1847. . . . We arrived at the outskirts of the city about 11 o'clock, A.M., halting for a short time while our officers, or Quarter-master, went to the city to find out our quartering place. They soon returned, and we then marched through the city of Jalapa, and passing out to the northern end of the city, we went into camp on the open field without any tents. It is about three miles from Jalapa, along the National Road.

. . . . .

Thursday, April 22, 1847. This morning is kind of cold, raining and drizzly, which had the effect of some of our men trying to make their way to the city,

and hunt better quarters. Having no tents we are exposed to all kinds of weather. A strong guard was ordered to be placed around our camp to keep the soldiers from going out. . . .

At noon orders were issued for every soldier to brighten his belt and musket, and clean his clothing; but the men say, "What is the use of cleaning our clothing as long as we are compelled to lay out in the rain and mud. We want our tents, oh, Israel!"

. . . . .

Sunday, April 25, 1847. This morning, or in fact all last night, was very cold and rainy, and those who had no shelter got soaking wet, and could be seen hugging up around the camp fires drying their blankets and clothing, and talking about the hard weather, exposure, suffering, &c.

At noon John Newman, Louis Bymaster and myself carried shingles and boards from a deserted ranch, and built ourselves a small shanty.

. . . . .

Tuesday, April 27, 1847. This morning, after a cold night's rest, our soldiers were busy in tearing down deserted ranches, and building themselves shanties to sleep under. Some could be seen bringing in shingles, others poles and boards; some were digging holes to plant the posts; some with saws, hammers and hatchets. All for to keep out of the cold rain and damp night air, which is very unhealthy at this time. . . .

Wednesday, April 28, 1847. This morning I don't see much of any importance going on, except that several New Yorkers were put in the guard-house for robbing a ranch and breaking and destroying all the things in it, also for disorderly and un-soldier-like conduct in camp. In fact, nearly all the New Yorkers have acted very badly and disorderly for some time. Fighting among themselves is a common occurrence; they think nothing of forming a ring and trying one another's muscles, and beating one another like so many brutes.

. . . . .

Thursday, April 29, 1847. . . . In the afternoon we were visited by an awful thunder storm, and never did I see it lightning sharper; it blew a perfect gale. It blew down some of the ranches, and nearly unroofed all the houses, blowing the boards and shingles high in the air, and for miles around. We, our mess, had to hold on to our shanty to keep it from blowing down. It stood it nobly against the howling storm, not budging an inch. We have had pelting rain and storm almost every day since our encampment; in fact, such soaking ones too, that I declare we almost forget how it looks when it is fair. No other news except that we are beginning to get tired of this camp, which is now styled, and somebody had a hand-board out "Camp Misery."

To-night the wind blows from the snow-top covered mountain Orazaba. It blows about our faces and ears as keen as a whistle, and you can hear some of the fellows cry out, "shut the door!" "Confound this wind, it's blowing in a fellow's face." "Shut up, there's no use quarrelling about the wind or the weather." Laughter, etc.

Friday, April 30, 1847. This morning it commenced raining again, and continued all day, making it very disagreeable for our soldiers, and particularly for those whose shanties blew down in yesterday afternoon's storm. In fact, some of our men are almost drowned out, and more particularly those who were in caves, they being dug down about a foot below the surface of the earth. Some were so sound asleep that they could hardly be wakened up, the water almost running into their mouths. Our shanty being high and level the water does us no harm. Our men are now clamoring and awaiting for our Quartermaster to bring our tents from Vera Cruz.

. . . . .

Tuesday, May 4, 1847. This morning Gen. Scott sent out the Surgeon-General for the purpose of examining our camp, and the condition of the soldiers. He was accompanied by several other doctors. They examined our quarters thoroughly, and they were not long in finding that our camp was really a camp we styled and named, "Camp Misery."

They reported to Gen. Scott the condition we were in, and the unhealthiness of the camp, and that the sooner the soldiers were removed the better it will be for the troops who are camped here.

. . . . .

Friday, May 7, 1847. This morning, sure enough, the rumors of last evening, that we would leave "Camp Misery," is true. About 9 o'clock, A.M., the drums began to beat. The soldiers all seemed pleased to get away from this camp, and hurried into line to answer roll-call. After a few complimentary remarks from our Captain, W. F. Small, a command came from Col. Wynkoop: "Forward! March!" And off we went with no regret and without weeping eyes.[43]

CAMP LIFE OF THE OFFICERS

Although the commissioned officers often underwent privations similar in kind (if seldom in degree) to those of the enlisted men, they unabashedly lived apart and in greater comfort. Brig. Gen. John A. Quitman was one of the outstanding volunteer officers. At the Battle of Monterey he commanded a brigade which included Col. William B. Campbell's First Regiment of Tennessee Volunteers and Jefferson Davis' Mississippi Riflemen. Quitman arrived at Camargo as Taylor's troops were concentrating there before moving on Monterey. In a letter to his wife and children he pictured the town and an officer's life in camp:

General Taylor's Headquarters near Matamoros

I write to you from my tent on the banks of the river San Juan, a branch of the Rio Grande. Fifty yards on my right is Gen[era]l Taylor's tent. On the other side of the town are encamped about 6,000 troops. The remainder are . . between this [place?] and the mouth of the river. The town of Camargo which contained about 6,000 inhabitants, was nearly washed away last spring by an immense flood in the river. . . .

I have suffered some inconvenience from using the warm river water. I have no fears however of my health & try to take care of it. I wish you could take a peep into my tent—dirt floor—two mess chests, one containing a grid-iron, tea kettle, sauce pan, frying pan, coffee & tea pot, ½ doz. coarse knives & forks &c. The other a little flour buiscuit, sugar, tea, coffee, &c, my trunk, 3 camp stools without backs, and what is quite a luxury a camp cot with two blankets on it. At one end hangs my saddle & holsters—at the other my sword, pistols & spy glass.[44]

After the Battle of Monterey had been won and Taylor's camp was again encamped at nearby Walnut Grove, Quitman continued his description of an officer's life.

We are still here waiting our time in ignoble ease. Those, who like my-self have charge of a camp of 2,500 men, without anything but camp duties to perform, have no enviable task.

My tent is near a beautiful spring gushing out of rocks. Live oaks and ebony trees, hang over it. Before me in full view at the distance of about ten miles is Mitre mountain one of the Sierra Madre. It derives its name from resemblance to a mitre. Although so distant it sometimes looks as if I could lay my hands upon it so near—such is the purity of the air. On my left is the Comanche saddle mountain 3,000 feet high. I had the hardihood to ascend its summit the other day. . . . Aside of the spring is Harry & Ceasar's [sic] tent. The first *faithful boy*, is now rubbing [down] Messenger in my view. I know not what I should do without Harry. On the 21st Sept. after I came from the battle he seized me by [the] hand for joy. He declares while far in the rear of my brigade, that the Mexicans kept shooting cannon balls at *him*. Sometimes he avoided them by dodging, sometimes by jumping & sometimes by laying flat on the ground. Ceasar, [sic] my cook, is faithful and gives me no trouble.[45]

Quitman's life was somewhat Spartan compared to that of some other general officers in the army. Patterson, when on the march, ordered three wagons to carry his equipment and that of his staff of six persons; a single wagon served two companies of soldiers. A volunteer complained: "You can't understand how a general and his staff could fill three large four-horse wagons with movables, when on the march; but if you could be present at the general's quarters, on encamping at night, you would be surprised at the amount of kitchen furniture (enough for a good-sized hotel), bags, vegetables, champagne baskets, and cases of bottles; carpet bags, mattresses, bedding, trunks, &c., taken out. You would think of prairie wagons loaded for Oregon." Quitman had his slaves as body servants; other Southern officers hired Mexican boys on almost the same terms. One Ohio officer engaged a boy (white) camp follower from the United States to cook for his mess while in camp on the beach near Vera Cruz. He described his mess as follows:

Fyffe,[46] Jamison [sic],[47] Howard,[48] Dr. McDonald[49] of Lancaster and myself form a mess together (*that is a family*). We have our own cooking utensils, table furniture, &c. We have a good cook. He is a[n] American boy, white, about 15 years of age, named Theodore Murray. He has no parents, but little education, cooks well, talks Spanish, and can steal like a young Greek, in fact he is just the boy for the army. He was out last campaign on the Rio Grande and was with Capt. Cutter from Covington, Kentucky; he makes good coffee, excellent biscuit[s] and splendid bean soup. We pay him $15 a month. Our expectations are that our boarding will cost us $25 each per month; this includes Theodore's pay, washing & eating.[50]

Brig. Gen. Caleb Cushing employed a cook, two waiters and two grooms. His young aide-de-camp, Lt. W. W. H. Davis, discussed his way of life in July 1847, when encamped on the battle site at Buena Vista. In a letter to his mother, Davis wrote:

The place of our encampment is one of the prettiest places in the world, and place and climate at home would make it almost a paradise. We are upon the broad table land of Mexico, some four or five thousand feet above the level of the sea, and surrounded on all sides by lofty mountains, whose tops assume every shape the fancy could possible [sic] desire. The plain is some four miles wide and many long with scarcely any improvements, and nothing to relieve the eye when riding over it, but deep and rocky ravines. We see only three things here. Mountain, sky and plain.

I suppose you would like to learn how I live, and all about my domestic concerns. The General [Cushing] and I live together and form one mess. We have a cook, two waiters, and two grooms for our horses. We have a tent on purpose for a dining room. We give money to our boys who buy the food, and cook it, when we eat it. We have tolerably good living, such as beef—pork, milk, bread, red peppers, squash, chickens, &c., &c., tomatoes, &c. We live well and have plenty to eat. We can't get up dinner in as good style as you can at home as every thing is done out doors. The General has a complete set of tin ware, a dozen pieces. We call it our silver service, as it is just as good. This can't break, so we have an advantage over good crockery. We had Gen. Wool and staff to dine with us a few days ago, when we had all our silver plate out.

. . . I have a marque[e] to myself which I have nicely arranged and neat as a pin. I have another for my office in which I do all my business. I have a clerk to assist me, and an orderly who runs errands for me. You would laugh to see me sometimes sitting down mending my old clothes.[51]

Some of the officers in the field, at least early in the war, enjoyed few of the comforts provided by marquees, servants, or other luxuries. The tent of Maj. John L. Gardner (Bvt. Lt. Col. and Col., Cerro Gordo and Contreras), 4th Regiment of Artillery, resembled that of Cromwell's Roundheads in its rugged simplicity. His friend Samuel R. Curtis described it:

On the South of the ridge [at Point Isabel], the slop[e] is very gentle and troops are encamped on the grass in various directions. The tent nearest the grass is that of Major Gardner. Let us call on him. He is the Commandant of this point and the region including Brasos Sa[i]nt Iago where my Regiment is encamped. I used to know the Major when I was a Cadet at West Point. He recognized me when I first met him and I will call now and see how he lives.

He is lounging on his cot. His tent is a common wall tent 12 feet square. His trunk and a box and his cot are all his household furnature. On a camp stove in front of him is a book. It is the Holy Bible. On entering the major receives us with the kindest hospitality. He has been here but a few days. He was ordered down from the far North East where he has left a most interesting family and arrived here since I did. . . . The Major accompanied us to the tent of my old friend Captain Swartwout.[52] . . . We dined all together —the subject of home, peace and war subjects well discussed as [the] mess chief provided [us] with bean soup, turtle stake, hard bread, and rain water. After dinner we went to the quartermasters department and saw many of the articles taken on the 8th and 9th [of May] from the Mexicans.[53]

If the officers enjoyed some comforts not shared with their men, there were times when they were not as well off. This was true of hospital care early in Taylor's campaign of 1846. Assistant Surgeon John B. Porter[54] mentioned this in his official correspondence.

Lt. Magruder, 1st Arty,[55] having irregular intermittent [fever], which attacks him at all hours of the day & night in consideration of the incessant rains and the worthlessness of our tents, which are no protection whatever against storms. I have the honor to recommend that he go to the town of Matamoros for the present or until his health is somewhat restored.

The present seems a proper time to allude to the situation of sick officers. They are not as well off when ill as the men, for the latter are provided with hospital tents, flies, &c., which in a great measure afford protection from the weather, whereas the officer in his wall tent of nearly one year's service, originally little better than gauze, is comparatively shelterless. It appears to me that some building ought to be procured for an offcer's hospital, and I have the honour to recommend that measures be taken to procure one as soon as practicable.[56]

WOMEN IN THE CAMPS

Although it was exceptional, officers occasionally were able to have their wives with them in the camps. At Camargo the army found that most of the upperclass Mexicans had left the town, and the sight of a gentlewoman soon became a rarity. A Tennessee volunteer, writing to his sister, commented: "The sight of our fair Tennessee damsels would be a god send in this land of swarthy faces and grim features. An American Lady, the wife of a regular officer, rode in front of our encampment the other evening, and had she been a wild animal from the shores of Africa or Bengal, she could not have attracted a more riveted gaze from our boys. . . ."[57] Officers sometimes brought their

Mexican mistresses into camp. Josiah Gregg mentions in his diary the amorous adventure of a faithless army surgeon, whose Mexican mistress followed the army from Chihuahua. Dressed in a man's clothing, she shouldered a musket and rode with her paramour. Gregg reported later that he frequently saw her in the surgeon's tent.[58] Samuel Chamberlain tried to have his Mexican concubine kept in camp as a laundress.[59]

The laundress was a traditional part of the United States army, fully recognized by army regulations, which assigned four of these camp women to each company. Early in his 1846 campaign, Taylor ordered the laundresses to be moved forward with the baggage to Matamoros. Often these women were wives of the rank and file, and the ration list sometimes provided for their children to come with them to the camps. After the capture of Vera Cruz, when Scott eliminated all surplus baggage for the march inland to the City of Mexico, orders barred camp women from the march. One of them, however, refused to remain behind. Henry Moses Judah recorded her plight in his diary:

[APRIL] 14 [1847] Co. "B" has for its camp woman the ugliest of her sex. Dutch to extremity, with her huge unseemly misshapen body, and her round ugly red face, she still perseveres in supposing that she keeps the flame of love undying in the breast of her man Clancy as she calls him. By the way, poor Clancy gets a whipping every little while. This woman was ordered to stay behind by Maj. Graham, but without letting herself be seen she had deposited her wardrobe and household furniture in a champagne basket, put it in the wagon, and trudged along on foot after her man Clancy. Upon her being seen by the Major, he ordered her to get into one of the empty wagons of the team then passing, and to go back to Vera Cruz, as he could not be bothered with women on such a march as this. Mrs. Clancy did not like the idea of such a forced separation and would not go. 3 men were ordered to accompany her to the wagon. One of them imprudently laid his hand on her arm, when in an instant her huge fist sent him sprawling on the ground, with a very red eye. Apparently satisfied with this exhibition of her prowess she accompanied the other two to the wagon, they by the way keeping at a respectable distance. The worst part of this was that her man Clancy sat among the men joining in their laugh, and [was] not at all disposed to interfere in her behalf. Such a look as she gave him. It foreboded many a hard thump; it breathed vengeance.[60]

THE SAGA OF "THE GREAT WESTERN"

Perhaps the best known "army woman" to emerge from the Mexican War was "The Great Western," who accompanied her husband when he joined the army and served as a laundress and cook in an officers' mess. She was

Numerous Engravings....12½ cts.

Mexican Treacheries and Cruelties.

INCIDENTS AND SUFFERINGS

IN THE

MEXICAN WAR;

WITH

Accounts of Hardships endured; Treacheries of the Mexicans; Battles Fought, and Success of American Arms;

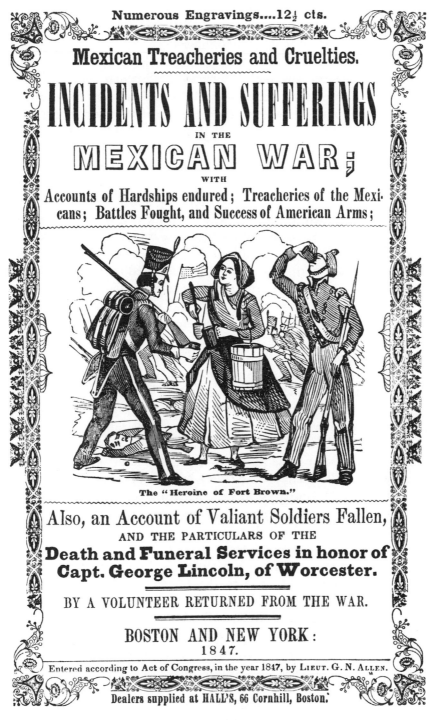

The "Heroine of Fort Brown."

Also, an Account of Valiant Soldiers Fallen,

AND THE PARTICULARS OF THE

Death and Funeral Services in honor of Capt. George Lincoln, of Worcester.

BY A VOLUNTEER RETURNED FROM THE WAR.

BOSTON AND NEW YORK:
1847.

Entered according to Act of Congress, in the year 1847, by LIEUT. G. N. ALLEN.

Dealers supplied at HALL'S, 66 Cornhill, Boston.

The Great Western

especially valiant during the bombardment of Fort Brown. She soon attained
the status of a legend as her reputation spread through Taylor's army. Lewis
Leonidas Allen was one of those who told her story:

Many of your readers have probably heard of a woman connected with the
regular army, the wife of an orderly sergeant, if my memory serves me. She is
familiarly known upon the Rio Grande as the *Great Western.* Some may have
supposed that this person only existed in fancy, but I have seen the Great
Western, and conversed with her while she was in Gen. Taylor's camp; and
also learned her history from childhood, which may be relied upon as authen-
tic.

It appears that she is of respectable parentage, and respectable connection.
In early life she married a soldier as young ladies will do when they take it
into their heads. Her husband being necessarily called away from home, and
deprived of the society of his family for a long period, and often upon the
frontiers in imminent peril, exposed to dangers, and doomed to undergo hardships, true to woman's nature, she determined to accompany him to camp;
hence, she emphatically chose the profession of arms for her future calling.

She is very highly respected by all who are acquainted with her, both officers and soldiers, and comfortably provided for, having her own quarters, pay,
and rations, and very useful, being appointed Matron of the hospital. She
administers to the immediate wants of the sick, wounded and dying. One
reason why she is called the Great Western is because of her height and size,
being a remarkably large, well proportioned, strong woman, of strong nerves
and great physical power, capable of enduring great fatigue. Another reason
is because of natural and moral courage, being very intrepid and reckless of
danger, and at the same time possessed of all the finer qualities which char-
acterizes her sex. When any of the troops are wounded or sick she manifests
the greatest care and sympathy in personally attending, at proper times to
all their wants—for woman never appears more lovely than when engaged in
her respective sphere, and which is more particularly her province, in bending over the couch of the sick and dying. . . .

When the army marched from Fort Jesup, in Louisiana, through Texas to
Corpus Christi, and from thence to the Little Colorado, where there was
great danger in crossing, she rendered great assistance; and, in one instance,
saved the lives of a number of soldiers who were crossing in a flatboat—which
sunk while she and her children were in it.

At the bombardment of Fort Brown, opposite Matamoros, she exhibited
great courage, and the most cool, daring intrepidity. The cannon balls, bullets, and shot, those sure messengers of death, were falling thick and fast
around her. She continued to administer to the wants of the wounded and
dying; at last the siege became so hot that a bullet passed through her bon-

net and another through her bread tray while she was preparing some refreshments for the men. Her marquee being a little distance from the men, they were obliged to watch their opportunity to go for their meals. Finally, they wished her to bring it to them; but, in her own language to me, she became very much offended, and indignant at their conduct, in making such a demand. After she had run such great risks, and periled her life to demand her to expose her life still more in carrying food from her tent to them was asking a little too much, and she begged to be excused, and upbraided them in very severe terms for their want of courage.

On the 4th of July last, at a national festival, an officer proposed the following sentiment, which was received with enthusiastic applause:

"*The Great Western*—One of the bravest and most patriotic soldiers at the siege of Fort Brown."

When I left Matamoros, the *Great Western* was pulling up stakes and preparing to push on to Camargo and Monterey.[61]

MEXICANS AND THE CAMPS

As the armies moved farther into Mexico, native women did more of the camp work. Although Taylor cautioned his officers against employing Mexican servants,[62] he did little to keep the natives from his camps; the forward movement of Taylor's army would have been difficult without their help. On Brazos Island, the Quartermaster hired "half naked Mexicans" to unload the ships; Mexicans manned steamboats on the Rio Grande; when the army marched from Camargo to Monterey, Mexican arrieros braved guerrilla reprisals to drive mules heavily laden with supplies; Mexicans served in the base hospitals at Matamoros, Vera Cruz and Jalapa. Each day, Mexican women came into American camps to vend their fruits, vegetables and other wares. There was irony in this, as Capt. John W. Lowe noted in a letter to his son:

We have skirmishes with them [the Mexicans] 5 or 6 miles from camp every few days, but others come into our Camp and sell us bread & cakes, pies, green corn, oranges and so on, but we have to pay for them. We have to give 3 cents for a potatoe; 4 cents for a sweet potatoe—2 cents for a small ear of corn and 12½ cents for 3 rolls of bread as large as your hand—eggs three cents a piece—a pint tin cup 25 cents, an iron tablespoon 12½ cents and almost everything else in proportion. I would rather pay more for oranges and less for other things.[63]

By the time Scott's army reached Jalapa the practice had become so commonplace that the same officer was able to write: "I can scarcely realize that we are in an enemies country, the Mexicans are passing my tent every minute

with sugar, bread, cheese, oranges, potatoes, onions &c., for sale. They have mingled so much with the Americans that they can understand us very well."[64]
. . At Jalapa, however, the venders did not always fare well in their dealings with the army. Once, having set up their huckster stands in "Camp Misery," they were set upon by Pennsylvania troops who were desperate after days of a near-starvation diet. Sergeant Oswandel reported the scene:

At noon the Cameron Guards, hailing from Harrisburg, Pa., belonging to the Second Regiment Pennsylvania Volunteers, marched up in front of Col. Wm. B. Roberts' tent, and told the Colonel that they wanted something to eat. The Colonel answered them by saying that he had nothing to give them. At this moment they made a rush on the Mexican huckster women, who have their stands throughout the camp, selling their things to the officers and soldiers, that is to those who have money left, and took nearly all the poor Mexican women had, and such a scrambling and rushing I never saw before. . . . The Officer of the Day tried to stop them from plundering the women, but all of no use. He might just as well attempt to stop thundering as to stop hungry mouths from being fed when there is something to eat. After they had plundered from the hucksters all they had they went to work and cleaned the huckster women out of "Camp Misery."[65] The eatables taken were then handed around from one to the other in the fellowship of good will. There was a marvelous wagging of jaws, and a volume of voices that much reminded one of the buzzing in a church fair.[66]

Those too poor to barter with the invaders were sometimes able to gain some benefit from the occupying army, though their harvest was lean. H. Judge Moore of the South Carolina Volunteers told of such an incident:

The town of Las Vigas[67] contains quite a fine church for a place of so small a population. . . . The houses (if houses they can be called) presented a very picturesque and uniform appearance, being built mostly of erect posts drove in the ground and lashed together with vines which supported a roof composed of flag or palm leaves tied together with strings made from the bark of the pulque plant. The earliest dawn of the morning of the 8th of May (the anniversary of the battle of Palo Alto) found our camp all in motion, and sounding the busy notes of preparation for the start, while crowds of lean, half-clad women and children were already hurrying to and fro through the quarters, picking up grains of corn and scraps of meat and bread, and tattered garments and worn out shoes which the soldiers had thrown away; and even the scattering blades of straw and fodder that were left about the wagon-yard were all taken care of and husbanded as though they were of the most intrinsic value.[68]

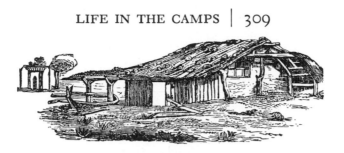

A Mexican Hut

Ubiquitous Sutlers

The Quartermaster Department had assistance from the sutler—not always welcome—in supplying the troops. The sutler was a merchant, a peddler of sorts, who followed the army from camp to camp; his business was hard, sometimes hazardous; and he often was unscrupulous and aimed only at maximum profits. The soldier knew he was being cheated but the sutler had the goods, and as long as the men had money, they bought.

John R. Kenly of the Maryland Volunteers described the activities and reception of a sutler:

That we were now approaching the end of our march was clear from the arrival of a sutler in camp from Tampico. He brought with him cigars and potatoes. All who had money, bought; without money they were not to be had; no kind of promise or entreaty was of any avail; no claim of former acquaintance either with self or friend was recognized by that sutler. He charged just as much as he thought he could get, and he did get high prices. My purchase of potatoes was soon in a camp-kettle, and I ate the first vegetable that I had had since leaving the ship last July, with the exception of the cabbage-palm; and these potatoes, with a tin-cup of vinegar, of which we had had none for a month past, gave me a relish for the cigars known only to those who have been long deprived of these necessaries of life,—a soldier's life.[69]

Gambling in the Camps

After months of waiting, when a regiment finally received its pay, gambling became the order of the day. The officers braced themselves for trouble as men with money in their hands, and not knowing quite what to do with it, played at "Old Sledge," faro and roulette. As Buhoup described it: " 'Click, click, here is a game you all can win at.' A fellow might be seen sitting with a blanket spread out before him, with cards displayed thereon, and himself shaking a chucklebox into fits."[70] Most of the dealers were from the ranks, but "blackleg" gamblers from New Orleans, Philadelphia and New York followed the army. *Dr. S. Compton Smith, an Acting Surgeon with Taylor's army, wrote a grim description of their operations. The army he observed was made up of various ingredients:*

There are the numerous employés of the quartermaster and commissary departments,—the artisans, the teamsters and mule-drivers; the clerks, facto-tums, and servants; the contractors, speculators, and letter-writers; as well as the blacklegs, whisky-sellers and pickpockets, with their coadjutors, the courtezans of the camp—all these elements form important components of the great whole.

The last-named gentry, in our army, did not confine their operations to the garrisoned towns, and the permanent camps; but were frequently found accompanying the trains, as they passed to and from our dépôts—often in the capacity of teamsters.

In some secret corner of their wagons, the montebank,[71] the faro-box, and the roulette-cloth, with its gilded figures and emblazoned eagle, the keno-urn, or the wheel of fortune, were snugly stowed away, side by side with the whisky-keg,—to be placed in tempting array upon the tail-boards of their wagons on arriving at the first camping-ground for the night. These men could accommodate themselves to any change of circumstances or any ostensible occupations, in order to carry on their game of plucking the poor soldier.

One would hardly recognize in the unkemped, coarsely dressed, and dirt-and-tar-begrimed teamster, mounted on the nigh mule of the rear span, and vociferously yelling to the little leader, as he springs to the ascent of the hill, the over-dressed and Frenchified swell, he had observed dealing the cards at the richly-laden monte-table of the "Dos Amigos," the evening previous. Yet it is the same man. The long, and, in spite of the dirt, which would disguise them, the delicate and supple fingers of the dealer are now all that remain by which he may be identified.

Yesterday, the troops were paid off a long-due installment, and, as a large escort accompanies the train, with the money in their pockets, our "professional gentleman" dons his teamster's suit, and presents himself at the office of the quartermaster for a "berth." His partners attend to "business" in the town and at the camp, while he follows to attend to their mutual interest on the road.

At night, after his team is stripped, watered, and fed, and his own supper of fried bacon and army-bread is hastily disposed of, he prepares for business. First, his private corner is examined; the whisky-keg is unrolled from the folds of blankets, which have protected it from the close inspection of the wagon-master, and deposited in some convenient place; as it is to perform an important function during the performances of the night. Then, if the night is calm, two empty porter-bottles are called into requisition to hold each a stump of a sperm candle. These are placed upon the ground, under the cover of some friendly clump of bushes which would hide the light from that part of the camp occupied by the commanding officer of the escort. The tail-board of the wagon is now unhinged, and laid upon the ground between the lights; a pack of Spanish cards, prepared beforehand, is placed upon the board in little piles symmetrically arranged, with "*caballo*," "*rey*," "*corona*," and "*espada*" uppermost. The dealer, seating himself with his legs doubled under him, and a bandanna handkerchief spread before him on which is piled in tempting array, his golden "bank,"—now makes proclamation of —"*free whisky to any gentleman who feels disposed to risk a quarter on a game, at which any one may easily make a fortune!*"

Men whose money weighs heavily in their pockets, and whose dusty palates long for the whisky, soon gather around the gambler. Down goes the money on the cards, and the whisky down the thirsty throats.

As the fiery "rotgut" inflames the brain, the bettors become more reckless; and their "anties" increase from quarters, to halves, and dollars. The dealer understands his business; he is a good judge of human nature, and knows who to "clean out" at once, and so dismiss half wild with the wretched liquor and his losses; and who to amuse and play with, as the cat toys with her little captive before she swallows him. The game vacillates and vibrates up and down the scale of luck; the bettor now losing, now winning, now gaining stake after stake. The dealer damns the cards, swears that fortune is against him, and calls for a new deal to change the luck. The new deal is made, and still the lucky bettor rakes down the silver. Emboldened by success, he now ventures an eagle. The cool, unexcitable gambler scarcely condescends to notice the gold; but, as luck *would* have it, it slips into the bank. There was no cheating—that the bettor could observe; it was all fair, only a turn of luck. He tries it again; and again he loses; and still loses, with an occasional turn in his favor. By this time, the game, with the help of the free whisky, becomes exciting; the bettor will make or break; down goes his entire pile on "kavallo"; the dealer makes a careless slang remark, while a close observer might detect a half-expressed smile of exultation on his skinny lips; and up comes the "woman"; the soldier is "cleaned out!" Cursing his *luck*, and more than half-crazed with the excitement of the liquor and the play, he seeks his blanket, from which he is soon aroused by the shrill, sleep-banishing notes of the reveille.[72]

RECREATION

Life in the camps was far from one of unbroken drill, poor food, bad water, and sickness. The men were permitted some latitude in amusing themselves outside as well as in the camps. At Corpus Christi hunting parties went out to shoot deer, geese, wild turkeys, "small birds without number," and an occasional panther. Along the lower Rio Grande, riding and racing captured wild horses finally led to an order from General Taylor forbidding the "running of loose horses about the Camps . . . between retreat and reveille." Almost a year later, however, the Massachusetts Regiment, according to a letter written to a Boston newspaper, was doing it in camp at Matamoros:

There is an abundance of sport going on in the camp; the jack-asses are plentiful about here, and the men require no instructions to mount them and run races. Wild horses are very cheap; the best can be bought for $10. Some of them are perfect beauties. I had one for which I paid $11; somebody stole him a few nights since. This morning I caught one on the prairie, wilder than old Nick himself, and full of life. Three or four of us managed to saddle and bridle him, in spite of his capers. After throwing several, I mounted him, and let him have the whip; the way he spread himself was a caution. We did not stop to give the countersign to the guard but went off like a locomotive under a full head of steam. He aimed right for a large drove of mules; before you could say Jack Robinson, we were in their midst. All I could do was to "freeze to him," as they say in Boston. John Gilpin's race was not a circumstance; in the course of half an hour he was covered with foam, and pretty well tired out.[73]

The volunteers also found excitement in the horsemanship and bull-baiting of the Mexican rancheros. John Blount Robertson, of the 1st Tennessee Regiment, recalled such experiences when he described an American soldier's recreations in Mexico:

The Mexicans gave fandangoes every Saturday night, and our officers and men would attend them now and then by invitation, but in sufficiently strong parties to overawe any treachery on the part of the Mexicans. . . .

A Mexican Ranchero

While on an excursion above our camp, and in the neighborhood of Mata-moras, some few of us had an opportunity of witnessing a sport which, I be-lieve is peculiar to the Rio Grande country, and is in lieu of the bull baits of the interior. A number of rancheros, well dressed and with their horses capari-soned with all their usual cumbersome trappings, had met together at a rancho, where some fifteen or twenty bulls had been confined in a cor[r]al [sic] or enclosure. After sipping freely of their mescal, smoking a few cig-garettos, and arranging the preliminaries, they mounted their horses and were drawn up in the road; the bulls were now driven out. Off they started in a run, when the first horseman dashed after them at full speed, and selecting the largest bull, galloped up to him and stooping lightly from his saddle, seized him by the tail, when, dexterously passing it under his leg he suddenly wheeled his horse about, and by a peculiar jerk brought the bull broadside to the ground, amidst the loud cheers and plaudits of his companions. Each of the other rancheros in turn then made similar attempts, but not always with like success, for sometimes a bull that had probably run the gauntlet half-a-dozen times before, would dash off in an oblique direction before his tail was fairly secured under the rider's leg, when the ranchero would be lifted from the saddle and hurled like a rocket into the air while his friends laughed and jested him without any sympathy for his misfortune. Whenever one failed in his attempt, the next in turn dashed off, until every bull was fairly thrown.[74]

THEATRICAL PERFORMANCES

Whenever they could get passes to visit nearby cities the men were likely to find theatrical performances of one kind or another. A touring company ar-rived with its mountebanks in the streets of Matamoros almost before the army went into camp. An American circus played for the troops (en route from Vera Cruz to the City of Mexico) in Jalapa. One observer noted: "The soldiers were delighted, and it reminded one of home to hear the familiar cries of boyhood uttered by them at the ring performances, the antics and the witty sayings of the clown; I am sure our men were as near happy as it is in the power of mortals to be."[75] When Scott's army reached Puebla, there were more elaborate dramas. H. Judge Moore of the Palmetto Regiment discussed them:

There are two very fine and spacious theatres in Puebla, the one near the "Plaza del Toro," on the western side of the city, was occupied dur-ing the stay of the American army by a company of American actors, under the proprietorship of Messrs. Hart and Wells, and assisted by some amateur actors belonging to the army. The circus was also a place of popular resort, which was gotten up by an association of Yankees from the land of steady habits, and was very well sustained and numerously patronized, and brought the public-spirited and enterprising proprietors quite a handsome dividend. Mrs. Morrison and Miss Christian, both celebrated actresses from the States, were on the stage almost every night, and command crowded houses to the last. The former was not only a fine actress and a splendid looking lady, but one of the best singers, decidedly, that I have ever heard. The latter appeared to be quite young, not exceeding fifteen, and was universally admired as a beauty; she wore Spanish gaiters, with small brass bells on the heels, and could out dance Macbeth's witches. She acted Pauline in the Lady of Lyons, and Corporal Styles acted Claude Melnotte, and were encored to the last.

The theatre which was occupied by the Spanish company was tolerably well patronized, the entrance money being only *uno real* (twelve and a half cents), while that of the American Company was fifty cents. The Spanish are very good actors, perhaps superior to ours as far as mere action and gesticulation are concerned; as to the merits of their pieces, I did not possess a sufficient knowledge of their language to enable me to form anything like a correct judgment. The costume of the actors was rich and gawdy in the extreme, but in this particular the actresses even excelled them, their dresses being in a perfect blaze with gold, silver, and diamonds.[76]

An astute theatrical manager at Puebla even invited a few of the men in the camps to play supernumerary parts in "Hamlet."[77] One of the battalions under Doniphan had its own dramatic society.[78] Col. Robert Treat Paine of the North Carolina Volunteers—who had faced mutiny on August 15, 1847 and shot one of his own men dead to quell it—was solicitous for the troops' pleasure some months later, and apparently was satisfied with a camp theater.

The regulars, and a few volunteer regiments also, had bands that played "The Star Spangled Banner," "Hail Columbia," "Yankee Doodle," and other patriotic tunes. Sometimes groups of musicians who had appeared at political meetings before the war now serenaded officers with their favorite songs. Except for fife and drum, there were few musical instruments among the volunteers, and they gathered instead in groups to sing before the commander's marquee on a Sunday afternoon or around the camp fires, or at "Texas Reveille," at the top of their lungs as soon as they awoke in the morning. The parody of "The Girl I Left Behind Me" became "The Leg I Left Behind Me" in derision at Santa Anna.[79] Gossip of the day and speculations about the war were often mixed during these evening sessions. Lt. Raphael Semmes told of one such session at Vera Cruz:

And as often as I awoke I heard the merry voices of our volunteers and teamsters, over their little campfires in the street, now singing short snatches of some favorite song, and now discussing the politics of their native country, and the merits of the Mexican war. As I dozed away again the words Texas, Rio Grande, Mr. Polk and General Scott intermixed with

"Molly is the gal for me!"

would strike with dying and dreamy cadences on the tympanum.[80]

READING IN THE CAMPS

In general, however, the simplest recreations were the most popular: surf bathing at Brazos Santiago or Vera Cruz, fishing in streams and the Gulf, playing ball on the parade ground, running foot races, jumping and wrestling. Some of the more thoughtful men read Mexican history and literature during their leisure hours[81]; many began to learn Spanish, but most of them, like Quitman, finally gave it up; a few, such as Daniel Harvey Hill, mastered it. Especially on long marches, like that of Wool, reading material was scarce; newspapers when they appeared were read and reread to tatters. At Matamoros, however, there were three newspapers being published during the early days of occupation. One of them, The American Flag, was hailed as "one of the most frequently quoted papers we know of on this continent."[82]

Except for local happenings, this was a gross exaggeration. Even more famous than the Flag was The American Star, published by the resourceful and indefatigable John H. Peoples,[83] who commandeered presses at Jalapa and other points as he accompanied Scott's army to Mexico City. Its first issue appeared in the capital only a week after the city's capture. During the occupation, Scott and other commanders made it the more or less official mouthpiece of the army. John Henry Warland, of Cambridge, Massachusetts, then edited it in parallel English and Spanish pages.[84] Officers in Scott's army often differed with its views, but sedulously read every issue. They knew, however, as did the rank and file, that their friends back home were getting more information from the Washington and New York newspapers than they were from either the army newspapers or the Spanish-language journals in Mexico.

Mail was criminally slow in arriving from the states. Often a soldier would answer mail call for months before his reward was a single letter. When he did receive letters or newspapers from home his pent up emotions usually broke loose in rejoicing. Thus, Lt. George W. Clutter[85] wrote his wife from a camp at Mier (August 1847): "On Friday morning last I received eight papers from you, on one of which you announced your arrival at home—the papers and the letters or writing on one of them was equal to a long letter—you cannot imagine the pleasure it was to pour over those papers after being so long absent. Send lots of them as they cost me nothing."[86] Capt. John R. Kenly while en route from Victoria to Tampico was even more affected by letters from home. He recorded in his journal (January 17, [1847]): "Last night after I had laid down in my blanket I was aroused by a report that an express had reached camp with a mail direct from the United States. I flew through the chaparral, scratching my hands and tearing my clothes, but was amply rewarded by receiving two letters from HOME, which I read over and over again before I turned in or closed my eyes."[87]

RELIGIOUS INFLUENCES

A request from the army for reading matter brought a response from the American Missionary Society, which sent four thousand Bibles to Taylor's army. The influence these Bibles had upon Taylor's men is hard to assess. There are numerous references to religious concern in the diaries and letters of the troops. On the other hand, as Burnett's regiment of New York Volunteers lay on shipboard, awaiting passage to Mexico from New York Harbor, one hard-bitten enlisted man cynically commented on the donation of Bibles to soldiers:

One or two days previous to sailing, orders were given to rig ourselves in our best toggery, that Gen. Gaines was expected to pay us a visit, &c. But, who should come but the Rev. Mr. Gallagher, with a lot of bibles & tracts,— though all very good in their way, and at a proper time,—but you might as well "throw physic to the dogs," as to give a bible to a soldier going to war. I never saw but one man read them, and he was crazy;—men only abuse and commit sacrilege at such times—for I pledge my honor, many were thrown over-board— others used for waste paper—the ballance were left upon the sand-hills of Vera Cruz, as it was impossible to carry them on a tramp, besides thousands of dollars worth of clothing that were thrown away. If, instead of bibles and tracts, the good people who so much desired the welfare of the men's souls, should have sent something for their bodies, many a life might have been saved, and perhaps, many a widow and orphan would now have prayed and blessed them. . . . Three cents worth of nourishment might have saved a life!—or the cost of a bible, laid out for the same purpose, would, perhaps have saved many lives.[88]

Both Protestant and Catholic chaplains accompanied the army,[89] and, as in all wars, some of the chaplains identified the national cause with the will of God. The Rev. Capt. Richard A. Stewart,[90] a Methodist minister and planter from Iberville Parish, Louisiana, combined (or confused) manifest destiny with religious exhortation and attributed to Providence an imperialistic design that encompassed not only possession of the North American continent but also the modification of the "character of the world." His voice was not only the voice of the expansionist extremists of his own day but was prophetic of similar appeals that the Rev. Josiah Strong and others would make forty or fifty years later when another outthrust would turn the eyes of the American people to other lands. *Thomas Bangs Thorpe* reported Capt. Stewart's sermon:

The Rev. captain took for his text: *If ye oppress not the stranger, the fatherless and the widow, and shed not innocent blood in this place, neither walk after other gods to your hurt.*

Then I will cause you to dwell together in this place, in the land I gave to your fathers for ever and ever. Jer. vii. 6, 7.

The comments and illustrations were apposite in the extreme, and suggested by the scenes around the speaker. He dwelt upon the incidents of the preceding month, and of the beautiful spectacle shown to the world by a conquering army, extending over a country its laws,—which were more benign, more liberal, more protecting, than those displaced by the fortunes of war. This, said the speaker, warming with his subject, is carrying out the spirit of the text,— this *"is not oppressing the stranger, or the fatherless, or the widow, or shedding innocent blood."* Such a peaceful conquest, he continued, worthily rivals the gallant feats of arms that shone forth on the fields of Pala [sic] Alto and Resaca de la Palma,—such a peaceful contest went beyond the effect of arms—it not only conquered the body, but carried willingly captive the mind. It was calculated to shed light over the dark borders of Tamaulipas,—to make its inhabitants embrace the blessings of freedom,— to open their eyes to the degradations of their own government, that enslaves alike their bodies and their minds.

The soldier-preacher then passed on to the second part of his text,—*"Then I will cause you to dwell in this place, in the land I gave to your fathers for ever and ever."* It would be impossible for us to give the slightest idea of the conclusion of this remarkable discourse. The Rev. speaker showed most plainly and beautifully, that it was the order of Providence that the Anglo-Saxon race was not only to take possession of the whole North American continent, but to influence and modify the character of the world,—that such was meant by *"the land I gave your fathers for ever and ever."* He stated that the American people were children of destiny, and were the passive instruments in the hands of an overruling power, to carry out its great designs; and beautifully illustrated this position by a rapid glance at the history of our nation in times past, and the present. He concluded by hoping that hostilities with Mexico would cease,—that wiser councils would govern at her capitol,—and that peace would again extend its wings over her distracted land; and with a truly eloquent burst of patriotism upon the Christian duty of every man's standing by his country, so long as a single foe remained in arms against her, he sat down, amidst deep, silent, powerfully suppressed feeling.[91]

CHILLS, MEASLES, AND YELLOW JACK

Disease—the Deadliest Enemy

The deadliest enemy of the United States army during the Mexican War was disease. The casualties on the battlefield were far from insignificant, but disease, led by yellow fever (the black vomit), dysentery, and diarrhea, was the great killer.[1]

Since killing and maiming are war's methods for achieving a victorious end, killing and maiming are inevitable. But the length and gravity of the casualty list is directly related to the army's medical branch, and the American medical service left much to be desired. The reasons for this were numerous. Some deficiencies were unavoidable. Although it had been suggested during the 1840's that insects played a part as carriers of yellow fever,[2] neither the cause nor anything but empirical means for treating the disease were known to medical science at the time; nor had medical practitioners isolated the causes of dysentery and diarrhea.

Shortcomings of the Medical Dept.

But the level of knowledge and skill were not entirely accountable for the deficiencies. Incompetence and indifference, if not the rule, were all too prevalent in both Washington and the theaters of war. A description of one surgeon as "a young man without experience and who in my opinion is for that reason incompetent to the discharge of the duties of the office in the higher branches of surgery particularly,"[3] might well have been applied to many of the army medics who, unsuccessful in private practice, had found refuge in the military—some as contract surgeons. But even the competent were handicapped. The worst trouble was the lack of doctors, but Surgeon General Thomas Lawson,[4] hardened by years of service in the field, was more likely to answer pleas for assistance with statistics and organization charts than with more doctors. Another difficulty was the disruption of the supply lines. From Camargo: "I have to inform you that 50 boxes of the New York supplies of medicines and hospital stores have been lost at the time of the sinking of the Col. Harney. . . . I sent 100 ounces of quinine to Monterey & this is all that is in the country. I think it would be advisable to have an order issued for the Medical Purveyor to supply the department with every article immediately required by purchase in New Orleans. I wrote to you a few days ago that I had received only 99 of 149 forwarded by Surgeon T. G. Mower."[5] From Santa Fe: "The Medical supplies sent from St. Louis have not yet all arrived, and many of the packages that have reached here were broken open, and some of their contents stolen."[6]

Remote posts, like those in California, were short of almost everything; only the greatest ingenuity met their needs. Asst. Surg. John S. Griffin[7] wrote from San Diego:

On the 14 Decr. [1846] I received an order from Genl. Kearney to make an estimate for such Medicines, Hospital Stores, &c. as would be required for six hundred men for four months; these troops were expected from New Mexico. The estimate to be sent to the Sandwich Islands, by Major Swords, Qr. Mr., U.S.A. to be filled. I was informed by the Medical officers of the Navy that the greater portion of the articles required could be obtained from the naval stores on the Islands—and that nothing could be expected from the U.S. Squadron on this coast, as their supplies had been exhausted.

Mattrasses were required for the reason that no hay or straw is to be obtained in the country for filling bed sacks, and at the time the estimate was made we could have no communications with the interior to procure wool for making mattrasses; the Hospital Department of the Navy could not supply the necessary bedding.

The most necessary articles of hospital furniture were required for the service of two posts; these articles could not be obtained on the coast.[8]

Some of the available equipment was almost unusable. Dr. Joseph K. Barnes, later to become Surgeon General during the Civil War, complained:

I have to report that none of the bedding, instruments, &c under my charge, although very old and much worn, have suffered from the effects of the climate. Having only a condemned hospital tent, rotten & ragged, it has cost much labor & vigilance to preserve the medicines, furniture &c. for which I am responsible.[9]

A few of the wounded were lucky enough to find transportation in a limited number of spring wagons, ordered by Surgeon General Lawson in lieu of civilian ambulances,[10] others were fortunate if they could be jolted along in the regular army wagons. Jacob S. Robinson discussed the plight of some of the wounded in Doniphan's command:

No medicines and no wagons are provided for the sick: we have to jumble them over the rocks and mountains in our broken wagons, among the camp kettles and pork barrels. A poor chance is this when one is sick; what can he expect but to die? Those who are well have to live on half rations and sleep in the open air; the sick have nothing to eat but salt pork and wheat meal or rather bran.[11]

Not widespread at first, disease nonetheless attacked the troops from the time of their enlistment, and the army was often unprepared. In New Albany, Indiana, Q.M. Samuel P. Heintzelman[12] complained:

I have the honor to enclose herewith a number of accounts for medicine, medical attendance and board and nursing the sick of the 3 regiments of the Indiana Vols whilst at the rendezvous at New Albany.

Soon after their arrival the measles broke out amongst them and there was no bedding to be obtained for a hospital, no surgeons and no medicine. It was considered best by the Agent appointed by the Governor to board them out in the town amongst the citizens. After a Quarter Master of the Army arrived there a temporary building was erected for a hospital and on the 2nd July an order was issued for all the sick to be removed to it and that no bills for board would be paid after that date, some few were probably too sick to be removed. Although Surgeons had been appointed in the meantime they have neglected to designate the cases in this situation.

Many of the accounts are deficient in dates and [in] others the charges are too high. Board under similar circumstances could be obtained in this place for the same class of men at from 37½ to 50¢ per day. I consider 50¢ per day for the sick & 37½ per day for the nurses as about a fair compensation. I respectfully recommend that they be paid with those reductions.[13]

UNHEALTHY RECRUITS

Among those who fell victims to disease were recruits who never would have been accepted had they been given a thorough medical examination. Many of them, primarily volunteers, were unfit for the rigors of military life when they enlisted. In 1847, Surg. S. G. I. De Camp wrote from Santa Fe, New Mexico:

A great number of Volunteers came to this country [i.e., to New Mexico] for the purpose of regaining lost health, and many of them have not done one day's duty since they left Missouri. I recommend that measures be taken to have examinations made as to the physical qualifications of Volunteers, *be-fore they are received into the service;* thousands of dollars have been paid to Volunteers in N.M. who have never rendered any service to the country, and who never expected to render any when they left home, as they have acknowledged to me.[14]

The valleys of the Ohio and its tributaries were subject to malaria and typhoid from the time of their earliest settlement. The fevers were often blamed on the riverboats which were thought to be bringing the pestilence from New Orleans, but the swamps and low-lying meadows of the Ohio, flooded in the spring, were breeding places for disease, and were so recognized at the time, though (as in Mexico) miasma rather than insects was held responsible. Whatever the cause, the presence of fever renders the image of the sturdy frontiersman false in so far as both backwoodsman and inhabitants of the river towns of the Ohio Valley were concerned. As a whole they were a sicklier lot than either "easterners" or the later settlers of the high plains. Lt. John P. Hatch complained of their lack of physical fitness in a letter written near Vera Cruz:

Our strength has been already much reduced by sickness not because the climate is unhealthy but because the men enlisted at the west have not the constitutions of those at the east; most of them have had the ague ever since they were born and cannot stand the hardships of a campaign. The Company I am now in was enlisted in the southern part of Indiana and they have lost two men since they came to Jeff. Bks. and two more will not live long. We had fourteen deaths in the regt. last month and there is not another Regt. of Regulars that lost half that number.[15]

There also were those who feigned illness to escape duty, and perhaps to secure a medical discharge. A surgeon described the problem:

I herewith enclos[e] a quarterly abstract of the sick of the the Army of the West for the Quarter ending Dec. 31st. Surgeon Richardson's[16] last quarterly report ought to be recd. with some allowance, I think. The command to which he belonged was proverbially healthy when compared with a larger portion of the Army where disease prevailed to an alarming extent. The men must have imposed on his good nature. I am convinced of this from the fact that when he left this place with Major Clark I examined eighteen men of one company left on sick report by him, and convinced myself that he had been grossly deceived by most of them.[17]

Sickness on the Rio Grande

An angry account of the ravages of sickness is to be found in a letter written by Col. Samuel R. Curtis from Matamoros and published in the Washington Daily National Intelligencer:

In my regiment there are 150 on the sick list. The same proportion at Camp Washington,[18] when you were there, would have made the list eight or nine hundred, as there was then under my command all the volunteers from the State, and five or six times the force I now command. My surgeon reports that, though the number continues large, there is evidently a change for the better, and almost every man is [now] on the mend.

It is considered a very hard battle, and a bloody one, that carries off ten per cent. of a given force. Very few battles of the many thousands the world has fought have risen above five per cent. But by disease and death I have seen my ranks already reduced from 780 to 620. And in some of the regiments, where they have guarded themselves less, or been more exposed, the regiments are reduced from 760 to 500. The number gone are not all dead. Hundreds pass down the river daily on their way home, having procured a certificate from their surgeon that they are attacked by incurable disease. They will many of them return home to their families emaciated, sick, and unable to toil. They are wounded soldiers who have met the pestilential foes of the South; and as much deserve the honor and care of their country as though the fatal shaft had been composed of lead.

So far as life and death are concerned, I would rather risk a battle once a week, with my regiment in the north, than remain in a climate so unnatural to them. But we do not repine—we do not complain. Those who stay, and those who die here, are doing so in the discharge of their duty. Of those who leave to return home, many will never reach there, but will find graves in the Gulf or river.[19]

The health problems of the American soldiers in the lower Rio Grande Valley were treated in detail in a quarterly report of Dr. J. J. B. Wright,[20] U.S. Army Surgeon in charge of the hospital at Matamoros.

Tho' the sickness & mortality . . are considerable . . . I need not say that a general rule, applicable to residents of the North on coming South many degrees of latitude, determines that they must suffer more or less, in the process of acclimation [sic]. This rule is subject only to rare exceptions, when emigrants from Northern latitudes arrive at a season of the year which affords opportunity for the system to accommodate itself to the new influences, by gradual exposure to their action—and when moreover the circumstances of their position enables them to adopt all the precautionary and preventive measures calculated to ward off disease,—when they can keep themselves within doors, and choose their mode of living. What then was to be expected when Volunteers—*sickly boys, and invalid men* (many of whom came into the service with a view *to improve* their impaired health) were suddenly transferred from the States of Ohio, Illinois & Indiana, in June, July & August, to a parallel of latitude South of 26°

These men, when they arrived at the mouth of the Rio Grande were for the first time in their lives subjected to all the dangers to health incident to camp life—half of them bivouacking at night, exposed to an almost tropical sun during the day—drinking brackish water, and compelled to subsist on the rations inartistically & carelessly cooked, and without vegetables, and, above all, suffering under the depressing influence of nostalgia. Under these circumstances, sufficient in themselves to decimate the whole Army of Volunteers, the measles broke out among them, and typhoid fever with its characteristic rosecolour eruption, and chronic diarrhoea opened each for itself a broad avenue to death. The report exhibits the fact that many died of Rubiola, but it may be pertinent to remark that it was rubiola supervening in almost all cases, a condition of the system prostrated by previous disease. I am not aware that any considerable number of the cases reported were due to causes in any way connected with local origin, unless the few cases of congestive fever are chargeable to such account. No case of yellow fever has occurred so far as my knowledge extends, tho' this town has frequently suffered from its ravages.

The Rio Grande has been swollen to an almost unparalleled degree this season, and immense ponds are still existent all around this town which were supplied from the overflowing river. From these an evaporation has been going on since the last of August, but no appreciable disease has occurred assignable to such origin. The discharges were granted to the Volunteers for causes much less important than are considered necessary to entitle the regular soldier to discharge. I am satisfied that I have done the State some service in granting so many certificates of disability *in these cases.*[21]

In a comprehensive review of the lower Rio Grande region's medical topography Dr. George Johnson[**] ascribed part of the cause to dietary deficiencies:

The troops that have, from time to time, sojourned at the Brazos, have been for the most part volunteers, and they have had much more to learn than the drill and discipline. They have been compelled to take a few lessons in the culinary art—particularly so far as related to the cooking of pork and beans— a knowledge of which was not obtained until the pains of colic had been experienced more than once. It would be fair to say that the beans of every volunteer regiment are not half cooked, for, at least, the first month of service. Besides, the young soldier is apt to indulge in every excess. He will lie down on the wet ground without his blanket. The old soldier is more prudent—he may drink a little too much whiskey (if he can get it), but he will not expose himself unnecessarily to the sun's heat at mid-day, in fishing or hunting. Neither will he eat the coarse and unwholesome food that a recruit will swallow with avidity. The old soldiers of our regiment were the only men who would not indulge in eating red fish, oysters and crabs, while on the island. They were influenced, in part, by the example of the Mexicans, who eschew these luxuries during the summer months.[23]

SCURVY IN THE CAMPS

Most of the army doctors agreed that a diet of hard bread, beef, bacon and beans offered the most wholesome food; the fresh fruits and vegetables of Mexico were excluded as a sure cause of diarrhea. Nevertheless the troops did feast on green corn, peaches, bananas, chili peppers, oranges and other products of the region.[24] A few of the doctors pointed out that the heavy, monotonous army diet invited scurvy. Pickles, sauerkraut and other antiscorbutics were "extra issues," but the disease still appeared at a camp across from Matamoros in June 1846. Asst. Surg. Grayson M. Prevost,[25] reported it:

A Vegetable Vender

I have the honor to submit to your notice a brief report concerning the health of the Troops of the 7th Regiment.

The men having subsisted for several months on the usual Commissary stores are beginning to suffer for want of variety in the articles of their diet.

The number of cases of decided scurvy in the Regt. is not very great, say eight or ten, but in many instances of patients labouring under other diseases, a scorbutic taint is very perceptable [sic] rendering the more prominent affections less amenable to treatment than they would be in constitutions otherwise healthy.

Whether the 7th Regt. suffers more in this respect than other portions of the Army I do not know, but as the evil is one likely to increase unless some addition can be made to the usual rations of the men, I deem it my duty to submit this report in hopes that by your recommendation suitable supplies of fresh vegetables will be ordered by the commissary genl. for the use of the Regiment.[26]

Later, S. G. I. De Camp, the able Surgeon at Santa Fe, advised Surg. Gen. Lawson:

Scurvy has recently made its appearance among the troops, produced I think from living entirely on bread & meat, the latter generally very poor, having been mutton until recently, but at my suggestion beef is now issued and the health of the men has improved. Vegetable diet is almost unknown in New Mexico, and to the men of Missouri where vegetables form a large part of the food, the change can not be other than prejudicial. When Regular troops are sent to this country I recommend that an abundant supply of garden seeds be sent with them, as there is every facility for good gardens.[27]

THE MENACE OF YELLOW FEVER

At Vera Cruz the specter of "yellow jack," the dread yellow fever or "black vomit," haunted Maj. Gen. Winfield Scott from the earliest days of his command in Mexico. Despatches to the Secretary of War, outlining his plans for the campaign, urged haste so that the soldiers might get away from the coastal plain before the season for yellow fever. The theme recurs in subsequent letters. But the task of assembling, supplying and transporting the army went slowly, and it was April 8 before the American forces advanced inland from Vera Cruz. Moreover, the port remained the army's supply base; fresh troops landed and paused there; others, whose term of enlistment ran out, returned there to await transportation home; and a hospital for the care of the sick and wounded was there. The general's worst fears were consequently realized; the "black vomit"[28] struck. The grim tale of sickness in the lower Rio Grande

Valley is repeated on the road from Vera Cruz to Mexico City—fevers, dysentery, diarrhea. Altitude, climate, and the season might affect the intensity of the fever but the incidence always remained high no matter where the army happened to be.

A report submitted in August 1847, by Dr. John B. Porter at Vera Cruz gave the number of patients in his hospital, the nature of their sickness and the mortality rate of the major killers. It shows yellow fever to be the deadliest, even though dysentery and diarrhea claimed more victims:

I have the honor to transmit Reports of sick & wounded in General Hospital [Vera Cruz] for the Quarter ending 30 June, 1847. It was my intention to have sent them many days ago, but on careful research I found there were some errors which ought to be corrected, and new Reports throughout have been made. I wish it to be distinctly understood that these Reports vary from those furnished in haste to the Medical Director, and that they are more correct.

. . . . .

I have made the following abstract of the most important, deaths per cent., &c.

REGULARS.—Total number of cases 1310
       "   "   fever cases 234
       "   "   yellow fever 112
       "   "   dysentery & diarrhoea 482
REGULARS.—Died of all fevers 26
       "   "   yellow fever 14
       "   "   dysentery & diarrhoea 84
     Total number of deaths 150
     Deaths per cent 11.45
       "   "   "   from all fevers 11.11
       "   "   "   from yellow fever 12.5
       "   "   "   from dysentery & diarrhoea 17.42
   Discharged   "   " 46
VOLUNTEERS.—Total number of cases 860
       "   "   all fevers 178
       "   "   yellow fever 14
       "   "   diarrhoea & dysentery 347
     Deaths. Total number 73
       "   "   from all fevers 9
       "   "   "   yellow fever 4
       "   "   "   dysentery & diarrhoea 33

[Volunteers]	Deaths—per cent.	8.45
	" " " from all fevers	5.05
	" " " " yellow fever	28.57
	" " " " dysentery & diarrhoea	9.51
	Discharged	12.67

Q.M. Dept.	Total number of cases	144
	" " " all fevers	86
	" " " yellow fever	52
	" " " dysentery & diarrhoea	40
	Deaths Total	30
	" " all fevers	18
	" " yellow fever	13
	" " dysentery & diarrhoea	7
	Deaths per cent	20.83
	" " " all fevers	20.93
	" " " yellow fever	25.00
	" " " dysentery & diarrhoea	17.50

Consolidated Report

Per cent of deaths	10.9
" " " " from all fevers	10.64
" " " " " yellow fever	17.41
" " " " " dysentery & diarrhoea	14.38

The per cent. of mortality from all fevers, yellow fever, and dysentery & diarrhoea is the per cent. of each class of cases respectively.

Considering the severe cases of bowel affection in April, when the hospital was first established; the epidemic influence in the last part of May & the whole of June; and the condition of the hospital at its organization, the mortality has been unexpectedly small.

. . . . .

You will see, Sir, that the Q.M. Dept. has suffered most. This is owing to the fact that the men employed in that Dept. are more exposed to the sun & rains than any others, and that they have more money to spend than the soldier, are less under restraint, and are much more dissipated. Moreover, they do not report sick under 2, 3, or 4 days; the soldier reports immediately.

It ought to be made apparent that the regulars have not suffered so much as would appear on paper. In the first place there is a great difference in the discharges per cent. Then, nearly all the vol[unteer]s left with their regiments (12-months' men) for the U.S. before the yellow fever broke out.[29]

DISEASES ON SCOTT'S MARCH

When Scott's Army moved inland, reports indicated that because the main body was in a healthy region of tablelands nothing but the "ordinary diseases" should be expected. But these included dysentery, diarrhea, and intermittent and typhoid fevers.[30] A memorandum which Asst. Surg. P. G. Jones[31] submitted to Scott's Medical Director in Mexico City provided a case study of a detachment of troops which he accompanied from New Orleans Barracks to Mexico City, as a specimen of the illnesses which could befall a unit of troops. The highest incidence of disease did occur while they were camped at Vera Cruz; but the number was still considerable on the march from Vera Cruz to the City of Mexico:

CITY OF MEXICO, JANY. 28, 1848.

Memorandum of cases treated by the undersigned from the 5th of December, 1847 to the 16th Decr. inclusive—being a detachment of recruits sent from New Orleans Barracks to Vera Cruz under my charge—to wit—(being 300 troops) Inflamatory fever 1; Mumps 12; Measles 11; Dysuria 1; Gonorrhea 1; Scald 1; Contusion 1; Dyarrhea 3; Cholic 1; Dysenteria 1; Total: 33.

Of this number 0 case was left at hospital at Tampico.

Memorandum of cases treated by the undersigned from the 17th of Decr., 1847 to the 25th January 1848 inclusive being 1,200 troops encamped at Camp Washington Vera Cruz—from 17th Decr. to 2d Jany. 1848—also 700 troops in the train from Vera Cruz to Mexico from 2d Jany. 1848 to 25th Jany. inclusive.

At Camp Washington—as follows—to wit—Dysenteria 50; Diarrhea 81; Measles 21; Mumps 18; Pneumonia 16; Gonorrhea 8; Syphilis 2; Fever Int[ermittent] 2; Cholera Morb. 8; Cholic 5; Del. Tremens 1; Ampt. finger 1; Total: 213.

On the march from Vera Cruz to Mexico as follows—from 2d Jany. to 25th Jany.—1848.

Diarrhea 108; Dysenteria 9; Cholera morbus 6; Cholic 4; Gonorrhea 3; Burns from powder 2; Ampt. finger 1; Fract. tibia 1; Dislocated humerus 1; Fever Int. 12; Fever contd 4; Total: 151.

Of this number I left 5 cases at the [General] Hospital at Vera Cruz and 13 cases at the different hospitals on the march from Vera Cruz to the City of Mexico.[32]

CAUSES OF ILLNESS

Accompanying Scott's army inland to Mexico City, Surg. Charles S. Tripler[33] analyzed the causes of illness among the troops. He found many contributing factors, but deficiency in the medical staff was not one of them:

Agreeably to your instructions of the 3d inst., I called together yesterday the medical officers of the 2d division for the purpose of consultation & the interchange of opinion upon the causes of the diseases now so extensively prevailing among the troops. I have now the honor to submit the result.

We consider the origin of the evils the inferior physical constitution of so many of the men that are enlisted for the service. In peace when we have comfortable quarters, good hospitals, abundance of clothing & bedding & no exposure for our men, the greatest care & caution are exercised in the inspection of recruits & it is seldom a man gains admission into the ranks, who is not qualified to perform the duties of a soldier. But in war, where a still greater degree of physical vigor in the soldier is required from the necessary privation & exposure to which he must be subjected, a relaxation in the scrutiny the recruit is submitted to, is winked at, & even encouraged with the effects of giving us armies on paper, filling our hospitals & embarrassing the operations of the Generals in the fields. It is undeniable that the recruits the Regiments of the Division have received within the last year have been of the most inferior description & it is among them the greatest proportion of disease has occured.

Another cause of disease is the necessary & rapid transition of climate. It is believed that few individuals in private life make a rapid transit from our climate to another without experiencing some disturbance of healthy function. This cause would of course operate to a greater extent among soldiers from the peculiarity of their circumstances & it is one that cannot be obviated.

Deficiency of clothing is another cause. In many & perhaps most instances this is the fault of the soldier himself. Men will throw away their clothing in a march to relieve their knapsacks, preferring future pain, disease & death to present fatigue—this evil has prevailed extensively in the march from Vera Cruz to Puebla.

The sudden & violent change of habits the recruit must undergo in becoming a soldier produces an unfavorable influence upon the power of his constitution to resist disease. This cause is also irremediable.

The neglect of personal cleanliness is another cause of disease. It is a fact that numbers of our men, particularly those reporting sick neglect to a shameful extent such attention as is necessary to health.

The quarters occupied by our troops are for the most part open to the weather; those which are within doors are small & ill ventilated apartments, the floors upon which the men sleep are of brick & at least one half on the ground floor, & necessarily damp. This is a palpable cause of disease. It has been mitigated to some degree by the issue of mats to the men.

The use of fresh provisions exclusively no doubt occasion disturbance of the digestive organs & swells the number of our cases of diarrhea.

The improvident use of the fruits of the climate occasions many cases & is a great impediment in the way of convalescence.

It is also thought that a proper attention is not given to the cooking of the rations. That the cooks are frequently careless in the performance of their duties & that bad cookery makes a doubtful diet positively injurious.

But an important reason for the increase of the number on the sick report may be found in the climatic influence. Ordinarily, men when relieved of disease rapidly recover strength of flesh & are able to return to duty. Here this is not the case—convalescence is astonishingly slow & an improvement, scarcely perceptible, is made from day to day in men who do not want any further medical treatment. Of this class are most of those now on the Surgeon's reports.[34]

Persistence of Disease

Disease persisted to the end, though in the Valley of Mexico typhoid appears to have supplanted diarrhea as the greatest menace. Surg. Timothy Childs,[35] with the Massachusetts Volunteers at San Angel, reported:

The Valley of Mexico in which we are stationed is fertile and beautiful— but not healthy—certainly not to the unacclimated. We have lost here about as many men as we have in all other places in Mexico put together. We reached here in December. In December we lost 1 man—in January, 7 men— in February, 10 men—and in March 4 men—in all 22.

We have had *Rubiola Erysipelas* of the most malignant kind. *Typhoid fever* and the devil and all—*Intermittent fever* too has been rife. I have had it myself no less than three times. Wounds do badly. A vast proportion of the amputations after the battles in the valley died—and of those that survived not one in ten would heal till they were sent out of the country. The Malaria which abounds here seems to give character to all the diseases—and in every case the typhoid symptoms showed themselves early. Of late, however, the health of the troops has improved—and our sick list has fallen down nearly one half.[36]

Even when fever did not ravage the camps and the health of the troops was pronounced "very good," as Dr. N. S. Jarvis[37] did at Monterey in August 1847, there would be added, almost as a matter of course, "with [the] exception of those never-failing diseases of armies viz. Diarrhea & Dysentery."[38]

In Monterey, California, Asst. Surg. Robert Murray[39] found that his veteran troops were healthy but that many of his newly arrived recruits were ill:

I have the honor to transmit the Quarterly Report of the sick at Monterey, Calif[orni]a. up to the 30th June. I am happy to be able to report the healthy condition of the troops at that Post. So far no case of fever has occurred among them & I am convinced that but few cases will take place, save among those recently arrived. At this place among 200 men who have been in the country some 18 months, but 2 or three cases of fever have occurred while of the 70 Recruits which arrived this spring some 15 or 20 have had fever & some very severely; two of them have died. A few cases are of the remittent type but most of them are real typhoid.[40]

In a bracing atmosphere above 7,000 feet, the troops at Santa Fe still succumbed to many diseases: typhoid, scorbutis, meningitis, gonorrhea, syphilis, and pneumonia—often fatal within a few hours.[41] The resident Surgeon, Samuel G. I. DeCamp, commented:

Fever from malaria is unknown among the natives of this place. But pleurisy, pneumonia, and rheumatism are said to be common in the winter months.

There are more diseased persons here than I ever saw in a town of this size. These cases have their origin in diseases produced from sensual habits of promiscuous sexual indulgence which is carried on here, to an extent that would scarcely be credited at a distance, and there are few persons among the natives who are believed to be free from venereal disease in one form or other.[42]

Solicitude of Generals

So throughout the Mexican War disease was prevalent: the lower Rio Grande Valley, the Valley of Mexico, Monterey, Vera Cruz, Buena Vista, Puebla, Santa Fe, and California—the pattern varied in detail and intensity but it was always an ugly one, and the records of the care of the sick and wounded do little to improve the picture.

The nonmedical branches of the army did what they could. Scott and (to an even greater degree) Taylor were solicitous of their men, especially the wounded. In the early months of the war Taylor wrote from Matamoros to Surg. R. C. Wood:

I was pleased to learn the wounded officers were on the mend & hope they will not only be able, but will very soon leave for their homes or friends in the North or elsewhere. At the same time I deeply regretted to hear the other wounded, the n. comd. officers & privates were not doing so well, & that some of them had died, no doubt owing in part to the effects of the dreadful storm you had soon after you returned, which prostrated your tents, and perhaps other covering which must have exposed them all to its violence, at any rate must have wet them through [and] through as far as it could be done, besides doing them other serious injury; but I trust you have since been able to make them as comfortable as circumstances would admit of, & I feel satis-[fied] you will do all in your power to restore them to health as soon as it can be done; I am sorry for want of hands that nothing has been done towards fitting up the *Long* for a hospital, as I supposed she was far on the way towards completion, but in this I fear I have been mistaken.[43]

An order issued at Buena Vista by Brigadier General Wool described measures taken by an army commander in the field to care for his sick and to prevent the further spread of disease:

The North Carolina Regiment is . . unprovided with the shelter and comforts necessary for the sick. In this regiment the Board [of Surgeons] suggested the propriety of pitching tarpaulins on frames, and whitewashing them outside, and also, as a general means of preventing a further increase of sickness suggests the exclusion of fruits, cakes, and indigestible vegetables, the building of ovens for baking good bread, and a change in the hour of morning drill, making it is early as practicable.

Brig. Gen. Cushing will take proper measures to have the above suggestions carried out.

Such of the sick as shall be designated by the Medical Director will be removed to Saltillo.[44]

Surgeon General Lawson's Defense

As "wagon loads" of patients arrived at Camargo and other staging points, surgeons worked themselves to the point of exhaustion, and General Taylor did his best, but neither the surgeons nor the general could cope with shortages ranging from space to doctors. Appeals to the Surgeon General in Washington were met by references to "the law of the land" and pompous bombast. In a reply to a request from General Taylor to grant a leave of absence to his Medical Director, Surg. P. H. Craig,[45] Surg. Gen. Lawson wrote:

Upon the subject of the scarcity of medical officers in the field, I have no hesitation in expressing the belief that the regular troops employed against Mexico have comparatively as large a number of medical officers as any other army in the world.

The laws of the land in former times, as on a late occasion, awarded two medical officers to a full regiment of about 750 men, or one medical officer to 375 men; and this proportion of medical officers to a consolidated regiment or body of 750 men has been found, from long experience, sufficient to meet the requirements of the service.

From the monthly returns in the adjutant general's office for May last (the latest report received), it appears that on the 30th of that month the strength of the army of occupation in officers and men was 3,938; and from the returns in the surgeon general's office it is found that there were at that time 24 medical officers serving with that army.

Now, if we divide 3,938 men, the strength of the command, by 24, the number of medical officers present with it, the result will give one medical officer to every 164 men, instead of 375, or 100 per cent. more of medical officers than is contemplated by the laws providing for the organization of the military corps.

If we give twelve medical officers to the 3,938 men in the field, which is the full complement recognized by law, we shall have, after furnishing one for medical director, two for a general hospital, and one to perform the duty of medical purveyor, still eight officers, or one-third of the whole number, in reserve to meet the contingencies of the service, the incidents and accidents growing out of active operations in the field.

Since the last return from the army, one medical officer has gone into the field with a body of recruits; two are now en route with detachments of the 2d infantry towards the theatre of action, and one is about to sail in a day or two with another portion of the 2d infantry for the seat of war.

In this way—that is, by sending a medical officer with each detachment of troops which goes into the field—the standard number of medical officers (originally large) will be kept up with the army of occupation.

To do more than this would be making a secrifice of military propriety and the public interest, to save a little labor to some of the medical officers, who, if the duties are equitably distributed among them, I am free to say, from analogy and from experience have not more to do than the government has a right to claim of them.

I know what a man can perform and ought to do in time of need. I have myself acted as medical director, medical purveyor, and attending surgeon to a body of troops, at one and the same time; nay more, I have frequently prescribed for 250 men a day; and I have a right to expect that those under my control will perform something like the same amount of duty.

As to the "exposure and privations incident to a camp life, making serious inroads upon a man's health," or his being "broken down by long and arduous service in the field," of less than one year's duration, I can scarcely entertain the idea.

Why, I never would permit myself to be sick when honor and duty claimed from me active exertion; but whether sick or well, I was never known to quit the field until called off by authority. It is very easy for an officer, who is called upon to do a little more duty than the very little service he has been accustomed to perform at a small military post, to speak in round numbers of the arduous duties, the privations and sufferings, he has experienced in the field, when a statistical examination into the matter will prove that his grievances are all imaginary—mere trifles, as light as air.

. . . . .

I have given all in the way of medical aid which military propriety, the customs of the service in like cases, and the actual wants of the army, seemed to require; but if they desire more medical officers they shall have them, with myself to boot, if acceptable, and I am borne out in the measure.[46]

ARMY HOSPITALS

One of the earliest acts of the Army Medical Division was to establish hospitals, which filled so rapidly with the sick and wounded that overcrowding, added to wasteful and extravagant practices of volunteer attendants, created numerous problems. Asst. Surg. John C. Glen[47] discussed some of his problems at the San Antonio Hospital:

As it is impossible to ascertain exactly what [medicines] have arrived and what have not, I was appointed to take charge of them, and relieved Asst. Sgn. Hitchcock who had only a day or two before relieved Surgn. Price of the volunteers. The former had taken no inventory of them and the latter was in charge too short a time to take any steps toward that end. I merely assumed charge of those which were in store at the time, a great deal having been issued already, and most of the things taken from the boxes. . . . I should have made my returns at the usual time but have been prevented by the necessity for my almost constant attendance at the General Hospital at this place. My sick have averaged nearly one hundred daily and I have been left with stewards, attendants, nurses, &c all new and unaccustomed to the duties and all *volunteers*. In the Purveyor's Department I have been compelled to weigh out, pack up, & label all the articles which I have issued, besides making out the papers with my own hands, labours which I think we were never intended to perform without the assistance of a clerk.

. . . . .

The General Hospital at this place has consumed a very large quantity of medicines and stores, much larger than would have been required for an establishment of the same kind for regular troops. The volunteer nurses and attendants being wasteful and extravagant, and requiring constant watching and attention in order to regulate their distribution of medicines and stores.

I would beg leave to inform you that I have received an order from General Wool to join him without delay with an additional supply of medical stores.

. . . . .

I shall leave at this place some articles of medicines, stores, &c., which Gen. Wool has directed me to turn over to Dr. Griffith, a private physician holding the appointment of Acting Asst. Surgeon from the General.[48]

Dr. S. G. I. De Camp reported similar problems from Santa Fe:

Soon after the arrival of Col. Price's Regt.[49] & the independt. Battalion,[50] it was found that the Genl. Hospl. was far too small to accommodate the sick, and at my suggestion another building was procured, and another Hospl. was established for Col. Price's command and placed under the immediate charge of Surgeon May.[51]

As the heavy trains of provisions came in, great numbers of teamsters and other persons in the Qr. Master's dept. arrived sick, and it became necessary to open a Hospl. for them.

A sufficient quantity of wool for matrasses and Mexican blankets have been purchased, and the sick are as comfortably provided for as the means in the country will allow.

The supply of medicines is very limited, and unless I receive this month what I wrote to St. Louis for by Capt. Murphy,[52] I shall be in a sad dilemma before spring. I have been enabled to procure small quantities from the merchants, but there is no more to purchase. Many of the leading articles are nearly expended, & cases of the worst form of disease are daily presenting themselves.[53]

Other hospitals in Texas and northern Mexico—Corpus Christi, Matamoros, Saltillo—were overcrowded, the treatment was frequently inadequate, and there was a shortage of doctors. But the most scathing attacks were made on the hospitals to which the sick and wounded of Scott's army were condemned. Vera Cruz was among the worst.

Surg. John B. Porter, Director of a Vera Cruz hospital, brought order out of chaos. He introduced strict regulations, demanded detailed reports, and tried to provide efficient care against great odds:

When this hospital was established I had not a single steward, and since have had sick, dishonest and incompetent ones; scarcely an attendant; few & incompetent (in the main) medical assistants; no ward master, and always a sick or incompetent one; not a kitchen, or sink, bunk, table, bench, spit box, close stool—in a word, there was nothing but the miserable sick. The condition of things was deplorable. On this point my best witnesses were the Surgeon General of the Army and Medical Director Harney.[54] . . . There being no sink about the place and the hospital filled with diarrhoea patients when it was first opened, the appearance of [the] hospital every morning was lamentable. There was no observance of order & regularity among the disorderly & half mutinous volunteers, and all was confusion. But by degrees this discouraging state of things was removed.[55]

Milton Jamieson, 5th Regiment of Ohio Volunteers, wrote an appalling account of conditions in the same hospital:

On the 17th [of October 1847] I visited the general army "Hospital." Three of Com. C, viz: Michael Wood, John Turner and Robert Thompson, were stricken down with disease, and had been placed in it. I called to see them but was unable to find any but Thompson. These young men were very unfortunate; they were taken down with diseases soon after they entered the service, and were never able to perform any duty. They would no doubt have made excellent soldiers, and all that they desired was good health. But in consequence of their continued illness, they were "honorably discharged" from the service of the United States, on a surgeon's certificate of disability, about the first of January, 1848.

I passed all through the hospital, and I hope never again to behold such horrid, ghastly and shocking pictures of humanity as there fell under my sight. Diseases of all kinds were prevailing there, from their mildest to their most malignant forms. Some were bearing the pains of their diseases with fortitude, some were screaming, some were praying to God to release them from their miseries, and others were raving maniacs, talking incoherently of parents, home and country. Some were so reduced in flesh that they looked more like walking skeletons than human beings—nay! their very bones could be seen "creeping through their flesh." Who but a Stoic could look upon these scenes, unmoved. The number of diseased victims in this hospital was seven hundred. I was informed that they died at the rate of eight or ten per day.

The breath is scarcely out of the body of the deceased before the "stewards" are rifling his pockets. It was a common expression there, that the man who entered one of the *general hospitals*, sick, with twenty dollars in his pocket, might as well "give up the ghost" at once; for the "stewards" would soon kill him with medicine; whereas, if he went there penniless, in nine cases out of ten he would recover from his disease. Many died from the want of proper attention.

Sometimes the physicians were extremely cruel to their patients. An instance of the barbarity of one of the surgeons at Vera Cruz was related to me by a member of Com. C, in whose veracity the utmost confidence can be placed, as having fallen under his observation while he was unfortunately confined in the hospital at that place. One poor fellow had been placed there, whose disease was so extremely painful that it kept him screaming pretty much all the time. His continued screams fell very [un]pleasantly on the ears of one of the surgeons. He sent the stewards to the poor victim several times to command him to "stop his noise." But his cries were altogether involuntary, and he could not repress them. When the surgeon saw that his commands were not obeyed, it made him very angry. He ordered the stewards to *"gag him!"* He could offer but a feeble resistance. And while they were tying on a block of wood to his mouth, his soul took its flight to another world. When they had obeyed this inhuman command, they beheld a *gagged corpse.* And in three hours afterwards it was resting in the silent tomb. This young man further informed me, that he understood that this matter reached the ears of the commanding officer at Vera Cruz, and he had this surgeon brought before a "Court Martial," who, upon its investigation, let him go "unwhipped of justice," by paying a small fine, and receiving a slight reprimand. I never learned this surgeon's name.[56]

The use of an existing structure as a field hospital was a practice common to armies for centuries. In September 1846, Taylor's surgeons selected "a strong stone building, which had been intended for a granary" at the edge of Cerralvo as a depot for surplus munitions and provisions, and the sick were left there too, under the care of a small garrison.[57] The Castle at Perote soon proved to be a dank and sickly place for Scott's wounded. Surg. Adam N. McLaren[58] told of this in his report to Washington:

I have the honor to transmit herewith a Report of the Sick, Wounded &c. of Regulars, for the month ending the 31st August 1847, also a monthly report of sick & wounded Volunteers ending the same period. The number of deaths which have occurred during the month, amount to one hundred & nineteen including Regulars & Volunteers, the number of deaths when the facts are known can be readily accounted for. A large majority of the cases who were admitted into the Hospital had contracted disease on the march from Vera Cruz to this place, many of them in fact were in a moribund state when recd., being without tents and almost destitute of clothing—they suffered severely on the march. Every wagon train that has passed this Post for Puebla has left a large number of sick in the lowest condition of filth & disease, crowding the hospital to an excess & far beyond our means of accommodation. We were obliged through necessity to occupy bombproofs as *sick wards* which are ill adapted for the reception of the sick, being cold & damp, besides badly ventilated. The number of sick & convalescents of Regulars and

Volunteers now remaining in Genl. Hospital amount to nearly 300 patients —they are generally doing well with some exceptions. Every comfort as far as practicable has been purchased for them in the way of diet—out of the Hospital Fund, and the strictest attention [has] been observed in the police and administration of medicines.[59]

CLINICAL INVESTIGATIONS

There was a brighter side. Dedicated physicians worked until they were exhausted; some with an interest in medical science, observed, collected data, and reported their findings. Although the war failed to produce any startling advance in medical knowledge or practice, it was not altogether unfruitful. If the army medical corps did not discover the causes of yellow fever, they helped establish that it was not contagious, and that it bore some relation to the presence of swamps and stagnant water. They also correctly guessed that impure water and diet were the chief culprits responsible for diarrhea and dysentery. Many of the surgeons probed into the causes of disease, its treatment and preventative measures.

Asst. Surg. Charles H. Laub[60] described the epidemic character and treatment of yellow fever at Vera Cruz:

Herewith I have the honor to enclose a quarterly report of sick and wounded . . U.S. Infy. stationed at this post for the qr. ending the 30th of June, 1847.

By this report you will observe that the Yellow Fever is established as one of the prevailing diseases of the city at this time, and although it can not be said as yet to have assumed the *Epidemic* character, nevertheless a considerable number of cases have occured, the mortality from which, I am happy to be able to say, up to this time is comparatively small (for hospital patients) the amt. of deaths from this disease being about 24 pr. ct. & that from all diseases about 5, a result which I believe will compare very favourably with the mortuary statistics of the southern cities of the U[nited] States during its existence in those subject to its visitation; that of New Orleans I am informed for a series of years being a fraction less than 50 pr. ct. With some exceptions the disease has been of a mild and tractable character, yielding in most cases if taken in its earliest attack, to the influence of full doses (15 to 25 grs) of quinine, with mercurials, aided by the general or local abstraction of blood, according to circumstances, together with warm mustards baths, mild purgatives if necessary, or enemas, iced or acidulated gum water as a drink in small quantities, the greatest reliance and apparent benefits being from the large doses of Quinine at the onset, and continued in smaller quantities, from 5 to 8 grs every 4 to 6 hours during the first 36 or

48 hours in arresting its progress, the mercurial being added with the view principally of discharging the contents of the bowels during that period.

Should this course, as it sometimes does, fail in producing a favourable termination or crisis, the subsequent treatment, a much less active one, has consisted in the administration of the various remedial agents, in combat[t]ing the local symptoms suggested by the diversified prominent features of the individual cases, such as the application of dry cups, cold applications, as iced water and v[i]n[e]gar to the head, fomentations or sponging with brandy (warm) or water, sinapisms & blisters, with warm Mustard Pediluria, together with the internal administration of the Camphorated Ammonia mixture or bi Carb Soda & Morphia, where there is much irritability of stomach, and at the same time keeping the bowels freed by mild enemas alone. In regard to the efficacy of the after treatment I am compelled to say that my experience & [I] believe that of most of the medical men here, has shown that little benefit has been derived from it; the cases in which we have had an opportunity of testing its remedial value, with but few exceptions, have terminated fatally.

A few of the cases from the commencement have assumed an aggravated character, the hemmorhagic tendency being developed in the sanguinous discharges from the mouth & anus, in connexion with the simultaneous ejection from the stomach of that fecutive accumulation, the Black Vomit, which with some of the resident Physicians appears to have given the distinctive appelative to this disease of the *vomitos* as differing in some respects with the Yellow Fever of New Orleans, but of which the evidence presented by the disease gives no corroboration. Other cases of more rare occurence of the peculiar character designated as the walking cases of Yellow Fever, have been observed, in which the patient although *fatally* affected, is nevertheless able, if allowed to *walk* about (in some up to a comparatively short time of his dissolution) a propensity too, in which he is sure to indulge, contrary to instruction, if not narrowly watched and prevented. Of these cases I have only to say that my experience affords additional evidence of the assertion of Professor Harrison of [New] Orleans, that they have almost invariably proved fatal, in defiance of all remedies & contrary to what might be expected, judging mainly from appearances to those who have never witnessed this uncommon form of the disease.

A singular symptom which I have not seen noticed by any writer on the subject, and which has been observed by myself as well as others here during the period of convalescence even as late as the 15th to the 25th day is the discoloration of the tongue throughout its center and in some cases over the entire upper surface of the organ, presenting the appearance as if it had been immersed in *Ink*, a circumstance for which I am entirely unable to assign any cause, but which has proved to be of minor importance, gradually disappearing with the improving tone of the system under the administration of the Aromatic Sulp. acid with Quinine in from one to two grs. doses, 2 or 3 times during the 24 hours. The general type of fever in the large proportion of cases has been that of an open *remittant* character, while *some* from the commencement of the attack have assumed or very early after degenerated into that of a typhoid condition, a state of things highly unfavourable, the mortality in such being greater, while the convalescence is always more tedious and protracted.

I have not spoken of the dietetic management in this disease because indeed little is necessary to be said on this subject, where an *entire restriction* from all articles of nourishment is strictly *required* and *enjoined* untill the period of convalescence is permanently established, when beef tea or chicken water may be allowed in small quantities, together [the following was written in but lined out, possibly by the author or by someone else—this passage is indicated by angle brackets] <with port wine, sangaree, brandy toddy, porter or ale as the ap[p]etite of the individual may prefer, together with the occasional use of the mineral acids.> When the cases have terminated fatally, death has taken place generally on the 5th day while the period occupied in the convalescence has been from 8 to 20 days.[61]

Hygienic Regulations

Dr. E. H. Barton,[62] also at a Vera Cruz hospital, became president of a sanitary board in that city. He promulgated hygienic rules for the city's inhabitants which were recommended for general use in tropical climates.

The *first* precept . . . is temperance, in every sense of that extensive term—but especially with regard to an indulgence in intoxicating drinks, and overtasking the digestive organs with strong and rich food, or that which is difficult of digestion, or green fruit—or very much of ripe fruit, if you are unaccustomed to it.

The *second* is in relation to exposure to the sun and night air: the first will be avoided as far as practicable, and particularly from 7 A.M. to 2 P.M., and the night air is the more dangerous from the increased susceptibility acquired by a previous exposure to the sun; and if necessarily in it, use flannel and be in motion while so exposed. Use every prudent means to avoid exposure to the rains and dampness now daily expected.

The *third* is in regard to your dress—rather be too warm than too cool—flannel to the skin is strongly advised; avoid indulging in the seductive but dangerous drafts or currents of air—watch carefully the first approaches of coolness or chill, and retire from it.

On the first signal of sickness—pain in the head, back and limbs, apply to a competent medical man, and obey his instructions implicitly. Use the warm and salt baths freely before your meals, or not sooner than three hours after; the first is most applicable when exhausted from fatigue.[63]

TREATMENT OF DIARRHEA

At Jalapa, diarrhea was one of the most fatal diseases. Dr. Otis Hoyt[64] studied it carefully, then discussed its treatment:

Generally the disease can be controlled by attending in the first instance to the secretions of the liver, which is generally deficient. Blue Mass usually is sufficient to accomplish this object. After the functions of the liver and skin have been restored, Opium and Ipecac, of each one grain, Gum Camphor three grains, and occasionally the addition of one half of a grain of Sulph. Cuprii[65] or two grains of Acet. Plumbi,[66] administered three or four times per day has in most cases been successfull in arresting the disease. There is one peculiarity, however, which deserves notice; that is when the men begin to recover they have extraordinary appetites, not for meat, bread, or other nutritious and wholesome food, but for all kinds of green vegetables, and it is almost impossible to keep such articles from them; and when they do get them they are sure to produce a relapse and as sure to terminate fatally. I do not know to what influence to attribute this inordinate or morbid appetite. The desire to obtain such articles of food sometimes amounts almost to monomania.

When a patient at . . first has been sick but a short time and frequently when the disease has been of slight character he becomes very frale [sic] and the lower extremities become o[e]dematus and indicating very great deficiency in the fibrin of the blood. This state is more particularly manifested in cases of intermittent and remittent fevers. I at first was induced to attribute it to the use of Quinine which we have been obliged to use freely as almost all diseases are inclined to assume an intermittent character—but on further investigation I found the same state of things to exist to nearly as great an extent in cases where no quinine is used. In cases where there is no oedema there is almost invariably a peculiar painful sensation of the feet and in some instances so severe as to prevent walking. The state of the atmosphere has a very material influence on the sick as regards the quantity of moistness it contains. When a rainy or cloudy day occurs we invariably have more deaths occur than when the weather is pleasant.[67]

BATTLEFIELD SURGERY

The most severe tests of the doctors' skill and devotion must have been the hours of surgery following a battle. Considering the limitations imposed upon them by the conditions, the surgical skills exhibited at times were remarkable. For example, Dr. Robert Crooke Wood, a surgeon with Taylor's army, in August of 1846 operated for an aneurism resulting from the puncture of a bayonet, and successfully secured the artery with two ligatures and a breach spring.[68]

At the Battle of Buena Vista the conduct of some of the volunteer surgeons drew unfavorable comment, but other army doctors faithfully administered to the wounded. Asst. Surg. Charles M. Hitchcock[69] described the battlefield care of the wounded:

As I had a number of stretchers or litters, I directed the different Medical Officers to have tent poles passed through these litters (as no other timber could be procured) and to have their hospl. attendants or other men detailed to carry the wounded to the tent or to the nearest place of shelter. (The battle field was perfectly bare of timber or undergrowth of any kind. Ravines and gentle slopes were our only protection.) From which place after they were dressed the spring wagons or ambulances were to carry them to a Ranch about two miles distant and near where the Qr. Master's train was stationed. Many of the Drs. left for the ranch without my instruction and one actually came into town. How he passed the lancers I have yet to learn. After the battle was over on the evening of the 23d I mustered all the Medical Officers that could be found and repaired to the Ranch for the purpose of performing such further operations as were considered necessary before taking them to Hosps. in town. But General Wool had taken a different view of things, and I was ordered after midnight with all the wounded, dead & dying into town. I accordingly set all the Drs. to work loading the wagons, or superintending the same and by 3 A.M. we got them into the churches. I gave the Medical Officers such further instructions, in regard to the further treatment and comfort of the wounded as seemed necessary and returned to the field where lo! Santa Anna was gone! After scouring the field in search of the wounded, and after dressing many of the enemy there, I returned to town to select suitable buildings and to arrange the hospitals. But Dr. Craig had just arrived and the Directorship fell into his hands.[70]

In spite of these efforts, the wounded often lay moaning on the field for hours. Herman Upmann was one of those who suffered at Buena Vista. His account vividly told of his anguish.

Late in the afternoon of the second day, the 23d of February, I was badly wounded in my right leg, just above the knee, by two bullets, carried away from the battlefield by two men, thrown on to a cart and carried to Buena Vista about a mile distant, where we were placed on the floor of the house and lay there until 11 P.M.. Then we were carried into town where the hospital has been fitted out in the town cathedral. Here I am at present lying on the floor beside a side-altar, covered over with an old carpet, a wooden image of the Virgin Mary as a pillow, and beside me on the floor as a writing-desk, a Lamb of God embroidered on gold upon white silk and fastened upon a frame of wood. The surgeon has raised my hopes high that I shall keep my leg.[71]

SURGICAL SKILLS IN HOSPITALS

An account of surgery in the hospitals after the Battle of Buena Vista was written by W. B. Herrick, M.D., Professor of Anatomy at Rush Medical College and Surgeon to the 1st Regiment Illinois Volunteers:

On the day of the battle, the wounded, after receiving such attention from the surgeons, as could, at the time and under the circumstances, be given to them, were removed from the field, some to Saltillo, others to the Ranchera de Buena Vista.

When, on the evening of that day, we arrived at the last named place, we found those of the wounded still living, the dying and the dead, crowded together indiscriminately, and presenting a melancholy picture of suffering and distress not easily described, and never to be forgotten.

As soon as circumstances would permit, such as were still living were selected from their less fortunate companions, placed in wagons in charge of the writer, and conveyed late at night to the large cathedral in town which had already been converted into a temporary hospital.

The time, both day and night, for the forty-eight hours after, was spent by the surgeons in attending to such wounds as had been overlooked on the field, in renewing the dressings of those requiring attention, and in performing amputations and such other operations, as, upon a re-examination of the cases, seemed to be required.

During the third, and a part of the fourth days subsequent to the battle, the wounded were removed from the large but crowded church to more convenient buildings, each capable of containing from fifty to one hundred patients.

In making this more permanent arrangement, those of the volunteers belonging to the same State, were, as far as was practicable, collected together in the same Hospital, and placed in charge of some one of their respective surgeons.

The wounded of the first and second Illinois regiments, consisting in all of nearly one hundred, in the proportion of about ten officers in their private quarters in different parts of the town to eighty or ninety privates collected together in one of the best and most commodious of the above named hospitals, came, in accordance with the plan adopted, naturally under our charge.

Myself, and so far as I know, all other surgeons in charge of hospitals, on making the proper requisitions were provided with assistants, attendants, hospital stores, provisions, &c., promptly, and to an extent creditable both to the officers in charge and to our country.

With regard to the subsequent termination and treatment of the cases under the charge of myself and others, it may be stated that most of the simple flesh wounds healed rapidly and kindly under the use of dressings of lint, changed once in twenty-four or forty-eight hours, with an occasional aperient, and a diet adapted to the case. In some few instances the tendency to inflammatory action was so great as to require general antiphologistic treatment, and the use of emolients, anodynes, and other soothing local applications.

The presence of foreign substances in the simplest wounds frequently caused protracted suppuration, and the formation of abscesses, and thus retarded their cure, in many instances for a long time.

Stimulants and tonics, such as brandy, wine, iron, and acids, were used freely by myself and others, and with ma[r]ked benefit in all cases of debility consequent upon profuse suppuration. (A friend who has observed the beneficial effects of such treatment in one or two cases of the kind, suggests the propriety of using astringents in the form of lotions or injections to moderate the profuse and debilitating discharge from extensive suppurating surfaces.)

The gun shot wounds in which bones were injured presented all the complications of compound comminuted fractures, and proved to be the most troublesome and difficult cases to treat. The practice usually adopted by us, was to search carefully for and extract all detached pieces of bone, cleanse the wounds, bandage the limb firmly to a point high above the injury, and then to apply splints to prevent motion, but so as, if possible, not to interfere with the renewal of dressings, or the exit of pus. Thick paste board splints, shaped properly, perforated opposite to the external wounds, moistened and adapted accurately to the limb thus injured, afforded, when dry, a most perfect and firm support, and were found, therefore, to answer better than any others the indications in such cases.

Shortening was, in a few instances, the necessary consequence of loss of portions of bone, but these were exceptions to the general rule, for in most cases of fracture, union took place without loss of motion or deformity.

. . . In a majority of instances, primary amputations were followed by favorable, and secondary, by unfavorable results. The principal reasons why this was the case are obviously the following: . . most of the amputations upon the field, the only ones truly primary, were performed upon individuals in good health, and under excitement, and, therefore, not in a condition to suffer from debility or nervous depression. The subjects of the subsequent operations, on the other hand, had become depressed both physically and mentally by profuse suppuration, pain, and want of rest, and were, therefore, cases in which unfavorable results are most generally expected.

Most of the amputations in the hospitals were performed after consultations, and were found to be indicated, in most cases, not by the severity of the injury, so far as could be determined by the first examinations, but by the appearance of general symptoms of an unfavorable character, in many instances, such as are consequent upon the absorption of pus.

It is a remarkable fact that upon making examinations in the only two cases which proved fatal after the first week under my care, one after amputation, balls were found lodged in cavities filled with pus, one at the upper, and the other at the lower extremity of the tibia.

In our opinion, the fatal termination of these cases, as indicated both by the symptoms and the examinations, was in consequence of the absorption of pus, for it must be admitted that pus globules, whether too large or not to be absorbed by uninjured vessels, might readily pass into the large venus sinuses, such as are found every where in large bones, when broken into as in the cases above cited.[72]

LACK OF ANTISEPSIS

The Mexican War was fought before Joseph Lister's contributions to medical science profoundly affected surgical techniques. Dr. Nathan S. Jarvis, in a case study which he submitted to the New York Journal of Medicine *illustrated this problem:*

The first annoyance which we experienced, and which no doubt exerted an injurious effect, was one little anticipated at the time. The moment a limb was amputated, numerous flies would light on the stump, and must have deposited their eggs, for when it became necessary to dress the stump, myriads of maggots were found buried in it, which could be expelled with great difficulty; rendering it necessary in some instances to re-open the flap, for their complete extermination. But a much more formidable enemy made its appearance in an erysipelatous inflammation of the integuments, covering the stump, which generally set in two or three days after the operation; and notwithstanding all the means to arrest it, most commonly ended in sloughing, and either proved fatal, or rendered a second amputation necessary. That some influence existed previously, either external or internal, from some cause conected with the state of the atmosphere, or habits of men, arising from diet or water, was manifest. The slightest wound or scratch became in every case a tedious ulcer; in some instances proving a cause for serious alarm. Apparently the most trifling wounds require an unusual time for healing, and even those that had previously healed would break out again, and present greater difficulty in their cure than in the first instance.[73]

With almost pathetic eagerness the use of disinfectants became a quest. Every rumor of an advance in this direction reached the field. For example, Mrs. Edward G. W. Butler wrote to her husband, Colonel Butler:

I see that some French chemist has invented a disenfecting fluid. I wish you had some of it in your camp.[74]

Indeed, General Scott himself took cognizance of such reports when he ordered 40 or 50 barrels of Labarraque's disinfecting liquid together with chloride of lime.[75]

At Puebla, Bvt. Brig. Gen. Thomas Childs, in his Orders No. 58, directed that lime and whitewash be freely used:

The prevalence of disease in this city, renders it necessary that the utmost attention should be paid to the cleanliness of the men and their quarters. Commanding Officers will daily detail strong police parties, with one Commissioned Officer at their head, and not only order, but see, that every place is thoroughly cleaned about the quarters, that sinks are dug, and no filth allowed in any other place, that lime and white-wash are freely used, frequent bathing of the men, hair cut short and the men kept shaved, precautions, which are in themselves, great preventives of disease and dirt. There is now no excuse for any beards; the troops are in garrison and have ample time to attend to their personal cleanliness.[76]

INOCULATIONS FOR SMALLPOX

Although there was an insufficient quantity of vaccine, and what little there was tended to deteriorate rapidly in the hot climate, in the end it nonetheless was used successfully to contain an incipient epidemic of smallpox which broke out at Mier and Monterey in the winter of 1847-48. Even so there were over a hundred cases before the vaccination checked its further spread.[77]

Surgeon Jarvis discussed his encounter with the disease in his report to Washington:

I regret . . to state that the small pox a few days since made its appearance among the troops at Mier and Dr. Moore under date of Jany. 6th says that there [are] already 20 or more cases. He writes in regard to its origin that the men are supposed to have contracted it in a deserted ranche where they remained all night and where it was subsequently ascertained the inhabitants had the disease.

A case made its appearance here in one of the men belonging to the escort of the last train and who came up from Mier. By immediately isolating the patient and cutting off all communication whatever we have succeeded thus far in preventing its extension. Unfortunately all the vaccine virus I had on hand altho preserved with great care has as yet proved inert and worthless. This may be ascribed to its rapid decomposition & deterioration from the heat of the climate, notwithstanding all the precautions taken to preserve it from such causes or agency.[78]

Introduction of Anesthesia

On the night of September 30, 1846, Dr. William Thomas Green Morton, a dental surgeon in Boston, successfully administered ether to relieve the pain of a patient whose tooth he extracted. An account of the successful use of ether appeared the next day in a Boston newspaper. Morton disguised the anesthetic under the name "Letheon," and he colored and perfumed it to avoid identification. Two weeks later he received an invitation from Dr. C. F. Heywood, House Surgeon to the Massachusetts General Hospital, to demonstrate his anesthetic on a surgical patient. Another successful use of anesthesia occurred, in a clinical exhibition of Dr. John C. Warren on October 16.[79] The story soon appeared in the Boston and Surgical Journal.[80] Surg. Gen. Lawson read this article, but did not immediately order the introduction of "Letheon" for the Army in Mexico.

Meanwhile, Morton's revelation gained attention in Europe—even crowding the importance of gun cotton and Leverrier's discovery of the planet Neptune in the public journals. The London Times, on January 21, noted that leading surgeons in London hospitals were performing operations with their patients "under the influence" of sulphuric ether, and eminent surgeons in Paris accepted it. Morton, aided by Warren, sent a lobbyist to Washington on behalf of his preparation. Dr. A. L. Peirson of Salem wrote in praise of ether to Caleb Cushing, in Mexico during August 1847:

I shall make no apologies [for] addressing you in reference to a subject which is of high importance, I trust, in your estimation as well as mine—I mean the relief of human suffering.

It has long been known to chemists that inhaling the vapor of ether would intoxicate, it has recently been discovered that it would produce insensibility to pain—even under the most excruciating surgical operations. This fact was fully ascertained by many operators in this part of the country as early as last November, & certainly, at the present period & in the present state of our knowledge on the subject, most practitioners would not feel justified in omitting to urge the inhalation of ether upon any one about to submit to a capital operation. In many cases in which I have used it & have seen it used, I have noticed no circumstance which would deter me from recommending it, but have hailed it as a glorious discovery, achieving in a harmless way, what we have in vain been long seeking, in the preparation of patients for undergoing operations, by the use of opium and other drugs.

These facts, perhaps, are already familiar to you thro' the public journals, & I refer to them to induce you to promote the application of so beneficent a means, in the surgical practice of your command. No doubt your surgeons already have made trials of the ether, & are prepared for its exhibition & I am not presumptuous enough to lecture them on their duties. But as we have received no account of its general introduction into the army now in Mexico, I have been induced to think a knowledge of the confidence which practitioners in chirurgery in this part of Massachusetts repose in its efficiency, might aid in rendering its use more general. I have used it in amputations of large limbs, in operations for strangulated hernia, in removing tumors and reducing dislocations, & have witnessed its effects in the hands of others, more or less satisfactorily.

. . . . .

The method of application is exceedingly simple, requiring only a sponge & pure ether. The sponge, partly saturated with ether, is held over the nose and open mouth of the patient. . . . Mrs. Hoyt who goes to join her husband Capt. Stephen Hoyt of the Massachusetts regiment, has kindly offered to take this letter, and to state some of the results of my experience in the use of the remedy which I have communicated to her. She has been made the subject of inhalation and can testify as to its effects.[81]

Dr. E. H. Barton, writing from Baltimore, urged upon Lawson a favorable consideration of the new anesthetic:

I take the liberty of introducing to you Mr. Warren a near relative of the distinguished surgeon of that name—of Boston—who visits Washington with the object of making some arrangement with the Government for introducing the important agent recently discovered at Boston for *suspending pain during Surgical operations.* If you have not met with the valuable papers, prepared by Dr. Bigelow, Warren, Heywood &c., &c., he will furnish you with them. They as well as their eminent authors completely take this agent from the domain of empiricism & put it in the ranks of the regular faculty—to whom is communicated its actual constituents. I know not why the man that exposes his life for the benefit & honour of his country should be denied the solace & comforter the citizen has—who undergoes operations under vastly different circumstances.

The papers show an extraordinary success & no injury. I have also witnessed it here, & hope to be in Washington before Mr. W. leaves to witness it there also.

Knowing your feeling for the sick & wounded, I trust neither your sympathies or influence will be withheld from an agent so important to humanity.[82]

Lawson ordered his medical purveyor in New York City, Surg. Thomas G. Mower, to study Morton's preparation and report to him on it. Mower did this on January 18. Morton was patenting his preparation and hoped to exploit it for commercial purposes. His importunities were rejected by both the war and navy departments. Morton's offer to the Navy, however, was a reasonable one: "We will send persons properly trained to give ether. Instruments will be furnished at cost. And the charge for the use of the Vapor will be nominal—two cents for each patient." Lawson, with the attitude of an old campaigner, said "The new substance is ill adapted to the rough usage of the battlefield!"

In the spring of 1847, however, Dr. Barton, who had so earnestly advocated ether to Lawson the previous December, went to Vera Cruz as a medical officer, taking with him a distinguished reputation as a surgeon and physician, especially in the treatment of tropical diseases; he also carried in his luggage the glove and tube needed to administer the anesthetic along with a supply of sulphuric ether. The Vera Cruz American Eagle described his use of it in surgery there:

A German teamster belonging to one of our trains . . had both of his legs horribly shattered by the accidental discharge of a musket, which had been carelessly loaded. He had been conveyed to the church of San Francisco, which is now occupied by us as a hospital, and after some days it was discovered that it would be necessary to amputate both his legs, so badly had they been shattered. On Friday last one was taken off, but it was found impracticable to proceed with the other immediately, and it was therefore deferred until next day, Saturday. In the meantime, Dr. Barton, a physician and surgeon of great reputation, arrived from the United States, via Havana, bringing with him an apparatus for the administering of the new and wonderful discovery in medicine, called the letheon, and was used by him prior to the operation, in presence of, and assisted by, Drs. Harney, Potter [sic][83] and Laub, with the most triumphant success. The unfortunate man was soon rendered completely insensible to all pain, and, indeed, to everything else, and the limb was removed without the quiver of a muscle.

The above operation was the first in which the letheon has ever been used in this country. Dr. Barton comes out to the army by special appointment of the President, and, we understand, will remain at this post, upon which we congratulate the unfortunate and diseased, as he brings a reputation for great skill and experience, which being added to our already excellent medical department, will make it worthy of great confidence.[84]

This was apparently the first use of ether in the Mexican War. The New York papers soon revealed that it was being administered to wounded men all along Scott's line. This was at least exaggerated; the surgeons did not mention the use of it in their reports. The following winter Lawson ordered a supply of chloroform for the Army to test its qualities in surgery.[85]

LIFELINES OF THE ARMIES

James Harrington, the English philosopher, likened an army to a beast that crawls on its belly. His theme was that whoever feeds the beast controls it and thereby commands the power to govern the state. This conclusion is debatable, but the comparison of an army to a beast that must be fed is apt; and it must also be clothed, transported, doctored, and armed. In times of peace the task is normally neither difficult nor urgent. But during war the beast's appetite expands a hundred or a thousand fold as it consumes stores ranging from rations to bullets, from quinine to wagons, from mules to ships. And as the beast grows more ravenous the time that may be allowed to lapse before feeding it diminishes.

In 1846, supply of the armed forces was shared by the Quartermaster, Subsistence and Ordnance departments. Subsistence was responsible for the procurement of rations and the administration of the depots where these were stored until needed; ordnance for supplying the troops with the weapons of war, guns, ammunition, sabers, etc.; and the quartermaster for clothing, equipment and transportation. It was this latter responsibility that made the Quartermaster General the key figure in maintaining the lifelines of the army, and as such he was frequently the butt of criticism not only for deficiencies in his own department but also for those concerned with subsistence and ordnance as well. Transportation was the critical point in supply because after materials were procured, packaged and if need be stored they still had to be shipped to the camps or theaters of war. As a consequence, poor quality, faulty packaging, spoilage and other deficiencies for which he was not in fact always re-

351

sponsible were often attributed to the Quartermaster General. This was the more unfortunate because his own shortcomings constituted a sufficiently heavy burden for one man to bear.

The Quartermaster's Department was created, eo nomine, in 1818. There had been officers responsible for supply prior to this time, but they had been attached to the armies in the field and made responsible to the field officers. During periods of peace they were inactive. The reorganization of 1818 created a continuously functioning office located in Washington. This put the Quartermaster General in direct contact with the Secretary of War, and though in theory the estimates of their needs still came from the field generals, the Quartermaster General was no longer responsible to them.

The first Quartermaster General appointed was Thomas S. Jesup,[1] the same Jesup who was serving in 1846 at the outbreak of the war with Mexico, and who was to continue to serve until 1860. Thus the department he headed was largely built by him and if it sometimes failed to meet the needs in 1846-1848 it should be remembered that it had been developed and financed during a period in which Congress had dealt parsimoniously with the army, and that it functioned reasonably well in serving a small army engaged in no activities more demanding than occasional clashes with Indians. But despite such allowances the fact remains that there were grave deficiencies in Jesup's department which he generally refused to acknowledge. It is probable that his sensibility to and intolerance of criticism was caused in part by his long tenure in office and the fact that during the Mexican War he was second only to Scott as the army's senior ranking officer.

The Subsistence Department was responsible for procuring food for the army and administering the depots where the provisions were stored until the Quartermaster's Department removed them for shipment. At the outset of the war the depots were in New York, New Orleans, Baltimore and St. Louis. These were too far from the camps and battlefields to serve efficiently and, beginning with San Antonio, Texas, new depots were added as the armies moved ever deeper into Mexico. Among these were Brazos Island, Camargo, Tampico, Santa Fe, Monterey (California) and others.

As in the case of the Quartermaster's Department, in 1846, Subsistence was structured much as it had been in 1818. And its chief, Bvt. Brig. Gen. George Gibson,[2] like Jesup, had been its chief officer since its creation.

The methods of procuring and handling weapons and munitions were similar to those employed by the other supply departments. On the whole there was less criticism of the Ordnance Department than of others. Its chief officer was Col. George Bomford.[3]

A serious obstacle to procurement for all these departments was the general prosperity of the country. There was an adequate market for American producers, processors and shippers. Consequently, supply was short and prices high. The shortage was particularly true of both oceangoing and river boats, a situation of especial gravity since with a few exceptions almost everything including the soldiers had to be transported to Mexico by sea or river.

In mid-nineteenth-century America there was no giant industrial complex and no "Pentagon" in the contemporary sense and hence no problem resulting from interrelationships between the two. On the contrary, American production was dispersed among small independent units scattered throughout the country. Thus the problem of understaffed army supply departments was to contract with numerous producers, assemble the goods at depots and transport them to their various destinations.

During the Mexican War the Quartermaster General's task was the more difficult because this was the first time the American army undertook a large-scale invasion deep into enemy country, the first time it occupied a foreign land, and the first time it was required to cross deserts and mountains to span a continent and penetrate a foreign country.

When the obstacles were competently surmounted, the Quartermaster General remained an unsung hero. When there was bungling, and there frequently was, the troops didn't like him because they were too cold, or too hot, or too hungry, or too ragged; the generals didn't like him because of his penury; his civilian bosses preached the virtue of thrift and warned against waste; suppliers of goods regarded him as an enemy because he curtailed their profits.

The relationship with the War Department was particularly difficult because the Polk administration tended towards a "pinchpenny" policy. The President wanted to win a big empire by means of a little war waged at small cost. Thus, early in 1847, the Secretary of War wrote to the Quartermaster General: "It appears to me that in some respects the preparations are large and I hope on reconsideration you will adjudge, larger than the exigencies of the service will require. . . There are some other articles specified in your list which in amount appear large."[4]

JESUP'S APPROACH TO SUPPLY PROBLEMS

Thomas S. Jesup was neither a genius nor a fool. He knew his business and worked hard at it, though he was inclined at times to solve some problems by assuring subordinates that there really was no problem at all. Thus he wrote from headquarters in New Orleans to Col. Henry Whiting[5] who was with the army of occupation in Mexico:

The subject of transportation should not give you the slightest embarrassment. You have ample means in the country and you must use them. The transportation required and used by the Army in Mexico is so enormous as to cause not only great embarrassment to the public service, but to cause a drain upon the treasury unparalleled in any other period of our history, or in any other service in the world. Not a single wheel sh[oul]d ever have been used in Mexico except for Artillery. The enemy uses none; and to make our operations effective we must do as he does. As to packing subsistence there should be no difficulty; the second office of the Commissary's Department is in Mexico. Require him to have his subsistence put up in such packages as shall be readily transported. He has certainly had time enough to have had the system of his department adapted to the circumstances of the country in which the war is going on. Have you made the proper representations to the Commanding General on the subject? If you have not, let it be done at once & let the General or the Subsistence department be responsible if the difficulty of which you complain be continued. All the drivers for company and regimental purposes should be taken from the Army.[6]

But Jesup's own problems were of a different magnitude. He described their dimensions and reports with considerable complacency, certain of his success in meeting them, in a letter to the Secretary of War:

In treating . . of some of the matters properly embraced in this report, it will become my duty to go back to a period anterior to, or coeval with, the commencement of the war with Mexico. That war, suddenly forced upon us by the acts of the enemy, found us entirely unprepared in men, as well as in the means of equipment and movement. The sums which I had asked for the purpose of filling the store-houses with military supplies had been refused; and as late as the 8th of May, 1846, the appropriations for the department were limited to the wants of our small peace establishment.

. . . . .

The expenditures of the department show how vast has been the amount of its business. From reports already received and accounts examined, it is ascertained that eleven thousand five hundred and forty-nine horses have been purchased for the artillery, cavalry, and for draught; and exclusively for transportation, twenty-two thousand nine hundred and seven mules, sixteen thousand two hundred and eighty-eight oxen, six thousand eight hundred and eighty-six wagons, fifty-four steam vessels, four ships, two barks, eight brigs, thirty-four schooners, and two hundred and one scows, life and surf boats, besides two or three hundred wagons and carts, four or five thousand pack mules, and several hundred sail and steam vessels that had been hired. These means, with the vast supplies required, have been collected from a territory exceeding in extent the whole of Europe. And the results of the proper application of them by the generals in command, have been a series of brilliant achievements unsurpassed in military history. Every movement has been an onward movement without a single check. With our nearest depots farther from the sources of supply than Algiers is from Toulon or Marseilles, we accomplished more in the first six months of our operations in Mexico, than France, the first military power in Europe, has accomplished in Africa in seventeen years. And heavy as the expenditures unquestionably have been, there is not another instance in the last two centuries in which so much has been accomplished by any other nation, in so short a time, with so small a force and at so little cost.

. . . . .

The estimates for the present fiscal year were made for a force of thirty-six thousand four hundred men. Taking into consideration the circumstances of the service at that time, and the measures then contemplated by the government, they were minimum estimates for that force. The department has been required to provide for more than fifty thousand men; and it also has been called upon to supply the deficiencies of other departments, and to provide horses and equipments for volunteer cavalry and artillery, neither of which was contemplated in the estimates. Besides, the high prices of breadstuffs in Europe, and the great demand for vessels to transport them, enhanced greatly the prices of forage and all other supplies, as well as of labor and freights. The consequence of all which will be an arrearage to be provided for, to enable the department to meet the demands upon it to the close of the year, which I estimate at five millions six hundred thousand dollars.[7]

MILITARY CRITICISMS OF THE QUARTERMASTER GENERAL

The warriors in the field, from private to general, did not always share the Quartermaster General's estimate of his achievement. In August 1846, only a few months after the outbreak of the war, Brig. Gen. John A. Quitman complained:

I am entirely out of patience with the tardiness of every movement. The quarter-master's department is wretchedly managed. The medical department worse. There are here no horse-shoes or nails, no iron to make them; and, though we have 6,000 men, there are no medicines. The twelve months troops are armed with refuse muskets, and their knapsacks, canteens, haversacks, and cartridge-boxes are unfit for service.[8]

A member of the engineers' company on the lower Rio Grande complained of the quality of both food and clothing in late 1846:

When our clothing came to us we were indeed surprised, for I am certain that our citizens would not bestow such upon the town's poor. It is coarse and not half made. . . .

In a short time we arrived at Brazos, and since that time . . we have lived wholly on southern pork, or bacon, and hard bread, which was not only stale, but mouldy, and full of bugs, worms, and even lice.[9]

The quality of supplies was not the only cause of complaint. An observer with Scott's army on the road to Mexico wrote:

Indeed I had frequent occasion to note the destruction of quarter-master property along the whole route arising from the incompetency of wagon-masters, the carelessness and drunkenness of teamsters, and the general want of organization and accountability in the crops.[10]

General Taylor was among the most virulent critics of the Quartermaster's Department and the Quartermaster General, when he declared on June 21, 1846:

I am perfectly disgusted with the way they are going on. I consider there is an entire breakdown in the Qr.M. department every where.[11]

Ten months later the general's attack was yet more violent and more personal:

As to Jesup, I have not looked on him as entirely sane.[12]

JESUP'S DEFENSE OF HIS POLICIES

Jesup admitted that his department left something to be desired and believed he knew both the reasons for its weakness and the remedy:

The quartermaster's department is far from being efficient; the officers are efficient individually, but they are not sufficiently numerous for the highly responsible and laborious duties that devolve upon them.[13] I earnestly recommend that four additional quartermasters, to be taken from the army, and ten additional assistants, to be taken from the subalterns of the army, be authorized by law; and I further recommend that a regimental quartermaster be appointed to each regiment, to be taken from the subalterns of the regiments respectively, with the same additional pay and emoluments as are now allowed to adjutants. This additional force would enable the department to perform every duty as it should be performed.[14]

The Quartermaster General's admission of inefficiency in his department was not rooted in a humble spirit, and he did not meekly bear criticism. Upon occasion his defense was in the best military tradition, a counteroffensive. He launched one against Taylor, and "others" in November 1846, as he discussed his problems in a letter to Col. Henry Whiting from New Orleans:

I am thus far on my way on a tour of inspection of the affairs of the Department. We have been denounced by Genl. Taylor, as well as by many other officers, and others, as I believe, most unjustly; and it is my purpose to investigate the facts and report them to the War Department. I shall then demand the most searching investigation, not only of my own conduct, but of that of the whole Department. I am willing to take upon myself and the Department the whole responsability [sic] that properly belongs to me and to it; but I mean that others shall bear the responsability that properly belongs to them. I received from Col. (now General) Twiggs a requisition for one hundred and ninety two horses and equipments; as well as I remember that is the only requisition I have received from the army in Mexico. Now every one with the slightest professional knowledge or experience knows it is the duty of the government to indicate the object to be accomplished in a campaigne [sic]; it is then the duty of the General who is to command to call for the means necessary to accomplish the object. If he waits for others to guess what he wants and fails to give orders, or make requisitions in time, the whole responsability rests upon him, and whatsoever the consequences he must bear it.[15]

Over a year later Jesup was even more caustic as he not only defended his own department but attacked the competence of "most" of the generals in the field:

In reply to the complaint of General Scott, in his despatch of the 25th of December, that Lieutenant Colonel Johnson's [sic][16] train had returned without one blanket, coat, jacket, or pair of pantaloons, the small depot at Vera Cruz having been exhausted by the troops under Generals Patterson, Butler, and Marshall,[17] respectively, all fresh from home, I have the honor to state that, if the facts are as set forth by General Scott, the responsibility lies at other doors than mine.

. . . . .

If the volunteers and new regiments went to Mexico without the proper supplies, that was the fault of those who commanded them. General Butler,[18] I understand, was specially directed to superintend the organization, equipment, and movement of the volunteer force. It was his business, not mine, to see that they were properly clothed and supplied; and neither he, General

Patterson, nor General Marshall had any right to take for their commands the supplies I had placed at Vera Cruz for General Scott's old regiments.

For the new regiments I had made timely arrangements, and would have sent to Vera Cruz, in November, a large supply of clothing, but I received, in October, a report from Captain Irwin,[19] the acting quartermaster general of General Scott's army, dated at the city of Mexico the 27th of September, of which the following is an extract: *"I have now a thousand people engaged in making clothing; the quality of the material is not so good as our own, and the price on the average is fifty per cent. higher. Still supposing the road between this and Vera Cruz to be entirely open, I think the government will lose little, if anything, by purchasing here. I shall be able to fill, in a very short time, every requisition which has been made on me, with clothing, which, though not exactly of our uniform, will be comfortable and good."*

This information, sir, was from a man who not only knew how to supply an army, by putting into requisition all the resources of the country around him, but was better qualified to command a large army than most of your generals in the field. The report of Captain Irwin delayed my action here [Washington], but, in December, I ordered from Philadelphia a supply of clothing sufficient for the whole army, regulars and volunteers.[20]

CHARTERING OF TRANSPORTS

The Quartermaster's Department fought its war on several fronts. Supplying the troops was its primary task but this frequently involved rearguard action against contractors and a parsimonious government. Virtually all contractors wanted larger profits and some delivered shoddy goods.

Ships to transport the army to Mexico were one of the first and most difficult problems to engage the Quartermaster General.

Early in the war the difficulties encountered in dealing with shipowners were reported to the Adjutant General's office by one of the most knowledgable American shipowners, George Law of Baltimore:

We are advised from New Orleans of the return there of the *Alabama* from a trip to Galveston, and that she has been chartered by the Qr. Master for *three months certain*, at the rate of $16,000 pr. month, the charterer to furnish fuel and water, on which charter the owners thought to clear at least $30,000, and so far as the New Orleans owners are concerned they won't show any disposition to sell, as they act as ship's husbands and earn a commission on all the monies for outlays & charters. Not so the Baltimore owners whom it does not suit to own property so far from their own control; and they have the power & would still sell without privilege of the above charter, should the dept. desire to purchase in [preference] to continuing to pay such commissions of Charter. There is a Spaniard now after the Schooner *Sea*, & has made an offer which will probably be accepted in course of tomorrow, as I have kept Messrs Henderson & Co. from selling as long as I could, still hoping the Government would move in the matter, & secure a vessel so suitable for their service, as you will perceive by the enclosed certificate of Major Bache,[21] who has just returned from a [month's?] cruise in the *Sea*, surveying the Southern Coast.[22]

Jesup complained to the Secretary of War about the uncooperative attitude of shipowners as he attempted to assemble vessels for the Scott expedition to Vera Cruz:

One of the steamers which the President and yourself desired me to purchase (the *Natchez*) was lost on the coast of Cuba in the gale of the 11th of October; and I think it extremely doubtful whether the other (the *Alabama*) can be purchased at a fair price. The owners, I learn, are holding her up for a charter with the government; and as there is no other boat on the gulf at all to be compared to her, they expect to make their own terms. She cannot be purchased, I am told, for less than $90,000, if for that. That sum is too much for her; and if a boat could be obtained at the north equal to her, I would not think of purchasing her at all. The *Southerner*, now running between New York and Charleston, is a new boat—is better than the *Alabama*, and is equal, in proportion to her tonnage, to the Cunard steamers. I was informed to-day that she could be purchased for about $100,000. She would not, unless from accident, require repairs for three years. The *Alabama* is an old boat, and is much dearer at $90,000, or even $80,000, than the other at $100,000. I have written to New York, and have had a letter written to Charleston, to ascertain the lowest sum for which she can be purchased. If operations commence south before we purchase, the *Alabama* will have to be chartered.

Had we foreseen the nature of the navigation of the Mexican coasts and harbors, and of the Rio del Norte, and built suitable steamboats several months ago, a million of dollars might have been saved by this time. We have now a sufficient number of boats that do very well for the river, but suitable lighters cannot be purchased, and must be built; and if we cannot obtain either the *Southerner* or the *Alabama*, a similar boat should be built for the gulf.

The distance we have to pass over is so vast, and the navigation so difficult, that the amount of transportation required is enormous. The distance from the Mississippi to the Rio del Norte is greater than from the latter to the Pacific ocean, or from the former to the Atlantic.[23]

Lt. Daniel Harvey Hill commented on the same problem in his diary:

Our difficulties seem to increase daily, it is almost impossible to get transports; in New Orleans, the immense rise in the price of cotton has called off many of them to the European trade. Besides few ship owners are willing to permit their vessels to sail with sealed orders as those are required to do, which come out to this coast upon the Vera Cruz expedition.[24]

The battle with the contractors of ocean transport continued throughout the war and was fought along the same lines, although the objective shifted from getting the soldiers to Mexico to getting them home. Maj. D. D. Tompkins, Quartermaster at New Orleans, told of his dealings with shipowners:

No one knows the difficulties I have had to contend against; for instance, last summer, when I was called upon for transportation for the returning Army from Mexico, a plan was set on foot at once by "Ship Brokers" in this City to compel the U. States through me to pay an exorbitant price for vessels. The thing was so apparent to me that I at once determined to send to Mobile, and did send a confidential agent there for this purpose; so soon as this was known, the whole affair fell to the ground, and their vessels were taken upon liberal terms, thereby saving as I claim from $60 to $100,000.[25]

SHODDY SUPPLIES

Gouging on price was bad; inferior products were far worse. Goods and services sold to the army often were inadequate in quality. Bakers in New Orleans were guilty of "a fraud upon the government." Capt. Amos. B. Eaton[26] disclosed these frauds in a letter from Matamoros:

I have to [report] to you that I have examined a lot of hard bread from the New Orleans bakeries delivered to the A.C.S. at this place a few days since in [the] putting up of which the bakers have committed what would seem to be a fraud upon the Government by very greatly increasing the tare of the barrels in which it is packed.

This lot of bread consisting of 1,140 barrels is marked to contain 83,445 pounds for which Lieut. Simmons,[27] the A.C.S. at this place, has made himself responsible by giving the usual receipts.

The tare on these barrels, marked (it being from several different bakeries) is not the actual [tare] of the barrel but every barrel is marked with "17" as the average tare whereas the true and correct average tare of this lot of 1,140 barrels is 22½ pounds—this I have arrived at by emptying and weighing several of the barrels . . of the several different bakeries.

Here then the baker is paid for 5½ pounds of bread on each barrel more than he has delivered and on this whole lot there is a deficiency of bread amounting to 6,270 pounds.[28]

Lt. Col. Aeneas Mackay,[29] the Deputy Quartermaster General at St. Louis, declared that the knapsacks he ordered there were supposed to be made from "linen canvas, well painted in oils." But a board of survey at Camargo found that the knapsacks and canteens which arrived there were unusable:

I had the honor to receive your letter of the 10th April, enclosing a report of a Board of Survey held at Camargo in Mexico, on a number of knapsacks & canteens condemned as being unfit for issue.

This report presents the following facts, viz. That 14 boxes containing 1,864 knapsacks were examined and found to be of the very poorest quality of material, very badly made, and too small for the wants of the soldier. And further states that the cotton of which many are made is coloured and the colouring matter stains and washes out with water. That they are not impervious to water, for the want of oil paint. That many of them are mildewed and rotten in consequence of their being packed whilst in a green and damp state. They also report the examination of 6 boxes containing 567 tin canteens, and find them imperfectly made.[30]

PROBLEMS IN PACKAGING

Inefficient packaging may not have been deliberately fraudulent but the loss it inflicted was serious. Concerning this problem, Q.M. Gen. Jesup wrote to Brig. Gen. George Gibson, Commissary General of Subsistence:

The amount of subsistence that becomes damaged is enormous. This arises from putting it up in barrels &c. which are not water tight, and the barrels and other packages are of an inconvenient size for transportation. All supplies for this army should be put up in sacks or packages of from eighty to a hundred pounds, but never exceeding the latter, so that they may be conveniently and expeditiously transferred from wagons or boats to mules. Bread, flour, beans, sugar, coffee, salt and bacon should be put up in India Rubber sacks; and salt pork, salt beef, vinnegar &c. should be put up in half barrels or kegs. This would cost you something more in the outset, but would save in the course of a campaign a hundred times this additional cost by the preservation of supplies which are now damaged. The efficiency of the army would be increased also, by avoiding the delay which always occurs in the reducing of packages, whenever it becomes necessary to change the means of transportation. Besides whenever packages be reduced you have to incur the expense of sacks, and you then lose the barrels in which your stores had been previously packed. I wish you would consider this matter. I feel great interest in the change, because my department, when supplies become damaged, is taxed with double transportation. I estimate that every ration of subsistence that reaches the army cost[s] from seventy five cents to a dollar. You may therefore readily imagine how important it is that every thing required for the Army should reach it in a sould [sic, sound] state, but be so put up as to be preserved in that state.[31]

TAYLOR'S TRANSPORTATION PROBLEMS

The Quartermaster General was responsible for the procurement and delivery of supplies, but, as Jesup insisted, the needs of the troops had to be determined by their commanders. The latter accepted the responsibility. Thus Taylor estimated his needs at Camargo and found transportation the chief problem:

It is necessary to look ahead if the present operations are to continue. The means of transportation now with the army are very inadequate. In the strait to which we were reduced, a resort was had to pack mules of the enemy's country. They answered a good purpose, and might answer every purpose, provided we could bring ourselves to make war as the enemy makes it. But this is probably out of the question. We have customs which neither the officer nor the soldiers will forego, excepting in cases of extremity. Our camp equipage, so comfortable and yet so cumbrous, our rations, so full and bulky, all must be transported. We will soon advance on Monterey with a column of some six thousand men, having some five thousand animals in all. This calculation embraces the train and pack mules. To provide subsistence and forage (meaning by the latter only grain, for it is now understood that there is no grass and not much fodder on the way, the continued heat having parched up every thing) will require large means of transportation. At least a thousand wagons ought to be on the route between the Rio Grande and Monterey. We have now less than two hundred. If the wagons are furnished (harness with them, of course), the mules can be purchased here at a low rate. I have not been informed what wagons are coming in. One hundred are directed to be stopped at the Brazos, where we have mules (lately purchased) to be put in them. The rest will come up here to make up as rapidly as possible the required train here.

About one hundred thousand rations of subsistence have been thrown forward to Serralvo. This has been done by packs and wagons, while the troops are coming up. As soon as they arrive, and the movement begins, these means will nearly all be engaged by the column, and the throwing forward additional stores to Serralva [sic] or other depots must cease, in a measure, until a new stand be made, and the means of transportation liberated from special purposes.[32]

SUBSISTING TAYLOR'S ARMY

Following the capture of Monterey, supply was a matter of the first importance. The Assistant Quartermaster General with Taylor's army, Col. Henry Whiting, reported to the Quartermaster's Department in Washington on the logistical problems of the Army of Occupation:

As soon as the armistice took place, General Taylor directed that some four or more hundred thousand rations of subsistence should be placed in deposite here. Immediate measures were taken to fulfil this order. All the pack mules remaining with the army were sent down to Camargo, and in due time brought up about eleven hundred cargoes (about three hundred pounds each); while the train, consisting of about one hundred and fifty wagons (a certain number were of course necessary with the troops), was despatched by detachments of fifty to the same place, for the same object. Captain Arnold[33] left the Brazos with a new train of one hundred and twenty-five wagons about the 1st of October, and reached Monterey the beginning of this month. Arrangements were also made with certain persons to employ pack mules in number to bring up from Camargo two thousand cargoes. These were in readiness to go down at any time after five days' notice, but were held back until it should be known that the cargoes were likely to be in readiness for transportation. All this has been done with the knowledge and approbation of the general, and the whole means of the department have been diligently employed all the time, except as to the number of pack mules. Double the number could have been had for the same purpose, had it been deemed advisable to engage them. But, after consultation with the general and with the subsistence department, it was thought that proper stores for packing (only certain articles can be packed to advantage) could not be had for more than the two thousand.

Before the last instructions from the government rendered it probable that the armistice would be suspended, General Taylor deemed it prudent to have the train greatly augmented, in anticipation of movements that would probably follow its termination. Accordingly, instructions were at once despatched to Matamoras to begin the purchase of tame mules; five hundred to be called for at once from the local authorities, as mules had previously been called for. This step was only preliminary to calls, to follow each other as fast as the animals could be obtained, to the extent of our wants. At the same time,

Captain Crosman[34] was directed to make purchases at Camargo with the same view. Captain Hill[35] had had standing instructions to set up all the wagons the mules sent out to him would enable him to do.

I make this statement in order that the department may know what has been doing to fulfil the calls of the general commanding. It must be borne in mind that the army and its followers here consume full two hundred thousand rations per month.[36]

LOGISTICAL PROBLEMS ON SCOTT'S LINE

Scott's situation was more difficult than Taylor's inasmuch as he faced greater logistical problems caused by a more vexatious supply line, a mountainous terrain and a tropical summer. He called attention to all of these in describing his needs in two letters of April 1847. The first of these was dated April 23:

We already occupy Perote, & shall soon occupy Puebla. Indeed we might safely take possession of Mexico, without a loss perhaps of one hundred men. Our dangers & difficulties are all in the rear between this place & V[er]a Cruz: 1. The season of the year—heat, & below Cerro Gordo, sand & disease; 2. An imposibility (almost) of establishing any intermediate post, say at the National bridge, or any other point—on account of disease, & the want of sufficient supplies within easy reach. 3. The danger of having our trains cut and destroyed by the exasperated rancheros, whose homes are thinly scattered over a wide surface, & whom it is almost impossible, with our small cavalry force, to pursue & to punish & 4. The consequent necessity of escorting trains, seventy odd miles up & the same down, with a meagre cavalry that must, from day to day, become from that intolerable service more & more meagre.

I have stated the situation of this advanced army strongly to show how infinitely important it is that we should, as speedily as possible, while the season may permit us, get up to this healthy region all *essential* supplies. Those supplies fall within the Ordnance, Quartermasters, Commissary, & Medical Departments. The Chief of each with me has been instructed to write to the proper chief at Veracruz accordingly and I desire you to give a rigid attention to those requisitions, & make yourself sure that as fast & as far as practicable, they be complied with. I put down myself in this place the supplies which I hold to be indispensable leaving the amount of each article to the respective chiefs here & at Veracruz. Viz—medicines & hospital stores, & clothing for troops, salt, ammunition, shoes for animals, & coffee. Articles only a little inferior in importance are—knapsacks, blankets, hard bread, bacon & camp kettles.[37]

Scott's second letter was written on April 28:

Breadstuffs, beef, mutton, sugar, coffee, rice, beans, and forage we may hope to find, though not in convenient places or in great abundance, on our line of operations.[38] For these we must pay,[39] or they will be withheld, concealed or destroyed by the owners, whose national hatred of us remains unabated. I shall continue to do all in my power to conquer that hatred, but cannot as yet promise myself success; and if I cannot enforce the utmost economy in the use of such supplies, by causing them to be collected and regularly issued by the proper departments of the staff, we shall further exasperate and ruin the country, and starve ourselves.[40]

KEARNY'S SUPPLY LINES

Supply for Kearny's invasion of New Mexico was insignificant compared to that of Taylor's and Scott's armies. The estimates were for an expedition of only about 2,500 men. But the trail across the plains was long and the Indian menace was real. Transport was thus more difficult than procurement of food and clothing. The Missouri Republican described the difficulties in the issue of August 18, 1846.

We understand, from a reliable source, that apprehensions are entertained at Fort Leavenworth, and by U.S. officers concerned, that the requisite supply of provisions cannot be forwarded to Gen. Kearney. Great exertions have been made by the Quartermasters at this place and at the Fort,[41] and through their agents and assistants, to procure the means of transportation. All the wagons which could be made or purchased have been bought and sent up to the Fort. A large number of wagons and teams—in fact nearly every one that could be had, have been bought in the upper country; yet with all these exertions, only provisions sufficient to supply for six months the men General Kearney has with him, have gone forward.[42] He expected to receive provisions for twelve months; and this amount will be necessary for the subsistence of his troops, for all the traders and persons acquainted with New Mexico concur in saying that provisions for such a force are not to be had in the provinces.

In addition to the troops with Gen. Kearney, Col. Price's regiment of about 1,000 men; Lieut. Col. Willock's extra battalion of about 500 men; Lieut. Col. [sic] Allen's battalion of the Mormons,[43] about 500, which, with teamsters, &c., &c., will make a body of about 2,500 men, have yet to go forward, and for these, but a small amount of provisions have been sent forward. Probably not more than sufficient to supply them on their march. In a few days, the regiment of Infantry now raising, will also be ready to march, and they also must be supplied. From the number of men yet to go, it is evident that the quantity of provisions which it will be necessary to send, even to furnish six months' supply, is much larger than the quantity already sent forward. To cross the prairies, it is necessary that the teams should leave by the middle, or at furthest, by the last of September. Teams leaving at that time may experience considerable difficulty in performing the trip. The season has been unusually dry, and there is great scarcity of water on the plains. If the fires break out early, which may be the case because of the drought, the teams may not be able to cross at all.

In view of the number of men going out, the difficulty of procuring transportation, the amount of supplies indispensably necessary, for the subsistence of the troops, the fact that teams cannot cross the prairies from the 1st of October until about the 1st of April following, are just causes for apprehension. We trust that these differences may be overcome by the energy and industry of the officers who have the matter in charge. As an evidence of the great demand for wagons, teams and drivers, the settlers have agreed to pay as high as fifteen cents a pound for the transportation of their stores. The government, we presume, will pay that much or more, by the time the cost of wagons, teams, drivers and the depreciation and losses of horses and wagons are added to the bill. If the requisite quantity of provisions is not forwarded, it may subject Gen. Kearney and his command to much inconvenience, if not totally defeat the purpose of the expedition.[44]

The Republican's apprehensions were well founded. In October, Lt. William N. Grier wrote from Santa Fe to the Commissary of Subsistence in St. Louis:

I regret to inform you that I am some what apprehensive that troops are daily arriving at this place much faster than the provisions intended for their use. The Asst. Commissary at Fort Leavenworth writes, under date of August 11th, that some six months' supply for a portion of the Army of the West was then in store at Fort Leavenworth awaiting transportation. I fear that (from all I can learn from those who are daily coming in), that the provisions intended for the Army now in this Territory will not all reach their destination this winter.

The several estimates for provisions were, I believe, for six months. The army now here must be subsisted for one year. It will therefore be necessary to make large purchases of flour here; I have already purchased about 60,000 pounds of flour at a very reasonable rate—about 3 cts. per pound—but it now demands a higher price, and will continue to do so as the wants of the army increase. There is no such thing as being able to get bidders for contracts for furnishing flour here, and *specie only* will procure it. When I arrived here, I procured about $5,000 in silver for my checks on the bank of St. Louis.

. . . . .

The Troops arrive at this place in advance of the provision trains, and the supplies on hand in my store room are very limited just now. The Battalion of Mormons arrived this evening and will not be able to resume their march for California until a provision train arrives—probably in six or eight days.[45]

Though the situation may have appeared serious to Capt. Grier in Santa Fe, the Commissary of Subsistence in St. Louis did not share his concern. In a letter to Brig. Gen. George Gibson in Washington, Maj. Richard B. Lee,[46] the Commissary in St. Louis, defending himself, blamed Indians, lack of discipline on the part of the troops, and insufficient military escort. And he did not seem to think it really mattered because he was sure that the Santa Fe country abounded in beef:

I enclose herewith an abstract of provisions forwarded from Fort Leavenworth to the Santa Fe army exclusive of three months' supplies taken on the march with each column of the Army. You will thus perceive that whatever may be the complaints on account of the failure of provisions, that no delinquency can be charged upon the Subsistence Department.

Every arrival from Santa Fe brings unfavourable accounts of the progress of the Quarter Master's trains of provisions, which added to the loss of fourteen wagons captured by the Indians and the advanced season of the year, may probably result in some failures and cut off from the Army a portion of the supplies, but as the country abounds with beef cattle and sheep, no serious results are to be apprehended.

. . . . .

As you are aware, one hundred and twenty thousand dollars in specie, principally gold, has been recently sent to the Disbursing Department at Santa Fe. These funds have been sent without a military escort, and in addition to the uncertainty of effecting a passage across the plains at this season, an opportunity offers itself to marauders from either border and to Indians a most tempting booty.

. . . . .

It is proper that I should suggest to your consideration the expediency of sending to Santa Fe early in the spring an additional supply of the most essential parts of the ration, as sugar, coffee, flour and bacon sides.[47]

Opinion in Santa Fe remained somewhat jaundiced even though there was no suggestion of dire need. A correspondent of the St. Louis Reveille complained:

The inner man sometimes feels a little solicitude here in consequence of the beggarly account of empty barrels, boxes and sacks in the commissary's storehouse. The ten wagon loads which I had the pleasure of bringing from Bent's Fort are pretty well exhausted already; and we have had no other arrivals, nor do we know when we shall have, though we know that ample stores are on the way. We have fresh beef plenty, furnished to the commissary under contract by a Frenchman from St. Louis, named Gosslein, [sic][48] I believe, who has been some three or four years in this country. The commissary department is under charge of Capt. Garrison,[49] recently appointed to the staff by the President—a citizen appointment, as I understand.

Some of the native flour issued by the commissary is miserable stuff—exceedingly coarse (perhaps fraudulently prepared by sifting out the finer portions), and operates constantly on the bowels of many persons. To this cause, concurring with bad quarters and exposure, much of the sickness in the army may be attributed.[50]

DEFICIENCIES IN OCEAN TRANSPORTATION

Some of the soldiers marched to Mexico but more went by water, and the vessels leased or purchased by the government often were unfit for use. The deficiencies and repair of vessels were all discussed in a letter from Col. Henry Stanton[51] to his superior, the Quartermaster General on December 13, 1846:

I am truly sorry to learn, as I do from the New Orleans papers, that my apprehensions and predictions in relation to the unfortunate *Neptune* have been so soon and so disasterously realized. Her fate adds another to the appalling list of disasters which have occurred to vessels of her class and character, along our coast during the last few months, and more than warrants all the repugnance which I have on so many occasions expressed to the purchase or employment in any way for sea or coast service of side wheel and side guarded steam boats. And I cannot but indulge renewed hopes that the last vessel of the description which the Department will ever be burthened with is now in service. So far as it depends on me such is most certainly the case.

The *Edith* I am also sorry to hear is unseaworthy from [a] defective or wornout boiler! after only one or two months service. Since she has been the property of the Government which is particularly unfortunate and from a casual examination of her boiler after her purchase I am not without apprehensions that the *Massachusetts* will ere long be placed alongside the *Edith.*

The Propellers *Washington, Ocean,* and *Ashland* are now undergoing thorough repairs by their late owners, which may be completed in a few days. When they will be dispatched, the former with coal and clothing for the Brazos, and the two latter with coal for Tampico, as I have, I believe, hereto-

Point Isabel from Brazos Santiago

fore advised you. I am now commencing what should, and would have been commenced weeks since could I have obtained the requisite instructions, preparations for the *grand expedition*.[52] the 140 boats of about 20 tons burthen, which I was directed about the 1st to have constructed within the month! and sent out! will I trust be ready in time. It was not until yesterday that I felt myself at liberty to commence even preparatory measures for providing the several transports for the heavy supply of Ordnance and Engineer stores ordered.[53]

Even if suitable vessels were obtained problems still remained. At Brazos Island the shallow water made lightering necessary, and payment of demurrage as the oceangoing vessels lay at anchor became an important item of expense. These and other difficulties were discussed in a memorandum written by Capt. John G. Tod, who was sent to Brazos Island by Jesup to investigate the situation in November 1846:

I embraced the opportunity afforded me on my recent visit to the Brazos de San Iago, to obtain such information and make such observations as I believed would be beneficial, if not interesting to the Department.

The bar at the Brazos has seldom over 8 feet water. Vessels drawing 7 feet can enter the harbor, which ought for the future be a *sine qua non* in all Charters or employment of Vessels for the Department.

The distance from the bar at the mouth of the Rio Grande to the bar at the Brazos is nine (9) miles.

It is about two (2) miles from the Brazos bar to the *depot* on the island where the vessels discharge their freight. By using one or two scows as a floating wharf and rigging an ordinary stage they discharge the freight from the lighters with great ease.

The vessels in the port are lightered by the steam boats, and the latter discharge the freight at the *depot* on the island; in some instances it is carried round to the mouth of the river. The steam vessel *Cincinnatti* [sic] is employed in carrying the supplies from the *depot*, or from the vessels in [the] port, to the mouth of the river.

The calculation of the cost of her transportation to the Department, estimating her charter, fuel &c.—and the number of barrels she carries, from the *Depot* on the Island, to the mouth of the Rio Grande, is found to be at the rate of $2.50 cts. per barrel freight. That is the average cost to the Government taking the *Cincinnatti* as an estimate.

The Lighterage outside depends so much upon wind & weather, that it is a difficult matter to arrive at any thing like an accurate estimate of the expense.

The Ship *Sophia Walker* was discharged or lightered entirely by the Steamer *Sea*. The cost to the Department, estimating it only so far as the Steamer *Sea* was concerned was found to be $3,500 (say three thousand and five hundred dollars). This I think is a higher average than the usual cost.

The demurrage of the shipping appears very enormous. The average cost to the Government of storage, taking the bulk of the cargoes of the shipping inside the Bar, is found to be about one dollar per month. Yet I do not know how this is to be remedied. The depot on the Brazos Island is situated on a point, or sandy flat, which is liable to be covered with water during a heavy northerly gale, particularly if it occurs after a blow from the N. Eastward & our northers along this seacoast mostly ensue after eastwardly gales, and may be looked for during the season, which continues until April, with as much certainty, as we calculate upon the sun's rising & setting.

Immense supplies, pork, beef, bread, flour, corn, hay, oats, waggons, supplies in boxes, and every thing else, is [sic] piled up all along the shore and about the Point or Neck, which composes the depot. I observed some few stages erected high enough to protect the supplies that were stored on them from the water. In other cases, pork & beef, and such articles as are not so liable to injury, form the ground tier & perishable articles are then stored on them. They are covered chiefly with tarpaulings [sic], or canvass, so as to form a roof, the ends open.

There must necessarily follow more or less loss & damage during these gales, come when they may. There are a few store houses, but very few in proportion to the magnitude of supplies on shore. There are some large store houses at St. Joseph's [near Corpus Christi] and as that depot is broken up, I do not see why the houses cannot be carried down to the Brazos & be put up. . . .

The depth of water at the mouth of the Rio Grande is about 3½ feet at low water & about 5 feet at high tide, some few tides have given as much as 6 feet over the bar, but it is not safe to calculate over 5 feet for vessels to enter the river. The *depot* at the river is situated about two (2) miles from the bar.

A train of some hundred waggons (oxen & mules) leave[s] the *depot* at Brazos Island, carrying supplies to the *depot* on the river. It is a heavy road, over a sandy plain, a distance of nine (9) miles.

Hundred[s] of waggons are standing about the depot of the island; and I found a great many on board the vessels in the harbor. Many of the former, I was told, was [sic] not worth the freight out from New Orleans, being worn out before they were obtained for the Department.

. . . . .

It is a small matter for the boats to carry the supplies a few miles as lighters. The loss of time in getting the cargo on board heretofore, and discharging the same, has caused the necessity of employing so many boats at a great expense to the Department. Now if they are made to work at night, so far as the receiving their cargoes or lightering the vessels in port are concerned, they will be able to do twice as much.[54]

The shortage of lighters appears to have been chronic, for Jesup called attention to this early in the war and demanded, ineffectually as it turned out, its immediate remedy.

It has been stated in this city by individuals who pretend to be acquainted with the facts, and to speak from personal observation, that such is the want of system in the discharge of the cargoes of vessels at Point Isabel that the demurrage is sometimes equal to three thousand dollars a day. This should be avoided. The transports, whether propelled by sails or steam might be so regulated as that not more than one or two at most should be in Port at the same time, and the cargoes be discharged as they arrive, so as to avoid any considerable amount of demurrage. If the evil exist to the amount stated it must be immediately remedied.[55]

Mexican Horses and Mules

Once landed in Mexico the army depended upon horses and mules (mainly mules) to carry their supplies and haul their wagons. Q. M. Gen. Jesup gave his attention to the matter during the first few weeks of the war, but two months later was apprehensive concerning his orders.

On the 22d of May last I requested you to send Captain Irwin to La Baca bay to superintend the formation of a depot at San Antonio de Bexar for about five thousand troops, principally mounted men, and informed you that

a competent train must be formed for that purpose; and I afterwards, in my instructions to Colonel Whiting, directed that such a train be formed. . . . I feel some apprehension that the train may not have been organized. I had counted largely upon it as auxiliary to the transportation of General Taylor's army; and I now call your attention to the subject, and I desire you, if a full train has not already been formed there, to have it done immediately. In addition to this train you will direct Captain Irwin to purchase in Texas at least two hundred ox, horse, and mule teams, with the wagons, harness, and yokes. The horses, mules, and oxen of that State being acclimated and accustomed to graze, will be better for our service than those on the way from the west. The volunteers I fear have not been supplied with sufficient trains; and it is doubtful whether wagons, harness, and mules will reach the scene of operations in time for the movement of the army. Send Captain Cross[56] also into Texas to purchase all the wagons, mules, and draught horses that can be obtained, and have them as early as possible on the Rio Grande.

Major Eastland[57] informs me that large numbers of well broke mules can be purchased at this season of the year in Louisiana. Purchase and send forward to the point in Texas where they can be most readily landed all you can obtain, as well as draught horses. Send agents to the Mississippi to purchase all that can be taken across by land, or be sent by water, as you may think best. Send all the wagons and harness you can purchase. I feel so much anxiety on this subject that I have concluded to send you a duplicate of this letter by an express. . . . How far can we avail of the mules and horses of Mexico?[58]

In August 1846, Jesup was informed that Mexican mules were admirably suited for the armies' needs but that the horses were not.[59] During the remainder of the war most of the mules required and some horses were purchased in Mexico.

General Scott made the following estimate of the number of mules and wagons needed for the advance from Vera Cruz to Mexico City, and suggested sources of supply.

A sufficient portion of the siege train for the reduction of the castle of Vera Cruz, though due more than a month, not having arrived, I can give no definite day for the advance of this army into the interior of Mexico, say by the national road hence, towards the capital. But I have every reason to hope that the heavy guns and mortars (or most of them), still due, may be here in time to enable the army to take the castle in, say, the next ten, or at the outside, fifteen days, when I shall take up the line of operations as above.

For that interior march, a very heavy baggage train, wagons and teams, and pack mules will be needed for the army, however greatly I may restrict the articles to be transported with it. For an army of at least 10,000 men, there will be needed, as early in April as practicable, means of transportation about as follows; say from 800 to 1,000 wagons, with five mule teams; say from 2,000 to 3,000 pack mules; say from 300 to 500 draught animals for a travelling siege train, including entrenching tools and pioneer tools.

Some of the draught animals, for all of the above uses, say two-thirds, we may hope to obtain in this vicinity and on our line of operations; but the wagons, and as many of the draught animals as possible, must be brought hither from our sources of supply—Tampico, the Brazos, and New Orleans.

In making the above estimate, reliance is placed on the country within reach of our line of operations; for forage, beyond five leagues from the sea coast; for bread stuffs, at thirty leagues; for three days in four, and for the meat ration, five days in six. Notwithstanding this reliance, it will be necessary to transport with us much hard bread and bacon, coffee, sugar, and salt, besides common tents, at the rate of three per company; some wall tents for the general officers and general staff, and the field and staff of regiments; a full supply of ammunition for artillery and small arms; medicines, some hospital stores, and the personal necessaries of officers; leaving many wagons for the transportation of the sick to the next depot, and pack animals as well as wagons, for gathering in forage and subsistence within (say) ten miles of our line of operations. The loss of draught animals may, no doubt, be readily replaced all along the line of operations by capture and purchase.

Besides the estimates above for land transportation, additional means must be found for a reinforcement of at least 10,000 men (new regiments and recruits), expected to join me in all the month of May, if not by the end of April.[60]

It was natural that the Mexicans should regard the invading Gringos as fair game (the American contractors did) and not only charge as much as they could get but frequently cheat in the bargain. A flagrant example of this is found in the traffic in wild horses described by Maj. Luther Giddings:

In consequence of the short allowance of mules, a great amount of baggage had necessarily to be abandoned [by General Taylor] at Camargo. But no complaints were heard on that account; indeed, the troops selected were all too glad to go, to stand upon the manner or order of their going. Such was their enthusiasm, that they would cheerfully have marched in their shirts alone rather than have missed the *fandango*, as they facetiously termed the anticipated battle at Monterey.

Taking advantage of our wants, a number of native horsedealers daily visited our camp offering mustangs and mules at prices previously unheard of in that region. These leather-clad jockeys were the most arrant knaves I ever encountered, and, in selling their animals, rarely failed to sell the purchaser also. The wild, half-broken mustangs generally escaped in a short time to their native chaparral, for, "the Unicorn could not be less willing to serve thee, or abide by thy crib"; or, if detained by strong halters, were often claimed by other Mexicans, who had doubtless shared the purchase money with the vendors. In the prevailing desire to conciliate the inhabitants and live up to the proclamation, these false claims of ownership were, in many cases, recognized upon the bare assertion of the claimant, and the property restored; perhaps to be re-sold and re-claimed again by the same villainous confederates. Indeed, it was ascertained that one notorious rogue had sold the same mustang to five different persons; the animal having escaped from each successively, and been re-captured by the same lasso.[61]

The Soldiers' Food

The greatest logistical task was feeding the army. Some of the food, especially beef, was bought from the Mexican people but much of it had to be bought and packed in the United States and shipped to the troops. The fare was simple. A statement of commissary supplies on hand at the principal depots on February 15, 1847 listed pork, bacon, flour, bread, beans, rice, sugar, coffee, salt, vinegar, soap and candles and noted fresh beef was to be supplied.[62]

Efforts also were made to include as "extra issues" some antiscorbutic foods, such as sauerkraut, limes, or pickled onions. With these, however, there were some specific problems. For example, at San Angel, the regimental commissary of the 7th Infantry listed seven hundred limes as wastage because they decayed so rapidly after being received that they were unfit for use.[63] Maj. Thomas W. Lendrum, Commissary of Subsistence at Baltimore, reported to the Commissary General during May 1847 that he was unable to purchase either sauerkraut or pickled onions on the market there; the best he could do was to substitute pickled cucumbers.[64]

In his Narrative of the Central Division or Army of Chihuahua, Brigadier General Wool's "Boswell," Jonathan W. Buhoup, commented on the quality of the soldiers' rations after Wool's army had penetrated into Mexico.

For the benefit of those who know not what a soldier's rations consist of, we will state that we here received three quarters of a pound of pork, bacon or beef per day. Generally, about the same time, we got one pound of beef per day for four days, and three fourths of a pound of pork or bacon the fifth day, and one pound of hard bread or flour, and coffee, salt and soap accordingly. But the beef we here received was very bad—so poor, as the soldiers say, that to throw it against a smooth plank it would stick.

· · · · ·

[At Monclova] food began to improve in quality a train having come to hand with Major Borland,[65] bringing provisions. We now commenced to draw one half American and the other half Mexican flour.[66] Our rations of coffee were increased, and we also drew three fourths of a pound of bacon per man. With these additional supplies, we fared tolerably well. It was amusing, indeed, to see the men practising economy, endeavoring to make their small allowance of bacon reach as far as possible. They generally boiled a small piece of it with the poor beef which we here received, in order to heighten its flavor, and then divided that piece of bacon among a mess of five or six men.[67]

ROLE OF THE BEEF CONTRACTORS

Purchasing cattle for beef to feed the army was the work of beef contractors appointed by the Army in Mexico.[68] One such transaction occurred when Scott's contractor bought from the agent of General Santa Anna, presumably with the latter's approval, near Vera Cruz, in April 1847. Maj. Henry L. Kinney,[69] Scott's beef contractor, wrote about the transaction:

I sent day before yesterday some Tennessee Cavalry with an understanding with their Col. that they were to have pay for their services for assisting in bringing in cattle for the use of the U.S. troop[s] at this place.

I made a contract with the agent of Genl. Santa Anna (the owner of the cattle) to supply our forces here with cattle as well as with horses & mules. Our contract was made in [the] presence of Genl. Worth allso with the knowledge & aprobation of Genl. Scott. The agent of Genl. Santa Anna (Dr. Manual Garcia) informed me a few days afterward that he had made Dr. Nicholas Dorich his agent & that he would deliver cattle, horses &c & receive pay for them and it has been by the request of the agent Dr. Nicholas Dorich that I have sent our men to drive in the cattle, with an understanding that the expenses I might incur should be deducted from the price agreed upon for the cattle. They have been up to this time paid to their satisfaction for the animals they have delivered. The marauding parties of Mexican[s] prevent the agents from delivering cattle & consequently I am obliged to get our own forces to assist in bringing them in [in] order to be able to supply your command with fresh beef.[70]

Capt. Amos B. Eaton, Commissary of Subsistence, reported on various problems of food procurement at Monterey and Victoria, including that of contracting for fresh beef:

I rec'd yours of the 27 of Dec. on the 17th inst. on our first days march from Victoria. We arrived here on the 25 inst. While at Victoria we had no very especial difficulties in the Sub. Dept. None which were not obviated. The greatest one arose from the absurdity of Lieut. Britton[71] in sending very illy assorted supplies to Monte Morales instead of forwarding to that place properly equalized quantities and rations of the different articles: for instance on the 16th of Dec. he sent 200,000 rations of beans & rice and only 38,000 rations of sugar. When the troops moved to Victoria, all the troops then at Monte Morales were taken from that place, of course the stores must be taken along, this involved the taking along [of] a good many loads of the vegetable rations, where there were not the other articles to issue with these articles. Previous to the arrival of the last train from Matamoras, I had purchased some salt and sugar to make up deficiencies. The salt was the coarse salt of the country, not very clean but still it would answer the purpose, price $8 per cargo (4½ bushels) the sugar was the "pelonci" of the country, a pretty good article, price $14 per cargo of 320 lbs. this sugar does passably well especially when it is *boiled with the coffee*.[72]

When the troops were finally ordered from Victoria to Tampico no more stores were required for them sufficient to subsist them to that point. The second Matamoras train after taking out a few barrels was ordered here; so long a route has broken the bbls. very much; the flour is in very bad condition.

. . . . .

While at Victoria I obtained the consent of the commanding General to making a new arrangement for obtaining fresh beef if I could do so without endangering the quality or the certainty of obtaining it. I accordingly made contracts with Mr. Isaiah B. Bigelow and Mr. Gallagher the former assigned to Genl. Patterson's and the latter to Genl. Twigg's Division. I enclose a copy of one of these contracts by which you will perceive that the price has been considerably reduced, and that should it not work advantageously it can be amended in ten days. *I am* sure from many accounts [and] calculations, that the Beef does not cost the contractor on an average a single mill over two cents per lb.—one cent clear profit is very ample compensation.

It appears to me clearly the better plan to make limited contracts so that the person who takes over can be himself present and superintend and manage his own business and now these results [are] an advantage which was not formerly the case, viz., there are many persons who are familiar with the mode of obtaining and issuing beef in this country who wish to take contracts of a limited extent and also will themselves remain with and superintend their business. I propose to make a separate contract for this position and perhaps another for the troops at and in the vicinity of Saltillo.

. . . . .

There is not a single ham in all these parts, if there are any below. I wish you would direct some to be invoiced to me or to the A.C.S. here so that they may not be stopped by the way. If it can be done I wish some *new hams* might be called for *from Baltimore,* now that we have a small force and abundance of transportation in this direction we can afford to call for all the articles composing the ration (or nearly so) without impropriety.[73]

INSPECTION OF SUPPLIES

Inspection of the supplies was an important, and frequently disappointing, task. Some months after his report from Monterey, Captain Eaton, now on Brazos Island, reported on one inspection to Major Seawell, Acting Commissary of Subsistence at New Orleans:

The cargo of the Schooner *Exit* has been delivered & I herewith enclose duplicate receipts corresponding with your invoices.

You have repeatedly invited a rigid inspection of the supplies purchased by you, believing that such inspection made here will greatly aid the purchasing officers in their efforts to receive none but the best quality, I shall readily embrace your request & endeavor, whilst I remain in charge of this depôt, to pass every article under my own eye.

The articles recd. by the *Exit* are generally good; the pork & sugar (so far as I have inspected them, having seen but one barrel of each), are very good[74]; the bacon appears now to be good, but whether it has been *thoroughly smoked,* & with the proper material of wood, is difficult to determine at present; the keeping quality of bacon mainly depends on this.

The soap is only passably good; it will not compare with several other brands now in the depôt, especially "W. Hull & Sons" from New York; have these gentlemen an agency in New Orleans?

The candles are New Bedford, where competition has run so high as to induce a deterioration in the material; they are as good as the common run of cheap sperm candles; the best in this depot are from the manufactory of "Samuel Judd's Sons." Have not those gentlemen also an agency in New Orleans?

The beans are, as a lot, inferior & somewhat more than half of them (69 barrels—207 bushels), I consider so decidedly inferior that they should not have been sold to the U.S. for the use of the Army; the most of them would at once be condemned by a Board of Survey; I therefore re-invoice them to you. . . . I have, I presume fully 500 barrels of beans as good as those now returned, which can never be issued. . . . Those returned are musty & quite unfit for issue, tho' there might be a barrel or two that, if issued to day, might answer.[75]

Though inspection was to be thorough it must also be prudent: whatever could be saved must be. Captain Eaton, although conscientious in his inspection, was aware of the Polk administration's desire to economize even at the risk of consuming questionable commissary supplies:

I trust that you will not too readily conclude that the bread you have on hand is unfit for issue. The bacon you have, ought, every barrel of it, to be overhauled, taken from the barrels, thoroughly scraped, pruned of the bad parts & then smoked (as you can very readily make a smoke house of some one of those apartments in rear of your storehouse) or, to have a handful or two of fine quick lime scattered inside the barrels & on the bacon as it is packed. A very great deal of bacon is condemned when the meat, through & through, is perfectly sound & sweet, merely because skippers are on it & much has fat run out of the pieces, making the barrel look bad.

I have sent you some bacon of our last receipts, though there is here 1,600 bbls. which is to be overhauled in the way I mention. The old bread you have ought to be immediately & thoroughly inspected before it is laid aside as unfit for issue. A Board of Survey will condemn any thing you place before them, I mean a careful inspection, barrel by barrel, made by yourself or under your immediate supervision.

The most of our supplies in the Country, and we have a very great supply, are old & we must all save to the U.S. what we can, without prejudice to the health of the soldiers.[76]

IMPURE DRINKING WATER

Water as well as food was a problem and one that the Commissary Department could do little about. There are many accounts of suffering and illness because of impure and unpalatable water.

George Furber, "The Twelve Months Volunteer," as he called himself, described an encampment on Christmas Day, 1846, at Santa Teresa on the march from Matamoros to Victoria:[77]

We continued the march, finding no water until about three P.M., when we arrived at a miserable collection of ranchos, on small, dry, barren knolls. . . . Here were tough times for men and horses.

The rancheros were on the knolls; in the little valley were three large holes, each about twenty-five feet across and six or eight feet deep, dug out to contain water; and such water as it was! It had a thick, green slimy scum over it, and in it thousands of green frogs; for it had been in the holes since the last rainy season; it was very warm; but that was not all: the water itself was green with slime, and would not settle, nor could the slime be separated from it by straining; the smell of it was nauseous, the taste ten times worse. Many although suffering, could not bear it near them; others, of stronger stomachs, got some down; with the author, and many others, it acted as an instantaneous emetic. The horses drank a little of it, and refused more.[78]

Along the Gulf Coast, near Vera Cruz, they dug holes, sank barrels, then scooped out "nasty brackish water" that seeped in through the moist sand. They mixed wine, brandy, lemon juice, or coffee with it, to neutralize its gall-bitter taste.[79]

CLOTHING DISPUTES

Clothing also created problems for the army. At the war's beginning the regulars were, of course, adequately supplied, but the federal government did not issue clothing to the volunteers until the end of January 1848. This meant that the individual soldier had to buy his own from quartermaster stocks with a clothing allowance. At first he had received a uniform from his state or a proud community. When hard usage, particularly on foot wear, wore out the original gear, the volunteers frequently were unable, unwilling, or both, to replace them.

An unusual incident was the "Camp Bergarra [Vergara] Mutiny" of the Massachusetts Regiment of Volunteers.

On the 18th [October, 1847] there was a mutiny in a part of the Massachusetts regiment that was encamped with us at Bergarra [sic], and which caused a good deal of excitement. I will give the cause of the mutiny and let the reader judge of its justness. Gen. Cushing ordered the regiment to throw away its "volunteer clothing" and take the "regular uniform." Some of the soldiers' old clothing was very good yet, and they did not want to throw them away, and be at the expense of purchasing new ones. Near one whole company refused to comply with the order, giving as their reasons for not so doing that their present clothing was good enough. Gen. Cushing immediately had them published, giving each man's names, as "cowards, and unworthy to march with the column to the interior," and ordered them to be confined in the castle of San Juan de Ulloa, to which place they were marched the next day.[80]

This, however, was atypical. Ordinarily the soldiers were eager to get equipment of any kind, and the need was frequently pressing.

On September 23, 1846 a correspondent of the Kentucky Observer reported on Col. Humphrey Marshall's regiment:

They are barefooted, and some of them literally without breeches, many without hats and coats.[81]

The following April, Quartermaster General Jesup wrote from aboard a steamer:

Several thousand men of Genl. Scott's army were reported entirely barefooted the morning I left Vera Cruz. March (31st) [1847].[82]

In April 1848 the complaints were still being sounded. This time, Capt. Kenton Harper, in Parras, complained in a letter to Col. John F. Hamtramck:

Many of the men are destitute of clothing. I had *nineteen* barefooted a few days ago, but I made an arrangement to supply them. Pantaloons are most needed.[83]

The generals and the Quartermaster Department did what they could and soldiers without pantaloons must have been rare, and lack of boots, while too frequent, was the exception rather than the rule. Stations were established where worn-out gear could be exchanged for new. Captured clothing was distributed at Jalapa.[84] Wool jackets and overalls, forage caps, flannel shirts and drawers, wool stockings, bootees, great coats, cotton shirts and blankets were issued to regulars at the Camargo depot in October 1846.[85]

A quite different sort of clothing problem presented itself after the army occupied Mexico City. Perhaps the Americans were trying to impress the natives, particularly the dark haired señoritas that some of them had dreamed of meeting in the Halls of Montezuma, but Scott's Inspector General, Ethan Allen Hitchcock, was unimpressed. He complained in the following report about unofficial dress affected by the Gringos there:

I have the honor to report that the Army dress appears to be continually diverging from the prescribed pattern. Some latitude has been rendered necessary from the absence of proper materials in this country, particularly in the colors of cloth, but this affords no excuse for officers, not entitled to them, wearing gold or silver lace on their pantaloons and there is no reason why the prescribed shoulder insignia of rank should be departed from. The evil in this latter case has found its way to non-commissioned officers & particularly to hospital stewards some of whom are wearing lace upon their shoulders & adopting fancy dresses of all kinds.

Some of the followers of the Army, such as wagon masters & perhaps some of the teamsters, are adopting dresses making it difficult to distinguish them from officers, a deception which is aided by the departure of officers themselves from the prescribed pattern.[86]

Army Ordnance

Feeding, clothing and moving the army were incidental to enabling it to fight. For this it had to be armed. This was the responsibility of the Ordnance Department, and on the whole it performed its duties well. Naturally, there were complaints. While the army was assembling at Corpus Christi, Lt. Braxton Bragg of the 3rd Artillery wrote to the Assistant Adjutant General. The West Pointer, though studiously polite, clearly implies that the Ordnance Department does not really know how the new mobile artilleryman should be equipped. He informs them:

I have the honor to report that I have received a Field Battery of two six pdr. guns & two twelve pdr. howitzers, with harness for horses & equipment & stores complete for the field. No swords have been supplied with this battery for the men, & no horse equipment for those mounted men out of the teams. Upon inquiry I learn that the ordnance depart. do not supply horse equipage except for the teams. To equip the Battery for service, they will require, 12 saddles, 12 bridles, 24 saddle blankets, 12 forage bags, 50 halters, 50 nose-bags, 200 yds. picket-rope & 12 [word illegible] singles. The number of horses absolutely requisite for constant service is 50. A tarpaulin of large size will also be requisite to protect the stores.

It must have been an oversight on the part of the Ordnance Department in not sending swords for the men. The use of muskets is inconsistent (indeed impossible) with that of movable artillery. Sixty artillery swords will be necessary then to complete the equipment of [the] men.

Accompanying this battery is a very large supply of surplus stores of every possible kind, filling an invoice of several sheets of fool [scap?] paper, which cannot be sent into the field without a train of several luggage wagons, and it will therefore be necessary to leave them with the quartermaster for storage or turn them in to the ordnance officer at this depot unless the Comdg. Genl. prefers this being kept with the battery. As his decision on this point must regulate my packing in some respect, I should like to be advised.

In my estimate for horses & equipments I include the officers of my command, as it cannot be expected they are to furnish their own horses & forage them when no allowance is made them for that purpose.

Please inform me what disposition is to be made of the Infantry equipment now in my possession.[87]

Flintlock Rifles

At the beginning of the war the flintlock rifle was still the standard weapon of the infantry regiments, though its effective range was only about a hundred yards, and it was unreliable in damp weather. No less than nine models of smoothbore flintlocks were made at government armories after 1800; most of these models were used in the Mexican War—the most famous was the Model of 1822. The flintlocks were both smoothbore and rifled, in various calibers, though the .69 caliber was the most widely accepted.[88] There were some of the Hall breech-loading flintlock rifles, .53 caliber, which had been patented in 1811. Both because it was tried and tested by experience, and because its flints were in generally adequate supply, many of the officers, including General Scott and not a few of the rank and file, preferred the flintlock "Deerslayer" rifle above all others. Company C, Florida Volunteers, let it be known through a formal petition that they would not be willing to surrender their accustomed weapons for strange percussion-type muskets. Capt. R. G. Livingston presented their case to Col. Jones M. Withers and received favorable consideration:

The undersigned commanding Co. (C) Florida Volunteers having applied to you and through you to the proper source for rifles for the use of my Company instead of muskets, the latter being the character of the arms now in their hands, respectfully submit[s] for your consideration the following statement of reasons for the change.

1st. The men composing this Company were raised upon the frontier in the fields of Florida where game is plenty and the rifle almost the exclusive weapon used for its destruction. 2d. My own personal acquaintance with the men and knowledge of their habits, enables me to state that (with the exception of two men) all of them are skilled in the use of the rifle and can be made more effective in an engagement with this kind of arm than any other that could be placed in their hands. 3d. Florida was for nearly seven years engaged in a guerilla warfare with the Seminole Indians which was but lately ended and the men composing this Company (with the exception of the two before mentioned) were almost continually engaged in the service, hunting Indians and used rifles almost, if not entirely exclusively during the whole war. 4th. The Company has been organized to serve during the War with Mexico, and although they are now accompanied by another Company from the same State, their period of service will expire in about 5 or 6 months, and there will remain but this one Company from that State and therefore, [it] must be attached to some other command which will probably destroy a military organization unless it be as a Rifle or Light Infantry Company. 5th. The Company has been organized only about two months, the whole of which time has been occupied (with the exception of 10 or 15 days) in being transported from the United States to this place and consequently have had no time for drill. They do not know or understand the use of the musket and would require not less than two or three months longer to enable them to do efficient service whilst with rifles they can do skilful, efficient and effective service immediately, and the undersigned as the commanding officer, does not hesitate to say that they can do as much execution with the rifle without more than 5 to 10 days drill as any troops now in the service of the United States either regular or irregular.

.   .   .   .   .

[endorsement]

I would respectfully add my request & recommendation to the change of arm desired by Capt. Livingston believing as I do that it would render this Company more usefull & efficient.

Very respectfully, &c.,
J. M. Withers
Lt. Col. Comdg. Batt.[89]

PERCUSSION MUSKETS

The percussion system of ignition came into the United States, however, in 1841, or just in time for the Model 1841 percussion musket, the Jager rifle, (more familiarly known as the Mississippi rifle) to be available for some regiments, including Jefferson Davis' 1st Mississippi Volunteers in the Mexican War. This was the first general-issue, United States army rifle designed and manufactured with the percussion system; it was .54 caliber, and originally made to fire a paper cartridge and spherical lead ball. Perhaps one reason why the Mississippi rifle was not still more widely used in the war was the uncertain supply of percussion caps. On one occasion Colonel Davis had to point out to Lt. John McNutt, an ordnance officer, that percussion caps were a necessary adjunct to percussion rifles.

Maj. Bradford[90] of the 1st Mi[ssissippi]. Vol. will hand you this. I have sent to your post to request you, if possible, to send me some rifle ammunition and percussion caps. We may get on without the ammunition having a small allowance of that furnished to the two rifle companies as originally armed, but now that the percussion rifles have arrived the caps are indispensable and we have none. By some means then I hope you can send us some caps and if it shall not greatly promote the public service, it will at least greatly oblige me, and inspire some additional confidence in the men.[91]

In spite of the preference for flintlocks the percussion musket did make its way into the armies. For example, in an ordnance return for Company "A", 4th Artillery, made on June 30, 1847, Capt. J. H. Miller accounted for eighty-seven percussion muskets, and only fourteen flintlock muskets.[92] The Mounted

Rifles had percussion muskets and Colt's army revolvers. The Hartford Courant was among those who praised the new Colt repeating arms:

These weapons are undoubtedly the most formidable and efficient, in the hands of mounted men, of any ever before used or constructed. Each arm is calculated to hold six charges, which may be fired in as many seconds, and again reloaded as quickly as an ordinary fire arm. The regiment of United States Mounted Rifles, for whom a thousand of these arms have been made by Mr. Colt, can, at the commencement of an engagement fire a volley of six thousand balls into an enemy's ranks, without loading, and afterwards load and fire at the rate of six thousand charges per minute! No force in the world five times as large can withstand such a terrific fire.[93]

A report issued by the Ordnance Department in November 1847, written by Lt. Col. George Talcott, Jr., not only expressed satisfaction with its performance but itemized the supplies it had delivered to the army.

In presenting the annual report of the principal operations of the Ordnance Department for the last fiscal year, I must before coming to details state in general that the existence of war during that period has imposed so great an amount of duty as to call for the constant and utmost exertions of all its officers.

. . . . .

The great quantity of arms and ordnance stores which it has been necessary to prepare and issue has compelled me to keep most of the ordnance officers at the arsenals on their appropriate duties. As many have been sent to Mexico as could possibly be spared for service in the field, although they constitute but a small portion of those who are anxious to participate in the labors, dangers, and glories of the armies in that country. Of the thirty-six officers composing the corps, an average of thirteen have been on service in Mexico.

Gun-cotton, the knowledge of which had just reached this country at the date of my last report, has been submitted to experiments to test its fitness as a substitute for gunpowder. The limited trials made have not shown it to be well adapted to use in firearms. Its explosive force, or bursting effect, is far greater than that of gun-powder; its nature, in this respect, assimilating more to that of fulminates, a property which seems well suited to mining purposes.

. . . . .

During the fiscal year there has been expended . . the sum of $40,064.94 . . . . applied to the purchase of 458,666 pounds of fused saltpetre, and 100,-000 pounds of brimstone. The stock of these materials, which have been provided and laid up in store during several years past, now amounts to

3,368,681 pounds of saltpetre, and 734,560 pounds of sulphur; enough to make about 45,000 barrels of new powder.[94]

The expenditures from the appropriation . . [for the purchase of gunpowder] have been $100,000.

The following quantities have been procured therewith: 468,182 lbs. cannon powder, 162,506 lbs. musket powder, 83,978 lbs. rifle powder, 10,000 lbs. pulverized nitre; and 5,000 lbs. mealed powder.

The expenditures at the armories, during the fiscal year, have been . . for the manufacture of arms, appendages, component parts, gauges, tools, &c., and purchase of materials for the same . . $426,153.39 . . . There have been made during the same period at Harper's Ferry armory 12,000 percussion muskets, with 39,809 appendages for the same, consisting of ball screws, screw drivers, wipers, spring vices, extra cones, and cone picks; and 3,054 percussion rifles, with 11,408 appendages. . . . There have been made at the Springfield armory, during the same period, 14,300 percussion muskets, and 201 musketoons, with 56,275 appendages for the same.

. . . . .

Besides the permanent armories and arsenals, depôts for supplying the troops in the field have been established at Point Isabel, Camargo, Monterey, Saltillo, and Vera Cruz, in charge of officers of this department.[95]

Inefficiency, dishonesty, lack of planning and pinchpenny economy often plagued them, but somehow the armies survived. They might have to travel on leaky tubs of vessels, ride emaciated mustangs, and follow Mexican mules, but in one way or another they were able to get the job done. As far as food was concerned, in the mud villages on the Rio Grande, the Halls of Montezuma, or the Palace of the Governors at Santa Fe, it was bread, beans, pork, and whatever beef was to be had on the hoof.

TRIUMPHS AND WOES OF THE VICTORS

An Army of Occupation

The American forces that conquered Mexico were the first United States army of occupation. Their experiences in this role were akin to those of other such armies in that life was conditioned primarily by their relations as victors with the civilian population and by the shroud of boredom and the yoke of army discipline, the latter growing more galling, and, for some, intolerable, when the battles were over. Dissensions among the commanders, who for long had chafed under forced cooperation, broke forth in a quarrel involving Scott and a cabal of discontented general officers, notably Pillow and Worth. With the help of Secretary Marcy, Scott's enemies managed to have him superseded in command by General William Orlando Butler, thus setting the stage for a highly publicized court of inquiry on the troubles of his army.

In general the conquered are not friends of the conquerers, and the Mexican people in 1846-1848 were not an exception. But the Mexicans, doing what they had to do, accommodated themselves to and made the best of, defeat. As a consequence there was a certain amount of peaceful and even friendly intercourse between the invading armies and the Mexican civilians.

From the beginning, the policy of the United States government was to win over, or at least to tranquilize, the people of the conquered land, and to turn them against their leaders. Taylor, early in the war, issued a Spanish proclamation (prepared for him in Washington) which declared that the war was against "tyrants and usurpers" who had "extort[ed] from the people the very money which sustains the usurpers in power." It was a policy of "divide and rule" explained by Secretary Marcy in a despatch to Taylor:

The proclamation which you were directed to spread among the Mexican people will have put you in possession of the views of the government in relation to the mode of carrying on the war, and also in relation to the manner of treating the inhabitants. . . .

The President has seen, with much satisfaction, the civility and kindness with which you have treated your prisoners, and all the inhabitants with whom you have come in contact. He wishes that course of conduct continued, and all opportunities taken to conciliate the inhabitants, and to let them see that peace is within their reach the moment their rulers will consent to do us justice. The inhabitants should be encouraged to remain in their towns and villages, and these sentiments be carefully made known to them. The same things may be said to officers made prisoners, or who may visit your headquarters according to the usages of war; and it is the wish of the President that such visits be encouraged; and also that you take occasions to send officers to the head-quarters of the enemy for the military purposes, real or ostensible, which are of ordinary occurrence between armies, and in which opportunity may be taken to speak of the war itself as only carried on to obtain justice, and that we had much rather procure that by negotiation than by fighting. . . . A discreet officer, who understands Spanish, and who can be employed in the intercourse so usual between armies, can be your confidential agent on such occasions, and can mask his real under his ostensible object of a military interview.

You will also readily comprehend that in a country so divided into races, classes, and parties, as Mexico is, and with so many local divisions among departments, and personal divisions among individuals, there must be great room for operating on the minds and feelings of large portions of the inhabitants, and inducing them to wish success to an invasion which has no desire to injure their country; and which, in overthrowing their oppressors, may benefit themselves. Between the Spaniards, who monopolize the wealth and power of the country, and the mixed Indian race, who bear its burdens, there must be jealousy and animosity. The same feelings must exist between the lower and higher orders of the clergy; the latter of whom have the dignities and the revenues, while the former have poverty and labor. In fact, the curates were the chief authors of the revolution which separated Mexico from Spain, and their relative condition to their superiors is not much benefited by it.

Between the political parties into which the country is divided, there must be some more liberal and more friendly to us than others; the same may be said of rival chiefs, political and military; and even among the departments there are local antipathies and dissensions. In all this field of division—in all these elements of social, political, personal, and local discord—there must be openings to reach the interests, passions, or principles of some of the parties, and thereby to conciliate their good will, and make them co-operate with us in bringing about an honorable and a speedy peace. The management of these delicate movements is confided to your discretion; but they are not to paralyze the military arm, or in any degree to arrest or retard your military movements. These must proceed vigorously. Policy and force are to be combined; and the fruits of the former will be prized as highly as those of the latter.

. . . . .

Availing yourself of divisions which you may find existing among the Mexican people—to which allusion has been made—it will be your policy to encourage the separate departments or States, and especially those which you may invade and occupy, to declare their independence of the central government of Mexico, and either to become our allies, or to assume, as it is understood Yucatan has done, a neutral attitude in the existing war between the United States and Mexico. In such of the departments or states as may take this course, you will give the inhabitants assurances of the protection of your army until the return of peace, so far as may be consistent with your military plans of operation. When peace is made, they may decide for themselves their own form of government.[1]

Dealings with Mexican Officials

American military commanders tried to deal with the people of the Mexican towns through their own officials—alcaldes and ayuntamientos.[2] At times this was successful, as, for example, when a small detachment of an Illinois cavalry company stationed at Matamoros pursued horse thieves to the town of Burgos. Lieut. Simon Doyle described the incident:

I will . . give you a sketch of a trip recently taken to Bourgos [sic, Burgos] a beautiful little town about 100 miles to the interior of this place. On the 8th Inst. I learned that two Mexicans were in Bourgos with 3 American horses. Thinking they mite be some of those lost by our Company I started at 2 P.M. with 25 men and on the 3[d] day after a hard ride through mountains half the way, we came sudently upon the town which is in a beautiful little valey through which the most beautiful little stream of water I ever saw is running, just at the town the two branches comes together, one of which is salt, the other fresh.

. . . . .

Our road or rather trail for we had to travel Indian file lais most of the way through the mountains and winds and turns around through passes and over the most accessable spurs and we came suddenly upon the town by turning round a spur of the mountain.

Thus you see we were in sight of and looking as it were down on the town before its inhabitants were aware of our approach, and such a scratching of gravel, cuting dirt and vamoosing for the shaparel was probably never seen about Bourgos, as took place about this time. Women runing and ringing their hands, children bawling as though a managerry of wild beasts had been turned loos in the mountains and were rushing with savage fury upon the town. As we passed [through] the streets we could see women and children peeping around the corners as though we were a monkey-show.

The alcaldy met us at the corner of the Palaza and said they were all friendly and upon being informed what we wanted said he would deliv[er] men & horses to us. He gave me a good house for quarters during my stay in town. And after the first day, the people having seen by our actions that we were not the savage *criters* for which they had at first taken us, I had many invitations to visit them, some of which I accepted, and I assure you I was never in my life more hospitably treated and at the same time I have no doubt if they were not a frade many of those who were showing such signs of friendship would have cut my throat for the clothes on my back. At the same time I think some of the Spanish population are really friendly to our government. Bourgos is the only place in Mexico that I have yet saw where I think I should like to live. It is a most beautiful town of 700 inhabitants, everything neet and clean, and the inhabitants look more like white folks than any I have yet seen, & I have a strong notion of comeing back there to live. There is the finest stream of water runing by the town I ever saw from which water is led through every door yard, it is large as crooked creek and falls over 100 feet in a mile near the town & has a perfect natural mill dam across it of stone 10 feet high as ever I saw. After a stay of one day and a half in Bourgos on Sunday morning the 12th we bid adieu to the good *folks* of that place and took up our return march for camp, fetching with us 3 Horses & 2 Mexican Prisoners. As we left the town the bells (3) on the church were chimed in most beautiful stile. What it was for I am unable to say, perhaps a signal for the peons or Indian portion of the citizens which during our stay in the place had been laying in the shaparel to return as Los Americanos had left the town.[3]

The alcaldes were spokesmen for the civilians. Correspondence of American military commanders is filled with complaints of outrages on the Mexicans, and other grievances. On the other hand, Americans frequently objected to what they thought were high-handed acts of the alcaldes. For example, Quartermaster General Jesup complained:

It has just been reported to me that the Alcalde at Matamoros has stopped the cutting of wood for the steamers employed upon the Rio Grande—this will stop our steamers if it be true. Our policy is wrong—we should organize governments wherever we go, and allow not one to exercise authority unless appointed by the Military Commander. If I had the right to exercise command for a short time, I would teach those gentry better than to interfere with our operations.[4]

Maj. Jubal A. Early, Acting Governor of Monterey, reported a conflict over authority with a Mexican official:

I send you two circulars from the Acting Governor of New Leon, one directing a collection of a tax and the other directing the payment of some money which had been collected before the battle of Monterey, avowedly for the purpose of defraying the expenses of the State Government. I did not know of the existence of these circulars until this morning, when I received information of them from some American. . . .

It struck me as being improper under existing circumstances that a public revenue should be collected in a territory occupied by the forces of the United States, which might be perverted to the purpose of aiding the enemy, and I therefore sent for Senor Prieto and had some conversation with him upon the subject, and he says that the revenue which he has directed to be collected is only intended for state purposes, such as the maintenance of the tribunals of justice &c. I told him that before issuing orders of the character of those in question, he ought to have submitted the matter to me in order that it might be submitted to the General Commanding, but he seems to be of the opinion that his government is entirely independent of the Military authority of the United States, and that it would be very humiliating to have his orders submitted to inspection before they could be issued,—and intimated that he could not acknowledge any such claim and if it was insisted upon he would be compelled to resign his office rather than submit to a course which he thinks would degrade his government in the eyes of the people.

My understanding is that while the Mexican authorities are allowed the exercise of their appropriate functions within certain bounds, yet that every thing must be subservient to the military supremacy of the United States, and for that reason I sent for Senor Prieto who is now exercising the functions of governor of New Leon and have obtained from him the circulars in question which I send to you in order that they may be submitted to the General Commanding.[5]

MARTIAL LAW

In various occupied cities—Matamoros, Tampico, and Vera Cruz—martial law prevailed, with military governors appointed to enforce it. The main elements of military rule were an unwritten code, written rules and the articles of war approved by Congress on April 10, 1806. Martial law applied only if an American were involved (i.e., a Mexican committing a crime against an American, an American against a Mexican, or an American against an American). In keeping with the policy of minimal interference in Mexican affairs, the code explicitly denied any jurisdiction to American officers or soldiers in the administration of justice by Mexican authorities in their own matters.[6] Enforcement varied, but at times it was strict, as at Matamoros when Colonel Cushing commanded the post.[7] His regimental adjutant wrote of Cushing's administration of justice there:

You can scarcely imagine the amount of labor we have done since we came here and while Col. Cushing had command of the Post. When he assumed command every thing was in disorder, and the town was filled with black-legs, and loafers in general. There was no such thing as order in the city. Murders and assassination, were nightly occurrences. In fact there was no effective government in the place. Col. Cushing went to work and established civil and military tribunals and at once put the city under martial law. An order was issued shutting up all grog shops and places where liquors were sold. We had considerable trouble and met with much opposition but we succeeded, and order was soon established. We also shut up all fandangoes, and public parties, closed the gambling rooms. A strong patrol was sent around the city every night after tattoo and every house closed and lights put out. We soon received the thanks of the Mexican population and deep curses from the rascals whose sport we had stopped. The Spanish consul refused to give up his liquor and we had to use actual force to get it. He threaten[s] to complain to his government. Now this is one of the most orderly places I was ever in, and the streets after 9 are as still as a church yard.[8]

At Vera Cruz, as soon as Scott's army moved into the city, Major General Worth became Military Governor, and issued the following rules:

Orders No. 3
1. The alcalde will forthwith cause all citizens of Vera Cruz, other than such as may receive special authority, to deliver up their arms into his custody; reports of the same to be made to these headquarters. 2. The alcalde will cause every "pulperias" to be forthwith closed, and none hereafter opened, except under special license. And none to be opened after 6 o'clock, p.m., when licensed. 3. The alcalde will require every citizen to apply for a letter of domicil, showing his occupation.

. . . . .

4. The Mexicans laws, as between Mexicans, will be continued in force, and justice administered by the regular Mexican tribunals. 5. In all cases

arising between American citizens of the army, or the *authorized* followers of the same, a military commission will be appointed to investigate the case. 6. All Mexicans will be allowed to enter and leave the city freely between reveille and retreat. 7. Soldiers on pass can enter the city by the gates of Mercy and Mexico, and at no other point, between the hours of 10, a.m., and 6, p.m.; at the latter hour all soldiers, not on duty with the guards, will retire from the city.[9]

ADMINISTRATION AT JALAPA

When Scott's army moved from Jalapa toward Mexico City, they left behind a garrison commanded by Maj. Thomas Childs, 1st Artillery.[10] When that city was later abandoned it became the center of guerrilla activity, but when reoccupied, the task of governing it fell to Col. George W. Hughes.[11] He became a successful administrator of occupied territory, but not without tribulations.[12]

Hughes was able to keep order at Jalapa by such drastic measures as those an unidentified corporal described in a letter to Dr. William Henry Grimes. Only a fragment has been preserved:

On the twenty fourth and twenty fifth of Nov. [1847] there was a little excitement in town. There were two Americans hung and two Mexican Officers shot. On the twenty fourth the two Americans was hung and on the twenty fifth the two Mexicans were shot. One of the Americans was a wagon master and the other a teamster. They were hung for killing a Mexican boy about ten years old. They shot one of his legs almost off and one of his arms. After they had got some distance from him, one said to the other go back and finish him, and he went back and shot the back part of his head almost off. They acknowledge that they disserved to be hung and advised those that he left behind him not to follow his example, to do their duty as soldiers and not assassinate an innocent Boy as they had done.

The Mexican Officers that was shot were taken prisoners at Vera Cruz and let go on Parol of Honor, and on the fifteenth of Nov. retaken by Col. Winekoop [sic Wynkoop] near this place. There were four Officers taken, one Col., Capt., two Lieut[s]. The Capt. and one Lieut. was shot on the twenty fifth. The Col. and other Lieut. was taken on to the City of Mexico to stand their trials, as the principal part of the witnesses were there. They will be shot at the City. There was twenty four men detailed to shoot them, twelve was taken from our company and I had to act as Corporal of the detail. I never heard a better fire in my life, it sounded as but one gun, they were shot in the lower plaza of the town. They were blindfolded and each of them led by an American Officer, and a Mexican Citizen, they were both in full uniform, and sat upon their coffins when they were shot, they both fell back at the same time and never moved. The bodies were given . . . [End of fragment].[13]

QUITMAN AS GOVERNOR

Scott once again decreed martial law when he entered Mexico City. This time he appointed Maj. Gen. John A. Quitman, Governor. Writing to his wife, Eliza, the new Governor described his office: "As Governor . . . I have not time for anything outside except to eat and sleep. I am obliged to keep the 6 officers of my staff, two secretaries, two interpretors and two clerks constantly employed. . . . I am Civil and Military Governor, that is in governing the city and Federal District, I possess absolute powers. I now sit in the great saloon of this beautiful Palace, behind me is my private parlor furnished magnificently and my bed room is the private study of the President."[14]

In the days which followed, Quitman's administration won praise from many upper-class Mexicans. Quitman's own thoughts, however, were those of a conqueror—an expansionist imbued with the spirit of manifest destiny— and he expressed his opinions on Mexico and its future in a "few hints" to Senator H. S. Foote:

The Mexican Army is disbanded. The whole country except where we govern is in confusion. No prospect of a new government being established. If we desire peace, there is no power & will be no legitimate one with which we can make it. What then is to be done. I speak to you boldly, as we spoke when the Texas question arose, hold on to this country. It is destiny, it is ours, we are compelled to this policy. We cannot avoid it. There are but three modes of prosecuting this war. One to increase our force to 50,000 men and overrun the whole country, garrison every state capital and take every considerable city. The second to withdraw our armies from the country & take up the proposed defensive line. The third, to occupy the line or certain points in it, keep the ports and this capital, & preserve an open communication with the sea ports.

The last is the true policy of the country. The first has the objection of being too expensive without the prospects of any good results. It would also demoralize the Army as a war of details always does. The second would be equally expensive & would protract the war indefinitely. The last is alone practicable and is forced upon us. If we abandon this Capital, in thirty days the officers and office holders now driven from their hives, would return & reestablish a strong military Government, whose bond of union would be preserved by our pressure upon the frontier. They would keep alive this distant war on the frontier from choice, force us into keeping up strong garrisons from the mouth of the Rio Grande to the Pacific, because from the centre they would strike a blow upon any part of the line before it could be reinforced. They would move on a semi-diameter, while our operations would be on the circumference. If on the other hand the 20,000 disbanded officers, the military aristocracy of this country, should not be able to establish a government—the country would be left in a state of absolute anarchy upon our withdrawal, & soon wasted, plundered & depopulated; it would become derelict, and be seized as a waif by some European power. Think you such a prize as this splendid country is, would be long without some claimant? England would be ready to throw an army here to protect her mining interests, or league with France to establish a monarchy here.

I do not exaggerate when I say that it would become derelict. How can it exist without a government. It is already wasted. Five out of its seven millions of inhabitants are beasts of burden, with as little of intellect as the asses whose burdens they share. Of the population of this city, 50,000 are leperos, with no social tie, with no wives, no children, *no houses.* Santa Anna was the only man who could even for a time keep together the rotten elements of his corrupt government. Here in this capital, we are in possession of all the machinery of that miserable contrivance which they called the Government. Out of it they cannot establish another. No sensible man in this country believes it. Then it follows that if we abandon this capital, either the official jackalls return and set up the old carcass of the state, or the country will become wasted, impoverished & ruined by anarchy, regarded as derelict, and seized upon by some foreign power. On the other hand with 10,000 men we can hold this capital & Vera Cruz & keep open a safe communication between the two points. Possessing the heart there would be no force to annoy us upon the frontier line we might choose to occupy.

The expenses would be less to hold this point & the frontier line than to occupy the latter & leave this as a rallying point for the opposition to our country. I mean to say it would require less men & less money & be attended with less difficulty & risk to keep this capital & the sea ports as a part of the policy of the defensive line than to adopt the latter purely. But by holding on to the sea ports and the capital and keeping open the communication, a large portion of the expenses of this mode of prosecuting the war would be drawn by very simple means from the Country. . . .

Let foreign goods be brought to this capital under our low system of duties, and we should sustain a moral conquest over this country which would soon bring us peace, unless indeed it should produce so violent a friendship for our institutions and government that we would be unable to shake off our amiable neighbors. An event I assure you not unlikely to occur. What then? Why the Old Fogy will say, as he has sung since the first new state was admitted, as he has said when Louisiana & Florida were purchased, and latterly when Texas was annexed, the Union is in danger. The country will be ruined &c. But I say take the prize. Take the mines, & the sugar & coffee plantations, the olive groves, the vineyards, the bellowing herds & bleating flocks that slake their thirst in the snows of Orizaba and Popocatepetl, and lie down at night beneath the cocoa groves of the vallies. Why refuse the country, that in addition to its mines, its plantations, its rich vallies and its jewelled mountains, possesses a treasure infinitely greater, the commercial philosophers stone, the power to tax the commerce of the world by the junction of the two oceans? But where am I? I jumped down on terra firma. Let us try the policy I advocate & not be alarmed because in process of time it may possibly result in extending our federation to the isthmus.[15]

SOLDIER'S VIEW OF MEXICO CITY

After Scott's army had firmly established itself in Mexico City and nearby towns, Sgt. J. Jacob Oswandel wrote of the beautiful valley, the grandeur of the public buildings, the pleasures and the problems of occupation:

You no doubt, like a great many others, have heard and read a good deal about Mexico, and particularly about the city of Mexico.

Mexico City

It is truly the most interesting city in this country. It fills a brilliant page in the history of that incomparable conquest of Cortez.

After its capture by the Spaniards, it was the residence of the viceroys of New Spain (as it was then called), and it is now the residence of its President, Congress and Supreme Court.

On approaching the city you behold one of the finest and most admirable views that can be brought before a human eye to see, and it will never be forgotten by anyone that ever entered it. No book's opinions or correspondence of tourists, that I ever read, can describe its romantic and magnificent sceneries. The beautiful valley expands as far as the eye can reach. Rich table-lands, with cultivated fields, and the city with its innumerable white domes and steeples. The snow-clad volcanoes Popocatepetl and Iscotafelt[16] a little distance to the left, with all its grandeur and extent, is indescribable.

Mexico (the Tennochtitlan [sic, Tenochtitlán] of the old Mexicans), was formerly surrounded by lakes, and was a dirty, low and unhealthy city, more than half covered with water, mud and other unmentionables.

The Spaniards drained and laid it out in squares and regular streets; built it up solid with neat, clean houses; two and three stories high. Many of them are fine mansions, with beautiful murmuring fountains, adorned with jete de eau, sparkling in the bright sun like brilliants.

The grand Catholic cathedral—a monument of art, a model of architecture, in a Roman style. On the corner is set in the stone calendar of the ancient Aztec, together with the baptistry.

The city is supplied with good and never-failing water, conducted in by an aqueduct from the Castle of Chapultepec, which fortress, on the 13th of September last, was stormed and captured by our gallant little army.

Cortez, in 1521, previous to capturing the city of Mexico, cut and partly destroyed this aqueduct. After which he rebuilt it more substantially and perfect.

The conquest of Mexico by Cortez has cost the Mexicans hundreds of thousands of lives. They were driven into their temple by droves, after which it was set on fire and all therein were burnt up alive.

The conquest has done one good thing—it has put an end to the annual sacrifice of twenty thousand to twenty-five thousand human beings, whose hearts were torn out by the barbarous Aztec priests on the piedra stone or sacrificial block, which is still preserved and placed in the museum of this city.

The Mexicans are celebrated for their fine leather work, the silver ornamental manufacture, their silk embroidery, gold and handsome jewelry. They are the most daring horsemen on this continent; they are in full national riding dress and trapping, and seated on a $400 to $500 silver-mounted saddle on a full blooded Mexican mustang.

Mexico is a great place for all kinds of people and amusements. In fact, it is spoken of as being one of the best show places known with the number of its population, which is about two hundred thousand.

There are, I think, seven theatres, including the Plaza d'Toro (Bull Pit). The principal theatres are the National, Santa Anna, some call it.* The second theatre in size is the Iturbide. This theatre is devoted to opera comique. The National seats three thousand, with a parquet, four circles and a gallery. They are lighted with some kind of oil, gas not having been introduced in this country.

I have read a great deal about Mexico, but I never read or heard of such temples and such fountains. What an Eden is this? To see such palaces, such portals, such Alameda parks and a host of other things, and how little it is appreciated by the thousands who daily behold and enjoy its beauties. Governed by good men and inhabited by an educated people, it would be the garden of the earth; but, at the same time, of all this richness staring you in the face, I would particularly request all new comers from the United States to fill their pockets with good gold and silver, and a good supply of it, for we are suffering awfully, and in particular us privates and corporals.

I see that Mr. Bensley's circus company has been augmented by a ballet and pantomine corps. It is [a] pleasant place for passing an afternoon or evening for those who are in the city. The bull fights on Sundays are the best of the season; Plaza de Toros is crowded, animals furious, *matadores* ditto, bulls second best. I was at this place of amusement on Sunday last. It is over four hundred feet in diameter, with an area of three hundred feet, and sitting and standing room for from eight to ten thousand spectators. The assailants are called *picadores*, and are on horseback, provided with a spear.

How odd it is and how odd it looks to see Mexicans and American soldiers mingling together in the streets and Alameda *Passo*, each observing every courtesy towards the other; that is amongst the respectable class; *ladrones* and *leperos* our men don't associate with. In fact it seems strange how quickly the people have forgotten their former queer notions in regard to our barbarians towards one another.* It is strange, indeed, but such is the fact. As I mentioned in my former letters, that when we first came into this country it was impossible to get acquainted with the ladies, but now they go to the theatre, circus, balls and other places of amusement and pleasurable time-killing, their faces gracing the occasion. No city under the starry tent of the Supreme General furnishes such a variety of *beldadz*, beauty, as the city of Mexico, and it would be a sin were the dear angels to hide their bright eyes and sweet lips from so many gallant admirers of their sex as are to be found in the American army.

*Thus in text.

There is an abundance of game, such as snipe, partridges, pheasants, pigeons, wild ducks and many other birds; of fish there is very little in the market, and are very high in prices during Lent; what there is of them are caught in the surrounding lakes of the city.

The closing of all the liquor stores at 6 o'clock in the evening (as ordered by Gen. Scott), has already had an admirable effect. The order was absolutely necessary to prevent the midnight assassination of our soldiers, an occurrence by-the-by that was getting to be entirely too frequent. No Mexican, I believe, however inclined, will attempt to take the life of an American soldier when sober, for most all the men that have been assassinated have been beastly drunk.[17]

SOCIAL LIFE IN THE CAPITAL

For the invaders victory was most rewarding in Mexico City. Unlike the "mud" villages the soldiers had seen on the Rio Grande, or even fever-stricken Vera Cruz, the City of Mexico was a great metropolis, one of the most magnificent cities of the western world. The citizens were more friendly—at least some of them—after an armistice relieved tensions. At last the beautiful señoritas who had dwelt in the heads of the men since the war began now were there. A young staff officer wrote:

GILBERT & GIHON

Window of a Private House

Watching the American
Troops Marching by

The march from Puebla here was made more pleasant by reason of having a beautiful Mexican girl with us, and under our protection. She had been in New York, seven years, receiving her education, and was returning to her parents in Mexico. She is very pleasant indeed and I sometimes feel almost inclined to make love to her. How would you admire a Mexican sister-in-law? This afternoon at 3 I dine with her.

The universal cry here is Peace!! Peace!! Peace!! An armistice has been concluded between the two governments, and all military operations have ceased. The olive branch and the white flag are the rage.

Since the armistice the city has become much gayer. Ladies who before confined themselves closely to their houses, now show themselves, radiant in smiles and beauty. They are very pretty, and even hardened soldiers cannot altogether withstand their fine black eyes and winning manners. They now come out to the theatres, and upon the public drives, and are not the least afraid of the American officers. I am going into a Mexican family to live during the rest of my stay in Mexico, for the purpose of learning the Spanish language. I intend to devote all my leisure time to Spanish, and hope to acquire a tolerable knowledge of it.[18]

While stationed at Puebla, young William Britton recorded in his diary some poignant impressions of his friendly relations with Mexican people:

March 9th [Puebla]. Well—have been so during the interval. The 5th, 6th, & 7th was the Carnival, a masked ball each night. I went the last night only— it caused me to wish myself at home. It was a grand sight and I had a number [of] friends present yet my mind was far far away and I felt solitary and alone.

[March] 28th. Well during the whole time except 2 days, during this month. I have been twice to the theatre with ladies as my companions (it is rarely the case that a Mexican lady of good standing will go to a place of amusement with an American. I think it is not caused by fear that their people will resent their friendship to us but because men who have been trusted have betrayed their trust). They were of Spanish origin and as light complexioned and pretty as those of my own native land—sociable and engaging in their manners yet my thoughts would in spite of my utmost endeavour wander to those I can never forget. . . .

[April] 22d. Well—left Puebla at noon. As I bade the family of Donna [Cuebeda?] farewell she presented me with a basket filled with refreshments to use on the journey. Arrived at and bivouacked in Amosoque at sun set, in company with Genl. [Lane?], he is on his way to Verra Cruse. Opened my present and found it filled with the choicest of confectionary. Believing as I do that this family are true Mexican I view them as among my best friends.[19]

When Britton reached Hacienda San Marco on his homeward journey, he wrote in the same vein to his brother on May 29, 1848 of his friendship with Mexican families:

On dress parade this evening it was officially announced that peace was actually made and that in a fiew days we would take up the line of march for home. . . . I have a letter from Pueblo. . . but it is in Spanish and I cannot translate it all . . . It is from the Mother of Pillar Vasques the young Lady who gave those presents of embroidery. Not a thing can ail me but the family here are ready to provide for me, a cup of chocolate is sent in to my room for me every morning before I am up. It comes with "Good morning [Señor Guillermo?]" "How are you this morning?" "How did you pass the night?" If the reply is "Well," their response is "Thanks be to God."[20]

Hostility in Occupied Cities

But all was not romance and friendship. There was a constant undercurrent of hostility. Countless small grievances could add up to a malaise, sometimes hard to detect but always there, as, for example, when overcrowding led to the use of homes for barracks, or when a brigade dammed up the water in an aqueduct passing through its camps, thereby cutting down the supply that reached Mexico City. While the army was in Puebla, rumors constantly fed distrust and seriously affected the psychology of Scott's army. This was apparent in the diary kept by Lt. Henry Moses Judah, who wrote:

16th [June?] 1847. . . . I was detailed as officer of the day about dusk. Gen. Worth got up an estampede, on the following grounds. He received an anonymous letter from a Mexican stating that he knew that there was a plan being formed between the guerrillas and the cut throats of the town, to surprise our guards, throw the city into disorder [i.e., Puebla], and murder all they could. He ended by saying that he did not wish his name to be known to his fellow countrymen. This plan seemed quite reasonable, for Puebla has the worst reputation of any town in Mexico; the knife is used more freely here, and the city contains at least 10,000 villains of the blackest dye, men who seldom work, but who live upon stealing, highway robbery and murder.

It is dangerous to go out after night, particularly for foreigners. Four of our men were stabbed today, one of my company by the name of Brown, after stabbing him in the back the infernal villains cut his throat. He is dead. Gen. Worth has issued an order, requiring extra vigilance of the guards, forbidding officers or men to appear on the streets without side arms, the men who go out on pass to go in parties of not less than 6, to keep together and be ac-

Mexican Robbers

companied by a non Comd. Offr. Col. Graham[21] ordered me to consider myself as Offr. of the Guard; and to remain with it all night. I posted two extra sentinels, and made the necessary arrangements in case of attack. I took a nap after daylight until breakfast.

17th. . . . I heard today a few of the numerous lies that have been circulated in advance of our march, and which are believed by the lower classes. After branding us in general terms with cowardice and barbarity it was reported that we sent to New Orleans from Tampico seven or eight shiploads of inhabitants as slaves, having previously branded them. That besides killing everything, even the dogs, we stuck little children at Vera Cruz upon the points of our bayonets. Such lies as these are circulated even by Santa Anna. Now compare our treatment of the Mexicans, with their intentions to us. After every fight and even during a battle have our men fed and watered their wounded enemies; never, have the[y] injured a fallen foe.

. . . On the field of battle they [the Mexicans] have not only killed the wounded but mutilated the dead. The[y] falsify and distort our most humane acts into the most lawless cruelty, and a foreigner here told me, that they now say all they want is to get the Yankees prisoners, we'll fix them, in other words we are going to cut their throats to satisfy our wounded pride, in not whipping them. When from the odds in our favor, we should have done

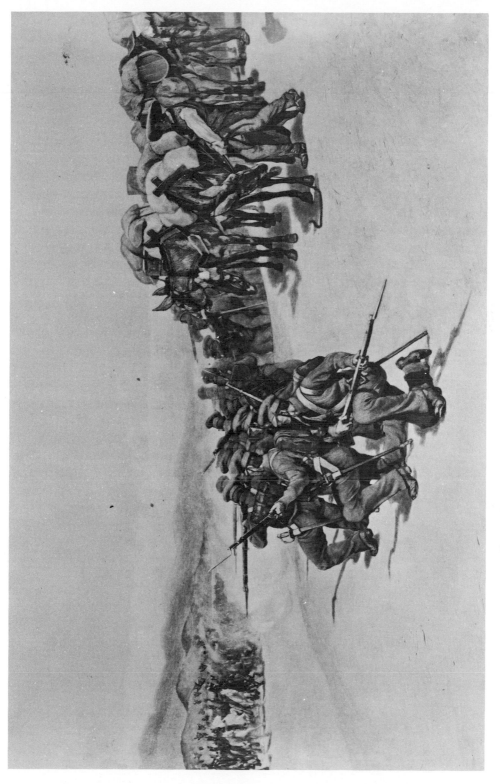

PLATE XXXI. Pack Train Attacked by Mexican Cavalry

PLATE XXXII. *Mexican Guerrillas*

so. Without law or order the community is one of the basest kind, and he who can pillage, plunder, and oppress the most from the President down, is the best fellow. Into a city of 80,000 inhabitants of such a character did our little Division of 3,000 men march, in my opinion one of the most impudent daring things on record.[22]

OCCUPATION OF CUERNAVACA

When about 1,300 men were sent as a detachment from Mexico City to occupy Cuernavaca, in February 1848, all the variants of occupation—from brutality to fraternization—were to be found in an account written by Lt. William D. Wilkins, Quartermaster of the 15th Infantry:

While we were comfortably seated at dinner in the Castle of Chapultepec, on the 1st of this month, an orderly from head quarters brought us a mandate to march on the 2nd [to Cuernavaca]. . . . We left the Castle of Chapultepec at 8 o'clock on the evening of the 2nd and marched all night until 4 in the morning. Our halting place was at the "Hacienda Portalis," one of those delightful country seats, adorned with all that wealth can furnish to the suggestions of taste, which are scattered over the lovely valley. Its inmates had just left it, and it pained me to see the abode of taste and comfort occupied and damaged by a rude soldiery. I thought how I would feel if my own happy home was polluted by a band of invaders and I was obliged to look on, an unwilling but helpless spectator of the scene. But the scene was a curious one. Large camp-fires were burning in the marble court-yard, muskets were stacked on rich carpets, and soldiers reposed in dirty-weary length on crimson sofas and velvet covered lounges. However, these are but part of the hardships of war; God grant that our land may never feel them.

Our next day's route for a few hours lay through the valley, but soon we arrived at the foot of, and had to commence ascending the grim ridge of rugged mountains, which encloses like a precious jewel the beautiful valley below. The ascent up this mountain was horrible. The road had long been destroyed by the rains, and a succession of ravines, water courses and small precipices left in its place. Up and over these our heavily laden waggons had to be forced, not by the mules alone, for a company was detailed to each wagon and officers and men worked diligently at the wheels. That night we spent in scattered parties on the rugged mountain's side, without fire, food or blankets, a poor contrast to our luxurious lodgings the night before.

It took us two days to travel some ten miles—but at last we reached the summit, and enjoyed an exquisite parting view of that earthly paradise, the valley of Mexico. How I wish that you could have left cold, snowy Michigan for a moment, and stood with me on the top of that old mountain. Earth cannot boast a fairer prospect than was extended below and it is well worth the trouble, the labor and the bloodshed which it cost us in getting to it. And it is always beautiful. No winter covers with a death-like pall, its green Savannas and strips the foliage from its olive and orange groves. It lies in the lap of perpetual summer, soft breezes continually play over it, and Heaven seems to smile benignantly on its fair creation. The next day's journey lay over an elevated plateau, nearly on a level with the clouds, and in the midst of wild yet beautiful mountain scenery. The atmosphere was very rarefied and the wind cold and piercing.

Our advanced guard had a lively chase after a small party of lancers, and succeeded in capturing two of their number. We encamped for the night at a little village just at the commencement of the descent of the mountain. The Mexicans had cut off the water, and our greatest comfort, coffee, could not be had. Our poor animals, also, after their long and thirsty march suffered exceedingly—and we lay down on our blankets in a very ill humor. We had not progressed far on the fifth day's march, when we were met by a deputation consisting of the Alcade and "Ayuntamiento"—or Civic Council of Cuernavaca who informed us that Genl. Alvarez[23] with a force of lancers had that morning evacuated the city—and who tendered us the hospitalities thereof, and offered to provide us with quarters. We accepted their offer, and consequently our entry was made peaceably, and to the great satisfaction of the citizens, who were amazed to find that the "Americanos" were not such savage barbarians as their cowardly rulers had represented us to be.

Cuernavaca (Anglicé "Cow's-horn") the capital of a state of the same name, is a town containing about eight thousand inhabitants, situated in the centre of a little valley of much lower altitude than the valley of Mexico, and consequently enjoying a much warmer climate. The country around supplies Mexico (from which it is distant about 60 miles) with fruit, and they raise immense quantities of sugar, and manufacture a great deal of "Aguardiente" a fiery, coarse sort of rum, Coffee, plaintains, bananas, tea, several kinds of spices, and even the bread fruit grow in the valley, which, even now in the winter month of February, looks like a tropical paradise. The town itself is a small affair, little one story houses embowered in orange or olive trees, straggle irregularly a[long] narrow, shady streets, their sociable balconies encroaching on its limits and inviti[ng] [a] passerby to an evening chat—a plaza in the centre of the place, surrounded by two story shops, and boasting a governor's palace and a fountain, is regarded by the people as a fine affair— and a noble old Cathedral embounded with a beautiful grove, are the most prominent features of the town.

A quiet, Sunday like stillness constantly reigns here, unbroken save by the rattling drum or melancholy bugle calling to Guard mounting—to drill or to evening parade. The people are unusually friendly and sociable, the Dons invite us into their houses, and produce their fragrant Havanas, and the dark eyed Señoritas chat, sing, ride or promenade with us, as if we were true Sons of Anahuac, and not heretic invaders and conquerors of their native land. One in particular, a lustrous eyed graceful girl who lives opposite my quarters, has, I think taken a fancy to a gentleman who shall be nameless, and, were it not for stronger and dearer ties at home, I might when I return introduce Señorita Constancia Gonzales—as "Mrs. Wilkins Jr." We are quartered here very pleasantly, some in convents, others with private families, and a few in barracks. The Major, the Adjutant and myself have a nice little house all to ourselves, plainly but neatly furnished—and I assure you we live very comfortably.[24]

The Pyramid of Cholula

A visit to the pyramid of Cholula at the time Scott's army occupied Puebla afforded a memorable experience for the travel-worn soldiers from the north who stood in wonder to gaze upon it. Capt. George T. M. Davis,[25] an aide-de-camp, recalled it in his Autobiography:

On the 31st [of July, 1847], by the invitation and great courtesy of General Scott, I was one of a party of which General Twiggs with an escort from his division formed a prominent feature, that visited the once vastly populous and ancient Indian city of Cholula.[26] It it seven miles from Puebla, and at the time of its conquest and devastation by Cortez was one of the largest cities in Mexico.[27] It was the theatre of that Spanish conqueror's most memorable military exploit; and after its conquest gave him an easy victory over Montezuma in occupying the Aztec capital. . . .

Erected upon that ancient site was a pyramid, 200 feet in height, and the base upon which it stood was of massive dimensions, covering, as we were told, forty-two acres of land and said to be the largest in the world, the pyramid itself[28] exceeding any of those of the Egyptians. On its crest the natives, previous to the conquest, had built their principal idol temple, and after its destruction by the Spaniards, they reared upon its ruins, in 1626, a large Catholic church. This temple many of us visited; it is called *La Iglesia de la Señora de las Remadies* [sic, *de los Remedios*]—The Church of the Lady of the Remedies. . . . The church was in a perfect state of preservation, though the storms and tempests and the vicissitudes of nearly two centuries and a quarter have beaten against its venerable walls, while within it was still resplendent in magnificence, and the grandeur of its architecture and its altars beyond compare. A number of small pictures, each commemorative of the death of some distinguished personage, many of them bearing the dates of 1752, 1761, 1765, 1772, and 1792 were suspended on one side of its walls, the two of most recent date being 1820 and 1829. The paintings (other than the above) were very fine, bearing the evidence of being the work of many of the old masters; and beneath its floors were several vaults in which reposed the remains of some of the most distinguished Spaniards of more than two centuries.

From that spot I counted the spires of no less than forty-three churches and chapels scattered over that vast space, with not over five thousand of its great multitudes spared, nine-tenths of whom are Indians, and the greater portion of them Catholics by profession. In most of those monuments to heathen-worship which I had counted, the walls were no longer vocal with pagan songs of praise or adoration, and their unbroken silence of ages remained still undisturbed, save only when the cry of the owls or the fluttering of the wings of the bats were heard, seeking a refuge from the storms, or a safe breeding-place and shelter for their young beneath those deserted roofs. Among the ruins of some of the oldest structures which tradition had established as such, I succeeded in finding, and took home with me, as mementoes of that instructive visit, the heads of three different idol-images worshiped by the Aztecs anterior to their conquest; and to which I attached a value not only for their antiquity, but as having been the only diety worshiped by a powerful race of human beings, then nearly if not quite extinct. Immediately preceding our departure, the band attached to General Twiggs's division (and which he had thoughtfully taken with his escort) was ordered by him to play in succession our three popular national anthems: "Hail Columbia," "Yankee Doodle," and "The Star Spangled Banner," and from the highest elevation of that famed Mexican pyramid the general's orders were executed in an inimitable style.[29]

CULTURAL EXCHANGES

William Hickling Prescott's The Conquest of Mexico *already had fired the imagination of the more literate among Scott's officers and men when his army pushed into the City of Mexico. Prescott, in turn, hoped that the rewards of Scott's victory might include such treasures as manuscripts and rare volumes which the conquerors might gather in by purchase, or otherwise. In April 1848, Prescott wrote to his friend, the scholarly Yankee general, Caleb Cushing:*

You have closed a campaign as brilliant as that of the great *conquistador* himself, though the Spaniards have hardly maintained the reputation of their hardy ancestors. The second conquest would seem, *a priori*, to be a matter of as much difficulty as the first, considering the higher civilization & military science of the races who now occupy the country. But it has not proved so—

and my readers, I am afraid, will think I have been bragging too much of the valor of the old Spaniard.

I hope we shall profit by the temporary possession of the capital, to disinter some of the Aztec monuments and MSS. The Spanish archives everywhere, both public and those belonging to private families in Old Spain and in the colonies, are rich in MSS. which are hoarded up from the eyes of the scholar, as carefully as if they were afraid of the truth coming to light. Of late these collections have been somewhat thinned in the peninsula. But such repositories must exist in Mexico, as Señor Aleman [sic][30], formerly Minister of Foreign affairs, has communicated some to me, and made liberal use of others in his own publications. If you meet with him you will see one of the most accomplished and clever men in Mexico. But I heard he was in disgrace, a year since, for his royalist predilections. Could you oblige me, by saying to him if you meet him—that I am very desirous of sending him my "Conquest of Peru," and if he can let me know how to do so, I shall do it at once with great pleasure. Have you met with either of the Mexican translations of my "Mexico?" The third volume of one of them is filled with engravings taken from old pictures of the time of the conquest—at least so it purports. This edition contains also some very learned and well-considered criticism on different passages of the work.[31]

In another letter to Cushing, John R. Bartlett,[32] bibliographer and bookdealer, who aided John Carter Brown in collecting his great library, pointed out the rich possibilities for a bibliophile in Mexico. Beyond that there was the need for a scientific survey of Mexico's natural wealth:[33]

My principle reason in writing you at this time is to call your attention to a subject to which I briefly alluded in my last; that of procuring early printed books on Mexico or other parts of America. Mr. Gallatin[34] has written to General Scott requesting him to purchase for [him] to the extent of $200 works of a particular class on Mexico. He has given a similar order to Lieut. Col. Emory, who leaves Washington in a few days for Mexico[35] and I would be glad to invest 3 or 400 dollars in the same way if opportunities should present themselves to you.

A great many grammars and dictionaries on the numerous languages of Mexico were published in the 17th & early part of the 18th century. These would be desirable for ethnological purposes. Then there are the works of Boturini,[36] Las Casas,[37] Barcia,[38] [Gomara?],[39] etc. which are desirable, Catechisms and other works including recent publications in the Mexican languages are also desirable, as they cost little. Ancient MSS I suppose are hardly to be had, still MSS and antiquities do exist in the convents & museums of the country and may be obtained under certain circumstances.

You[r] familiarity with the subject will make it unnecessary to say more. But if you can expend the sum named to advantage, I will feel obliged to you & will pay your draft for the same. It would not do to pay the high prices these books command in England. The Ethnolog. Soc. or Mr. Gallatin want the principal part—the remainder two or three of our large collectors will be glad to get.

Where you are now stationed there is no field for antiquarian research, though you may perchance fall in with some antiquarian treasures, an account of which would be interesting to our Eth. Society. Any communication from you would be acceptable.

We have received some contributions of interest and value from Lieut. Col. Emory & other officers who were attached to General Kearney's California expedition. These will be embodied in Mr. Gallatin's Memoir in our new volume.[40] Lieut. Col. Fremont has also promised us a contribution as soon as his trial is ended, though I fear it will be late for our volume.

All the departments at Washington as well as the officers of the army have tendered to Mr. Gallatin of the Ethnolog. Soc. any papers, maps, &c in their power and the Topographical Bureau has lately sent some MSS of interest relating to the aborigines.

I like your suggestion much for a scientific survey of the northern provinces of Mexico recently acquired by us, and have mentioned the subject to some of my friends in Congress, who approve of it. There are doubtless treasures there in ores and minerals—in botany—antiquities &c which would well repay us for a systematic and scientific exploration of the country. *Nothing would please me better than to engage in such an expedition* and when the proper time comes, we must see what can be done.

. . . . .

When we are in quiet possession of our conquests and know what part we are to keep, the question will doubtless be asked, what is there in the country so conquered. The question can only be answered by sending proper persons to examine and report.[41]

Cushing had already anticipated Prescott and Bartlett. He had in mind a study of Mexico, and cultivated the acquaintance of the Mexican scholar-politician, Lucas Alamán. That Alamán was willing to cooperate, not only by providing him with facts but also with an indoctrination in political affairs, became apparent in a note addressed to Cushing on February 10, 1848:

I have the pleasure of sending to you
1. The registro trimestre where you will find at the page marked something about maguey and pulque, and every where some information interesting to you about several points.

2. A memoir about maguey as writ[t]en by D. Govi. Mariano Sanchez y Mora (the anagram of his name at the title of the pamphlet) Count del Peñasco.

3. The voyages of Beltrami the volume which contains Mexico.[42] You can find in it many notices about buildings, paintings and other things. Their [sic] not worth much credit, being very charlatan. I will explain [to] you the cause of being myself very hardly treated by him.

4. A memoir in my own defence,[43] in which there is much information about the government of General Bustamante at his first epoch[44] when I was employed as a member of his Cabinet.

5. A newspaper very fresh containing at the marked place the *denouement* of my direction of industry .

The two last I beg you to keep for you[rself], and I should be glad to offer to you the t[h]ree first pieces, were they not the only copy I have.

I return with many thanks the newspaper you left me yesterday and to-morrow Friday at eleven o'clock I shall await for you [at the hospital up town?] to have the pleasure to present you to Count de la Cortina[45] at Calle de Juan Manuel.[46]

THE ARMY AND THE CHURCH

The Catholic church, at times, served as a conciliatory bond to link victor with vanquished. When the fighting was over, Catholics of the invading army were accepted as members of the faith, a tolerance sometimes extended to all Christians. At Vera Cruz, General Scott himself held a candle during Easter Sunday mass in the cathedral, where a week before the domes of the churches had been excellent targets for his mortars. The American Eagle of Vera Cruz (occupation newspaper) carried the story:

On [Easter] Sunday morning last we entered the church on the Plaza, and were gratified to see so full attendance of our officers and men. In rather an obscure place, on the left hand side of the aisle, sat Gen. Scott, and a number of his friends. The General appeared devout and pious, and not like the many of us who go to such places to pass an idle hour. The entrance of the General we are told created no little astonishment amongst the natives and he was readily known and whispered about as the Commander-in-chief of the Americans.

. . . . .

The scene in the church on Easter Sunday, was indeed one of interest and solemnity. Many who the week before were sending death shots at each other now, standing and kneeling together, communed with the same God. We noticed that much deference was paid to our General, and that he was the first one to whom a long lighted candle was handed. He received it solemnly and held it, for a time, lighted in his hand. This was also pleasing to the citizens and from all appearances they seemed to think that at least we were not *all* the devils they had pictured to them.[47]

Some months later, when Capt. John W. Lowe of Ohio visited a church in the same city he found equality before God and wished that it might be the same in the United States.

This is Sabbath afternoon . . . . To get out of the noise of the camp, I this morning rode up to the City and went to Church; there were several churches open, two of which I attended. They were beautiful, heavy buildings but rather tawdry and tinselled in the inside; the floors were of marble in small diamond slabs, small organ galleries and few seats. One thing in particular pleased me much and that was, *the equality of all ranks before the altar of God.* For here I saw kneeling on the marble pavement for more than 15 minutes, the haughty Castillian in whose veins flowed the pure blood of the Cortes, the yellow Aztec, the stupid Indian, and the decrepid negro, altogether, side by side; the distinction of races, of color, of wealth, of rank was disregarded or unknown and they all seemed to regard each other, at least in the Sanctuary, as equal before God. In one instance (and I am satisfied it was of common occurence) I saw a beautiful young, fair, Spanish girl, evidently of the higher class, kneeling, and just in front of her, was an old negro beggar in the same attitude, while at the side of the negro was a Castillian gentleman and his little son (about Tom's age) all devoutly offering up their prayers to Almighty God without even a thought of "Negro pews" or "poor seats." And then I wished that it were so in my own, my native land, where we boast that all men are *free and equal*.[48]

All who went to the Catholic mass did not have Lowe's sensitive perception. In Mexico City, a young aide to General Cushing admired the magnificence of the churches, but sneered at what he styled "the flummery" of the rituals:

I remained in . . [Mexico] City eleven days, during which time I had an opportunity to view some of its much boasted magnificence. . . . There has been many extravagant things said about it, though I think it would be called magnificent by any one. The cathedrals and convents particularly are the places of vast wealth and elegance. In the church of Gaudaloupe, four miles from town, there are huge silver railings which would cause you all to stare with amazement.

That one church combines more that is beautiful and rich than any thing I have ever seen in my life. There they hold the annual religious festival in honor of "Our Lady of Gaudaloupe" who as tradition has it, appeared there many years ago very mysteriously to an Indian, and in addition to all this, the church sprang from the rock in a single night. Very marvelous indeed! ! ! This same Lady of Gaudaloupe is the patron Saint of all Mexico, and can do many wonderful things. You would think she was held in high estimation if you were to see the use she is put to. She is connected with all their associations of life, and even the butchers have her placed in a conspicuous place in their shops that she may bless the beef.

You have no idea of the flummery that we see here every day, all of which the Mexicans call religion.[49]

Quarters for the Troops

In Puebla, Mexico City, and surrounding towns, some of Scott's regiments were quartered with the clergy. It was a welcome experience for Lt. Daniel Harvey Hill at Pachuca, who thought it was his first comfortable billet in Mexico. A rigid Presbyterian, Hill wrote: "I left the Convent of San Francisco with some regret. I had quite an extensive acquaintance with the Monks & found them af[f]able and sociable though extremely ignorant & superstitious. Besides there was a Romance about my life in the Monastery. I slept on a Friar's plank bed in a Friar's cell and ate off a Friar's table. Over my door was the inscription "Hail Mary, Most Pure Conceived Without Sin." Below this inscription was an exhortation to say these mysterious words as the mere repeating them would be rewarded with many indulgences."[50] Another officer, quartered at San Angel, observed: "The old Padres take it kindly since there is no help for it."[51] But in Puebla, a sergeant in Engineer Company A thought there was real camaraderie, plus generous rents:

My last letter to you was written from this city and dated 8th & 12th [of] June last past. In said letter I stated that our Company was quartered in a castle just outside the city limits. Since then we have moved into town & occupy splendid *apartments* in a monastery by permission of the monks, who get a rent for the same rivalling the rents you pay in N.Y.—$90 per Month, pretty good rent to pay to accomodate one little Compy. Behold us then daily, hourly, mingling with the Mexican priesthood on terms of the greatest intimacy, occupying splendid apartments in the heart of their Sanctum Sanctorum, strolling with them through their extensive grounds, inspecting and commenting on their eligent [sic] buildings, courts, fountains; on their manners, customs and costumes. The monks are a jolly set of fellows, not at all backward in drinking or *gambling* with our men; in singing, or swearing in English which some of them can do perfectly, it being no sin as English is not Latin or Spanish either. The church of this city is amazingly rich, owning as I am credibly informed one-third of the entire city. The cathedral, the principal church, is much the finest I ever saw. All the monks are officiating priests. The order in whose midst we are is called the order of St. Francisco.[52]

Trade Follows the Army

The rewards of victory might also include profitable ventures for Mexican venders and Yankee merchants who followed in the wake of the armies. No sooner had Taylor entered Matamoros, in May 1846, than a swarm of merchants appeared in the city, aided by Secretary of the Treasury Robert J. Walker whose circular of June 11 permitted American vessels carrying products of the United States to enter captured Mexican ports without paying duties.[53] Thomas Bangs Thorpe described the thriving commerce on the lower Rio Grande:

The high price of cotton goods in Matamoros, owing to the Mexican tariff, is well known. Several enterprising "Yankees" since General Taylor has taken possession of the city have "moved in," and opened stores and are selling goods on "cheap principles," about one third of the usual Mexican prices, but double the usual American prices. It is an amusing scene to witness the crowd around these stores, composed of the mixed people of the city. Finely dressed women, rancheros, naked Indians, and negroes, all eager to purchase goods.

. . . . .

This river, under the influence of American enterprise, is assuming a very busy appearance. The steamers Frontier and Cincinnati have arrived at Matamoros, giving the port of the town a lively appearance. "River front lots" will soon become valuable in that city, and stores will be erected on the water's edge.[54]

As the New Orleans Delta pointed out, it was a two-way trade, especially after Scott's army had penetrated into the region of tropical products. The "fruits of victory" then appeared on the New Orleans market:

Our late operations in Mexico have opened to us the fruit markets of Jalapa. We observe several varieties of melons, figs, and other fruits in our markets, and at the fruit stores, from Vera Cruz. Large quantities are brought over by every ship. They find a ready sale in our market. The valley of Jalapa is famous for its delicious fruits. The pine apple produced there is the finest in the world.[55]

POLICY OF ECONOMIC CONTRIBUTIONS

It was President James K. Polk himself who declared that the Mexicans should be required to pay for the war, either through trade or by a levy of economic contributions. He explained his views in a message to the Secretary of the Treasury:

The government of Mexico having repeatedly rejected the friendly overtures of the United States to open negotiations with a view to the restoration of peace, sound policy and a just regard to the interests of our own country require that the enemy should be made as far as practicable to bear the expenses of a war of which they are the authors, and which they obstinately persist in protracting.

. . . . .

In the exercise of . . unquestioned rights of war, I have, on full consideration, determined to order that all the ports or places in Mexico which now are, or hereafter may be, in the actual possession of our land and naval forces by conquest, shall be opened, while our military occupation may continue, to the commerce of all neutral nations, as well as our own, in articles not contraband of war, upon the payment of prescribed rates of duties, which will be made known and enforced by our military and naval commanders.

While the adoption of this policy will be to impose a burden on the enemy, and at the same time to deprive them of the revenue to be derived from trade at such ports or places, as well as to secure it to ourselves, whereby the expenses of the war may be diminished, a just regard to the general interests of commerce, and the obvious advantages of uniformity in the exercise of these belligerent rights, requires that well considered regulations and restrictions should be prepared for the guidance of those who may be charged with carrying it into effect.[56]

UNLOCKING MEXICAN SPECIE

Q. M. Gen. Thomas S. Jesup encouraged the War Department to permit trade with the Mexicans. It would unlock Mexican specie needed to command that country's resources:

I respectfully submit for the consideration of the War Department the propriety of permitting citizens of the United States, as posts are taken and occupied by our troops on the Gulf, to enter with merchandise for the purpose of trading with the Mexicans. All articles that could be used against us in war might be prohibited. If the sale of tobacco, dry goods, &c., were permitted, the disbursing officers in Mexico could obtain, either for treasury notes or drafts, all the specie they would require there, without the expense or risk of transporting it thither; and we could often command the resources of the country in labor and means of transportation through our merchants, when the people of the country would be afraid to deal directly with public officers.[57]

FREEDOM FROM THE ALCABALA

If the occupying army drew wealth from Mexico, it also freed the laboring and productive classes from the burdens of the alcabala and other oppressive taxes. A writer in the American Star *commented with emphasis upon conditions in Mexico City:*

From the first moment we landed on the shore at Vera Cruz to our arrival in this capital [Mexico City], the rights of both person and property have been respected; all supplies of flour, grain, meat, &c., which the service required, were purchased and paid for at even higher prices than those paid by the citisens of the country. During the whole period that our forces have been in the valley of Mexico we have paid to the agriculturist from five to seven dollars per cargo for barley, and from eight to ten dollars for corn, whilst at the same time, in this capital, a tariff was promulgated by the Authorities, which limited the price of barley to three and a half dollars, and that of corn to seven dollars. In Vera Cruz, Jalapa, Perote and Puebla we gave liberty to the laboring and productive classes by abolishing the odious system of Alcabala or tax on labor, by which both the producer and consumer are benefitted: the first is able to sell the fruits of his labor without any restraint or taxation, and the consumer is enabled to purchase the fruits of the earth at their legitimate prices, viz., the cost of production.

The municipal authorities of those places have been taught a useful lesson, and compelled to resort to the democratic system of levying taxes on property, with a view to sustain the police and government of their respective cities which were hitherto sustained by a tax on labor. We regret that in this city of palaces, the municipal authorities have been permitted even temporarily to sustain their police and government by levying an Alcabala duty, or tax on labor. The poor Indian who presents himself at the gates of the city with a basket of fruit, a dozen of eggs, a few fowls, or a load of charcoal, is obliged to pay a tax before he enters, and if he has not the money with him, he is made to deposite with the guard either a part of his produce, or some article of clothing, until he can effect a sale and return with the money to redeem the article pledged. In consequence of this tax, he is obliged to advance the price of his produce to the poor artizan who consumes it, and by this indirect mode of taxation, sustains the police and government of this magnificent city.

The population of the city is estimated at 200,000, of which number some twelve thousand, or 6 per centum, are free holders; they are in possession of all the wealth and power by which they have hitherto managed to keep in force and monarchical custom of Alcabala or tax on the poor laborer, who, although not worth a dollar in the world, is made to contribute as much for the support of the municipal government as his rich neighbor who may be worth millions. The injustice of this mode of taxation must be obvious to every one, and we sincerely hope that the causes which gave rise to the temporary continuation of this most unrighteous (Alcabala) tax on labor, will be speedly removed, and the free sale and consumption of the fruits of the earth fully established, by which measure the laboring classes will be taught to consider us in the same light as their neighbors of Puebla, Vera Cruz, &c. —That is to say, as benefactors and not destroying enemies.[58]

Scott's Assessments

Incidental benefits might accrue to the Mexican people, but the Polk administration, faced with a war-cost deficit, was determined to make the Mexicans pay for the war, either by seizing their country's products, through tax revenues, or by levying contributions (assessments) upon the conquered land. Scott discussed the problem in his Memoirs:

Early in the campaign I began to receive letters from Washington, urging me to support the army by forced contributions. Under the circumstances, this was an impossibility. The population was sparse. We had no party in the country, and had to encounter the hostility of both religion and race. All Mexicans, at first, regarded us as infidels and robbers. Hence there was not among them a farmer, a miller, or dealer in subsistence, who would not have destroyed whatever property he could not remove beyond our reach sooner than allow it to be seized without compensation. For the first day or two we might, perhaps, have seized current subsistence within five miles of our route; but by the end of a week the whole army must have been broken up into detachments and scattered far and wide over the country, skirmishing with *rancheros* and regular troops, for the means of satisfying the hunger of the day. Could invaders, so occupied, have conquered Mexico?

The war being virtually over, I now gave attention to a system of finance for the support of the army and to stimulate overtures of peace. The subject required extensive inquiries and careful elaboration. My intention was to raise the first year about twelve millions of dollars, with the least possible pressure on the industry and wealth of the country, with an increase to fifteen millions in subsequent years.[59]

To carry out his plan, Scott levied an assessment of $150,000 on Mexico City almost as soon as his army began its occupation. Government-owned tobacco, captured in the city, was distributed among the soldiers, although internal revenues were to remain temporarily with the municipal authorities. Scott's policy on these matters was indicated by the following endorsement (Sept. 21):

I approve the written suggestions; that is to say; that the receipts of the post office, & other internal sources of revenue, remain to the city; that the external sources (receipts at the Custom houses or gates) also remain with the city; & in respect to the captured tobacco, that part be distributed in kind & the remainder be disposed of to the municipality as proposed within. As to the mode of distribution in kind (the whole army sharing alike) Major General Quitman will please submit a projet.

Tobacco not belonging to the Mexican government, & which may hereafter be brought into the market, may be disposed of by the City authorities, as heretofore.

The first instalment of the contribution which was to have been paid in, yesterday, is not yet forthcoming: If it be not soon paid in, let the municipality be informed that the receipts at the gates & other sources of income shall be seized into the hands of the army.[60]

On December 15, Scott issued his comprehensive General Order No. 376, which gave notice that the army was about to occupy various parts of the Republic of Mexico and required that all Mexican taxes owed to the federal government of Mexico should be paid over to the Americans for the support of the army of occupation. Scott's order read:

1. This army is about to spread itself over and to occupy the Republic of Mexico, until the latter shall sue for peace in terms acceptable to the Government of the United States.

2. On the occupation of the principal point or points in any State, the payment to the Federal Government of this Republic of all taxes or dues of whatever name or kind, heretofore—say in the year 1844—payable to or collected by that Government, is absolutely prohibited, as all such taxes or dues will be demanded of the proper civil authorities, for the support of the Army of Occupation.

3. The State and Federal District of Mexico being already so occupied, as well as the States of Vera Cruz, Puebla and Tamaulipas, the usual taxes or dues heretofore contributed by the same to the Federal Government, will be considered as due and payable to this army from the beginning of the present month, and will early be demanded of the civil authorities of the said States and District, under rules and penalties which shall be duly announced and enforced.

4. Other States of the Republic, as the Californias, New Mexico, Chihuahua, Coahuila, New Leon, &c., &c., already occupied by the forces of the United States, though not under the immediate orders of the general-in-chief, will conform to the prescriptions of this order, except in such State or States where a different system has been adopted with the sanction of the Government at Washington.

5. The internal taxes or dues referred to are—1. direct taxes; 2. duties on the production of gold and silver; 3. melting and essaying [sic] dues; 4. the tobacco rent; 5. the rent of stamped paper; 6. the rent on the manufacture of playing cards; and 7. the rent of post offices.

6. The rent of national lotteries is abolished—lotteries being hereby prohibited.

7. Import and export duties at the ports of the Republic, will remain as fixed by the Government of the United States, except that the exportation of gold and silver in bars or ingots (plata y oro en pasta) is prohibited until further instructions of [the] Government on the subject.

8. All imported articles, goods or commodities, which have once paid, or given sufficient security for the payment of duties to the United States, at any port of entry of the Republic, shall not again be burdened with any tax or duty in any part of the Republic occupied by the forces of the United States.

9. The levying of duties on the transit of animals, goods or commodities, whether of foreign or domestic growth, from one State of this Republic to another, or on entering or leaving the gate of any city within the Republic, will, from and after the beginning of the ensuing year, be prohibited as far as the United States forces may have the power to enforce the prohibition. Other and equitable means, to a moderate extent, must be resorted to by the several States and city authorities, for the necessary support of their respective Governments.

10. The tobacco, playing card and stamped paper rents, will be placed for three, six or twelve months, under contract with the highest bidders, respectively, for the several States; the State and Federal District of Mexico being considered as one. Accordingly, offers or bids for those rents, within each State, or any one of them are invited. They will be sent in as early as possible, sealed, to the headquarters of Commanders of Departments, except for the Federal District and State of Mexico.[61]

THE PACHUCA EXPEDITION

At the end of December an assessment equal to four times the direct taxes paid in 1843 was levied upon the states. Although it was collected only in Mexico City and Vera Cruz, and the total proceeds were less than $4,000,000, Scott sent three detachments to prepare for the levy in other places—one to Cuernavaca, another to Toluca, and the third to Pachuca, fifty miles northeast of Mexico City and near the great mines of Real del Monte. Scott knew that a large amount of silver bullion was soon to be brought to the assay office at Pachuca; to prevent Mexican officials from seizing it, he despatched a force to forestall them and to aid in collecting the duties on precious metals. Lt. Thomas Williams, 4th Artillery, discussed the Pachuca expedition and other problems of military occupation in a letter of December 27:

We are again ourselves, & ready to move forward with the moving spirits of the century. Already, looking to permanent occupation, the Americans here, have held three public meetings on the practicability of constructing a rail-road from this Capital to Vera Cruz.

The subject of the revenues of Federal Mexico has deeply engaged Genl. Scott for some weeks, & as the subject is developed, from time to time, those revenues will be taken into our own hands.

The first expedition to the interior for that object, will move towards the mines of Pachuca or Real del Monte—in a few days. These mines are the property of individual foreigners who pay a percentage on all silver & gold assayed—to the Mexican Govt. our object is to collect that percentage.

Other detachments will be made towards San Luis & Zacatecas, perhaps, so soon as the *half clad* troops, *just arrived from the U.S.*, can be provided with some indispensable jackets &c.

I think there will be no *peace*, consequently no indemnity by Mexico, & therefore will have to help ourselves, whence will come, first, occupation, & next annexation. The President (in his message recd. Christmas) disavows that the government of the U.S. ever entertained the purpose of annexation. But such must be the end, inevitable, of all these things. I regret that the event cannot be postponed for 30 years. A commercial intercourse, on our part, for that period, with this people is necessary to their regeneration, & preparation for our more advanced civilization & liberal ideas of government. . . .

In coming years the advance upon & entrance of the capital of Mexico by the little army under General Scott will be *written*—blazoned—as the great event—the epoch—of the 19th century; & as not surpassed by any military achievement in *all* previous history.[62]

Mexican Guerrillas

GUERRILLA WARFARE

The force sent to Pachuca and Real del Monte also searched for Mexican guerrillas. Guerrilla warfare came naturally to the Mexicans; they had used it in their war for independence, and against both Taylor and Scott. Helped by their familiarity with the land, the guerrilleros could travel light, strike quickly, and then vanish into the chapparal. Guerrilla tactics, however, rarely were geared to any large strategy—their assaults were sporadic—but after the fall of Mexico City they continued to harass Scott's line of communications for some months. One of their most colorful leaders was Padre Jarauta, an ex-divinity student, who eventually was shot for revolutionary activities in 1848. Daniel Harvey Hill, with the detail at Pachuca, recorded in his journal the hunt for Jarauta and his band:

Jany. 17th, [1848] 9 P.M. I have just received orders to be ready to march tomorrow morning on a secret expedition. I have been let into the secret, though few other officers know anything about it. We are to make a forced march for Tulancingo a large town some thirty miles from here, where 'tis said General Paredes and the notorious Guerrilla Chief, Father Garaute [sic, Jarauta] are recruiting troops. Our force will consist of my section of Artillery and about seventy men, fifty of these Dragoons, the others Infantry soldiers mounted for the occasion.

Jany. 21st. We have just returned (forty miles distant) after a harassing but fruitless chase in search of Padre Garaute and Genl. Paredes. Our preparations for the march were all made on the night of the 17th, and at 8 A.M. on the following morning we started, giving out that Col. Withers[63] was going to visit an English Hacienda some fourteen miles beyond Mineral Del Monte and wished to take with him a large escort. Mineral Del Monte is some three thousand feet above this place and the road leading to it is exceedingly narrow and in many places there are frightful ravines so close to it that the least false step of one of my horses would have precipitated horses, cannon & carriages hundreds of feet below. Many careless riders have been dashed to atoms in these ravines. We made a short halt in Mineral Del Monte, a mining town of ten thousand inhabitants. 'Tis built on a very rugged site. All the houses have shingle inclined roofs, the only roofs of the kind that I have seen in Mexico. In fact Mineral Del Monte is essentially an English town with English houses, English manners & customs. We saw in the streets a great number of crossbreeds, English & Mexican. Many of the English have married Mexican women but far the greater number have their mistresses.

For the next fourteen miles after leaving the Mineral we were descending and then found ourselves in the Valley of Puebla. The whole country through which we passed this day is in the English interest and the English employ. We passed thousands of mules & asses laden with wood & other materials for the town. Occasionally after passing through a wild & barren defile we would be cheered by the sight of a fine English farm-house or a pretty Mexican village.

A little before sunset we halted at an English Hacienda near a town called Huasca. Here we fed our horses, got something to eat for ourselves and then lay down on the floor and wrapped up ourselves in our own blankets until after eleven at night. We then roused up and proceeded on our march with a Mexican as guide, who was compelled under pain of death to show us the way. The road was exceedingly bad and as my harness was old & worn out, our march was slow and tedious. However by daylight we had made twenty miles & then found ourselves in sight of Tulancingo. We entered it at a brisk trot and then found to our mortification that the enemy had fled a few hours before. Garaute had three hundred (300) men with him & was supported by the population of a town of ten thousand inhabitants and yet thought himself unable to fight a hundred (100) Yankees. Truly this people have an exalted opinion of our fighting qualities.

Soon after we entered, the Ayuntamiento or City Council was called together and Col. Withers demanded of that body why they had given countenance and support to a robber chief when they well knew that Genl. Scott had declared all guerrilleros outlaws and they and all who gave them aid &

comfort worthy of death. The Ayuntamiento replied that Father Garaute came their [sic] with an order from the Mexican Government for arms, men and horses and that he had the physical power to enforce the compliance with the order however unwilling they may have been to give him assistance. They said that the venerable Priest had released forty-four criminals from the prison and had committed many excesses and the town had not the power to restrain him. Col. Withers and all his officers were so little satisfied with the excuse of the Ayuntamiento that they determined to lay a contribution on the town of ten thousand dollars. But 'twas decided not to demand the money until the next day when we were ready to march, lest there should be an insurrection that night.

[In] spite of our fatigue another officer and myself wandered all over the town. The people evinced none of that fright and abhorrence so usual on the first entrance of the American troops into any town. Crowds of little boys followed us desirous to see what sort of animals the Yankees were. Many lovely girls were also curious to see the "Monsters of the North" and presented themselves at their windows and their balconies. Among others was a daughter of Genl. Paredes,[64] a very pretty girl. We bowed to her several times in the course of our ramble. Tulancingo is the prettiest town that I have seen in Mexico and the inhabitants appear to be more enlightened and consequently more liberal and sociable than the majority of Mexicans.

The night of the 20th, we spent as the preceding night, on the floor wrapped up in our blankets. The next morning the Ayuntamiento was summoned again and we subordinate officers were much surprised to learn that Col. Withers had changed his mind with reference to the contribution. It seems that the night before he was waited upon privately by a deputation of the citizens who requested him to change his Head-Quarters to that place. This so flattered the Colonel that he abated of his fury and gave up all thought of the assessment. We were no little mortified at this evidence of weakness in our commanding officer.

About sunset that night we reached the English Hacienda where we halted two nights before. We again put up there and several of us went by the invitation of Mr. Rule, the Director of the Mines, to the Hacienda of Don Ignacio Castelaso and there were most handsomely entertained. Mr. Rule, the English Director, has been twenty-three years in Mexico and as he speaks the language like a native and is immensely wealthy, he has more power with the Mexicans than ever [an] English Nabob had on his Indian estates. The next morning we visited near the house of Senor Castellaso [sic] a remarkable fountain of water, the source of the River Panuco [sic] or River of Tampico. We remained several hours in Mineral Del Monte that day. Most of the officers dined with Mr. Arthur, a wealthy Englishman, whilst I dined with a Mexican by the invitation of an Englishman. I observed that the

Mexican had in good part adopted the English mode of cooking and had English vegetables on his table.

Jany. 23d. Yesterday, with another officer, I rode around the Valley for many leagues and visited three Haciendas, though we ran no little risk of being captured by rancheros or guerrilleros.

. . . . .

Jany. 29th, 11 P.M. I am again going out hunting guerrilleros. We are to start after midnight and will have a long ride but I do not know where to nor how far. These wretches, the guerrilleros are getting more and more impudent every day. They are swarming all around us and their object now seems to be to murder all of us at Pachuca and all the English at Real Del Monte, and then plunder the mines. The population of this town is getting more and more hostile every day and they have become so bold as to stab our soldiers and stone our officers in broad daylight. Our force is too small and we have every prospect of having a blood[y] time before many days.

Jany. 30th. We have returned from our night expedition in search of the guerrillero Falcon.[65] We expected a bloody action but not a shot was fired. We started last night about two o'clock and moved off in profound silence across the mountains. The moon had just risen and the hour, the wild scenery, the pale moonlight, the character of the excursion all gave a romantic tinge to this journey which I can never forget. Notwithstanding the exceeding roughness of the mountain path, we reached the Hacienda where Falcon was supposed to be, some twelve miles distant, before 'twas day. The Bird had flown in haste. And now our soldiers began committing every class of disorder incident upon a sack. What a profanation of the holy Sabbath morning! We remained at the Hacienda an hour or two and then without breakfast took a longer route for Pachuca. For a couple of miles we skirted the edge of a magic mountain overgrown with most enormous cactus and then entered a lovely valley dotted with Haciendas. The heat was now very oppressive and the dust almost unendurable. We had suffered a great deal the night before from cold while crossing the mountain, but now we suffered still more from the heat. We reached Pachuca at 12 M. having ridden thirty miles through cold, heat and dust without any food.[66]

CRIME AND PUNISHMENT IN THE ARMY

For the Americans in the Mexican War there was victory, and for those not killed or wounded there were assorted compensations. But since it was a war, there was another, seamy side, and for most of the soldiers when viewed individually (rather than collectively as a victorious army), this side was predominant. Although they had volunteered to go to war, and by far the greater number of them honored their commitments by creditably sustaining hard-

ship and battle, and behaved as well as soldiers in a hostile country are apt to behave, they did not like the army, they did not like war, and generally speaking they did not like Mexico or the Mexicans. This was the majority: disliking the job, resenting the discipline and caste system of the army, and wanting to get out and go home.

Summaries of court martial trials held in the field are replete with lists of infractions and the punishments prescribed. For the most part these were traditional military sentences that differed little from those of Washington's army during the American Revolutionary War. A private found guilty of drunkenness on duty forfeited six dollars of his pay and stood on a barrelhead "every alternate two hours for five successive days from reveille to retreat." Another, for the same offense, received twenty days at hard labor, and carried "a weight of fifty pounds from retreat until twelve o'clock every night"; his forfeit was twelve dollars. Sleeping while on guard brought demotion for a corporal, forfeit of his pay for the term of his enlistment, and work at hard labor with a twenty-four-pound weight attached to a leg. Others received brands: HD (for Habitual Drunkard), W (for Worthless); heads were shaved, and in extreme cases the culprit was drummed out of camp. An enlisted man found guilty of stealing clothing stood on a barrel with a board bearing the phrase "Great coat thief" suspended from his neck. The wearing of an iron yoke, ball and chain, and similar punishments usually were remitted when the army broke camp.

Resentment of the rank and file against these punishments ate deeply into the morale of the armies. One protest came from a Pennsylvania volunteer stationed at Matamoros late in the war:

We are under very strict discipline here. [Some of] our officers [are] very good men but the balance of them are very tyrannical and brutal toward the men. They go out and get drunk every night and raise the very devil. They strike the men with swords and abuse them in the most brutal manner possible for a human being to be treated. And if a poor soldier should be caught drinking a glass of liquor he is bucked and gagged and if he says one word protesting his innocence they have him taken to the lake and water thrown in his face by pails full untill he is nearly drowned. Many a poor soldier has been discharged after a long and severe illness [caused] by this water being thrown on him. There is now one in the Hospital in town raving crazy and lashed to his bed . . [because of] this water. There is another poor being cramped so he walks half bent by this water and several other cases I could mention and all by this accursed water.

Another way of punishing men [is that] they have a hole dug under-ground, tight and dark with the e[x]ception of a small particle of light [which] comes through a crack in the door. [Those put in there] sleep on the cold ground as they allow them no blanket in there. In short it is [a] back house and alltogether [the prisoners are allowed] 3 crackers and water a day. One man, a fifer, was sentenced for 30 days after having 400 pails of water thrown on him and all his crime was running through the guard. Many instances of this kind occur daily and to night on drill an officer laid a soldier's skull open with his sword, and the poor man is now suffering from it in the Hospital in camp.

Our Captain is a good man. He seeks every opportunity to search for the interest and welfare of his company. He will not see them abused or misused in any way when it is in his power to prevent it. His name is Joseph A. Yard of Trenton, for a long time keeper of the Mercer County prison. He was also a custom house officer in New York. His character is well known throughout New Jersey. He is a well educated man and a religious man, and loves his men as though they were his children. Two Captains of our regiment fought a duel at Camargo about 3 weeks ago, Capt. Wilkin of New York[67] and Capt. Collett[68] of Burlington, New Jersey in which Collett was killed. He was taken into the church at Burlington as a member previous to his departure for Mexico. He was the most wicked man to swear during the short stay he made here I ever saw and very ugly to his men. In short put the officers in the tenth regiment all in a bag and shake them up, I do not know which would come out first but I think they would all come out together.

I wish a man of good standing would inform them men at Washington of the brutality of these officers now in Mexico, but there is no use of a soldier writing to them as no notice would be taken of it, but these are facts if they do come from a soldier. They have never had any hold of me yet and I have no reason to lie about it but I have a heart and feeling for my brother Americans who came out here under arms in defence of their country and in a foreign country not congenial to our health. But the time may come and that soon when officers and men will stand on equal footing. The men seem to form an opinion that some of the officers will soon depart from this world. . . . A soldiers life is very disgusting.[69]

Paine's Mutiny

The root of most grievances was imbedded in the nature of the army itself. The American soldier was an individualist, whether from a farm, a farm-market town, or a larger city; one man might be richer than another but he was not any better. He was accustomed to order his life in his own way. As a soldier he readily recognized the need for obeying orders in battle or on the march but he resented camp discipline and any implication of being inferior to his officers in any sense except that of military rank. In northern Mexico, after Taylor's departure for the United States, General Wool took over the army on the Saltillo line. Except for guerrilla raids, the fighting in that sector was over, and the men settled down to sit out the war in a hostile land, with very little to do. It was in such situations as this that morale was lowest and the incidence of insubordination and crime the greatest. Rigid discipline, imposed in part to counter the ennui, produced a mutiny on the night of August 15, 1847. The mutineers were from Virginia, Mississippi and North Carolina regiments of volunteers. The object of their rebellion was Col. Robert Treat Paine.[70]

"Paine's mutiny" had greater significance than its purely military aspect would seem to warrant. It illuminated the whole problem of the military establishment and its administration. How to enforce discipline on volunteers commanded by regimental officers many of whom had been elected by the men themselves and whose military training was not sufficient to merit respect from the soldiers they commanded? What to do with idle troops in an enemy's land? The outcome of the affair also was interesting. General Wool sustained Colonel Paine and discharged dishonorably two lieutenants who refused to obey their colonel's orders during the hectic night of August 15. A military court of inquiry vindicated Paine and confirmed Wool's action. But the discharged lieutenants carried their case to President Polk in Washington.

The President and Secretary Marcy, influenced perhaps by the unpopularity of Paine and public opinion in North Carolina, and judging that, since the fighting was over in northern Mexico, ballots were more important than bullets, restored the lieutenants' commissions. Thus the military court of inquiry upheld military caste and discipline while the President sided with the "boys" and the voters back home. Paine was adjudged to be justified in killing a mutineer and his subordinates were pardoned for refusing to aid him in quelling the mutiny. It was the sort of thing that gave ammunition to the many critics, both in and out of the army, of "Mr. Polk's war."

Col. Robert Treat Paine's account of the mutiny, written in a letter to his wife, was a graphic statement:

15th [August]. The mail has come without tidings from my Dear, Dear Wife. A long, very long week has closed, & it was the more slow in its completion because knowing that you would start in a day or two after your letter of the 14th of July I did not much think that you would in the hurry — — — — — — [sic]

My life! Oh God what a change has come over the spirit of my dream since I wrote the last unfinished sentence! It is now the 23rd Aug. & since the night of the 15th I have been bewildered in mind at occurences that have taken place. My own regiment! yes the troops to take charge of whom I set at naught even the feelings of my dear wife have banded with the soldiers of other regiments to assassinate me. . . . I had submitted to endless insults from crowds of the Va. and Miss. Volunteers & purposely avoided taking notice of them save on one or two occasions when my duty required it to be noticed. So long as their animosity towards me was confined to empty threats & insulting noises I bore it with what patience I could, at all events. I made no effort of myself to punish the offenders, my only course towards them was to report their conduct to Gen. Wool & to their immediate commanding officers.

On the night of the 14th inst. emboldened I suppose by my apparent disregard of their insults, a mob of more than an hundred Virginia Volunteers entered my camp & there during my temporary absence & in the presence of some of the officers & most of the men of my regiment committed a riot within a few feet of my tent uninterrupted. Col. Fagg[71] & Major Stokes[72] were at the time both sick. Emboldened by this success, & combining with persons from the Miss. Regt. they commenced at dusk on the evening of the 15th to parade my streets in bands of from five to twenty or more & it soon became apparent that they intended some evil. One of these bands numbering some 20 or more as I sat at supper passed within a few feet of my tent door, muttering insults as they passed & I sprang up & rushing out siezed [sic] two of them, whom I reported to their Col., Hamtramck.[73] They were Virginia Volunteers & he ordered them to be confined with the Provost Guard. The soldiers of his regiment then were ordered not to come into my camp & for half an hour every thing was quiet. It was during this interval of quiet that I sat down to finish writing to you & was startled by the information that there were men prowling around my tent with concealed arms.

I immediately sprang up & gave orders for a quarter guard of eight men to be detailed & sentinels to be posted near my tent, to stop & examine all strangers & suspicious persons. In attempting to detail the guard, the men of K company positively refused to obey the order & on going into the quarters of that company I found the men in a state of open mutiny against me & that they were aided & countenanced by the men of A company. I immediately though not without difficulty had the ringleaders arrested & sent to the Provost Guard. Persons now under the cover of darkness, it was about 8 o'clock, began to stone me, with rocks of size sufficient to have killed me had I been struck. My field officers were both sick a bed, the Lieut. Col. very ill & Capt. Shive[74] whom I shall ever remember for his loyalty and devotion to his duties was dying. Surrounded by these dangers & difficulties, would you, can you, believe that every officer, even my adjutant Lieut. Singleton[75] & Lieut. White [76] remained quietly in their tents neither offering nor affording me the least assistance. They knew what was going on & either through fear for themselves or indifference to my fate kept out of the way. I was not however without friends. Lieuts. [sic] Singleton & White & all of my nom-com staff except the Qr. Master Sergeant C. C. Battle gave me such support as they could.

It was now after tattoo when every soldier is required by the regulations to be at his company quarters yet bands of other soldiers were parading my streets & holding consultations with my troops. I made several ineffectual attempts to arrest some of these persons, but they escaped uttering threats & curses against me as they fled. The numbers of rocks thrown at me increased & followed me wherever I turned. I saw now that the time for prompt and decided action had arrived & that summary steps must be taken to put a stop to this thing & to preserve my life; for I was not permitted to remain in my tent unmolested. The number & strength of the mutineers increased every moment. I sent down to the extreme left of my regiment for assistance, having lost all confidence on [sic, in] the loyalty of the men in the right wing & they too refused to come.

I saw that I was abandoned to my fate by both officers and men & I determined to meet it as became a man. I went to my tent (now after nine o'clock) and arming myself with a brace of pistols I went out determined to act promptly. I went into the right wing of my encampment & warned the men that I was determined to put a stop to the mutiny & ordered them all to their tents telling them of the danger they ran in being out & of the violation of orders they committed in remaining in their streets & upon a volley of stones being thrown at me I ran to the front of the encampment to discover the perpetrators of the outrage. Again I was warned that persons were armed & had come into my camp to take my life & that my guard was not to be depended on & I replied, then let them take it. During all the time for nearly two hours my Drum Major Saml. Roquas, a native of Missouri & enlisted by me at Camargo, had followed me like a shadow & now for the first time spoke. When I replied let them take my life, he said "Col. I fear they will do it; but they shall have mine also." I told him to go to his tent, that one man could render me little assistance & he was exposing his life unnecessarily. "No," said he, "Sir & I know my duty is to assist you & I beg to share your danger." I then passed along the front of my encampment & through the left wing where every thing appeared quiet & I stopped at the tent of Capt. Shive. I found him insensible & breathing his last.

As I started towards my tent only a few steps distant I was met by one of the music[ians] (Stubbs by name) a drummer boy, he appeared in great alarm telling me that a large crowd of men were coming, towards my tent from the Virginia camp. I called to Lieut. Singletary[77] to bring to my assistance 20 men of his Company, telling him of my danger & urging him to bring up the men with all speed. He showed a reluctance to execute the order that astounded & disgusted me & I started to meet the crowd alone, no not alone for Roquas was still faithful. I had proceeded not more than forty steps, when I saw the crowd in the Officers street of D Company—they were engaged in low & earnest conversation & were to the number of thirty or more. I walked up & saw they wore the uniform of the Va. & Miss. troops. At the distance of eight paces I challanged the crowd—no answer was returned. I challenged a second & third time & received no answer. There was an evident show of resistance & I drew my pistol & advanced quickly upon the crowd, repeating in quick succession the words halt or I will fire. The crowd gave way & scattered in different directions, uttering threats as they ran. I continued to advance on that part of the crowd which retreated down the street towards the front of the encampment & ordering them repeatedly to halt or I would fire. I discharged my pistol at the distance of some ten or fifteen paces into the crowd. One man fell, he was a man of my own regiment belonging to one of the companies in which the mutiny first showed itself, another man exclaimed, Oh! God damn him, he has shot my hand. The first lived until morning. The ball passed through his body & entered the hand of the latter a Va. Volunteer, producing a flesh wound. He was no doubt from his bad character one of the ring leaders in the mutiny & his officers expressed great regret that the ball had not passed through him. I did not intend to kill & purposely lowered my pistol to take effect below the body; but I suppose I was decived in its direction by the darkness. I regret the death of Bradley, since he was but a youth & probably persuaded into his crime by others; but from what I have since learned & what further occured that night I feel satisfied that the death of this man, saved my own life & that of many others in the Regiment.

At the report of the pistol the non-com officer in charge of the guard ordered them to my assistance & a portion of them deserted the guard. The regiment was called out under arms & obeyed very reluctantly & the officer in command of the Company on the extreme right adjacent to the Va. camp suffered the soldiers of that regiment to flock into my camp without resistance. I posted myself in the officers street determined to brunt the storm alone, my adjutant was getting the companies under arms & Lieut. White had gone at the call to turn out his company. Lieut. Singletary had not come nigh me & did not afterwards attempt to offer any excuse for not obeying my order to bring a force to my assistance. Mr. Buck[78] was in camp at the time & seeing the state of things there ran over to Gen. Cushing & in two or three minutes the Gen. & his staff were with me. Several officers of the Va. Regt. also ran up & offered their assistance & the Gen. ordered a line of sentries to be thrown between the three encampments. Capt. Robinson[79] of the Va. Regt. begged me to retire to my tent assuring me that I was in great danger of being killed; but I refused to go & just then Gen. Wool came over with his staff & guard & insisted on my going to his quarters. I went over & remained about an hour & returned to my tent guarded by regular soldiers. The thought was indeed most humiliating that I should have to look for aid in such an hour, beyond the limits of my own regiment. The Gen. insisted on my retaining his guard through the night but I declined. I was willing still to trust another guard of my own troops, or preferred to be without one. Major Stokes came out at the discharge of the pistol & was very active in forcing the men to a discharge of their duty. I retired to bed about one o'clock & no further disturbance occurred.

Not one of my officers however except the major, the adjt. & Lieut. White came near me & early the next morning I received a note written by Lieut. Pender & signed by every Company officer in camp save the two above mentioned, calling upon me to *surrender*, yes *surrender* my Commission. I sent this paper over to the Gen. & he immediately issued an order denouncing the mutiny & dishonorably discharging from the service Lieuts. Pender[80] and Singeltary [sic, Singletary] & private Hunter of my Regt. and the wounded man of the Va. regiment. He wrote a note requesting to see me & when I went he told me that every officer who signed the paper requiring me to surrender my commission was guilty of mutiny & would be dishonorably discharged unless they withdrew their names from the paper. I begged him to give them time for reflection & he promised 48 hours & in the mean time required of them an explicit obedience to my orders & a faithful discharge of their duties. The day, the 16th, passed off quietly. The men I thought seemed to feel ashamed of their conduct towards me the night previous & raised their hats whenever they passed me. The daily exercises were gone through with us as usual & the order above referred to was read at parade. On the morning of the 17th all the officers of the regiment who had signed the note the day previous except four sent in their resignations. Three of the staff who had signed had requested to have their names stricken off & had written to me a note of apology. Two of the signers Capt. Kirkpatrick[81] and Lieut. Dunham[82] came early on the 17th & assured me that in signing the request for me to yield my commission they were actuated solely by kind feelings towards me & by a regard for my personal safety & that had I left the regiment they intended to have left with me. . . . & they all on the 17th withdrew their resignations & desired to have their names stricken from the first note.[83]

Lt. Josiah S. Pender, one of those discharged after the mutiny, gave the other side of the story in a letter to Brig. Gen. Caleb Cushing:

As you had the kindness to promise me, to exert your influence, to have the matter wherein I am grossly and unjustly charged with divers acts of fearfull import calculated to brand an innocent man with dishonour, brought to a fair, just and impartial investigation; being driven forth, in the night and dreary rainy night, laboring under indisposition in an enemies country my life exposed, without being previously named or notified. I had not the opportunity during the short and excited conversation I had with you; having just been branded with dishonour without a hearing, without an investigation contrary to all rules of Government even the most despotic for even among despots they make a semblance to do justice, even the midnight assassin is allowed a trial a hearing of his case and is an officer of the army of our Grand Republic to be denied that which is accorded to the most ignominous. My mind labouring under those reflections I did not probably, for I scarcely know what I said, explain my position to you in as lucid a manner as I otherwise should have done; therefore I concluded to make this statement with such references of testimony as will with any unbiassed [sic] mind be sufficient to show that my conduct instead of being reprehensible has been praiseworthy as being active and energetic in the performance of my duty.

In the first place at the time I had the conversation with you at your quarters not having the time to peruse the orders for my discharge having been notified to leave forthwith I understood you to say that my discharge was based on the fact that the paper or petition which was sent to [the] Colonel and on which my name appeared was of a mutinous & seditious character. I do not pretend to debate this point but can only say that it was not so intended by the Officers—but was done from the purest motives from a sincere desire for the welfare of our Regiment—its reputation and the reputation of our State.

Our Colonel having perpetrated acts highly derogatory to the post he holds some of [them being of] so ludicrous a nature as to become a jest & laughing stock among the Officers of our Brigade—whereupon the Company Officers unanimously adopted & signed the following caption to a petition requesting the Colonel to resign. It was also signed by three of the Staff Officers who were not otherwise interested than from a sincere desire for the honor of the Regiment.

. . . .

The causes that produced these feelings that required in our estimation that the Colonel should withdraw from the Regiment are as follows.

That he the Colonel did not treat the Officers of the Regiment with the respect they were entitled to. That they were frequently subjected to arrest and close arrest for the most trivial circumstances, that he had endeavoured to weaken the authority of the commanders of companies. That he did on one occasion at Taylor's camp attack a private with his fists, because the said private did not take his cap entirely off having touched his cap to the Colonel, declaring that he should take his jacket off if he demanded it. That he did on batallion drill at Buena Vista attack a private with the following abusive language—"You God damn rascal what are you doing with your hands in your pocket" following these words with a blow of his sabre "I will cut your God damned head off" retiring a few moments he returned remarking that he appeared to be mad that the next time he would give him something to get mad about, that he would stick his sword in him. That he did at Camp at Buena Vista order the Drum Major to strike down a soldier with a heavy stick of wood and having the same enforced without any just provocation.

Instances of oppression and abuse are numerous but being aware of the caution necessary in preferring charges against a superior in rank, I shall not state anything that I cannot satisfactorily prove which if I fail in I am willing to hear all the ignominy and reproach that mortals can devise.

. . . . .

I can safely say that every means was resorted to in the power of the officers of our Regt. to get quietly on with our Colonel at length his conduct became so galling to some few that our resignations were tendered & returned with unbecoming remarks endorsed on them. We then preferred charges with the same success being treated with silent contempt or [unwanted?] neglect. Whereupon the Officers unanimously agreed to send in the petition before referred to, believing that a general expression from the Officers disapproving his conduct would either cause him to resign, or change his course of conduct, both towards his officers & men.

In the same paragraph our men are charged with mutiny and I am happy to say that in my opinion & in fact in the opinion of all the officers there was no disposition to mutiny among the men. It was looked upon by all as a kind [of] spree or frolic on the part of Virginians & Mississippians what [sic] was in progress before the Colonel fired his pistol. . . .

The same order also speaks of the assassination of our Colonel, the first I ever heard of it was in that order. I know that there is not a man in our Regiment that would secretly do him personal injury. I have a better opinion of the men from the "Old North State." That he is disliked by both men & officers is universally known, and I would say to those who have accused our Regiment with mutiny either directly or indirectly that such was not their intention, that they respect the Col. of the N.C. Regiment though they do not the man.

Citizens of the "Good Old North State" to leave their families & the comforts of life expose themselves to this pernicious climate and for what, that they might be a disgrace to her—'tis false! we came to do honor to her & we will sacrifice our lives on that Altar.[84]

DESERTION

Desertion was an even more serious problem than mutiny. The causes were numerous. Some of these were the sort that are common to all wars: violent distaste for military life, disenchantment with the "romance and glory" of battle, bitter resentment over real or fancied wrongs, and flight to escape just punishment for crimes. Less conventional were the "turncoats" who deserted to the enemy. Some of these undoubtedly deserted to the enemy because, having fled in a hostile country, they had no other place to go. But ideology and greed also played a part.

There were a great many recent European immigrants in the United States army. Most of these were Irish and Germans, many of them Roman Catholics. Their devotion to their faith was deeply rooted in their heritage. And they had come to America to earn a better living. The Mexican government, knowing this, directed propaganda at both conscience and pocketbook.

Within a month after Taylor reached the Rio Grande, General Mariano Arista, commander of the Mexican army, issued at Matamoros (on April 20, 1846) a proclamation containing "advice to the soldiers of the United States army." This was in effect an invitation to the rank and file of Taylor's army to desert. Arista's "advice" possibly had some effect. At least Taylor's problem of desertion became so bothersome that he discussed it in a despatch to the Adjutant General of the United States army at the end of May 1846:

In reply to your communication of the 8th instant, calling for information relative to deserters who were shot near Matamoras, I have to state that soon after my arrival on the Rio Grande the evil of desertion made its appearance, and increased to an alarming extent; that inducements were held out by the Mexican authorities to entice our men from their colors, and that the most efficient measures were necessary to prevent the spread of this contagion. As our deserters by merely swimming the river were at once in the enemy's lines, pursuit and apprehension with a view to trial were out of the question. I therefore deemed it my duty, and warranted by the hostile attitude of the Mexicans, whose commanders assumed that a state of war existed, to give orders that all men seen swimming across the river should be hailed by our pickets and ordered to return; and in case that they did not return, that they would be shot. These orders were verbally given to the several commanders on or about the 1st of April. I annex a description of two soldiers who are supposed to have been shot under this order,[85] remarking that it was impossible in the first instance to identify the individual with absolute certainty while in the act of crossing the river; and, in the second, to ascertain whether he were actually killed, the occurrence taking place at night. I beg leave to add, that these measures seem to have checked and nearly stopped the practice.[86]

Later, at Monterey, enough regulars deserted from Taylor to form an artillery battalion in the Mexican army, known as the San Patricio Battalion or The Irish Legion. It carried a standard on one side of which was the Mexican coat of arms and the motto: "Long Live the Republic of Mexico"; on the other side was the figure of St. Patrick. In March 1847, the Adjutant General in Washington advertised rewards for 1,011 deserters. Later that year Santa Anna, in a broadside, again offered farms and a good life in Mexico to deserters. This broadside declared:

The President of the Mexican Republic to the troops engaged
in the Army of the United States of America.

The circumstances of war have brought you to the beautiful valley of Mexico, in the midst of a wealthy and fertile country. The American Government engaged you to fight against a country from which you have received no harm; your companions have after the battle received and shall only receive the contempt of the United States and the scorn of the nations of civilized Europe that, quite surprized, see that that government seek engagements for their battles in the same manner as they look for beasts to draw their carriages.

In the name of the Nation I represent, and whose authority I exercise, I offer you a reward, if deserting the American standard you present yourselves like friends to a nation that offer you rich fields and large tracts of land, which being cultivated by your industry, shall crown you with happiness and convenience.

The Mexican Nation only look upon you as some deceived foreigners and hereby stretch out to you a friendly hand, offer you the felicity and fertility of their territory. Here there is no distinction of races, here indeed there is liberty and not slavery; nature here plentifully sheds its favors and it is in your power to enjoy them. Rely upon what I offer you in the name of a nation; present yourselves like friends and you shall have country, home, lands; the happiness, which is enjoyed in a country of mild and humane customs; civilization, humanity and not fear address you through me.

General Quarters in the Peñon, August the 15th 1847
Antonio Lopez de Santa-Anna[87]

End of the San Patricio Battalion

At Buena Vista and again at Churubusco, the San Patricio Battalion fought with the courage of desperation, even to the point of killing Mexican comrades who attempted to display a white flag at Churubusco. About eighty were captured, and Capt. George T. M. Davis, an aide-de-camp to Scott, told of their trial and punishment:

After their surrender to General Twiggs a military commission was organized under a general order issued by General Scott for their trial as "deserters from the United States Army" in time of war, the penalty for which, under

Battle of Churubusco

the "Articles of War," was death. The whole forty-two were tried, convicted and sentenced to be hung, subject, of course, to the approval of the general-in-chief; and the record of their conviction was transmitted to him for his approval, modification or rejection. The general held this under advisement several days, giving to the case of each of the condemned a rigid and impartial consideration. When his order was promulgated, carrying into effect the findings of the military commission, he had in part modified the findings as follows: 27 were ordered to be hung on the 10th of September, 1847; 14 were to be stripped to the waist of their pantaloons, and to receive fifty lashes each on their naked backs, and to be branded with the letter D high up on the cheek-bone, near the eye, but without jeopardizing its sight; 1 was unconditionally pardoned: 42 total.

Intense dissatisfaction, and an earnest remonstrance among the officers of the army in general, followed at the commutation of the sentences of the fourteen from death to whipping and branding, more particularly in the case of Riley,[88] who was in command of the Mexican Battalion of St. Patrick, composed entirely of deserters from the United States Army, over one hundred strong; and who, from his rank at the time of his desertion, his general intelligence and influence, was believed by our officers to have been the principal cause of the desertion of the others. It was urged upon General Scott that it would be far preferable that every one of the rest of the forty-two condemned deserters should be pardoned rather than that Riley should escape death, more especially as we were in possession of the knowledge of the high estimate placed upon him as an officer by the enemy. The importance attached to saving his life was attested by the unwearied efforts that had been made by the whole Catholic priesthood within our lines to procure his liberation by exchange or ransom. It was held that if his life was spared from any cause it would, in their judgment, be attributed by the enemy to fear on our part, and its tendency would be to produce a more stubborn resistance, and increase our difficulties in taking the City of Mexico.

General Scott listened with dignified patience and courtesy to the arguments with which he was stormed to drive him from his position and induce him to abandon the modification he had made in the finding of the military tribunal that had condemned Riley to death. . . . With great terseness and eloquence of expression General Scott in a very few words disposed of all that had been urged against commuting Riley's death sentence, and put to confusion those who, in the best faith and with the most patriotic motives, had asked him to swerve from what he regarded to be the clearly defined spirit and letter of the Articles of War, and concluded by declaring that, sooner than the life of Riley should be taken, under the finding in his case of the military commission which had tried and condemned him to death, he (General Scott) would rather with his whole army be put to the sword in the assault he was about to make upon the gates of the City of Mexico! . . .

The facts upon which the action of General Scott was taken were simply these: Riley and his co-deserters, whose sentences he had commuted from death to whipping and branding, deserted during or immediately after the battle of Palo Alto, and before the United States had declared war against Mexico. Under the provisions of the "Articles of War," deserters in times of peace can receive no greater punishment than whipping and branding, as the penalty of such desertion[89]; whereas, in time of war the punishment of desertion is death upon conviction of the offender. And as Riley did not desert in time of war (the United States not then having declared war against Mexico), to hang him in pursuance of the finding of the military court which tried and convicted him would have been nothing less than military judicial murder.

The twenty-six other deserters who were hung deserted after we declared war, and richly merited the fate the Articles of War inflicted upon them. On September 10th those of the condemned whose sentence was death were hung. The fourteen that were to be whipped and branded, were tied up to trees in front of the Catholic church on the plaza, their backs naked to the waistband of the pantaloons, and an experienced Mexican muleteer inflicted the fifty lashes with all the severity he could upon each culprit. Why those thus punished did not die under such punishment was a marvel to me. Their backs had the appearance of a pounded piece of raw beef, the blood oozing from every stripe as given. Each in his turn was then branded, and after digging the graves of those subsequently hung, the fourteen were drummed out of camp to the tune of the "Rogues' March." I should have prefaced this revolting scene with the statement that all the generals, with their respective staffs, were required to be present, but for which order nothing on earth could have influenced my witnessing what I did.

The sixteen who were executed at our camp were launched into eternity at one and the same moment, each being dressed in the uniform of the enemy in which he had been captured, the white caps being drawn over their heads. The scaffold was about forty feet in length, consisting of heavy string-pieces of timber supported by large square uprights, one at each end and a third in the middle, mortised into the stringer; it was fourteen feet high and erected upon an open plain or field. Two prisoners were placed at the extreme end of a transportation wagon, to which was attached a pair of our fleetest, best-broken mules, which were handled by the most expert drivers in the service.

The teams were alternately headed to the east and west, with the ends of the wagons to which they were attached arranged in line, with mathematical precision, directly under the nooses suspended from the stringer. The drivers were mounted upon the saddle-mule of each team, ready to make an instantaneous start at the tap of a drum as the signal. In the front of the prisoners were arranged five Catholic priests in their canonicals, with a crucifix in one hand, engaged in appropriate devotional services, from the time the prisoners were stationed at the tail end of the wagons until they were swung off. Seven out of the sixteen hung being communicants of the Roman Catholic Church, their bodies after death were delivered into the custody of the priests to be buried in consecrated ground; the other nine were buried immediately under the scaffold where they were hung. They all, but one, died without a struggle; the exception, who was named Dalton, was literally choked to death.

The remaining sixteen, of whom eleven were hung and five whipped and branded, were executed at Miscoac, under the direction of Colonel Harney, who was in command of that place; but as I did not witness the execution I can enter into no details as to what transpired. The prisoner who was pardoned owed his deliverance from death to a singular and touching incident. He was an old man of three score years, and had been a loyal and faithful soldier for many years in the United States army until he was tempted and fell under the evil influence and example of Riley. In the same company with himself was his eldest son, who had attained the meridian of the allotted period of man's life, and was still in the service of his country. The son had refused to desert, or to become a traitor to his flag. This circumstance was brought to the notice of General Scott mainly through my instrumentality, but without any expectation or design that it would in any way influence the action that followed. The deserter condemned to death was unconditionally pardoned, and the only reason assigned by General Scott for this act of unexpected clemency was given in these few words: "In the hour of the greatest temptation the son was loyal and true to his colors."[90]

In spite of the mass execution of the San Patricio Battalion, desertions continued after Churubusco. The total number of deserters during the war, according to Heitman's statistics, was 9,207 (5,331 regulars and 3,876 volunteers) out of 39,197 casualties from all causes.[91] Boredom, dislike of the army; for some, disapproval of the particular war, hunger for home—these were more or less common and accepted by the great majority of the soldiers with no more grumbling than was to be expected; brutality, crime, mutiny and desertion were the exceptions but they were part of the record written by the war.

WAR AMONG THE GENERALS

There was, however, yet another episode which threatened to rob Scott's army of its prestige and to dissipate its success. That was a controversy between Scott and a cabal of his officers—especially Worth and Pillow—abetted by Secretary Marcy. Animosities which had been held down by the need to cooperate in the field, flared up after the army entered Mexico City. Pillow was the chief instigator. His reports of the Battle of Contreras and Chapultepec in effect made him the hero and reduced Scott to something of a supernumerary. In a letter to his wife after Contreras, Pillow did not minimize his achievements. He wrote: "My friends at Nashville . . . will doubtless soon have full accounts of the battle through letters and official reports. Now I can only say, my part was far more brilliant & conspicuous than I myself in my most sanguine moments ever hoped for."[92] When Pillow's official reports (dated August 24 and September 18) came to Scott's attention, the commanding general politely requested his field commander to make certain changes. Pillow, President Polk's former law partner, was well aware that earlier in the campaign Scott had quarreled with Secretary Marcy and had accused the Polk administration of withholding proper support from his expedition. He now not only refused to "correct" his reports, but, in addition, instigated and probably himself wrote under the nom de plume "Leonidas," letters which appeared in the New Orleans Delta. Pillow also discovered that Major General Worth and Colonel Duncan were ready to join him in his fight. A second letter, for which Duncan claimed authorship, although he *did not in fact write the passage in it that Scott objected to, implied that Worth, not Scott, had chosen the route around Lake Chalco for the approach to Mexico City. Scott then issued his General Orders No. 349 interdicting such newspaper stories by his officers. Recriminations followed. Scott arrested Worth, Duncan and Pillow. Worth and Pillow appealed to Washington. The bitterness of the squabble was evident in a letter written by Pillow after his arrest:*

On the day before yesterday I was arrested by Genl. Scott. My offence consisted in an official letter of mine to the Government in which he professes to think my language was not *respectful* towards him. My letter I know made the *blood fly.* It was however true as I am prepared to show. He has violated the Law & outraged every principle of justice in regard to myself, & I feel very confident of *flooring him.* He cannot sustain *himself*—nor will the Govt. I am sure, sustain him. He is offended with me for opposing his views in connection with the *fatal armistice* & that hostility is the real motive under which he has acted, though he seizes hold of this letter of mine as a *pretext.* He has by this conduct and by his out-rageous orders, produced a burst of indignation throughout the army. Genl. Worth has preferred charges against him upon which he must be *tried* by this Government. I expect & have applied to the Govt. to be ordered to the United States immediately for Trial myself. I feel very confident the Govt. will order me home for Trial, & I feel almost as sure that Scott will be also. He is the most malignant man I ever saw. He has taken offence for nothing and is now so much blinded by passion, that he has betrayed himself into acts so much in violation of law and military usage, that he is clearly in the wrong and I can show it to the world. I will blow him higher & kill him deader than did the *"hasty plate of soup"* letter or *"the fire in front & fire in rear."*

You need not have the least *uneasiness.* The whole affair will produce much excitement & newspaper discussion at home; but it will prove ultimately great to *my advantage.* My enemies seem determined to make me a *great man* whether *I will* or not. If I have any knowledge of the American people & of the signs of *the times*—the affect of the proceeding[s] will be [to] place me more *prominently* and more favourably before the nation, and will result even more to my advantage than do my successes in the valley, but when coming as it does immediately upon the news of my brilliant successes, it will startle the public and as soon as the facts come to light, will show a degree of *malignaty* in Scott, as *black* and *attrocious* as *ever disgraced* a fiend.

. . . . .

Genl. Scott has issued a most scandalous order—in violation of every principle of law—of his powers & of military usage. That order was aimed at myself and Genl. Worth, & was intended to gratify Scott's *private hate.* About this order of Scott's, Genl. Worth has preferred *charges* against Genl. Scott, for which Scott has this moment arrested him. This is enough. It was all that was wanting to *destroy him* & to give me the means of *undoubted triumph.* Worth is a Whig of high character for gallantry & great popularity in the United States, and has always been a protege of Scott & has done more to give Scott character than any man in the army. In the Whig party, at home, Worth has 3 friends to Scott's one. This arrest of Worth makes the *issue between Two Whigs* and will therefore prevent the matter assuming a party character at home & will relieve the Govt. from all embarrassment as between myself & Scott. The Taylor Whigs, who constitute at least two thirds of the party—will aid in crushing Scott. Worth's friends will *join in.* Col. Duncan, a most popular & Gallant officer who is arrested for the same cause, will *join*—the *Democracy* and the Govt. will now *let loose* upon him, and all these *elements* at work, with his out-rageously *violent* & *illegal* acts & orders & *blunders*—we will kill him so dead that he will never know what *hurts him.* I only wanted this last step to be taken. He before stood upon the very brink of the *prescipice* [*sic*]. He had to take but one more step to plunge into the bottomless abyss of deep public condemnation. That step *he has taken.* This has given me joy *inexpressable.*

Scott has become so enraged that he is *stark blind.* I now feel fully able to tell you of the course which the Govt. will take. It will certainly order Scott, myself, Worth and Duncan all home *for trial* and will therefore by removing Scott from the command of this army render him powerless for evil, & will place Butler in command of the army.[93]

Just as angry, and wholly contemptuous of Pillow, was a letter written by Lt. William Montgomery Gardner of the 2d Infantry:

There has come to light a number of letters written by officers of the army for *publication* which have created indignation not only among most of the junior officers of the *old Army* but has even extended to the General Head Quarters. I refer to the letters of Leonidas, Veritas, &c.—I will inform you of a fact which will serve in some measure to explain the appearance in print of some truly romantic, affecting and unique productions.

Some *distinguished* officers of our army, and I am glad to say the practice is confined to a very few, have and have had during the whole of this war in their employment a parcel of letter writers, who for a consideration blow the trumpets of their patrons in the principal papers of the United States, thereby creating impressions on the people at home totally at variance with truth and history, for example *Leonidas* says that Genl. Pillow was the hero of Contreras, when said Pillow was not within hearing of said battle, said battle having been fought against his expressed disapprobation. . . .

I know that my letters to you will not appear in a public journal, consequently I will give you my private opinion of some of the distinguished offices of our *mustang army*. I opine that Gideon Pillow is about as consum-[m]ate an ass, as any army, modern or ancient, has ever been inflicted with. The illustrious Cadwallader [*sic*][94] is a likeness of friend Gideon as perfect as nature, rather more perfect than nature perhaps, that is he is most essentially a perfect natural fool. He is one of those fools who is a fool for want of sense, the most confounded of fools—to express myself elegantly and in an intelligent manner. He is just like Pillow but a little more so. Genls. Quitman and Shields are gallant and talented men, and perfect gentlemen. Genl. Worth is a good officer but has such an inordinate desire for the applause of the *mob*, that he will stoop to things that no officer or gentlemen should be guilty. As for the rest of them I don't know them, Genl. Smith is perhaps next to General Scott in military talent. There exists at present a lively indignation among all *honorable officers* on account of the base falsehoods which have appeared in print in the U.S. concerning the brilliant operations of our armies in this valley. The most stupid and worthless have been most lauded.[95]

A court of inquiry was organized. The Polk administration then removed Scott from his command and replaced him with Maj. Gen. William Orlando Butler. Eventually all of the charges were withdrawn, except those against Pillow. But Scott by then had become a martyr in the eyes of his men—even those who had been unwilling to acknowledge his greatness before then. His departure was compared with that of Bonaparte's leave-taking from his old guard at Fontainebleau. One of his Lieutenants wrote: "Grey haired officers and rugged soldiers wept when they parted from their General, and a host of officers followed him to the Peñon, to obtain one word from, or exchange one look with their hero and their idol."[96] Lt. George B. McClellan belatedly discovered he had underrated his commander, and in a letter to his mother, had nothing but praise for "noble old Gen. Scott":

The Court of Inquiry is now in session. The accusations of that ungrateful Worth against Gen. Scott are withdrawn, also those of Scott against Col. Duncan—but the Pillow case is now under investigation. Our noble old Gen. Scott is coming out of it most magnificently, Pillow is getting mired worse & worse every day—he has already been proved to be a liar, a scoundrel & a mean, pitiful rogue. You cannot imagine the feeling in the old regular army in reference to Gen. Scott. No general ever possessed the hearts of his troops to a greater extent than does Gen. Scott today. Before his conduct in reference to this persecution of the administration I never thought him to be a great man—but now I do believe that he is really a very great man.[97]

Eventually the Court of Inquiry, loaded with pro-Polk officers, transferred its hearing to the United States, and found Pillow not guilty of writing the "Leonidas" letters, though it did not support his interpretation of the Battle of Contreras. By then there was genuine concern that the feud among the generals might have serious repercussions upon the peace settlement. On February 2, 1848, Nicholas Trist had signed the Treaty of Guadalupe Hidalgo; on March 10, by a vote of 38 to 14 the United States Senate confirmed it, but an exchange of ratifications with Mexico did not come until May 30. A brother of Col. John W. Geary[98] of Pennsylvania wrote to him of the Pillow case and of momentous European events which might be related to peace making:

You men in Mexico, I tell you, cannot be too well fortified at every avenue by which envenomed envy & slander can assail you. There are a host of calves at home, with a vicious propensity to eat your laurels. Give them a chance & they will war upon you like Bulls of Bashan. Do not understand me as charging your countrymen with ingratitude. The mass are grateful & proud of your heroism. This is true irrespective of party. But many who would battle for the loaves & fishes, will not be guilty of raising mortals to the skies though ready to drag angels down.

Quite a general & exciting interest is felt in the proceedings of the "Court of Inquiry." I have read the charges against General Pillow & the testimony of Freaner[99] & Trist. If Pillow cannot invalidate their testimony, I would not be Pillow for North America. Should the charges be true a more contemptible scoundril lives not. . . . I solemnly aver that if one half the specifications against Pillow be true, I would prefer association with horse thieves to that with him & those who take his part.

Think me not a rash unjust prejudger of the case. I say not Pillow is guilty nor do I wish him so. If on the other hand Gen. Scott fails & Pillow triumphs, the lustre of all his greatness will be deeply tarnished. These unhappy contentions among the superior officers of the Army are deeply mortifying, must greatly lessen our army in the esteem of foreign nations, & will, I fear, result in disaster to our affairs in Mexico. Our latest intel[l]igence leaves the ratification of the treaty doubtful. . . . The revolutions in Europe will damp the ardor of the monarchic party [in Mexico], if not wholly subvert the designs of Paredes. The effect of this may be to expedite peace. . . . Republicanism has become endemic in Europe. France took the disease the natural way & nearly all the nations have caught it from her. Doubtless there was a predisposition that way. Even the old Northern Bear has had a chill & a shake & Metternich has been compelled to retire to the salubrious shades of privacy. Even *unser gutter konich von* Prussia has found his subjects ungrateful, and ready to make him as one of them. In short thrones have become precarious, crowns thorny, kingship unpopular. It is almost certain that this year will terminate, except in Russia, absolutism in Europe. The power of the people is rocking the political institutions of the old world with more than earthquake violence & if there be but wisdom to build up equal to the power to throw down a blessed day dawns on the world.[100]

While the Mexican Congress fenced, the army of occupation fumed, anxious to go home, or to get on with it and complete the conquest. Lt. William D. Wilkins voiced these belligerent opinions about what he regarded as a job still to be done:

We had some hopes that the ratification of the Treaty by our Senate would infuse a little spirit into the sluggish souls of the Mexican Congress, but those hopes have vanished. They seem to be no nearer a quorum than they were two months ago. I am now anxiously looking for the Re-commencement of hostilities, for I despair of peace, long for activity, and hate the inaction of garrison life. The Army generally, are disgusted with the course which [the] Govt. has taken towards Mexico. The squeamish tenderness with which we have treated her, the frequent armistices we have granted, destroying thereby, the fruits of our hard earned victories, the "modus operandi" of the war, which makes Mexico richer and more prosperous than she would be under her own Government, are all so many incentives to them, to prolong the contest.

We do not want Mexico. Its annexation to our country would be productive of far more evil than good, but if we want to close the war, we must commence a new system. We must teach them that if we are just, magnanimous and liberal, we know, also, how to be terrible. Impose crushing contributions, burn every town that offers resistence, blow up their churches and take no prisoners, and they will soon humbly sue for terms. War should be the last resort of nations, but when once commenced, it should be waged in earnest. Half way measures never lead to success. A very singular idea is prevalent amongst many well informed Mexicans. They believe that a powerful party in the U.S. have got up a "pronunciamento" against the Government, which will result in Mr. Polk's being removed and the army withdrawn from Mexico.[101]

The Future of Mexico

Lt. Edmund Bradford had a more balanced view as he surveyed the Mexican scene a short while before the final acceptance of the treaty. He was, however, certain that manifest destiny would yet have its way:

I am most happy to inform you that peace is now looked upon as certain by almost all the officers and intelligent Mexicans; indeed, by this time I expect the Treaty has been ratified by the Senate and House of Deputies, and only wants the signature of the President.

By the latest accounts from Queretaro, we learn that the Committee on Foreign Relations had been appointed, and that all the members composing it are decidedly in favor of peace. Immediately after the Treaty was presented to Congress, it was referred to the Committee and by it returned to Congress last Saturday. The message of Peña-y-Peña,[102] at first produced a great deal of dissatisfaction, but this was soon dissipated by the clear, able and sensible speech of Señor Rosa,[103] who placed before the Congress the deplorable state of the country, without money, arms or men, and in the end by conclusive arguments convinced them of the utter impossibility of carrying on the war with anything like success. He concludes his discourse by stating that there exists among the Indians a spirit to rise against the whites (Mexicans & Spaniards) and exterminate them, and that in order that the Government may be enabled to bring all its energies to bear to suppress the insurrections of the Indians in Yucatan and the south of the State of Mexico, it is absolutely necessary that the Treaty should first be ratified. More than two-thirds of Congress are in favor of peace, and it is said that Rosa by his speech has made many converts of those in favor of war. Even those who have exerted themselves to destroy the present administration have given up all hope of doing anything now, but boast loudly of what they will do so soon as the American Army shall have left the country.

A revolution, supposed to be gotten up by the influence of Paredes, lately broke out in San Luis Potosi; but by the energy of the Gove[r]nor it was put down the same day. The last heard of this revolutionist, he was in Aguascalientes and Zacatecas endeavoring to concoct a revolution against the general government. As yet he has met with very little success. The people place no reliance on what he says. Since the great events which have occured in Europe, he has abandoned his project of creating a monarchy in Mexico, and is now in favor of a military dictatorship.

I cannot agree with you, my dear Sir, that Peña-y-Peña merely offered the Treaty in order that he might gain time to collect his scattered forces and arrange the internal affairs of the nation, so that at the end of the armistice, he might be in a position to renew the war. I firmly believe the President (who is a sensible man) has seen the folly of further resistance, and has acted in perfect good faith since the appointment of the Commissioners to treat with Mr. Trist. For the last three months, I have closely watched the events which have been taking place in the Republic, and I have for a long time felt convinced that the majority of the people are in favor of peace and that a great exertion would be made to obtain it. The Government will not ask for more time, but will either ratify or reject the Treaty as modified by the U.S. Senate. Should the war be continued, Mexico will find herself in no better condition to prosecute it than she was before the Armistice, whereas, we are far better prepared. Our force has been greatly augmented by recruits, the men are acclimated, and therefore better able to endure the hardships of a campaign. The new regiments and volunteers are drilled, the Depots well stored, arrangements have been entered into to supply the troops with as much money as may be required—indeed everything is prepared either to commence active operations, or in the event of peace, to make a rapid movement to the United States.

When peace shall have been made, I do not think Mexico will again be anxious to enter into war with us. I have no doubt that in twenty years all the country lying between the Rio Grande and the Sierra Madre will be annexed to the U.S. and this will be accomplished without a war, if our country shall not interfere. All the northern States are even now almost ripe for a revolution, and if the Mexican government does not grant them many more privileges than it has heretofore, they will in a few years declare themselves independent and ask to be admitted into our Union. Mexico with a population of which three fifths are ignorant, superstitious Indians, can never form a solid government. The only means by which she can ever attain a respectable place among nations is to introduce colonies of foreigners and to give to each a certain quantity of her useless land. In this way the Indians would obtain labor—and by seeing so many luxuries around them, the desire of possessing them would be created, which would cause them to throw off their indolent habits.[104]

RETURN OF THE HEROES

The majority of the people back home regarded their fighting men in Mexico as heroes. But there were some exceptions—those who believed war was degrading and bound to brutalize the soldiers engaged in it—for these the returning hero would be less human, more bestial then when he left. "The recent accounts of the success of the American arms under General Scott at Mexico are calculated to cause regret in the minds of all men of principle. But glory, glory, glory, whether the cause is just or not, is what most warriors strive for," wrote John Langdon Sibley, assistant librarian at Harvard, in 1847.[1]

A New England clergyman voicing the sentiments of many who were hostile to the war in his region condemned, in a Thanksgiving Sermon, the invasion of Mexico as a criminal assault on an all but helpless neighbor, and warned of its demoralizing effect on the warriors who fought in it:

But our course in this matter has [a] . . point of similarity to the course of Ahab towards Naboth. He took advantage of his weakness; and because he was the stronger, he robbed him of that which had been refused to his covetous demand. So have we used the power of this great nation against our weaker neighbor, and in taking possession of Texas without the consent of its rightful owners we have become a criminal party in the fraud and robbery which were designed in its original revolt. It is idle to deny that our government would never have made Texas a part of our territory if it had belonged to a nation equal in power with ourselves. We first coveted those fair fields,

445

and then in the spirit of robbery seized them because our arms were longer and stronger than the arms of Mexico.

. . . . .

The brutal spirit which it [the war] excites—the bad passions which it cherishes, tend to unhumanize all who are engaged in it. It tends to deaden the moral sense of those who rejoice in its bloody victories, or even become familiar with its dreadful carnage. It is the embodiment of all evil, it is the image of Badness, fiercely opposing with its own carnal weapons the influence and the ends of Goodness. More directly and more rapidly than any other evil, it leads those who engage and delight in it to the deep disgusts and sottish corruptions of moral death.[2]

An anonymous author spelled out the demoralizing effects of war on the soldier and saw him upon his return not as a hero but as potentially vicious and a source of criminal infection for others.

Think then of the demoralizing and degrading effect of war on the great mass of those employed as soldiers. How are they employed? What is their great business? What is the purpose for which they are enlisted, and equipped, and drilled in the use of arms? Their employment is—the end for which they are subjected to all that rigid discipline is—to kill their fellow men; to kill those who personally have done them no injury, and whose only crime against the country that causes them to be killed, is that they are in the service of the country that gave them birth and that attempts to give them its protection.

How can such an employment have any other than a demoralizing and degrading effect on the masses of the army, the rank and file that do the drudgery of slaughter? Think of the inevitable temptations and the many brutalizing influences of the camp, the march, the siege, the storm, the pillage. Who would not shudder at the thought of having a son or a brother exposed to all those dreadful influences? After a while those men, or rather as many of them as shall outlive their respective terms of service, will be disbanded and distributed over the country, to carry with them every where the infection of the vices they have acquired in Mexico, and to waken unthinking minds, in country bar-rooms and in all the haunts of village idlers, to a savage thirst for wild adventure and for the violence and license of a soldier's life.[3]

CAMPS AS BREEDERS OF CRIME

In the eyes of at least one observer, writing in The New Englander and Yale Review after the war was over, the worst fears of its critics were realized:

This war has introduced crime and vice among us. A camp is the notorious home of unbridled passions. Soldiers in a foreign country feel that they are removed from all the restraints of civil law, and whenever the barrier of military discipline can be passed, unrestrained indulgence is sure to be sought. No one can know, until he has witnessed it, the hardening influence of war upon the characters of those who are engaged in it. He, who under the name of glory can coolly blow out the brains of his fellow man, or urge a bayonet into his bosom, has taken a lesson in blood, the effects of which he has rarely the ability or disposition to shake off. . . . Soldiers are commonly drawn from that class of society who most need the checks of civil law. Having been removed from its authority for a time, it is difficult for them to assume again the character of peaceable citizens. Martial law no longer holding them in restraint, they are too apt to feel a spirit of reckless defiance. And this inhumanity and lawlessness are scattered over the land. Its breath is infection, its touch is contagion. It breeds a moral miasma in every community which comes within its influence.

The war has excited and encouraged among our people the spirit of conquest in which it had its origin.[4]

PRAISE FOR THE GRINGOS

Not all critics of the war shared this concern over its effect on the character of the men who fought it. The Massachusetts Legislature condemned the war, but lavishly praised its heroes—especially General Zachary Taylor, who they undoubtedly already saw as a Whig candidate for the presidency. Nor did the critics themselves go unchallenged. Their moral admonitions and political charges were alike rejected; their motives were impugned. At least one fierce opponent believed they should be hanged and damned, in that order. E. V. Everhart wrote from Washington, D.C., to his friend, Col. John W. Geary in Mexico:

I crave your pardon for not writing you long since. While Congress was in session, the result of their deliberations on the Army bill &c was enveloped in so much doubt that I chose to postpone my intention until something definite should occur. . . . I am satisfied there has been too much lenity shown the "yaller skinned" scoundrels, and that the only way to conquer is to strike home—make them feel all the horrors, wants, and miseries of a war they so eagerly sought to bring about. Every town taken should be pillaged and erased to the ground. Prisoners of war should be sent north—the army *supply* itself, and the spoils go to the Victors. I would as soon think of keeping faith with a rattlesnake as to trust a Mexican—their *name* is perfidy itself.

I am humiliated, the country is indignant at the conduct of Congress in so long postponing action upon the increase of the Army. Had the President's recommendations been complied with the Ten Regiments would now be in the field, and old Zack would be succored from the peril his senior officer has put him in. I will not be astonished if Tom Corwin[5] is burnt in effigy all over the country. His speech was the quintessence of toryism—profusely interlarded with fiendish slanders of our brave soldiers—who he said were ready to perpitrate every outrage—rape-arson-murder were the only deeds he saw proper to accredit them with. Such a libeller of his country men should—ought, not only to be hung in effigy—he ought to be hung by the neck until he was dead—and then handed over to the Devil to be roasted through all eternity. Nor was he the only renegade in the Senate—he was supported by almost the entire federal party, and received "aid and comfort" from some from whom better things were, and had a right to be expected.

Besides these congressional advocates of Mexico—the federal press in this city, and many of its contemporaries throughout the country, groaned, and still groans with black-hearted falsehoods against their own government, and daily expressions of sympathy for the Mexicans. It is enough to make one's blood boil, to see those things. Our Country at war—our brave men & officers rallying under our flag—yielding the quiet & happiness of home—wife, children, friends, business, and welcoming even death itself, while at our Capitol, men clothed with representative power—pretending to speak for millions of freemen, are denouncing the war as "unholy—unjust and damnable," and by implication, at least, proclaiming to our enemy that the American army is made up of infidels, robbers, and cut-throats, because if the war is such as they describe it, none other than such would engage in it. The [Washington] *National Intelligencer* teems with abuse of the war, now and then, it is true, faintly praising our brave army, but always ending with denunciations of the cause they are engaged in. If this office was in any other city in the Union it would be torn down *instanter*, but it's tone is admirably adapted to the sentiment of the majority of the resident citizens in town. All they want to make them actual tories is the chance to commit the overt act.[6]

Heroes' Welcome

Public sentiment in general, though less extreme, was undoubtedly pro-war, and the returning warriors were greeted as heroes rather than dupes or potential criminals.

The first to come home were the volunteers whose term of enlistment expired before the war was over. They were warmly welcomed in most places. For example:

Nashville is really now a most splendid city. The Volunteers from Mexico are expected in a few days. A great barbecue is to be given—speeches made—the town to be illuminated—the hills to be lighted up with bon fires and every thing else done to show respect to the Volunteers.[7]

An unidentified lady writing from Cincinnati on July 8, 1847, described to a relative in New England a sober account of the volunteers' homeward journey up the Mississippi River from New Orleans:

We arrived here two weeks since, and had a very pleasant passage up, ten days from New Orleans. It so happened that we saw all the parade[s] at the different towns on the river and in New Orleans on account of the returning volunteers; and the funeral ceremonies in honor of Clay,[8] McKee,[9] Vaughan [sic][10] and two other officers who were killed at the battle of Buena Vista, and whose bodies were now on their way to their friends. I saw the Mississippi Volunteers march in procession to hear the oration delivered by Mr. Prentiss.[11] I could not get near enough to him to hear his remarks. The next day a large procession paraded the streets following the bodies, which were placed on board the steamer *Ringgold*, for Louisville. We left the next day, and when we arrived at Vicksburg the military were out, and on the bank of the river, to receive the Mississippi Volunteers, or what was left of them. Out of nine hundred, only three hundred lived to return. Poor fellows, they looked as though they had seen hard service; they were sun burnt, and many appeared as though they were not long for this world. We had 275 passengers, most of them returned volunteers. When we passed a large town they saluted the boat to welcome the volunteers. The *Ringgold* arrived a few hours before us, but we were in time to see the procession come down to the Louisville Canal to receive the bodies of the lamented Clay and the four other officers. There were five hearses, three of them with four horses and two of them with two horses. It was indeed solemn to see the procession and hear the music, and one could not but feel that death was in our midst. A volunteer died on board our boat; he was one of the Baltimore volunteers, and has left a wife and two children to mourn his untimely end.

On arriving here we were saluted from a town directly across the river, in doing which a cannon burst and killed one man instantly, and another had both his arms blown off. The day before two were killed while firing off the same cannon; they were all returned volunteers—two of them returned only the day before they were killed. I should think there were more than a thousand people at the landing all shouting and cheering, and the volunteers returning the compliment in the same manner. All was excitement. From their appearance one would suppose the volunteers had had enough of Mexico, but, strange to tell, some are expecting to return. If you could hear some of them relate their hair-breadth escapes it would make the hair rise on your head.[12]

The soldiers were greeted no less warmly in Charleston, South Carolina, when the war was over:

The celebration of the reception of the returned Volunteers of the Palmetto Regiment from Mexico, whither they had been gallantly fighting for their country. It was a day of rejoicing throughout the city—Bells ringing, Flags flying. The entire military were out. Swords were presented the Cols. of the Regiment, and officers of the Charleston Company—A[dley] H. Gladden Colonel—Wm. Blanding—Capt., A[rthur] M. Manigault, Lieut., Lewis Robertson, Lieut., [Ralph] Bell Lieut.

A grand Dinner was given in the Park. In afternoon a "Regatta took place off the Point Garden"—and at night a Grand Torch light Procession marched through the principal streets to the Gardens where a splendid display of Fire Works took place.[13]

PLIGHT OF THE MASSACHUSETTS REGIMENT

Bells ringing, flags flying, and convivial banquets marked the return of many of the heroes. The homecoming of others evoked a more complex reaction. That of the Massachusetts Volunteers is an example. They had been under the command of Caleb Cushing, an able lawyer, successful diplomat, controversial politician, and rankly amateur soldier. They followed Scott's army in the campaign from Vera Cruz to Mexico City, and though they gathered no laurels on the battlefield they had suffered sickness and death from disease. Some did not want to come back to Massachusetts at all. But they were brought back: "The Massachusetts Regiment. Col. Wright,[14] left Albany yesterday morning, and arrived at their camp-ground last night. . . . They muster about 330 men, some 300 having died in Mexico," and their arrival precipitated a storm described in the columns of the Cambridge Chronicle:

The wretched plight in which the surviving soldiers of the Massachusetts Regiment have been permitted to return, has occasioned a general outburst of indignation. During the past week, thousands of people have visited the camp, and but few, we opine, have left it without a conviction that the volunteers have been most brutally treated. We know that men in their circumstances are prone to magnify their grievances, and on that account we do not implicitly credit all they say of themselves and their officers. Yet, without a word from any of them, it is easy to see that they are the victims of the grossest neglect; and, if a tithe of their complaints be grounded in truth, no whitewashing process known to political science can save the heartless perpetrators of so many indignities from the excoriating lash of an indignant public opinion.

Why, we ask, were these volunteers permitted to come home, as it were, in disgrace? What acts of insubordination, what crimes have they committed, to justify this treatment? If the speeches at the late reception dinner can be relied on, these men have done all that brave soldiers could do to merit the praises of their officers and entitle them to the thanks of the government. Yet they are hurried through a distance of near three thousand miles, in the hottest season of the year, after the fatiguing marches of a prolonged campaign, without change of clothing and with hardly provisions enough to keep soul and body together; ashamed of themselves and the wonderment of all; haggard in countenance, bent in body, depressed in spirits, and altogether representing the tattered remnants of a spectral army rather than the laurelled heroes of a successful war. Was there any necessity for this? Who, that is familiar with discipline in the regular army, will say there was? Was it done that the personal adornments of the high officers, those who get the emoluments and all the glory, might be set off, by the contrast, in greater brilliancy? We cannot believe it.

Who are to blame? Some say the soldiers were improvident. Is that an excuse for the treatment they have received? For what are the officers commissioned? To see that their men are properly disciplined, protected from their own inadvertencies, and at least treated with humanity. A regular officer would sooner cut off his right hand than assign the improvidence of his men as an excuse for his own neglect. The government is bound to look into this matter. Let us know if Gen. Cushing, who was hissed at the reception dinner by some of these maltreated volunteers, deserved that insult. Let us know how far Col. Wright is to be held guiltless. Tell us how the commissaries of this regiment have acquitted themselves. Charges of the most serious nature against one and all of these military officials, drop daily from the lips of the volunteers. Those against Gen. Cushing are too disgusting to be repeated. If true, they should consign him to the lowest deep of infamy.[15]

The Mexican War was probably more unpopular in Massachusetts than in any other state in the Union. This was partly because of conviction that it was an unjust "dirty little war," and partly from partisan politics. The Whigs were strong in the state and for many of them the aversion to the war was less because it was unjust than because it was Mr. Polk's Democratic-party war. Thus the foregoing account from the Cambridge Chronicle may have been more than tinged by political or moral prejudice. John Langdon Sibley, however, though opposed to the war, was not a politician, and his comments on the heroes upon their return were not public statements but entries in his private diary. On the whole he confirmed the report of the Chronicle and recorded Brig. Gen. Cushing's unpopularity with his men:

[July] 20 Thursday [1848] . . . . After tea walked about one mile & a half from the College [Harvard] to the corner this side of what is called the Brighton Rail Road Crossing, on the way to Brookline to see the remains of the Massachusetts Regiment, which arrived there yesterday from Mexico, via New Orleans and the inland route. They were occupying buildings a short distance from the corner, on the Eastern side of the road which leads toward Boston. They numbered about two thirds as many as when they left for Texas. They were ragged, dirty worn down by fatigue, several of them sick & half starved. Of Caleb *Cushing* they spoke in terms of unexceptional hostility. Of Z. *Taylor* they were enthusiastic, to a man. Of their sufferings they gave thrilling descriptions. Although they were engaged in no action, there did not seem to be one of the many with whom I conversed, who was not rejoiced to have got back. Most of them seemed to be very young, or broken down old men. Thousands of people were thronging to the place from Boston & vicinity, & all appear to be satisfied that there is no fun in going to war.

[July] 22 Saturday [1848]. The troops were entertained with a dinner at Faneuil Hall. The escort is said to have been splendid & the contrast between the two very striking. Speeches were made at the dinner table & when *Caleb Cushing*, their General, rose he was so hissed & whistled at, that during the eight or ten minutes that he had the floor, they drowned what he said by their noise, & several of the troops left the hall. They give most disgusting & outrageous accounts of his treatment of them.[16]

Soldiers' Rewards

Cushing, however, and Polk's administration were not without their champions. A pro-Polk newspaper attacked the reports of the soldiers' miserable condition and listed the material benefits bestowed by a grateful nation:

As much has been said about the destitution and poverty of the Volunteer Regiment, we feel bound to present its actual state and prospects in a few words. Our citizens have had an opportunity of ascertaining by personal observation, that the stories told of their looks and dress have been atrociously exaggerated, their own hearty cheers have attested the strength of their feeling towards their officers. But we have been told that the regiment has been badly treated by the Government, and were virtually beggars. This is infamously untrue. These men have now due them two months' wages: by a bill which has just passed, or will soon pass, Congress, they are entitled to three month's additional pay; besides which, their land scrip is worth from

115 to 120 cash in the market now, or 200 dollars intrinsic value, with a prospect of soon rising to 500 dollars. But let us take the lowest estimate: 2 months' wages, at $11 per month, $22.00; 3 months' do at $11 do; $33.00; land scrip, $115.00: total $170.00.

We wish from our heart that the compensation had been twice as great, but we undertake to say in honor to our government, that no army ever mustered out of service was better paid than that of the United States.[17]

PROBLEMS OF DEMOBILIZATION

Wherever the truth lay, it is evident that the homecoming of the Massachusetts Volunteers was not altogether a gala affair. This must have been particularly galling to many among them who had not wanted to come back at all.

This opposition to coming home was not peculiar to soldiers from Massachusetts. The Mexican War stimuated, rather than checked, the Westward Movement, and many of the soldiers, officers and men wanted at the war's end to go West, particularly to California; others had been attracted by some section of the country they had passed through and wished to settle there. There was also a financial motive for many. If they were demobilized in New Orleans, and were given the fare home, they could travel more cheaply on their own and thus save the difference, or spend it in some other way.

In May 1848, when the troops were about ready to leave Mexico, young Capt. William W. H. Davis, at San Angel, drafted a letter to William L. Marcy, Secretary of War:

We have learned with much surprise, that upon the conclusion of peace, the Mass. Volunteers, together with the other Regiments of the old Volunteer Division, are to be shipped to their respective states before being mustered out of the Service of the United States.

Against this we, the Commissioned Officers of the First Mass. Infantry enter our respectful protest, and ask that the same course as heretofore adopted may be pursued, and the Regiment be discharged at New Orleans.

We will give briefly our reasons why we are not satisfied to be mustered out of service where we were mustered in.

In the first place, we are of the opinion that the Act of Congress providing for the mustering of Vols. out of service, and giving both officers and men a certain allowance of travelling fees, never contemplated that the troops should be shipped to their homes before being discharged, and thereby lose this allowance. The spirit and true meaning of the law is in our opinion, that the troops shall be mustered out of service at the nearest convenient point in the United States, and allow them the benefit of their travelling expenses. The provision for this allowance is convincing proof to us that this was the intention of the framers of the bill, together with the practice under it, in discharging the 12 month volunteers at New Orleans.

With all due respect we are free to say that we do not think it would be doing justice to the officers and men to deprive them of this allowance when no public benefit can be accomplished, and the good of the service in no manner promoted. We have now been in Mexico nearly fifteen months with just pay enough to support ourselves decently, and have looked forward to our allowance when discharged, as a means to clothe ourselves with one suit for the civil walks of life. Without it we will return home after having served our country long & well, poorer by far, then when we enlisted under her banner.

The men will be in a worse condition than ourselves. They will not be enabled to clothe themselves with decent clothing without disposing of their land scrip, which should be avoided, when it can be done as easily as in this case.

In addition we do not wish to be compelled to return to Mass. against our desire, and if the Regt. is not to be mustered out at New Orleans, we will be compelled to ask to be discharged individually at Vera Cruz. Not more than one third of our number are from Mass. and we desire at least the privilege of returning home without a long sea voyage. Many of us have friends and relatives through the South and West whom we have a strong desire to visit, and some even now have made arrangements to take up their abode in these new regions. At least one half of the men of the Regiment, with the peculiar spirit of the New England race, intend to seek their fortunes in the fertile regions of the South and West, and have looked to the small allowance they would receive if discharged at New Orleans as the foundation of their fortune & their fame. The non-payment of this sum would be a serious matter to them, and it would change the destiny of many for life. It would be hard indeed to compel them to receive their discharge two thousand miles away when they might be set free at the very threshold of their new career, without any detriment to the government. Several intend fixing their fortunes in Mexico, and have already made engagements at high wages. Most surely nothing should be done to fetter the enterprise of our countrymen.

There are dangers too in being shipped to Boston at the season at which we will most probably embark, which the administration may have overlooked. It will be in the middle of the yellow fever season, and in our opinion would be highly improper and unwise to confine men closely in ships for the time it would require to reach Boston.

The men would necessarily be closely packed, deprived of comforts which would enable them to take measures against the fever, and in fact, their situation would almost invite the disease. The troops should be kept in this confined situation no longer than the greatest emergency would require—and we know of none which would require three weeks extra exposure, the difference between the passage to New Orleans and Boston. The administration I am sure can have no desire to expose anew the lives of men who have already repeatedly exposed them in their country's cause.[18]

Col. James H. Lane, commanding the 5th Indiana Volunteer Regiment, together with his lieutenant colonel and eighteen other officers of the regiment, wrote in a similar vein to Maj. Gen. W. O. Butler:

We the undersigned officers of the 5th Regt. Inda. Voltrs. having understood unofficially that the department thought of mustering our Regt. out of service in Inda., beg leave respectively to file this protest against any such arrangement for the following reasons, viz. The men of our Regt. when mustered understood it as a part of the contract that they were to be mustered out at this place [i.e., at New Orleans]. That they have now been traveling on government transports & and are exhausted in strength & spirits—are entirely out of money and some have not sufficient apparel to cover their nakedness and none have a change—and that the health of the men imperiously require[s] a change of clothing as well as a change of diet—that the men desire to meet their friends, not in their present filthy state, but as Gentlemen who have discharged their duty to their country—that a large portion of the Regt. do not wish to return to Inda.—if taken they would have to pay their own traveling expenses to the west—that 5 Companies of the Regt. belong on the Wabash & in the north of the State & that if the Ohio River is low these five companies entire would return by way of St. Louis or Shawneetown—for the reasons above, believing it would be unjust, cruel & oppressive we file this our solemn protest.[19]

Easy Profits from Veterans

Not all those who greeted the returning heroes were present to do them honor. Congress had voted land warrants to the veterans of the war. At the end of 1847 the land office reported: "7317 Mexican bounty land warrants, for 160 acres each have been issued, and 1,120 for 40 acres—in all 1,215,840 acres, of which only 3,520 acres have been located." Smelling profit, the vultures gathered, and one of them wrote Caleb Cushing:

A friend of mine H. A. Goldsborough of this city, for some time Chief Clerk in the Bureau of Clothing & provisions, is acting as agent for getting through the papers of the returned volunteers. They could not come here to attend to the business themselves without much expense and he prepares &

obtains all necessary papers for them at $10 each & will undertake to sell their land warrant, if they so desire. If you could recommend him to Col. Wright, or any of the Massachusetts regiment, you would oblige me much. *As there is a violent probability I should receive one half his fee.* Can you do this?[20]

Nor did the speculators wait until the war's end or content themselves with greeting the victim when he got home. They intercepted him at New Orleans. Correspondents of the New York Commercial Advertiser *and St. Louis* Union *witnessed the speculators at work at the Louisiana port of debarkation when the volunteers came home in June 1847 and reported:*

June 16 [1847] Washington

The speculators have, it seems been very busy at New Orleans in gathering up the fragments that fall from Uncle Sam's table, in the shape of land warrants for discharged soldiers. These warrants are convertible into treasury scrip for one hundred dollars, bearing six per cent. interest and payable in ten years. Each of the soldiers lately discharged at New Orleans has become entitled to land scrip convertible into stock. Speculators from the north have had agents in New Orleans for the purchase of this scrip. Large amounts have been expended in these purchases, and the soldiers were doubtless greatly benefited thereby; because, in their situation, a certain sum in hand was of more value than double the sum a year or two hence. The purchased soldiers' certificates came to the pension office, and the chief of that bureau has adopted such a construction as to render it scarcely possible for any speculator to obtain any advantage from these purchases, or even to avoid an almost total loss of the amount invested.

As proof of this I may mention, for the information of all parties concerned, that, a day or two ago, a person came here from New Orleans with five hundred of these soldiers' certificates, convertible into stock worth some fifty three thousand dollars. Col. Edwards applied to the five hundred certificates the square and compass of his legal construction, and threw out and rejected the whole five hundred certificates, on one point and another, with the exception of twenty-three. But these twenty three certificates which were made special pets were perhaps even worse treated than those that were rejected.

. . . . .

It is a well known fact that immense fortunes were made out of the poor soldiers who shed their blood in the revolutionary war by speculators who preyed upon their distresses. A similar system of depredation was practised upon the soldiers of the last war. And now we find by the "St. Louis Union" of the 8th ult. that the sharpers are already at work at N. Orleans, waiting for the volunteers as they return from the war, and pouncing upon them the moment they land in the city. We call upon all our brethren to warn the volunteers of the tricks and frauds which will be practised upon them in all parts of the country, and to put them upon their guard against all these harpies. . . .

In conversing with the gallant Illinoisians who have just returned from General Scott's army, we were sorry to learn that many of the privates, whilst in New Orleans were induced to sell their certificates. Not knowing the importance of retaining those evidences of their service, they parted with them to sharpers, who, regardless of the soldiers' welfare, extorted of them the bounty to which they were entitled. Each of those privates is entitled to 160 acres of land, and yet many of them sold their bounty for less than fifty dollars. We learn that there is a set of persons in New Orleans who make it a regular business to seize upon the returning volunteers, and buy their certificates for a trifling sum. It is thus they filch from men who have been battling for their country the fruits of a nation's gratitude. In most cases gross imposition is practised. If a volunteer parts with his certificate, knowing its value, no one has a right to complain; but if deceived as to its importance, he is outrageously wronged, and the Shylock who abuses him deserved unmitigated execration.[21]

Post-War Careers of the Gringos

The heroes were home. What was their future? The volunteers were re-absorbed into civilian life and disappeared as a distinct group. There were too few of them to cause economic or social dislocation or to exercise power as a veterans' pressure group. To be sure, the Aztec Club, formed by officers in Mexico City itself, held reunions, as did other veterans' organizations,[22] but with the exception of pensions and land grants these emphasized nostalgic memories of the campaigns. Buena Vistas, Cerro Gordos, Pueblas, El Pasos, Montezumas, Montereys, Churubuscos appeared also on maps of the United States. The cultural ties, so tentatively established during the military occupation, were perpetuated to some extent by relics, artifacts, and descriptions brought home. But, except for California and to a lesser degree New Mexico, other concerns soon crowded out the fascination of Mexican life. The regulars, too, returned to more or less remote military posts.

Of course there were exceptions. The war made Zachary Taylor President of the United States and the presidency did to him what the Mexicans couldn't—killed him. Winfield Scott missed the presidency, but he was the Whig candidate in 1852, only to be defeated by another, though less renowned, Mexican War general, Franklin Pierce. The old soldier, however, rallied from defeat at the polls and remained the ranking general of the United States army until after the outbreak of the Civil War.

YOUNG PROFESSIONALS LOOK TO THE FUTURE

Finally there was another group that was not to sink into the nameless obscurity of civilian life. It was composed of the young lieutenants and captains, most of them professional soldiers, who were to return to the battlefield and become the heroes, North and South, of the Civil War. Grant, Lee, Sherman, and many others were on the threshold of their military careers, and it may be fairly said that it was they, particularly the engineers and artillery officers, who contributed most to the American victories. To Taylor and Scott, warriors of an earlier generation, must go the credit for reorganizing and placing confidence in the young professionals of a new military age.

Able as they were, however, the young men could be wrong. Bvt. Capt. George B. McClellan was among the most professional of the professionals and none of them had greater zest for military life or studied it more diligently. Yet in a memorandum on military organization drafted in 1848 and based on his experience in the Mexican War, he wrote:

The greatest Military men of ancient & modern times have regarded it as no useless waste of time and labour to commit to paper for the benefit of posterity those principles which they conceived necessary to be known and followed in order to ensure success. These were no empty theories proceeding from the teeming brains of politicians & parvenus, but sage precepts issuing from men who should be regarded as oracles in their own profession; they resulted from a cool, clear, dispassionate review of the reasons by which they had been actuated in the trying moments of a long and eventful career, & of the results of their inductions.

None of these men have ever claimed to be Generals by intuition; they have not been ashamed to confess that they owed their knowledge of their profession, & consequently their success, to a close, searching study of the history & deeds of those who preceeded them—from their own experience they looked upon it as a duty to place in the hands of their successors the conclusions which had been forced upon them by the study & practice of a life time. For this age, for this country, has been reserved the happy privilege of producing that wonderful phenomenon, that strange enigma, that monstrosity of "natural General." Eureka! Eureka! Well may we exclaim! We have solved the problem—we have capped the climax! Oh age of all ages! Nation of all Nations! We await with joy the loud exclamations of an admiring world, to thank us. We have proved that as Nature makes noblemen, she also makes soldiers. We have proved that mere men of yesterday—Generals, Colonels, Captains & Lieutenants, taken from the village Court House, from the low bar room, from behind the counter and from the workshop, men who are as innocent as the lamb unborn of the slightest tincture of military knowledge—

that these men put in command of others equally ignorant, utterly unable to handle their arms, have rushed from victory to victory, with a speed & certainty before unknown in the annals of the world! *They*—these men of yesterday—have done all this! There were sometimes near them—probably in the rear—some Divisions commanded & officered by men who had gone through the farcical forms of a Military Education, well drilled & disciplined— but these if we are to judge by official reports have done mere nothing.

We hope before we have concluded to stamp the falsehood on this monstrous lie—to show that the old regulars have ever led & the others followed, to show too how different would have been the results had these new regts. been officered & commanded by graduates of the military academy. We also hope to show wherein the military precepts to which we have already alluded have not been followed & what would have been the present state of affairs had this war been conducted in strict accordance with the true principles of military operations. All this [is] in no spirit of faultfinding, but merely in the hope of doing some little* towards disentangling the truth, & exposing errors that we may profit in the next war by the dearly bought experience of that which now exists— & throw off the great incubus of folly under which we labor, & from which there seems so little hope of ever freeing ourselves.

First, as to the organization of our army.

It must have struck every observing mind capable of discrimination that the period of enlistment is too short, and that the Volunteer system renders it almost impossible to fill the ranks of the line with respectable and intelligent men. It is barely possible to make a decent soldier even of Infantry in 5 years, much less of Engineers, Artillery and Dragoons—granting that a man at the end of his enlistment is a fine soldier, we then lose his services in 9 cases out of 10 and his place is filled by a raw recruit who in turn leaves the service just as he becomes fit to remain in it. It is well known that a great prejudice exists among our native born citizens against enlisting in the regular army—consequently they prefer to volunteer. To remedy these evils let no volunteers be accepted except in case of the actual invasion of our soil by a foreign power; let the period of enlistment be extended to 15 years. . . . And any deficiency in recruits should be in time of war supplied by drafts. Last [but] not least, if Citizens must be appointed they should in every case go in below those already in service—that is to say as 2nd Lts., not as Generals.[23]

This was the man who was to play a vital part in the organization and training of the Army of the Potomac in the Civil War—the great citizens' army that was to fight through to victory and that was composed largely of the despised volunteers.

*Thus in text

NOTES

NOTES TO CHAPTER I

1. The legally authorized force was 7,590, but the number of men in service was fully a thousand less than that figure.

2. J[oel] R. Poinsett, War Department [Washington, D. C.] to [President Martin Van Buren], Dec. 5, 1840, Letters Sent from the Secretary of War to the President, Record Group 107, National Archives. Hereinafter, Record Group will be abbreviated as RG and National Archives as Nat. Arch.

3. Von Steuben received his military education in the service of Frederick the Great of Prussia. The complement of sixty-four noncommissioned officers and privates continued until the War of 1812, when the number was increased to one hundred. The French school of tactics which came into vogue with Napoleon emphasized that discipline could make a company of that size controllable by one captain. At Secretary of War Marcy's suggestion, Congress in 1846 again ordered the army to be so constituted. See, "New Organization," *Niles' National Register*, Vol. 70 (Jul. 11, 1846), pp. 292-293.

4. Marcy also suggested that the President should be authorized to fill up the companies to eighty men, and that a mounted regiment of riflemen or dragoons should be added to the regulars. After much debate, Congress during that session did pass a bill which authorized the Regiment of Mounted Riflemen which developed into the 3d Cavalry of later years. W[illiam] L. Marcy, Report of the Secretary of War, Nov. 29, 1845, *Congressional Globe*, 29 Cong., 1 Sess., Dec. 2, 1845, pp. 13-15.

5. [George Ballentine], *Autobiography of an English Soldier in the United States Army* (New York: Stringer & Townsend, 1853), pp. 30-31, 35.

6. In 1845, the United States Army consisted of fourteen regiments, ten companies each. A considerable part of this army was at Fort Jesup (twenty-five miles southwest of Natchitoches, Sabine County, Louisiana) when the order came to advance to Corpus Christi. The units stationed there at that time were the 3d and 4th Infantry regiments and the 2d Dragoons. By November 1845, over half the Army was in Texas. Secretary of War Marcy explained in his annual report that it was "the ill-will of the Government of Mexico" which had "set on foot . . . extensive preparations to invade and subjugate Texas," once that Republic had agreed to accept terms of annexation to the United States which had induced the United States to act. Taylor received instructions "to repel Mexican aggressions, and protect the country from Indian invasions, to regard the Rio del Norte [Rio Grande] as its western boundary, and to select a position . . . with reference to this frontier."

7. William Walker of Evansville served during the Mexican War as a captain, 2d Regiment of Indiana Volunteers. He was killed at the Battle of Buena Vista.

8. Ja[me]s Whitcomb, Indianapolis, to William L. Marcy [Washington, D.C.], Sept. 11, 1845, Letters Received, Secretary of War, Registered Series, RG 107, Nat. Arch.

461

9. The reference is to Bvt. Brig. Gen. Zachary Taylor and his force which had been sent to Corpus Christi in the summer of 1845.

10. Humphrey Marshall, Louisville, to [Thomas] J. Read, Louisville, Sept. 14, 1845, Letters Received, Secretary of War, Registered Series, RG 107, Nat. Arch.

11. The authorized number of volunteers was not called up at once. As in previous Indian wars, it was thought desirable to call troops from the states which were most accessible to the area of conflict. On May 19, a circular from the War Department called upon eleven states for volunteers to serve at once. Of these there would be twenty-two regiments, a total of 3,945 horse and 13,208 foot soldiers. The eleven states and the troops requisitioned were: Tennessee (789 horse, 1,554 foot), Kentucky (789 horse, 1,554 foot), Illinois (2,331 foot), Indiana (2,331 foot), and Ohio (2,331 foot); each received calls for three regiments. Arkansas (789 horse, 388 foot), Texas (789 horse, 388 foot); each was requested to provide one and one-half regiments. Mississippi (777 foot), Alabama (777 foot), and Missouri (789 horse), each was called upon for a regiment. An additional thirty-nine regiments, a total of 24,486 infantry volunteers, were to be enrolled but not called into service until they received further notice. These were distributed among the states as follows: New York, 7 regiments; Pennsylvania, 6; Virginia, 3; Maryland and Louisiana, 2 each; Maine, Massachusetts, New Jersey, North Carolina, South Carolina, Michigan, Iowa, and Wisconsin, 1 each; New Hampshire, Rhode Island, Connecticut, Vermont, Delaware, Florida, and Alabama, from each one-half a regiment.

12. [John Blount Robertson], *Reminiscences of a Campaign in Mexico, By a Member of the Bloody-First . . .* (Nashville: J. York & Co., 1849), pp. 57-60.

13. Wheat was mistaken in his opinion that no cavalry would be accepted from Tennessee. Four days after he wrote this, a War Department circular called upon Tennessee for 789 horse troops. Wheat served as 2d Lt. in the Regiment of Tennessee Mounted Volunteers, and also as Capt. of the Tennessee Company of Mounted Volunteers which was attached to the Regiment of Maryland and District of Columbia Volunteers.

14. Probably Lt. Nimrod R. Porter, Adjutant of the Regiment of Tennessee Mounted Volunteers who died April 21, 1847 at Plan del Rio, Mexico.

15. C[hatham] R[oberdeau] Wheat, Memphis, to George [Maney], [May] 15, 1846, John Kimberly Papers, Southern Historical Collection, The University of North Carolina Library, Chapel Hill. Hereinafter, this depository will be cited as So. Hist. Col., NC.

16. W[illiam] T. Dickinson, Shady Grove [Virginia], to Maj. Langhorne Scruggs, June 17, 1846, Langhorne Scruggs Papers, Duke University Library, Durham, North Carolina. Hereinafter this depository will be referred to as Duke.

17. Jubal Anderson Early graduated from West Point and was 2d Lt. 3d Art. in 1837. He served in the Florida War against the Seminole Indians, was 1st Lt. on July 7, 1838, but resigned the same month. He was Counsellor of Law at Rocky Mount, Virginia, from 1840 to 1846; after the Mexican War he was Commonwealth Attorney, 1848-1852. During the war he was Major in the Virginia Regiment of Volunteers (from Jan. 7, 1847), Acting Governor of Monterey, May-June, 1847, and Acting Inspector-General of Cushing's Brigade, 1847.

18. Lindsay M. Shumaker was commissioned and served as 1st Lt. in the Virginia Regiment of Volunteers.

19. W[illia]m T. Dickinson, Shady Grove [Virginia], to Maj. Langhorne Scruggs, Dec[embe]r 30, 1846, Langhorne Scruggs Papers, Duke.

20. The New York State Senate, however, took no action on this proposal.

21. Nashville *Whig*, May 19, 1846.

22. Louisville *Journal*, May 21, 1846, cited in *Niles' National Register*, Vol. 70 (May 30, 1846), p. 202.

23. G. M[ott] Williams, Washington, D.C., to J[ohn] R. Williams, Detroit, May 15, 1846, John R. Williams Papers, Burton Historical Collection, Detroit Public Library. Hereinafter, this depository will be referred to as Burton.

24. One reason given was that the government did not seem to be determined enough to carry the fighting to the gates of Mexico City, but instead would be satisfied with far less than that.

See, E. F. Smith, Hertford, North Carolina, to [Josiah Townsend Smith], Charlottesville, Virginia, June 10, 1846, Josiah Townsend Smith Papers, Duke. E. F. Smith wrote: "I have nothing new to tell you. Nothing has occurred to disturb the monotony of this dull place save on yesterday we had a circus here—rather a poor affair. The war at first caused a little excitement—but that has subsided as, in the opinion of all, it has been brought to a close. If it has not, we shall possibly get up a Troop of horse and offer our services to the Government—our company is increasing rapidly—but it is not large enough at present for service. . . . If the Government has a serious idea of invading Mexico and carrying the war to the very gates of the city I think we shall raise the requisite number and take a chance."

25. In New England the ratio of enlistment to white population was 1 in 2,500; in the South Atlantic states it was 1 in 1,080; in the North East Central states it was 1 in 255; in the South East Central states it was 1 in 140; in the North West Central states it was 1 in 110; in the South West Central states it was 1 in 33. In part, however, these regional differences reflected the policy adopted by the War Department early in the war, i.e. the decision not to call into immediate service volunteers from some of the regions.

26. David Campbell of "Montcalm," Abingdon, was governor of Virginia from 1837 to 1841. He had been a supporter of Andrew Jackson, but split with Van Buren and became a Whig.

27. William Bowen Campbell was Colonel of the 1st Regiment of Tennessee Volunteers in the Mexican War. He had studied law under David Campbell, and had fought as a volunteer Captain in the Florida Indian War. In 1851, he was elected Governor of Tennessee, the last Whig governor of that state. During the Civil War he was a Unionist, and for a time a Brigadier General in the Union Army.

28. On Nov. 16, 1846, Secretary Marcy issued a call for nine more volunteer regiments (6,750 men). These regiments were to come from Massachusetts, New York, Pennsylvania, Virginia, North Carolina, South Carolina, Mississippi, Louisiana, and Texas—one regiment from each state. Florida (on Nov. 27) received a call for a company, and, in December, Pennsylvania was requested to provide a second regiment.

29. David Campbell, "Montcalm" [Virginia], to [Col. William B. Campbell], Dec. 7, 1846, David Campbell Papers, Duke.

30. *Id.* to *id.*, Jan. 14, 1847, *Ibid.*

31. Capt. Patrick M. Henry, Regiment of North Carolina Volunteers.

32. Probably Peter Scales, 1st Lt., Regiment of North Carolina Volunteers.

33. Possibly Lt. Sewell L. Fremont, 3d Artillery.

34. Maj. Samuel Ringgold, 3d Art., mortally wounded at Palo Alto, died May 11, 1846.

35. Juliana [Paisley] Gilmer diary MS, Greensboro, North Carolina, entries of Jan. 5, 10, 1847, Duke. See also, William D. Valentine diary MS, entry of Dec. 30, 1846, So. Hist. Col., NCa. Valentine wrote: "on yesterday the militia of Hertford county [North Carolina] was summoned at the seat of justice to obtain volunteers. All day the drums and fifes and occasional speeches to our men's patriotism were exciting, encouraging and stimulating the men to volunteer to fight. Eight men, only eight, volunteered. They receive the thanks of the county and of the state. . . . They deserve more than they perhaps will ever receive."

36. [Recruiting Poster] "VOLUNTEERS," Feb. 1, 1847, in Caleb Cushing Papers, Manuscript Division, Library of Congress, Washington, D.C. Hereinafter, this depository will be referred to as DLC.

37. "Rough and Ready," Cambridge [Mass.] *Chronicle*, June 10, 1847.

38. Capt. Edmund L. Dana, 1st Regiment of Pennsylvania Volunteers.

39. [Broadside] Francis L. Bowman, Brigade Inspector, 2d Brigade, 8th Division, P[ennsylvania] M[ilitia], Wilkes-Barre, Pa., "VOLUNTEERS! . . ." Nov. 23, 1846, in Yale University Library, The Beinecke Rare Book and Manuscript Library, New Haven, Conn. Hereinafter, this depository will be referred to as Beinecke. Francis L. Bowman, the author of this broadside, was a major in the 1st Pennsylvania Volunteer Regiment during the Mexican War.

40. The question had been debated in Congress, whether the volunteers called for under the act of May 13, 1846 "for twelve months, or during the war," could be retained in service

longer than a year, even for ten or twenty years if necessary, or whether the "twelve months" limitation was imperative and "during the War" applied only if the war should last less than a year. See, "The Commanding General," *Niles' National Register*, Vol. 71 (Dec. 26, 1846), p. 262.

41. [Broadside] W. P. Richards, Science Grove, North Carolina, "To the Volunteers of Davidson," Nov. 25, 1846, Western Americana MSS, Beinecke.

42. The Philadelphia nativist riots grew out of the Philadelphia school board's decision to permit Catholic pupils to use the Douay version of the Bible and to be excused from Protestant religious exercises. By the spring of 1844, the controversy evolved into election riots, and, in May, culminated in mass meetings, street fighting, the burning by mobs of homes in an Irish neighborhood, and more violence which militia troops finally quelled after some thirty persons had been killed.

43. Morris Longstreth, Whitemarsh, to James Buchanan, May 31, 1846, James Buchanan Papers, Historical Society of Pennsylvania, Philadelphia. Hereinafter, this depository will be referred to as Hist. Soc. Pa.

44. Capt. John S. Barker, Regiment of Massachusetts Volunteers.

45. Nathan Burdit, Boston, to Caleb Cushing, Feb. 13, 1846 [sic, 1847], Caleb Cushing Papers, DLC.

46. Regiment of Virginia Volunteers; its Colonel was John F. Hamtramck Jr.

47. There was no Capt. Smith in the Virginia Volunteer Regiment.

48. Lt. John K. Cooke, Virginia Regiment of Volunteers.

49. James Miller, Virginia Regiment of Volunteers, to Lt. Col. Thomas B. Randolph, Virginia Regiment of Volunteers, China, Mexico, May 10, 1847, Jubal A. Early Papers, DLC.

50. Ward Benjamin Burnett graduated from West Point and was 2d Lt. 2d Art., April 1, 1834, and resigned, July 31, 1836. He was Col. of the First New York Volunteer Regiment on Dec. 3, 1846.

51. "Corporal of the Guard," *The High Private, With a Full and Exciting History of the New-York Volunteers* (New York: [no pub.], 1848), pp. 7-10, 14-16, 19-20, 22, 25. On inside of the front cover, this statement: "Entered according to an Act of Congress, in the year one thousand eight hundred and forty-eight by Albert Lombard."

52. John Bell [War Department, Washington, D.C.] to [John Tyler], June 29, 1841, Letters Sent from the Secretary of War to the President, RG 107, Nat. Arch. John Bell's warning was echoed in a statement made by Lt. William Montgomery Gardner, 2d Inf., in Dec. 1847. Gardner wrote: "There are a great number of superannuated and infirm officers who are born[e] on the role as effective who are unable to stand the hardship of an active campaign." See, Lt. William Montgomery Gardner to his brother, Dec. 4, 1847, William Montgomery Gardner Papers, So. Hist. Col., NCa.

53. Cadmus M. Wilcox, *History of the Mexican War*, ed. Mary R. Wilcox (Washington: Church News Pub. Co., 1892), pp. 115-116. Cadmus Marcellus Wilcox, born in North Carolina, was graduated from West Point and was Bvt. 2d Lt., 4th Inf. to July 1, 1846, and 2d Lt., 7th Inf. for the remainder of the Mexican War.

54. Gideon Johnson Pillow, a former law partner of President Polk, was Brig. Gen. of Volunteers, July 1, 1846, and Maj. Gen., Apr. 13, 1847.

55. Lt. James Stuart was Bvt. 2d Lt., Mounted Rifles, on July 1, 1846 and 2d Lt., Oct. 9, 1847. He won two brevets in the Mexican War—for Contreras and Churubusco and for Chapultepec.

56. Wilcox, *Mexican War*, pp. 113-114.

57. Grant graduated from West Point and was Bvt. 2d Lt., 4th Inf., July 1, 1843; 2d Lt., 7th Inf., Sept. 30, 1845; 1st Lt., 4th Inf., Sept. 16, 1847, and regimental quartermaster from Apr. 1, 1847 to July 23, 1848. He won two brevets in the Mexican War—for Molino del Rey and Chapultepec.

58. George Brinton McClellan graduated second in his class from West Point and was Bvt. 2d Lt., Engineers, on July 1, 1846, 2d Lt. on Apr. 24, 1847. His two Mexican War brevets were for Contreras and Churubusco and for Chapultepec.

59. This was an exaggerated, erroneous report of the Battle of Palo Alto, fought on May 8, 1846. For an account of this engagement, see Chapter II.

60. Nativist prejudices against Germans and others were frequently found in the Army. For example, when selections were made to fill up Capt. Kendrick's company of the 2d Art. in the spring of 1848 "the principle of selection was to take native Americans and others to whom the [English] language was familiar." Out of forty chosen, there were but two Germans, although more than three-fourths of the body of recruits from which the choice was made were Germans. See Lt. Col. John Munroe, 2d Art., Chapultepec, to Capt. George Deas, A.A.G., 1st Div., May 2, 1848, Letters Received, Army of Occupation, AGO, RG 94, Nat. Arch. Prejudice was not confined to anti-German feeling. A slave named "Dan" who ran away from his master and passed himself off as a white man, enlisted in the Voltigeurs at New Orleans; when found out he was "dishonorably discharged from the service of the United States without pay or allowances." This was at Vera Cruz. See Lt. Col. H[enry] Wilson, commanding at Vera Cruz, to Brig. Gen. R[oger] Jones, Adj. Gen., Washington, D.C., Apr. 4, 1848, Letters Sent, Headquarters Vera Cruz, Nov. 20, 1847—July 14, 1848, copybook, Persifor F. Smith Papers, Hist. Soc. Pa. "Unless recommended by quite extraordinary qualifications," no "naturalized citizen" was permitted to enlist in the Engineer companies. See Col. Jos[eph] G. Totten, Washington, D.C., to Capt. A. J. Swift, Corps of Engineers, West Point, N.Y., May 19, 1848 (copy), George B. McClellan Papers, DLC.

61. General Mariano Arista who commanded the Mexican forces against Taylor's army at Palo Alto and Resaca de la Palma.

62. George B. McClellan, United States Military Academy, West Point, to his sister, May 3-13, 1846, George B. McClellan Papers, DLC.

63. Secretary of War Marcy wrote in his annual report for 1845: "The distribution of troops. . . . in small detachments and skeleton companies along our widely-extended lines of frontier, prevented the acquisition of much practical knowledge essential to a high state of discipline and efficiency. By this opportunity [i.e. the opportunity to concentrate at Corpus Christi], regiments and battalions long separated have been brought together within the same chain of sentinels, and instructed in all the practical duties of camp and field service."

64. Lt. J[ohn] P. Hatch, camp near Corpus Christi, to his sister, Oct. 14, 1845, John Porter Hatch Papers, DLC.

65. *Id.* to *id.*, Oct. 28, 1845, *ibid.* John Porter Hatch was Bvt. 2d Lt., 3d Inf. July 1, 1845; he transferred to the Mounted Rifles on July 17, 1846, and was 2d Lt., Apr. 18, 1847; from Nov. 1, 1847 to May 1, 1850 he was regimental adjutant. During the Civil War he was Bvt. Brig. Gen. and Bvt. Maj. Gen. of Volunteers. He won the Medal of Honor for bravery at the Battle of South Mountain in 1862.

66. Ethan Allen Hitchcock was born at Vergennes, Vermont in 1798; his father was a distinguished lawyer, and his mother was a daughter of Ethan Allen. He graduated at West Point, and in 1842 was Lt. Col. 3d Inf. During the Mexican War he was brevetted Col. for Contreras and Churubusco, and was Bvt. Brig. Gen. for Molino del Rey.

67. Lt. Col. E[than] A[llen] Hitchcock, Ship *Massachusetts* off Lobos [Island], to Rev. Theodore Parker, West Roxbury, [Mass.], Feb. 27, 1847, Ethan Allen Hitchcock Papers, DLC.

68. Col. William B. Campbell, Camp near Jalapa, to [David Campbell], Apr. 25, 1847, David Campbell Papers, Duke.

69. Samuel H[enry] Starr, Vera Cruz, to [Mrs. Eliza Starr, New York City], Apr. 5, 1847, Samuel Henry Starr Papers, Bixby Collection, Missouri Historical Society, St. Louis.

70. Shorter terms of service, more lenient discipline, service in a company with friends and neighbors, and bounties all were inducements to sign up with the volunteers.

71. Acts of Congress at the beginning of the war authorized a regular army of 17,812 officers and men, but in Nov., 1846, only 10,690 were in the service—two regiments of dragoons, one of Mounted Riflemen, four artillery (although most of the artillery was fighting as infantry), eight infantry, and Company A of Engineers. The support troops were those in the Ordnance Department, Corps of Engineers, Corps of Topographical Engineers, Medical Department, Pay Department, Commissary Department, Adjutant General's Department, Quartermaster Department, and Purchasing Department. By Nov. 1847, the strength of the Regular Army was given as 21,686, but officers in Mexico derided that figure as grossly excessive with respect to *effective*

troops available for service. In Nov. 1848, the Army again had been reduced to 10,035. To the 6,562 officers and men in the Army at the beginning of the war (May 1846), 35,009 men and 1,016 officers were added by enlistment (to July 5, 1848); this made a total of 42,587 that served in the Regular Army during the war. Of these, however, 30,954 actually were engaged in the war. The total number of troops employed by the United States, including Regulars, Volunteers and Navy, was 112,230.

72. See William M. Tredway, Washington, D.C., to Jubal Anderson Early, Dec. 9, 1846, Jubal Anderson Early Papers, DLC. Tredway wrote: "I do not think . . that there will be any increase of the regular army. The volunteers have done so well that I believe Congress will prefer to rely upon them, for any increase of our force. . . . There is serious objection to increasing the regular army because it will be difficult to reduce it in time of peace.

73. David Campbell, "Montcalm," Virginia, to [Col. William B. Campbell], Feb[ruar]y 6, 1847, David Campbell Papers, Duke.

74. The Ten Regiments were: 3d Regiment of Dragoons, Col. E. G. W. Butler; 9th Regiment of Infantry, Cols. T. B. Ransom, J. M. Withers, and H. L. Webb; 10th Regiment of Infantry, Col. R. E. Temple; 11th Regiment of Infantry, Cols. M. C. Meigs, E. D. Keyes, and W. S. Ketchum; 12th Regiment of Infantry, Cols. L. D. Wilson, and M. L. Bonham; Thirteenth Regiment of Infantry, Cols. R. M. Echols and J. J. Fay; Fourteenth Regiment of Infantry, Col. William Trousdale; Fifteenth Regiment of Infantry, Col. G. W. Morgan; Sixteenth Regiment of Infantry, Cols. Franklin Pierce, J. W. Tibbatts; Regiment of Voltigeurs and Foot Riflemen, Col. T. P. Andrews. The aggregate number of recruits in the new establishment was 10,562; 5,200 of these recruits were organized and on their way to Mexico within sixty days after the opening of the recruiting rendezvous. A supplementary act of Mar. 3, 1847, authorized the organizing of the ten regiments into "Brigades and Divisions, with portions of the regular Army, or of the Volunteer forces, if expedient, and the appointment of (and not exceeding) two Major Generals, three Brigadier Generals, and other officers."

75. An act of July 19, 1848, however, provided "that all officers of the Old Army, appointed to any of the additional Regiments, shall be restored to their former Regiments or Corps, as additional Officers of the grades to which they would have succeeded, and to fill the first vacancies therein."

76. See, Nelson McClanahan, New Orleans, to John McClanahan, Jackson, Tenn., June 19-21, 1847, McClanahan-Taylor Papers, So. Hist. Col., NCa.

77. Ibid.

78. Col. W[illia]m S. Harney, Commanding Brigade, Headquarters of the Cavalry Brigade, to Capt. H. L. Scott, A.A.A. Genl., Headquarters of the Army, Oct. 23, 1847, Letters Received, Army of Occupation, AGO, RG 94, Nat. Arch.

79. Raphael Semmes, The Campaign of General Scott in the Valley of Mexico (Cincinnati: Moore & Anderson, 1852), pp. 202-203.

80. Kenly later was major, Regiment of Maryland and District of Columbia Volunteers.

81. On Aug. 18, 1846, General Taylor in an order issued at Camargo divided his force of regulars into two divisions. The second division, under Bvt. Brig. Gen. William J. Worth, was made up of the 5th, 7th and 8th Regiments of Infantry, Bvt. Col. Thomas Childs' Artillery Battalion, C. F. Smith's light troops, and Duncan's and Mackall's batteries; also acting under Worth's orders were Blanchard's company of Louisiana Volunteers and McCulloch's mounted Texas Rangers. The strength of the division was about 1,800 men.

82. Adj. Gen. Roger Jones, in his report of Nov. 30, 1847, wrote: "While probably not more than ten companies of the four regular artillery regiments are serving with their appropriate arm— the other thirty-eight being armed and equipped as infantry—there are two batteries with the main army in Mexico served by ordnance men (with several officers), and one by a company of the Regiment of Maryland and District of Columbia Volunteers." See Senate Executive Document, No. 1, 30 Cong. 1 Sess., p. 80.

83. John R. Kenly, Memoirs of a Maryland Volunteer. War With Mexico (Philadelphia: J. B. Lippincott & Co., 1873), p. 98.

84. Maj. Gen. Winfield Scott, "The Brassos," to [William L. Marcy], Jan. 16, 1847, William L. Marcy Papers, DLC, Col. Joseph G. Totten, Chief of Engineers, held opinions quite in sympathy with those of Scott. See Totten, Washington D.C., to Capt. J. F. K. Mansfield, "Army in Mexico, Corps of Engineers," July 7, 1846, Totten copybook, Office of the Chief of Engineers, RG 77, Nat. Arch. Totten wrote: "In [the] future there will be a larger proportion of the Army as ignorant & inexperienced as men can be; and the want of military knowledge will not be confined to the rank & file but will belong equally to the officers of a large portion of the force up to generals inclusive; for this want, & the want of reciprocal confidence which it must beget—the courage, though so exuberant, and indeed so genuine, as well as so common among our countrymen, will not afford compensation."

85. The total number of volunteers engaged in the Mexican War (including militia troops) was 73,260—3,131 officers and 70,129 enlisted men. See Francis B. Heitman, *Historical Register and Dictionary of the United States Army* (Washington: Government Prtg. Office, 1903), Vol. I, p. 282. See also Thomas H. S. Hamersly, *Complete Regular Army Register of the United States For One Hundred Years (1779-1879)* (Washington, D.C., T. H. S. Hamersly, 1880), p. 204 (second paging). Hamersly's figures differ slightly from those of Heitman. According to Hamersly, participation by states in the volunteer force was as follows: Alabama, 3,026; Arkansas, 1,323; Florida, 370; Georgia, 2,132; Illinois, 6,123; Indiana, 4,585; Iowa, 253; Kentucky, 4,842; Louisiana, 7,947; Maryland and District of Columbia, 1,355; Massachusetts, 1,057; Michigan, 1,103; Mississippi, 2,423; Missouri, 7,016; New Jersey, 425; New York, 2,396; North Carolina, 935; Ohio, 5,536; Pennsylvania, 2,503; South Carolina, 1,077; Tennessee, 5,865; Texas, 8,018; Virginia, 1,320; Wisconsin, 146.

86. Commenting on the May 13, 1846 act, Secretary of War Marcy wrote: "The law . . . requires that volunteers furnish their own clothing. . . . Such as are already uniformed need not change; such as are not, and contemplate uniforming, are at liberty to adopt such as they think proper; but it is advisable that all who may be called into service adapt their dress, as nearly as circumstances will permit, to the nature of the service that may be required of them, and to the character of the country and climate where they may have to serve. . . ." (William L. Marcy to William F. Giles, House of Representatives, Washington, D.C., May 19, 1846, cited in *Niles' National Register*, Vol. 70 (May 23, 1846), p. 181. In lieu of uniforms the volunteers of some states received commutation money with which to buy clothing and equipment as they needed it. This amounted to $42 per soldier in the Illinois regiments, and caused the editor of *Niles'* to comment that if the volunteer received the whole sum for clothing for a twelve months' tour of duty in advance, "the harpies that always hang around a camp watching for soldiers' pay" would get most of the commutation money, and the poor volunteers would be barefooted and barebacked too before they reached the City of Mexico. See "Payment for Clothing," *Ibid.* (July 11, 1846), p. 294. Although the clothing depots of the regulars in Mexico had been ordered by General Taylor to issue no clothing except undress uniforms, the officers of the new Massauchsetts Regiment of Volunteers requested that the following be authorized as dress uniforms (the officers themselves to pay for them): single breasted grey coat, white collar, white sleeve cuffs two and a half inches deep, and skirts trimmed with white. They also hoped to have swords and epaulettes of the regular army pattern. (See Caleb Cushing, Boston, to Gov. George N. Briggs, Boston, Feb. 5, 1847, Caleb Cushing Papers, DLC.)

87. Battalion of Maryland and District of Columbia Volunteers, under Lt. Col. William H. Watson (killed at Monterey), was six companies; four recruited in Maryland and two in the District of Columbia.

88. "From the Palmetto Regiment," letter signed "Dan," dated at Island of San Antonio de Lizardo, Mexico, Mar. 9, 1847, Charleston *Mercury*, Apr. 1, 1847.

89. The name of the Regiment of Kentucky Cavalry Volunteers (Col. Humphrey Marshall) was adopted from the title of a popular song, "The Hunters of Kentucky," which lauded the Kentucky rifles who had stood with Jackson against the British at the Battle of New Orleans. It was symbolic of the traditional American confidence in the fighting qualities of the citizen-soldiers —especially the straight-shooting frontiersman. It was therefore ironic that the Mexican War

brought into question, more than any previous conflict, the prowess of civilian volunteers in the army. The citizen as warrior from the Revolutionary Minute Man to the volunteer Gringo in the Mexican War, did not yield easily his place in American folklore, but the campaigns of Taylor and Scott, at least in some degree tarnished the luster of his reputation. On the "Hunters of Kentucky" as a symbol in the Jacksonian era, see, John William Ward, *Andrew Jackson, Symbol for An Age* (New York: Oxford University Press, 1962), pp. 13-29.

90. "Volunteer Army," *Niles' National Register*, Vol. 70 (Aug. 22, 1846), p. 386.

91. Private Alexander Doniphan, Co. C, Missouri Mounted Volunteers, was elected Col. of that regiment on June 18, 1846. For a further account of Doniphan's Mexican War career, see Chapter III.

92. Nelson McClanahan, New Orleans, to John McClanahan, Jackson, Tenn., June 19-21, 1847, McClanahan-Taylor Papers, So. Hist. Col., NCa.

93. Brig. Gen. John Ellis Wool was Capt., 13th Inf., Apr. 14, 1812; Bvt. Col. after the Battle of Plattsburg (Sept. 11, 1814); Inspector-General from 1816 to 1841; Lt. Col., 6th Inf., May 20, 1820, and Brig. Gen., June 25, 1841. He was brevetted Maj. Gen. for Buena Vista during the Mexican War; and in the Civil War was Maj. Gen. in the Union Army, May 16, 1862. He retired on Aug. 1, 1863.

94. Col. George Croghan had been Inspector General since 1825.

95. Col. Archibald Yell, Regiment of Arkansas Mounted Volunteers. He was killed at Buena Vista.

96. Lt. Col. George Talcott, Jr., was Lt. Col., Ordnance, on May 30, 1832, Col. and Chief of Ordnance, Mar. 25, 1848, and Bvt. Brig. Gen. for his services during the Mexican War. He was, however, dismissed from the Army on July 10, 1851.

97. Brig. Gen. John E. Wool, Cincinnati, to W[illia]m L. Marcy, Washington, D.C., June 7, 1846, William L. Marcy Papers, DLC.

98. Sam[ue]l R. Curtis, Adjutant General's Office, Columbus, Ohio, to his wife [Belinda Curtis, Wooster, Ohio], May 21, 1846, Samuel R. Curtis Papers, Beinecke. Samuel Ryan Curtis graduated from West Point and was commissioned, July 31, 1831, Bvt. 2d Lt., 7th Inf. After frontier duty at Fort Gibson, Indian Territory, he resigned on June 30, 1832. In civilian life he was a civil engineer and practiced law; he was an officer in the Ohio militia (Colonel, 1843-1845), and from May 20 to June 24, 1846 he was Adjutant General of Ohio "for the special purpose of mustering and organizing the State's quota of volunteers for the Mexican War." He then became Col. of the 2d Ohio Regiment of Volunteers. After that regiment was mustered out in June 1847, he served on Brig. Gen. Wool's staff as Acting Asst. Adj. Gen., and was civil and military Governor of Camargo, Mexico.

99. Alexander Konze was mortally wounded at Buena Vista. So inspiring was his personality that after his death a fellow private, Herman Upmann, wrote from a hospital bed in Saltillo that, "while awaiting upon the field on the night of the twenty-third of February the renewal of the attack by Santa Anna, the thought was most consolatory to several of his [Konze's] comrades, that death on the next day might make them companions of Miltiades, of Socrates, and of Konze." Lt. Nathaniel Niles, 2d Illinois Volunteers, wrote a eulogy that appeared in the Boston *Evening Post*: "In the same part of the field [at Buena Vista] . . another fell, pierced by a lance, whose name is worthy of a place in the rolls of fame—Private Alexander Konze, of Company H, 2d regiment of Illinois. . . . His conduct on the field was most soldierly, cool, calm, deliberate, and [he was] prompt in obeying orders. His courage was conspicuous, even in the moment of his death, when he refused to surrender. Except a brother in South America, he left no relatives on this continent. His widowed mother lives in Bueckeburg, in Hanover, near to his native city— Hamburg. He received a splendid education in the universities of Jena and Goettingen. He had been but a year in the United States when he joined our regiment in Alton. . . . He was twenty-seven years of age and probably the most learned man in the army. His knowledge of philology was accurate and profound. Such was his familiarity with the Latin, that by one day's examination of a Spanish grammar he was able to read this cognate language with facility. Many pleasant hours have we spent together in rambling over the plains and mountains of Mexico, while he filled his haversack with new plants to send to Germany, and which his knowledge of botany often

enabled him to class in their several genera and species. A better or braver heart never beat its last on a field of battle. . . . This man died for a country of which he was not a citizen; shall it be said that he, the republican son of Germany, was not a true American?"

100. Fourth Regiment of Illinois Volunteers, commanded by Col. Edward D. Baker.

101. James Semple (1798-1866) was United States Senator from Illinois, 1843-1847, but was not a candidate for renomination in 1846; after Mar. 3, 1847 he returned to Alton where he engaged in the real estate business. A Democrat in politics, it seemed likely that he might, like other leading Democrats, be given a colonel's commission. He did not, however, command an Illinois regiment or participate in the Mexican War.

102. Maj. James L. D. Morrison, later promoted to Lt. Col., 2nd Illinois Regiment of Volunteers.

103. A[lexander] K[onze], Alton, Illinois, to Editor, Milwaukee *Wisconsin Banner*, July 2, 1846, cited in Milwaukee *Wisconsin Banner*, July 18, 1846 (typescript copy), Alexander Konze Papers, State Historical Society of Wisconsin, Madison, Wisconsin. Hereinafter, this depository will be referred to as Wis. Hist. Soc.

104. Kenly, *Maryland Volunteer*, p. 77.

105. James Crabb to Henry H. Keeling, July 14, 1846, Western Americana MSS, Beinecke.

106. Col. Humphrey Marshall.

107. Probably Pierce M. Butler, later Col., South Carolina Volunteer Regiment ("Palmetto Regiment").

108. Col. William R. McKee, 2d Regiment of Kentucky Volunteers; he was killed at Buena Vista.

109. "Volunteers," *Niles' National Register*, Vol. 70 (July 25, 1846), pp. 325-326.

110. The Polk administration's appointment of members of Congress to the command of volunteer regiments brought forth this criticism from Joel R. Poinsett, a former Secretary of War: "If the measures of the Democratic administration are to serve as future precedents, the power & patronage of the Executive will hereafter be excessive." J[oel] R. Poinsett, "The Homestead," to Go[u]v[erneur] Kemble, Cold Spring, New York, July 27, 1846, Gilpin-Poinsett Papers, Hist. Soc. Pa.

111. "Illinois Volunteers," St. Louis *Missouri Republican*, July 7, 1846.

112. Isaac Smith, *Reminiscences of a Campaign in Mexico* (Indianapolis: Chapman & Spann, 1848), p. 6.

113. Apparently this was a unique arrangement, but numerous independent companies served from various states during the Mexican War.

114. Kenneth McKenzie, Covington County, Mississippi, to Duncan McLaurin, Richmond County, North Carolina [n.d. fragment of a letter], Duncan McLaurin Papers, Duke.

115. Daniel C. McKenzie, to Duncan McLaurin, May [date obliterated], 1847, *Ibid.*

116. Lt. T[homas] Williams, Headquarters of the Army, Ship *Massachusetts* off Lobos Island, to J[ohn] R. Williams, Detroit, Feb. 28, 1847, John R. Williams Papers, Burton. Lt. Thomas Williams, 4th Art., was aide-de-camp to General Scott; Bvt. Capt. for Contreras and Churubusco, and Bvt. Maj. for Chapultepec.

117. Col. John C. Hays, 1st Regiment of Texas Mounted Rifle Volunteers.

118. Col. George T. Wood, 2d Regiment of Texas Mounted Rifles.

119. Governor James P. Henderson was Maj. Gen., Texas Volunteers.

120. [Luther Giddings] *Sketches of the Campaign in Northern Mexico* (New York: Published for the author by George P. Putnam & Co., 1853), pp. 96-97. Giddings was Maj., 1st Regiment of Ohio Volunteers.

121. Brantz Mayer, *History of the War Between Mexico and the United States* (New York: Wiley & Putnam, 1848), pp. 158-160.

122. Dr. S. Compton Smith was an 'Acting Surgeon,' i.e. a surgeon under contract, to Taylor's army.

123. The Mounted Company of Capt. Mabery B. Gray.

124. S. Compton Smith, *Chile Con Carne; or, The Camp and the Field* (New York: Miller & Curtis, 1857), pp. 292-295.

125. T. M. Cook to William H. Leevis, Oct. 12, 1847, Western Americana MSS, Beinecke.

126. Ephraim Kirby Smith, *To Mexico With Scott. Letters of Captain E. Kirby Smith to His Wife*, ed., Emma Jerome Blackwood (Cambridge: Harvard University Press, 1917), p. 17. This letter was dated at Corpus Christi, Texas, Sept. 18, 1845.

127. The 2d Regiment of Ohio Volunteers was reconstituted the 5th Regiment, but Lowe and other officers still continued to identify it as the 2d Ohio. Lt. Col. William Irvin of the 2d Regiment became Col. of the 5th Regiment.

128. Lt. William Howard was 2d Lt., 5th Ohio Volunteers.

129. Capt. John W. Lowe, Steamer *Trenton* on the Mississippi River, to Mrs. Manorah F. Lowe, New York City, Sept. 26, 1847, John W. Lowe Papers, Dayton and Montgomery County Public Library, Dayton, Ohio. Hereinafter, this depository will be referred to as Dayton.

130. Sir Edward Pakenham, commander of British troops near New Orleans, was killed on Jan. 8, 1815 while attempting to carry General Jackson's position by assault.

131. Brig. Gen. John E. Wool with troops from the Upper Mississippi Valley was en route to the Texas coast; from there he would march inland to San Antonio de Bexar.

132. Port LaVaca, Texas, on Lavaca Bay, adjoining Matagorda Bay, and about twenty-five miles southeast of Victoria. A[lexander] K[onze], Camp Crockett near San Antonio de Bexar, to the editor of the Milwaukee *Wisconsin Banner*, Sept. 10, 1846, cited in Milwaukee *Wisconsin Banner*, Nov. 2, 1846 (typescript copy), Wis. Hist. Soc.

133. The John Kreitzer diary, in the Historical Society of Pennsylvania library, has been transcribed in longhand from some earlier draft; the society accessioned this journal in 1920, but it has been unable to provide any further information on its origins. Anyone using the Kreitzer diary immediately becomes aware of a close parallel in wording when he compares its entries with those of the printed journal of J. Jacob Oswandel (*Notes of the Mexican War, 1846-47-48* Philadelphia: [no pub.], 1885). Private Kreitzer, a printer by trade, and Sergeant Oswandel were both in Company C of the 1st Pennsylvania Volunteer Regiment. Oswandel mentioned Kreitzer (spelling his name Kritser) in his journal. In his entry for Wednesday, Dec. 29, 1847, Oswandel writes: "one of our members, named John Kritser, a printer, works on [*The American Star*, a soldiers' newspaper published at that time in Mexico City]." In comparing the journals of these soldiers the similarity is so great that it becomes difficult to avoid a conclusion that one of them used the diary of the other. That of Oswandel, however, is more sophisticated—more polished—than the Kreitzer diary; Oswandel's also is more extensive, and his published "notes" include letters, etc. That of Kreitzer seems more artless, and perhaps is less derivative. In an entry of Dec. 24, 1846, Kreitzer discusses a "poney purse"; Oswandel in relating the same incident seems to misinterpret the term. Possibly Oswandel may have used and embellished Kreitzer's diary in his *Notes*.

134. This is an error, a confusion of town names. Greensburg is in Westmoreland County, east southeast of Pittsburgh. The town he passed through probably was Dauphin.

135. Capt. Turner G. Morehead.

136. Capt. William F. Small.

137. Col. Francis M. Wynkoop, 1st Regiment of Pennsylvania Volunteers, enlisted as a Private (age 28 years), in Company B, 1st Pennsylvania Volunteers, on Dec. 1, 1846, at Pottsville; he was elected Col. of the regiment on Dec. 18, 1846.

138. Capt. James Nagle commanded Company B.

139. John Kreitzer Journal MS, 1846-1848, entries of Dec. 9-23, 1846, Hist. Soc. Pa.

140. Dr. Charles Luzenberg, an Austrian physician from Verona, Italy, opened this hospital where soldiers were treated; he had no official status, having been barred from a surgeon's appointment to the war because of political involvements. Other members of the medical profession in New Orleans, especially Dr. E. D. Fenner, assisted the Army Surgeons. The editors are indebted to Mrs. Virginia Gray, Assistant Curator of MSS, Duke University Library, for information on medical conditions in New Orleans during the Mexican War. They are especially grateful to her for permission to read her excellent MS on the subject.

141. Tho[ma]s N. Love, "Remarks on Some of the Diseases Which Prevailed in the 2d Regt.

Mississippi Rifles for the First Six Months of Its Service," *The New Orleans Medical and Surgical Journal*, Vol. 5 (July, 1848), pp. 3-6.

142. This was an occupation newspaper published after the capture of the city. For more on soldier newspapers, see Chapter VI.

143. "Injustice to Volunteers," *Matamoros American Flag*, Jan. 17, 1847.

144. Capt. Charles R. Crowninshield, Massachusetts Regiment of Volunteers.

145. Lt. Col. Edward W. Abbott.

146. Col. Caleb Cushing.

147. Lt. W[illiam] W[atts] H[art] Davis, to his mother [Mrs. Amy H. Davis], "Davisville" [Doylestown], Pa., Feb. 13, 1847, W. W. H. Davis Papers, Beinecke.

148. Lt. John C. Cremony, 2d Lt. of Massachusetts Regiment of Volunteers.

149. Lt. W[illiam] W[atts] H[art] Davis, Ship *Remittance* at sea, to his mother [Mrs. Amy H. Davis], Mar. 6, 1847, W. W. H. Davis Papers, Beinecke.

NOTES TO CHAPTER II

1. Bvt. Brig. Gen. Z[achary] Taylor, Comdg. Army of Occupation, Corpus Christi, to the Adjutant General of the Army [Roger Jones], Washington, D.C., Aug. 15, 1845 (copy), Letters Sent, General Zachary Taylor's Headquarters, AGO, RG 94, Nat. Arch. Zachary Taylor was 1st Lt. 7th Inf., May 3, 1808; Capt., Nov. 30, 1810, and Maj., 26th Inf., May 15, 1814. He was honorably discharged on June 15, 1815, but reinstated as Maj., 3d Inf., May 17, 1816, and, after a number of transfers, was Col., 1st Inf., Apr. 4, 1832. He was Bvt. Brig. Gen. for distinguished service in the war against the Seminole Indians (1837), and was Bvt. Maj. Gen. for the battles of Palo Alto and Resaca de la Palma. He was Maj. Gen. on June 29, 1846, and resigned on Mar. 4, 1849 when he became President of the United States.

2. William Jenkins Worth was 1st Lt., 23d Inf., Mar. 19, 1813; Col., 8th Inf., July 7, 1838; Bvt. Brig. Gen., Mar. 1, 1842 for his services as a commander in Florida, and was Bvt. Maj. Gen. after Monterey. He died May 7, 1849.

3. Alexis DeTocqueville, *Democracy in America*, ed. Richard D. Heffner (New York: Mentor Books, 1961), p. 276.

4. Bvt. Brig. Gen. W[illiam] J. Worth, Corpus Christi, to Surgeon General [Thomas] Lawson, Washington, D.C., Nov. 1, 1845, Thomas Lawson Papers, DLC.

5. Taylor's Orders No. 14, Corpus Christi, Sept. 26, 1845, brigaded the "Army of Occupation." The 8th Inf. and companies of artillery serving as infantry were the 1st Brigade under General Worth. (On Sept. 28, 1845, another order incorporated the detachments from the various regiments of artillery into the Artillery Battalion to be commanded by Bvt. Lt. Col. Thomas Childs.) The 2d Brigade was made up of the 5th and 7th Regts. of Inf. The 3d and 4th Regiments of Inf. constituted the 3d Brigade. The 2d Drags. remained a separate command, as did four companies of artillery with batteries.

6. Along the coastline from the Nueces River (nearly to the Rio Grande) lay Padre Island—a narrow ridge of sand separated from the mainland by Madre Laguna. Opposite the southern end of this island Point Isabel jutted out from the shore into Laguna Madre and faced a strait—Brazos Santiago—which separated Padre and Brazos Islands. Brazos Island was a treeless expanse of sand; the only village on it had been destroyed by a hurricane and tidal wave. When Taylor's transports arrived their crews found it inhabited by one Mexican family and a herd of goats. At the other side of Brazos Island there was another narrow strait, named Boca Chica, but it was only fifty yards wide and, like Brazos Santiago, was deep enough only for light draught vessels. The shoals around Brazos Island were littered with wrecks. At first only a few sheds were erected on Brazos Island; most of the supplies were heaped up in the open air. But eventually a complex of structures formed a major supply base there. At Point Isabel (only five miles away) there were fortifications which Taylor's men began to erect; they covered some fifty acres, and soon were given the name Fort Polk.

7. It took alternating battalions from each brigade (altogether twenty-four hundred men) thirty days to construct the fort. The walls of its magazine were built of pork barrels filled with sand, piled up seven tiers thick and covered with timbers; over all this they piled sand ten feet high. Taylor's Orders No. 62, May 17, 1846, designated this work as Fort Brown, "in memory of the gallant commander who nobly fell in its defense."

8. Joseph King Fenno Mansfield was Capt., Engineers, July 7, 1838, and was Bvt. Maj. for Fort Brown; Bvt. Lt. Col. after Monterey, and Bvt. Col. for Buena Vista. During the Civil War he was Brig. Gen. (Union Army) on May 6, 1861, and died, Sept. 18, 1862 of wounds received at the Battle of Antietam.

9. General Pedro de Ampudia, a native of Havana, began his career as an infantry cadet in a Spanish regiment, Apr. 24, 1818. He commanded the Mexican Army at Monterey, and led a brigade at Buena Vista. At the Battle of Cerro Gordo he repulsed the first American attack on El Telégrafo hill. For the Battle of Cerro Gordo, see Chapter V.

10. [Lt. John P. Hatch], "Camp opposite Matamoros," to his sister, Apr. 3, 1846, John Porter Hatch Papers, DLC.

11. The 7th Inf., with Companies I, 2d Art. and E, 3d Art., remained to form the garrison at Fort Texas; Capt. Mansfield of the Engineers also stayed at the Fort with Maj. Jacob Brown. The rest of Taylor's army moved out on May 1—Maj. George A. McCall with an elite detachment of light troops (drawn from the various units) at noon, the other troops about 2 P.M. Those under Col. David E. Twiggs' command were in the following order: one company 2d Dragoons, 5th Inf., Ringgold's artillery, 4th Inf., 3d Inf., two companies 2d Dragoons. Worth had tendered his resignation in pique over promotion and brevet rank and Taylor had given him leave of absence until May 31. Bvt. Lt. Col. William G. Belknap therefore was in command of the 1st Brigade. On the march, Belknap commanded the 8th Inf., Duncan's artillery, the Artillery Battalion, and two companies of the 2d Dragoons.

12. Maj. Jacob Brown of Massachusetts was Maj., 7th Inf., Feb. 27, 1843. He died May 9, 1846 from wounds received on May 6.

13. Capt. Edgar S. Hawkins was Capt., 7th Inf., Nov. 10, 1829, and Maj., 1st Inf. on Feb. 16, 1847. He was Bvt. Maj. for the defense of Fort Brown.

14. Capt. Samuel Hamilton Walker, was Capt. Texas Mounted Rangers on Apr. 11, 1846; Lt. Col., June 24, 1846; Capt. Mounted Rifles, May 27, 1846, and killed at Huamantla. See Chapter V for Walker at Huamantla.

15. Lt. Charles Hanson, was 1st Lt., 7th Inf. on Mar. 16, 1844; Capt., Feb. 16, 1847, and was killed at the Battle of Contreras.

16. Lt. Braxton Bragg of North Carolina was 2d Lt., 3d Art., July 1, 1837; 1st Lt., July 7, 1838; Capt., June 18, 1846. He was Bvt. Capt. for the defense of Fort Brown; Bvt. Maj. after Monterey, and Bvt. Lt. Col. after Buena Vista. Bragg's battery was Company E, 3d Art.; it served as light artillery but was not so designated until 1847. During the Civil War, Bragg was a General in the Confederate States Army and commanded the Army of Tennessee.

17. Capt. E[dgar] S. Hawkins, commanding post, Fort Taylor, Texas [Fort Brown], to Capt. W. W. S. Bliss, A. A. A. G., Army of Occupation, Texas, May 10, 1846, *Congressional Globe*, 29 Cong., 1 Sess., appendix, pp. 681-682.

18. Alternate battalions of each brigade worked on the entrenchments under the supervision of their officers; the morning battalions worked from 6:30 A.M. until 12:30 P.M., the evening battalions from then until 6 P.M.

19. Matamoros was across the Rio Grande from Fort Brown, but Taylor was not merely trying to return to Fort Brown—he was marching at the enemy. See Taylor's Orders No. 58, Point Isabel, May 7, 1846: "The Army will march at 3 o'clock today in the direction of Matamoros. It is known that the enemy has recently occupied the route in force—if still in position, the General will give them battle. The commanding General . . . wishes to enjoin upon the battalion of Infantry that their main dependence must be on the bayonet."

20. Lt. Jeremiah Mason Scarritt of New Hampshire graduated fifth in his class at West Point and was 2d Lt., 6th Inf., July 1, 1838; 2d Lt., Engineers, July 7, 1838; 1st Lt., July 1, 1839, and Bvt. Capt. for Monterey. He died June 22, 1854.

21. Col. Joseph Gilbert Totten, graduated from West Point and was 2d Lt., Engineers, July 1, 1805; he was Col. and Chief Engineer on Dec. 7, 1838. During the Mexican War his brevet was for Vera Cruz (Bvt. Brig. Gen.).

22. Duncan's battery was Company A of the 2d Art. James Duncan was Capt., 2d Art. on Apr. 16, 1846; Bvt. Maj. for Palo Alto; Bvt. Lt. Col. for Resaca de la Palma, and Bvt. Col. for Monterey. He died July 3, 1849 at Mobile, Alabama.

23. Capt. Charles Augustus May was 2d Lt., 2d Drags. on June 8, 1836, and Capt., Feb. 2, 1841. He won three brevets in the Mexican War—for Palo Alto, Resaca de la Palma, and Buena Vista.

24. Capt. John Page was 2d Lt., 8th Inf., on Feb. 13, 1818; he transferred to the 4th Inf. in 1821 and was Capt. on Apr. 30, 1831. He died July 12, 1846 of the wounds he received at Palo Alto.

25. Probably Lt. Roland Augustus Luther, 2d Art.

26. Bvt. Capt. William Wallace Smith Bliss, Taylor's son-in-law and Asst. Adj. Gen. since 1839, was ninth in his class when he graduated from West Point in 1833. As an adjutant he was invaluable to Taylor and the army. He won two brevets—for Palo Alto and Resaca de la Palma, and for Buena Vista.

27. Lt. Randolph Ridgely of Maryland was 1st Lt., 3d Art., on July 17, 1838; regimental adjutant, 1838-1841, and Asst. Adj. Gen. on July 7, 1846. He was Bvt. Capt. after Palo Alto and Resaca de la Palma. On Oct. 27, 1846 he died at Monterey as the result of a fall from his horse.

28. Gen. R. Diaz de la Vega commanded the second brigade of the Mexican Army at Resaca de la Palma.

29. Lt. J. M. Scarritt, Point Isabel, to Col. J. G. Totten, Washington, May 12, [1846], Letters Received, Office of the Chief of Engineers, RG 77, Nat. Arch.

30. Lt. Edmund Kirby Smith was 2d Lt., 5th Inf., July 1, 1845; 2d Lt., 7th Inf., Aug. 22, 1846. He received brevets for Cerro Gordo and Contreras and Churubusco. In the Civil War he was a general in the Confederate States Army.

31. Lt. Edmund Kirby Smith, Matamoros, to Mrs. Frances K. Smith, May 20, 1846, Edmund Kirby Smith Papers, So. Hist. Col., NCa.

32. Lt. Jenks Beaman, "Camp of the Army of Occupation at Matamoras, Mexico," to Mrs. C. R. Mallory, West Poultney, Vermont, May 29, 1846, Jenks Beaman Papers, Houghton Library, Harvard University, Cambridge, Mass. Hereinafter, this depository will be referred to as Houghton. Jenks Beaman was a native of Vermont. He was 2d Lt., 4th Inf., Dec. 31, 1842, and 1st Lt. on Nov. 27, 1846. He died at Vera Cruz, May 6, 1848.

33. Maj. Gen. Z[achary] Taylor, Matamoros, to Dr. R[obert] C. Wood, Fort Polk [Point Isabel], Texas, July 14, 1846, in *Letters of Zachary Taylor from the Battlefields of the Mexican War; Reprinted from the Originals in the Collection of Mr. William K. Bixby, of St. Louis, Mo.* (Rochester, New York: The Genessee Press, 1908), p. 28.

34. Lt. Col. Henry Wilson was Ens., 32d Inf., May 17, 1813, and Lt. Col., 1st Inf., June 14, 1842. He was Bvt. Col. for Monterey. After the occupation of Vera Cruz he became commander and governor at that city.

35. Independent Company of Texas Volunteers (Mounted Company) commanded by Capt. John T. Price.

36. Lt. George H. Thomas was 2d Lt., 3d Art., July 1, 1840 and 1st Lt., Apr. 30, 1844. He won brevets for Monterey and Buena Vista. During the Civil War he was Maj. Gen. (Union Army), and won fame as "The Rock of Chickamauga."

37. Gen. Antonio Canales.

38. Most of the volunteers left Matamoros by July 30, but part of the Baltimore Battalion did not begin its march until Aug. 15.

39. Kenly, *Maryland Volunteer*, pp. 61-63.

40. General Francisco Mejia was General-in-Chief, Army of the North, after Arista.

41. Taylor's Orders No. 99, Camargo, Aug. 17, 1846.

42. The afternoon of Aug. 18, a brigade consisting of the Artillery Battalion (eight companies), Duncan's light artillery, and six companies of the 8th Inf. was ordered to march on the nineteenth

to Cerralvo, enroute to Monterey. Also on the afternoon of the eighteenth, General Taylor reviewed all his regulars. On the eighteenth the Artillery Battalion crossed the San Juan River to camp on its left bank; the next morning the 8th Inf. also went over, and by that afternoon (the nineteenth) the whole brigade was striking tents for the march. It began about sunset when the Artillery Battalion and Duncan's battery moved out. On the advance, see Taylor to Wood, Aug. 19, 1846, *Bixby letters*, pp. 43-44.

43. Brig. Gen. David Emanuel Twiggs of Georgia was Capt., 8th Inf., Mar. 12, 1812; Lt. Col., 4th Inf., July 15, 1831; Col., 2d Drags., June 8, 1836, and Brig. Gen., June 30, 1846. After Monterey he was Bvt. Maj. Gen. During the Civil War he was (1861-1862) Maj. Gen. in the Confederate States Army; he died July 15, 1862. Taylor's Orders No. 49, Apr. 22, 1846, defined Twiggs' command, as follows: "The command of Col. Twiggs, comprising the cavalry [i.e. 2d Dragoons] and 2d Brigade of Infantry [5th and 7th Regiments] will be styled the 'Right Wing of the Army of Occupation.' "

44. Smith's description of Taylor's army differs somewhat from the organization set forth in an order by Taylor on the same day that Smith's letter was written. According to Taylor's Orders No. 98, the regulars were grouped into two divisions. The First Division was commanded by Twiggs and consisted of the 1st, 3d and 4th Regiments (Infantry), the batteries of Bragg, Ridgely and Webster, and four companies of the 2d Dragoons under May. Also attached to this division were the Baltimore Battalion and Capt. William R. Shivors' foot company of Texas Volunteers. Twiggs' command numbered nearly two thousand men. The Second Division, under Worth, had the 5th, 7th, and 8th Infantry regiments, the Artillery Battalion ("red legged infantry" commanded by Childs), and Duncan's and Mackall's batteries. Also there was an elite company of light troops commanded by Capt. Charles F. Smith, Blanchard's company of Louisiana Volunteers and McCulloch's Texas Rangers. Worth's division added up to about eighteen hundred men. On August 20, Taylor issued another order (General Orders No. 100) which split the volunteers into two divisions, one commanded by Maj. Gen. William Orlando Butler, the other by Maj. Gen. Robert Patterson. The three brigades of the 1st Volunteer Division were commanded by Brig. Gen. Thomas Marshall, Brig. Gen. Thomas L. Hamer, and Brig. Gen. Joseph Lane. The brigade commanders of the 2d Volunteer Division were Brig. Gen. James Shields, Brig. Gen. Gideon J. Pillow, and Brig. Gen. John A. Quitman. (All the Brig. Gens. had been appointed pursuant to an Act of Congress approved June 26, 1846.) It was the 1st Volunteer Division, known as the "Field Division," which moved with the Army to Monterey. It included the 1st Regiment of Mississippi Volunteers (Mississippi Rifles, commanded by Col. Jefferson Davis), the 1st Kentucky, the 1st Tennessee, and the 1st Ohio Regiments, in all two thousand men. In addition, Henderson's brigade of Mounted Texas Rangers, comprising the regiments of Hays and Wood, not quite one thousand men, acted as an independent brigade, but later in the campaign were attached to Worth's division. The army with which Taylor moved on Monterey was under seven thousand men. The volunteers left behind "for instruction and camp service" were to be subjected to a "rigid system of police and discipline." The volunteer regiments that went on the march were reduced to five hundred men each, exclusive of officers; they left behind "all sick and disabled men and all who shall not be deemed capable of undergoing the fatigues and privations of the campaign."

45. Lt. Edmund Kirby Smith to his mother, Aug. 18, 1846, Edmund Kirby Smith Papers, So. Hist. Col., NCa.

46. The allowance of transportation for the march was one wagon to each division and brigade headquarters; four pack mules to the field officers and staff of each regiment or battalion; one pack mule to the officers of each company, if not more than three; and one pack mule to every eight noncommissioned officers, musicians and privates. Three wagons were assigned to each regiment for the transportation of water, but when the Army reached Cerralvo, Taylor decided that these wagons were no longer needed for water and ordered them turned over to the Quartermaster's Department. Two wagons also were allotted to each regiment for the transportation of articles that could not be packed on mules.

47. Ulysses S. Grant, *Personal Memoirs of U.S. Grant* (New York: Charles L. Webster & Company, 1885), Vol. 1, pp. 104-106. As Taylor's army moved toward Monterey and Torrejon's

Mexican cavalry could be seen in the distance, the Mexican mule-drivers became less willing to go forward. Kenly wrote (*Maryland Volunteer*, pp. 94-95): "We passed through the village of Agua Frio, and just beyond it saw the enemy's cavalry; it was doubtless the same force which had preceded us all the way from Seralvo [*sic* Cerralvo], and was said to be the cavalry of General Torrejon. I had noticed that our arrieros had changed their appearance and demeanor very materially within the past two or three days. From some knowledge of their language, I was enabled to make myself understood by them and could gather the purport of what they said, and was on pleasant terms with the chief of those attached to our battalion. At first he was cheerful and communicative, but since our halt at Marin was taciturn and gloomy. I was near him when he caught a glimpse of his countrymen, the cavalry of Torrejon, and upon my soul I pitied him. He was very much alarmed; and what could I say to him by way of encouragement? I was not surprised to hear during the day that a number of these muleteers had made an effort to escape by leaving their mules and cargoes to shift for themselves and taking to the chaparral; but Colonel Kinney, of Corpus Christi, who was the contractor, . . . headed them off and brought them back."

48. The reference here is to the Texans' Mier expedition of 1842. In Nov. 1842, ordered by President Sam Houston, a force of about 750 men left San Antonio with Gen. Alexander Somervell as their commander on an incursion across the Rio Grande into Mexico. The next month part of this raiding party stayed on in Mexico, elected William S. Fisher leader, then fought and finally surrendered to a superior Mexican force at Mier. When the prisoners were being marched to Mexico City some of them escaped, but they were recaptured within a week. One-tenth of them were executed and others were taken to Perote Fortress. Some died there, others escaped, and the last of them were released in 1844. Thomas J. Green, one of the officers wrote an account in his journal of this expedition.

49. As the Army moved toward Monterey, Henderson's brigade, beginning Sept. 18, formed the advance of the Army. See Taylor's Orders No. 120, Sept. 18, 1846.

50. Major [Luther] Giddings, 1st Ohio Volunteers Camp near Monterey, Mexico, to "Messrs. Comly," publishers of the Dayton (Ohio) *Journal*, cited in *Niles' National Register*, Vol. 71 (Nov. 14, 1846), p. 167.

51. Capt. William S. Henry of New York was Bvt. 2d Lt., 3d Inf., July 1, 1835 and Capt., May 18, 1846. He won a brevet at Monterey.

52. Capt. Electus Backus, 1st Inf., was Bvt. Maj. after Monterey. He died June 7, 1862.

53. Taylor ordered (General Orders No. 111, Aug. 31, 1846) the Baltimore Battalion to be brigaded with the 1st Inf. After Monterey, the Battalion became part of General Quitman's volunteer brigade.

54. Lt. Col. John Garland, 4th Inf., won two brevets in the Mexican War; he was Bvt. Brig. Gen. after Contreras and Churubusco.

55. Capt. William George Williams, Topographical Engineers, died of wounds received at Monterey.

56. Maj. Henry L. Kinney was Division Quartermaster with the Texas Volunteers but seemed to be omnipresent. It was on his land that Taylor established his camp at Corpus Christi in 1845. When the mule train moved from Camargo to Monterey, Kinney was in charge of it. In assigning to Kinney "the general charge of the conductors of the mule supply train," Taylor's Orders No. 103 provided that Kinney would receive his orders only from the Commanding General and the Quartermaster Department. Kinney also was guide, beef contractor, and aide to both Taylor and Scott in their campaigns, and even acquired some of the Army's surplus equipment at the end of the war.

57. Maj. William W. Lear, 3d Inf., died Oct. 31, 1846 from wounds received at the Battle of Monterey.

58. Capt. Joseph Hatch Lamotte, was 1st Lt., 1st Inf., July 11, 1833, and Capt. July 7, 1838. He was Bvt. Maj. after Monterey.

59. Capt. John M. Scott, 1st Inf., was Bvt. Maj., for Monterey.

60. There was a controversy over the credit due for the taking of the tannery involving the claims presented by Backus on behalf of himself and his regulars and rival claims by Brig. Gen.

Quitman's volunteer brigade. Among the volunteers also, there was a dispute between Col. William B. Campbell, 1st Tennessee Volunteers, and Col. Jefferson Davis of the Mississippi Rifles over the part played by their respective regiments in the action. For this dispute, see Col. William B. Campbell, Camp near Monterey, to Allen A. Hall, Nashville, Sept. 25, 1846, cited in Nashville Whig, Oct. 1846; Bailie Peyton, New Orleans, to Col. William B. Campbell, Nov. 5, 1846; Id. to Jefferson Davis, Nov. 3 1846 (copy); Jefferson Davis to Bailie Peyton, Nov. 1, 1846 (copy), all in David Campbell Papers, Duke.

61. Electus Backus Journal MS, Burton.

62. Brig. Gen. John Anthony Quitman was Brig. Gen. of Volunteers on July 1, 1846; Bvt. Maj. Gen. after Monterey, and Maj. Gen. on Apr. 14, 1847. He died July 17, 1858.

63. Lt. Col. Mirabeau B. Lamar was Inspector General of the Texas Volunteers.

64. W[illiam] S[eaton] Henry, Campaign Sketches of the War With Mexico (New York: Harper and Brothers, 1847), pp. 206-209.

65. Capt. Charles Ferguson Smith, was 2d Lt. 2d Art., July 1, 1825; Instructor of Infantry Tactics at West Point, 1829-1831; Commandant of Cadets, 1838-1842; Capt., 2d Art., July 7, 1838. He received three brevets for his services in the Mexican War—for Palo Alto and Resaca de la Palma, Monterey, and Contreras and Churubusco. During the Civil War he was Maj. Gen. of Volunteers (Union army), Mar. 21, 1862, and died Apr. 25, 1862.

66. Capt. John Benjamin Scott, 4th Art., was Bvt. Maj. for Palo Alto and Resaca de la Palma.

67. Capt. Henry McKavett, 8th Inf.

68. Lt. William Whann Mackall, 1st Art., was regimental adjutant, 1840-1841, and Capt., Aug. 20, 1847. From Dec. 29, 1846 he was Bvt. Capt. and Asst. Adj. Gen. to Bvt. Maj. Gen. Worth. During the Mexican War he won two brevets—for Monterey and for Contreras and Churubusco.

69. Lt. George Washington Ayers, 1st Lt., 3d Art., Dec. 20, 1845, Bvt. Capt. for Monterey, and killed at the Battle of Molino del Rey, Sept. 8, 1847.

70. Capt. John Rogers Vinton, 3d Art. For more on Capt. Vinton, see Chapter IV.

71. Lt. John Frederick Roland, 2d Art., was Capt. on Mar. 3, 1847. He won two brevets—for Palo Alto and Resaca de la Palma, and Monterey.

72. Maj. John Munroe, born in Scotland, was Capt., 4th Art., Mar. 2, 1825; Maj., 2d Art., Aug. 18, 1846, and won brevets for Monterey and Buena Vista. He died Apr. 28, 1861.

73. Lt. Edmund Bradford, "Plaza Monterrey, Mexico," to Miss Caroline Bradford, Philadelphia, Sept. 27, 1846, Bradford Papers, Western Americana MSS, Beinecke. Bradford was 1st Lt., 4th Art. During the Civil War he was Maj. and Asst. Inspector General, Conferedate States Army.

74. "Touching Incidents," Louisville Journal cited in Niles' National Register, Vol. 71 (Dec. 19, 1846), p. 242.

75. Having returned to Mexico from exile, Santa Anna, on September 17, 1846 was appointed Commander-in-Chief of "The Liberating Army" and urged forward troops to prepare for Taylor's army. On Sept. 28, after praying at the Guadalupe shrine, Santa Anna himself set out on the campaign.

76. "Letter from General Taylor," Maj. Gen. Z[achary] Taylor, Monterey, to [n.n.], Nov. 9, 1846, New York Express cited in Boston Advertiser, Jan. 25, 1847.

77. For the orders to Butler, see Taylor's General Orders No. 159 (Dec. 12, 1846).

78. Col. John J. Hardin, 1st Regiment of Illinois Volunteers, was killed at the Battle of Buena Vista.

79. Col. William H. Bissell, 2d Regiment of Illinois Volunteers.

80. Col. Humphrey Marshall, see Chapter I for Marshall and his regiment.

81. Capt. John Macrae Washington, 4th Art., was Maj., 3d Art., Feb. 16, 1847, and Bvt. Lt. Col. after Buena Vista.

82. Maj. Benjamin L. E. Bonneville, born in France, was a West Point graduate and Maj., 6th Inf. He won a brevet for Contreras and Churubusco.

83. Col. William Selby Harney, 2d Drags., was Bvt. Brig. Gen. for Cerro Gordo.

84. Col. Sylvester Churchill of Vermont was Maj., 3d Art., Apr. 6, 1835, and Col. and Inspector General, June 25, 1841. He was Bvt. Brig. Gen. after Buena Vista.

85. Lt. Nathaniel Niles, correspondent of the Boston *Evening Post*, "Camp at Buena Vista, Coahuila, Mexico," to [n.n.], Boston *Evening Post* cited in *Niles' National Register*, Vol. 72 (May 8, 1847), p. 156.

86. Capt. Thomas West Sherman, 3d Art.; he was Bvt. Maj. after Buena Vista.

87. Jonathan W. Buhoup, *Narrative of the Central Division or Army of Chihuahua, Commanded by Brigadier General Wool* . . . (Pittsburgh: M. P. Morse, 1847), pp. 111-114. Buhoup was in the Regiment of Arkansas Mounted Volunteers.

88. "Gen. Taylor and [the] Army," Exeter [New Hampshire] *News-Letter*, May 3, 1847. Citing a letter from an officer of the Ohio volunteers to the editor of the Cincinnati *Chronicle*.

89. Lt. Col. (later Col.) William Weatherford succeeded Col. John J. Hardin (killed at Buena Vista) as commander of the 1st Regiment of Illinois Volunteers.

90. Commanded by Col. William H. Bissell.

91. Brig. Gen. Joseph Lane.

92. Capt. Enoch Steen, 1st Drags., was Bvt. Maj. after Buena Vista.

93. Lt. Col. John Selden Roane, Regiment of Arkansas Mounted Volunteers, became Col. of that regiment after Col. Archibald Yell was killed at Buena Vista. Roane was a Brig. Gen. in the Confederate States Army during the Civil War.

94. Maj. Willis A. Gorman 3d Regiment of Indiana Volunteers, became Col. of the 4th Regiment of Indiana Volunteers, and was wounded at Buena Vista. He was Brig. Gen. of Volunteers (Union Army) in the Civil War.

95. Lt. John Paul Jones O'Brien, 2d Lt., 4th Art., on July 1, 1836; 1st Lt., July 7, 1838; he was Capt. and Asst. Quartermaster, Jan. 18, 1847-May 16, 1849. For his services at Buena Vista he was brevetted Maj.

96. Gen. Juan José Miñon.

97. Maj. Xerxes F. Trail.

98. Col. William A. Bowles, 2d Regiment of Indiana Volunteers.

99. Capt. Albert Pike, Regiment of Arkansas Mounted Volunteers; he was a Brig. Gen. in the Confederate Army during the Civil War.

100. Lt. John Fulton Reynolds, 3d Art., was Bvt. Capt. after Monterey and Bvt. Maj. for Buena Vista. During the Civil War he was a Maj. Gen. of Volunteers (Union Army) and was killed July 1, 1863 at the Battle of Gettysburg.

101. Brig. Gen. John E. Wool, Headquarters, Camp Taylor, Agua Nueva "twenty miles south of Saltillo," to Maj. W. W. [S.] Bliss, Asst. Adj. Gen., Mar. 4, 1847, *Senate Executive Documents*, No. 1, 30 Cong., 1 Sess., pp. 145-149.

102. [G. N. Allen], *Mexican Treacheries and Cruelties; Incidents and Sufferings in the Mexican War* . . . (Boston and New York: [no. pub.], 1847), p. 4.

NOTES TO CHAPTER III

1. George Bancroft, United States Navy Department, Washington, to Commander John D. Sloat, Commanding United States naval forces in the Pacific, June 24, 1845, House of Representatives. Exec. Doc., No. 60, 30 Cong., 1 Sess., p. 231. Sloat became Commodore in 1862.

2. Roger Jones began his career as a 2d Lt., Marine Corps, Jan. 26, 1809; he was Adj. Gen. in 1818 and Brig. Gen. in 1832. He was Bvt. Maj. Gen. in 1848 for his services in the Mexican War, and died July 15, 1852.

3. Richard Bland Lee of Virginia graduated from West Point and was 3d Lt., 3d Art., June 1821, a Capt. in 1836, and transferred to the Commissary Dept. in 1838. He was Maj. and Commissary of Subsistence in 1841. He was Commissary of Subsistence at St Louis in 1845 and remained in that post throughout the Mexican War. During the Civil War he was a Col. in the Confederate States Army. He died in 1875.

4. Josiah Gregg, *The Commerce of the Prairies*, first published in 1844, has been republished, unabridged, with introduction by Archibald Hanna. (Lippincott: [1962]), 2 vols.

5. Maj. R[ichard] B[land] Lee, C[ommissary] of S[ubsistence], St. Louis, to Brig. Gen. [Roger] Jones, Adjutant General [Washington, D.C.], Sept. 4, 1845, Letters Received, Records of U.S. Army Commands, Dept. of the West, RG 98, Nat. Arch.

6. Bvt. Brig Gen. George Gibson had been Commissary General of Subsistence since 1818. For further discussion of Gibson's part in the Mexican War, see Chapter VIII.

7. Maj. R. B. Lee, Commissary of Subsistence, St. Louis, to [Bvt.] Brig. Gen. George Gibson, Commissary General of Subsistence, Washington, D.C., Dec. 9, 1846, Letters Received, Office of the Commissary General of Subsistence, RG 192, Nat. Arch. Lee wrote: "The report was written upon the spur of the occasion and so hastily that I did not keep a copy [of] the original draft . . . this accounts for my failure to furnish you with a copy, as I had none to send."

8. Col. Stephen Watts Kearny was Col., 1st Drags., July 4, 1836 and Brig. Gen., June 30, 1846. He was brevetted Maj. Gen. for meritorious conduct in the New Mexico—California campaign of 1846-1847.

9. Brig. Gen. Roger Jones, Adjutant General, Washington, D.C., to Maj. R[ichard] B[land] Lee, St. Louis, May 14, 1846, Letters Received, Records of Army Commands, Dept. of the West, RG 98, Nat. Arch.

10. 1st Regiment of Dragoons.

11. Kearny assembled about 1,660 troops at Ft. Leavenworth. Included were: Kearny's 1st Dragoons, the 1st Regiment of Missouri Mounted Volunteers (1,860 men with Alexander W. Doniphan as Col.), Battery A of Artillery from St. Louis, and another company under Capt. Woldemar Fischer—these formed a battalion commanded by Maj. Meriwether L. Clark. In addition Kearny had two companies of volunteer infantry, the Laclede Rangers (Mounted), fifty Delaware and Shawnee Indians, and, on orders from Washington, a Catholic Priest who spoke Spanish.

12. "Important News From Washington," St. Louis *Missouri Republican*, May 22, 1846.

13. Bvt. Capt. John Charles Frémont left St. Louis in Apr. 1845, with sixty men on an expedition to California and Oregon. By December 1845, he was encamped near Sutter's Fort, California. His passage to California was not disturbed by conflicts with the Indians.

14. John S. Tutt, Fort Leavenworth, to J[ames] A. Tutt, May 27, 1846, James A. Tutt Papers, Duke.

15. [James K. Polk, draft of instructions], to Col. S[tephen] W. Kearny [ca. June 2, 1846], William Larned Marcy Papers, DLC.

16. Maj. Thomas Swords, was a quartermaster. On May 30, 1848 he was Bvt. Lt. Col. for meritorious service while serving in the enemy's country.

17. Lt. Rufus Ingalls, 1st Drags., was Capt. and Asst. Q.M. on Jan. 12, 1848. He was brevetted for the conflicts at Embudo and Taos. During the Civil War he was Brig. Gen. of Volunteers (Union Army).

18. Lt. Jeremy F. Gilmer, "Santa Fe Road, Cow Creek, 250 miles from Independence, Mo." to Capt. George L. Welcker, Corps of Engineers, Washington, D.C., July 23, 1846, Lenoir Family Papers, Group II, So. Hist. Col., NCa. Lt. Gilmer graduated fourth in his class at West Point and was 2d Lt., Engineers, July 1, 1839; 1st Lt., Dec. 29, 1845, and during the Mexican War supervised the construction of Ft. Marcy at Santa Fe. From 1861 to 1865 he was a Maj. Gen. in the Conferedate States Army.

19. The camp he left was near Ojo de Vernal (Bernal); it was a little over eight hundred miles from Fort Leavenworth.

20. San Miguel was near the right bank of the Pecos River, about twenty miles southwest of Las Vegas, and about one-third of the way from Las Vegas to Santa Fe.

21. Capt. Dámaso Salazar. But the leader who enlisted a force of about one thousand New Mexico militia and prepared to oppose Kearny's force at Apache Pass was Capt. Antonio Manuel Chavez.

22. Gen. Manuel Armijo was "Governor" of New Mexico from Jan. 1824 to Aug. 1846.

Technically New Mexico had no governor although the administrator, who was under direct orders from Chihuahua, kept the title.

23. Capt. Luis Salazar. He was later released.

24. Maj. Meriwether Lewis Clark was appointed to the command of the battalion of Missouri Artillery on July 1, 1846. He graduated from West Point and was Bvt. 2d Lt., 6th Inf., July 1, 1830, but resigned in 1833. During the Civil War he was Col. and Aide-de-Camp in the Confederate States Army.

25. "Diary of an Officer of the 'Army of the West,'" *Niles' National Register*, Vol. 71 (Oct. 10, 1846), pp. 91-92.

26. Rio Vigita, thirty miles south of Santa Fe.

27. Col. Alexander W. Doniphan and the First Regiment of Missouri Mounted Volunteers.

28. Glorietta Pass.

29. Lt. Col. Charles Frederick Ruff, 1st Missouri Mounted Volunteers, was 1st Lt., 1st Drags., in July 1838, but resigned on Dec. 31, 1842. He was Capt., Mounted Rifles, July 7, 1846, and Bvt. Maj., Aug. 1, 1847, for San Juan de los Llanos.

30. Capt. Waldemar Fischer, Clark's Battalion of Missouri Artillery.

31. [Pvt. Andrew T. McClure?], Company "E," 1st Regiment of Missouri Mounted Volunteers, Rio Vigita, to his wife, Aug. 22, 1846, Getty Papers, New Mexico State Records Center and Archives, Santa Fe, New Mexico.

32. The officer was Lt. Richard S. Elliott, 1st Lt., Clark's Battalion, 1st Missouri Volunteers. He wrote under the nom de plume "John Brown" for the St. Louis *Reveille*.

33. Lucius Falkland Thruston, born in Kentucky, had been in New Mexico since 1827. Kearny appointed him Prefect at Santa Fe after the American occupation began there. He was a citizen of Mexico and knew well the Spanish language and the people of the region.

34. Col. Samuel C. Owens, a trader from Independence, Jackson County, Missouri. He had joined Kearny in July at Bent's Fort.

35. Maj. Edwin Vose Sumner was 2d Lt., 2d Inf., Mar. 3, 1819; Capt. 1st Drags., Mar. 4, 1833; Maj., 2d Drags., June 30, 1846, and Lt. Col. 1st Drags., July 13, 1848. He won two brevets in the Mexican War—for Cerro Gordo and Molino del Rey. During the Civil War he was Maj. Gen. of Vols. and Bvt. Maj. Gen. for the Battle of Fair Oaks. He died Mar. 21, 1863.

36. Thomas Fitzpatrick, one of the most famous of the mountain men and guides in that era. He had been Fremont's guide across the plains in 1845 and had been Kearny's guide also in 1845 before he became guide to the Santa Fe expedition. Later he carried despatches from Kearny and Stockton to Washington.

37. [Lt. Richard S. Elliott] "John Brown," "Capture of Santa Fe!" Correspondence of the St. Louis *Reveille*, Aug. 18, 1846, St. Louis *Reveille*, Sept. 28, 1846.

38. "Our Army in New Mexico," correspondence dated at Galisteo, New Mexico, Aug. 23, 1846, *ibid.*

39. M. L. Baker, Santa Fe, to Mrs. Hugh Martin, New York City, Sept. 13, 1846, Western Americana MSS, Beinecke.

40. General Manuel Armijo.

41. Tomé was served in 1846 by a priest from Valencia, six miles north of there. At the time Kearny visited Tomé it probably was Father José de Jesus Cabeza de Baca.

42. "General Kearney's Expedition to Tonie [*sic*, Tomé]," letter from a Captain in Kearny's force, dated at Santa Fe, Sept. 13, 1846, in *Niles' National Register*, Vol. 71 (Nov. 7, 1846), p. 145. Kearny took with him on this trip down the Rio Grande his personal staff, Capt. Burgwin's Dragoons, five hundred volunteers under Lt. Col. Ruff, one hundred fifty artillerists of Maj. Clark's battalion, and four howitzers under Lt. Davidson. See Dwight L. Clarke, ed., *The Original Journals of Henry Smith Turner* (Norman: Univ. of Okla. Press, 1966, p. 75. Capt. Henry Smith Turner, 1st Drags., was one of those who accompanied Kearny and may have been the author of this letter, although there is nothing in his diary for these dates to indicate that he wrote it.

43. Lt. J[eremy] F. Gilmer, Corps of Engineers, Santa Fe, to Capt. [George L.] Welcker, Washington, D.C., Nov. 6, 1846, Lenoir Family Papers, Group II, So. Hist. Col., NCa.

44. John Henry K. Burgwin was Capt., 1st Drags., and mortally wounded at Taos Pueblo, Feb. 4, 1847; he died three days later.

45. Correspondence of St. Louis *Missouri Republican*, dated at Santa Fe, Dec. 5, 1846, cited in *Niles' National Register*, Vol. 72 (Mar. 6, 1847), p. 8.

46. Among those involved were Manuel Chavez, Nicolas Pino, Tomás Baca, Diego Archuleta, and the Curate of Taos, Antonio José Martinez. Col. Price, on discovering the plot, placed Chavez and Pino under arrest; the others fled. After a trial, Chavez and Pino (defended by Capt. Angney of Price's staff) were acquitted of treason charges, it being argued that being Mexican citizens they could not be convicted of treason against the United States.

47. Kearny appointed Charles Bent to be Governor of New Mexico.

48. Maj. Benjamin B. Edmonson, 2d Regiment of Missouri Volunteers.

49. Ceran St. Vrain (1798-1870), explorer and fur trader, born near St. Louis, joined with Charles Bent in 1830 to form the mercantile house of Bent and St. Vrain, later Bent, St. Vrain and Co.

50. Capt. William B. Angney, Independent Company of Missouri Volunteers.

51. Capt. Benjamin F. White, 2d Regiment of Missouri Volunteers.

52. Capt. Samuel H. McMillan, 2d Missouri Volunteer Regiment.

53. Capt. Thomas Barber, 2d Missouri Volunteer Regiment.

54. Capt. William Y. Slack, 2d Missouri Volunteer Regiment.

55. Capt. William C. Halley, 2d Missouri Volunteer Regiment.

56. Lt. Elias W. Boone, 1st Lt., 2d Missouri Volunteer Regiment.

57. Lt. Clarendon J. L. Wilson, 2d Lt., 1st Drags. He was brevetted for the conflicts at Embudo and Taos, and died in Albuquerque, Feb. 21, 1853.

58. Embudo is on the Rio Grande River about twenty-eight miles southwest of Taos.

59. Lt. Joseph McElvain, 2d Lt., 1st Drags., accidentally killed at Albuquerque, July 12, 1847.

60. Lt. Oliver Hazard Perry Taylor graduated from West Point and was Bvt. 2d Lt., 1st Drags., July 1, 1846; 2d Lt., Feb. 1847. He was brevetted for Embudo and Taos, and received a second brevet for Santa Cruz de Rosales.

61. Trampas is twenty-five miles south and slightly west of Taos.

62. Chamisal is about three miles northeast of Trampas.

63. Lt. Alexander Brydie Dyer was 2d Lt., 3d Art., July 1, 1837; 2d Lt., Ord., July 9, 1838, and 1st Lt., Mar. 3, 1847. He won a brevet for Santa Cruz de Rosales.

64. Lt. Francis Hassendeubel, 2d Lt., Clark's Battalion, Missouri Volunteers.

65. Lt. William B. Royall, 1st Lt., 2d Regiment Missouri Volunteers.

66. Lt. George E. Lackland, 2d Lt., 2d Regiment Missouri Volunteers, died Feb. 16, 1847.

67. Col. Sterling Price, commanding the [United States] Army in New Mexico, to [Brig. Gen. Roger Jones] Adj. Gen., Washington, D.C., Feb. 15, 1847, Senate Exec. Doc., No. 1, 30 Cong., 1 Sess., pp. 520-525.

68. "From Santa Fe," correspondence of the St. Louis *New Era* dated Oct. 10, 1847, cited in Boston *Advertiser*, Dec. 2, 1847.

69. "From Santa Fe and California," St. Louis *Missouri Republican*, Sept. 7, 1847.

70. *Ibid.*, citing Santa Fe correspondence.

71. Capt. Thomas B. Hudson, Clark's Battalion of Missouri Volunteers.

72. Capt. Richard H. Weightman, Clark's Battalion of Missouri Volunteers.

73. Capt. Monroe M. Parsons, 1st Missouri Mounted Volunteers.

74. Lt. Samuel M. Sprowl, 2d Lt., 2d Missouri Volunteers.

75. William H. Richardson, *Journal of William H. Richardson, A Private Soldier in Col. Doniphan's Command* (Baltimore: Printed by J. Robinson, 1847), pp. 60-63. William H. Richardson was a private in Capt. Thomas B. Hudson's Company, Clark's Battalion, Missouri Volunteers.

76. Susan Shelby Magoffin, *Down the Santa Fe Trail. The Diary of Susan Shelby Magoffin, 1846-1847*, ed., Stella M. Drum (New Haven: Yale University Press, 1926), pp. 228-229. Diary entry of May 23, 1847.

77. John Collins was a Missouri trader who had undertaken with a party of twelve men to get through to Brig. Gen. Wool at Saltillo, and returned to Chihuahua on Apr. 23.

78. Capt. John W. Reid, 1st Regiment of Missouri Mounted Volunteers.

79. Lt. Col. David D. Mitchell, 2nd Regiment of Missouri Volunteers.

80. A[dolphus] Wislizenus, *Memoir of a Tour to Northern Mexico* (Washington: Tippin & Streeper, Printers, 1848), pp. 62, 70-72, 74. This was published as Senate Miscellaneous Document No. 26, 30 Cong., 1 Sess.

81. [untitled article], Matamoros *American Flag*, June 7, 1847.

82. General Angel Trias.

83. Lt. John Love, 1st Drags., was Bvt. Capt. for the Battle of Santa Cruz de Rosales.

84. Lt. A[lexander] B[rydie] Dyer, Chihuahua, to Maj. J[ubal] A. Early, Virginia Regiment of Volunteers, Saltillo, Apr. 5, 1848, Jubal Anderson Early Papers, DLC. Trias surrendered at Santa Cruz de Rosales with forty-two of his officers.

85. Gillespie crossed Mexico to Mazatlán pretending to be a merchant; he arrived in Monterey on Apr. 17, 1846.

86. General José Castro.

87. Capt. John B. Montgomery.

88. General Mariano Guadalupe Vallejo.

89. Capt. John Grigsbey, California Volunteers.

90. Bvt. Capt. John C. Frémont, Mission of Carmel, Alta California, to Thomas Hart Benton, Washington, D.C., July 25, 1846, *Niles' National Register*, Vol. 71 (Nov. 21, 1846), p. 191.

91. Lt. MacRae came to California as a despatch bearer; he later was ordered to report for duty on the *Erie*, once a sloop-of-war and after that a Store Barque. This vessel, mounting four 12-pounders, had a crew of fifty men; she was converted into a cruiser, so Lt. MacRae found that he was 1st Lt. on a fighting ship after all. He wrote his letter discussing the situation in California after the *Erie* had put to sea.

92. Lt. Archibald MacRae, U.S. Ship *Erie* at sea, to his brother [John C. Macrae?], Oct. 25, 1845 [sic, 1846], Hugh Macrae Papers, Duke.

93. George Bancroft, United States Navy Department, Washington, to Commander John D. Sloat, commanding U.S. Naval Forces in the Pacific, May 15, 1846, House of Representatives Exec. Doc., No. 60, 30 Cong., 1 Sess., pp. 235-236.

94. William Mervine commanded the sloop-of-war *Cyane* in 1845.

95. Commander John D. Sloat, Ship *Levant* at sea, to George Bancroft, Secretary of the Navy, Washington, D.C., July 31, 1846, House of Representatives Exec. Doc., No. 60, 30 Cong., 1st Sess., pp. 258-259.

96. Lt. Archibald MacRae, U.S. Ship *Erie* at sea, to his brother [John C. MacRae?], Oct. 25, 1845 [sic, 1846] Hugh MacRae Papers, Duke.

97. Commander Samuel F. Dupont.

98. Governor Pio Pico.

99. Thomas O. Larkin.

100. Commodore Robert F. Stockton, Ciudad de los Angeles, to George Bancroft, Washington, D.C., Aug. 28, 1846, House of Representatives Exec. Doc., No. 60, 30 Cong., 1 Sess., pp. 265-266.

101. See, John McHenry Hollingsworth, *The Journal of Lieutenant John McHenry Hollingsworth of the First New York Volunteers (Stevenson's Regiment), September 1846-August 1849* (San Francisco: California Historical Society, 1923), pp. 2-6. More properly the 7th New York Regiment.

102. Capt. Benjamin D. Moore, 1st Drags., was killed Dec. 6, 1846 at the Battle of San Pasqual.

103. Capt. Archibald Gillespie, earlier a bearer of despatches, was Maj., California Volunteers and Bvt. Maj. for the Battle of San Pasqual. He brought about thirty-eight men with him from San Diego.

104. Brig. Gen. S[tephen] W[atts] Kearny, San Diego, to Brig. Gen. Roger Jones, Adj. Gen.,

Washington, D.C., Dec. 12, 1846, cited in *Niles' National Register*, Vol. 72 (May 15, 1847), p. 170.

105. John Mix Stanley, an artist, had been added to Kearny's staff as a draughtsman at Santa Fe, just before Kearny's expedition left for California.

106. Acting Lt. Edward F. Beale, the frigate *Congress*.

107. Lt. Thomas C. Hammond, 2d Lt., 1st Drags., killed at San Pasqual.

108. The force was about eighty men, commanded by Andrés Pico, brother of the California Governor.

109. Capt. Abraham Robinson Johnston, 1st Drags.

110. "General Kearny," letter of John M. Stanley, dated at San Diego, Jan. 19, 1847, cited in St. Louis *Reveille*, May 10, 1847.

111. Frémont did move southward from Monterey with four hundred men and was in the San Fernando Valley, just north of Los Angeles, on Jan. 11, 1847.

112. Stockton was commander-in-chief of this expedition, but Kearny was commander of the troops. The force was composed of sailors from the *Congress*, *Savannah*, *Portsmouth*, and *Cyane*; there were sixty men from Kearny's 1st Dragoons, and sixty mounted riflemen commanded by Capt. Gillespie.

113. General José Maria Flores.

114. Bvt. Maj. W[illiam] H. Emory, *Notes of a Military Reconnaissance from Fort Leavenworth, in Missouri, to San Diego in California*, Senate Exec. Doc., No. 7, 30 Cong., 1 Sess., pp. 118-122. Emory was 1st Lt., Top. Engineers, on July 7, 1838. He was Bvt. Capt. for the Battle of San Pasqual, and Bvt. Maj. for San Gabriel and the Plains of Mesa. During the Civil War he was Brig. Gen. of Volunteers and Maj. Gen. of Volunteers, Union Army.

NOTES TO CHAPTER IV

1. Correspondence of the New Orleans *Picayune* cited in *Niles' National Register*, Vol. 71 (Nov. 14, 1846), pp. 164-165.

2. Jesup had been Q. M. Gen. since May 8, 1818. For further discussion of Jesup and his career, see Chapter VIII. Jesup and Taylor had quarreled over Taylor's charges that the Quartermaster Department had not supported him efficiently in his Rio Grande-Northern Mexico campaign.

3. Bvt. Maj. Gen. Th[omas] S. Jesup, "Brassos San Iago," to Col. Henry Stanton, Asst Q. M. Gen., Washington, D.C., Dec. 28, 1846, Thomas Sidney Jesup Papers, DLC.

4. Bvt. Maj. Gen. John A. Quitman, "Camp Allen near Monterey," to Robert J. Walker [Secretary of the Treasury, Washington, D.C.], Nov. 18, 1846, Western Americana MSS, Beinecke.

5. "Letter from General Taylor," Maj. Gen. Z[achary] Taylor, Monterey, to [n.n.], Nov. 9, 1846, New York *Express* cited in Boston *Advertiser*, Jan. 25, 1847.

6. Conner was Commander in Chief of the Home Squadron, 1846-1847; he was superseded by Commodore Matthew C. Perry on Mar. 21, 1847.

7. As late as Sept. 1846, however, Secretary of War Marcy seriously considered operations inland from Tampico. See William L. Marcy, War Department, Washington, to Gen. Zachary Taylor, Sept. 1, 1846, Western Americana MSS, Beinecke. Marcy wrote: "It is intended to make a descent upon the Gulph coast of Mexico as soon as the season shall have so far advanced as to render it safe in regard to the health of our troops. Our attention is turned to Tampico as one of the places for the attack. It may be important to take that place and hold possession of it and the surrounding country with reference to your line of operations. Though our information is not so full and accurate as we desire in relation to the interior of the country in the vicinity of Tampico yet it is such as induces us to believe that this will be an important position to be occupied to facilitate the future prosecution of the war."

8. Arthur Campbell, Washington to [David Campbell, "Montcalm," Abingdon, Virginia], Nov[ember] 15, 1846, David Campbell Papers, Duke.

9. Lt. William T. Withers was 2d Lt., 2d Kentucky Regiment of Volunteers.

10. Lt. William T. Withers, Headquarters 1st Div., Monterey, to Dr. Montgomery W. Boyd, Nov. 10, 1846, Western Americana MSS, Beinecke.

11. It was with great reluctance that Marcy and Polk came to this conclusion. Even when Scott was about ready to leave on his expedition to the Gulf, Marcy opposed the idea of any move inland from Vera Cruz into the Valley of Mexico.

12. Winfield Scott, born near Petersburg, Va., in 1786, was a Capt. Light Art., May 3, 1808; Lt. Col., 2d Art., July 6, 1812; Col., Mar. 12, 1813; Brig. Gen., Mar. 9, 1814, and Maj. Gen., June 25, 1841. From July 5, 1841 to Nov. 1, 1861, he was General-in-Chief. His brevets were Bvt. Maj. Gen. for Chippewa and Niagara in the War of 1812, and Bvt. Lt. Gen. for his services in the Mexican War. In Washington, Scott had greater political prestige than any other military man of his day. In 1839 he had received thirty-nine votes on a rollcall at the Whig presidential convention. Six feet four inches tall and of massive build, he was an impressive figure. Strength of character and personal charm were, however, to some extent balanced by a certain arrogance, verboseness, and passion for petty details. In the early stages of the war, Scott quarreled with Polk and Marcy over administrative and strategic matters, and political considerations doubtless created dissensions also, with the result that Scott, complaining that he would be subjected to "fire in the rear" did not take the field in 1846. It was Marcy who finally convinced Polk that Scott should lead the Vera Cruz expedition of 1847. Taylor was rapidly emerging as a leading Whig candidate for the presidency in 1848, and was out of favor; an attempt to make Thomas Hart Benton, a leading Democrat, general-in-chief had failed in Congress; none of the Democratic field commanders seemed to be the right man, and although Scott was a powerful Whig he did not have the popularity of Taylor, and he was a capable commander. Scott, however, from the beginning of the campaign, complained that he did not receive unstinted support from the Polk administration.

13. Maj. Gen. Winfield Scott, Headquarters of the Army, New Orleans, to Commodore D[avid] Conner, U.S. Navy, commanding blockading squadron off the coast of Mexico, Dec. 23, 1846, House of Representatives, Exec. Doc., No. 60, 30 Cong., 1 Sess., pp. 842-843.

14. Maj. Gen. Robert Patterson was Capt., 32d Inf. during the War of 1812. He returned to military service as Maj. Gen. of Volunteers, July 7, 1846. Late in Dec. 1846, about 1,500 volunteers under his command (two regiments of Illinois infantry and a Tennessee cavalry regiment), marched from Matamoros to Victoria, and from there to Tampico, where Patterson was for a time in command, after it had been taken by the Navy and held temporarily by small detachments of regulars. In the Scott expedition against Vera Cruz he commanded the Volunteer Division.

15. Brig. Gen. James Shields was Brig. Gen. of Volunteers on July 1, 1846. He was severely wounded at Cerro Gordo. During the Civil War he was Brig. Gen. of Volunteers (Union Army).

16. Part of the Regiment of Louisiana Volunteers, Col. Louis G. DeRussy commanding, was shipwrecked on the coast of Mexico opposite Lobos Island on Feb. 6, 1847. After being threatened with capture by the Mexicans, the regiment finally made its ways to Tampico to rejoin Scott's army.

17. Col. William Gates was Col., 3d Art. on Oct. 13, 1845. He was left in command at Tampico and remained there for the duration of the war.

18. Lumsden, one of the editors of the New Orleans *Picayune*, writing from Tampico, Feb. 20, 1847, cited in "War With Mexico," *Niles' National Register*, Vol. 72 (Mar. 20, 1847,) pp. 35-36.

19. For the misfortunes of this regiment on its way to war, see Chapter I.

20. Capt. Francis Taylor commanded Company K, 1st Art.

21. Anton Lizardo was a deep harbor about fourteen miles southeast of Vera Cruz and about two hundred miles from Lobos Island.

22. Capt. John L. Saunders.

23. Maj. Gen. Winfield Scott, Headquarters of the Army, Ship *Massachusetts*, off Lobos, to W[illiam] L. Marcy, Secretary of War [Washington, D.C.], February 28, 1847, House of Representatives, Exec. Doc., No. 60, 30 Cong., 1 Sess., pp. 896-898.

24. Correspondence of Philadelphia *North American*, dated at Island of Lobos, Gulf of Mexico, Feb. 7, 1847, *Niles' National Register*, Vol. 72 (Mar. 13, 1847), pp. 21-22.

25. Capt. John R. Vinton of Rhode Island had a long and honorable career in the regular Army. He graduated from West Point and was 3d Lt., Corps of Artillery in July, 1817; 2d Lt. in Oct. 1817, transferred to the 4th Art. in 1821, and to the 3d Art. later that year. He was Capt. on Dec. 28, 1835. After Monterey he was Bvt. Maj.

26. Sacrificios Island is a small isle in the Gulf three miles south of Vera Cruz; it was used by the Aztecs for sacrificial rites.

27. Capt. John R. Vinton, Steamer *Massachusetts* off Lobos Island, to his mother, Feb. 27, 1847, John R. Vinton Papers, Duke.

28. Brig. Gen. Persifor F. Smith was Brig. Gen. Louisiana Volunteers, May 15, 1846; Col., Mounted Rifles, May 27, 1846; Bvt. Brig. Gen. after Monterey and Bvt. Maj. Gen. for Contreras and Churubusco. He died May 17, 1858.

29. Electus Backus Journal MS, Burton.

30. Bvt. Maj. George Archibald McCall, 3d Inf., had won distinction in Worth's command during the Florida Indian War. He was Asst. Adj. Gen. with the rank of Bvt. Maj., on July 7, 1846, and Maj., Dec. 26, 1847. He won two brevets early in the war—for Palo Alto and Resaca de la Palma. During the Civil War he was Brig. Gen. of Volunteers in the Union Army.

31. Bvt. Maj. George A. McCall, Steamer *Alabama* off Anton Lizardo to [M-----], Mar. 7, 1847, cited in George Archibald McCall, *Letters From the Frontiers* (Philadelphia: J. B. Lippincott & Co., 1868), pp. 475-476.

32. Capt. Alexander Joseph Swift, Company A, Engineer Corps had been sent to France to study French military engineering practices after the Mexican War began; he returned and became first commander of the newly established Company A, engineer soldiers. He died at New Orleans on Apr. 24, 1847.

33. Lt. George Henry Talcott, 1st Lt., Ord., 1838; Capt. on Mar. 3, 1847, and Maj., Voltigeurs, Apr. 9, 1847—Aug. 28, 1848. He was brevetted after Molino del Rey.

34. Capt. Alvin Edson, at Vera Cruz, commanded three companies of Marines temporarily attached to the 3d Artillery.

35. William G. Temple, "Memoir of the Landing of the United States Troops at Vera Cruz in 1847," in Philip Syng Physick Conner, *The Home Squadron Under Commodore Conner In the War With Mexico* (Philadelphia: [no pub.], 1896), pp. 63-69.

36. See R. R. Pegram, Norfolk, to P. S. P. Conner, Feb. 28, 1884, Philip Syng Physick Conner Papers, Hist. Soc. Pa.

37. This was during the "Pastry War" between France and Mexico. The French blockaded the port of Vera Cruz for seven months; after that Admiral Baudin bombarded the city.

38. Capt. Robert E. Lee, Company A, Engineers, had been chief engineer in Wool's column during the march from San Antonio to Saltillo in 1846. He received three brevets for his services during Scott's campaign of 1847.

39. Lt. Henry Lee Scott of North Carolina was Capt., Feb. 16, 1847. He was General Scott's adjutant and one of his most effective advocates, and received two brevets during the Mexican War. From 1855 to 1861 he was Lt. Col. and Aide-de-Camp to Bvt. Lt. Gen. Scott; May 14, 1861 he was Inspector General and Col., but retired with Scott on Oct. 30, 1861. He died Jan. 6, 1886. For H. L. Scott's defense of General Scott's conduct of the Mexican War, see Henry Lee Scott, New York, to [n.n.], June 10, 1853, 26 pp., Western Americana MSS, Beinecke.

40. Winfield Scott, *Memoirs of Lieut.-General Scott* (New York: Sheldon & Company, 1864), Vol. 2, pp. 421-425. Scott also may have had in mind the results of experiments carried out at Old Point Comfort, which seemed to indicate that the walls of the fortress could withstand shells fired at pointblank range. See Joel R. Poinsett, War Department, Washington, D.C., to [President Martin Van Buren], Dec. 5, 1840, Letters Sent from the Secretary of War to the President, RG 107, Nat. Arch. Poinsett wrote: "It may be proper here to remark that the capture of the castle of St. Juan d'Ullua at Vera Cruz, has led many persons to suppose that stone revetments might be destroyed by shells. This is incorrect. After that event, I caused experiments to be made at Old Point Comfort, by firing, at point blank range against a stone wall erected for

the purpose; and the shells broke against it, making very little impression. . . ." He was referring to the capture of San Juan de Ulloa by the French during the Pastry War.

41. Lt. T[homas] Williams, Headquarters of the Army, Camp Washington, near Vera Cruz, to [John R. Williams], Detroit, Mar. 13, 1847, John R. Williams Papers, Burton.

42. Capt. William Wing Loring of North Carolina and Florida was 2d Lt., Florida Volunteers, June 16 to Aug. 16, 1837 in the Florida Indian War; Capt., Mounted Rifles, May 27, 1846; Maj., Feb. 16, 1847, and Lt. Col., Mar. 15, 1848. He won two brevets in the Mexican War, and during the Civil War was Maj. Gen. in the Confederate States Army.

43. Capt. Stevens T. Mason of Virginia, was Capt., Mounted Rifles, on May 27, 1846. He died, May 15, 1847, of wounds received at the Battle of Cerro Gordo.

44. Bvt. Capt. William Alburtis of Virginia was Bvt. Capt. for gallantry in action during the Florida Indian War (in 1841), and 1st Lt., 2d Inf., on July 1, 1839. He was killed before Vera Cruz on Mar. 11, 1847. See *Journal of Francis Collins, An Artillery Officer in the Mexican War,* ed. Mary Clinton Collins, in *Quarterly Publications of the Historical and Philosophical Society of Ohio,* Vol. 10 (April and July, 1915), pp. 50-51. Collins wrote in his journal: "At the time Captain Alburtis was killed, our division was at a halt, waiting for the removal of some obstructions in front. Availing himself of this oportunity he [Alburtis] had seated himself on a log, and was reading a letter which he had received a short time before from home; while thus engaged a cannon ball took off his head."

45. Capt. Winslow F. Sanderson was Capt., Mounted Rifles, May 27, 1846. He won one brevet in the Mexican War.

46. Capt. John Smith Simonson during the War of 1812 was a Capt. in the New York Volunteers; he was Capt., Mounted Rifles, and Bvt. Maj. for Chapultepec in the Mexican War.

47. Capt. Benjamin Stone Roberts had been 1st Lt. in the 1st Drags., but resigned in 1839; he was 1st Lt., Mounted Rifles on May 27, 1846, and Capt. Feb. 16, 1847. He won two brevets in the Mexican War. During the Civil War he was brevetted for Valverde, New Mexico, where he was Col. of the 5th New Mexico Inf., at Cedar Mountain, and the 2d Battle of Bull Run, Union side.

48. Capt. John Bankhead Magruder, was Capt., 1st Art. He won two brevets in the Mexican War—for Cerro Gordo and Chapultepec, and was Maj. Gen., Confederate States Army, during the Civil War.

49. Brig. Gen. D[avid] E. Twiggs, Headquarters Second Brigade of the Army, Camp at Vergara, near Vera Cruz, to Capt. H. L. Scott, A.A.A.G., Mar. 15, 1847, Senate Exec. Doc., No. 1, 30 Cong., 1 Sess., pp. 245-246.

50. Commodore Matthew C. Perry was vice-commander of the Home Squadron, and commander of the steamer *Mississippi* which sailed from Norfolk on Mar. 6, 1847. On Mar. 21, he succeeded Commodore Conner as commander of the Home Squadron.

51. Capt. William P. Bainbridge of Kentucky, 4th Art., Bvt. Maj. after Cerro Gordo.

52. Lt. John H. Miller, 4th Art., was Capt. on Mar. 3, 1847, and Bvt. Maj. for his part in the defense of Puebla.

53. Lt. Edmund Bradford, "Camp of Investment in rear of Vera Cruz," to Caroline Bradford, Philadelphia, Mar. 27 [1847], Edmund Bradford Papers, Western Americana MSS, Beinecke.

54. Lt. Col. Francis S. Belton, 2d Lt. in the 1st Light Dragoons, Mar. 27, 1812, was Lt. Col., 3d Art., Oct. 13, 1845; he was brevetted for Contreras and Churubusco (one brevet).

55. Col. F[rancis] S. Belton, "Camp Washington before Vera Cruz," to his wife and son, Mar. 22, 1847, Edmund Kirby Smith Papers, So. Hist. Col., NCa.

56. "Mexican Narrative of Events At the Heroic City of Vera Cruz, While Besieged by the American Army," published at Jalapa, 1847, cited in *Niles' National Register,* Vol. 72 (May 8, 1847), p. 149.

57. "War With Mexico," Citing New Orleans *Delta, Ibid.* (Apr. 17, 1847), p. 100.

58. Midshipman Thomas B. Shubrick, Midshipman United States Navy on Mar. 3, 1841, served with the Navy Battery in the siege of Vera Cruz and was killed by a cannon shot on Mar. 25, 1847.

59. Lt. Col. E[than] A. Hitchcock, Camp Washington near Vera Cruz, to [Miss Elizabeth Nicholls, Georgetown, D.C.], Mar. 27, 1847, Ethan Allen Hitchcock Papers, DLC.

60. Lt. Peter V. Hagner was 1st Lt., Ordnance, May 22, 1840. He won brevets at Cerro Gordo and Chapultepec. In 1865 he was again brevetted, for his services in the Ordnance Department (Union Army) during the Civil War.

61. Lt. Peter V. Hagner, "Camp before Vera Cruz," to Mary M. Hagner [his sister], Annapolis, Md., Mar. 30, 1847, Peter Hagner Papers, So. Hist. Col., NCa.

NOTES TO CHAPTER V

1. An Act of Congress, published in a War Department general order (No. 14), March 27, 1847, invited the men in these regiments to reenlist for the duration of the war. When this order reached Scott's headquarters, he immediately sent it to the volunteer regiments concerned. They were: the Tennessee Cavalry, 3rd and 4th Illinois volunteer infantry regiments, the 1st and 2d Tennessee Infantry, the Georgia Infantry, and the Alabama Infantry.

2. Maj. Gen. Winfield Scott, Headquarters of the Army, Vera Cruz, to W[illiam] L. Marcy, Secretary of War, Washington, D.C., Apr. 5, 1847, House of Representatives Exec. Doc. No.60, 30 Cong., 1 Sess., pp.909-911.

3. William Higgins, Birmingham [Michigan?], to William Carter, Defiance, Ohio, Jan. 14, 1848, Western Americana MSS, Beinecke.

4. Ballentine, *Autobiography*, pp.169-170.

5. It was three miles in a straight line from Cerro Gordo to the river crossing, but by the circuitous road it was twice that far.

6. This brigade was made up of the Third Regiment of Illinois Volunteers (Col. Ferris Foreman), the Fourth Regiment of Illinois Volunteers (Col. Edward D. Baker), and the First Regiment of New York Volunteers (Col. Ward B. Burnett).

7. Pierre Gustave Toutant Beauregard (during the Mexican War he usually signed his name merely G. T. Beauregard) graduated second in his class at West Point and was 2d Lt., 1st Art., on July 1, 1838; 2d Lt., Engineers, July 7, 1838, and 1st Lt., June 16, 1839. He won two brevets in the Mexican War—for Contreras and Churubusco, and for Chapultepec. He was a general in the Confederate States Army, 1861-1865.

8. Lt. Franklin Gardner, 7th Inf., was Bvt. 1st Lt. for Monterey.

9. Capt. Edward Jenner Steptoe, was Capt., 3d Art. on Mar. 3, 1847. He won brevets for Cerro Gordo and Chapultepec.

10. Lt. Hachaliah Brown was 1st Lt., 3rd Art. on Mar. 3, 1847, and Bvt. Capt. for the affair at Medelin, near Vera Cruz, Mar. 25, 1847.

11. Lt. Truman Seymour was 2d Lt., 1st Art. on Mar. 3, 1847. During the Mexican War he won brevets for Cerro Gordo and for Contreras and Churubusco. He was Bvt. Maj. Gen. (Union Army)on Mar. 13, 1865 after having won no less than six brevets in the Civil War.

12. Lt. Zealous Bates Tower graduated first in his class at West Point and was 2d Lt., Engineers, July 1, 1841. He won three brevets in the Mexican War.

13. Lt. Theodore T. S. Laidley was 1st Lt., Ord., Mar. 3, 1847. His Mexican War brevets were for Cerro Gordo and the defense of Puebla.

14. Maj. James C. Burnham, First Regiment of New York Volunteers (Burnett's Regiment).

15. Lt. Roswell Sabin Ripley was Bvt. Capt. for Cerro Gordo and Bvt. Maj. after Chapultepec.

16. Bvt. Col. Bennet Riley was Lt. Col., 2d Inf., Dec. 1, 1839; Bvt. Col. for the Battle of Chokachatta, Florida, June, 1840; Bvt. Brig. Gen. for Cerro Gordo, and Bvt. Maj. Gen. for Contreras and Churubusco. He died June 9, 1853.

17. Capt. William Wall, 3d Art.; he died Aug. 13, 1847.

18. Col. Edward D. Baker.

19. According to Scott's report, his total force in action at the Battle of Cerro Gordo and in

reserve was 8,500 men; he estimated Santa Anna's army at 12,000. The American casualties were 431 men (63 killed); the Mexican loss was put at 1,000—1,200.

20. Winfield Scott, Headquarters of the Army, Jalapa, to W[illiam] L. Marcy, Secretary of War [Washington, D.C.], Apr. 23, 1847, Senate Exec. Doc., No.1, 30 Cong., 1 Sess., pp.261-263.

21. Scott and his troops in describing the Battle of Cerro Gordo frequently gave that name to the hill which dominated the scene. More accurately this hill, on whose summit there was a tower, was El Telégrafo.

22. "The Hardships of War," correspondence of New York *Commercial Advertiser* cited in Cambridge [Massachusetts] *Chronicle,* June 3, 1847.

23. They were on La Atalaya hill.

24. These were volunteers from General Shields' brigade assisted by engineers and others.

25. "The Hardships of War," correspondence of New York *Commercial Advertiser*, cited in Cambridge [Massachusetts] *Chronicle,* June 3, 1847.

26. Col. William S. Harney's brigade (1st Brigade, 2d Division) was made up of the Mounted Rifles, 1st Artillery, and 7th Infantry.

27. Bvt. Col. Thomas Childs was Maj., 1st Art., Feb. 16, 1847. He was Bvt. Col. for Palo Alto and Resaca de la Palma, and Bvt. Brig. Gen. for the defense of Puebla, Sept. 13—Oct. 12, 1847. He was Military Governor of Puebla, Sept.—Oct., 1847.

28. Capt. Edmund Brooke Alexander, 3d Inf., was twice brevetted for Mexican War duty.

29. Lt. Col. Joseph Plympton, 7th Inf., was Bvt. Col. for Cerro Gordo.

30. Col. W[illiam] S. Harney, 2d Drags., commanding 1st Brigade, Jalapa, to Lt. W. T. H. Brooks, A.A.A.G., 2d Division [Jalapa], Apr. 21, 1847, Senate Exec. Doc., No.1, 30 Cong., 1 Sess., pp.280-281.

31. On and near La Atalaya.

32. Lt. Gustavus Woodson Smith, 2d Lt., Engineers, won two brevets in the Mexican War— for Cerro Gordo and for Contreras and Churubusco. He was a Maj. Gen. in the Confederate States Army, 1861-1865.

33. The number is exaggerated but Santa Anna did send two regiments as reinforcements.

34. "The Battle of Sierra Gordo," letter dated at Jalapa, Mexico, May 5, 1847, New Orleans *Courier,* June 7, 1847.

35. Col. William T. Haskell, 2nd Regiment of Tennessee Volunteers.

36. The attack was supposed to be against the Mexican right flank positions, just north of the Rio del Plan.

37. Jalapa *American Star,* Apr. 29, 1847, cited in Oswandel, *Notes,* pp. 135-136.

38. Lt. Col. E[than] A. Hitchcock, Acting Inspector General, Jalapa, Mexico, to Maj. Gen. Winfield Scott, Jalapa, Apr. 23, 1847, Ethan Allen Hitchcock Papers, DLC.

39. J. H. P. Jalapa, to [n.n.], Apr. 20, 1847, cited in Vera Cruz *American Eagle,* Apr. 28, 1847.

40. Convolvulin from the convolvulus (bindweed or morning-glory) forms about ninety percent of jalap resin.

41. Waddy Thompson.

42. Scott had discovered that only a few of the volunteers wished to reenlist after their one-year term of service; he therefore requested the Q.M. at Vera Cruz to prepare transports for 3,000 troops as soon as possible. On the discharge of the volunteers, see Capt. H. L. Scott, A.A.G., Headquarters of the Army, Jalapa, to [Bvt.] Col. Henry Wilson, Commanding, Vera Cruz, May 3, 1847, and [Winfield Scott] General Orders No.135, May 4, 1847, cited in House of Representatives Exec. Doc., No.60, 30 Cong., 1 Sess., pp.955-957.

43. "Letters From Mexico," Boston *Advertiser,* May 29, June 1, 1847. These letters were published under the by-line "From our own correspondent" and signed "K."

44. General Pedro de Ampudia commanded at El Telégrafo on Apr. 17 when the first American attack was repulsed.

45. General J. J. de Landero.

46. General Juan Morales.

47. Bvt. Maj. Gen. William J. Worth, Headquarters of the 1st Division, Perote, to Capt. H.

L. Scott, A.A.A.G., Headquarters, Jalapa, Apr. 22, 1847, Senate Exec. Doc., No.1, 30 Cong. 1 Sess., pp.300-301.

48. This was the Black Bean Episode which involved the Texans taken prisoner at Mier in Dec. 1842. Victims selected by lot were those who drew black beans from a jar containing 176 beans. Seventeen men who drew the black beans signifying death were shot on Mar. 25, 1843. The other prisoners were taken to Perote.

49. General Guadalupe Victoria, President of Mexico, 1824-1829.

50. Nelson McClanahan, City of Mexico, to John McClanahan, Jackson, Tenn., Dec. 8, 1847, McClanahan-Taylor Papers, So. Hist. Col., NCa.

51. Bvt. Maj. Gen. W[illiam] J. Worth, signed by Capt. J. C. Pemberton, aide-de-camp, Headquarters, Puebla, to Capt. H. L. Scott, A.A.A.G., Headquarters of the Army, Jalapa, May 15, 1847 (copy), House of Representatives Exec. Doc., No.60, 30 Cong., 1 Sess., pp.994-995.

52. Anahuac, the Valley of Mexico, sometimes used as synonymous with New Spain. The "hosts of Anahuac" were the Aztecs.

53. 75,000 to 80,000 would have been more accurate.

54. H. Judge Moore, Scott's Campaign in Mexico (Charlestown [South Carolina]: J. B. Nixon, 1849), pp.96-98.

55. Probably Maj. John Lind Smith, Engineers, who was Bvt. Lt. Col. for Cerro Gordo and Bvt. Col. for Contreras and Churubusco. The Spooner mentioned here may have become Capt. of the Spy Company.

56. [Ethan Allen Hitchcock], Fifty Years in Camp and Field, Diary of Major-General Hitchcock, U.S.A., W. A. Croffut. (New York and London: G. P. Putnam's Sons, 1909), pp.259, 263-265.

57. To distinguish themselves from the Mexican guerrillas, they wore red bands ("bloody flags") around their hats. That they were faithful to their promises is not remarkable, for, as Lt. Edmund Bradford remarked, "if any of them were taken by the Mexicans, they would certainly be hung." See Lt. Edmund Bradford, Vergara, to John M. Tazewell [Norfolk, Va.], Jan. 2, 1847, Edmund Bradford Papers, Western Americana MSS, Beinecke.

58. Henry Moses Judah Journal MS, entry of Aug. 17, 1847, DLC. Judah was 2d Lt., 4th Inf., Apr. 19, 1846, and 1st Lt., Sept. 26, 1847. He won brevets for Molino del Rey and Chapultepec. During the Civil War he was Brig. Gen. of Volunteers, Union Army.

59. Elisha Kent Kane (1820-1857) was Asst. Surg., U.S. Navy in 1842; later he served with the Coast Survey and was with the first Grinnell expedition to the arctic, 1850-1851, and commanded the second Grinnell expedition (1853-1855).

60. General Juan José Gaona, Commandant at Puebla and Governor of Perote fortress in 1847.

61. E[lisha] K[ent] Kane, Assistant Surgeon, United States Navy, Mexico [City], to Maj. Gen. W[illiam] O. Butler, Commanding [U.S. Army, Mexico City], Mar. 14, 1848, Letters Received, Army of Occupation, AGO, RG 94, Nat. Arch.

62. Tlascala is twenty-one miles north of Puebla.

63. Lt. Raphael Semmes, The Campaign of General Scott in the Valley of Mexico (Cincinnati: Moore & Anderson, 1852), pp.165-167. Lt. Semmes, of the U.S.S. Porpoise was a volunteer aide to General Worth. During the Civil War he commanded the Sumter and the Alabama in the Confederate States Navy.

64. Lt. George Maney, "San Augustine near City of Mexico," to his father [Thomas Maney, Nashville], Sept. 6, 1847, John Kimberly Papers, So. Hist. Col., NCa. George Maney was in the 3d Drags.

65. El Peñon was surrounded by water, connected with the road only by a causeway; it was "defended by twenty different batteries, having embrasures for fifty-one guns, besides an infinity of infantry breastworks." See George Wilkins Kendall, The War Between the United States and Mexico. Illustrated by Carl Nebel (New York: D. Appleton & Co., 1851), p.27.

66. Capt. James Louis Mason was Capt. Engineers, Apr. 24, 1847. He won two brevets—for Contreras and Churubusco and for Molino del Rey.

67. Lt. Isaac Ingalls Stevens graduated first in his class at West Point and was Bvt. 2d Lt.,

Engineers, July 1, 1839; 1st Lt., July 1, 1840, and received two brevets in the Mexican War—Contreras and Churubusco and Chapultepec. In the Civil War he was Col., 79th New York Volunteers; Brig. Gen. of Vols. and Maj. Gen. of Vols. He was killed at the Battle of Chantilly, Sept. 1, 1862.

68. There were, however, reasons for rejecting this route. The road to Mexicaltzingo ran westward from Los Reyes, just south of El Peñon. The town of Mexicaltzingo was six miles south of Mexico City, connected with it by a causeway, and near the northern end of Lake Xochimilco. Mexicaltzingo was strongly fortified; an advance from there into the city would have to be made over the causeway, raked by artillery fire, or along the canal from Lake Xochimilco, an approach which also would be much exposed to Mexican guns.

69. Capt. R[obert] E. Lee, Ayotla, to Maj. J. L. Smith, Chief Engineer, U.S. Army, Mexico, Aug. 12, 1847, Letters Received, Office of the Chief of Engineers, RG 77, Nat. Arch.

70. General Gabriel Valencia commanded the Mexican forces at Padierna (Contreras). Born in Mexico City, he began his military career in 1810 as a cadet in the provincial cavalry of Tulancingo. On two occasions he was Commanding General of the Department of Mexico and Tulancingo. He marched to Texas as a Q.M. in Bravo's army in 1836, and in 1839 was Chief of Staff of the Mexican Army.

71. Lt. Col. William Montrose Graham, 11th Inf. He was killed at Molino del Rey.

72. Capt| Philip Kearny, 1st Drags., was Bvt. Maj. for Contreras and Churubusco. In the Civil War he was Brig. Gen. of Vols. and Maj. Gen. of Vols. (Union Army), and was killed at the Battle of Chantilly, Sept. 1, 1862.

73. [Bvt.] Capt. R[ichard] S. Ewell, Vera Cruz, to Ben [S. Ewell], Lexington, Virginia, Nov. 25, 1847, Richard S. Ewell Papers, DLC. Ewell was 1st Lt., 1st Drags., Sept. 18, 1845, and Bvt. Capt. for Contreras and Churubusco. He was a Lt. Gen. in the Confederate States Army.

74. Capt. Seth Barton Thornton, killed Aug. 18, 1847.

75. 4th Art.

76. Capt. Simon Henry Drum, Capt., 4th Art., killed Sept. 13, 1847 during the assault upon Mexico City.

77. See Chapter II.

78. Lt. Daniel Harvey Hill Diary MS, entries of Aug. 18-23, 1847, So. Hist. Col., NCa. Hill graduated from West Point and was Bvt. 2d Lt., 1st Art. on July 1, 1842; 2d Lt., 4th Art. on Oct. 13, 1845; 1st Lt.; Mar. 3, 1847. His Mexican War brevets were for Contreras and Churubusco, and for Chapultepec. He resigned from the Army in 1849. During the Civil War he was Lt. Gen. in the Confederate States Army.

79. Lt. William Montgomery Gardner, Mexico City, to his brother, Oct. 24, 1847, William Montgomery Gardner Papers, So. Hist. Col., NCa. Gardner was 2d Lt., 2d Inf.; he was Bvt. 1st Lt. for Contreras and Churubusco. During the Civil War he was Brig. Gen. in the Confederate States Army.

80. Capt. Ephraim Kirby Smith, 5th Inf., died Sept. 11, 1847 of wounds received at the Battle of Molino del Rey.

81. This was the battalion commanded by Bvt. Lt. Col. Charles Ferguson Smith. It was made up of two companies from the 2d Art., one from the 5th Inf., and one from the 8th Inf.

82. Capt. William Hoffman.

83. Bvt. Maj. William Reading Montgomery, brevetted for Palo Alto and Resaca de la Palma; he was Bvt. Lt. Col. after Molino del Rey.

84. Charles Ferguson Smith was Bvt. Lt. Col. for Monterey and Bvt. Col. for Contreras and Churubusco.

85. Patrick Alden Farrelly was 2d Lt., 5th Inf., and Bvt. 1st Lt. for Contreras and Churubusco.

86. Capt. Ephraim Kirby Smith, Tacubaya, to [his wife], Aug. 22, 1847, in Smith, *To Mexico With Scott*, pp.197-204.

87. Kendall, pp.50-51.

88. Bvt. Maj. Isaac I[ngalls] Stevens, *Campaigns of the Rio Grande and of Mexico, With Notices of the Recent Work of Major Ripley* (New York: D. Appleton and Co., 1851), pp.82-84.

89. General Ignacio Mora y Villamil was General Engineer, General Staff. After negotiating the armistice he was one of the commission that attempted to discuss peace terms.

90. General Benito Quijano.

91. Capt. Henry Constantine Wayne was 1st Lt., 1st Art., from 1842 to 1851; he also had the staff rank of Capt. and Asst. Q.M. on May 11, 1846. He was Bvt. Maj. for Contreras and Churubusco. During the Civil War he was Brig Gen., Confederate States Army.

92. Pierre Gustave Toutant Beauregard, Diary of the Mexican War MS, DLC.

93. Capt. Benjamin Huger, Ordnance, won three brevets in the Mexican War—for Vera Cruz, Molino del Rey and Chapultepec. During the Civil War he was Maj. Gen. in the Confederate States Army.

94. Col. Newman S. Clarke, 6th Inf.

95. Capt. George Wright, 8th Inf., was Bvt. Lt. Col. for Contreras and Churubusco, and Bvt. Col. for Molino del Rey, where he was wounded.

96. Lt. Col. James Simmons McIntosh, 5th Inf., brevetted for Palo Alto and Resaca de la Palma where he was seriously wounded; he was killed at the Battle of Molino del Rey.

97. Lt. John Gray Foster, Bvt. 2d Lt., Engineers, won brevets for Contreras and Churubusco, and for Molino del Rey. He was a Maj. Gen., Union Army, on Mar. 13, 1865.

98. The Light Battalion of Bvt. Col. Charles Ferguson Smith.

99. General Juan Alvarez, commanding the Mexican cavalry, was later criticized for not executing some of the movements he was expected to carry out.

100. Col. Timothy Patrick Andrews was Major and Paymaster, May 22, 1822; Col., Voltigeurs, from Feb. 16, 1847 to July 20, 1848, and Bvt. Brig. Gen. for Chapultepec.

101. Maj. Edwin Vose Sumner, 2d Dragoons.

102. General Juan José Andrade.

103. Maj. Martin Scott, 5th Inf., won two brevets in the Mexican War.

104. Maj. Carlos Adolphus Waite, was Maj. 8th Inf., on Feb. 16, 1847; he won brevets for Contreras and Churubusco and for Molino del Rey. He was Brig. Gen., Union Army, on Mar. 13, 1865.

105. Semmes, Campaign, pp. 324-331.

106. Capt. Silas Casey, 2d Inf., won brevets for Contreras and Churubusco and for Chapultepec. During the Civil War he was Brig. Gen. of Vols. and Maj. Gen. of Vols. (Union Army).

107. Maj. John Lind Smith.

108. Capt. Samuel Mackenzie, died Oct. 19, 1847 in Mexico City.

109. Pierce had been injured in a fall from his horse on the 19th; he attempted to mount again before the Battle of Churubusco but fainted and fell from the saddle.

110. The Brigade of Col. Newman S. Clarke, or the 5th, 6th and 8th Inf. regiments.

111. Capt. Gabriel René Paul was Bvt. Maj. for Chapultepec. During the Civil War he was Col., 4th New Mexico Inf., and Brig. Gen. of Vols. (Union Army). He was Bvt. Brig. Gen. for Gettysburg.

112. Capt. James Miller.

113. Capt. Benjamin Stone Roberts.

114. Lt. James Stuart.

115. Maj. Gen. Winfield Scott, Headquarters of the Army, National Palace of Mexico, Mexico City, to W[illiam] L. Marcy, Secretary of War, Sept. 18, 1847, Senate Exec. Doc., No.1, 30 Cong., 1 Sess., pp.376-379.

116. Candelaria garita. This was about two and one half miles east of Tacubaya and a mile south of the City. Chapultepec was two miles southwest of Mexico City.

117. Lt. George W. Morgan.

118. Lt. Barnard E. Bee was 2d Lt., 3d Inf. He won brevets for Cerro Gordo and Chapultepec. In the Civil War he was Brig. Gen. (Confederate Army) and was killed at the First Battle of Bull Run.

119. The role of the Marines at Chapultepec became a controversial issue. On behalf of the Marine Corps it was argued that General Quitman ordered the Marine contingent to halt before

it could attack, that its ammunition failed, and that between thirty and fifty of the Corps led by Capt. Terrett did distinguish themselves. For the Marine's side of the controversy, see Bvt. Maj. John G. Reynolds, *A Conclusive Exculpation of the Marine Corps in Mexico . . .* (Washington, D.C.: Stringer & Townsend, 1853), 124 pp.

120. General Nicolás Bravo, Commander General and Governor of the Department of Mexico; Santa Anna also named him Commander General of Puebla, and afterward Chief of the Southern Defense Line of Mexico City (1847).

121. General José Mariano Monterde, second in command (under Bravo) at Chapultepec. He was wounded and taken prisoner. He had directed the fortification of Chapultepec and the Tacu-baya line. A third general also was taken prisoner at Chapultepec, namely General José Maria Diaz Noriega. General Juan Nepomuceno Perez was killed there.

122. Lt. Daniel Harvey Hill Diary MS, entry of Sept. 14, 1847, So. Hist. Col., NCa.

123. Lt. Calvin Benjamin, 1t Lt., 4th Art.

124. Lt. Henry Jackson Hunt, 1st Lt., 2d Art. was brevetted for Contreras and Churubusco, and for Chapultepec. He was Brig. Gen. of Vols. and Maj. Gen. of Vols. (Union Army) during the Civil War.

125. Polkos were four elite militia companies formed in Mexico City during 1846.

126. Lt. Sidney Smith, 1st Lt., 4th Inf., died Sept. 16 from wounds received on the 14th.

127. George W. Kendall, correspondence of the New Orleans *Picayune*, City of Mexico, Sept. 14, 1847, New Orleans *Picayune*, Oct. 14, 1847.

128. "Chapultepec Taken . . .," New York *Sun*, Oct. 5, 1847, cited in *Niles' National Register*, Vol.73 (Oct. 9, 1847), pp.89-90.

129. Lt. William D. Wilkins was 2d Lt., 15th Inf. on Apr. 9, 1847 and 1st Lt. on Aug. 20, 1847. He was Regimental Quartermaster from Jan. 12 to Aug. 7, 1848. His Mexican War brevet was for "gallant and meritorious conduct in the several affairs with guerrillas at Paso Ovejas National Bridge and Cerro Gordo, Mexico, on 10, 12, and 15 Aug., 1847."

130. Capt. Samuel P. Heintzelman, in 1846, transferred from the Q.M. Dept. to line duty. He was in the 4th Inf., and won a brevet for Huamantla.

131. El Peñal was forty-three miles from Perote.

132. Lt. William D. Wilkins, Puebla, to [Ross] Wilkins [Detroit], Oct. 22, 1847, Ross Wilkins Papers, Burton.

NOTES TO CHAPTER VI

1. Capt. J[ohn] W. Lowe, "Camp near Vera Cruz, Mexico," to his son [Owen Thomas Lowe, New York City], Oct. 21, 1847, John W. Lowe Papers, Dayton.

2. S[amuel] R. Curtis, Camp Washington [Cincinnati, Ohio] to his wife [Belinda Curtis, Putnam, Ohio], June 3, 1846, Samuel R. Curtis Papers, Beinecke.

3. *Id.* to *id.*, June 5, 1846, *ibid.*

4. [Lt. Daniel Harvey Hill], "The Army in Texas," *Southern Quarterly Review*, Vol. 9 (Apr., 1846), pp. 448-450.

5. Lt. Thomas Ewell, 1st Lt., Mounted Rifles, was killed at the Battle of Cerro Cordo.

6. Lt. Thomas Ewell, "Camp Page, mouth of the Rio Grande," to Ben [Prof. Benjamin S. Ewell, Lexington, Virginia], Feb. 12, 1847, Richard Stoddard Ewell Papers, DLC.

7. *Ibid.*

8. William Hunter Churchill, 3d Art., was Bvt. Capt. for Palo Alto and Resaca de la Palma.

9. [Benjamin Franklin Scribner], *Camp Life of a Volunteer. . .* (Philadelphia: Grigg, Elliot and Co., 1847), pp. 21-28, 33, 41.

10. John R. McClanahan, "Camp of the Avengers, Texas," to his brother [James McClanahan?], Aug. 15, 1846, McClanahan—Taylor Papers, So. Hist. Col., NCa.

11. Dr. John J. B. Hoxey, Surgeon, Battalion of Georgia Volunteers, commanded by Lt. Col. Isaac G. Seymour.

12. [Lt. John Forsyth], "Pleasures of Soldiering," Richmond *Enquirer* cited in *Niles' National Register*, Vol. 71 (Sept. 26, 1846), p. 55.

13. William H. Prescott, *History of the Conquest of Mexico*, ed. by John Foster Kirk (Philadelphia: J. B. Lippincott Co., 1873), Vol. 1, p. 322.

14. Lt. Simon Doyle was 2d Lt., First Independent Company of Illinois Mounted Volunteers, commanded by Capt. Adams Dunlap.

15. [Lt.] S[imon] Doyle, "Camp Rio Grande near Matamoros," to James Doyle, Rushville, Illinois, Oct. 13 [1847], Doyle Papers, Beinecke.

16. Lewis Leonidas Allen was Chaplain to the St. Louis Legion (Regiment of Missouri Volunteers), commanded by Col. Alton R. Easton. Allen, however, was from New Orleans. His observations were first published as a series of letters to the St. Louis *American*.

17. The Louisville Legion, First Regiment of Kentucky Volunteers, commanded by Col. Stephen Ormsby.

18. Sixth Regiment, Smith's Brigade of Louisiana Volunteers; its Col. was Edward Featherstone.

19. Col. Alton R. Easton of the St. Louis Legion.

20. Lt. Col. Ferdinand Kennett, St. Louis Legion.

21. Dr. George Johnson, Surg. of the St. Louis Legion. For Dr. Johnson's observations on health problems along the lower Rio Grande, see Chapter VII.

22. Col. Bailie (also spelled Balie) Peyton, 5th Regiment, Louisiana Volunteers.

23. L[ewis] L[eonidas] Allen, *Pencillings of Scenes Upon the Rio Grande* (New York: [no pub.], 1848), pp. 25-26.

24. Lt. Daniel Harvey Hill Diary MS, So. Hist. Col., NCa.

25. Col. Balie Peyton, Camp Peyton near Burrita, to Gen. Z[achary] Taylor, Camp near Matamoros, June 27, 1846 (fair copy), Letters Received, Army of Occupation, AGO, RG 94, Nat. Arch.

26. of Louisiana Volunteers.

27. Bernardo Garza, Antonio Treneria, O. F. Janes, "Camp Peyton near Burrita," to Col. Balie Peyton, June 26, 1846 (fair copy), Letters Received, Army of Occupation, AGO, RG 94, Nat. Arch.

28. Col. Henry R. Jackson, Camp Belknap near Burrita, to Miss Martha J. R. Jackson, Monroe, Georgia, August 9, 1846, Jackson—Prince Papers, So. Hist. Col., NCa.

29. Maj. Charles J. Williams, Regiment of Georgia Volunteers.

30. Capt. John McMahon.

31. Capt. Allison Nelson.

32. Capt. Harrison J. Sargent.

33. Capt. Daniel H. Bird.

34. Fourth Regiment of Illinois Volunteers.

35. "From the Savannah *Republican*, Georgia Regiment, Camp near Camargo, Sept. 7th," cited in *Niles' National Register*, Vol. 71 (Oct. 10, 1846), p. 88. For Col. Jackson's account of the riot see Col. Henry R. Jackson, Camp near Monterey, to his sister, Miss Martha J. R. Jackson, Monroe, Georgia, Oct. 19, 1846, Jackson—Prince Papers, So. Hist. Col., NCa. The aftermath of the riot was the General Court Martial of Capt. John McMahon. See Taylor's Orders No. 132, Camp near Monterey, Oct. 17, 1846. McMahon was charged with drunkenness on duty and mutinous conduct in his attack upon Col. Baker. The court found McMahon guilty and ordered him to be cashiered. But because of the "favorable recommendation of the court and the palliating character of the testimony" the sentence was remitted, and McMahon was ordered to "resume his sword."

36. For descriptions of Worth's and Twiggs' divisions at this time, see Chapter II.

37. Giddings, *Sketches of the Campaign*, pp. 74-75.

38. The Volunteer Division.

39. "A General's Orderly in Mexico," *Colburn's United Service Magazine and Naval and Military Journal*, Vol. 78 (May, 1855), Part II, pp. 78-80.

40. Brig. Gen. John E. Wool, by Irvin McDowell, A.A.G., General Orders No. 326, June 22, 1847.

41. George C. Furber, *The Twelve Months Volunteer* (Cincinnati: J. A. and U. P. James, 1848), pp. 417-422.

42. George F. Ruxton, *Adventures in Mexico and the Rocky Mountains* (London: John Murray, 1847), pp. 175-176.

43. Oswandel, *Notes*, pp. 140, 142, 144, 146-148, 155, 159.

44. Brig. Gen. J[ohn] A. Quitman, "Camp at Carmargo," to Louisa and F. H. Quitman, Aug. 18, 1846, John A. Quitman Papers, So. Hist. Col., NCa.

45. Bvt. Maj. J[ohn] A. Quitman "Camp Allen near Monterey," to his wife [Mrs. Eliza Quitman], Nov. 22, 1846, *ibid.*

46. James P. Fyffe, 1st Lt., Fifth Ohio Regiment of Volunteers. But they always called their Regiment the Second Ohio.

47. Lt. Milton Jamieson, 2d Lt.

48. Lt. William Howard, 2d Lt.

49. Dr. George T. McDonald, Asst. Surg.

50. Capt. J[ohn] W. Lowe, "Camp near Vera Cruz, Mexico," to [Mrs. Manorah F. Lowe, New York City], Oct. 17, 1847, John W. Lowe Papers, Dayton.

51. Lt. W[illiam] W. H. Davis, "Camp near Buena Vista," to Mrs. Amy H. Davis, July 28, 1847, W. W. H. Davis Papers, Beinecke.

52. Capt. Henry Swartwout, 2d Art., and Curtis were classmates at West Point.

53. Col. Sam[ue]l R. Curtis, "Brasos Santiago," to his wife [Belinda Curtis, Mount Vernon, Ohio], July 29, 1846, Samuel R. Curtis Papers, Beinecke.

54. Dr. John B. Porter of Connecticut was Asst. Surg., Dec. 1, 1833, and Maj. and Surg. on Oct. 4, 1846.

55. John Bankhead Magruder.

56. Asst. Surg. J. B. Porter, Artillery Battalion, 1st Brigade, near Matamoros, to Lt. Col. T[homas] Childs, Commanding Artillery Battalion, June 24, 1846, Letters Received, Army of Occupation, AGO, RG 94, Nat. Arch.

57. John R. McClanahan, Camargo, to his sister, Mrs. James R. Taylor, Jackson, Tenn., Oct. 25, 1846, McClanahan—Taylor Papers, So. Hist. Col., NCa.

58. Josiah Gregg, *Letters and Diaries of Josiah Gregg*, ed. Maurice Garland Fulton (Norman: University of Oklahoma Press, c. 1941-1944), Vol. 2, pp. 117-118. Josiah Gregg, trader and physician, was with Wool's column on its march from San Antonio to Buena Vista. He then served as a volunteer surgeon.

59. Samuel E. Chamberlain, *My Confession* (New York: Harper and Brothers, 1956), p. 215. Samuel Emery Chamberlain was a private in Company E, 1st Dragoons, from Sept. 8, 1846 to Mar. 22, 1849. During the Civil War he was Capt., Maj., Lt. Col. and Col. of the 1st and 5th Mass. Cavalry, and on Feb. 24, 1865 was Brig. Gen. of Vols.

60. Henry Moses Judah Journal MS, entry of [Apr.] 14, [1847], DLC.

61. Allen, *Pencillings*, pp. 22-24.

62. Bvt. Maj. Gen. Zachary Taylor, Matamoros, General Orders No. 77, June 17, 1846. These orders read: "It has been represented to the Commanding General by the authorities of Matamoros that Mexican servants who according to the custom of the country are paid in advance, have in several instances left the service of their masters and taken up refuge in the American camp. The General wishes to caution officers and all persons connected with the Army against the employment of such servants and to say that where recognized and claimed on this side of the river, they will in all cases be given up to their former masters."

63. Capt. J[ohn] W. Lowe, Camp near Vera Cruz, Mexico," to his son [Owen Thomas Lowe, New York City], Oct. 21, 1847, John W. Lowe Papers, Dayton.

64. *Id.* to his wife [Mrs. Manorah F. Lowe, New York City], Nov. 9, 1847, *ibid.*

65. For Camp Misery, see *ante*, p. 297-299.

66. Oswandel, *Notes*, p. 154.

67. Las Vigas was a village about half way from Jalapa to Perote.

68. Moore, *Scott's Campaign*, p. 74.

69. Kenly, *Maryland Volunteer*, pp. 225-226.

70. Buhoup, *Narrative*, pp. 109-110.

71. For a brief discussion of the game of monte which had "become part of the very nature of the inhabitants of Southern America," see Brantz Mayer, *Mexico As It Was and As It Is* (Third rev. ed., Philadelphia: G.B. Zieber & Co., 1847), p. 78.

72. Smith, *Chile Con Carne*, pp. 321-325.

73. "Massachusetts Regiment," [no name], Camp Massachusetts, Matamoras, Mexico, to [no name], Apr. 13, 1947, in *Bunker Hill Aurora*, cited in Boston *Advertiser*, May 11, 1847.

74. Robertson, *Reminiscences of a Campaign*, pp. 94-95.

75. Kenly, *Maryland Volunteer*, p. 381.

76. Moore, *Scott's Campaign*, p. 123.

77. Oswandel, *Notes*, p. 236.

78. Frank S. Edwards, *A Campaign in Mexico with Colonel Doniphan* (Philadelphia, Carey and Hart, 1847), pp. 70-71.

79. When Scott's troops came upon Santa Anna's estate, El Encerro, located between Jalapa and Vera Cruz, they were supposed to have found Santa Anna's wooden leg in a carriage because of his hasty flight from the scene. Santa Anna had a leg amputated during the "Pastry War" with France in 1838.

80. Semmes, *Campaign*, p. 51.

81. During the first summer of the war, fifteen New York publishers "contributed a very excellent library to the army on the Rio Grande." Among the publishers that sent books were: Harper & Brothers; Burgess, Stringer & Co.; Wiley & Putnam; Saxton & Miles; Baker & Scribner; M. W. Dodd; Davis Mead; and Stanford & Swords.

82. "The American Press and Printers," Niles' *National Register*, Vol. 71 (Jan. 16, 1847), p. 308; Lota M. Spell, "The Anglo-Saxon Press in Mexico, 1846-1948," *The American Historical Review*, Vol. 38 (Oct. 1932), pp. 20-31.

83. Peoples had associates in his publishing enterprise. See Oswandel, *Notes*, p. 145.

84. See, seven pages of MS notes by John H. Warland tipped into the *American Star* file at Houghton Library, Harvard University. See also, John Langdon Sibley, Library Journal MS, entry of July 11, 1873, Massachusetts Historical Society. The editors are grateful to Mr. Edward S. Wallace for suggesting to them the existence of the Warland MS.

85. Lt. George W. Clutter was 1st Lt., 13th Inf., on Apr. 9, 1847; he was Regimental Adjutant from Aug. 9, 1847 to Feb. 1, 1848.

86. Lt. George W. Clutter, Camp near Mier, Mexico, to his wife [Mrs. Sarah M. Clutter, Wheeling, Virginia], Aug. 8, 1847, Western Americana MSS Beinecke.

87. Kenly, *Maryland Volunteer*, p. 211.

88. *High Private*, pp. 45-46.

89. For other aspects of religion in the Army, see Chapter IX.

90. Capt. Richard A. Stewart was in the Third Regiment of Smith's Brigade of Louisiana Volunteers. Thorpe gave his name as Stuart.

91. T[homas] B[angs] Thorpe, *Our Army on the Rio Grande* (Philadelphia: Carey and Hart, 1846), pp. 171-172.

NOTES TO CHAPTER VII

1. The total number of men (regulars and volunteers) killed in action was 1,192; died of wounds, 529; accidental deaths, 361; and died of disease, 11,155. Heitman, II, p. 282.

2. Dr. Josiah Clark Nott was a physician and ethnologist; after 1835 he practiced medicine in Mobile, Alabama, and with George R. Gliddon wrote *Types of Mankind*, published in 1854. For

Nott's paper on yellow fever, see *The New Orleans Medical and Surgical Journal*, Vol. 4 (Mar., 1848), pp. 563-601.

3. Col. John Francis Hamtramck Jr., to [Maj. Gen. Zachary Taylor], [undated fragment of a letter], John Francis Hamtramck Jr. Papers, Duke.

4. Thomas Lawson of Virginia was a Surgeon's Mate in the United States Navy on March 1, 1809, but resigned on January 12, 1811. He then became a garrison Surgeon's Mate, and, on May 21, 1813, Surgeon of the 6th Inf.; he transferred to the 7th Inf. in 1815, and was Staff Surgeon on June 1, 1821. On Nov. 30, 1836, he became Surgeon General of the United States Army and retained that commission until his death, May 15, 1861. He was Bvt. Brig. Gen. for his Mexican War services.

5. Asst. Surg. J[ohn] B. Wells, Medical Purveyor, Camargo, Mexico, to Surg. C[lement] A. Finley, Medical Director, Army of Occupation, Monterey, Mexico, November 3, 1846, Letters Received, Army of Occupation, AGO, RG 94, Nat. Arch. Surgeon Thomas Gardner Mower of Massachusetts was the Army Medical Department's Medical Purveyor in New York City.

6. Surg. Samuel G. I. DeCamp, Santa Fe, to Dr. Th[omas] Lawson, Surgeon General, April 14, 1847, Letters Received, Office of the Surgeon General, RG 112, Nat. Arch. Surgeon Samuel G. I. DeCamp was Asst. Surg., October 10, 1823; Maj. and Surg. on Dec. 1, 1833, and retired in 1862. Surgeon DeCamp was at Fort Leavenworth from August, 1845 to June, 1846. He then accompanied the Kearny expedition to Santa Fe, where he was stationed until Sept. 1847.

7. Asst. Surg. John Strother Griffin was in the medical service of the United States Army from 1840 to 1854. Griffin was in the Kearny expedition to New Mexico, and from there went to California where he was assigned until June 1853.

8. Asst. Surg. John S. Griffin, San Diego, to Surg. Gen. Th[omas] Lawson, Washington, D.C., May 5, 1847, Letters Received, Office of the Surgeon General, RG 112, Nat. Arch.

9. Asst. Surg. Joseph K. Barnes, Camp Matamoros, to Surg. Gen. Thomas Lawson, Washington, D.C., July 3, 1846, *ibid*. Dr. Joseph K. Barnes was one of a number of young surgeons who served in the Mexican War and later became Surgeons General of the United States Army. He was Asst. Surg. on June 15, 1840 and Brig. Gen. and Surg. Gen. on Aug. 22, 1864.

10. Maj. Gen. Th[omas] S. Jesup, Q.M. Gen., Steamer *New Orleans*, to Lt. Col. Th[omas] F. Hunt, Deputy Quartermaster General, New Orleans, Feb. 12, 1847, Thomas Sidney Jesup Papers, DLC.

11. Jacob S. Robinson, *A Journal of the Santa Fe Expedition Under Colonel Doniphan* (Princeton: Princeton University Press, 1932), p. 38. Robinson wrote this entry in his journal while Doniphan was in the Navajo country, New Mexico.

12. Samuel P. Heintzelman was Capt. and Asst. Q.M. from July 7, 1838 to June 18, 1846. During the Civil War he was Maj. Gen. of Volunteers in 1862 (Union Army).

13. Capt. S[amuel] P. Heintzelman, Asst. Q.M., Louisville, to Surg. Gen. Tho[ma]s Lawson, Washington, D.C., July 17, 1846 (fair copy) Samuel P. Heintzelman Service Letters MSS, Samuel P. Heintzelman Papers, DLC.

14. Surg. S[amuel] G. I. DeCamp, Santa Fe, to Dr. Th[omas] Lawson Surg. Gen., Apr. 14, 1847, Letters Received, Office of the Surg. Gen. RG 112, Nat. Arch.

15. [Lt. John P. Hatch], Camp At Vegara [sic. Vergara], Vera Cruz, to his father, P. Hatch, Oswego, New York, Apr. 7, 1847, John Porter Hatch Papers, DLC.

16. Surg. Robert F. Richardson of Illinois was a Surgeon of Volunteers from July 7, 1846 until his honorable discharge on June 30, 1847. He was surgeon to Clark's Battalion of Missouri Volunteers.

17. Surg. S[amuel] G. I. DeCamp, Santa Fe, to Dr. Th[omas] Lawson, Surg. Gen., Feb. 16, 1847, Letters Received, Office of the Surgeon General, RG 112, Nat. Arch.

18. Camp Washington was the rendezvous camp at Cincinnati.

19. "Return of Volunteers," Col. Samuel Ryan Curtis, Matamoros, to [n.n.], Sept. 7, 1846 [extract] cited in Washington *National Intelligencer*, Oct. 16, 1846.

20. Dr. Joseph Jefferson Burr Wright of Pennsylvania was Asst. Surg. on Oct. 25, 1833, and Maj. and Surg., Mar. 26, 1844; he served until his retirement in 1876.

21. Surg. J[oseph] J. B. Wright, Matamoros, "Quarterly Report of the Sick and Wounded at General Hospital, Matamoros, Mexico, for the Quarter Ending [the] Thirtieth [of] Sept. 1846," AGO, RG 94, Nat. Arch.

22. Johnson was Surgeon of Volunteers from July 25 to August 25, 1846.

23. Surg. George Johnson, "The Medical Topography of Texas and the Diseases of the Army of Invasion," cited in *Boston Medical and Surgical Journal*, Vol. 36 (May 19, 1847), p. 311.

24. Capt. J[ohn] W. Lowe, Camp near Vera Cruz, to [O. T. Fishback, Batavia, Ohio], Oct. 14, 1847, John W. Lowe Papers, Dayton.

25. Grayson M. Prevost of Pennsylvania was Asst. Surg. from Dec. 31, 1845 to June 7, 1848.

26. Asst. Surg. G[rayson] M. Prevost, Camp opposite Matamoras, to Surg. P[resley] H. Craig, Med. Dir., Army of Occupation, June [n.d.] 1846, Letters Received, Army of Occupation, AGO RG 94.

27. Surg. S[amuel] G. I. DeCamp, Santa Fe, to Dr. Th[omas] Lawson, Surg. Gen., Apr. 14, 1847, Letters Received, Office of the Surgeon General, RG 112, Nat. Arch. Garden seeds were sent as requested to DeCamp.

28. Although some attempts were made to distinguish "black vomit" as a different disease, the consensus of medical opinion seemed to be that it was yellow fever, and that the fever in Vera Cruz was identical to the type known in New Orleans.

29. Surg. J[ohn] B. Porter, Vera Cruz, to H. L. Heiskell, Acting Surg. Gen. [Washington, D.C.], Aug. 27, 1847, Reports on Sick and Wounded by U.S. Army Surgeons, 1846-1848, AGO, RG 94, Nat. Arch.

30. "Sickness in the U.S. Army in Mexico," *The New Orleans Medical and Surgical Journal*, Vol. 4 (July, 1847), p. 140. The writer of this article reported: "As to General Scott's division, we hear of nothing but the ordinary camp diseases; dysentery, diarrhoea, intermittent and typhoid fevers, beyond Vera Cruz. The main body is doubtless in a very healthy region on the table lands."

31. Philip G. Jones of Indiana (born in Maryland) served as Asst. Surg. of Volunteers from Sept. 22, 1847 to July 20, 1848. He was Regimental Surgeon to the Fifth Regiment of Indiana Volunteers.

32. Asst. Surg. P[hilip] G. Jones, Molino del Rey, Mexico, to Dr. [Richard S.] Satterlee, Mexico [City], Feb. 29, 1848, Reports on Sick and Wounded by U.S. Army Surgeons, 1846-1848, AGO, RG 94, Nat. Arch.

33. Charles S. Tripler of New York was Asst. Surg., Oct. 30, 1830; Maj. and Surg., July 7, 1838. During the Civil War he was for a time Medical Director of the Army of the Potomac; Bvt. Col. on Nov. 29, 1864, and Bvt. Brig. Gen. in 1865.

34. Surg. Charles S. Tripler, Medical Director, 2d Division, Puebla, to Surg. Gen. [Thomas] Lawson, Headquarters of the Army, Puebla, July 6, 1847, Letters Received, Office of the Surgeon General, RG 112, Nat. Arch.

35. Surg. Timothy Childs, of Pittsfield, Mass., served from Feb. 16, 1847 to July 27, 1848 as Asst. Surg. to the Massachusetts Regiment of Volunteers.

36. Surg. T[imothy] Childs, Mass. Vol. Regiment, San Angel, to [Surgeon Otis Hoyt], Jalapa, Apr. 10, 1848, Otis Hoyt Papers, Wis. Hist. Soc.

37. Dr. Nathan S. Jarvis, Surg. to the 3d Art. superintendant of the General Hospital at Taylor's Corpus Christi base in Sept. 1845; in Dec. 1846 Taylor consolidated the general hospitals in Monterey and placed Jarvis in charge of them. (See Taylor's Orders No. 7, Corpus Christi, Sept. 3, 1845 and No. 156, Camp near Monterey, Dec. 10, 1846.) Jarvis was Asst. Surg. Mar. 2, 1833 and Maj. and Surg. on July 7, 1838. He served as Surg. until his death, May 12, 1862.

38. Surg. N[athan] S. Jarvis, Medical Director, Monterey, Mexico, to Dr. H. L. Heiskell [Asst. Surg. Gen.], Washington, D.C., Aug. 10, 1847, Letters Received, Office of the Surgeon General, RG 112, Nat. Arch.

39. Asst. Surg. Robert Murray of Maryland began his service as Asst. Surg. on June 29, 1846; he was Maj. and Surg. on June 23, 1860, and finally was Brig. Gen. and Surg. Gen., Nov. 23, 1883; he retired in 1886. Murray was stationed in California from May 1847 to Sept. 1850; he returned to California in 1857 and remained there until 1861.

40. Asst. Surg. R[obert] Murray, Pueblo de los Angeles, to Dr. Th[oma]s Lawson, Surg. Gen., Washington, D.C., July 30, 1848, Letters Received, Office of the Surgeon General, RG 112, Nat. Arch.

41. Surg. D[aniel] Turney [Santa Fe], "Quarterly Report of Sick and Wounded of Battalion of 1st Regiment of Illinois Volunteers Infantry, Santa Fe, New Mexico for the Quarter Ending Mar. 31, 1848," AGO, RG 94, Nat. Arch. Turney wrote: "The type of the diseases this quarter have been decidedly Typhoid. Most of the fatal cases of Pneumonia were complicated with Tetanus, in a few hours becoming profoundly Typhoid. A few cases of sudden death have also occurred from meningitis. Scorbutis, syphilis & gonorrhea have prevailed to an alarming degree."

42. Surg. S[amuel] G. I. DeCamp, Santa Fe, to Dr. Th[omas] Lawson, Surg. Gen., Oct. 12, 1846, Letters Received, Office of the Surgeon General, RG 112, Nat. Arch.

43. Bvt. Maj. Gen. Z[achary] Taylor, Matamoros, to Surg. R[obert] C. Wood, Fort Polk, Texas, June 21, 1846 *Bixby letters*, p. 11. See also Taylor's Orders No. 111, Camargo, Aug. 31, 1846 which ordered Surg. Wood and Surg. Wright, at Matamoros, "to hire such private physicians as may be required for the wants of the service in their respective hospitals." Also Taylor's Orders No. 113, Camargo, Sept. 4, 1846 by which he directed Maj. Gen. Patterson to see to it that "necessary provisions for the sick" were made in the camps and hospitals of the volunteers. Surg. Robert C. Wood was General Taylor's son-in-law and confidant. Wood was Asst. Surg., May 28, 1825; Maj. and Surg. on July 4, 1836; Col. and Asst. Surg. Gen. (Union Army) from 1862 to 1865. During the Mexican War, Wood was at Fort Polk (Point Isabel) from June, 1846 to March, 1847, then at New Orleans Barracks until June, 1848.

44. Wool's Orders No. 384, by Lt. W[illiam] B. Franklin, A.A.D.C., Buena Vista, Aug. 2, 1847, (fair copy), Caleb Cushing Papers, DLC.

45. Surg. Presley H. Craig was a veteran of many years' service in the Army Medical Department. He had been a Surg's. Mate in the 22d Inf. on July 6, 1812; Asst. Surg., June 1, 1821, and Maj. and Surg. on July 13, 1832. In 1846 he was Medical Director of Taylor's army and although his health was badly impaired stayed with that Army until June 1848. He died soon after the war ended—on Aug. 8, 1848.

46. Surg. Gen. Th[omas] Lawson, Surgeon General's Office, [Washington, D.C.], to Brig. Gen. R[oger] Jones, Adj. Gen., U.S.A., July 29, 1846, "Remarks of the Surgeon General on the Letter of Surgeon P. H. Craig, Medical Director, Army of Occupation, Asking for a Leave of Absence, With the Endorsement of General Taylor Thereon . . . ," House of Representatives Exec. Doc., No. 60, 30 Cong., 1 Sess., pp. 415-417.

47. Dr. John C. Glen of South Carolina was in the Army Medical Department from June 22, 1839 until his death on Feb. 14, 1848. From Nov. 1846 to Mar. 1847 he was in San Antonio.

48. Asst. Surg. John C. Glen, San Antonio, to Surg. Gen. Thomas Lawson, Washington, D.C., Oct. 24, Dec. 1, 1846, Letters Received, Office of the Surgeon General, RG 112, Nat. Arch.

49. Second Regiment of Missouri Volunteers; it had about 1,000 officers and men.

50. Battalion of Missouri Volunteers commanded by Lt. Col. David Willock—about 300 men.

51. Asst. Surg. Win S. Way was with the Second Regiment of Missouri Volunteers.

52. Capt. William S. Murphy, Clark's Battalion of Missouri Volunteers, and also Independent Company of Missouri Volunteers.

53. Surg. S[amuel] G. I. DeCamp, Santa Fe, to Dr. Th[omas] Lawson, Surgeon General, Jan. 5, 1847, Letters Received, Office of the Surgeon General, RG 112, Nat. Arch.

54. Surg. Benjamin Franklin Harney was Surg., 3d Inf. on Aug. 17, 1814, Maj. and Surg., 1821.

55. Surg. J[ohn] B. Porter, Vera Cruz, to H. L. Heiskell, Acting Surg. Gen., Aug. 27, 1847, Reports on Sick and Wounded by U.S. Army Surgeons, 1846-1848, AGO, RG 94, Nat. Arch.

56. Milton Jamieson, *Journal and Notes of a Campaign in Mexico* . . . (Cincinnati: The Ben Franklin Printing House, 1849), pp. 26-27.

57. Kendall, p. 5.

58. Surg. Adam Neill McLaren, born in Scotland, was Asst. Surg. in 1833, and Maj. and Surg. on June 30, 1839. At the end of the Civil War he was brevetted Lt. Col.

59. Surg. A[dam] N. McLaren, Perote Castle, to The Medical Director of the U.S. Army at General Headquarters, Mexico [City], Sept. 3, 1847, AGO, RG 94, Nat. Arch.

60. Asst. Surg. Charles H. Laub entered the Army Medical Department on Nov. 30, 1836; he was Maj. and Surg., Oct. 17, 1854.

61. Asst. Surg. C[harles] H. Laub, Vera Cruz, to H. L. Heiskell, Asst. Surg. Gen., Washington, D.C., July 3, 1847, Letters Received, Office of the Surgeon General, RG 112, Nat. Arch.

62. Dr. Edward H. Barton, a well known physician, became an army surgeon on March 3, 1847. He was Regimental Surgeon of the 3d Dragoons. He resigned Jan. 29, 1848.

63. "Means of Preserving Health At Vera Cruz," *Boston Medical and Surgical Journal*, Vol. 36 (July 14, 1847), p. 484.

64. Dr. Otis Hoyt, Surgeon of Volunteers, was Regimental Surgeon to the Massachusetts Regiment of Volunteers. During the Civil War he was Surgeon to the 30th Wis. Infantry.

65. Copper sulfate.

66. Lead acetate.

67. [Dr. Otis Hoyt] "Monthly Report of the Sick and Wounded Men Admitted into the General Hospital at Jalapa, Mexico, December, 1847" (fair copy), Otis Hoyt Papers, Wis. Hist. Soc.

68. Robert Crooke Wood Diary MS, entry of Aug. 26, 1846, Trist-Wood Papers, So. Hist. Col., NCa.

69. Charles M. Hitchcock of Maryland was Asst. Surg. on Aug. 17, 1835.

70. Asst. Surg. C[harles] M. Hitchcock, Saltillo, to [Thomas Lawson], Surg. Gen., Washington, D.C., Mar. 11, 1847, AGO, RG 94, Nat. Arch.

71. Herman Upmann, hospital at Saltillo, to his uncle [D. Upmann, Milwaukee], Feb. 25, 1847, cited in Milwaukee *Wisconsin Banner*, Apr. 17, 1847 (typescript copy), Alexander Konze Papers, Wis. Hist. Soc. He recovered; after the war he fell into a pond while intoxicated and was drowned.

72. W. B. Herrick, "Surgery in the Hospitals After the Battle of Buena Vista," *Illinois Medical and Surgical Journal*, Vol. 4 (1848), pp. 416-417.

73. Surg. N[athan] S. Jarvis, "Surgical Case at Monterey," *New York Journal of Medicine* cited in *The Western Lancet*, Vol. 6 (May, 1847), p. 102.

74. Mrs. Edward G. W. Butler to Col. Edward G. W. Butler, Point Isabel, Sept. 16, 1847, Edward G. W. Butler Papers, Duke. Col. Edward G. W. Butler graduated from West Point and was 1st Lt., 4th Art., on Nov. 6, 1823, but resigned his commission and retired from the Army in 1831. On Apr. 9, 1847 he became Col. of the 3d Dragoons.

75. Capt. A[bner] R. Hetzel, Asst. Q.M., "Brassos San Iago," to Maj. Gen. Th[omas] S. Jesup, Q.M. Gen., New Orleans, Jan. 29, 1847 (fair copy), Hetzel Letterbooks, 1846-1848, RG 92, Nat. Arch. Labarraque's solution is a sodium hypochlorite solution having the germicidal value of available chlorine.

76. [Bvt. Brig. Gen.] Thomas Childs, Orders No. 58, by Maj. O[scar] F. Winship, Department Headquarters, Puebla, Mar. 28, 1848 (fair copy), General and Special Orders Puebla, AGO, RG 94, Nat. Arch.

77. "Sickness in the U.S. Army in Mexico," *The New Orleans Medical and Surgical Journal*, Vol. 4 (July, 1847), p. 140.

78. Surg. N[athan] S. Jarvis, Monterey, to Dr. H. L. Heiskell, Asst. Surg. Gen., Washington, D.C., Jan. 17, 1848, Reports on Sick and Wounded by U.S. Army Surgeons, 1846-1848, AGO, RG 94, Nat. Arch. See also, *id.* to Tho[ma]s. Lawson, Surg. Gen., Feb. 26, 1848, Letters Received, Office of the Surgeon General, RG 112, *ibid.* In this statement which accompanied his Monthly Consolidated Report for January, Jarvis spoke of the prevalence of variola among the troops. The Surg. of the 16th Inf. had reported 36 cases of variola and varioloid; the Surg. at the General Hospital, Monterey, reported eight cases of smallpox in a detachment of 3d Drags. which formed an escort to a train from Mier. Jarvis succeeded in procuring a supply of vaccine and took steps to vaccinate all who previously had not been vaccinated.

79. Dr. Crawford W. Long had employed ether when he removed a tumor from the neck of a patient on Mar. 30, 1842, but this operation had not been widely publicized.

80. See, Victor Robinson, *Victory Over Pain, A History of Anesthesia* (New York: Henry Schuman, 1946), pp. 119-129.

81. Dr. A. L. Peirson, Salem, Mass., to Brig. Gen. Caleb Cushing, Aug. 31, 1847, Caleb Cushing Papers, DLC

82. Dr. E. H. Barton, Baltimore, to Dr. [Thomas] Lawson, Surg. Gen., Dec. 16, 1846, Letters Received, Office of the Surgeon General, RG 112, Nat. Arch.

83. Probably this is a typographical error. Dr. John B. Porter doubtless was the Surgeon who assisted Barton.

84. "Surgery At Vera Cruz," *Vera Cruz American Eagle* cited in *Boston Medical and Surgical Journal*, Vol. 36 (July 7, 1847), pp. 466-467.

85. "Chloroform in the United States Army," *The Western Lancet*, Vol. 7 (Feb. 1848) p. 128.

NOTES TO CHAPTER VIII

1. Thomas Sidney Jesup was 2d Lt., 7th Inf. on May 3, 1808; Maj., 19th Inf., April 6, 1813; Lt. Col., 3d Inf. on Apr. 30, 1817, and Brig. Gen. and Q.M. Gen., May 8, 1818. He won two brevets in the War of 1812—for Chippewa and Niagara, and was Bvt. Maj. Gen., May 8, 1828 for "ten years faithful service in one grade."

2. George Gibson was Capt., 5th Inf. on May 3, 1808; Col. and Quartermaster General for the Southern Division, April 29, 1816, and Commissary General of Subsistence from April 18, 1818 to Sept. 29, 1861 (his death date). He was Bvt. Brig. Gen. in 1826 and Bvt. Maj. Gen. for his Mexican War services. From 1777 to 1842 there was an office of purchases—Commissary General of Purchases, but after 1842 the functions of that office were those of the Commissary General of Subsistence.

3. Lt. Col. George Bomford was 2d Lt. of Engineers, July 1, 1805, and Col. and Chief of Ordnance on May 30, 1832. He died Mar. 25, 1848. In 1847, Lt. Col. George Talcott, Jr., assumed many of the Chief's duties, and was Bomford's successor in Mar., 1848. The Ordnance Department, first established under an Act of May 14, 1812, did not exist as a separate department from 1821 to 1832; it was merged into the Artillery by an Act of Mar. 2, 1821. On Apr. 5, 1832, another Act set it up as a separate department.

4. William L. Marcy, Secretary of War, Washington, D.C., to [Bvt.] Maj. Gen. Thomas S. Jesup, Quartermaster General, Feb. 8, 1847, Thomas Sidney Jesup Papers, Duke.

5. Col. Henry Whiting was Cornet, Light Drags., on Oct. 20, 1808; Maj. and Q.M., Feb. 23, 1835, and Col. and Asst. Q.M. Gen., Apr. 21, 1846. He was with Taylor's army and was Bvt. Brig. Gen. for Buena Vista. He died Sept. 16, 1851.

6. [Bvt.] Maj. Gen. Th[omas] S. Jesup, Q.M. Gen., New Orleans, to Col. H[enry] Whiting, Asst. Q.M. Gen., Headquarters of the Army of Occupation, Mexico, Jan. 13, 1847 (fair copy), Letters Received, Correspondence of Col. Henry Whiting, Office of the Q.M. Gen., RG 92, Nat. Arch.

7. [Bvt.] Maj. Gen. Th[oma]s S. Jesup, Q.M. Gen., Washington City, to W[illiam] L. Marcy, Secretary of War [Washington, D.C.], Nov. 24, 1847, Senate Exec. Doc., No. 1, 30 Cong., 1 Sess. pp. 544, 548-550.

8. Brig. Gen. [John A.] Quitman, Camargo, to Gen. F. Huston, Aug. 24, cited in John Francis Hamtramck Claiborne, *Life and Correspondence of John A. Quitman . . .* (New York: Harper & Brothers, 1860), Vol. 1, pp. 241n-242n.

9. "The Sappers and Miners," New London *Advocate* cited in *Niles' National Register*, Vol. 71 (Jan. 9, 1847), p. 304.

10. Semmes, *Campaign*, pp. 202-203.

11. Bvt. Maj. Z[achary] Taylor, Matamoros, Mexico, to Surg. R. C. Wood, Fort Polk, Texas, June 21, 1846, *Bixby letters*, p. 13.

12. *Id.*, Monterey, to *id.*, New Orleans, Apr. 4, 1847, *ibid.*, p. 96.

13. After the Acts of May 13, 15, and 19, and June 18 and 26, 1846, the Q.M. Department's roster was as follows: Q.M. Gen., two Asst. Q.M. Genl.'s, two Deputy Q.M. Genl.'s four Q.M.'s and twenty-eight Asst. Q.M.'s. Thirteen of the Asst. Q.M.'s were taken from the line of the Army.

14. [Bvt.] Maj. Gen. Th[omas] S. Jesup, Q.M. Gen., Brazos San Iago, Texas, to W[illia]m L. Marcy, Secretary of War, Washington City, Dec. 27, 1846, House of Representatives Exec. Doc., No. 60, 30 Cong., 1 Sess., pp. 568-569.

15. [Bvt.] Maj. Gen. Th[omas] S. Jesup, Q.M. Gen., New Orleans, to Col. H[enry] Whiting, Asst. Q.M. Gen., Headquarters of the Army of Occupation, Camargo or Monterey, Mexico, Nov. 4, 1846 (fair copy), Letters Received, Correspondence of Col. Henry Whiting, Office of the Q.M. General, RG 92, Nat. Arch.

16. Lt. Col. Joseph Eccleston Johnston was 1st Lt., Top. Eng., July 7, 1838; Capt. on Sept. 21, 1846, and Lt. Col., Voltigeurs, Apr. 9, 1847 to Aug. 28, 1848. He won brevets for Cerro Gordo and Chapultepec. During the Civil War he was a general, Confederate States Army.

17. Thomas Marshall of Kentucky was a Brig. Gen. of Volunteers from July 1, 1846 to July 20, 1848.

18. William Orlando Butler was Maj. Gen. of Volunteers from June 29, 1846 to Aug. 15, 1848.

19. James R. Irwin was Capt. and Asst. Q.M. from July 7, 1838. He died Jan. 10, 1848.

20. [Bvt.] Maj. Gen. Th[omas] S. Jesup, Q.M. Gen., Washington City, to W[illiam] L. Marcy, Secretary of War, Washington City, February 18, 1848, House of Representatives Exec. Doc., No. 60, 30 Cong., 1 Sess., pp. 1251-1252.

21. Possibly Maj. Hartman Bache, Topographical Engineers. Alexander Dallas Bache was Superintendent of the U.S. Coast Survey from 1843 to 1867.

22. George Law, Baltimore, to Brig. Gen. R[oger] Jones, Adjutant General [Washington, D.C.], May 20, 1846 (fair copy), Letters Received, Correspondence of Col. Henry Whiting, Office of the Quartermaster General, RG 92, Nat. Arch.

23. [Bvt.] Maj. Gen. Th[omas] S. Jesup, Q.M. Gen., New Orleans, to W[illiam] L. Marcy, Secretary of War, Washington City, Nov. 7, 1846, House of Representatives Exec. Doc., No. 60, 30 Cong., 1 Sess. p. 564.

24. Daniel Harvey Hill Diary MS, entry of Feb. 11, 1847, So. Hist. Col. NCa.

25. Maj. Daniel D. Tompkins, Q.M., New Orleans, to [Bvt.] Maj. Gen. Tho[ma]s S. Jesup, Q.M. Gen., Washington City, Nov. 2, 1848 (fair copy), Daniel D. Tompkins Letterbooks, Office of the Quartermaster General, RG 92, Nat. Arch. Maj. Tompkins was 3d Lt., Ordnance, July 1, 1820; Capt. and Asst. Q.M., July 7, 1838, and Maj. and Q.M., July 22, 1842. He was Bvt. Lt. Col. for his services during the Mexican War.

26. Amos Beebe Eaton was Bvt. 2d Lt., 4th Inf., July 1, 1826 and Capt. and Commissary of Subsistence, July 7, 1838. He was Bvt. Maj. for Buena Vista. From June 29, 1864 until his retirement, May 1, 1874, he was Brig. Gen. and Commissary General of Subsistence.

27. Probably Lt. Seneca Galusha Simmons, 1st Inf.

28. Capt. A[mos] B. Eaton, Commissary of Subsistence, Matamoros, to Lt. Col., J[oseph] P. Taylor, Asst. Commissary General of Subsistence, Matamoros, Dec. 5, 1846, Amos Beebe Eaton Papers, Beinecke.

29. Mackay was Lt. Col. and Deputy Quartermaster General, Apr. 21, 1846. He was brevetted Col. for his Mexican War services. He entered the Army as Asst. Deputy Commissary of Ordnance on Mar. 12, 1813.

30. Lt. Col. Ae[neas] Mackay, Deputy Q.M. Gen., St. Louis, to Col. Henry Stanton, Asst. Q.M. Gen., Washington, May 22, 1847 (fair copy), Western Americana MSS, Beinecke.

31. [Bvt.] Maj. Gen. Th[omas] S. Jesup, Q.M. Gen., Brassos St. Iago, Texas, to Brig. Gen. George Gibson, Commissary General of Subsistence, Jan. 2, 1846 [sic 1847], Letters Received, Office of the Commissary General of Subsistence, RG 192, Nat. Arch.

32. Col. Henry Whiting, Asst. Q.M. Gen., Camp at Camargo, Mexico, to [Bvt.] Maj. Gen. Thomas S. Jesup, Q.M. Gen., Washington City, Aug. 28, 1846, House of Representatives Exec. Doc., No. 60, 30 Cong., 1 Sess., pp. 679-680.

33. Capt. Ripley Allen Arnold, 2d Drags., was Capt. and Asst. Q.M. from May 11, 1846 to Mar. 10, 1847. He was brevetted Maj. for Palo Alto and Resaca de la Palma.

34. Capt. George Hampton Crosman, was Capt. and Asst. Q.M., July 7, 1838, and Maj. and Q.M., Mar. 3, 1847; he was brevetted for Palo Alto. For his services in the Quartermaster Department (Union Army) during the Civil War he was Bvt. Brig. Gen. and Bvt. Maj. Gen.

35. Capt. James Madison Hill was Capt., 8th Inf., Sept. 28, 1840 to June 18, 1846; he was Capt. and Asst. Q.M. from July 7, 1838. He died June 29, 1849.

36. Col. Henry Whiting, Asst. Q.M. Gen., Camp near Monterey, to Col. Henry Stanton, Asst. Q.M. Gen., Washington, D.C., Nov. 5, 1846, House of Representatives Exec. Doc., No. 60, 30 Cong., 1 Sess., pp. 683-684.

37. Maj. Gen. Winfield Scott, Jalapa, to Bvt. Col. [Henry] Wilson, Commander and Governor, Vera Cruz, Apr. 23, 1847, Henry Wilson Papers, Beinecke.

38. With overland transportation severely restricted, there was a tendency for large quantities of stores intended for Scott's army to pile up at Vera Cruz. Even a glut of provisions occurred there, as the army found itself depending upon the country for a considerable part of its food. (See, Maj. W[ashington] Seawell, New Orleans, to Brig Gen. George Gibson, Washington, June 23, 1847, Letters Received, Office of the Commissary General of Subsistence, R.G. 192, Nat. Arch.) Seawell cited a letter from Lt. Johnson, A.A.C.G., at Vera Cruz, as follows: "If you will take my opinion on the matter I would advise you by no means to forward more stores here until a requisition is made from this place—there is a large quantity on hand here, and but little demand or means of transportation to the interior. Lieut. Blair writes me that he has at Jalapa, beans, rice, sugar, and salt in great abundance; that he can keep Perote supplied with them, and that Puebla can supply itself with the same. He also states that a large quantity of flour can be obtained in the interior and requests me to send him bread, meat, soap and candles. The army, it is understood, subsists (as far as the article of meat is concerned) mainly on fresh beef. From these facts it appears to me that there are too many provisions ordered to this place. A supply mainly of bread, meat, salt, coffee, sugar, soap, and candles, with a small proportion of other articles thrown in here *gradually*, so as to meet the current issues, would in my opinion be entirely sufficient."

39. Although the prices paid were sometimes excessive, Scott's commissaries were able to buy most of the articles needed to subsist the Army after it left Vera Cruz. Capt. John B. Grayson, Asst. Commissary of Subsistence, listed the prices paid for some of the articles on the ration list after the occupation of Mexico City had begun. He wrote: "The price of the ration here is 32¢. We are paying for flour now, 9¢ p[er] lb. Coffee 23 & 24¢, sugar 10¢, rice 10¢, soap 16¢, tallow candles 30¢, vinegar 40¢, gallon; hams 28¢, hard bread from 13¢ @ 14¢. Salt beef 16¢, fresh d° 10¢. Beans, I have not purchased any yet but suppose they will cost from $3 @ 4 p[er] bushel. Salt is the most extravagant article, ranging from 10¢ [to] 13¢ p[er] lb.—*my disbursements for the last quarter amount to nearly half a million of Dollars.* [Italics added by editors.]" Capt. John B. Grayson, Asst. Commissary of Subsistence, City of Mexico, to [Brig.] Gen. George Gibson, Commissary General of Subsistence, Washington, D.C., Oct. 16, 1847, Western Americana MSS, Beinecke.

40. Maj. Gen. Winfield Scott, Jalapa, to W[illiam] L. Marcy, Secretary of War [Washington, D.C.], Apr. 28, 1847, House of Representatives Exec. Doc., No. 60, 30 Cong., 1 Sess., p. 944.

41. Fort Leavenworth.

42. According to a memorandum of Lt. William E. Prince there were sent to Santa Fe from Fort Leavenworth, exclusive of what each column carried with it to Bent's Fort, the following quantities of subsistence: flour, 1,229,772 lbs.; hard bread, 51,530 lbs.; pork, 396,000 lbs.; bacon, 140,045 lbs.; fresh beef, 700 beeves at an average weight of 500 lbs. each; beans, 921 bu.; rice, 49,277 lbs.; coffee, 60,517 lbs.; sugar, 107,672 lbs.; tallow candles, 1,820 lbs.; sperm candles, 1,876 lbs.; soap, 20,266½ lbs.; salt, 508 bu.; molasses, 3,372 gals.; vinegar, 3,055 gals.; pickles, 800 gals. See, "Provisions forwarded from Fort Leavenworth, Mo., to Santa Fe, New Mexico, exclusive of a supply taken with each column to carry them to Bent's Fort, according to the report of Lt. William E. Prince, A.C.S.," enclosed in Maj. R. B. Lee, St. Louis, to Brig. Gen. G[eorge]

Gibson, Com. Gen. of Subsistence, Washington, D.C., Dec. 9, 1846, Letters Received, Office of the Commissary General of Subsistence, RG 192, Nat. Arch.

43. The battalion made up of Mormons exiled from Nauvoo, Illinois, who had gathered at Council Bluffs. There they had planned to emigrate to California, but at the invitation of the United States government they enlisted in the Army and went to Fort Leavenworth. From there they marched to Santa Fe, and eventually continued on to California, where they arrived in Jan. 1847. The first commander of the battalion was Capt. James Allen, 1st Dragoons.

44. "Santa Fe Expedition," St. Louis *Missouri Republican*, Aug. 18, 1846.

45. Lt. [*sic.* Capt.] W[illia]m Grier, Santa Fe, to Maj. R[ichard] B. Lee, Commissary of Subsistence, St. Louis, October 9, 1846, Letters Received, Department of the West, Records of United States Army Commands, RG 98, Nat. Arch. Capt. William Nicholson Grier was 1st Lt., 1st Drags., April 14, 1838 and Capt., Aug. 23, 1846. He won a brevet at Santa Cruz de Rosales.

46. For further discussion of Maj. Richard B. Lee, see Chapter III.

47. Maj. R[ichard] B. Lee, Commissary of Subsistence, St. Louis, to Brig. Gen. George Gibson, Commissary General of Subsistence, Washington, D.C., December 9, 1846, Letters Received, Office of the Commissary General of Subsistence, RG 192, Nat. Arch.

48. Herbert Gosselin.

49. Capt. Amos F. Garrison was Capt. and Asst. Commissary of Subsistence of Volunteers, June 26, 1846 to Nov. 30, 1848.

50. [Lt. Richard S. Elliott] "John Brown," "Letters From New Mexico," Santa Fe, New Mexico, Nov. 3, 1846, in St. Louis *Reveille*, Jan. 11, 1847.

51. Col. Henry Stanton of Vermont was 3d Lt., Light Art. on June 29, 1813; Col. and Asst. Q.M. Gen., July 7, 1838, and Bvt. Brig. Gen., Jan. 1, 1847, for his services during the Mexican War. He died Aug. 1, 1856.

52. Scott's Vera Cruz expedition, see Chapter IV.

53. Col. Henry Stanton, Asst. Q.M. Gen., Washington, D.C., to [Bvt.] Maj. Gen. T[homas] S. Jesup, Quartermaster General, New Orleans, Dec. 13, 1846, Thomas Sidney Jesup Papers, Duke.

54. Memorandum of Capt. John G. Tod, Nov. 16, 1846, in Thomas Sidney Jesup Papers, DLC.

55. [Bvt.] Maj. Gen. Th[omas] S. Jesup, Q.M. Gen. [Washington, D.C.], to Col. Henry Whiting, Asst. Q.M. Gen., Headquarters of the Army, on the Rio del Norte, Mexico, July 1, 1846 (fair copy), Letters Received, Correspondence of Colonel Henry Whiting, Office of the Quartermaster General, RG 92, Nat. Arch.

56. Capt. Osborn Cross was Capt. and Asst. Q.M., July 7, 1838; Maj. and Quartermaster, July 24, 1847. He was in the Quartermaster Department (Union Army) during the Civil War and was Bvt. Brig Gen. in 1865.

57. Maj. Thomas B. Eastland, Maj. and Quartermaster of Volunteers, June 26, 1846 to Mar. 3, 1849.

58. [Bvt.] Maj. Gen. Th[omas] S. Jesup, Q.M. Gen., to Lt. Col. T[homas] F. Hunt, Deputy Q.M. Gen., New Orleans, July 19, 1846, House of Representatives Exec. Doc., No. 60, 30 Cong., 1 Sess., pp. 601-602.

59. Col. Henry Whiting, Asst. Q.M. Gen., Matamoras Mexico, to [Bvt.] Maj. Gen. Tho[ma]s S. Jesup, Q.M. Gen., Washington City, Aug. 17, 1846, *ibid.*, p. 678.

60. Maj. Gen. Winfield Scott, Headquarters of the Army, Camp Washington before Vera Cruz, "Memoranda for Brevet Major General Jesup, Quartermaster General," Mar. 19, 1847, *ibid.*, p. 913.

61. Giddings, *Sketches of the Campaign*, pp. 100-101.

62. Lt. Col. J[oseph] P. Taylor, Assistant Commissary General of Subsistence, Matamoros, to Brig. Gen. Geo[rge] Gibson, Commissary General of Subsistence, Washington, D.C., Feb[ruar]y 15, 1847, Letters Received, Office of the Commissary General of Subsistence, RG 192, Nat. Arch.

63. Lt. Henry Little, San Angel, to [Brig. Gen. George Gibson, Washington, D.C.], Sept. 3, 1847, *ibid.*

64. Maj. T[homas] W. Lendrum, Baltimore, to Brig. Gen. George Gibson, Washington, D.C.,

May 26, 1847, *ibid.*; see also, Capt. A[mos] B. Eaton, New York City, to *id.*, June 5, 1846, *ibid.*, on the scarcity of pickles and onions in New York City during June 1846.

65. Maj. Solon Borland, Regiment of Arkansas Mounted Volunteers.

66. In June, 1846, Lt. Col. J. P. Taylor, Assistant Commissary General of Subsistence, suggested to the Commissary General that the troops should be given small hand mills with which to grind Mexican corn. Taylor wrote: "Should the army be thrown on their own resources for subsistence while advancing into the interior of Mexico, grain will be found, I am told by Captain Sanders [of the Engineers] in abundance in the vicinity of Saltillo & Monterey, and would it not be advisable to supply the troops with small hand mills in order to crack or grind their corn. The Mexicans use stones for that purpose, and in Texas every family is supplied with a small steel mill, not much larger, I believe, than a coffee mill to make their meal." (See, Taylor to Gibson, June 20, 1846, Letters Received, Office of the Commissary General of Subsistence, RG 192, Nat. Arch.) Before Capt. Amos B. Eaton left New York City to become Gen. Taylor's commissary of subsistence, he purchased several mills for Taylor's army. Two of these were broken in being erected; the other one finally arrived in Saltillo. (Eaton to Gibson, July 13, Aug. 4, 1846, *ibid.*, and *id.* to Lt. Thomas Donaldson, Saltillo, Mar. 22, 1847, Amos Beebe Eaton Papers, Beinecke). It is doubtful, however, that Eaton ever succeeded in having much corn ground in his mill, for the troops strongly resented using them. Wool's army offers an illustration of this. Flour was in such short supply when Wool's force encamped at San Antonio that General Wool hesitated to condemn flour which otherwise would have been rejected. (W. J. Newton, San Antonio, to Brig. Gen. George Gibson, Nov. 23, 1846, Letters Received, Commissary General of Subsistence, RG 192, Nat. Arch.) It was certain that Wool would have to rely during at least a part of his long nine hundred mile march to Saltillo on Mexican corn. He therefore issued steel mills (one to each company) and nine ears of corn daily to every man, so that he could grind his own meal. The response to this was violent indignation against such menial labor by soldiers; there was even a mock trial which ended in a demand that the "Corn Laws" be repealed, followed by a general melee. All of it was semi-humorous, but the regulation was repealed. (Buhoup, *Narrative*, pp. 67-72.)

67. Buhoup, *Narrative*, pp. 35, 79-80. The amount of beef and bacon varied according to circumstances. The Arkansas Mounted Volunteers, for example, when in camp near San Antonio received three-sevenths beef and four-sevenths bacon; when the train was cut off from those troops because of high water, the ration was entirely beef, but at other times, when the beef ration was not to be had, the entire issue was bacon. See G. W. Parkes, Arkansas Mounted Cavalry, Camp Wool near San Antonio, Texas, to [n.n], Sept. 14, 1846, Letters Received, Office of the Commissary General of Subsistence, RG 192, Nat. Arch.

68. See, Register of Beef and Fresh Meat Contracts, 1821-1855, Commissary General of Subsistence, RG 192, Nat. Arch. This register presents in tabular form the beef contracts made between June 1, 1846 and Apr. 1, 1848 by representatives of the Commissary General of Subsistence and various beef contractors. A total of twenty-four contracts are listed. These were made at San Antonio, Port LaVaca, Bent's Fort, Santa Fe (2), Reynosa, Tampico (2), Vera Cruz (6), Puebla (3), Cerralvo (2), Mexico City (2), Cordova, Nopalucan, and Cedras. Obviously the list is incomplete, but the data is representative. Among the beef contractors were: W. J. Riddle, San Antonio; L. T. Clinkenbeard at Bent's Fort; W. S. Smith and Herbert Gosselin at Santa Fe; H. L. Kinney, Wood & Bigelow and R. H. Leitch at Vera Cruz; Kinney, again, at Cordova; Benj. Woodson at Cerralvo; H. W. Birdsall at Puebla, and others. The duration of the contracts was from one month to a year or more—some of them were for "optional" periods or an unstated time. Prices paid for beef on the hoof varied from 2¢ (E. D. Smith's contract at Reynosa which was famous for its fine black cattle) to 10¢ per lb. paid in Mexico City and Puebla. At Vera Cruz, Kinney made contracts to supply Twiggs' and Worth's division at 6¢ per lb., and on the same day Wood & Bigelow received a contract there to supply Gen. Patterson's volunteer division at 4¢ per lb. After Dec. 28, 1846, Gosselin, at Santa Fe, delivered mutton instead of beef; mutton also was purchased (for 12½¢ per lb.) in Puebla and Mexico City.

69. For further discussion of Maj. Kinney's role in the war, see Chapter II.

70. Maj. H[enry] L. Kinn[e]y, Beef Contractor, to [Lt.] Col. [Henry] Willson [*sic*, Wilson], "Governor of Vera Cruce," Apr. 29, 1847, Henry Wilson Papers, Beinecke.

71. Lt. Forbes Britton was 1st Lt., 7th Inf., on July 7, 1838 and Capt., Feb. 16, 1847.

72. On the purchase of Peloncillo to make up deficiencies in the ration of Taylor's army, see Capt. A[mos] B. Eaton, Camp Agua Nueva, to Capt. M. R. Patrick, A.C.S., Saltillo, Feb. 6, 1847, Amos Beebe Eaton Papers, Beinecke. Eaton instructed Capt. Patrick: "I wish you or Lieut. Donaldson to purchase the best 'Peloncillo' to be had at Saltillo, and thus keep our sugar ration good until supplies are rec'd. from Monterey. If this article cannot be had at Saltillo at all and the A.C.S. at Monterey is behindhand in sugar, I will direct him to purchase 'Peloncillo' sufficient to make good his deficiency of American sugar, as it is better for us to furnish this article than to fail in this ration." Capt. Stephen Hoyt, A.C.S., Regimental Commissary of the Massachusetts Volunteer Regiment, bought Peloncillo at Matamoros and also while on a march from Camargo to Monterey on the authority of his commanding officer's order. See, Capt. Stephen Hoyt to Brig. Gen. George Gibson, June 30, 1847, Letters Received, Office of the Commissary General of Subsistence, RG 192, Nat. Arch.

73. Capt. A[mos] B. Eaton, Commissary of Subsistence, Camp near Monterey, Mexico, to Col. J[oseph] P. Taylor, Assistant Commissary General of Subsistence, Matamoros, January 27, 1847, Amos Beebe Eaton Papers, Beinecke.

74. This unfortunately was not always the verdict on the pork given to the troops. Lt. Darius N. Couch, for example, complained to Brig. Gen. Gibson about the pork at Point Isabel in July, 1847. Couch wrote: "The large wastage of pork is accounted for from the fact that most of the pork issued is of the flimsy stuff known as swill pork. This article will from my own observation when in the field lose from five- to six-tenths in cooking." Lt. D[arius] N. Couch, Point Isabel, to [Brig.] Gen. George Gibson, Commissary General of Subsistence [Washington, D.C.], July 4, 1847, Letters Received, Commissary General of Subsistence, RG 192, Nat. Arch.

75. Capt. A[mos] B. Eaton, Commissary of Subsistence, Brazos Island, to Maj. W[ashington] Seawell, Acting Commissary of Subsistence, New Orleans, July 16, 1847, Amos Beebe Eaton Papers, Beinecke. Seawell was Bvt. Maj. for services in the Florida Indian War, and Maj., 2d Inf., Mar. 3, 1847.

76. *Id.* to William Scott Colquhoun, Subsistence Agent [Matamoros], July 13, 1847, *ibid.* Colquhoun was a civilian employee; he had been a Lt., 7th Inf., on Dec. 31, 1822, but had been cashiered in 1829.

77. These were Maj. Gen. Patterson's troops, but the resentment of the men for the hardships they endured on this march was directed largely against Brig. Gen. Gideon J. Pillow, the second in command.

78. Furber, *Twelve Months Volunteer*, pp.280-281.

79. Capt. J[ohn] W. Lowe, Camp near Vera Cruz, to [O. T. Fishback, Batavia, Ohio], Oct. 14, 17, 1847, John W. Lowe Papers, Dayton.

80. Jamieson, *Journal*, pp.27-28.

81. "From the *Kentucky Observer* of October," *Niles' National Register*, Vol. 71 (Oct. 24, 1846), p.122.

82. [Bvt.] Maj. Gen. T[homas] S. Jesup, steamer *Alabama* below New Orleans, to Col. Henry Stanton, Asst. Q.M. Gen., Washington City, Apr. 7, 1847 (fair copy), Thomas Sidney Jesup Papers, DLC.

83. Capt. Kenton Harper, Parras, to Col. [John F. Hamtramck Jr.], Apr. 4, 1848, John Francis Hamtramck Jr. Papers, Duke. Capt. Harper of the Virginia Volunteer Regiment was commanding in Parras.

84. Maj. Gen. [Robert] Patterson, by [Lt.] W[illiam] H. French, A.A.A.G., Jalapa, General Orders No. 11, May 1, 1847.

85. "Memo of Returns of Cl[o]thing received and issued at the Camargo Depot of Clothing by L[ewis] T. Jamison, Acting Mil[itary] Store Keeper, October 26, 1846," Letters Received, Army of Occupation, AGO, RG 94, Nat. Arch. Jamison had been a Capt., 5th Inf., on Oct. 31, 1836,

but was dismissed from the service on Dec. 31, 1838. See also, Taylor's Orders No.133, 135, Camp near Monterey, Oct. 18, 25, 1846. Regular clothing depots were established at Point Isabel and Camargo. The supply train which brought the clothing issued at Camargo (as per the October memo) was believed by Taylor to have provided sufficient clothing to issue to each of the regulars one of the following: Wool jackets, overalls, flannel shirts, stockings and boots (the allowance of boots was four pairs per year, later increased to five pairs); the quartermasters also issued forage caps, flannel drawers, camp kettles, and mess pans. Only undress uniforms were issued.

86. Lt. Col. E[than] A[llen] Hitchcock, Mexico [City], to Maj. Gen. Winfield Scott, Mexico [City], Dec. 6, 1847, Ethan Allen Hitchcock Papers, DLC.

87. Lt. Braxton Bragg, Comdg. Co. E, 3d Art., Camp near Corpus Christi, Texas, to Capt. W[illiam] W. S. Bliss, [A.] Asst. Adjt. Gen., Sept. 12, 1845, Letters Received, Army of Occupation, AGO, RG 94, Nat. Arch.

88. "Buck and ball"—or one ball and three (sometimes two) buckshot made up the cartridge fired from muskets and rifles, but Taylor ordered that in instruction and guard service only the ball should be used. Every man received orders to carry twenty-four rounds of ammunition in his cartridge box; on the march from Camargo to Monterey, Taylor increased this to forty rounds per man.

89. Capt. R. G. Livingston, Commanding Co. C, Florida Volunteers, Camp Bergarra [sic, Vergara], Mexico, to Col. J. M. Withers, Oct. 17, 1847, in Caleb Cushing Papers, DLC. Col. Jones Mitchell Withers was Lt. Col., 13th Inf. on Apr. 9, 1847 and Col., 9th Inf., Sept. 13, 1847. He was Maj. Gen., Confederate States Army, 1861-1865.

90. Maj. Alexander B. Bradford.

91. Col. Jefferson Davis, mouth of R[io Grande], to Lt. [John] McNutt, Ordnance Officer [month is missing—sheet torn], 20 [1846], Western Americana MSS, Beinecke.

92. "Return of Ordnance and Ordnance Stores . . . June 30, 1847," Burton.

93. "Colt's Rifles," Hartford *Courant* cited in Cambridge [Massachusetts] *Chronicle*, Dec. 2, 1847.

94. After the Battle of Buena Vista there were complaints from some of the gunners that the powder used by them was inferior to that of the Mexican Army.

95. Lt. Col. G[eorge] Talcott [Jr.], Ordnance office, Washington, D.C., to W[illiam] L. Marcy, Secretary of War [Washington, D.C.], Nov. 20, 1847, Senate Exec. Doc., No. 1, 30 Cong., 1 Sess., pp. 680, 683-686.

NOTES TO CHAPTER IX

1. W[illiam] L. Marcy, Secretary of War, Washington, D.C., to Maj. Gen. Zachary Taylor, July 9, 1846, House of Representatives Exec. Doc., No. 60, 30 Cong., 1 Sess., pp. 155-158.

2. The *alcaldes* were the mayors; they had judicial as well as administrative powers. *Ayuntamientos* were municipal government councils.

3. Lt. S[imon] Doyle, Santa Teresa [south of Matamoros] to [Margaret Doyle, his sister, Rushville, Illinois], Mar. 15, 1848, Doyle papers, Beinecke.

4. Bvt. Maj. Gen. Th[omas] S. Jesup, Q.M. Gen., Brazos Santiago, to Col. Henry Stanton, Washington, D.C., Feb. 28, 1847, Thomas Sidney Jesup Papers, DLC.

5. Maj. J[ubal] A. Early, Monterey, to Maj. W[illiam] W. S. Bliss, A.A.A.G., June 17, 1847, Western Americana MSS, Beinecke. Early was Acting Governor of Monterey, May-June 1847, and Acting Inspector of Brig. Gen. Cushing's brigade, 1847.

6. Nevertheless, there were numerous complaints that Mexicans were arbitrarily jailed by American commanders for minor offences. See, for example, *Gregg diary*, Vol. 2, p. 210, for the case of Cecilio Flores, who was imprisoned in Saltillo for forty-eight hours because he was found drunk in the streets by a patrol "while American soldiers were to be seen continually staggering and swaggering about the streets in shameful intoxication."

7. Col. Caleb Cushing and his Regiment of Massachusetts Volunteers were at Matamoros during the spring of 1847.

8. Lt. W[illiam] W. H. Davis, Matamoros, to John H. Davis, Philadelphia, May 5, 1847, W. W. H. Davis Papers, Beinecke.

9. Maj. Gen. W[illiam J.] Worth, Governor [of Vera Cruz], by Lt. W[illiam] W. Mackall, A.A.G., Orders No. 3, Mar. 30, 1847, House of Representatives Exec. Doc., No. 60, 30 Cong., 1 Sess., p. 932.

10. Childs was Military Governor of Jalapa from April to June, 1847.

11. Col. George Wurtz Hughes was Capt., Top. Eng., July 7, 1838, Lt. Col., Maryland and District of Columbia Volunteers, Aug. 4, 1847, and Col., Oct. 1, 1847. He won two brevets in the Mexican War—one for Cerro Gordo, and the other for meritorious conduct while serving in the enemy's country (at Jalapa).

12. Col. George W. Hughes, Jalapa, to Brig. Gen. C[aleb] Cushing [San Angel], Feb. 3, 1848, Caleb Cushing Papers, DLC.

13. [n.n.], Jalapa, to Dr. W[illiam] H. Grimes, Dec. 14, 1847, William Henry Grimes Papers, Duke.

14. Maj. Gen. John A. Quitman, National Palace, Mexico City, to his wife [Eliza Quitman], Sept. 19, 1847 (typescript copy), John A. Quitman Papers, So. Hist. Col., NCa.

15. Id. to H. S. Foote, Oct. 15, 1847, ibid. Henry Stuart Foote was United States Senator from Mississippi.

16. Probably he was describing Iztaccihuatl.

17. Oswandel, Notes, pp. 453-456.

18. Lt. W[illiam] W. H. Davis, Mexico City, to his sister, Elizabeth W. Davis, Mar. 14, 1848, W. W. H. Davis Papers, Beinecke.

19. William Britton Diary, 1847-1848, MS, Wis. Hist. Soc.

20. William [Britton], Hacienda San Marco, to his brother, May 29, 1848, William Britton Papers, Ibid.

21. Lt. Col. William Montrose Graham.

22. Henry Moses Judah Journal MS, entries of June 16—17, 1847, DLC.

23. General Juan Alvarez.

24. Lt. William D. Wilkins, Cuernavaca, to [Ross] Wilkins, Detroit, Feb. 16, 1848, Ross Wilkins Papers, Burton.

25. Davis was in the 2d Regiment of Illinois Volunteers.

26. The religious center of the Toltecs, see Prescott, Conquest of Mexico, Vol. 2, pp. 3-10, for the classic description.

27. See, The Bernal Díaz Chronicles, trans. and ed., Albert Idell (Garden City: Dolphin Books, Doubleday & Company, Inc. [1956]), pp. 127-143.

28. The pyramid of Quetzalcoatl built by the Toltecs. Prescott called it "the most colossal fabric in New Spain."

29. George T. M. Davis, Autobiography of the Late Col. Geo. T. M. Davis, Captain, and Aid[e]-de-Camp, Scott's Army of Invasion (Mexico), From Posthumous Papers. Published By His Legal Representatives (New York: Press of Jenkins and McGowan, 1891), pp. 184-186.

30. Lucas Alamán (1792-1853), leader of the conservative landed aristocracy and clergy in Mexican politics, had favored monarchy and military dictatorship over liberalism. He was an adviser to Guadalupe Victoria, the real ruler of Mexico during the Bustamente administration (1830-1832), and held office under Santa Anna and his followers. One of his biographers (Arturo Arnáiz y Freg) has called him "a Metternich in an Indian world." Alamán was a distinguished scholar, author of a five-volume History of Mexico, organizer of the Mexican archives, and founder of the National Museum.

31. W[illia]m H. Prescott, Boston, to Brig. Gen. Caleb Cushing, Apr. 7, 1848, Caleb Cushing Papers, DLC.

32. John Russell Bartlett, of Providence, Rhode Island, from 1836 to 1850 operated a bookstore (in partnership with Charles Welford) and a publishing house that specialized in travel

books, located on the ground floor of the Astor Hotel in New York City. His establishment was the meeting place for a literary group that included Albert Gallatin, Brantz Mayer, Ephraim George Squier and others interested in history and ethnology. With Gallatin, Bartlett aided in the founding of the American Ethnological Society. After the Mexican War Bartlett was a member of the Mexican Boundary Commission. From 1855 to 1872 he was Secretary of State, in Rhode Island.

33. John Russell Bartlett wrote one such survey. See, John Russell Bartlett, *Personal Narrative of Explorations and Incidents in Texas, New Mexico, and California, Sonora and Chihuahua, Connected With the United States and Mexican Boundary Commission During the Years 1850, '51, '52, and '53* (New York: D. Appleton, 1854), 2 vols.

34. Albert Gallatin (1761-1849), then nearing the end of an eventful career, had been Secretary of the Treasury under Jefferson and Madison, a negotiator of the Treaty of Ghent (1814), and later U.S. Minister to France and Great Britain. This Swiss-born statesman had long been interested as a scholar in the American Indian. In 1844 he had been one of the prime movers in the organization of the American Ethnological Society.

35. Bvt. Maj. Emory (he was not Bvt. Lt. Col. until 1857 or Lt. Col., 1st Cav. until 1861) had returned to Washington from California with his "Notes of a Military Reconnaissance . . ." In response to a Senate Resolution of December 9, 1847, Secretary of War Marcy on December 15 had submitted Emory's report to the Senate, where it was ordered to be published. Emory then went to Mexico to join Scott's army.

36. Benaducci Lorenzo Boturini (ca. 1702-1750). His most notable work was *Ideal de Una Nueva Historia General de la America Septentrional* . . . (Madrid: Imps. de J. de Zuñiga, 1746). The Boturini pre-Columbian manuscripts, including the Boturini copy of the Veytia Tarascan calendars eventually (in 1898) went in large part to the Bibliotheque Nacionale.

37. Bartolomé de las Casas, Bishop of Chiapa (1474-1566). Spanish Dominican missionary and historian. He wrote *Brief Relation of the Destruction of the Indies* (1552) and *Historia General de las Indias* which, however, was not published until 1875.

38. Andrés González de Barcía Carballido y Zuñiga (1673-1743). His most significant work— *Historiadores Primitivos de las Indias* (3 vols.) —was published six years after his death.

39. Francisco López de Gómara (1510-1560?), author of *La Historia General de las Indias* (Antwerp: Juan Steelsio, 1554).

40. Gallatin already had demonstrated his interest in the region by publishing "Notes on the Semi-Civilized Nations of Mexico, Yucatan, and Central America," in Vol. I (1845) of the *Transactions of the American Ethnological Society*. See also, Albert Gallatin, New York, to Lt. W. H. Emory, Washington, D.C., Oct. 1, 1847, in Appendix No.1, Emory, *Notes Of A Military Reconnaissance*, p. 127. In Vol. II, of the American Ethnological Society's *Transactions*, Gallatin, only a year before his death, had an introduction to "Hale's Indians of North-West America and Vocabularies of North America."

41. John R. Bartlett, New York, to Brig. Gen. Caleb Cushing, Jan. 7, 1848, Caleb Cushing Papers, DLC.

42. Giocomo Constantino Beltrami (1779-1855), *Le Mexique* (Paris: Crevat [etc.], 1830), 2 vols.

43. Lucas Alamán, *Defensa del Ex-Ministro de Relaciones Extranjos: D. Lucas Alamán, en La Causa Formado Contra El y Contra los Ex Ministros de Guerra y Justicia de Vice-Presidente D. Anastasio Bustamante* (Mexico [City]: Impr. de Galvano cargo de M. Arevado, 1834), 126 pp.

44. General Bustamante was President of Mexico for the first time from 1830 to 1832.

45. José Justo Gómez, conde de la Cortina (1799-1860) was a distinguished Mexican scholar of that era. He was President of the Mexican Geographical and Statistical Society.

46. Lucas Alamán [Mexico City], to Brig. Gen. Caleb Cushing, Feb. 10, 1848, Caleb Cushing Papers, DLC.

47. "Easter Sunday," Vera Cruz *American Eagle*, Apr. 6, 1847.

48. Capt. J[ohn] W. Lowe, Camp near Vera Cruz, to [Mrs. Manorah F. Lowe, New York City], Oct. 10, 1847, John W. Lowe Papers, Dayton.

49. Lt. W[illiam] W. H. Davis, San Angel, to his sister, Elizabeth Davis, Jan. 11, 1848, W. W. H. Davis Papers, Beinecke.

50. Daniel Harvey Hill Diary MS, entry of Jan. 7, 1848, So. Hist. Col., NCa.

51. Lt. W[illiam] W. H. Davis, San Angel, to his sister, Elizabeth Davis, Jan. 11, 1848, W. W. H. Davis Papers, Beinecke.

52. Samuel Starr, Puebla, to [Mrs. Eliza Starr, New York City], July 7, 1847, Samuel H. Starr Papers, Bixby collection, Missouri Historical Society.

53. R[obert] J. Walker, Secretary of the Treasury, "Circular to Collectors and other officers of the customs," [Washington], June 30, 1846, House of Representatives Exec. Doc., No. 60, 30 Cong., 1 Sess., pp. 158-159.

54. Thorpe, Army on the Rio Grande, pp. 165, 172.

55. "The Fruits of Victory," New Orleans Delta, June 13, 1847, cited in Niles' National Register, Vol. 72 (July 3, 1847), p. 281.

56. "Important Documents," James K. Polk, Washington, to Secretary of the Treasury [Robert J. Walker], March 23, 1847, cited in Washington Union, Apr. 1, 1847.

57. [Bvt.] Maj. Gen. Thomas S. Jesup, Q.M. Gen., Headquarters Quartermaster General's Department, New Orleans, to W[illiam] L. Marcy, Secretary of War, Washington City, Nov. 26, 1846, House of Representatives Exec. Doc., No. 60, 30 Cong., 1 Sess., pp. 565-566.

58. "The March of Our Army From Vera Cruz to Mexico," Mexico City American Star, Sept. 25, 1847.

59. Scott, Memoirs, Vol. 2, pp. 552-553.

60. Maj. Gen. Winfield Scott, endorsement, Sept. 21, 1847, cited in Lt. G[eorge] W. Lay, Headquarters of the Army, Mexico City, to Maj. Gen. [John A.] Quitman, Sept. 21, 1847, John A. Quitman Papers, Houghton.

61. Maj. Gen. Winfield Scott, by Capt. H. L. Scott, A.A.A.G., Mexico City, General Orders No.376, Dec. 15, 1847, cited in New Orleans Courier, Jan. 7, 1848.

62. Lt. T[h]om[as] Williams, Headqtrs. of the Army, Mexico [City], to J[ohn] R. Williams, Dec. 27, 1847, John R. Williams Papers, Burton.

63. Col. Jones Mitchell Withers, 9th Inf.

64. General Mariano Padres y Arrillaga, President of Mexico from January to July, 1846; he went into exile in 1847.

65. General Ignacio Garza Falcon.

66. Lt. Daniel Harvey Hill Diary MS, entries of Jan. 17, 21, 29, and 30, 1848, So. Hist. Col., NCa.

67. Capt. Alexander Wilkin was Capt. 10th Inf. on Apr. 9, 1847; he resigned Mar. 6, 1848. During the Civil War he was Capt., Maj. and Lt. Col. (Union Army) and was killed at the Battle of Tupelo, Mississippi on July 14, 1864.

68. Capt. Joshua Wallace Collett, Capt. 10th Inf., Apr. 9, 1847, was killed in a duel with Capt. Wilkin on Jan. 21, 1848.

69. W[illia]m P. Tomlinson, 10th Inf., "Camp near Matamoras," to John G. Spencer, Attleborough, Pennsylvania, Feb. 15, 1848, Western Americana MSS, Beinecke.

70. Col. Robert Treat Paine, Regiment of North Carolina Volunteers.

71. Lt. Col. John A. Fagg, Regiment of North Carolina Volunteers.

72. Maj. Montfort S. Stokes, Regiment of North Carolina Volunteers.

73. Col. John Francis Hamtramck Jr., Regiment of Virginia Volunteers.

74. Capt. Martin Shive; he died Aug. 16, 1847.

75. Capt. Spyers Singleton.

76. Lt. Nixon White.

77. Lt. George E. R. Singletary.

78. Oel A. Buck was Adjutant, Regiment of North Carolina Volunteers.

79. Capt. William M. Robinson.

80. Lt. Josiah S. Pender.

81. Capt. William E. Kirkpatrick.

82. Lt. Thomas W. Dunham.

83. Col. Rob[er]t T[reat] Paine, Headquarters North Carolina Regiment of Volunteers, Brigade of Infantry, Buena Vista, Mexico, to [Mrs. Robert Treat Paine, Edenton, North Carolina], Aug. 13-30, 1847, Robert Treat Paine Papers, So. Hist. Col., NCa.

84. Lt. Jo[siah] S. Pender, Saltillo, to Brig. Gen. Caleb Cushing, Aug. 18, 1847, Caleb Cushing Papers, DLC.

85. The annexed description of the deserters, supposedly shot in attempting to cross the Rio Grande, was for Carl Gross, Private, 7th Inf., Compy. I, born in France, who deserted on Apr. 1; and Henry Laub, private 5th Inf., Compy. D, born in Switzerland, who deserted on Apr. 5. See, House of Representatives Exec. Doc., No. 60, 30 Cong., 1 Sess., p. 303.

86. Bvt. Brig. Gen. Z[achary] Taylor, Headquarters of the Army of Occupation, Matamoras, to [Brig. Gen. Roger Jones], Adjutant General of the Army, Washington, May 30, 1846, *ibid.*, pp. 302-303.

87. Antonio Lopez de Santa-Anna, "To American Troops in Mexico," Aug. 15, 1847, Peñon, Beinecke.

88. Sergeant John Riley (also spelled Reilly, Rylly, and O'Reilly), Company K, 5th Inf., was said to have deserted earlier from the British army when stationed in Canada. He enlisted in the United States Army, and for a time was drill sergeant at West Point before going to Mexico. He deserted in Apr. 1846.

89. In 1830, Congress passed legislation which eliminated the death penalty for desertion in time of peace. See, *U.S. Stats. at Large*, Vol. 4, p. 418.

90. Davis, *Autobiography*, pp. 224-228.

91. Heitman, Vol. 2, p. 282.

92. Maj. Gen. Gideon J. Pillow, Mexico City, to his wife [Mrs. Mary E. Pillow, Columbia, Tenn.], Aug. 27, 1847, Western Americana MSS, Beinecke.

93. *Id.* to *id.*, Nov. 25, 1847, Dreer Collection, Hist. Soc. Pa.

94. Brig. Gen. George Cadwalader, of Pennsylvania, was Brig. Gen. of Vols. on Mar. 3, 1847 and Bvt. Maj. Gen. for Chapultepec. During the Civil War he was Maj. Gen. of Volunteers, Union Army.

95. Lt. W[illiam] M[ontgomery] G[ardner], Mexico City, to his sister, Nov. 22, 1847, William Montgomery Gardner Papers, So. Hist. Col., NCa.

96. Lt. William D. Wilkins, Cuernavaca, to [Ross Wilkins], Detroit, Apr. 22, 1848, Ross Wilkins Papers, Burton.

97. Capt. George B. Mc[Clellan], Mexico City, to his mother, Mar. 22, 1848, George B. Mc-Clellan Papers, Series II, DLC.

98. Col. John W. Geary was Capt., 2d Pa. Inf., Dec. 21, 1846; Lt. Col., Jan. 7, 1847, and Col., Nov. 3, 1847. He was Mayor of San Francisco in 1850 and Territorial Governor of Kansas (1856-1857). During the Civil War, he was Brig. Gen. of Vols. and Bvt. Maj. Gen. in 1865. From 1867 to 1873 he was Governor of Pennsylvania.

99. J. L. Freaner was correspondent of the New Orleans *Delta*, the newspaper in which the "Leonidas letters" appeared.

100. Edward [N. Geary] to [Col. John W. Geary] Apr. 20, 1848, John W. Geary Papers, Beinecke.

101. Lt. William D. Wilkins, Cuernavaca, to [Ross Wilkins], Detroit, Apr. 22, 1848, Ross Wilkins Papers, Burton.

102. Manuel de la Peña y Peña was interim President of Mexico, 1847-1848.

103. Luis de la Rosa. Earlier Rosa had advised Santa Anna not to negotiate with Trist.

104. Lt. Edmund Bradford, Pachuca, to [John Tazewell], May 19, 1848, Edmund Bradford Papers, Western Americana MSS, Beinecke.

NOTES TO CHAPTER X

1. John Langdon Sibley Diary MS, Vol. 1, p. 134, entry of Sept. 20, 1847, Massachusetts Historical Society.

2. Eli Edwin Hall, *Ahab and Naboth; or the United States and Mexico . . . A Discourse . . . Thanksgiving of 1846* (New Haven, Connecticut: [no pub.], 1847), pp. 13-15.

3. "The War With Mexico," *The New Englander and Yale Review*, Vol. 5 (Oct. 1847), pp. 610-611.

4. Charles T. Porter, *Review of the Mexican War* (Auburn, New York: Alden & Parsons, 1849), pp. 162-163. In his preface, Porter denied that he was writing a political tract; he professed that he was avoiding the subject of slavery and declared that the war had not resulted from any plot to extend slave territory. The war spirit, he believed, was not confined to any one section of the country; the responsibility for it rested upon all the American people.

5. Thomas Corwin, of Ohio, was United States Senator from 1845 to 1850. He was one of the most outspoken critics of the war. In his sensational antiwar speeech, delivered on the floor of the Senate, he said that if he were a Mexican he would respond to the plea that the United States needed more room for expansion with the words: "Have you not room in your own country to bury your dead men? If you come into mine, we will greet you with bloody hands and welcome you to hospitable graves." See, Frederick Merk, *Manifest Destiny and Mission in American History* (New York: Vintage Books, Random House, c. 1963), p. 93.

6. E. V. Everhart, Washington, D.C., to [John W.] Geary, Mar. [24], 1847, John W. Geary Papers, Beinecke.

7. John Campbell, Nashville, to his sister [Betsey], May 28, 1847, David Campbell Papers, Duke.

8. Henry Clay Jr., Second Regiment of Kentucky Volunteers, was killed at the Battle of Buena Vista.

9. Col. William R. McKee.

10. Lt. Edward M. Vaughn, 1st Lt. and Adjutant, Regiment of Kentucky Cavalry Volunteers.

11. Sergeant Smith Prentiss, widely known as an orator, and, from 1845, practicing law in New Orleans. He was a member of the U.S. House of Representatives (1838-1839), and from 1832 to 1845 was an attorney in Vicksburg. He was a New Englander by birth.

12. "Returning Volunteers," Cambridge [Massachusetts] *Chronicle*, Aug. 5, 1847.

13. Robert Rowland Diary MS, entry of July 28, 1848, Duke. Col. Pierce M. Butler, the original commander of the regiment, had been wounded twice then killed in the Battle of Churubusco. Its Lt. Col., James P. Dickinson, also died from wounds received at Churubusco.

14. Col. Isaac H. Wright. He had become Col. of the regiment after Caleb Cushing was promoted to Brig. Gen.

15. "The Returned Volunteers," Cambridge [Massachusetts] *Chronicle*, July 27, 1848.

16. John Langdon Sibley Diary MS, Vol. 1, p. 177, entries of July 20, 22, 1848, Massachusetts Historical Society.

17. [Newspaper clipping], "Condition and Prospects of Volunteers," and Sam J. Bridge [Boston], to Brig. Gen. Caleb Cushing, July 24, 1848, Caleb Cushing Papers, DLC. See also [Broadside], dated Mar. 4, 1847, signed J. L. Edwards, Commissioner of Pensions, William Alexander Hoke Papers, So. Hist. Col., NCa.

18. [Capt. William W. H. Davis], San Angel, to William L. Marcy, Secretary of War, Washington, D.C., May 13, 1848 [draft of a letter], W. W. H. Davis Papers, Beinecke.

19. Col. J[ames] H. Lane, Commanding 5th Indiana Volunteers, and twenty other signatures, New Orleans, to Maj. Gen. W[illiam] O. Butler, July 6, 1848, Letters Received, Army of Occupation, AGO, RG 94, Nat. Arch.

20. Ch[arle]s W. March, Washington [D.C.], to Brig. Gen. Caleb Cushing, July 18 [1848], Caleb Cushing Papers, DLC.

21. "Soldiers' Bounties," *Niles' National Register*, Vol. 72 (July 10, 1847), pp. 298-299, citing New York *Commercial Advertiser*, Washington correspondence of June 16, and St. Louis *Union*, July 8, 1847.

22. The most important veterans' organization of the rank and file (as well as officers) was the National Association of Mexican War Veterans, organized considerably after the war, 1874, and lasting until about 1897. Alexander Kenaday was one of its chief organizers. It was concerned largely with pensions, though at times it did espouse other issues. Unlike the Civil War veterans' Grand Army of the Republic which lined up with the Republican Party, the Mexican War veterans' organization seemed to lean toward the Democratic Party. See, Wallace Evan Davies, "The Mexican War Veterans As An Organized Group," *Mississippi Valley Historical Review*, Vol. 35 (Sept., 1948), pp. 221-238.

23. Bvt. Capt. George B. McClellan, "Memorandum on military organization," [draft], Jan. 4, 1848, George B. McClellan Papers, DLC.

ILLUSTRATION SOURCES

Plates I, III, IV, VII, VIII, XI, XII, XIII, XVI, XVII, XVIII, XX, XXI, XXII, XXIII, XXIV, XXV, XXVI, XXVII, XXVIII, XXIX, XXX, XXXI, and XXXII are courtesy of the Library of Congress. Plates II, V, VI, X, and XIX are used by permission of Duke University Archives. Plate XV is reproduced from a photograph by Joseph Klima made from the Burton Historical Collection, Detroit Public Library.

The figures throughout the text are from the following books and sources. Those on pp. 32, 117, 134, 136, 137, and 372 are from Doniphan, A. W., *Doniphan's Expedition*, Washington, D.C.: GPO, 1914. Those on pp. 55, 197, 203, 218, 226, 297, 324, 350, 386, 396, 419, 434, 444, and 460 are taken from Frost, John, *The Mexican War and its Warriors*, New Haven & Philadelphia: H. Mansfield, 1848. Those on pp. 158, 160, and 163 are from Emory, W. H., *Notes of a Military Reconnoissance*, 30 Cong., 2 Sess., Exec. Doc. No. 7, Washington, D.C.: Wendell & Benthuysen, 1848. Those on pp. 63, 67, 142, 300, 312, 369, and 399 are from Thorpe, T. B., *Our Army on the Rio Grande*, Philadelphia: Carey & Hart, 1846. Those on pp. 65, 80, 97, 99, 177, 187, 205, 209, 211, 215, 237, 245, 252, and 267 are from Mansfield, Edward D., *The Mexican War: A History of its Origins*, New York: A. S. Barnes & Co., 1848. Those on pp. 150, 153, 261, 309, and 402 are taken from Frost, John, *Perilous Adventures by Land and Sea*, Chicago & New York: Belford, Clarke & Co., 1848. Figures 14, 43, and 45 are used by permission of the Library of Congress.

INDEX

515

Typefaces used in this book
are Linotype Electra, 11 point leaded 2 points,
with display in handset Melior.
Printed by offset on 60-lb. Warren's 1854.
The binding is Holliston Zeppelin.
Designed by Frank Mahood.